John Ridewall, *Fulgencius metaforalis*

EXETER MEDIEVAL TEXTS AND STUDIES

Series Editors: Richard Dance and Eddie Jones
Emeritus Editors:
M.J. Swanton (founder)
Marion Glasscoe
Vincent Gillespie

John Ridewall,
Fulgencius metaforalis

RALPH HANNA

LIVERPOOL UNIVERSITY PRESS

First published in 2023 by
Liverpool University Press
4 Cambridge Street
Liverpool
L69 7ZU

Copyright © 2023 Ralph Hanna

Ralph Hanna has asserted the right to be identified as the author of this book in accordance with the Copyright, Designs and Patents Act 1988.

All rights reserved. No part of this book may be reproduced, stored in a retrieval system, or transmitted, in any form or by any means, electronic, mechanical, photocopying, recording, or otherwise, without the prior written permission of the publisher.

British Library Cataloguing-in-Publication data
A British Library CIP record is available

ISBN 978-1-83764-475-9

Typeset by Carnegie Book Production, Lancaster
Printed and bound by CPI Group (UK) Ltd, Croydon CR0 4YY

Lectio caelestis placeat tibi, lectio salutis,
    medela mentis, lux iterque vitae.
Picta poetarum fuge carmina, quae venena fundunt
    luxus lutosi polluuntque puros.
Morales libros lege, perlege, corde lecta scribe;
    legas agendo quod facis legendo,
ne culpet factum tua lectio, ne manus loquela,
    ne scandalizent facta vocis usum …

John of Garland,
Parisiana poetria 7.55

God did not redeem man's soul
for the sake of a *cywydd* or an *englyn*.
Your songs, you minstrels,
are nothing but nonsense and vain voices,
and inciting men and women
to sin and falsehood.
Praise of the flesh which carries the soul
to the devil is no good thing.

Dafydd ap Gwilym,
'The Poet and the Grey Friar'
(who speaks)

Contents

Abbreviations	ix
Preface	xi
Introduction	1
The author: on John Ridewall	1
The *Fulgencius* and its dissemination	2
The use and influence of the text	9
Constructing *Fulgencius*: Ridewall's library	13
Editing *Fulgencius metaforalis*	14
Appendix: notes on the manuscripts	23
Bibliography	29

Fulgencius metaforalis: Text and translation

Book 1

[1] Idolatry	38
[2] Saturn/Prudence	56
[3] Jupiter/Love and Friendship	74
[4] Juno/Memory	94
[5] Neptune/Intelligence	110
[6] Pluto/Foresight	128
[7] Apollo/Truth	162
[8] Phaeton/Ambition	192
[9] Mercury/Eloquence	220
[10] Danae/Modesty and Women's Greed	240

[11]	Ganymede/Sodomy	250
[12]	Perseus/Courage	260
[13]	Alceste/Marital Continence	278

Book 2

[1]	Paris/Injustice	294
[2]	Minerva/Contemplative Life	312
[3]	Juno/Worldly Life	338
[4]	Venus/The Life of Pleasure	358

Appendix: Two inserted discussions	374
Textual notes	377
The A tabula	415
A brief commentary	427
Indexes	433
Biblia	433
Auctoritates	435

Abbreviations

Biblia	all texts are identified by the abbreviations of the Stuttgart Vulgate
BL	The British Library, London
C1, C2	Ridewall's commentary on Augustine, *De civitate Dei*: Oxford, Corpus Christi College, MSS 186 [prologue-book III] (C1) and 187 [books VI–VII] (C2)
CJC	*Corpus Iuris Canonici*, ed. Emil L. Richter *et al.*, 2 vols, 2nd edn (Leipzig, 1879–81)
CUL	Cambridge University Library
DCD	Augustine, *De civitate Dei*, ed. *PL* 41
Etym.	Isidore of Seville, *Etymologiae*, ed. *PL* 82
Fulg	Fulgentius, *Mitologiae: Opera*, ed. Rudolf Helm (Leipzig, 1898), 1–80
JBWW	*Jankyn's Book of Wikked Wyves Volume 2: Seven Commentaries ...*, ed. Traugott Lawler (Athens GA, 2014) [*JBWW* 1 (Athens GA, 1997) cited occasionally]
L	(largely in collations, as the text of Marciana, MS Z lat. 494) *Fulgentius metaforalis: Ein Beitrag zur Geschichte der antiken Mythologie im Mittelalter*, ed. Hans Liebeschütz, Studien der Bibliothek Warburg 4 (Leipzig and Berlin, 1926)
Mart	Remigius of Auxerre, *Commentum in Martianum Capellam*, ed. Cora E. Lutz, 2 vols (Leiden, 1962–85) [only a single reference to volume 2, those to volume 1 unmarked]
MLGB3	Richard Sharpe, James Willoughby *et al.*, *Medieval Libraries of Great Britain*, the website mlgb3.bodleian.ox.ac.uk, which incorporates and extends the earlier print versions, ed. N. R. Ker and Andrew G. Watson

MF	Chris L. Nighman *et al.*, 'The Electronic *Manipulus florum* Project', the website https://manipulus-project.wlu.ca
PG	*Patrologia Graeca*
PL	*Patrologia Latina*
Polyc.	John of Salisbury, *Polycraticus*, ed. *PL* 199
SC	R. W. Hunt *et al.*, *A Summary Catalogue of Western Manuscripts in the Bodleian Library at Oxford*, 7 vols in 8 (Oxford, 1895–1953)
Sharpe	Richard Sharpe, *A Handlist of the Latin Writers of Great Britain and Ireland before 1540*, Publications of the Journal of Medieval Latin 1 (Turnhout, 1997)
TNA, PRO	The National Archives, Public Record Office, Kew
VM3	ps.-Albrecht/ps.-Alexander Neckam/Mythographus Vaticanus III, *Poetarium siue Scintillarium poetarum*, *Scriptores rerum mythicarum Latini tres Romae nuper reperti*, ed. Georg H. Bode (Celle, 1834), 152–256
Walther, *Sprich.*	Hans Walther, *Proverbia Sententiaeque Medii Aevi: Lateinische Sprichwörter* ... , 6 vols (Göttingen, 1963–69)

Preface

I began contemplating this project in summer 2013 and began going after it in earnest during spring 2019, in an investigation of MS Bodley 571. But, in the main, this edition is a product of being locked down and, as a consequence, of the enormous debt I owe to the kindness of others. It is always customary to thank librarians for access to the books in their care, but it is more than imperative in the current circumstances. I think here first, impersonally, of Bodley's Librarian Richard Ovenden for making so many electronic sources available online and for facilitating the free reproduction of many others. I am also particularly indebted to Julian Reid, the archivist at Corpus Christi College, Oxford. Julian voluntarily wasted a number of his afternoons to provide me with an enormous number of images of Ridewall's Augustine commentary, many underwriting my essay 2021b, as well as bits in the notes and commentaries here.

While I had many of my own images, mainly of Bodley 571 and Cambridge, Queens' College, MS 10, for the latter of which I have been indebted to Tim Eggington's welcome and generosity, I couldn't have got on without those supplied by others. Estelle Gittens at Trinity College, Dublin provided me one-day service in March 2020 (quite by accident, mine was the first request Trinity received when they announced a free imaging service). James Freeman at Cambridge University Library has been extraordinarily generous, not to mention extraordinarily prompt, with images from Pembroke College, MS 230 and CUL, MS Ii.2.20, as has Laura Carnelos with the Eton College MS. Calum Cockburn, a graduate at University College, London, deserves special thanks for not just checking, as I had asked, but sending me a complete set of images from BL, MS Royal 7 C.i. I am, as always, indebted to the crew at Rare Books and Manuscripts in Bodley's Weston Library; in addition to their usual prompt provision of books *in situ*, they have provided images from MS Auct. F.3.5 and filled in my set from Bodley 571, as well as preparing for me free scans of useful secondary material. Thank you, Oliver House and Hannah Carson, Ernesto Gomez, Angie Goodgame, Gillian Humphreys, Neil Iden, and Nicola O'Toole. In addition, I am grateful to David Morrison at Worcester Cathedral and Richard Gameson at Durham Cathedral for answering queries about their MSS.

I am also much in the debt of two scholars, both now unfortunately departed, who introduced me to and, over many years, sustained my interest in Ridewall. The late Judson Allen was an enthusiastic companion in the Bodleian years ago and made Ridewall a figure central to his views of 'late medieval ethical poetics'. And Nigel Palmer's pursuit of Ridewall (and diagrammatic imagery generally) in late medieval *praedicabilia* has been inspirational.

As always, I am indebted to the team at Liverpool University Press for disseminating my work. First, as always, to my Exeter Medieval Texts editors, Vincent Gillespie and Richard Dance; and to my editor at the press, Clare Litt. To my copy editor, Patrick Brereton. And, of course, to the heroic Rachel Clarke, who has thoroughly outdone herself on this occasion, setting my files with such elegance and precision and making a silk purse from a pig's ear.

Introduction

This volume seeks to fill a gap produced by a century-old error of omission. In 1926 the formidable scholar Hans Liebeschütz published a fine introductory study of medieval mythography. As a centrepiece of his demonstration he offered a text of the Oxford Franciscan John Ridewall's *Fulgencius metaforalis* (the readings of his text are here designated L). Unfortunately, Liebeschütz did not recognise that his presentation, predicated on Venice, Biblioteca Marciana, MS Z lat. 494 (1790), was a partial one. This copy of Ridewall's text, although in an English hand of s. xiv ex., offers only a fragment of the work, roughly one-third of the whole. Since Liebeschütz, although his omission has been reasonably thoroughly discussed and universally recognised, only a single supplement to his text has appeared.[1] I here provide a fuller account of Ridewall's text, both re-editing, from a small group of manuscripts, those portions Liebeschütz printed and extending them to include the full text as most usually transmitted.

The author: on John Ridewall

'Ridewall was 54th regent master to the Oxford Franciscans about 1330. He was at Bâle on 28th Oct., 1340. That is all we know about his life.'[2] References

---

[1] Palmer 2005 includes an important edition of Ridewall's 2.4, discussed pp. 14–16. Liebeschütz's edition is accompanied by images from a derivative version of the text (see further pp. 3–6) in Biblioteca Apostolica Vaticana, MS Palatinus latinus 1066. For a similar image, here illustrating VM3, see Panofsky–Saxl, fig. 40 at 261 (BAV, MS Reginensis latinus 1290, c. 1420), and note their provocative comments, 228, 230, 251–58, 268. Throughout, I refer to Ridewall's text in the medieval spelling 'Fulgencius' and reserve 'Fulgentius', or the abbreviation 'Fulg', for the late antique author. All my references to the text below have the form 'mythography number/line'; those that refer to book 2 are prefaced by '2.' Thus, 2/15 would refer to a discussion of Saturn, but 2.2/15 to one of Minerva.

[2] Smalley 1956, 140, citing Little 170–71; neither Catto nor A. B. Emden's *Biographical Register* has extended this account. Smalley's discussions, including 1960, 109–32, 312–21, never address the *Fulgencius*, although she offered venomous

to him throw up a huge number of variant spellings for his name (Sharpe 901); these include substantial evidence that the second element may have been *-vall* or *-vaus* – i.e., a derivative of Latin *uallis* or its French reflex, not of Old English *weall*.[3] The sporadically recorded 'Musca' must be a nickname, suggesting a small, hyperactive individual (cf. Latin *musca* 'fly').

As Sharpe's bibliographical account (301–02) indicates, Ridewall is known to us as a commentator, scriptural and otherwise; much of the biblical exegesis has been lost and survives today only in citations, principally through his Oxford colleague Robert Holcot OP (see *Robert Holcot*, 225 and n.45, and pp. 9–10 below). My acquaintance with Ridewall's writing, beyond the *Fulgencius*, rests upon selective, yet extensive, reading in the author's texts. This partial account must remain so, because the sheer size of my first source will rebuff any effort at continuous reading. I present frequent analogues from two additional works: the commentary on Augustine's *De civitate Dei*: Oxford, Corpus Christi College, MS 186, fols 1–3ᵛ, 59–75ᵛ, 85–89 (the prologue, 2.4–15, 25–27 in Ridewall's capitulation), and ibid., MS 187, fols 9ᵛ–65 (6.2–9 in Ridewall's capitulation) (about 75,000 words);[4] and the commentary on Walter Map's *Epistola Valerii ad Rufinum*, ed., from all known MSS, *JBWW*, 51–119 (about 9,000 words).

The *Fulgencius* and its dissemination[5]

The mythography, *The metaphorical Fulgentius*, survives in 14 known continuous copies, all but one originally of English provenance.[6] These were

---

opinions about comparable pictorial *distincciones* in her various discussions of Robert Holcot, e.g. 1960, 165–83. See further *Robert Holcot*, 223–30.

[3] Cf. the two familiar North Yorkshire monastic sites, Rievaulx and Jervaulx, 'Ryedale' and 'Uredale', respectively.

[4] I am particularly grateful to the archivist Julian Reid for supplying me extensive images during lockdown. For accounts of these companion volumes, see R. Thomson, 93. They date from late s. xv med., i.e. the 1450s or 1460s, not Thomson's 's. xiv in.' I can only be selective, because, between them, the two books include something approaching 350,000 words (and treat only five of Augustine's 22 books, all of which the author apparently once intended to comment). Ridewall's capitulation differs from that of his source; I have added references to the *PL* edition of the original.

[5] For the best general introduction, see Allen 1979. His 1971 is the only protracted discussion of Ridewall's method and its implications, but should probably be read in concert with Green.

[6] I allow Sharpe's listing (302) to provide particulars, and refer to the copies by their current repository or collection. For fuller and more detailed references, see the 'Appendix' pp. 23–27.

produced throughout the entire run of the later Middle Ages. The oldest is probably Queens' (**Q**), post-1354 but probably of the 1360s; it is closely followed by Dublin (**I**, a dated manuscript, 1375×80) and Royal, which is written in hands that appear reasonably contemporary with the preceding pair. At the other chronological extreme stands the one 'foreign' book, Trier, from s. xv ex., although about half the surviving copies are of s. xv.

However, this primary circulation is dwarfed by that of an excerpted version, the *Compilatio exemplorum Anglicorum* identified by Palmer.[7] He enumerates 81 copies, all but one continental and primarily from 'German-speaking lands'. In this presentation, the excerpted text appears among a variety of other exemplaristic materials, including a version of the *Moralitates* ascribed to Ridewall's Oxonian comrade, the Dominican Holcot. In its fullest (and best-organised) form, this includes summary versions drawn from the entire text, excepting Ridewall's 1.11 (Ganymede), and in the order of his text.

As Palmer demonstrates, this derivative text probably predates any of the extant full manuscripts.[8] While this collection must have drawn on insular sources, the actual compilation might well have been done in a continental centre, the Ridewall materials among Palmer's 'Imagines' derived from an exported copy of the *Fulgencius*. One might note, however, the appearance of one small excerpt from this collection at Worcester Cathedral, MS F.154, fol. 144^v (a discontinuously produced volume also including a full text of *Fulgencius*; see p. 27).

Discussions of *Fulgencius* have been bedevilled by suspicions of the integrity of what we have received. These largely stem from Liebeschütz's presentation: did he print a full integral text or one truncated for reasons not immediately evident? Does the text represent some form of 'rolling revision', Ridewall having released (or allowed the promulgation of) a sequence of interim versions? Or is, indeed, Liebeschütz's Venice manuscript all that Ridewall wrote and the remainder the product of another hand (or hands)?[9]

---

[7] 1991, particularly 147–50.

[8] For example, he cites (149) a Prague manuscript dated 1367, already in a heavily redacted form. On the large number of Prague examples, see 157 and 171; like Malachy the Irishman, available in Prague in a manuscript dated 1379, this transmission speaks to established links between England/Oxford and Bohemia predating the well-known and widely discussed migration of Wycliffite texts. Cf. the provenance of the Berlin MS, p. 13.

[9] See Chance 438–39 n.85 (and for appropriate assessments of her contribution, Wetherbee 1997 and Friedman) and Dinkova-Bruun 2012, 319, 320, 323 n.24. The latter knew only the Royal MS. For useful analyses, see Allen 1979, 25–28; Palmer 2005, 228.

The mythography proper is extant, in gross terms (all copies are plainly working with much the same materials at the verbal level), in five forms:

[a] six chapters, concluding with Pluto: only L, the Venice manuscript printed by Liebeschütz.

[b] eleven chapters, concluding with Ganymede: only CUL Mm.1.18.

[c] twelve chapters, concluding with Perseus: three copies: Berlin, Queens', and Royal.

[d] a two-book presentation, the first of 13 mythographies, the second of four: in all nine remaining copies,[10] except that:

[e] Dublin, Pembroke, and apparently the copy underlying the *Compilatio*, which lacks any analogues, omit 1.11 (Ganymede). It was almost certainly omitted in this place in the exemplar underlying Bodley. There its absence is marked by a marginal note at the conclusion of 1.10 (10/144, fol. 115vb): 'Hic deficit mithologia de gaimede que habetur in fine post picturam ueneris'. As this note indicates, the text is copied separately following 2.4 (Venus, elsewhere the end of the text).[11]

Palmer's *Compilatio* was known to Liebeschütz, who published accounts of its textual order in a variety of manuscripts (56–57). Only a minority of these copies reflects anything like that order on offer in any of the surviving consecutive copies of *Fulgencius*. However, in Palmer's account, the fullest and most carefully organised manuscripts of the *Compilatio* present their derivative versions in two blocks, those he designates 'Imagines A', 18–31

---

[10] Although CUL Ii.2.20 is not quite complete, lacking 2.4/170–244; the text breaks off in mid-column, with the first sentence in Venus [6], and with 'etc.' in the inner margin.

[11] Not only the reference at 10/97 to Perseus as 'undecima mithologia', but the scribe's difficulties in numbering the remaining chapters of book 1 strongly imply that the omission is inherited. Perseus (1.12) is 'duodecima mithologia' at the head (12/1, where both Dublin and Pembroke read 'undecima') but 'undecima' at the end (12/280); Alceste (1.13) is 'duodecima mithologia' in both positions (13/1, 254). These readings imply that the Bodley scribe (or his exemplar) sought to accommodate his text to the absence of the chapter. In this reconstruction, the marginal note must be a belated signal for readers and the text of Ganymede from a source alien to that the scribe transmits elsewhere. See 7/1n for a more widespread (and unrelated) difficulty in numbering Ridewall's chapters.

and 'Imagines B', 23–24. In the second set of selections, *Fulgencius* 1.8 (Phaeton) and 1.5 (Neptune) appear out of sequence from the remainder, but in 'Imagines A' the textual order and contents, omitting, of course, 1.11 (Ganymede), are comparable to those of the fullest versions.[12]

This is convincing information, although scarcely probative. Palmer's *Compilatio* is an excerpt collection, or sequence of such, and many of his copies do not present the 'Imagines' at all. Moreover, as excerpts, such a collection was persistently subject, in its turn, to excerption, users taking what they felt of use (and in any order that might have appeared convenient).[13] Indeed, it is possible that Palmer's ideal order reflects not the 'original' *Compilatio* but a user who arranged some version of it so as to reflect an extensive text of *Fulgencius*.

In this context, Allen's suggestion, drawing on Liebeschütz's presentation of selected manuscripts of the *Compilatio*, is unlikely to convince. From this evidence, Allen sought to demonstrate that there had been a textual version that began where Liebeschütz's left off – at the juncture between 1.6 (Pluto) and 1.7 (Apollo). Unfortunately, this turns out to be yet another example of Palmer's general point about the vagaries of excerpt collections.

A number of Liebeschütz's copies indeed begin with their excerpted version of 1.7 (Apollo). However, in most of the published examples this selection is succeeded by Phaeton, Pluto, and Neptune – i.e., *Fulgencius* 1.8, 6, and 5. The displaced Pluto (1.6) is firmly part of Liebeschütz's text, and Phaeton and Neptune (1.8 and 5, the latter again part of Liebeschütz's text) are simply those portions customarily transmitted separately in Palmer's 'Imagines B'.

Moreover, this presentation continues with materials integral to the text Liebeschütz presents. In these copies, Neptune is succeeded by the selective presentations from *Fulgencius* 1.4, 3, and 2 (and eventually the condensed chapters derived from book 2). The evidence points toward a disordered more or less full text and one that, only accidentally, appears to correspond to a textual situation elsewhere. In fact, the fuller unexcerpted manuscripts imply that, if there were any break in the work, it should fall much later than the end of the Venice manuscript (and of Liebeschütz's text), at the end of Perseus (1.12). I cannot explain this fact, although it would be consonant with a decision to restrict the discussion to figures overtly representing 'vices and virtues', rather than including 'lives', the

---

[12] See the tables at Palmer 1991, 163 and 167.

[13] Cf. Palmer 1991, 142, 149, on the disorder and vagaries of transmission; for the following paragraph, see Allen 1979, 30–32. Although that discussion is relatively open to possible partial transmission, Allen categorically accepted the whole text as Ridewall's at 1982, 222.

subject of book 2, and further predicated on seeing Danae (1.10) and Alceste (the omitted 1.13) as inherently repetitive accounts of women's chastity.[14]

While one cannot be definitive, I think these arguments over the extent of the text reflect a confusion about a very basic point. Were Liebeschütz's edition not to have existed as a century's worth of access to *Fulgencius*, I cannot see that this problem would ever have emerged. Print has an enshrining power, and it produces a confusion between an editor's presentation and a medieval author's work. In this instance, it seems to me to have enshrined an accidental single-manuscript presentation as if it were The Textual Tradition, rather than considering that Liebeschütz unfortunately stumbled upon a manuscript that deviated from all other transmissional evidence.[15]

That majority evidence corresponds to the grossest statements one might offer about the 17-chapter version commonly promulgated. This is consonant with an authorial decision to comment each chapter of Fulgentius's book 1 and the very lengthy opening chapter of book 2, and, as appropriate in a commentary, in the same authorial order.[16] Although, in his account, all his materials represent 'fabulae', there is a distinct break in Fulgentius's presentation here. After his 2.1, although the moralising tenor of his mythography does not change, Fulgentius concentrates upon 'fabula' in its usually accepted sense, 'mythic narrative'. For example, 2.2–4 moralise various episodes from Hercules's career: his love for Omphale, the pursuit of Cacus, the battle with Antaeus.[17] In contrast, while such

---

[14] The vicissitudes of the Ganymede chapter (1.11) seem to me quite other. A plausible benign explanation would emphasise the clear juncture, created by excision, that links Danae (1.10) with her heroic son Perseus (1.12). However, given the scabrous material here, suppression of Ganymede is more apt to reflect deliberate bowdlerisation. One should compare the handling in confessional manuals of inquiries into a penitent's possibly having engaged in 'the sin against nature'. On this point, confessors are encouraged to proceed with circumspection – more apt to be encouraging sexual experimentation than communicating detestation of sin.

[15] Moreover, as one would expect, collation reveals Liebeschütz's text as less than total. Its omissions range from single words (e.g. 1/89, 97) through phrases (e.g. 1/112–14, 118–19) up to parts of four sentences (2/445–50, a bit of homeoarchy accidentally replicated in Bodley 571).

[16] Note Ridewall's persistent references to Fulgentius's 'processus' and 'littera'.

[17] The last is the subject of the oldest appropriation of Fulgentius I have found, c. 1280, at *Malachy* 1576–94 (and cf. Malachy's depiction of the Fulgentian attributes of Mercury at 825–37). Of course, Malachy was a Franciscan (and following through on the Fulgentian reference to *ymagines deorum* Ridewall reproduces at 2.1/146–50). On the persistence of such imagery in Franciscan texts see Palmer 1983, 180–84.

narratives are scarcely absent from the account, the preceding materials are centred upon analyses of single figures, strongly pictorial and driven by the attributes assigned to each. This portrayal runs all the way from the introduction of Saturn (cf. Fulg 1.2, 18/10–13, with 2/70–81) to the conclusion of Venus (Fulg 2.1, 40/21–24, cited at 2.4/224–27). Moreover, as I will argue in my commentary, Ridewall imposes a coherent pattern on the materials selected. I would argue that Liebeschütz's Venice MS represents a deliberately excerptive effort, largely the presentation of the traditional 'master-virtue' Prudentia.

As Allen saw, the strongest evidence for Ridewall's single authorship comes from repeated recourse to the same cited authorities. Such behaviour would join segments that an insistence on Liebeschütz's edition as The Text would render separate. Rambam's *Guide/Dux* provides one example (a citation early on in 1/14, but also at 7/49). Moreover, two of these repetitions involve texts one would describe as exceedingly rare. Hyginus appears at 3/275, but also at 11/130 and 12/249; there is but a single reference to a copy in the *Corpus* of medieval library catalogues presented in *MLGB*. Yet more telling are dispersed citations from Robert Grosseteste's translation of the Greek lexicon *Suda* at 6/91 and 11/26; this work survives only fragmentarily, but Oxford Greyfriars owned both the Greek manuscript from which Grosseteste had translated and a complete copy of his translation.[18]

More fundamentally, Ridewall's own words suggest that L represents a deliberately truncated account, basically an analysis of the 'master-virtue' Prudentia. After all, in his brief *accessus* at the head, Ridewall promises not just virtues but the opposed sins as well. Both get equal billing in that account and, consequently, the authorially imagined text should include something like Phaeton (1.8) or Venus (2.4).

So far as I can see, there is but a single moderately plausible argument for either multiple authorship or serial authorial promulgation of the text.

---

[18] The *Corpus*'s Hyginus does not actually come from a traditional medieval library, but UO24.37a, a printed book at Oxford, Corpus Christi College, s. xvi in. Cf. Brumble's slightly inaccurate comment, 'Hyginus (fl. before 207 AD), *Fabulae* and *Poetica Astronomica*, were unknown from about the 6th century until his work was published in Basle in 1535' (420). However, the text was also cited by 'the Digby 221 mythographer' (Allen 1970), as well as by Alexander Neckam, and there's a further English copy in Cambridge, Trinity College, MS R.15.32. Grosseteste's Greek manuscript of the *Suda* is now Leiden, Bibliotheek der Rijksuniversiteit, MS Vossianus Gr. F.2, and the only extensive fragment of his translation in a MS probably from Greyfriars, Bodleian, MS Digby 11. For further discussion, see the entry in the 'Index fontium', Hunt 1955, and the reference to another rare Grosseteste translation, also available at Greyfriars, at 6/95 and the textual note.

This would be predicated upon a considerable amount of repetitiousness, materials invoked in *ipsissima verba*, at different points. For example, an extensive discussion of Ulysses's travails, cited from Apuleius, appears at both 2/86 and 12/57; or Boethius's 1m7.20–31 is cited at both 1/135 and 7/491. These might be construed as independent efforts, clumsy efforts to extend Ridewall's work, while plagiarising some of his more memorable moments.

However, as 'plausible' implies, I don't find this argument of much weight. Ridewall clearly had favourite passages to which he returned. The citation from Boethius appears again in his Augustine commentary, for example, and, as I will argue in my commentary, is central to Ridewall's concerns. Moreover, Ridewall's *ordinatio*, a sequence of chapters addressing this virtue or that vice, presupposes that readers might most routinely consult the text selectively and topically; in the process, they might overlook relevant materials Ridewall had disposed elsewhere. The repetitions would, in this reading, as do Ridewall's abundant cross-references – the Augustine commentary reveals them as almost a definitive authorial 'tic' – compensate for an account otherwise rigorously segmented.[19]

A particularly pregnant example appears in a reprise of a passage from Chrysostom, first cited at 6/159 and repeated, with a cross-reference to the earlier account, at 10/120. The first occurrence represents Ridewall's most explicit and extended discussion of the prominent sin Avarice (although it is certainly one emphasis in the Juno of 2.3). However, in the Fulgentian argument, the citation is subordinated beyond discovery; the extensive description of Cerberus/Avarice (it covers 6/122–244) forms a subsidiary discussion, buried within a chapter ostensibly devoted to *prouidencia*/Foresight. Moreover, the citation is particularly resonant when repeated in its second context, a discussion of Danae's alleged 'corruption' by gold; Chrysostom offers a stridently feminised portrayal of the vice ('domina ... meretrix ... Nunquam pudet'), one thus particularly appropriate in a discussion of female virtue destroyed. On the basis of examples like these, I find no compelling reason to question the integrity of the text's majority transmission.[20]

---

[19] For the Boethius citation, see C2 fol. 23ᵛ and my discussion at p. 430; I consider the genre and use-value of *Fulgencius* at pp. 10–11, 415–16, 431. A sample cross-reference from Ridewall's commentary on Augustine, C2 fol. 22: 'Et de ista materia loquitur Augustinus libro 19° istius uoluminis, capitulo 25° ... sicud bene deducit Augustinus, libro 19° istius uoluminis, capitulo prius allegato'. (The reference connects the discussion of Augustine's 'uera religio non a terrena aliqua ciuitate instituta est' in *DCD* 6.4, cols 179–80, with the refutation of an essentially Stoic view that the pursuit of virtue is an end in itself at col. 656.)

[20] Cf. 2.3/3–4n.

The use and influence of the text

Catto asserts that Ridewall's 'work had little circulation, mainly in Oxford and among Franciscans'. While this is certainly true of Ridewall's spottily preserved biblical exegesis and his Augustine commentary (academic texts of a sort in which Catto was deeply invested), it profoundly misrepresents Ridewall's influence. Similarly, Catto underestimates the quality of his library.

There is one qualification, partially supportive of Catto's views, to be added immediately. While Ridewall's non-exegetical works, as I will show, were widely circulated, they passed as those of yet another medieval 'quidam' (quite the opposite of the pan-European name-recognition accorded Robert Holcot). Here the case of the commentary on Walter Map's *Dissuasio* is telling. This is the most widely circulating of the seven separate commentaries on Map's 'epistola'; it is transmitted in 15 manuscripts (four of them continental). Its author is identifiable only because Cambridge University Library, MS Ff.6.12, fol. 159^v, offers the colophon, 'Explicit exposicio Ridewas'. The ascription is authoritative, on the basis of textual detail (see the textual note to 2.4/61–62 *Tayde*) and the local affiliations of the Cambridge manuscript: it was used in Oxford, in the early fifteenth century, to produce another copy of Alan of Lille's *Anticlaudianus*, BL, MS Royal 8 A.xiii. No other reader was so fortunate, and while, as I will show, Ridewallian moments are commonplace across Europe, they were never known as his.

There is ample evidence for Ridewall's circulation in 1330s Oxford. For example, as I have already indicated, Robert Holcot, on several occasions, refers to his contemporary. One of these examples is well known; in his commentary on minor prophets, Oxford, Balliol College MS 26, fol. 38^v (on Os 9), he reproduces Ridewall's full division for 'idolatria'.[21] But this citation, unacknowledged as such, represents only the tip of the iceberg. References to Ridewall, mainly to the biblical commentaries, are dotted through Holcot's texts. For example, in the same manuscript, fol. 122^v (on So 3:2), Holcot says he is building on one of Ridewall's accounts, 'quod in parte ait Prudencius de pictura Spei, et magister Iohannis Rideualensis addit'. Or, on Ioel 2, in Gray's Inn, MS 2, fol. 47rb (Balliol, fol 58^v has omitted part of the text):

> Unde Augustinus, 10 *Confessionum*, capitulo 2, 'De Oreste et Pilade quod traditur, si non fingitur, quod uellent pro inuicem simul mori, quia morte peius erat eis non simul uiuere'. Magister Iohannes Rid' dicit quod unus optulit se pro alio ad immolandum in templo Eufegenie.

[21] Cf. 1/204–11 with the excerpt at Smalley 1960, 173–74.

The citation is *Confessiones* 4.6.11 (*PL* 32:697–98), and this comment must emerge from Ridewall's lost exegesis, probably on one of those passages discussing 'amici' in Proverbs. But Holcot's report directs one to texts with which Ridewall, who cites at least four other works of Ovid, was surely familiar, the extensive accounts of the two friends in Taurus at *Tristia* 4.4 and *Ex Ponto* 3.2.

The *magister sermonum* Siegfried Wenzel presents another contemporary Oxford citation (2008, 301). This appears in the concluding sermon in a lecture course on Lombard's *Sentences* delivered by the Dominican Ralph Frisby. The opening of Frisby's first division offers an extensive yet selective development of four of the attributes Ridewall ascribes to Jupiter, here as a figure for charity.

I have already discussed the next evidence for the text's circulation. This is its excerption in Palmer's *Compilatio*, whether at home or abroad, and the head of an extensive continental circulation.

Slightly later – probably early in the 1340s – Ridewall's text appears prominently in the Benedictine Pierre Bersuire's Paris revision of his *Ovidius moralizatus* (*Reductorium morale*, book 15). Bersuire had originally composed the work, a fable-by-fable commentary on the *Metamorphoses*, indiscriminately offering readings both *in bono* and *in malo*, in Avignon in the 1330s. At that point, of course, Ridewall may not yet have composed *Fulgencius*, but Bersuire found his text in Paris and cited from it, particularly in his opening chapter, 'De formis figurisque deorum'. He did not, as he says explicitly, know his author's name.[22]

By the later fourteenth century there is reasonably abundant evidence of the text's circulation among the audience for which it was intended: preachers. Wenzel (2005, 293–94) offers summary evidence from a little later, in the fifteenth century, for the general currency of materials at least comparable to Ridewall's. He cites 'three dozen uses' of similar Oxonian materials, elaborate pictorial divisions (not all will be Ridewall's, but some Holcot's), across nine sermon collections, and has overlooked a tenth, which he published subsequently. I would think this almost certainly underestimates the evidence, given that Wenzel does not seem to have consulted unpublished portions of *Fulgencius*.[23]

---

[22] For Bersuire's initial reference to *Fulgencius*, see the translations at Minnis and Scott 369; W. Reynolds 66–67 (with facing page Latin, perhaps a more available version than Engels's editions, as is Ghisalberti 87–101). W. Reynolds 72–75 provides one extensive passage explicitly from Ridewall, largely Bersuire's organisation of a description through citation of Ridewall's divisions. For the 60-odd manuscripts of Bersuire's full text (versions not distinguished), see Coulson–Roy no. 2 (24–27) and Engels.

[23] See further Delcorno, with some interesting methodological observations.

I simply point to two of Wenzel's published examples. An Oxford academic sermon from Wenzel's 'W' (c. 1400) uses the first four divisions of Ridewall's Minerva (1995, 313). More striking is the material in Cambridge, Jesus College, MS Q.A.13 (James 13, 'J/5–18' at Wenzel 2005, 523). At one point, this preacher cites 'the commentator on Fulgentius, book 2', and his quotation, which is *not* a pictorial division and has thus escaped Wenzel, is surely from 2.2/336–51 (Wenzel 2008, 285).

However, a development of the argument later in this sermon (287–89), Apollo's palace in Ovid, *Metamorphoses* 2, as the city of this world – the preacher's theme is Ac 9:6 'Ingredere civitatem' – is very probably the fruit of further reading in *Fulgencius*. Phaeton (1.8) is unique in Ridewall's text as being constructed virtually whole-cloth from Ovid's account, not Fulgentius's, with extensive citations, cf. 'qualiter Pheton intrauit aulam solis et palacium', followed by *Metamorphoses* 2.32–34 (note 'hac ... arce', 8/26). Ridewall's appearance here is an early and dispersed example; this sermon celebrates the inclaustration of a named anchorite and will have been preached in western Norfolk or Suffolk shortly after 1377. There are yet earlier and further dispersed examples; as Wenzel notes, John Waldeby, a famous York Augustinian preacher who d. 1372, cites Ridewall in his annual cycle, the *Novum opus dominicale*.[24]

A similar Yorkshire example comes from just after the turn of the century. A 'John de Foxton, capellanus' was inspired to extend Ridewall's divine images to include not all the virtues but all the planetary gods, with illustrations. His *Liber Cosmographiae*, so far as it is possible, pillages *Fulgencius* extensively – and, once he had run out of Ridewallian material, Foxton constructed his own imitative versions to present the remaining planets. Foxton apparently donated the unique copy of his work, Cambridge, Trinity College, MS R.15.21, to the tiny house of Trinitarian friars in Knaresborough.[25]

---

[24] See Hanna 2005–06, with some discussion of Nicholas Philipp, Franciscan of King's Lynn, one of Wenzel's examples in his 2005 discussion. To the references assembled in that essay, add TNA, PRO, C143/397/13: the feoffees (?) of the now-inclaustrated Alice Huntingfield's late husband, 1380/1, granted 'Huntingfieldhall manor' in East Bradenham to the prior and convent of St Edmund's (cf. C143/410/7, 1390/1, where the abbey received further rents in the manor). As I will shortly indicate, Bury were already in possession of a copy of *Fulgencius*, and the house had an anchorhold in the cemetery, at least at times with a woman recluse. For an edition of Waldeby's reference, see Akae 254–56.

[25] See *John de Foxton*, chs 65–66 (168–76) and 70 (180–85), materials from Jupiter and Saturn, respectively. The edition incorporates all Friedman's earlier publications on the text; for Foxton, see Sharpe 251; for the illustrations, see further Scott 2:114–17.

It is possible, although not readily demonstrable, that the St Albans monk Thomas Walsingham (d. c. 1422) used Ridewall in constructing his *De archana deorum* (so Clark 2004, 182, 196). The difficulty here is Walsingham's extensive debt to mythographic tradition, particularly the mapping of his argument upon Bersuire's presentation. His reliance upon the same sources to which Ridewall continuously returned, notably VM3 and Mart, renders any demonstration difficult, particularly in the context of Walsingham's encyclopedic tendencies.

Another contemporary example emerges from considerably further afield. Domenico di Bandino (d. 1418) was an Aretine encyclopedist. He spent much of his active career, 1381-99, teaching in Florence, where he numbered no less than Coluccio Salutati among his friends. In his encyclopedic writings he frequently cites Ridewall, although, as apparently also Waldeby, he did not know the author and believed he was citing the late antique author, not his commentator.[26]

MLGB3 shows at least further interest in the text, if not explicit examples of its use. Half the extant manuscripts have secure medieval institutional provenances, widely dispersed, both geographically and in terms of professional affiliation:

CUL Ii.2.20: from Norwich Cathedral OSB;[27]

Cambridge, Pembroke College: a medieval College book [= *Corpus* UC43.113-14];[28]

Dublin: from Cambridge OESA;

Durham: from Carlisle Cathedral OSA;

Eton: a medieval College book;[29]

Royal: from Ramsey (Hunts.) OSB (also in the 1542 inventory of Henry VIII's library as *Corpus* H2.135);

Worcester Cathedral: a medieval Cathedral book.

[26] See Hankey 192, 194.

[27] In addition, another medieval Norwich Cathedral book, now Norwich Cathedral, MS 2, s. xv², with substantial chunks of Palmer's *Compilatio* (excerpted *Fulgencius* at fols 164-72), includes at fols 188-89 a brief excerpt from the head of the full text (1/1-49).

[28] In *MLGB3*, entered as 'Fulgentius', not 'Ridewall', as are a dozen other books from late fourteenth- or fifteenth-century catalogues, all potentially examples of this text, rather than the late antique one on which it comments (analogous to Bandino's confusion).

[29] An Oxonian's bequest to a fellow of Eton after 1477, with Malachy (probably a Franciscan staple), and earlier in an Oxford loan-chest. See further Hanna 2017.

In addition, the Berlin MS has a provocative institutional provenance. From 1422 it belonged to the Dominican convent at Soest (Westphalia). It was donated by Jakob von Soest, who had earlier been a theology student in Prague, which was, as I have noted, an early centre for circulation of Palmer's excerpted version of the text.

MLGB3's *Corpus* also records a number of copies now lost:

Bury St Edmunds OSB, cited by Henry Kirkstede, s. xiv med. (K520.1);

Oxford, All Souls College, c. 1433 and later (UO7.429, etc.);

Oxford OESA, c. 1430 (F35.4);

York OESA, 1382, two copies (FA8.351b and FA8.490m).

Both the first and the last of these are provocative. Wenzel's inclaustration sermon may derive its materials from the same copy Kirkstede saw, and both Waldeby and John de Foxton are apt to have used one of the copies from the York Augustinians.[30]

Finally, Dinkova-Bruun has presented a late fifteenth-century example. Notes in British Library, MS Cotton Titus D.xx offer an analogue to Palmer's *Compilatio*. This writer provides selective excerpts from throughout *Fulgencius*, in this case including materials from the Ganymede chapter.[31] In all, this is an extensive enough showing, certainly an indication that Ridewall's reach substantially exceeded the currently visible transmission of his text. Moreover, I am certain that it remains an extremely partial account. In the absence of the full text, citations in unpublished medieval sermons have probably escaped notice. Similarly, the currently burgeoning studies of mythographic materials in later medieval poetry will probably unearth further examples. My bibliography below is deliberately extensive, designed to direct attention to further possible examples.

Constructing *Fulgencius*: Ridewall's library

I have taken up Ridewall's sources elsewhere (2021b) and will return briefly to the issue in the commentary below (pp. 428–31). Here I wish only to emphasise two points, both concerning Ridewall's 'learnedness' (or its opposite). First, there is a disparity between Ridewall's mythographic

---

[30] See further Palmer 1991, 147–48 n.37, for references to two copies at Erfurt, Collegium Amplonianum, s. xv in. (a library with a number of other Oxonian texts).

[31] For details of the manuscript, see Dinkova-Bruun 2013 and Copeland 2011.

knowledge, which is decidedly limited, and the deeply learned use to which he puts it, his 'metaphorical' commitments. These are customarily expressed through citations, particularly profuse in his Augustine commentary, that reveal the author's tactile familiarity with an extensive and varied library collection.

Second, just as Ridewall's mythographic knowledge appears limited to what he could glean from a few commonplace sources, he also relied, although I think only marginally, on compendia. At least some of his citations have clearly been lifted from the popular collection of *dicta*, Thomas of Ireland's *Manipulus florum*.[32] Here the most provocative example appears at 8/258, the ascription of a citation to Bernard, *Exposicio regule beati Benedicti* 3.7, certainly not a work from Bernard's canon and an attribution implausible on its face. However, the same citation, with the same ascription, down to the capitulation, appears as *MF* prelacio bl, and the source remains otherwise unidentified. However, as I argued in 2021b, Ridewall's consultation of *MF* was at best peripheral, and, in the main, he vindicates both inquisitive reading in a range of sources and high standards of scholarly competence, predicated on an extensive library, presumably that at Oxford Greyfriars.

Editing *Fulgencius metaforalis*

Palmer (2005, 228) provides the only useful conspectus of the relations between the manuscripts. Considering the full copies, only those extensive enough to include his text, 'Venus' (2.4, the concluding discussion), he finds the transmission developed through three branches:

α	B	γ
Worcester	Durham	I Trinity
Pembroke	Auct.	Trier
O Bodley		
Eton		

(in the form W[P(OE)])

I have found Palmer's textual materials inspiring, and have used them to guide my (covid-limited) researches. These have included detailed examination of a representative of each of Palmer's groups, O (= α), A (= β), and I (= γ). In addition, although I have not inspected it thoroughly, I have consulted the

---

[32] I'm particularly indebted to Dinkova-Bruun (2013, 328 n.8), who spotted *MF* iusticia et iustus y (ascribed to Cassiodorus on Ps 14) as underlying 2.1/141 and set me off on this investigation.

still not clearly affiliated Queens'. Like Royal and Berlin, this largely Ovidian volume ends Ridewall's *Fulgencius* with Perseus, but it may well be the earliest surviving copy of the work. In addition, **Q** looks suspiciously like the kind of book that might have emerged from a mendicant background, and, along with Liebeschütz's Venice manuscript, which includes his brief commentary on the Apocalypse as well as the truncated *Fulgencius*, it is the only surviving manuscript with more than one of Ridewall's works. (Q also includes the commentary on Map's *Dissuasio*.)

My examination of Palmer's edition leads, however, to some qualifications. These are in excess of the normal caveat, that the textual situation in an isolated portion of a text may not be typical of the whole. Palmer's report of manuscript relations plainly must rely upon his collations, those readings deemed erroneous, removed from the text and consigned to his apparatus; agreements among manuscripts in readings thus identified as errors provide the evidence that underlies his report of the transmission.

My inspection of this material produces a measure of befuddlement. First, even from my limited survey, the collation is incomplete; while the odd unrecorded variants I have discovered may be quirks of individual copies (and thus valueless for mapping transmission), one cannot be certain that is the case *ex silentio*. However, Palmer's collations present more serious problems.

Fundamentally, *Fulgencius* is a text for practitioners, a guide for individuals looking for exemplary material for sermon amplification. Certainly, the available evidence of the text's circulation I have cited above, the extensive list of copies with institutional affiliations, implies that the text found that practitioner audience. As I have argued elsewhere (*Malachy* 25–27), this is a situation in which usefulness trumps textual integrity; practitioners tend to record what they have received in forms they find convenient, not necessarily those they have received.

On that earlier occasion, I outlined a range of commonplace variations that are scarcely worth cluttering up a collation with, much less attempting to analyse. These include such matters as word-order, variation among the conjunctions and particles that connect sentences and clauses, variation among prepositions (and the cases that follow them), the presence or absence of punctuational features such as 'scilicet' and 'id est', simple synonymous substitutions, variations of verb prefixes and of tenses, the presentation of authorities, and the forms of references. As a result of this freedom in reproducing the text, many variants are simply indifferent; they do not necessarily reflect a stemmatic vertical transmission but a paraphrasal presentation in a form deemed usefully equivalent to what has been received. These choices may, obviously enough, get transmitted vertically, but equally, because commonplace substitutions, may be completely independent and only accidentally converge with their similars.

I have called such readings 'indifferents', because they are generally similar in their purport to other forms of the text and because, as variants, they cannot be 'resolved'. That is, one such reading cannot clearly be shown to have been the source of the others. In such a situation, the editorial recourse is conventionally 'follow one's copy-text'; that is, in the absence of any certainty, provide the perhaps questionable reading of that manuscript whose forms one is reproducing. But just as such a printed reading remains questionable, so also do all its alternatives, and in a situation in which rectitude and error remain indeterminate such readings cannot contribute to a transmissional genetic analysis.

Again befuddlement. From Palmer's report one cannot determine the extent to which variations of this type have underwritten his report of the transmission. However, a number of readings I would identify as 'indifferent' appear in his text to rectify what Palmer identifies as errors in his copy-text W. Examples would include 29/21 concomitantur/comitantur, 32/23 significat/figurat, 50/39 picture/picture de dea Ueneris nudacione.[33]

In addition, at least some of Palmer's evidence is predicated upon taking as authorial readings ones that, in my analysis, are simply errors. At 20/16 deportata/delata, although Fulgentius may read the latter, in line 52 Ridewall describes this action as *deportacione*, the linked variant *equor* is alien to Ridewall's usage, and, at best, the reading is probably indifferent. In 35/26 Palmer suppresses *inimica*, although that is the reading both of Jerome's text and of Palmer's citation version. At 67/52 famosa/famosa et formosa, the added phrase is scribal; it represents what I call a 'doublet of doubt', an instance where a scribe, faced with an ambiguous abbreviated form, inscribes his confusion and allows the reader to choose between alternative interpretations.

Insofar as Palmer's stemma depends upon a sequence of choices like these, one cannot repose utter trust in its value. Moreover, my investigation across the manuscripts strongly suggests that the tradition is basically bifid, α and β only; my examination of the γ representative I finds that its independence is illusory, that it is a conflated text, one predicated upon both other groups, and that the concurrence of its readings with those of α or β offers no independent support for either. I would say, as preface to my analysis, that the pool of significant variants is not particularly extensive, a reflection of a text not in wide circulation and generally copied for professional use (and thus, within limits I have already suggested, fairly carefully).

---

[33] The number preceding the solidus is the line number in my edition of 2.4; that following, of Palmer's edition of 'Venus'. However extensive – and thus significant – the last variant may appear, it represents a commonplace scribal desire for conclusiveness; cf. *Malachy* 36–37.

For those portions of the text Liebeschütz edited (= L), his copy appears closest to **A**. As a survey of the collations printed below will show, in the first six mythographies **AL** agree in erroneous readings where **IO** appear correct on around 55 occasions. These testify to the common descent of this pair of MSS.

I have surveyed **Q** from that manuscript's presentation of just over 3500 words, 1/121–235 and 3/191–94/187 and spot-checked elsewhere.[34] This MS is decidedly not a copy of Palmer's α, but related to **AL** (its agreements with **I** are attenuated). The scribe of **Q** frequently introduces advanced variants not paralleled in the other manuscripts examined: e.g., 1/163 Scriptura **AIL**, scripta **Q**; 1/166 *om.* primus ydolatra (**I** *om.* the second word); 1/167–68 ortam esse] incepisse; 1/168–69 *om.* rex Babilonis; 1/170 exhibebat] fecit, etc.[35] However, a number of agreements in error represent a stronger statistical showing for **Q**'s β exemplar than do the **AL** materials I have just cited. My survey has been predicated upon only 3500 words, less than a quarter of the full sample I have used in surveying **AL** agreements. On 17 occasions **Q** shares an erroneous reading with either **A** or **L** or both; on another three occasions, where it is not erroneous, **Q**'s reading shows that it cannot be derived from a source common with **IO**. (On a scaled basis, this showing would be equivalent to about 80 agreements of **AL**.) A distinct minority of examples show agreements in error with **O** or **I** (4× and 3×, respectively); however, in five of these seven cases the erroneous reading also appears in **A** or **L** as well.

However, one should note that **Q** is incomplete, lacking 1.13 and all of book 2, and that, on this showing, its evidence is *déjà lu*. It will be of only minimal help for those portions of the text provided by Liebeschütz, for there, when it is not, as frequently, independently deviant, it simply reproduces that text or that text as supported by **A**. Particularly given its frequent individual idiosyncrasies, I have chosen not to present its readings, although I will return to them briefly at p. 22.

On the customary stemmatic rule of 'complementary evidence', one might expect that **I** and **O** would form a pair with shared transmission. Certainly, over the portion of the text that Liebeschütz printed, **I** agrees with **O** more often than any other copy. The collations include 27 unambiguous examples of agreement, with another 11 examples where the pair agree in error in the presence of a single β copy. However, there is a considerable

---

[34] The intervening materials appeared on the now-lost two central bifolia of the first quire in this MS.

[35] I would particularly note 4/126, where **Q** reads 'Zepopum' for 'Theopompum'. This is a reasonably common misrepresentation of the **Q** exemplar's 'Þeopopum' (Latinate scribes often exchange 'þ' and 'ȝ'/'z'). The English graph appears rarely across Ridewall's writings, here cf. 8/48 ȝouialem.

amount of scattering evidence to qualify this conclusion. The pair OL appears in erroneous agreement on 12 occasions and the pair AO on five. One might further compare the variants at 1/71 (very probably convergent error, rather than vertical transmission), 1/90, 1/204, and 2/12.

Moreover, however strong the showing of I's relationship with O, it is overwhelmed by I's numerous agreements with either A or L in erroneous readings. AI occur together in error on 35 occasions, in this case unambiguous evidence roughly as strong as that supporting IO. In addition, IL agreements in error appear on about 20 occasions. And there are frequent examples of all three copies in agreement, 14 over the first 600 lines of the text. (These are not necessarily erroneous testimony to β, but arguably right readings where I have taken O as functionally indifferent variation.) But these examples strongly suggest that I does not represent an independent version of the text, as Palmer argued, although its propensity to join with O remains at this point puzzling.

However, this is far from the full story. On p. 249, marginally by 2.3/318 *emungat munera*, I's scribe, Adam Stockton, OESA of Cambridge, has written a note: 'respice bene istam partem folii, quia est aliqualiter facta' (recheck carefully this part of the leaf, because this part has been done in some different way). While there is no sign that Adam followed through on this bit of self-instruction, it does indicate his access to, and his detailed familiarity with, at least two versions of the text. He apparently recognised that they differed significantly at this point.

There was good reason for Adam to pause here, for his note immediately precedes the single certain interpolation I have found in my survey. As this passage appears in O, the chapter concludes with a reasonably lengthy passage from Alan of Lille and a shorter one from Peter of Blois, both excoriating courtly flatterers. In Adam's exemplar at this point, however, both passages had been extended, plumped up with additional materials mainly, but not exclusively, derived from adjacent materials in the *originalia*.[36] The result is disproportionate, a considerably longer chunk of citation than anywhere else in the work; on that basis, I identify it as interpolation, enthusiasm for a topic that routinely animates clerical authors. The first of these additions also appears in A, a fact that would indicate that, whatever Adam's possible affiliation with an α copy (O) in those portions of the text Liebeschütz edited, he was at this point copying from a manuscript affiliated with β. (On the absence of the second passage from A, see p. 22.)

This is far from the only example of such consultation of multiple exemplars in I. Blatant evidence for such behaviour becomes apparent almost immediately after Liebeschütz's version of the text ends. Assuming

---

[36] On these texts, see further the introduction to the textual notes on the Appendix, p. 413.

A and Q to adequately represent β, at the head of 1.7 (Apollo), that version of the text adopted an idiosyncratic chapter numeration; this is partially reproduced, on occasion as overtly corrected readings, in I. (See the full discussion, in the textual note to 7/1, pp. 393–94.) In addition, a dispersed set of minor erroneous readings offers further testimony to Adam's access to both textual versions, even as his text continues generally to reflect α affiliations. A sample of such readings would include:

7/24 nouem partes] nouem uel decem A, nouem partes uel decem I, Q here as O (see the textual note);

7/130 uirtutis ueritatis] ueritatis AI (ueritatis *over eras.* I) and Q (see the textual note);

8/143–45 Et² ... habenas] *om.* A and Q, *added marg.* I;

8/183 donacionem] de[a]cionem (= ? deificacionem) A, \de/[i]nacionem I, Q here as O (see the textual note);

8/298 tuta] tua A and Q, tuta *over eras.* I; and

12/270 filii Excelsi omnes] *om.* A, *over eras.* I (Q has ended at 12/198).

Many of these examples are associated with overt signs of correction. I is difficult to read at the best of times, in large measure because of persistent idiosyncratic abbreviations (it was, after all, copied for private use). But difficulties abound because of a heavy level of correction, much through zealous erasure that renders original readings usually irrecoverable. Inferentially, these represent places where Stockton had originally copied from his β source, but replaced its reading with that of his α one – or, irritatingly, the reverse. My collations will indicate a substantial number of examples, but only a selection from a persistent practice (my report generally restricted to occasions where significant variation occurs elsewhere).

I return for a moment to the variation I have cited above from those portions of the text Liebeschütz edited. Normally, genetic affiliation is subject to two tests: a demonstration of numerical superiority, but *also* a demonstration of consistency, that agreements in variation occur at roughly the same rate across the full text. The readings I have summarised above would fail any such second test. Although agreements of AI and IL are numerically strong, there are significant gaps in their occurrence: in those portions of the text Liebeschütz edited, only two examples appear in 1/101–2/55, and none in 2/170–3/94 or in 4/112–5/22. I would further note that eight of the 20-odd agreements of IO appear in these portions. (See also the textual note to 4/112–13.)

One might at this point return to Stockton's note by the interpolation on p. 249. This would seem to indicate that, although he had access to two textual versions, he was unable to access both of them simultaneously. Given that much of his copying explicitly occurred while he was on the road, Stockton copied the text in chunks from two different exemplars, one of which stayed in his house and the other of which travelled with him. (And he was not particularly careful about which was providing copy on any given occasion.) His erasures and other corrections represent his *post hoc* effort to accommodate the pair's readings.[37]

One should, I think, conclude that **I** offers little independent evidence about Ridewall's text. Generally, it will confirm, on an unpredictable basis, what one can learn from those two branches already in evidence and from which it has derived its readings. In editorial terms, this means that, insofar as Palmer has constructed his text of 'Venus' through a stemmatic logic, the results will remain subject to doubt. Palmer's three-branched stemma, in which I represents a separate line of descent γ, will have directed his resolution of the variants: in this situation, stemmatic theory dictates that, where two branches agree against a third, their reading is presumed correct. Removing the third branch, Palmer's γ, provides no such assurance. On the basis of the MSS I have examined personally, coupled with the gross dimensions of the text each copy conveys,[38] I would tentatively suggest the following revised stemma:

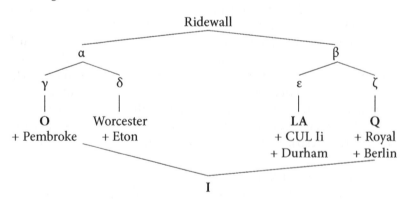

[37] I would simply note in this regard that the appearance of striking and flagrant β errors at the opening of 1.7 is overdetermined. At this point, Adam clearly was following his β exemplar; in the first 700+ lines from the head of 1.7, there are 21 agreements of **AI** (all but three of these readings also appear in **Q**), but only one of **IO**.

[38] So far as I have investigated, the varying dimensions of the text reflect archetypes available to the scribes: e.g. trial collations of CUL Ii.2.20 and Royal from around 3400 words (9/258–12/39) would affiliate these versions with **AQ**.

Wherever variation has occurred, there are no directives, only two competing readings, and the text can be determined only through editorial *ingenium*. Of course, Ridewall's frequent citations very often offer decisive evidence; with one exception, discussed in the notes to 8/149ff., these are verbally precise and can be used to determine the anterior reading. For better or worse, and with a substantially narrower range of variants than were at Palmer's disposal, that is the course I have followed here.

I present the text in the form of O/MS Bodley 571 (although I have moved its deferred copy of Ganymede to the position it has in the other copies, as 1.11). My general form of presentation follows that adopted in *Malachy*. In addition to the variants excluded from the collation there, I have adopted the same rules of transcription (*Malachy* 9 n.8) and cite references to patristic writings from *PL*, not 'more authoritative' editions (*Malachy* 35 n.56).[39] However, to the classes of variants excluded there I have added a large number of indifferent variations ceaselessly repeated and, in their frequency, perhaps peculiar to this text.[40] These include frequent 'de deo/dee' as either 'deo', 'dee', or inappropriately intruded 'de' before either; alternation between 'quomodo', 'qualiter', and 'quare'; similarly, variations involving 'patet per' ('p3 p'/'patet'/'per'); alternation between 'fingo' and '(de)pingo' (and whether either, or other references to 'images', require the clarifying subject 'poete'); variation between 'prudencia' and 'prouidencia'; between forms of 'nomino' and 'noto'; between various forms of 'ueritas' and 'uirtus'; between those of 'questio' and 'conclusio'; between forms of 'dico', 'doceo', 'debeo', and the adjective 'durus' (the last usually misreadings of 'dnr' [= dicuntur] as 'dure'); variation among adverbs such as 'bene' and 'pulcre' (or their absence) in the introductions to citations; between verbs indicating an authorial statement, whether 'pono', 'dico', 'recito', 'tango', 'tracto', or 'ostendo'; whether Fulgentius speaks 'in littera' or not; whether a verse inset is 'metrice' or 'in hiis uersibus' or not; alternation between such introductions as 'Sequitur X-a mithologia de' and 'X-a mithologia est de'. Although I discuss the most flagrant examples in my notes, I generally ignore misnumbering of mythographies or their constituent parts. In all these situations, unless it is plainly wrong, I present my copy-text O with no further comment.

I have routinely made two changes to O's text. On the one hand, I have tried to eliminate all those O readings I identify as the 'doublets of doubt' I have mentioned above. Second, O's exemplar seems routinely to have presented the form 'metho^a', invariably as the title to VM3. The scribe has inconsistently expanded the form (first at 4/103) as '*Methaphora*', rather

---

[39] On this point, cf. Hudson 18.
[40] Cf. Allen 1979, 26–27, where, in a discussion of a brief passage, he recognises the difficulty, but hasn't extensive enough material to address it critically.

than the intended '*Methologia*'. This I have silently corrected; although on Palmer's showing (2005, 228 note to line 14), this may still be erroneous, and limited to O+Eton, all other copies reading plural *Mithologiis*. Since the reference is clear (and the variation among those I would identify as 'indifferent'), I have let (corrected) O stand as copy-text.

Ridewall's frequent references to authority, part of the introduction to his citations, deserve a general comment. In practitioner texts of this sort these routinely show substantial variation. In these openings, O appears to offer substantially fuller references than the other copies, e.g. at 1/167 'capitulo 36 super Genesim', 5/52 'ad Romanos 2º', or 5/65 'illud Ysaie primo'. Instructively, the latter two of these examples only clarify what should have been apparent to any reasonably sophisticated reader, and the scribes who omit them may have found them extraneous.

However, this suppression of overt references has been carried to an extreme in A. This manuscript generally retains Ridewall's citations and, indeed, relatively frequently preserves their *ipsissima verba* where IO vary. However, A equally generally suppresses identification of sources and/or specific references. This behaviour is somewhat cavalier, since A frequently omits a second citation that follows another in short order, as well as a certain amount of interstitial material. This routine suppression of adjacent citations would explain why A includes only part of the interpolated passage mentioned above.

In this situation, the related copy Q is valuable. My survey of Q shows A's suppression of references as not a property of β but a decision unique to A's presentation. Its scribe/owner was apparently more interested in *sententiae* than in their sources. For example, Q contains most of 11/20–36, absent in A, although that is marked by a variety of scribalisms and an apparent eye-skip between 33 apparatum and 38 Uerum. Its variations from O include: 30–31 comatulis … nitorem] *om.*, 31 histrionibus] histrioni, 32 procis] *om.*, 39 quam … est] *om.*, 39 nugis] magis, 40 insertam] intractam, 41 manifestis] manifestius, 44 turpitudinem operantes] turpiter operatus. (Thus, Q confirms O's attribution in 11/28, *Suda*.) A good many of these represent minor variants of a type I have eliminated in the published collations.[41]

Ridewall's text is not particularly problematic in general substance. Whatever their vicissitudes, the MSS appear to be conscientiously reproducing similar materials. In only a couple of places, perhaps most notably 2.1/257–65 and a few bits like 6/109–47 or 6/360–418, does the

---

[41] Substantially the whole also appears in CUL Ii.2.20 and in Royal, although the latter lacks the *Suda* reference. Royal also agrees with Q's erroneous readings at 31 histrioni, 41 manifestius (these two readings also in CUL), and 44 operatus; for 32 procis] *om.* Q, it offers 'gerens profert'.

reproduction approach outright paraphrase. There is also minimal interpolation, limited to the two passages I present as an Appendix. The scribes are, however, susceptible to any variety of confusion, and they are particularly maladept when presented with verse. For example, in 1.8 (Phaeton), extensive citations from Ovid often left them at sea, and their confusions carried over as they copied surrounding materials.

My edition is followed by the expected sequence of notes addressing textual difficulties. I divide these by the text's chapters and use this broken display to outline Ridewall's commentative dependence on Fulgentius. It's time to lay to rest Smalley's silly characterisation of the author as a 'forger of fancies, disguised as antiques' (1960, 131). Ridewall is, within limits, a conscientious reporter of his late antique source and knew a variety of comparable presentations, as I indicate in my textual notes (mainly examples from the commentary on *DCD*). Moreover, he is apt to have believed that he was 'historicising', following classical precedent; see further the note to 2.1/146.

Preceding the Commentary, I offer one further piece of annotation. A, as some other copies of the text (e.g. Pembroke), accompanies the text with a 'tabula', a selective topical indexing tool. As I previously did in presenting selections from Holcot, I provide this annotational aid. It is particularly important to do so in this context, since Ridewall's pictorialism has produced a range of arguments that his work is to be valued for its 'memory diagrams'. Providing a 'tabula' is a gesture antithetical to such arguments; such an indexing aid presupposes conventional research procedures, the presence of the book and the ability to turn its leaves to find relevant materials. See further *Robert Holcot*, 223–30.

So far as I am able, I identify Ridewall's cited sources as footnotes to the facing-page translation of the text. For that third of the text that he printed, I have largely adopted Liebeschütz's identifications, although I have checked them all and adjusted them as appropriate. For those from classical texts, I have used the handy editions provided in the online 'Latin Library', www.thelatinlibrary.com. The volume concludes with an index that groups all Ridewall's biblical citations and all his *auctoritates*, arranged alphabetically by author.

Appendix: notes on the manuscripts

(a) copies used in this edition

A   Oxford, Bodleian Library, MS Auct. F.3.5

Membrane. Fols 223. Comprised of seven separate manuscripts, all s. xv. Only relevant is the fourth of these, fols 35–79. The sixth part, fols 108–97, has John of Wales, *Communiloquium*; and the seventh, fols 198–223, a Middle English commentary on Boethius's *Consolation*, book 1 only, predicated on Chaucer's translation. Two other portions, fols 26–34 and 80–107, include works ascribed to Peter of Blois.

s. xv in./med. Fols 45. Overall 270 mm × 190 mm (writing area 180–85 mm × 115–20 mm). In double columns, 42–46 lines to the page. Written in secretary bookhand.

The single text, succeeded by an alphabetical table (fols 76va–78va) and table of chapters (fol. 78vb). Fol. 79 is blank.

COLLATION 1–3^{12} 4^{12} (lacks 10–12, probably excised blank leaves). All leaves in the first half of each quire signed with a letter and arabic numeral (quires *a–d*), usually boxed; regular catchwords, also boxed.

BINDING A medieval binding of whittawed skin.

PROVENANCE Came to the library, from an unrecorded source, before 1602.

Previously described *SC* 2684, 2.1, 492.

O   Oxford, Bodleian Library, MS Bodley 571

Membrane. Fols 270 + vi (numbered 271–75, with the rear pastedown). Comprised of two separate manuscripts, both s. xv^{½} or s. xv med. Overall 260 mm × 190 mm. In anglicana with secretary *a* and *g*.

Manuscript A
Booklet 1 = fols 1–162, then extended (and certainly one, perhaps two, mediate extensions)

Writing area 190 mm × 140 mm. In double columns, 34 lines to the page.

[1] Fols 1ra–82vb: Pierre Bersuire, *Ovidius moralizatus* (i.e., *Reductorium moralium* 15). Ends incomplete, with the following two leaves cut out, an apparent production break.

[2] Fols 83ra–136va: John Ridewall, *Fulgencius metaforalis*. Fol. 136vb is blank.

[3] Fols 137ra–60va: A topical index to Bersuire's moralisations.

COLLATION 1^8 2–7^{12} 8^{12} (lacks 3 and 4, cut out after fol. 82) 9–14^{12}. Signed *f-r* [quire 12, to fol. 136 = *r* [10]; fols 137–38 [*r* 11–12] are also signed *a* 1–2, and are succeeded by quires doubly signed, *b/s* and *c/t*). All leaves in the first half of each quire signed, usually in arabic, although roman v and vj appear universally. In addition to the *in medias res* signatures, there is a note in catchword position, fol. 160^v: '18 quater(ni)'; as *SC* notes, Booklet 3 was originally planned to head the manuscript (the consecutive +, a-r = 18 quires).

Nominal Booklet 2 = fols 161 (the end of the prec.)–190

[4] Fols 161^(ra)–90^(vb): (Ps.-)John of Wales, *Ars predicandi*; manuscripts listed Harry Caplan, *Medieval* Artes Praedicandi: *A Handlist*, with supp., 2 vols (Ithaca NY, 1934–36), no. 62, and cf. nos 7, 71 (1:13–14, 5–6, and 15, respectively). Followed by excised leaves, with one broad unnumbered stub.

COLLATION [begins on the final two leaves of Q14] 15–16^(12) 17^(8) (lacks 5–8, stubs). Signed *v, x, –*.

Booklet 3 = fols 191–256

Writing area 195 mm × 135–40 mm. In double columns, 35 lines to the page. Where rules are legible, written above top line.

[5] Fols 191^(ra)–236^(vb): ps.-Albrecht/'Alberic of London', *Scintillarium poetarum* (VM3).

[6] Fols 237^(ra)–256^(vb): A commentary on Ovid, *Metamorphoses*, inc. 'Cum omnis corporum transmutacio', according to Coulson-Roy no. 79 (p. 45), unique. There are only three words in the final column, preceding the quire sews and an excised leaf.

COLLATION 18–22^(12) 23^(12) (lacks 7–12, apparently excised). Signed +, *a-e*.

Manuscript B = fols 257–70

Writing area 195–200 mm × 130 mm. In double columns, 44 or 45 lines to the page. A different scribe writing a contemporary anglicana.

[7] Fols 257^(ra)–69^(va): An alphabetical bestiary, inc. 'Iulius Solinus dicit quod aquila', identified T. Kaeppeli, *Scriptores Ordinis Praedicatorum Medii Aevi*, 4 vols (Rome, 1970–93), no. 1571 (2:105) as part 1 of William Jordan OP, *Summa praedicantium* (but see Sharpe 779). In addition to Kaeppeli's citation of this copy and that of Oxford, Merton College, MS 68, the text also appears in Lincoln Cathedral Library, MS 40.

[8] Fol. 269^(vb): an excerpt from Augustine, *Soliloquies*; fol. 270^r is frame-ruled, but the whole leaf is blank.

COLLATION 24^(12) 25^(2). Q24 signed originally with leaf-numbers only, not in the hand of the remainder, with *f* added in plummet; Q25 signed only on the first (and only written) leaf '1'. Followed by six blank flyleaves (a quire of six, including the rear pastedown). Fol. 275^v, the last numbered leaf, has a note in same hand as earlier, 'vj quater(ni)' (its reference unclear, perhaps a reference to Booklet 3?).

PROVENANCE An acquisition of 1605×11. The binding, *pace SC*, reversed calf, s. xvi/xvii or xvii in., has a rubbed armorial. *SC* identifies the arms with Richard Eedes (1554–1604). He appears as Richard Eads in *ODNB*;

he was a noted court preacher and eventually dean of Worcester, who died before he could fulfil an appointment as one of the Oxford team of translators of the King James Bible. Bodley's librarian, Thomas James, was his first cousin, and his portrait appears in the frieze of the Upper Reading Room. He donated £ 13 1/2 *m.* to the Bodleian in 1601. The upper board pastedown is from MS, from a parallel-text Psalter, displaying all three versions, s. xv in.

Previously described *SC* 2019, 2.1, 166–67.

I   Dublin, Trinity College, MS 115

A fine description appears at Marvin L. Colker, *Trinity College Dublin: Descriptive Catalogue of the Mediaeval and Renaissance Latin Manuscripts*, 2 vols (Aldershot, 1991), 1:238–44. For further discussion, see Hanna 2023, 111–12.

Q   Cambridge, Queens' College, MS 10

An extensive description and discussion at Hanna 2023, 133–50.

(b) published formal descriptions of other copies

Berlin: Gerard Achten, *Die theologischen lateinischen Handschriften in Quarto der Staatsbibliothek Preussischer Kulturbesitz Berlin, Teil 1* (Wiesbaden, 1979), 66–69.

Cambridge Ii: Montague R. James's otherwise unpublished description of the late 1920s is available on a link from CUL's iDiscover (https://idiscover.lib.cam.ac.uk/), s.v. Ridewall. The manuscript joins three originally separate books, bound together in the Middle Ages; that with *Fulgencius* also includes Bersuire's *Ovidius*.

Cambridge Mm: Like A, a binding of extensive unrelated fragments, again seven in all. The first, fols 1–28, has a commentary on Martianus Capella, dubiously attributed to Bernard Silvester (membrane, s. xiii^1); the fifth, fols 103–21, Map's *Dissuasio*, with Nicholas Trevet's commentary (membrane, s. xv). *Fulgencius*, preceded by Fulgentius, occupies the sixth unit, fols 122–67, mixed membrane and paper, s. xv: 1–4^{10} 5^6 (lacks 5, assigned fol. 166).

Cambridge Pembroke: Montague R. James, *A Descriptive Catalogue of the Manuscripts in the Library of Pembroke College, Cambridge* ... (Cambridge, 1905), 208–09, currently being replaced by Rodney M. Thomson. Fols 81–164 (from the opening of *Fulgencius*) are separate from the remainder, and the whole three booklets.

Durham: Thomas Rud (d. 1732), *Catalogus Manuscriptorum Ecclesiae Cathedralis Dunelmensis* (Durham, 1825), 242–43 (*Fulgencius* appears between John of Wales's *Legiloquium* and Bersuire's *Ovidius*), to be replaced by Richard Gameson's in-progress catalogue.

Eton: N. R. Ker, *Medieval Manuscripts in British Libraries*, 4 vols (Oxford, 1969–92), 2:726–28 (as James had pointed out earlier, three separate manuscripts).

Norwich Cathedral 2 (see n.27): Ker, *Medieval Manuscripts*, 3:529–30.

Royal: see Hanna 2016 (four scribes in 13 booklets, *Fulgencius* the sole text of the ninth of these, fols 311–38; extensive parallels in content with other *Fulgencius* manuscripts).

Worcester: Rodney M. Thomson, *A Descriptive Catalogue of the Manuscripts in Worcester Cathedral Library* (Cambridge, 2001), 104–06. The description requires some supplement; the volume gathers eight separate production-units, ending at fols 16 (ps.-Albrecht/VM3), 48 (John of Wales's *Breviloquium* + Map's *Dissuasio* + *Fulgencius*), 120, 144 (ending with a bit from Palmer's *Compilatio*), 168, 192, 203, and 277.

Bibliography

For Ridewall's sources see the 'Index fontium'.

Primary texts

ps.-Albrecht/'Albericus'/VM3, *Mythographe de Vatican III*, tr. Philippe Dain (Besançon, 2005).

Berchorius, Petrus (Pierre Bersuire), *Reductorium morale, Liber XV, cap. I. De formis figurisque deorum naar de Parisije druck van 1509: Werkmateriaal*, [ed. J. Engels] (Utrecht, 1960) [the Avignon version of the text].

—, *Reductorium morale, Liber XV, cap. I. De formis figurisque deorum textus e codice Brux., Bibl. Reg. 863–9 critice editus: Werkmateriaal 3*, [ed. J. Engels] (Utrecht, 1966) [the revised Paris version].

—, see also W. Reynolds.

Fasciculus morum: A Fourteenth-Century Preacher's Handbook, ed. tr. Siegfried Wenzel (University Park PA, 1989).

Holcot: *Robert Holcot, Exegete: Selections from the Commentary on Minor Prophets ...*, ed. Hanna (Liverpool, 2021a).

Innocent III (Lotario dei Segni), *De miseria condicionis humane*, ed. Robert E. Lewis, The Chaucer Library (Athens GA, 1978).

John de Foxton's Liber Cosmographiae (1408): An Edition and Codicological Study, ed. John B. Friedman, Brill's Studies in Intellectual History 5 (Leiden, 1988).

Malachy the Irishman, On poison*: A Study and an Edition*, ed. Hanna (Liverpool, 2020).

Neckam, Alexander, *Commentum super Martianum*, ed. Christopher J. McDonough (Florence, 2006).

Peter Comestor, *Lectures on the* Glossa Ordinaria, ed. David M. Foley and Simon Whedbee, Toronto Medieval Latin Texts 37 (Toronto, 2021).

Ridewall, John, 'Commentary Two: John Ridewall', *JBWW* 51–119.

Salutati, Coluccio, *De laboribus Herculis*, ed. B. L. Ullman, 2 vols (Zürich, [1951]).

La Somme le roi *par Frère Laurent*, ed. Édith Brayer and Anne-Françoise Leurquin-Labie, SATF (Abbeville, 2008).

Thomae Walsingham De archana deorum, ed. Robert A. van Kluyve (Durham NC, 1968).

Studies

Akae, Yiuchi, *A Mendicant Sermon Collection from Composition to Reception: The* Novum Opus Dominicale *of John Waldeby, OESA, Sermo 7* (Turnhout, 2015).

Allen, Judson B., 'An Anonymous Twelfth-century "De natura deorum" in the Bodleian Library', *Traditio* 26 (1970), 352–64.

—, 'Commentary as Criticism: The Text, Influence, and Literary Theory of the "Fulgentius Metaphored" of John Ridewall', *Acta Conventus Neo-Latini Amstelodamenis ...*, ed. P. Tuynham *et al.* (Munich, 1979), 25–47.

—, *The Ethical Poetic of the Later Middle Ages ...* (Toronto, 1982).

—, *The Friar as Critic: Literary Attitudes in the Later Middle Ages* (Nashville TN, 1971).

Baswell, Christopher, *Virgil in Medieval England ...* (Cambridge, 1995).

Bejczy, István P., *The Cardinal Virtues in the Middle Ages: A Study in Moral Thought from the Fourth to the Fourteenth Century* (Leiden and Boston, 2011).

Besson, Gisèle, 'D'Albéric au Pseudo-Albrecht. Date et origine du troisième Mythographe du Vatican', *Fleur de clergie. Mélanges en l'honneur de Jean-Yves Tilliette*, ed. Olivier Collet *et al.* (Geneva, 2019), 815–47.

Bloomfield, Morton W., *The Seven Deadly Sins ...* ([East Lansing MI], 1952).

Boswell, John, *Christianity, Social Tolerance and Homosexuality* (Chicago IL, 1980).

Brown, Emerson, 'Biblical Women in The Merchant's Tale: Feminism, Antifeminism, and Beyond', *Viator* 5 (1974), 387–412, at 399–403 (esp. 401 n.50).

Brown, Peter, *Power and Persuasion in Late Antiquity: Towards a Christian Empire* (Madison WI, 1992).

Brumble, H. David, 'Let Us Make Gods in Our Image: Greek Myth in Medieval and Renaissance Literature', *The Cambridge Companion to Greek Mythology*, ed. Roger D. Woodard (Cambridge, 2007), 407–24.

Burnett, Charles S. F., 'A Note on the Origins of the Third Vatican Mythographer', *Journal of the Warburg and Courtauld Institutes* 44 (1981), 160–66.

Camargo, Martin, 'Beyond the *Libri Catoniani*: Models of Latin Prose Style at Oxford University ca. 1400', *Mediaeval Studies* 56 (1994), 165–87.

—, '"Tria sunt": The Long and the Short of Geoffrey of Vinsauf's *Documentum de modo et arte dictandi et versificandi*', *Speculum* 74 (1999), 935–55.

Cameron, Alan, *Greek Mythography in the Roman World* (New York and Oxford, 2004).

Carley, James P., 'John Leland at Somerset Libraries', *Somerset Archaeology and Natural History* 129 (1985), 141–54.
Catto, Jeremy, 'Ridevall (Musca), John', *Oxford DNB*.
Chance, Jane, *Medieval Mythography Volume 2: From the School of Chartres to the Court at Avignon, 1177–1350* (Gainesville FL, 2000).
Clark, James, 'The Friars and the Classics in Late Medieval England', *The Friars in Medieval Britain*, ed. Nicholas J. Rogers, Harlaxton Medieval Studies 19 (Donnington, 2010), 142–51.
—, *A Monastic Renaissance at St. Albans …* (Oxford, 2004).
Copeland, Rita, ed., *The Oxford History of Classical Reception in English Literature: Volume 1: 800–1558* (Oxford, 2016).
—, 'Producing the *Lector*', *Medieval and Early Modern Authorship*, ed. Guillemette Bolens and Lukas Erne (Tübingen, 2011), 231–49.
—, and Ineke Sluiter, eds, *Medieval Grammar and Rhetoric …* (Oxford, 2009).
Coulson, Frank T., and Bruno Roy, *Incipitarium Ovidianum: A Finding Guide for Texts in Latin Related to the Study of Ovid …*, Publications of the Journal of Medieval Latin 3 (Turnhout, 2000).
Daniel, Norman, *Islam and the West: The Making of an Image*, rev. edn (Oxford, 1993).
Delcorno, Pietro, '"Christ and the Soul are Like Pyramus and Thisbe": An Ovidian Story in Fifteenth-Century Sermons', *Medieval Sermon Studies* 60 (2016), 37–61.
Dinkova-Bruun, Greti, '*Imagines Deorum*: Christianizing Mythography in MS Cotton Titus D.xx', *Archives d'histoire doctrinale et littéraire du moyen âge* 79 (2012), 313–34.
—, 'Medieval Miscellanies and the Case of Manuscript British Library, Cotton Titus D.XX', *Medieval Manuscript Miscellanies: Composition, Authorship, Use*, Medium Aevum Quotidianum Sonderband 31, ed. Lucie Doležalová and Kimberly Rivers (Krems, 2013), 14–33.
Dronke, Peter, *Fabula: Explorations into the Uses of Myth in Medieval Platonism*, Mittellateinischen Studien 9 (Leiden, 1974).
Echard, Siân, '"Iubiter et Iuno": An Anglo-Latin Mythographic Poem …', *Journal of Medieval Latin* 4 (1994), 101–17.
Edwards, Robert, 'The Heritage of Fulgentius', *The Classics in the Middle Ages*, ed. Aldo S. Bernardo and Saul Levin, Medieval & Renaissance Texts & Studies 69 (Binghamton NY, 1990), 141–51.
Elliott, Kathleen O., and J. P. Elder, 'A Critical Edition of the Vatican Mythographers', *Transactions and Proceedings of the American Philological Association* 78 (1947), 189–207.
Engels, J., 'L'Edition critique de l'*Ovidius moralizatus* de Bersuire', *Vivarium* 9 (1971), 19–24.
Friedman, John B., review of Chance, *Speculum* 77 (2002), 1254–57.
Fumo, Jamie C., 'Commentary and Collaboration in the Medieval

Allegorical Tradition', *The Handbook to the Reception of Ovid*, ed. John F. Miller and Carole E. Newlands (Chichester, 2014), 114–28.
—, *The Legacy of Apollo: Antiquity, Authority and Chaucerian Poetics* (Toronto, 2010).
Fyler, John M., 'Pagan Survivals', *A Companion to Chaucer*, ed. Peter Brown (Oxford, 2000), 349–59.
Ghisalberti, Fausto, *L'"Ovidius Moralizatus" di Pierre Bersuire* (Rome, 1933).
Gould, Thomas, *The Ancient Quarrel between Poetry and Philosophy* (Princeton NJ, 1990).
Graf, Thomas A., *De subjecto psychico gratiae et virtutum secundum doctrinam scholasticorum usque ad medium saeculum XIV*, 2 vols (Rome, 1934–35).
Green, Richard H., 'Dante's "Allegory of the Poets" and the Medieval Theory of Poetic Fiction', *Comparative Literature* 9 (1957), 118–28.
Hankey, A. Teresa, 'The Library of Domenico di Bandino', *Rinascimento* 8 (1957), 177–207.
Hanna, Ralph, '"Classicizing Friars", Miscellaneous Transmission, and MS Royal 7 C.i', *Journal of the Early Book Society* 19 (2016), 97–123.
—, *Looking at Medieval Books: Learning to See* (Liverpool, 2023).
—, 'Lost Libraries: The Case of the Oxford Franciscans, c. 1330–40', *Journal of the Early Book Society* 24 (2021b), 37–60.
—, 'Nicholas Kempston and his Books', *The Library* 7th ser. 18 (2017), 418–27.
—, 'Verses in Sermons Again: The Case of Cambridge, Jesus College, MS Q.A.13', *Studies in Bibliography* 57 (2005–06), 63–83.
Hays, Gregory, 'The Date and Identity of the Mythographer Fulgentius', *Journal of Medieval Latin* 13 (2003), 163–252.
Heinze, Theodor, and Sotera Fornaro, 'Mythography', *Brill's New Pauly* (Leiden, 2006), accessed 14 May 2021 <http://ezproxy-prd.bodleian.ox.ac.uk:2197/10.1163/1574- 9347_bnp_e815110>.
Herbert, J. A., *Catalogue of Romances in the Department of Manuscripts in the British Museum, Vol. 3* (London, 1910).
Hexter, Ralph, 'The *Allegari* of Pierre Bersuire: Interpretation and the *Reductorium Morale*', *Allegorica* 10 (1989), 51–84.
Hodapp, William F., *The Figure of Minerva in Medieval Literature* (Woodbridge, 2019).
Houser, R. E., *The Cardinal Virtues: Aquinas, Albert, and Phillip the Chancellor*, Medieval Sources in Translation 39 (Toronto, 2004).
Hudson, Anne, 'Wyclif's Books', *Image, Text and Church, 1380–1600: Essays for Margaret Aston*, ed. Linda Clark et al. (Toronto, 2009), 8–36.
Hunt, R. W., 'The Library of Robert Grosseteste', *Robert Grosseteste Scholar and Bishop ...* , ed. D. A. Callus (Oxford, 1955), 121–45.
—, ed. rev. Margaret Gibson, *The Schools and the Cloister: The Life and Writings of Alexander Nequam (1157–1217)* (Oxford, 1984).

Kahr, Madlyn M., 'Danaë: Virtuous, Voluptuous, Venal Woman', *The Art Bulletin* 60 (1978), 43–55.
Kamuth, Stephanie G., and Rita Copeland, 'Medieval Secular Allegory: French and English', *The Cambridge Companion to Allegory*, ed. R. Copeland and Peter T. Struck (Cambridge, 2010), 136–47.
Katzenellenbogen, Adolf, *Allegories of the Virtues and Vices in Mediaeval Art ...* (London, 1939).
Laistner, M. L. W., 'Fulgentius in the Carolingian Age', *The Intellectual Heritage of the Early Middle Ages: Selected Essays*, ed. Chester G. Starr (Ithaca NY, 1957), 202–15.
Lawler, Traugott, 'Langland Translating', *Answerable Style: The Idea of the Literary in Late Medieval England*, ed. Frank Grady and Andrew Galloway (Columbus OH, 2013), 54–74.
—, 'Medieval Annotation: The Example of the Commentaries on Walter Map's *Dissuasio Valerii*', *Annotation and its Texts*, ed. Stephen A. Barney (New York, 1991), 94–107.
Lehmann, Paul, *Pseudo-antike Literatur des Mittelalters*, Studien der Bibliothek Warburg 13 (Berlin, 1927).
Little, A. G., *The Grey Friars in Oxford*, Oxford Historical Society 20 (Oxford, 1892).
Lottin, Odon, *Psychologie et morale au XIIe et XIIIe siècles*, 6 vols in 8 (Louvain, 1942–60).
McCall, John P., *Chaucer Among the Gods ...* (University Park PA, 1979).
Minnis, A. J., *Chaucer and Pagan Antiquity* (Cambridge, 1982).
—, and A. B. Scott, *Medieval Literary Theory and Criticism c.1100–c.1375* (Oxford, 1988).
Morrisey, Jake W., 'Anxious Love and Disordered Urine: The Englishing of *Amor Hereos* in Henry Daniel's *Liber Uricrisiarum*', *Chaucer Review* 49 (2014), 161–83.
Newhauser, Richard, *The Treatise on Vices and Virtues in Latin and the Vernacular*, Typologie des sources du Moyen Age occidental 68 (Turnhout, 1993).
Palmer, Nigel F., '"Antiquitus depingebatur". The Roman Pictures of Death and Misfortune ... ', *Deutsche Vierteljahrsschrift für Literaturwissenschaft und Geistesgeschichte* 57 (1983), 173–239.
—, 'Bacchus und Venus. Mythographischer Bilder ... ', *Literatur und Wandmalerei II: Konventionalität und Konversation*, ed. Eckart C. Lutz et al. (Tübingen, 2005), 189–235.
—, 'Das Exempelwerk der englischen Bettelmönchen: ein Gegenstück zu den *Gesta Romanorum*?', *Exempel und Exempelsammlungen*, ed. Walter Haug and Burghart Wachinger (Tübingen, 1991), 137–72.
Panofsky, Erwin, and Fritz Saxl, 'Classical Mythology in Medieval Art', *Metropolitan Museum Studies* 4 (1932–33), 228–80.

Rahner, Hugo, tr. Brian Battershaw, *Greek Myths and Christian Mysteries* (New York and London, 1963).

Rathbone, Eleanor, 'Master Alberic of London, "Mythographus Tertius Vaticanus"', *Mediaeval and Renaissance Studies* 1 (1941–43), 35–38.

Reynolds, L. D., *The Medieval Tradition of Seneca's Letters* ([London], 1965).

Reynolds, William, 'Selections from *De Formis Figurisque Deorum*', *Allegorica* 2 (1978), 58–89.

Rivers, Kimberley A., *Preaching the Memory of Virtue and Vice ...* (Turnhout, 2010).

Robertson, D. W. Jr, 'A Note on the Classical Origins of "Circumstances" in the Medieval Confessional', *Studies in Philology* 43 (1946), 6–14.

Rouse, Richard H. and Mary A., and R. A. B. Mynors, *Registrum Anglie de Libris Doctorum et Auctorum Veterum*, Corpus of British Medieval Library Catalogues 2 (London, 1991).

Scott, Kathleen L., *Later Gothic Manuscripts, 1390–1490*, Survey of Manuscripts Illuminated in the British Isles 6, 2 vols (London, 1996).

Seznec, Jean, tr. Barbara F. Sessions, *The Survival of the Pagan Gods ...* (New York, 1953).

Sharpe, Richard, 'The English Bibliographical Tradition from Kirkestede to Tanner', *Britannia Latina ...*, ed. Charles Burnett and Nicholas Mann, Warburg Institute Colloquia 8 (London and Turin, 2005), 86–128.

Sjöström, Henning, 'Magister Albericus Lundoniensis, Mythographus Tertius Vaticanus: A Twelfth-Century Student of Classical Mythology', *Classica et Mediaevalia* 29 (1968), 249–64.

Smalley, Beryl, *English Friars and Antiquity in the Early Fourteenth Century* (Oxford, 1960).

—, 'John Ridewall's Commentary on *De Civitate Dei*', *Medium Ævum* 25 (1956), 140–53.

—, 'A Quotation from John Ridewall on *De Civitate Dei* by William Woodford', *Medium Ævum* 33 (1964), 21–25.

Southern, R. W., 'Towards an Edition of Peter of Blois's Letter-Collection', *English Historical Review* 110 (1995), 925–37.

Thomson, Rodney M., *A Descriptive Catalogue of the Medieval Manuscripts of Corpus Christi College Oxford* (Cambridge, 2011).

Thomson, S. Harrison, *The Writings of Robert Grosseteste, Bishop of Lincoln, 1235–1253* (Cambridge, 1940).

Tinkle, Theresa, *Medieval Venuses and Cupids: Sexuality and Hermeneutics in English Poetry* (Stanford CA, 1996).

Tuve, Rosemond, *Allegorical Imagery: Some Medieval Books and Their Posterity* (Princeton NJ, 1966).

Wahlgren, Lena, *The Letter Collections of Peter of Blois: Studies in the Manuscript Tradition* (Göteborg, 1993).

Wenzel, Siegfried, 'Academic Sermons at Oxford in the Early Fifteenth Century', *Speculum* 70 (1995), 305–29.
—, *Latin Sermon Collections from Later Medieval England ...* (Cambridge, 2005).
—, *Preaching in the Age of Chaucer: Selected Sermons in Translation* (Washington, 2008).
Wetherbee, Winthrop, 'Learned Mythology: Plato and Martianus Capella', *The Oxford Handbook of Medieval Latin Literature*, ed. Ralph J. Hexter and David Townsend (Oxford, 2012), 335–55.
—, review of Chance, *Speculum* 72 (1997), 125–27.
Willoughby, James, 'The Transmission and Circulation of Classical Literature: Libraries and Florilegia', Copeland 2016, 96–113.
Windeatt, Barry, 'Afterlives: The Fabulous History of Venus', *Traditions and Innovations in the Study of Middle English Literature: The Influence of Derek Brewer*, ed. Charlotte Brewer and B. Windeatt (Woodbridge, 2013), 262–78.

Fulgencius metaforalis
Text and translation

Book 1

[1]

Intencio uenerabilis uiri Fulgencii in sua *Methologia* est sub tegmine fabularum a poetis fictarum describere diuersa genera uiciorum et uirtutum eis appositarum, ut sic [cognita] uirtutum honestate et uiciorum deformitate, inducat auditores ad uirtutum
5 exercitacionem et uiciorum detestacionem. Nisi enim fabule tales poetice ordinarentur ad mores, theologi de eis se non deberent intromittere, sed eas pocius sicut uanas et friuolas deuitare. Et de hoc bene tangit doctor Ieronymus in epistola de filio prodigo et Hugo, *De archa Noe* libro 4, capitulo 8.
10 In primo ergo capitulo primi libri describit originem ydolatrie, que cum transcendit + cetera uicia magnitudine malicie, ideo ab isto peccato, uelut omnium criminum capitaneo, auctor iste sens[u]it inchoandum. Per eam enim fit a creatura maxima iniuria creatori; et ideo Rabi Moyses in libro quem
15 uocat *Matrem philosophie*, loquens de isto uicio et ostendens quante sit coram Deo displicencie, dicit sic, capitulo 33: 'Scias, cum inspexeris in tota lege et in libris prophetarum, non inuenies quod ira uel furor uel indignacio attribuatur Deo, nisi pro ydolatria, [nec uocatur inimicus Dei uel angustiator uel
20 odiosus], nisi pro ydolatria'. Hec ille. Istius ergo uicii originem et originate continuacionem tangit Fulgencius, dicens per amorem deordinatum istud uicium primo habuisse ortum et inicium. Unde concordat cum eo Augustinus, libro 41 *De ciuitate Dei*, qui dicit capitulo ultimo, quod 'Du[as] ciuitates + duo fecerunt amores.
25 Terrenam ciuitatem fecit amor sui | usque ad contemptum Dei;

---

1 fol. 83ʳᵃ • Intencio] Institucio L 2 fictarum] factarum A 3 sic cognita] cognita L, sic O 5 uiciorum] uirtutum *over eras.* A 6 de] de in I 8 doctor] om. L • epistola] eᵒ (= ? ego) A
10 primo ... primi] principio L 10–12 describit ... peccato] de peccato ydolatrie L 11 cum] *om.* AI • transcendit] *adds* omnia O 12 criminum] peccatorum A 13 sensuit] censuit L, sensiit O 19–20 nec ... odiosus] *om.* O 19 angustiator (-ur IL?)] *emended to* angelorum L 21 originate] originis (*over eras.*) O, originati L 23 eo Augustinus] Augustino AIL • De ... Dei] *om.* A 24 Duas ... duo] Due ... duos O 25 fol. 83ʳᵇ

[1]

In his *Mythography*, the wise man Fulgentius's intention is to describe the diverse species of sins and the virtues opposed to them. He does this through the *integumen* of the fables invented by the poets. As a consequence, having shown the propriety of the virtues and the ugliness of the sins, he impels his audience to exercise the virtues and to hate the sins. For unless such poetic fables are directed toward appropriate behaviour, theologians should not mess with them, but much rather avoid them as empty and frivolous. Jerome, in his letter about the prodigal son, and Hugh of St Victor, in *On Noah's ark* 4.8, treat this point well.[1]

[10] Therefore, in the first chapter of book 1, Fulgentius describes the origin of idolatry. He determined that he should begin with this sin because it surpasses all the others in the great extent of its malice and is, as it were, the general in command of all crimes. For through idolatry, a created being does the greatest injury to its creator. Therefore, Rambam, in his book called *The mother of philosophy*, speaking of this sin and showing how much it displeases God, says in chapter 33, 'You should recognise, if you have looked carefully in the complete Law and in the prophetic books, that you will not find wrath or fury or indignation attributed to God except in the case of idolatry. Nor is anyone called the enemy of God or His afflictor, or hateful, except in this case.' So he says.[2] Therefore Fulgentius treats the origin of this sin and its further continuation; he says that this sin first had its origin and beginning from disordered love. For this reason, Augustine agrees with him, in *On the city of God* 14, where he says in the final chapter, 'Two kinds of love have made two different cities. Self-love, to the point of disdaining God, has made the earthly city;

---

[1] Jerome, epistola 21.13 (*PL* 22:384–86); and Hugh, *ibid.* (*PL* 176:674).
[2] *Dux neutrorum* 1.36 (p. 51).

celestem ciuitatem fecit amor Dei usque ad contemptum sui'.
Hec Augustinus.

Ab isto ergo deordinato amore sui ortum habuit hoc genus
uicii, sicut ostendit Fulgencius, recitando quandam historiam
quam narrat quidam Grecus de ciuitate Lacedom[oni]orum, qui
fuit scriptor antiquarum historiarum, cui nomen Doffanes, ut
habent libri multi. Iste enim in libris antiquitatum quos scripsit
narrat de quodam uiro diuite Egipcio, cui[us fuit] nomen
Sirophanes. Qui filium genuit quem amore deordinato dilexit,
quia ultra quam debuit; qui filius, uiuente patre, mortuus est.
Pro cuius morte, pater ultra quam secundum rectam racionem
debuit, dolens et desolatus fuit. Amor enim deordinatus causat
dolorem deordinatum, quia tantus est dolor de re amissa,
quantus [fuit] amor in ea habita, sicut docet Augustinus. Iste
igitur Cirophanes, in sui doloris remedium, filii sui ymaginem
fieri fecit in domo sua; quam ymaginem uocauit 'ydolum'.
Est autem 'ydolum' quasi uerbum compositum ex + Greco et
Latino: *ydos* enim + Grecum est idem quod 'forma, species, uel
figura'. Unde 'ydolum' quasi 'species seu forma doloris'; 'dolor'
autem est uocabulum Latinum. Fuit enim ista ymago figura
filii, qui patri amore deordinato laboranti fuit materia dolendi.
Isti autem ymagini omnes qui erant de familia domini, aut
coronas solebant plectere, aut flores inferre, aut odoramenta
succendere. |

Nota apud antiquos ista tria consueuerunt fieri [diis]. Nam
apud [istos] paganos fuerunt uarie deorum differencie, ut tangit
Augustinus in suis libris, in *Ciuitate*, ut patet libro 7, et alibi
similiter. Uocabant enim aliquos deos lares, id est deos

---

27 Hec Augustinus] *om.* A, Augustinus I
30 Lacedomoniorum] Lacedomorum AIO   31 cui nomen] et uocatur AL
31–32 cui ... multi] *om.* I   31 Doffanes] Cyrophanes A   32 scripsit] scri‖bit A,
scripsitur L (*emended*)   33 quodam] *om.* I • cuius fuit nomen] cuius erat
nomen A, cui nomen O   35 ultra] ultima I • est] fuit AIL   36–37 ultra ...
debuit] ultra rectam racionem A   37 et] *om.* IL • fuit] m^{is} fuit I   39 fuit] est O
41 fieri] super (*emended to* sibi) L   42 ex] ex uerbo O   43 Grecum] est Grecum
et O   44 figura] signa I • quasi] id est AI   45 figura] signum (*corr. from*
signum) I   46 dolendi] condolendi A; reuolendi, *corr. to* redolendi I   47 erant]
adds in domo L   48 solebant] consueuerunt AIL • inferre] inserere A
49 succendere] accendere I • fol. 83va
50 tria] tripliciter I • diis] diis suis A, *om.* O   51 istos] *om.* O • deorum]
donorum A, *over eras.* I   53 similiter] *om.* I • deos¹] *adds* suos A, alios I, *adds*
deos L • deos²] *om.* A; dictos I

love of God, to the point of disdaining oneself, has made the heavenly city.'³ So Augustine says.

[28] Fulgentius shows that this variety of sin had its origin in this disordered love. He repeats a story told by a Greek from Sparta, an author of ancient histories named Dophanes, as many books say. In the books of antiquities that he wrote, Dophanes tells about Sirophanes, a rich Egyptian.⁴ He had a son whom he loved in a disordered way, because he loved him more than was appropriate, but then the son died before the father. The grieving father was devastated by his son's death, beyond what right reason would allow. For disordered love produces disordered grief; as Augustine teaches, one grieves to the same extent from having lost something as one loved it when one possessed it.⁵ Therefore, Sirophanes, as a cure for his grief, had an image of his son made for his house and called that image 'an idol'. The word 'idol' is, as it were, a compound from Greek and Latin ones, for *ydos* is a Greek word and means the same as 'appearance, shape, or representation'. For this reason, the word 'idol' means 'the appearance or the shape of sorrow' – and *dolor* 'sorrow' is a Latin word.⁶ This image was a representation of the son, who was the subject of the grief that the father was suffering from his disordered love. All the members of this lord's household were accustomed to wreathe crowns or bring flowers or burn sweet-smelling things for this image.

[50] Notice that ancient people were accustomed to do these three things for their gods. For among the pagans, there were different classes of gods, as Augustine discusses in his books, most explicitly in *On the city*, book 7, but elsewhere as well.⁷ For they called some gods Lares or

---

³ *Ibid.* 14.28 (*PL* 41:436).

⁴ Fulg 1.1 (15/20–17/18). Most of the paragraph, along with lines 45–48 and 68, reproduced VM3, Prooem. (152–53).

⁵ Presumably Augustine teaches this in many places; L has no note.

⁶ Cf. Isidore, *Etym.* 8.11.13–14 (*PL* 82:315).

⁷ *Ibid.* 7.1 ff. (*PL* 41:193ff.).

domesticos, [seu] penates. Alii uocabantur dii [selec]ti, qui erant dii magis principales; unde dicebantur '[selec]ti', quasi 'seorsum electi'. Alii fuerunt [dii] magis + communes, sicut patet per Augustinum. Et secundum istas tres differencias deorum, fuerunt tria genera cultuum et honorum, qui diis [select]is fuerunt corone plectende et offerende in signum singularis excellencie. Sed diis pena[t]ibus decuit odoramenta succendere; unde dicebantur 'dii ignis', qui erant quasi priuati et domestici unius familie. Sed diis communioribus consueuerunt flores inferre, qui communiter oriuntur in rure, quia pagani talia terre nascencia solent illis diis attribuere, sicut tangit Augustinus, *De ciuitate Dei*.

Ut ergo serui patrem defuncti filii placarent, ipsi filio mortuo deitatem attribuebant et eum consimili cultu cum diis colebant. Consueuerant eciam serui aliqui culpis grauibus irretiti, ut offensam domini uitarent et penam delicto debitam declinarent, ad predictam ymaginem confugere et ab ea territi timore ueniam postulare.

Nota ergo qualiter Fulgencius iuxta [ser]iem huius historie, ortum ydolatrie [a]scribit amori deordinato. Pater excessiue laborans amore filii, fecit fieri simulacrum filii mortui. Idem eciam pater ex [eodem] amore deordinato complacuit | in cultu et honore diuino exhibito filio suo mortuo, et ideo Fulgencius, designans excessum paterne affeccionis, dic[it] in littera quod pater iste filium suum ardencius diligebat 'quam paternitas exigebat'.

Nota eciam secundo, quomodo Fulgencius attribuit continuacionem ydolatrie adulacioni et timori. Illud enim, quod affeccio inordinata adinuenit, adulacio co[ntinu]auit et timor indebitus et deordinatus. Qualiter omnis adulator sit [ydolatra],

---

54 seu] Alii uocabantur O   54, 55 selecti] celesti O   54–55 qui ... quasi] id est I
56 dii ... communes] magis communiores O   58 et honorum] *om.* A • selectis] selecticis A, celestis O   60 penatibus] penaribus O • decuit] docuit (*emended to* debuit) L   61 quasi] *om.* I • familie] confamilie I   62 communioribus] communibus A • inferre] inserere A   63 rure] uere L
65 mortuo] defuncto A   66 deitatem] diuinitatem I, *adds* uel diuinitatem L • colebant] solebant I   67 aliqui] domus L • irretiti] heretici I   68 delicto] delicti AI
71 seriem] finem AOL   72 ascribit] describit IO   73 fieri] sibi L   74 eodem] *om.* O • deordinato placuit] filii I • fol. 83vb 75 designans] ad designandum AIL
76 dicit] dicens O • pater] *om.* A   77 ardencius] amore ardenter L
 • quam] ultra quam AL • paternitas] *om.* A • exigebat] exhibebat A, *adds* uel exhibebat L
78 secundo] *om.* I   80 continuauit] comminicauit O   81 sit ydolatra] sit O, nocet L

Text and translation: Book 1 [1] Idolatry 43

Penates, and these were peculiar to a household. They called others 'the chosen gods', and they were the greater and more important ones; for this reason, they were called *selecti* 'chosen', as if they were *seorsum electi* 'chosen apart from the rest'. Other gods were more common, as Augustine shows. In accord with these three classes of gods, there were three kinds of worship and of honours. Crowns were to be woven and offered to the select gods as a token of their unique excellence. But it was appropriate to burn sweet-smelling things for the Penates; for this reason, they were called 'the gods of fire', because, as it were, they were the private household gods of a single family. But the pagans were accustomed to bring flowers to the more common gods. This is because flowers commonly spring up in the countryside, and the pagans customarily attributed the growth of such things from the earth to these gods, as Augustine discusses in *On the city of God*.

[65] Therefore, to please the father of the dead son, his servants ascribed divine status to the son and worshipped him through a ritual analogous to that used for the gods. Also any servants accused of serious failings were accustomed to flee to this image and, terrified with fear, to ask for mercy from it. In this way, they might avoid their lord's displeasure and avoid the punishment appropriate to their offence.

[71] Notice also how, following the plot of this story, Fulgentius ascribes the rise of idolatry to disordered love. For the father, suffering excessively for love of his son, had a simulacrum made of the dead son. Also the father, from this disordered love, was satisfied by the worship and the divine honour shown his dead son. Therefore Fulgentius, identifying this as an excess of paternal love, says explicitly that this father loved his son more ardently than being a father required of him.[8]

[78] Notice secondly how Fulgentius attributes the continuation of idolatry to flattery and fear. For disordered affection introduced a behaviour that flattery and inappropriate and disordered fear extended.

---

[8] Fulg 1.1 (16/3).

44   John Ridewall, *Fulgencius metaforalis*

tangunt isti antiqui pagani, Secillius [Balbus] et alii, sicut recitat
Carnotensis in suo *Policratico*, sic dicens, 'Egregie quidam
Secillius Balbus [in]quid, "Imperator Auguste, in eo maxime
85   elucet prudencia tua, quod isti adulatores nondum te insanum
reddiderunt [omnino] qui, ut tibi applaudant, non solum diis
iniuriam faciunt, sed tibi ipsi et populo. Deorum siquidem
minuunt reuerenciam, quos parificant tibi; te uero arguunt
insipientem, dum condicionis repugnante natura, parem te
90   [numin]ibus persuadere presumunt; [n]ota supersticionis [inur]unt
populo, qui mortales deos pro immortalibus persuadent esse
colendos. Si ergo sapis +, Auguste, in deorum hostes insurges, et te
deorum docebis esse cultorem, si deceptores istos exterminaueris,
qui tui sunt excecatores et deorum contemptores"'. Hec ille.
95   Ecce, qualiter adulacio ydolatriam exsequitur, que ut
dictum est, ab amore deordinato oriebatur, qualiter uero timor
inordinatus sit executor illius uicii illiciti et peruersi cultus, tangit
Fulgencius et allegat uersum poete Petronii, qui dicit, 'Prim[u]s in
orbe deos fecit inesse timor'. Et cum isto uersu Petronii concordat
100   Stacius, *Thebaido*, qui eadem uerba ponit, | libro 3, quasi in fine.
Et uersum illum al|legat Cassiodorus super psalmum *Deus, Deus
meus, respice*. Quante uero malicie sit talis timor deordinatus
tangunt sancti. Unde glossa Augustini super illud psalmi,
Incensa igni et suffossa, sic dicit, 'Omnia peccata criminalia fiunt
105   uel propter cupiditatem ardentem, et i[s]ta uocantur "[peccata]
incensa igni"; uel propter timorem male humilitantem, et talia
dicuntur "peccata suffossa". Perscrutemini ergo consciencias,
interrogate corda [u]estra, utrum poss[i]nt esse peccata, nisi aut
timendo aut cupiendo. Omnia ergo peccata due res faciunt in
110   homine, scilicet cupiditas et timor'. Et de isto nota Hugonem, *De
sacramentis*, libro 2, parte 13ª, capitulo 2º: 'Duo sunt, inquit,

---

82 Secillius] Ce|lilius A • Balbus] *om.* O 84 inquid] *an extra minim* A,
quid O 86 omnino qui ut] *blank* A, qui ut O 89 parem] *om.* L 90 numinibus]
blank A, fluminum (?) I, muneribus O • persuadere] *om.* A • presumunt]
prestituunt A • nota] vota (*sic*) AIO, notam L • inurunt] irruunt A, ingerunt
IO, irruunt dum L 91 esse] omnes A 92 sapis] *adds* es O 93 docebis] doces L
94 excecatores] execatores I
95 adulacio ... que] timor ... qui A 97 sit] sicud eciam I • uicii] *om.* L • illiciti]
om. I 98 Primus] Primos O 99 isto uersu Petronii] hoc I 100 Tebaido]
Thebaidus A, de paidos I, Thebardus L • fol. 84ʳᵃ 101 uersum] *om.* I
102 malicie] *add* causa IL 103 tangunt] *add* eciam AIL 105 ista] illa I, ita O
• peccata] *om.* O 106 male] malicie I • humilitantem] humilitatis A
108 uestra] uestras *after* consciencias O • possint] possunt O

The ancient pagans, Caecilius Balbus and others, treated every flatterer as if he were an idolater, as John of Salisbury, bishop of Chartres, tells in his *Polycraticus*, saying, 'One Caecilius Balbus put it excellently when he said, "Emperor Augustus, your prudence shows forth most powerfully in that flatterers have never reduced you to complete insanity. In their effort to praise you, they not only injure the gods, but you yourself and the people. For they diminish the reverence due to the gods, whom they make your peers; they prove that you are stupid, so long as they attempt to persuade you that you are equal to the gods, rejecting the nature of your mortal condition; they brand the people with the mark of superstition, in persuading them that they should worship mortals, instead of the immortals, as gods. Therefore, since you are wise, Augustus, you should rise up against these enemies of the gods, and you will teach yourself to be a worshipper of the gods, if you eliminate these deceivers. They are blinding you and showing contempt for the gods." So he says.[9]

[95] See: Fulgentius treats how fear follows from idolatry – recall, as I've said, that it sprung from disordered love – and how disordered fear enacts this illicit sin of perverted worship. He cites a verse of the poet Petronius, 'Fear first made the gods exist in this world', and Statius agrees with this verse of Petronius, when he offers the same words at the end of *Thebaid* book 3.[10] And Cassiodorus cites the same verse in his commentary on Ps 21:2, *O God, my God, look upon me*.[11] Holy men also discuss how such disordered fear may be of so great malice. For this reason, Augustine glosses *Things set on fire and dug down [shall perish at the rebuke of thy countenance]* (Ps 79:17), 'All vicious sins come about either on account of burning desire, and these are called "sins set on fire"; or account of fear that wrongly humbles, and those are called "dug down sins". Therefore you should diligently examine your consciences, ask your hearts, whether sins can exist unless one fears or desires. For two things produce all human sins, desire and fear.'[12] On this point, notice Hugh of St Victor, *On the sacraments* 2.13.2, where he says, 'There are two motions

---

[9] *Polyc.* 3.14 (PL 199:507).
[10] Fulg 1.1 (17/3), citing Petronius frag. 27.1, echoed at *Thebaid* 3.661.
[11] Cassiodorus, *Expositio in Psalmos* 21 (PL 70:153).
[12] *Enarrationes in Psalmos*, on Ps 79:17 (PL 36:1026).

motus cor[d]is, quibus anima racionalis ad omne quod facit agendum impellitur. Unus est timor; alter est amor. Hec duo, cum bona si[n]t, omne bonum efficiunt. Per timorem enim mala cauentur; per amorem bona excercentur. Cum ergo mala sunt, omnium malorum causa existunt. Per timorem uero malum a bono receditur; per amorem uero malum mala perpetrantur. Sunt ergo duo hec quasi porte due per quas mors et uita ingrediuntur: mors, quando apperiuntur ad malum; uita, quando ad bonum reserantur'. Hec Hugo.

Et applicando ad propositum, ista duo, secundum Fulgencium, induxerunt homines ad colendum ydolum, amor seu cupiditas placendi patri construenti ymaginem filii mortui, et timor seu pusillanimitas paciendi. Quia malefactores timuerunt pati penas eis iuste pro peccatis debitas, ideo ut eas euaderent, ydolatriam commiserunt. Sed adulatores fecerunt ex cupiditate placendi illud, quod timidi fecerunt ex timore penas | debitas sustinendi. Sic ergo finitur prima methologia Fulgencii, in qua agit auctor de ydolatrie adinuencione et adinuente continuacione.

Uult enim Fulgencius ostendere, quomodo iste quattuor passiones principales in homine, de quibus loquitur Boecius, libro primo *De consolacione*, ducunt homines ad peccatum, et hoc loquendo de maximo genere peccati, quando non reguntur recta racione. Et sunt iste passiones amor, dolor, spes, et timor. Unde Boecius, libro primo, metro ultimo, sic dicit:

Tu quoque, si uis / lumine claro / cernere uerum, / tramite recto / carpere callem, / gaudia pelle; / pelle timorem, / spemque fugato, / nec dolor assit. / Nubila mens est / Uinctaque frenis / Hec ubi regnant.

Applicando ad propositum Fulgencii, nimi[u]s amor, per quem nimis gaudebat homo ille Egipcius de filio suo, fuit una passio

---

112 cordis] corporis O, *om*. I   112–14 quod ... omne] *om*. L   113 impellitur] expellitur A   114 sint] sunt I, sit O • sint ... bonum] sunt omnia bona I • efficiunt] faciunt siue efficiunt I, efficitur L   115 ergo] autem hec duo A
116 omnium ... existunt] omne malum efficiunt A   118 porte] partes A, *over eras*. I   118–19 porte ... malum] *om*. L   119 apperiuntur] operantur A
120 reserantur] referuntur L • Hugo] Augustinus A
122 ydolum] *a corr. from* deum [*blank*] A   123 mortui] *adds* constructi L
125 euaderent] cauerent A   127 fol. 84rb 128 finitur] *illeg. eras*. I
129 adinuente] de eiusdem A
133 reguntur] regulantur a L   136 lumine claro] clarum lumen A • cernere] dicere L   137 pelle²] *om*. AL   139 Uinctaque frenis] *om*. A
140 nimius] nimis O   141 nimis] uiuus A, *om*. I

of the heart that drive the rational mind to do everything that it does. One is fear, and the other love. These two, when they are good, bring about all good, for through fear, we beware evils, and through love, we perform good deeds. However, when they are evil, they are the cause of all evils. Evil fear draws back from the good, and evil love performs evil acts. Therefore these two are like two gates through which both death and life enter – death, when they are opened to evil; life, when they are opened to good,' So Hugh says.[13]

[121] Applying these opinions to the topic at hand: according to Fulgentius, these two have drawn people to idol-worship: love or desire for pleasing the father who constructed the image of his dead son, and fear or cowardice about enduring pain. Because malefactors feared suffering the punishments they justly deserved for their transgressions, to avoid them, they committed idolatry. But flatterers, from the desire to please, did the same thing that fearful people did from the fear of undergoing deserved punishment. So Fulgentius's first mythography ends; in it this author treats the invention of idolatry and its continuation.

[130] Fulgentius wishes to show how people's four principal passions lead them to sin, and he speaks here of the greatest kind of sin, when people are not ruled by right reason. Boethius speaks about these passions in *On the consolation* 1, and they are love, sorrow, hope, and fear. In the final poem of book 1 he says:

Therefore, if you wish / to know truth / with a clear sight / and to seize the way / in a direct path, / drive away both / joy and fear, / flee hope and / deny a place to sorrow. / Where these rule, / the mind is clouded, / conquered and in chains.[14]

Applying these verses to Fulgentius's point, unduly excessive love, through which the Egyptian Sirophanes rejoiced excessively in his son, was one

[13] *De sacramentis* 2.13.3 (*PL* 176:527).
[14] *Consolatio* 1m7.20–31.

deordinata in eo. Et istud gaudium excess[iu]um sequebatur +
dolor nimius et immoderata desolacio de filio mortuo. Sequebatur
eciam in eo temerata presumpcio, quam presumpcionem uocat
145 Boycius spem, nam propter uerba adulatorum credidit filium suum
deificatum. Sed in seruis reis et criminosis fuit quarta passio,
scilicet timor deordinatus; qui, ut possent penam eis debitam pro
sceleribus euadere, uolebant cultum soli Deo debitum exhibere
creature. De deordinacione autem talis timoris plura loquitur
150 Augustinus in suo originali *Super Iohannem*, omelia 21ª.
  Notare autem possumus [in ista prima methalogia]
quomodo Fulgencius in suo processu concordat cum Sacra
Scriptura, Sapiencie 14. Ibi enim Scriptura, describens ortum
ydolatrie, quasi idem | dicit cum ista narracione. *Inicium*, inquit,
155 *fornicacionis est exquisicio ydolorum, et adinuencio illorum*
corrupcio uite est. Non enim erant ab inicio, neque erunt in
perpetuum. Superuacuitas enim hominum hoc adinuenit. Acerbo
enim cum luctu dolens pater, cito sibi rapti filii fecit ymaginem; et
illum qui tunc quasi homo mortuus fuerat, nunc tanquam deum
160 *colere cepit, et constituit inter seruos sacra et sacrificia. Deinde*
interueniente tempore, et conualescente iniqua consuetudine,
hic error tanquam lex custoditus est, et tirannorum imperio
colebantur figmenta. Hec [Scriptura].
  Hic tamen notandum est dubium de processu auctoris. Nam
165 ipse recitat ydolatriam incepisse ab Egipciis, quia iste Cirophanes
primus ydolatra Egipcius fuit. Magister tamen in historiis,
capitulo 36 super Genesim, dicit primam ydolatriam ortam
esse a Babiloniis. 'Mortuo enim Belo, cuius filius fuit Ninus rex
Babilonis, iste Ninus in solacium doloris fecit fieri ymaginem
170 patris, cui tantam exhibebat reuerenciam, quod quibuslibet reis
[qui] ad eam confugi[ssent] parceret. Proinde homines de regno
diuinos honores ymagini illi ceperunt inpendere; et sicut ab
ydolo Beel cetera ydola traxerunt originem, sic et ab eius nomine
diriuatum est generale nomen ydolorum. Sicut enim dictus est

---

142 excessiuum] excessum O   143 dolor] unus dolor O • immoderata]
  inordinata A   146 quarta] *om.* L   149 plura] pulcre L
151 in ... methalogia] *om.* O   154 fol. 84ᵛᵃ • Inicium] Quicunque L
  163 colebantur] celebrantur A • Scriptura] ibi O
166 ydolatra] *om.* I   166 historiis] historia A   167 capitulo 36 super Genesim]
  om. AIL   168, 169 Ninus] unus, unus rex A   169 solacium] remedium A
  • doloris] dolorum suorum I • fieri] *om.* L   171 qui ... confugissent] ad eam
  confugientibus O   172 diuinos] dignos A   173 Beel] *om.* A, Beli I • traxerunt]
  ceperunt A

disordered passion in him. And an unduly excessive sorrow and immoderate unhappiness from his son's death followed this excessive joy. A blemished presumption – Boethius calls it hope – also followed, for on the basis of flatterers' words, he believed that his son had been made a god. But the fourth passion, disordered fear, was in his guilty and criminous servants; to avoid the punishment they deserved for their crimes, they chose to show a creature that worship that is appropriate to God alone. Augustine speaks a great deal in his composition *On John*, homily 21, about the disorder associated with such fear.[15]

[151] I can point out how Fulgentius's argument in this first mythography agrees with that in Scripture, Sap 14:12–16. There Scripture, describing the birth of idolatry, says much the same thing as Fulgentius's story does: *The beginning of fornication is the devising of idols, and the invention of them is the corruption of life. For neither were they from the beginning, neither shall they be forever. For by the vanity of men they came into the world. For a father, being afflicted with a bitter grief, made to himself the image of his son, who was quickly taken away. And him who then had died as a man, he began now to worship as a god and appointed him rites and sacrifices among his servants. Then in process of time, wicked custom prevailing, this error was kept as a law, and statues were worshipped by the commandment of tyrants.* So Scripture says.

[164] Here, however, one should notice a doubtful point about our author's argument. For he tells that idolatry began with the Egyptians, since the first idolator Sirophanes was an Egyptian. Yet the Master of the Histories, Peter Comestor, in his Genesis 36, says that idolatry first arose among the Babylonians. 'After Bel's death, his son Ninus, king of Babylon, had an image of his father made to relieve his sorrow. He showed such reverence to it that he would spare any guilty person who had fled to the image. For this reason, the people of his kingdom began to devote divine honours to this image, and just as other idols followed the original one, Beel, the general name for idols, was derived from his name. For just as

---

[15] *In Iohannis euangelium* 43.7 (PL 35:1708).

John Ridewall, *Fulgencius metaforalis*

175 Belus ab Assiriis, sic et alie naciones, secundum ydeomata lingue sue, dixerunt Beel, alie Baal, alie Baalim, alie Belphegor, alie Belzebub'. Hec | Magister ibidem. Et accepit ab Ysidoro et aliis auctoribus, ex quorum dictis uidetur quod primi ydolatre non fuerunt Egipcii, sed pocius Assirii siue Babilonii. Nota eciam quod
180 Ysodorus recitat unam [antiquam] opinionem ab illo Prometheo, sicut patet 8 *Ethimologiarum*, capitulo 11, que est 'opinio gentilium dicencium Prometheum primum simulacra hominum de luto finxisse, et ab eo natam esse artem fingendi statuas et ydola. Sed apud Grecos', ut dicit Ysidorus, 'Cecrops primus omnium ydola
185 reperit, aras constituit, uictimas immolauit, [nunquam talibus antea uisis] in Grecia'. Hec ille.
   Dicendum tamen quod auctor iste non intendit texere historiam, sed pocius methologiam, sermonem scilicet fabulosum et apologicum, ordinatum ad descripcionem
190 uiciorum et uirtutum. Unde *mithos* Grece idem \quod/ 'fabula' Latine. Et ideo non curat de ueritate historie, apud quam gentem primo incepit hoc genus uicii. Sibi enim sufficit ut ostendat, quare ydolatria oritur ex passionibus hominis deordinatis, cuius[modi] sunt amor et dolor, timor indiscretus et temeritas
195 presumpcionis. Alia tamen est responsio, quod gens Egipciorum est [gens] antiquissima. Sicut patet ex *Tymeo* Platonis et ex aliis historiis antiquis, precessit enim ista gens gentem Assiriorum multis annorum milibus. Tamen dicta Ysidori et aliorum + uerificantur, non quod simpliciter fuerit illud ydolum primum
200 quod \a/ Nino fuit factum, sed fuit primum uicinis gentibus pro tunc notum.
   Notari eciam hic potest qualiter antiqua pictura poetica huius maximi peccati, scilicet ydolatrie, concordat cum processu

---

175 Belus] Bolus A   176–86 dixerunt ... ille] *om., but added at foot of prec. page so far as* 180 Ysidorus, *then partially repeated in consecutive copy* I
176 alie Baalim] *om*. AI   177 fol. 84vb • Magister] multiter (?) I • ibidem] in historiis AIL • aliis] *adds* historiis et L   179 Babilonii] Babilonici I
180 antiquam] aliam AI, *om*. O • Prometheo] Prothomero A   181 gentilium] gencium L   182 Prometheum] Prothomeum A   183 finxisse] fecisse et finxisse I
184 Cecrops] Eycropys A   185–86 nunquam ... Grecia] *om*. I, nequaquam istius mundi rebus in Grecia nusquam O
187 tamen] *om*. L • iste] *add* Fulgentius AIL   190 mithos] michos A, mithologia I
191–92 apud ... uicii] sed I   193 oritur] ortum habeat A   194 cuiusmodi] cuius O   195–201 Alia ... notum] *added at page foot* I   195 responsio] racio I
196 gens] *om*. O   198 aliorum] *adds* auctorum O   199 a Nino] astino I
202 qualiter] aliter A • antiqua] *om*. I

the Assyrians called it Belus, other nations, in accord with the forms in their own language, named theirs Beel or Baal or Baalim or Belphegor or Beelzebub.' So the Master of the Histories says there,[16] and he drew his account from Isidore and other authors. From their writings, it appears that the first idolators were not Egyptians, but rather Assyrians or Babylonians. Also notice that Isidore, *Etymologies* 8.11, repeats an ancient opinion about a certain Prometheus; 'there's a pagan opinion that Prometheus shaped the first simulacrum of humans out of mud, and from his act developed the art of shaping statues and idols.' But Isidore says that 'among the Greeks, Cecrops was the first person of all who discovered idols, constructed altars, and made sacrifices, activities never before seen in Greece.'[17] So he says.

[187] Yet one should say that Fulgentius does not intend to compose a history, but rather a mythography. That is a species of writing devoted to fables and anecdotes, constructed to describe sins and virtues. For this reason, the Greek word *mithos* is the same as Latin *fabula* 'fable'. Therefore Fulgentius does not care about the factual issue, among what people this kind of sin first began. For his purpose, it is sufficient to show how idolatry had its beginning in disordered human passions; love, sorrow, undiscerning fear, and bold presumption are examples. However, there is another response to this doubtful point, namely that the Egyptians are the most ancient of peoples. As is evident from Plato's *Timaeus* and other ancient histories,[18] this people predated the Assyrians by many thousand years. Nevertheless the opinions of Isidore and others are verified, not because the first idol was made by Ninus precisely, but it was the first well known at the time to neighbouring peoples.

[202] Also here one can notice how the ancient poetic picture of this greatest sin, Idolatry, agrees with

---

[16] *Historia scholastica*, Genesis 40 (PL 198:1090).
[17] *Etym.* 8.11.8–10 (PL 82:315).
[18] Chalcidius 22B, his translation of *Timaeus* 21e–22b.

52   John Ridewall, *Fulgencius metaforalis*

        Fulgencii in serie istius methologie. Hec enim fuit apud a[nt]iquos
205   pictura ydolatrie:
           [1] mulier notata,
           [2] oculis orbata,
           [3] aure mutilata,
           [4] cornu uentilata, |
210   [5] uultu deformata,
           [6] et morbo uexata.
        [1] Pingebatur enim in f[igu]ra mulieris, meretricis et male fame
[et fornicarie], quia sicut dicit quedam glossa super 14 capitulo
libri Sapiencie, hoc est pessimum genus fornicacionis, quo anima
215   recedit a Deo et fornicatur cum ydolis.
        [2-3] Secundo, [ista ydolatria] pingebatur ceca et auribus
destituta, nam adulacio fuit ex[ceca]trix ydolatrie ex amore
deordinato adinuente. Adulacio enim est excecatrix hominum,
sicut pulcre tangit Carnotensis in suo *Policratico*, libro 3,
220   capitulo 4: 'Adulator, omnis uirtutis inimicus, quasi clauum figit
in oculo illius, cum quo sermonem conserit; [eo] quod magis
cauendus est, quo sub [aman]tis specie. Nocere non desinit,
donec racionis obtundat acumen, et modicum illud luminis quod
uidebatur adesse extinguat. Ad hoc auditorum aures obturat, ne
225   audiant uerum; quo quid esse [poterit] perniciosius, non facile
dixerim'.
        [4] Tercio, [ista ydolatria] pingitur malefica et exilio profuga
ac de crimine lese maiestatis conuicta, et ideo merito cornu
uentilata. Ipsa enim est maxima creatoris [iniuria similiter]
230   ad ostendendum, quod timor seruilis fuit una de causis
continuantibus ydolatriam. Et malefici, quibus conuenit cornubus
uentilari, ydola coluerunt, sperantes se per talem cultum
habituros refugium et remissionem suorum [delictorum], sicut
patet \per/ Fulgencium.

   204 antiquos] aliquos AOL   207 orbata] olbata I   209 fol. 85ra 211 et … uexata]
      uerbo taxata I   212 figura] forma O • mulieris] muliebri mulieris scilicet I
      213 et fornicarie] et fornica(cionis?) I, *om.* OL • dicit] *om.* L
   216 ista ydolatria] *om.* OL   217 excecatrix] executrix IOL   220 clauum] oculum L
      221 conserit] confert A, conferit I • eo quod] eoque A, ideoque I, quod O
      222 amantis] sanctitatis O   223 obturat] *om.* A   225 quid] *adds* aliquid A
      • poterit] *om.* IO, possit L
   227 ista ydolatria] ista I, *om.* OL   228 conuicta] uicta I   229 iniuria similiter]
      inimica semper O   231 ydolatriam] *adds* \nota quod/ I   233 delictorum]
      scelerum O   234-36 patet … merore] *om.* I

Fulgentius's account in the sequence of his mythography. For idolatry was depicted by ancient writers as:

[1] designated a woman,
[2] deprived of eyes,
[3] with a mutilated ear,
[4] blown by a horn,
[5] with a deformed face,
[6] and tormented by illness.

[1] For idolatry was depicted in the shape of a woman, a fornicating whore well known for her evil, because, as a gloss on Sap 14 says, the worst kind of fornication is when the soul withdraws from God and fornicates with idols.[19]

[216] [2–3] Second, idolatry was depicted as blind and deprived of ears, because flattery blinded idolatry, once it had been invented from disordered love. For flattery blinds people, as John of Salisbury says neatly in *Polycraticus* 3.4, 'A flatterer is the enemy of all virtue. He, as it were, sticks a nail in the eye of the person on whom he scatters his speech; and the more loving a flatterer appears to be, the more he should be avoided. A flatterer does not cease hurting a person until he dulls all the penetration of reason and extinguishes whatever bit of light appeared to be present. In addition, he stops up his hearers' ears, lest they hear the truth; it would not be easy for me to say what might be more damaging.'[20]

[227] [4] Third, idolatry is depicted as a witch, driven into exile, convicted of the crime of injuring royalty – and therefore properly blown about by a horn. For idolatry similarly shows the greatest injury to the creator, because servile fear was one among the causes of perpetuating idolatry. Wizards, who are appropriately blown about with horns, worship idols, in the hope that, through this ritual, they will have a haven and absolution for their crimes, as Fulgentius shows.

---

[19] Glossa on Sap. 14:12 (*PL* 113:1178).
[20] *Ibid.* (*PL* 199:481).

[5] Quarto, depingitur hec fornicaria uultu + deformata, tanquam tristis et merore confecta, in signum quod una de causis ydolatrie fuit dolor et mesticia deordinata.

[6] Quinto, pingitur hec fornicaria, morbo fatigata. Pingitur enim uexata quadam | infirmitate, que dicitur *amor ereos*. Qui est amor excessiuus et indiscretus, qui egrotare facit amantem, secundum quod docet commentator super 8^m *Ethicorum*, in signum quod ex amore deordinato et indiscreto, et excessiuo ortum habuit istud grauissimum + peccatum, sicut prius patuit per Fulgencium.

---

235 uultu] *adds* turpata uel O   **236** tanquam … confecta] *om.* A • confecta] confracta I
239 fol. 85rb **242** et indiscreto] *om.* I   **243** peccatum] genus peccatum O • prius] *om. and adds after* Fulgencium **244**, tractatorem presencium I

[**235**] [5] Fourth, this harlot idolatry is depicted with a deformed face, as if sad and formed in sorrow, an indication that among the causes of idolatry were sorrow and disordered grief.

[162] [6] Fifth, this harlot idolatry is depicted as exhausted by illness. For idolatry is depicted as racked by the disease called *amor hereos*. That is an excessive and indiscriminate love that makes the lover ill, as the commentator on Aristotle's *Nicomachean Ethics* 8 teaches.[21] This is an indication that this most grievous sin had its origin in disordered, indiscriminate, and excessive love, as Fulgentius has already made clear.

---

[21] *Ibid.* 8.3 (1156ab); L identifies the commentator as Averroes.

[2]

Secunda mithologia Fulgencii est fabula Saturni, in cuius serie intendunt Fulgencius et alii poete describere uirtutem prudencie. Ab ea enim inter ceteras uirtutes incipit auctor iste, quia ipsa est, sicut patet per commentatorem 6° *Ethicorum*, rectrix et auriga
5 omnium aliarum uirtutum. Unde Fulgencius allegat hic illum [antiquum] auctorem Apollophanem, quem dicit uocasse in suo carmine Saturnum 'diuinum sensuum et creatorem omnium'. Uiri enim prudencia prediti computati erant inter gentiles in numero numinum et deorum, sicut patet \per/ Lactancium, cuius
10 sentencia ponitur in glossa super librum Sapiencie, 14 capitulo. Et de isto tangit Seneca in suis epistolis, sicut patet epistola 76, ubi allegat dictum illius antiqui auctoris Sex[t]i, qui 'solebat dicere Iouem non posse plus quam bonum uirum'. Unde, sicut ibi deducit Seneca, 'Deus non uincit uirum sapientem et prudentem felicitate,
15 etsi uincat eum etate', hoc est duracionis diuturnitate. Et poeta Iuuenalis, '\Nulla numen abes[t]/, si sit prudencia, sed te / nos facimus, Fortuna, deam celoque locamus'.

Qualiter eciam prudencia sit creatrix omnium, sicut Saturnus, patet, quia ipsa est recta racio omnium agibilium.
20 Unde poete fingunt, sicut patet ex Ouidio, libro primo *De transformatis*, | quod regnante Saturno, seculum fuit aureum, uolens intelligere quod illo tempore omnia fieba[n]t uirorum sapiencium consilio, sicut patet per illum auctorem antiquum Possidonium, cuius sentenciam recitat Seneca in quadam
25 [epistola], dicens, 'In illo seculo quod aureum perhibent, penes sapientes regnum fuisse Possidonius iudicat. Hii continebant manus, et infirmiores a ualidioribus tuebantur; suadebant et dissuadebant, utilia atque inutilia monstrabant. Horum prudencia, ne quid deesset suis, prouidebat; fortitudo eorum

---

1 Fulgencii] *om.* I   4 rectrix] retrix I   6 antiquum] *om.* IO   • uocasse] *om.* A
7 diuinum] dominum I   • sensuum] sanctum A   8–13 Uiri … uirum] *marg.* I
9 numinum] *blank* A, *illeg.* I   9–10 cuius sentencia] *om.* I   11 in … patet] *om.* I
12 antiqui] *om.* I   • Sexti] Sexii AOL   13 Iouem] racionem A   • sicut ibi deducit] *om.* I   16 numen] inuenit I   • abest] abesse IOL
21 fol. 85va 22 omnia fiebant] fiebat A, omnia fiebat IO, fiebat … [reg]no L uirorum] *om.* A   23 sapiencium] sapientum A, discretorum et sapientum I
25 epistola] *om.* O   • perhibent] exhiberet A   regnum] regimen A
25–31 quod … Seneca] *om. and added at the page foot* I

56

[2]

Fulgentius's second mythography is the fable of Saturn, in the course of which Fulgentius and other poets intend to describe the virtue Prudence.[1] Among all the virtues, my author begins with it, for prudence, as the commentator on Aristotle's *Nicomachean Ethics* 6 makes clear, is the director and charioteer of all other virtues.[2] For this reason, Fulgentius invokes here the ancient author Apollophanes, whom he says called Saturn in his poem 'divine and the origin of all the wits'.[3] For the pagans accounted men endowed with prudence among the supernatural powers and the gods, as Lactantius makes clear – his opinion appears in a gloss on Sap 14.[4] And Seneca treats this in his letters, particularly epistle 76, where he invokes a saying of the ancient author Sextus, 'who was accustomed to say that Jupiter could be no greater than the good man'. For this reason, as Seneca deduces there, 'God cannot exceed a wise and prudent man in happiness, although he may do so in age', that is, in his persistent existence.[5] And the poet Juvenal says, 'If prudence is present, no supernatural power is absent; however, we ourselves make Luck a goddess and place her in heaven.'[6]

[18] How prudence, just like Saturn, is the creator of all things is evident, for this virtue is right reason controlling all our actions. For this reason, poets feign, as is evident from Ovid, *Metamorphoses* 1, that so long as Saturn ruled, it was a golden age.[7] Ovid wants us to understand that at that time all things were done in accord with wise peoples' counsel. This is also evident from the ancient author Posidonius; Seneca repeats his opinion in one of his letters, saying, 'In that age that people regard as golden, Posidonius judges that power was in hands of wise men alone. They restrained their hand, and the stronger nurtured the weaker; the wise persuaded and dissuaded, demonstrating which things were useful and which useless. Their prudence provided for them, so that they lacked nothing; their courage

---

[1] Fulg 1.2 (17/10–18).
[2] Cf. 2.2 (1104b).
[3] Fulg 1.2 (18/8–10).
[4] *Ibid.*, 1480 edn, 2:737b.
[5] Epistula 73.12–13.
[6] *Satyra* 10.365–66.
[7] *Metamorphoses* 1.89–112.

30 arcebat pericula; benificia horum augebat ornabatque subiectos'. Et multa alia dicit ibi Seneca. Quia ergo tempore Saturni omnia regebantur prudencia, [ideo significanter] prudencia creatrix dicitur omnium ad aureum seculum pertinencium.

 Nota eciam, secundum quod tangit Fulgencius, [iste Saturnus] dicitur Pollucis filius. Et apud poetas Pollux significat humanitatem; unde Saturnus dicitur filius Pollucis, id est humanitatis. Luce enim prudencie destituti pocius inter bestias et bruta animalia quam inter homines sunt computandi. Et hoc tractat commentator super librum *Ethicorum*, ostendens quomodo nomen et uocabulum hominis principaliter conuenit intellectui, qui dicitur homo interior. Corpus uero hom[o] habet commune cum bestiis. Et ideo corpus humanum ab auctoribus Ysidoro et aliis dicitur homo exterior, quia corpori non competit nomen humanitatis, nisi extrinseca denominacione | ab humanitate anime racionalis, que est homo interior. Et de isto nota Ieronimum, *Super Ezechielem*; et Crisostomum super Mattheum in *Opere perfecto*, et Boecium, *De consolacione philosophie*. Omnes isti uolunt quod homo qui non regitur [recta] racione in numero hominum non sit ponendus, sed pocius [irracionabilium] bestiarum. Unde dicit Crisostomus [in originali 4], 'Cum calcitres ut azinus, saltes ut taurus, hinn\i/as in mulieres ut equus, castrimargiam paciaris ut ursa, inpingues carnem ut mulus, memor es mali ut camelus, rapias ut lupus, irascaris ut serpens, percucias ut scorpio, dolosus sis ut uulpes, uenenum malicie obserues ut aspis \et/ uipera, qualiter potero te inter homines numerare, non uidens in te caracterem talis nature'? 'Certe', dicit Crisostomus, 'fera omni deterior est qui talis est'.

 Et nota hic significanter quomodo poete per Pollucem, Saturni patrem, intelligere uolunt humanitatem. Pollux enim dicitur quasi 'luce pollens'. Modo illud quod potissime pollet et preualet in homine est lux siue lumen racionis et intelligencie, sicut tangit Tullius in suo libro *De senectute*, allegans dictum

---

 30–31 188–89 pericula ... Seneca] *om*. A 30 benificia] bene I, beneficiencia L 31 tempore] tunc L 32 ideo significanter] *om*. O

34 secundum quod] quomodo AIL 34–35 iste Saturnus] *om*. O 35–37 Et ... humanitas] *om*. I 35 Pollux] *add* Pollucis AL 38 bruta animalia] cetera animancia L 41 homo] *om*. A, hominis O 43 competit] conuenit (?) I 44 fol. 85vb 48 recta] *om*. O 49 irracionabilium] *om*. O 50 in originali] Morali I • in ... 4] *om*. O 52 carnem] *om*. L • mulus] sus et mulus A 56 caracterem] caracteres AIL 57 deterior] pessima I

58 significanter] *om*. AI 60 pollet] *adds* et lucet A

repelled dangers; their kindnesses improved and ornamented their inferiors.' Seneca says many other relevant things there.[8] Therefore, because in Saturn's time everything was ruled by prudence, this virtue is significantly called the creator of all those things that identify the golden age.

[34] Also notice that, following what Fulgentius says, Saturn is called the son of Pollux. Among the poets, Pollux indicates humanity; for this reason, Saturn is called the son of humanity.[9] For those deprived of the light of prudence are accounted among the beasts and brute animals, rather than among humanity. The commentator on Aristotle's *Ethics* discusses this; he shows how the word and title 'humanity' directly answers to intellect, what is called the 'inner person'. For humanity has a body in common with the beasts, and therefore Isidore and other authors call the human body the 'outer person'.[10] For the noun 'humanity' does not pertain to the body, except as an external denotation derived from the human nature of the rational soul, the 'inner person'. On this point, notice what Jerome says in his commentary *On Ezechiel*, and Chrysostom in his *Perfect work* on Matthew, and Boethius in *On the consolation of philosophy*.[11] All these authors wish to show that a person who is not ruled by right reason should not be placed in the category 'human', but rather that of the irrational beasts. For this reason, Chrysostom says in homily 4, 'When you stomp on things like a jackass, leap about like a bull, whinny after women like a stallion, suffer gluttony like a bear, become fatty-fleshed like a mule, recall bad things done you like a camel, seize things like a wolf, grow angry like a snake, strike like a scorpion, are deceitful like a fox, follow poisonous malice like an asp or a viper, how can I place you in the category "human", when I don't see in you any mark of that nature?' Chrysostom says, 'Certainly, a person like that is worse than any savage beast.'[12]

[58] Notice here that it is significant how the poets wish to understand 'the human' through Pollux, Saturn's father. For Pollux means something like 'being powerful through light'. Now the thing that is strongest and most powerful in a person is the light of reason and intelligence, as Cicero says in *On old age*, where he cites a saying from

---

[8] *Epistula* 90.5.
[9] Fulg 1.2 (17/17–19).
[10] *Nicomachean Ethics* 9.8 (1168b–69a); *Etym.* 11.1.6 (*PL* 82:398).
[11] Jerome, *Super Ezechielem* 1.1 (*PL* 25:22); *Consolatio* 2p5.24–29 (and cf. 4p3.15–23).
[12] *In Matt.*, hom. 4 (*PG* 57:48). Also cited *Fasciculus morum* 514/134–40.

60 John Ridewall, *Fulgencius metaforalis*

Archite Tarentini. Qui consueuit dicere 'nichil prestancius datum homini a Deo racione et discrecione'. Et de hoc tangit Seneca, [in
65 quadam epistola, et est in aliquibus libris] 78, '[Omnia bono suo constant]. Uitem fertilitas commendat et sapor uinum, uelocitas [ceruum]. Sed quid est optimum in homine'? querit Seneca et respondet, 'Racio; hac enim antecedit animalia et deos sequitur. Racio ergo perfecta proprium hominis bonum est'. Hec ille.
70 Notandum est [ulterius] hic pictura posita a Fulgencio de Saturno, nam pingitur:
[1] Opi maritatus,
[2] senio | grauatus,
[3] capite uelatus,
75 [4] falce sept[r]atus,
[5] uultu desolatus,
[6] pudendis orbatus,
[7] prole cibatus.
Iste sunt septem proprietates, quas Saturno Fulgencius
80 attribuit, licet Remigius in commento super Marcianum plures sibi attribuat.
[1] Uideamus ergo quomodo ista sit pictura [uirtutis] prudencie, que merito dicitur Opi maritata, id est auxilio et subuencioni. Semper enim conuenit prudencie subuenire et
85 auxilium ferre tempore indigencie, sicut [de hoc pulcre] tractat Apuleius [in libro suo] *De deo Socratis*, ubi allegat Omerum dicentem Ulixem semper habuisse prudenciam comitem. 'Quam prudenciam poetico ritu', ut dicit Apuleius, 'Homerus uocauit Mineruam. Ista autem prudencia comitante, Ulixes
90 omnia horrenda subiit, omnia aduersa superauit, quippe ea adiutrice Sciclopis specus introiit, sed egressus est; Sol[i]s boues uidit, sed abstinuit; ad inferos demeauit, sed ascendit; eadem prudencia comite Cillam preternauigauit, nec [er]eptus est;

---

63 Qui] *add* Architas IL • consueuit] solebat A   64–65 in … libris] in quadam epistola I, epistola O   65–66 Omnia … constant] boto suo O   66 constant] sucristant I   67 ceruum] *corr. to* crini<bus>? O
70 ulterius] *om.* O   70–71 de … pingitur] *om.* A   71 nam pingitur] qui apud poetas pingitur sic iste Saturnus I   72 maritatus] maturatus A   73 fol. 86ra
75 septratus] stipatus A, septizatus O   79 proprietates] *om.* I • Saturno] de Saturno A, *om.* I   80 attribuit] ponit A
82 uirtutis] *om.* O   83 merito] *om.* L   85 ferre] facere L • tempore] *om.* A   85–86 de … suo] tractat Apuleius O   86 Apuleius] Achilleus A   87 semper] fingitur A   88–89 Homerus … Mineruam] *marg.* I   91 Solis] Solus O
93 ereptus] deceptus O

Architas of Taranto. Architas used to say that 'nothing God gave humanity was more outstanding than reason and discretion.'[13] Seneca discusses this in the epistle numbered 78 in some copies, 'All things are worthwhile for the good appropriate to them. Fertility commends the vine and tastiness wine, as its speed does the deer. But', Seneca asks, 'what is the best end in a person?' and he replies, 'Reason, for by this power, we have precedence over the animals, and we follow the gods. Thus, perfect reason is humanity's proper end.'[14] So he says.

[70] One should further notice this picture of Saturn that Fulgentius offers,[15] for he is depicted:

[1] married to Ops,
[2] bowed down by age,
[3] with covered head,
[4] with a sickle as sceptre,
[5] with a mourning face,
[6] deprived of his genitals,
[7] fed with his offspring.

These are the seven properties Fulgentius assigns to Saturn, although Remigius, in his commentary on Martianus Capella, gives him still more.[16]

[82] [1] Let us see how this might be a picture of the virtue Prudence. This virtue is properly said to be married to Ops, that is to aid and assistance. For it is always appropriate to prudence to offer assistance and to bring help at a time of need, as Apuleius discusses in *On Socrates's god*. There he cites Homer, who says that Ulysses always had prudence as his partner, and as Apuleius says, 'Homer, following the style of poets, calls prudence Minerva. With prudence's aid, Ulysses endured terrifying things and triumphed over all his hardships. For with prudence's aid, he entered the Cyclops's cave, but came out again; he saw the oxen of the sun, but refrained from eating them; he passed down to Hades, but ascended again; with his partner prudence, he sailed past Scylla, but was not snatched away;

---

[13] *De senectute* 12.40.
[14] *Epistula* 76.8–9.
[15] Fulg 1.2 (17/10–12).
[16] Mart 5.22 (73/3–11), for example.

[C]aribdi conceptus, retentus non est; Circis poculum bibit,
nec mutatus est; ad Lotho[fage]s accessit, nec remansit;
Siren[a]s audiuit, nec accessit'. Hec Apuleius Maudorensis de
uirtute prudencie et eius suffragiis. Unde conuenienter dicitur
Opi maritari. Nota Ops, Opis, de qua loquuntur poete, est dea
frugum et uocatur tali nomine pro sua opitulacione, qua
opitulatur hominibus in humane uite sustentacione.

[2] Secunda pars picture est etatis maturitas, quia Saturnum
poete fingunt senem et etate maturum. | Uirtus enim prudencie
reperitur in senibus, et non in iuuenibus, dicente Aristotele in
suis *Topicis*, 'Nemo iuuenes eligit duces, eo quod constet eos non
esse prudentes'. Et nota quomodo isti poete dixerunt Saturnum
deum temporis; unde uoca[ba]tur ab aliqui\bus/ Cronos. Est enim
cronos Grece [idem quod] 'tempus' Latine, et hoc quia prudencia,
per Saturnum designata, requirit tempus, quia prudencia requirit
magnam experienciam, que non habetur, nisi in magn[i] spacio
temporis. Notari autem possunt hic ea que dicit Tullius, libro
De senectute, de prudencia senum: 'Non uiribus', dicit Tullius,
'aut [ueloc]itate aut celeritat[e] corporis res magne geruntur, sed
consilio, auctoritate, et sentencia; quibus non modo non orbari,
sed augeri senectus solet'. Hec ille. Ambrosius eciam in suo
Exameron, omelia 9[a], dicit quod senectus ipsa est in bonis moribus
dulcior, in consiliis utilior, ad constanciam subeunde mortis
paracior, et ad reprimendas libidines forcior. Si ergo plus habeat
senectus de consiliatiua, sequitur quod plus habeat de prudencia,
sicut patet ex 6 *Ethicorum*.

[3] Tercia pars picture est de capitis uelamine. Ad litteram
apud antiquos paganos, philosophi et sapientes prudencia prediti
consuerunt incedere uelato capite, id est pilliato, in signum et
testimonium honoris et reuerencie, que debetur isti uirtuti. Et
de isto essent notande historie gentilium tractantes de habitu
et uestimentis philosophorum et uirorum prudencium. Et nota hic,
que narrat Alexander Nekham | in suis *Methologiis* de flaminibus

94 Caribdi conceptus] *om.* A   94–95 Caribdi ... mutatus est] *after 96* accessit O
95 mutatus] ututatus (?) I • Lothofages] Lothocagos O   96 Sirenas] Sirenes O
• Apuleius Maudorensis] *om.* A   97 prudencie] *om.* L
102 fol. 86[rb]   104 constet] *om.* A   106 uocabatur] uocatur O   107 idem quod] *om.* O
109 experienciam] *adds* temporis A • magni] magno O   112 uelocitate]
nobilitate O • celeritate] celeritatibus IOL   113 sentencia] sciencia AI
116 dulcior] direccio L
121 apud] *adds* Latinos, *expunged* O   122 consuerunt] solebant L   122–23 id ...
uirtuti] *marg.* I   122 signum et] *om.* A   125 et uestimentis] *om.* AI   126 fol. 86[va]

Text and translation: Book 1 [2] Saturn/Prudence 63

although caught by Charybdis, it did not hold him; he drank from Circe's cup, but was not transformed; he approached the Lotus-eaters, but did not stop; he heard the Sirens, but did not submit to them.' That is what Apuleius of Madauros says of the virtue prudence and of the support it gives.[17] For this reason, Saturn is appropriately said to be married to Ops. Notice that Ops (the genitive is Opis), about whom the poets speak, is the goddess of the crops, and she is called that because of her *opilacio* 'assistance', for she aids people in supporting human life.[18]

[101] [2] The second part of the picture describes Saturn's mature age, because the poets depict him as old and mature in years. For the virtue of prudence is found in old people, and not in youths, as Aristotle says in his *Topics*, 'No one chooses their leaders from youths, because it is a property of youths not to be prudent.'[19] And notice how the poets called Saturn the god of time; for this reason, some called him Chronos. For *chronos* in Greek means the same thing as 'time' in Latin,[20] and this is appropriate because prudence, identified with Saturn, requires time. Prudence requires extensive experience, and one does not gain it except through an extended period of time. In this regard, one can notice the things Cicero says, in *On old age*, about the prudence of old people: 'Great deeds are not brought to conclusion by strength or speed or bodily swiftness, but through good counsel, authoritative knowledge, and wise thought. These qualities are in no way removed in old age, but increased.'[21] So he says. Ambrose also, in his *Hexameron*, homily 9, says that age is sweeter in its good behaviours, more useful in its counsels, more prepared for constancy in facing death, and stronger in repressing desires.[22] Therefore if age should have greater consultative powers, it follows that it should have greater prudence, as is evident from *Nicomachean Ethics* 6.[23]

[120] [3] The third part of the picture concerns the veil on Saturn's head. Addressing the literal sense, among the ancient pagans, philosophers and wise men endowed with prudence were accustomed to walk about with their heads veiled, that is with a cap, as an indication of and witness to the honour and reverence that this virtue merits. On this point, one should notice the histories of the pagans that treat the dress and clothing of philosophers and prudent people. And notice here what Alexander Neckam tells in his *Mythology* about the pagan flamens,

---

[17] *De deo Socratis* 24.
[18] Fulg 1.2 (17/16–17).
[19] *Topics* 3.2 (117a).
[20] Fulg 2.1 (39/19–40/1).
[21] *De senectute* 6.17.
[22] *Hexameron* 1.8.31 (PL 14:140).
[23] *Ibid.* 6.8 (1142a).

gentilium, qui fuerunt sacerdotes paganorum, quomodo fuerat nephas eis incedere discooperto capite propter reuerenciam status. Unde in diebus festiuis necesse fuit eis uelare caput c[um] pell[e]is; aliis uero temporibus, propter magnitudinem caloris [et estus] fugiendam, utebantur filo, quo capita religabant, ne nudo capite incederent. Unde dicti sunt flamines +, quasi filamines. In testimonium ergo honoris et reuerencie, que uiris prudencia preditis et morum honestate conspicuis debebatur, incedebant tales persone uelato capite. Nota quod secundum Remigium, in commento suo super Marcianum, *De nupciis Mercurii*, istud uelamen capitis Saturni pingitur [glaucum, id est] uiride, et hoc in signum quod prudencia nunquam marescet, sed semper uirescet.

[4] Quarta pars picture est de falcis deportacione. Loco enim sceptri differt Saturnus falcem curuam in manu sua. Ad prudenciam enim pertinet regnare; tales enim digni sunt regimine. Unde et Socrates, qui Apollinis oraculo fuit sapientissimus iudicatus, asseruit tunc demum res puplicas beatas fore, quando philosophi uiri, scilicet prudencia prediti, eas regerent aut rectores earum studere sapiencie contigisset, ut recitat Carnotensis in suo *Policratico*, libro 4. Ubi adducit Scripturam, Prouerbiorum 8, ad eandem materiam, que dicit, loquens in persona sapiencie, *Per me reges regnant et principes imperant et potentes discernunt iusticiam*.

Prudencia ergo, in signum regiminis et regie dignitatis, | portat sceptrum, sed in signum magnifice largitatis defert sceptrum ad modum falcis recuruatum, ut omnes ad se posset attrahere et panem potumque sapiencie cunctis largissime ministrare. Nota hic Scripturam, Prouerbiorum 9, ubi Salomon, utens colore rethorico qui Grece dicitur *prosapeia*, Latine uero 'confirmacio', introducit Sapienciam conuiuium ordinantem et indifferenter omnes indigentes ad illud inuitantem. Unde dicit

---

129 cum pilleis] cum palleis A, c'a | pellis, *over eras.* O   130 et estus] *om.* O
131 filo] [*blank*] A   132 flamines] *adds* \sacerdotes/ O • flamines ... filamines] flamies L   136 Marcianum] librum I   137 glaucum id est] *om.* O, glaucum et L
138 marescet] marcet IL • uirescet] uiret AIL
140 differt] defert AL • Saturnus] prudencia AI   141 tales ... regimine] *om.* I
• sunt regimine] sunt sunt regnare A   143 iudicatus] *om.* A • tunc] sunt I
• demum] tunc (*repeats*) A • beatas fore quando] bonas fore retulisse quando siue L   144 prediti] *adds* uel prudencie dediti L   144–48 aut ... iusticiam] *marg.* I   146–47 ad ... sapiencie] *om.* I   148 discernunt] decernunt AL
149 dignitatis] deitatis (?) I • fol. 86vb   152 cunctis largissime] omnibus (cunctis A) largiter AI   154–55 qui ... confirmacio] *illeg. marg.* I • confirmacio] consolacio A   156 illud] conuiuium AIL

their priests, how it had been prohibited for them to walk about with uncovered heads on account of the reverence due to their office. For this reason, on festival days, they were required to veil their heads with caps; at other times, so as to avoid the great heat, they used only a cord that they tied around their heads, lest they should walk around bareheaded. For this reason, these priests are called *flamines*, as if they were *filamines* 'marked out by a cord'. Thus, as witness to the honour and reverence that was owed to people endowed with prudence and outstanding in their virtuous behaviour, such people walked about with their heads veiled.[24] Notice that, according to Remigius, in his commentary on Martianus's *On Mercury's marriage*, this veil on Saturn's head is depicted as green in colour, as an indication that prudence never withers but is always growing afresh.[25]

[139] [4] The fourth part of the picture shows Saturn carrying a sickle, for he carries along in his hand, instead of a sceptre, a curved sickle. It is a property of prudence to rule, and prudent people are worthy of rule. For this reason, Socrates, whom Apollo's oracle judged the wisest, asserted that commonwealths would be blessed only when philosophers, that is those endowed with prudence, would rule them or when it might chance that their directors would be eager for wisdom, as John of Salisbury repeats in *Polycraticus* 4.[26] He there cites Scripture on the same subject, Prv 8:15–16, where it says, speaking in the person of Wisdom, *By me kings reign and princes rule, and the mighty decree justice.*

[149] Therefore prudence, as a token of rule and royal dignity, carries a sceptre. However, as a sign of grand generosity, the virtue bears a sceptre shaped like a curved sickle, so that it can draw everyone to it and serve the bread and drink of wisdom to all in the most open-handed way. On this point, notice Scripture, Prv 9:2–5, where Solomon uses the rhetorical figure called *prosopopeia* in Greek, *confirmatio* 'the proof' in Latin. There he introduces Wisdom arranging a banquet and inviting to it all those in need, without distinction. Thus, he says

---

[24] VM3 6.34 (196/9–28).

[25] A correction of VM3 (?), although 1.1 has 'caput glauco amictu coopertum' (153/19; similarly, 1.4 [154/30]). I find no such information in Mart, but see the headnote to this chapter in the textual notes.

[26] *Ibid.* 4.6 (PL 199:525).

quod *Sapiencia miscuit uinum, posuit mensam, et misit ancillas suas ut uocarent ad arcem et ad meniam ciuitatis: "Si quis est paruulus, ueniat ad me". Et insipientibus loquta est, "Uenite,*
160 *comedite panem meum et bibite uinum quod miscui uobis".* Similiter Prouerbiorum 8, Sapiencia clamitat et prudencia dat uocem suam, dicens, *O uiri, ad uos clamito; intelligite paruuli astuciam, et insipientes animaduertite.* Ecce: falx prudencie siue sapiencie, qua nititur alios ad se trahere pro eorum comodo
165 et salute. Nota [quomodo], eundo ad litteram, Saturnus iste ideo depingitur cum falce, quia ipse primus in Ytalia docuit homines agros colere et cultos serere et satos metere, et hec omnia fecit uirtute prudencie mediante. Ideo poetice describitur falcem gestare.
170   [5] Quinta pars picture est de uultu[s deieccione seu] desolacione et iuxta ficcionem poeticam, bene conuenit uirtuti prudencie. Sicut enim narrant historie gentilium, aliqui + fuerunt uiri philosophici | prudencia preclari, qui consueuerunt continue lacrimari, considerantes et considerando compacientes hominum
175 mundanorum uicia et studia omni uanitate plena, sicut tangit Iuuenalis poeta et eciam Seneca. Unde Iuuenalis, loquens de Eraclito, qui sic consueuerat [continue] uicia hominum et uana facta deplorare, dicit sic metrice: 'Mirandum est, unde ille oculis sufficeret humor'. Seneca eciam in libro *De tranquilitate animi*,
180 loquens de isto Eraclito, dicit quod sibi uidebatur quod omnia, que homines mundi agunt, erant miserie. Et ideo flebat continue ex compassione.
    Narrat Seneca ibidem de Democrito philosopho, quomodo ipse ridebat continue, quia sibi uidebatur quod omnia, que
185 homines mundi agunt, erant inepcie facta, scilicet friuola, fatua, et uana, et ideo deridebat ea. Et ideo Seneca uidetur magis approbare factum Democriti semper ridentis quam factum Eracliti semper

---

157 posuit] proposuit AL   160 comedite] emite I   161 Similiter] Unde signanter I, Quare L   161–63 et … animaduerite] *om.* A   165 salute] solacium I   165 quomodo] tamen O, tamen quomodo L   • quomodo … litteram] *om.* I   • litteram] *add* et historiam AL   167 homines] *om.* I   168–69 poetice … gestare] poetice falcem depingitur deportare AL, sic cum falce depingitur I
170 de uultus] *om.* A   • uultus … seu] uultu O, *adds* desolatus A   171 uirtuti] *om.* I   172 aliqui] *adds* enim O   • aliqui … fuerunt] fuere aliqui IL   173 uiri philosophici] philosophici *marg.* I   • fol. 87ra 176–79 Iuuenalis … Seneca] *om.* I   177 continue] *om.* AO   177–78 uicia … facta] *om.* I   178 facta] *adds* hominum L
183 etc. Democrito] Demetrio A   187 factum] *om.* I

that *Wisdom hath mixed her wine and set forth her table. She hath sent her maids to invite to the tower and to the walls of the city: 'Whoever is a little one, let him come to me.' And to the unwise, she said, 'Come, eat my bread and drink the wine which I have mingled for you.'* Similarly, in Prv 8:4–5, Wisdom cries out, and prudence adds her voice, saying, *O ye men, to you I call. O little ones, understand subtlety, and ye unwise, take notice.* See: prudence or Wisdom has a sickle, with which she attempts to draw others to herself for their benefit and salvation. Notice, returning to the literal sense of Fulgentius's text, how Saturn is depicted with a sickle because he was the first to teach people in Italy to till the fields, to sow crops there, and to reap what they had sown.[27] He did all this by means of the virtue prudence, and for this reason, he is described in poetry bearing a sickle.

[170] [5] The fifth part of the picture concerns Saturn's dejected and mourning face; according to poetic fiction, this is appropriate for the virtue prudence. For, as histories of the pagans tell, there were some philosophers renowned for their prudence who were accustomed to weep continually, when they considered and, as they did so, pitied the sins of worldly people and their enthusiasms, filled with every sort of vanity. The poet Juvenal discusses this and so does Seneca. For this reason, Juvenal speaking of Heraclitus – he had been accustomed to lament continuously over people's vices and their empty deeds – says in a verse, 'It's a marvel where his eyes got enough moisture.'[28] Seneca also, in *On a tranquil mind*, speaking of Heraclitus, says that it appeared to him that every thing that worldly people do conduced only to wretchedness. Therefore he wept continually out of pity.

[183] In the same passage, Seneca tells about the philosopher Democritus. He laughed continually, because it appeared to him that everything that worldly people do represent acts of folly, frivolous, foolish, and empty. Therefore he laughed at them. Seneca appears to commend more Democritus's action, always laughing, than he does Heraclitus's, always

---

[27] Fulg 1.2 (17/13–16).
[28] *Satyra* 10.32.

flentis. Unde sic dicit Seneca: 'Democritum pocius imitemus quam Eraclitum. Hic Eraclitus, quociens in puplicum [processerat],
190 flebat; ille ridebat. Eraclito omnia que agimus uidebantur miserie; Democrito inepcie uidebantur. Sed human[i]us est', dicit Seneca, 'deridere uitam quam deplorare'.

   Sed notare debemus quod, quomodocumque sit de dicto Senece, factum Eracliti magis consonum est modo uiuendi Cristi
195 quam factum Democriti. Unde dicit Iohannes Crisostomus, omelia 6ª *Super Mattheum*, 'Nichil ita conglutinat Deo sicut lacrime, quas dolor peccati et amor uirtutis effundunt'. Et sequitur, 'Si tu huiusmodi lacrimas effundis, Domini tui Ihesu Cristi imitator eris. Flentem autem Cristum frequenter inuenies,
200 nunquam uero ridentem, sed nec leuiter subridentem saltem uel gaudentem. In cuius rei gracia, o Cristiane, in | chachinnum laxaris et defluis? Qui tantorum tui sponte factus es causa meroris, ante illud terribile tribunal Cristi staturus et summa examinacione racionem pro cunctis tuis actibus redditurus.
205 Idcirco multa nobis de luctu loquitur Cristus, et be[atifican]do lugentes et comminando ridentibus. Non enim propterea sepius in unum conuenimus, ut in decentibus resoluamur cach\i/nis, sed ut gemamus pocius et regnum ex hoc gemitu futurum hereditemus'. Hec Crisostomus. Laudo ergo et approbo plus
210 Eraclitum mundi miseriam deplorantem quam Democritum cachinantem.

   [6] Sexta pars picture est de Saturni castracione, nam poete fingunt eum castratum. Nam ad prudenciam pertinet reprimere uoluptatem ueneriam, quia nichil magis est perniciosum
215 prudencie quam delectacio illa deordinata carnalis lasciuie. Nam ut dicit Aristoteles, 7 *Ethicorum*, ipsa uoluptas carnis rapit intellectum spisse sapientis. Et ideo Augustinus, primo libro *Soliloquiorum*, loquens de ista uoluptate et ostendens quam

---

189 etc. Eraclitum] Eraclium A   189–90 Hic … Eraclito] *om.* I   189 processerat] exibat O   190 uidebantur] *om.* I   191 humanius] humanum magis A, humanus O
193 de dicto] deduccio L   194–95 Senece … factum] *om.* I   194 est] *adds* uite et L
196 ita conglutinat] igni (?) conglutinat tantum I   197–98 lacrime … lacrimas] *om.* I   200 saltem] *om.* A   201 In] Sequitur A, Et sequitur L • cuius] cicius A
• fol. 87ʳᵇ   202 sponte] tantorum I   203 meroris] malorum A • staturus et summa] stratus et cum I   205 luctu … Cristus] luculenta I • beatificando] benificendo O   207 decentibus] *adds* rebus L • resoluamur] laxemur A
209 hereditemus] habeamus A • et approbo] *om.* I
212 reprimere] remouere I   312 ueneriam] carnis I • perniciosum] periculosum L
216 spisse] sponte, *emended* L

weeping. For this reason, he says, 'We ought to imitate Democritus, rather than Heraclitus. He, as often as he went out in public, wept, but Democritus laughed. For Heraclitus, all that we do appeared wretchedness, but it appeared folly to Democritus. But', Seneca says, 'it is more humane to ridicule someone's behaviour than to despair over it.'[29]

[193] But we should notice that, no matter what Seneca may say, Heraclitus's behaviour resembles more closely Christ's way of life than Democritus's does. For this reason, John Chrysostom says, *On Matthew*, homily 6, 'Nothing binds us so closely to God as the tears that pour forth from our sorrow for our sins and from our love of virtue.' And he adds, 'If you pour out tears of this kind, you will be imitating your lord Jesus Christ. For you will frequently find Christ weeping, but never laughing, not even once smiling frivolously nor rejoicing. For what reason, O Christian, do you slip away and become loosened in laughter? You are rather, through your own volition, made a cause of sorrow by so many slips, destined to stand before Christ's terrifying judgement-seat and to render an account for all your actions under the strictest interrogation. For this reason, Christ speaks to us a great deal about weeping, both blessing those who weep and threatening those who laugh. Consequently, we do not most often gather together to be relaxed by decorous laughter, but rather so that we may lament and through this sighing, become heirs of the kingdom to come.' So says Chrysostom.[30] Therefore, I praise and commend more Heraclitus, who lamented the world's wretchedness, than I do Democritus, who laughed at it.

[212] [6] The sixth part of the picture concerns Saturn's castration, for the poets depict him as castrated. It is appropriate for prudence to repress sexual desire, for nothing is more destructive to prudence than the disordered delight of fleshly licentiousness. For, as Aristotle says, *Nicomachean Ethics* 7, fleshly desire insidiously carries away a wise person's intellect.[31] Therefore Augustine, *Soliloquies* 1, speaking of this desire and showing how

---

[29] Ibid. 15.2.
[30] *In Matthaeum homiliae* 76 (PG 57:69) (L).
[31] Ibid. 7.6 (1149b).

inimica sit prudencie, sic dicit: 'Nichil michi tam fugiendum quam concubitum esse decreui. Nichil enim sencio quod magis ex ar[c]e deiciat animum uirilem quam blandimenta feminea corporisque ille contactus, sine quo uxor haberi non potest'.

Et de isto nota Tullium in suo libro *De senectute*, ubi ostendit quomodo senectus in homine ideo maioris est laudis et reuerencie, quia etas illa caret uoluptat[is] uener[ee] feditate. Unde ex priori proprietate prudencie, scilicet quod pingitur senio grauata, sequitur ista proprietas, scilicet quod ipsa moraliter sit castrata, hoc est im[m]unis a uoluptate | deordinata lasciuie carnalis. Unde sic dicit Tullius: 'O preclarum munus senilis etatis, siquidem illud aufert a nobis quod in adolescencia est uiciosissimum! Nullum sane capitaliorem pestem Architas Tarentinus dicebat a natura datam hominibus quam uoluptatem. Cumque Deus homini \nichil/ mente, \enim/ racione, prestancius dedisset, huic diuino muneri nichil tam inimicum censuit quam uoluptatem. Nec enim libidine dominante, temperancie locum dixit esse, neque in uoluptatis regno uirtutem posse consistere. Nemini enim censuit fore dubium [quin], tamdiu dum homo uoluptate gauderet, cum nichil agitare mente, nichil racione, nichil cogitacione eum consequi posset. Que uoluptas, si maior esset et longius duraret, omne [animi] + lumen extingueret'.

Nota ergo quomodo, propter istam incopossibilitatem inter uirtutem prudencie et deformitatem carnalis lasciuie, poete finxerunt Saturnum, per quem uirtutem prudencie describere uoluerunt, castratum. Notandum eciam ulterius quomodo poete fingunt [Saturnum castratum a propria prole, id est a Ioue. Per Iouem enim, ut patebit inferius, intellexerunt poete uirtutem amoris et beneuolencie, quia ergo prudens et sapiens subtrahit se uoluntarie pro Dei et honestatis amore a carnis uoluptate. Ideo Saturnum castratum dixerunt a Ioue.

---

220 Nichil ... sencio] enim nichil esse L • ex arce] exacte I, ex arte O
222 contactus] contrarius A • sine ... potest] *om.* I
223 ostendit] dicit L 224 laudis] *om.* A 225–26 etas ... pingitur] *om.* I
225 uoluptatis uenereel] uoluptate Ueneris O 228 immunis] *an extra minim* I, *a minim short* O • fol. 87va • lasciuie] lacune I 230 quod ... uiciosissimum] adolescenciam uiciosissimam L 231 pestem] *om.* I 233 diuino] dominio (?) O
234 muneri] numeri I, uerum L • censuit] sensit I 236 uoluptatis] uoluntatis (?) I 237 quin] *om.* OL 240 animi lumen] *adds* et bonum A, cum lumine IO, animi bonum L
241 incopossibilitatem] impossibilitatem AL 245 fingunt] *adds* significanter I
245–50 fingunt ... fingunt] fingunt OL 247 beneuolencie] uni molencie I

inimical it is to prudence, says, 'I thought that there is nothing I should avoid so much as sexual intercourse. I think there is nothing more likely to cast a noble spirit down from its citadel than women's charms and contact with their bodies, without which one cannot have a wife.'[32]

[223] And on this subject, notice Cicero in his *On old age*, where he shows how old age is worth greater praise and honour, precisely because that time of life lacks the foulness of sexual desire. For this reason, this characteristic of prudence follows from the preceding one, that the virtue is depicted bowed down by age. Prudence is morally castrated, that is, it is immune to the disordered desire of fleshly licentiousness. For this reason, Cicero says, 'O the outstanding gift of old age, that it takes away from us what is most vicious in our youth! Architas of Taranto truly said that nature gave no more deadly plague to humanity than desire. Since God gave people nothing more outstanding than mind or reason, he thought nothing so inimical to this divine gift as desire. He said further that, so long as desire rules, there is no place for temperance, and that virtue may not co-exist where desire commands. He further considered that no one could doubt that, so long as a person rejoiced in desire, he might not exercise his mind at all, nor engage in anything reasonable or thoughtful. For desire, if it becomes greater or endures longer, extinguishes the light of the spirit completely.'[33]

[241] Therefore notice, because of the inability of the virtue prudence and the deformity of fleshly licentiousness to co-exist, how the poets depicted Saturn, whom they wished to describe as the virtue prudence, as castrated. Notice further how the poets describe Saturn as castrated by his own son, Jove. For through Jove, as will become evident below, the poets understood the virtue of love and kindness; therefore a prudent and wise person voluntarily restrains himself from fleshly desire in order to love God and virtue. Therefore they said that Saturn had been castrated by Jove.

---

[32] *Ibid.* 1.10 (*PL* 32:878).
[33] *Ibid.* 12.39–41.

250   Notandum est eciam ulterius quomodo poete fingunt] Saturni uirilia in mare proiecta a Ioue et inde [dicunt] deam Uenerem generatam. Sicut enim docet Remigius in commento super librum *De numpciis*, poete dicunt duplicem deam | Uenerem. \Unam, quam [dicunt] deam ordinate et caste delectacionis; aliam esse
255 Uenerem/, quam ponunt deam lasciuie et carnalis uoluptatis. Applicando ergo ad propositum, intelligendum est quod amor Dei separat a prudencia uoluptatem ueneream et proicit eam in mare contricionis: *magna*, dicit Ier[emia]s, *uelut mare contricio tua*. Et de istis membris uirilibus in hoc mari proiectis nascitur Uenus, id
260 est bona, sancta, et ordinata delectacio. Peccator enim, secundum Ambrosium, de peccato debet dolere et de dolore semper gaudere.

[7] Septima pars picture est de Saturni refeccione, nam poete fingunt Saturnum proprios filios in cibum assumpsisse. Et hec est septima proprietas prudencie: seipsam reficere et refectam,
265 nutrire suis propriis actibus, qui actus dicuntur filii. Talis habitus filius enim dicitur, quia 'fit ut ille'; et ideo, quia actus uirtutis conformiter est factus iuxta inclinacionem, talis habitus ideo dicitur poetice eius filius. Ist[e] autem fili[u]s dicitur cibare patrem suum, et pater hunc filium fingitur deuorare et comedere, quia
270 sicut cibus nutrit, auget, roborat, et perficit corpus comedentis, sic usus uirtutis nutrit uirtutem et eam reddit intenciorem, robustiorem, et perfecciorem, sicut patet per beatum Augustinum, *Super Iohannem*, omelia 5^a. Ubi loquens de caritate, dicit quod 'Caritas primo nascitur, et ipsa nata, per usum nutritur, nutrita
275 roboratur, et roborata perficitur'. Et quod ipse dicit de caritate, hoc idem intelligendum est de prudencia et quacumque alia uirtute. Et sic finitur intellectus moralis secunde mithologie.

---

250 ulterius ... poete] quomodo I   251 dicunt] *om.* O   253 fol. 87vb 254 dicunt]
  om. O • delectacionis] delectoris (?) I   255 carnalis] carnis I
  256 intelligendum] dicendum I   258 Ieremias] Ieronimus IO   259 uirilibus ...
  mari] sic I • Uenus] *om.* A   260 sancta] conscia I   260-61 Peccator ... dolore]
  om. L   261 gaudere] *om.* A
265 habitus] *om.* I   266 fit] sit A   267 inclinacionem] intimacionem A
  268 filius ... filius] filius I • Iste ... filius] Istis autem filiis O   270 perficit]
  reficit A   273 dicit] *om.* I   277 intellectus moralis] *om. (with nom.)* IL

[250] Notice further how the poets depict Jupiter throwing Saturn's genitals into the sea and say that the goddess Venus was born from them. For as Remigius teaches in his commentary on *On the marriage*, the poets say that the goddess Venus has a double aspect. They call one of these a goddess of orderly and chaste delight; but there is a second Venus, whom the poets identify as the goddess of licentiousness and fleshly desire.[34] Therefore, applying this to the matter in hand, one should understand that the love of God cuts sexual desire away from prudence and throws it into the sea of contrition; Tr 2:13 says, *Great as the sea is thy contrition*. The good Venus, the one who represents proper holy and orderly delight, is born from the genitals thrown into this sea. For, according to Ambrose, a sinner ought to lament over his sin and continually rejoice in his lament.[35]

[262] [7] The seventh part of the picture concerns Saturn's refreshment, for the poets depict Saturn as having eaten his own sons.[36] This is the seventh characteristic of prudence, to refresh itself and being refreshed, to be nourished by its own actions – those actions are called its sons. For a person's virtuous disposition is called their son, because *fit ut ille* 'it is made just as the person is'. Therefore, because a virtuous act comes about in accord with one's inclination, such a disposition is called poetically one's son. However, people say that the son feeds his father, and the father is depicted as eating and devouring the son, because just as food nourishes, augments, strengthens, and perfects the body that eats it, so practising virtue nourishes the virtue itself and renders it more intense, stronger, and more perfect. Augustine makes this evident in *On John*, homily 5, where he is speaking about charity, and says, 'First love is born, and then, once it is born, it is nourished by practising it; it is strengthened by having been nourished, and perfected by having been strengthened.'[37] What he says there about charity should be understood as true of prudence or any other virtue. This concludes the moral sense of the second mythography.

---

[34] Mart 37.4 (135/32–36/3).
[35] Cf. *De virginibus* 3.5.23 (*PL* 16:226–27).
[36] Fulg 1.2 (18/1–2).
[37] *In epistolam Ioannis ad Parthos* 5.4 (*PL* 35:2014).

[3]

Sequitur tercia mithologia de Ioue, potissima prole Saturni, id est uirtutis prudencie. Per Iouem enim poetice uirtus amoris designatur et beniuolencie. Unde secundum Fulgencium, Iubiter lingua Greca + Zeus dicitur, quod in lingua nostra Latina | idem sonat quod 'calor siue uita'. Amor autem ignis; amor eciam ordinatus uita est. 'Scio', dicit Hugo, alloquens animam suam in suo libro *De arra anime*, 'quod uita tua dilec[cio] est'. Eciam quod amor ignis est, docent sancti et mundi philosophi, sicut patet ex Dyonisio in suo libro *De angelica ierarchia*. Patet eciam ex poetica pictura, qua solet Amor depingi cum pharetra iacula continente ignita. Et hic notandum est quod, sicut recitat Fulgencius, opinio fuit Eracliti quod calor uitalis est principium [uiuendi] in rebus uiuentibus. Et sic, moraliter loquendo, amor rectus, uirtus scilicet caritatis, est principium bene operandi. Opera enim omnia extra caritatem facta reputantur mortua, quia ad habendum uitam eternam sunt inutilia et infructuosa. Et ideo congrue Iubiter, qui gerit figuram amoris et beniuolencie, nominatur istis nominibus, scilicet nomine uite et caloris.

De pictura autem poetica dei Iouis notare possumus + quod Iubiter iste pingitur:

[1] uertice curuatus,
[2] arena locatus,
[3] aquilis stipatus,
[4] cum palma sceptratus,
[5] et auro uelatus;
[6] uultus est amenus
[7] et color [serenus];
[8] fulmen iaculatur
[9] et cornu cibatur.

Iste sunt nouem + partes picture poetice caritatis sub ymagine dei Iouis, quibus correspondent nouem proprietates beniuolencie et amoris.

---

1 potissima] propriissima A   4 Zeus] zelus O   fol. 88[ra]   • sonat] est I   6 dileccio] dilecta O   7 docent] *om.* A   9 ierarchia] sarthia A   12 uiuendi] *om.* O   18 caloris] amoris I

19 poetica] *adds* caritatis sub ymagine L • possumus] *adds* ad presens O   20 Iubiter ... pingitur] *om. and* 30–33 *here* A   27 serenus] *om.* O   30 partes] proprietates O • poetice ... ymagine] *om.* A   30–31 poetice ... Iouis] Iouinialis L, *adds* Iouialis I

74

[3]

The third mythography, which follows, concerns Jove, the strongest offspring of the virtue prudence, Saturn. In poetic terms, Jove indicates the virtue of Love and friendliness. For this reason, according to Fulgentius, Jupiter is called Zeus in Greek; in our Latin, this means the same as 'heat or life'.[1] Indeed, love is a fire, and orderly love is life. Hugh of St Victor, addressing his soul in *On the soul's pledge*, says, 'I know that your life is love.'[2] Also both holy men and worldly philosophers teach that love is fire, as is evident in Dionysius's *On the angelic hierarchy*.[3] This is also evident from the poets' image, in which Cupid/Love is customarily depicted with a quiver that contains flaming darts. Here one should notice that, as Fulgentius reports, Heraclitus held the view that vital heat is the life-giving principle in all living things. Thus, in moral terms, properly governed love, that is the virtue of Charity, is the principle that underlies doing well. For all works performed without charity are considered dead, because they are without profit and useless for attaining eternal life. Therefore Jupiter, who presents the image of love and friendliness, is appropriately named through the nouns 'life' and 'heat'.

[19] We can notice that in the poetic picture of the god Jove, Jupiter is depicted:
[1] with a curved head,
[2] situated in sand,
[3] surrounded by eagles,
[4] with a palm-tree as sceptre,
[5] and veiled in gold;
[6] his countenance is pleasant
[7] and his colouring bright;
[8] casting forth a thunderbolt
[9] and fed from a horn.

These are the nine parts of the poetic picture of charity, in the image of the god Jove. They correspond to nine characteristics of friendliness and love.

---

[1] Fulg 1.3 (18/15–18).
[2] *Ibid.* (PL 176:951).
[3] *Ibid.* 15.2, but a rather more general reference.

[1] [Nam Iubiter pingitur cum uertice curuato, quia pingitur cum capite arietis. Et bene conuenit uirtuti beniuolencie et amoris], que uirtus est capitalis et principalis inter ceteras uirtutes. 'Aries' enim dicitur ab *ares* Grece, quod est 'uirtus' Latine, et ideo caput istius uirtutis est arietinum ad significandum dignitatis et perfeccionis excessum, quem habet caritas in ordine omnium aliarum uirtutum. De cuius dignitate tractat Augustinus in diuersis | locis, sicut 15 *De trinitate*, ubi dicit quod nullum est donum excellencius isto Dei dono. Et apostolus dicit *Maior horum*, id est uirtutum, *est caritas*. Et in sermone suo *De laude caritatis*, multa tangit Augustinus de dignitate et excellencia istius uirtutis; et super canonicam Iohannis plura tangit Augustinus de singulari excellencia caritatis.

[2] Secunda pars picture est de Iouis situacione, nam poete uocant eum [Am]on, id est arenosum. Unde ut recitant poete, Iubiter iste potissime colitur in arenis Libie, ubi est solenne templum deo [Am]oni, Ioui scilicet, dedicatum, sicut tangit Lucanus in sua poesi. Et istud est proprium amoris ueri et beniuolencie se ostendere pro loco et tempore necessitatis siue indigentie. 'Necessitas enim probat amicum', ut dicit Cassiodo[r]us. Et Ysodorus, *De summo bono*, dicit quod 'in prosperitate incerta est amicicia; nescitur enim aut persona aut prosperitas diligatur'. Et ideo poeta, loquens de amicicia ficta et simulata, dicit, 'Cum fortuna manet, uultum seruatis, amici; / cum cecidit, turpi uertitis ora fuga'. + Ergo arena locus est aduersitatis, quia in arena consueuerunt apud antiquos gladiatores pugnare et se mutuo interficere, ideo locus uere amicicie a poetis ponitur in arena. Et ideo significanter dicit Seneca in quadam epistola quod 'Ille turpiter errat, qui amicum querit in atrio uel in aula'. Et de isto multa essent notanda que dicit Scriptura Sacra, sicut patet in Prouerbiis, in Ecclesiastico, et in aliis locis.

31-35 Nam ... amoris] *om.* O   32 capite] uertice I   37 arietinum] arieticum A
38 omnium] *om.* I   40 fol. 88rb 41 horum] *adds* id est L   44 plura] pulcra I
44-45 de ... caritatis] *om.* I
47 Amon, 49 Amoni] Arnon, Ar|noni O   48 poete] *om.* I   52 amicum ... dicit] probat ut I   53 Cassiodorus] Cassio|domus O, *adds* libro [*blank*] A, *adds* facit amicum libro amiciarum I, *adds* libro L   54 amicicia] *adds* ficta et simulata A
56 ficta] fucata L • et simulata] *om.* A   57 Ergo] Quia ergo AIOL
58 consueuerunt] solebant A • apud antiquos] *om.* A   61 turpiter] *om.* L
63 dicit ... et] tangit Prouerbiis et I

[33] [1] Jupiter is depicted with a curved head, because he is depicted with a ram's head. This is appropriate for the virtue of friendliness and love, for that virtue is the head and principal among the various virtues. For the word *aries* 'ram' is derived from the Greek *ares*, which means 'virtue' in Latin,[4] and therefore the head of this virtue is ramlike to indicate the excessive worthiness and perfection that charity possesses among the rank of all the virtues. Augustine treats this worthiness in various places, for example in *On the trinity* 15, where he says that there is no divine gift more excellent than this one. And Paul says (1 Cor 13:13) that *the greatest of these*, that is, of the virtues, *is charity*. In his sermon *In praise of charity*, Augustine treats many things concerning the worthiness and excellence of this virtue, and he treats more instances of charity's unique excellence in his discussion of John's catholic epistles.[5]

[46] [2] The second part of the picture concerns Jove's location, for the poets call him Amon, which means 'sandy'. For this reason, as poets report, Jupiter is most carefully worshipped in the sands of Lybia, where there is a holy temple dedicated to the god Amon or Jove, as Lucan mentions in his poem.[6] It is a characteristic of true love or friendliness to show itself in a place and occasion of necessity or hardship, for, as Cassiodorus says, 'Necessity tests which friend is true.' Isidore, *On the highest good*, says that 'friendship remains uncertain in good times, for then one does not know whether it is the person or their prosperity that is being loved.' Therefore, a poet speaking about love that is feigned or simulated, says, 'Friends, while Fortune is stable, you serve another's face; / when she has fallen, you turn in flight from the shameful lips.'[7] Sand is a place of hardship, because among the ancients, swordsmen were accustomed to fight and kill one another in a 'sandy' arena; therefore, the poets identify the place of true friendship with sand. Seneca says significantly in a letter that 'The person who seeks a friend in an entryway or hall errs shamefully.'[8] And one should notice many things that Holy Scripture says on this subject, particularly in Prv, Sir, and elsewhere.[9]

---

[4] *Etym.* 12.1.11 (*PL* 82:426).

[5] Respectively, *De trinitate* 15.18 (*PL* 42:1082); sermo 350 (*PL* 39:1533–34); *In epistolam Ioannis ad Parthos* 5.4 (*PL* 35:2014).

[6] *Pharsalia* 9.511ff.

[7] Actually Peter of Blois, *De amicitia Christiana* 1.14 (*PL* 207:885) [= *MF amicicia ai*, ascribed to 'Cassiodorus in quadam epistola']; followed by Isidore, *Sententiae* 3.29 (*PL* 83:702); Petronius, frag. 80.9.

[8] *Epistula* 19.11.

[9] L cites scriptural parallels as Prv 14:20 and 19:4, 6; Sir 13:25; Ps 37:25.

[3] Tercia pars picture est de Iouis | administracione. Nam poete fingunt aquilam armigerum dei Iouis, et ideo pingitur a poetis uallatus undique aquilis, sicut magnus dominus consueuit circumdari suis armigeris. Quomodo autem istud conueniat uirtuti caritatis, pulcre docent auctores. Nam, ut docet Plinius in *Historia naturali,* in aspectu et auditu aquile terrentur omnes aues alie, et ex terrore aues, que sunt predales, cessant a predacione. Ap[plic]ando ergo ad uirtutem caritatis, docet Hugo de Sancto Uictore in sua exposicione super regulam beati Augustini, quomodo demones, qui in Scriptura aliquando d[icunt]ur aues et celi uolucres, quia sunt in celo et in aere caliginoso, ut docet Haymo – iste, inquam, aues 'nichil tantum timent in hominibus quam caritatem. Si distribuerimus totum quod habemus pauperibus, hoc diabolus non timet, quia ipse nichil possidet. Si ieiunamus, hoc ipse non metuit, quia cibum non sumit. Si uigilamus, inde non terretur, quia sompno non utitur. Sed si caritate coniungimur, inde uehementer expauescit, quia hoc tenemus in terra quod ipse in celo seruare contempsit. Hinc est quod sancta ecclesia terribilis, ut castrorum acies ordinata describitur, quia sicut hostes timent quando uident aciem bene ordinatam et coniunctam ad bellum, ita nimirum diabolus expauescit, quando conspicit spirituales uiros armis \uirtutum armatos in caritate concorditer uiuere'. Hec iste. Significanter ergo uirtus caritatis/ uallata depingitur undequaque aquilis pro timore quem [undique] incutit demonibus et malignis spiritibus.

[4] Quarta pars picture de Iouis est sceptracione. Unde pingitur | sceptrari cum arbore palme in signum uniuersalis potencie et uictorie, quam poete solent deo Ioui pre diis ceteris attribuere. Unde nomen Iouis idem significat quod 'uniuersalis uis'. Iouis [uis] enim, secundum poeticam ymaginacionem, se extendit uniuersaliter ad omnia, tam celestia quam terrena. Unde sibi attribuitur triumphus et uictoria tam de diis, quam eciam de hominibus, et \hac/ ex causa sceptro depingitur palmeo.

---

65 fol. 88va 71 terrentur] tractantur (?) I • aues] uolucres A • et ex terrore] in tantum quod I • terrore] timore A • predales] aues prede L
73 Applicando] Replicando A, Am|pliando O   75 dicuntur] dure O
81 uehementer] ualde A   87 armatos] munitos L   89 undique] *om.* O • incutit] incitat A, incurrunt I

91, 92 sceptra-] sceptriza- L   92 fol. 88vb 94 uniuersalis] uniu I   diis] *om.* A
95 uis] *om.* O • ymaginacionem] ymaginem IL   96 terrena] terrestria A
98 et hac ex causa] *om.* I

[65] [3] The third part of the picture concerns Jove's management, for the poets depict the god Jove with an eagle as a squire bearing arms. They show him defended on every side by eagles, just as a great lord is usually surrounded by his knights. Moreover, authors neatly teach how this detail might be appropriate for the virtue of charity. For Pliny teaches in his *Natural history* how all the other birds are terrified by the sight or sound of an eagle, and in their fright, other birds, even ones of prey, should stop their hunting.[10] In applying this detail to the virtue charity, Hugh of St Victor teaches in his commentary on the rule of St Augustine about the devils. In Scripture, they are sometimes called 'birds' or 'the fowls of heaven', because they are in the sky and in smoke-filled air, as Haymo teaches.[11] These (figural) birds, Hugh says, 'fear nothing in people so much as they do charity. If we have given everything that we have to the poor, the devil is not afraid, because he owns nothing. If we fast, he does not fear this either, because he does not take food. If we engage in vigils, he is not afraid, because he does not need sleep. But if we are joined in charity, he is violently terrified, because we uphold in earth what he disdained to preserve in heaven. Thus, the holy church is described as terrifying, as if it were the properly arranged battle-array associated with an encampment, for just as enemy forces are afraid when they see a well-ordered army ready to join battle, likewise it is no wonder if the devil is afraid when he spots spiritual people armed with the virtues as their weapons and living, with a single accord, in charity.'[12] So Hugh says. Thus, it is significant that the virtue charity is depicted defended on every side by eagles because of the fear that it everywhere instils in devils and evil spirits.

[91] [4] The fourth part of the picture concerns Jove's sceptre. He is depicted as having a sceptre from a palm-tree, as a token of his universal power and victory, which poets customarily assign to Jove before the other gods. For this reason, the name Jove means the same as 'universal strength'. For Jove's strength, according to what the poets imagine, extends universally to all things, both heavenly and earthly. For this reason, his attributes include triumph and victory, over both gods and humans, and for this reason, he is depicted with a palm-like sceptre.

---

[10] Unfound.

[11] E.g. *Homiliae in evangelia de tempore* 22 (*PL* 118:164), or *Commentaria in cantica aliquot*, 'Canticum Moysi' (*PL* 116:712).

[12] *Ibid.* 1 (*PL* 176:883).

Testantur enim auctores quod arbor palme talis est nature quod nullo onere uult succumbere; quamcumque enim graui pondere deprimatur, ad tempus licet succumbat, tamen tandem supra pondus se erigit et triumphat.

Nota de ista palme proprietate loquitur Alexander Nekham, libro suo secundo in tractatu de arboribus, ubi dicit quod 'uictores in suis triumphis palmam gestare consueuerunt, eo quod hec arbor, oneribus quantumlibet magnis impositis, non uincitur nec frangitur'. Et nota bene Carnotensem, libro suo 5 *Policratici*, capitulo 5º, de ista proprietate palme, ubi allegat Aristotelem, in 7 libro *De problematibus*, et Plutarcum, 8 *Memorabilium*. Et peroptime proprietas ista conuenit caritati et amori, qui amor uincit omnia. Unde apud poetas fuit solenne prouerbium, 'Amor uincit omnia', quia uincit Pan, qui apud [Grecos] fingitur 'deus omnium' uel 'deus tocius', quem poete ponunt captum amore Siringe, puelle pulcherrime. Sicut et nos dicimus Dei filium, uictum amore nature humane, in + Uirginis uterum corporaliter descendisse.

Et hic essent notanda multa que tangunt doctores catholici de potencia et triumphali uictoria caritatis. Nam Hugo in suo libro *De laude* | *caritatis*, alloquens eam sic dicit: 'Magnam uim habes, o caritas; tu sola Deum trahere potuisti de celo ad terras. O quam forte uinculum tuum, quo et Deus ligari potuit, et homo ligatus tuis uinculis, iniquitatis uincula disrumpit. Nescio quid maius in laudem tuam dicere possum quam quod Deum de celo traxisti et homines de terra ad celum subleuasti. Et ibidem nota, quod caritas facilius Deum uincit quam homines. Quia quo constat Deum magis esse b[eat]um, eo magis est Deo debitum amore uinci et a caritate superari. Unde, ut amor facilius homines uinceret, prius Deum superauit, adducens Deum uinculis alligatum, adducens Deum sagittis suis uulneratum, ut amplius puderet homini caritati resistere, cum uideret ipsam de Deo triumphasse. Nullum enim uinculum Eum ad columpnam tenuisset, si caritatis uinculum defuisset'. Hec ille.

---

103 loquitur] *om.* A 106 oneribus] honoribus A 109 et ... *Memorabilium*] *om.* A 110 peroptime] per omnia I 111 poetas] *om.* A 111–12 Unde ... omnia] *om.* L 112 Pan] Paulam A, Pana I 112–13 apud ... uel] *om.* L 112 Grecos] poetas OL 113 captum] add et uictum AI 114 puelle] uirginis I 115 Uirginis] uirgi|ginis O 116 corporaliter] *om.* A

119 fol. 89ʳᵃ 124–26 de terra ... Quia] *om.* I 126 beatum] bonum O 128 homines] *om.* I 129 Deum¹ ... Deum²] Deum L 131–32 Nullum ... defuisset] *om.* AIL

For authors testify that it's a characteristic of the palm-tree not to sink down under any load; for however heavy the weight with which it is pressed down, although it may sink for a time, in the end it raises itself up against the weight and triumphs.

[103] Notice what Alexander Neckam says about this characteristic of the palm-tree, in the tract about trees in his second book, that 'victors were accustomed to carry a palm-tree in their triumphs, because this tree, however heavy the loads imposed on it, is never broken or conquered.'[13] And notice what John of Salisbury says in *Polycraticus* 5.5 about this characteristic of the palm; he there cites Aristotle, *On problems* 7, and Plutarch, *Things deserving memory* 8.[14] This most desirable characteristic is appropriate for charity and love, since love conquers all things. Thus, the poets had an often-repeated proverb, 'Love conquers all things', because it conquered Pan. Among the Greeks, Pan is feigned to be 'the god of all things' or 'the god of all', and yet the poets present him as overcome by the love of the very beautiful maiden Syrinx.[15] Likewise, we say that the son of God, conquered by his love of human nature, descended bodily into the Virgin's womb.

[117] And here one should notice many things that catholic doctors discuss about charity's power and triumphant victory. Hugh of St Victor, in his *Praise of charity*, addressing this virtue, says, 'O charity, what great strength you have! You alone were able to draw God from heaven to earth. O what a strong chain you have! With it, you were able both to bind God and, having bound humanity with your own chains, to break apart the chains of iniquity that bound them. I don't know what greater thing I can say in your praise than that you drew God from heaven and raised up humanity from earth to heaven. And notice here that charity conquers God more easily than it does humans. For insofar as it is a divine property to be more blessed, it is more incumbent upon God to be conquered by love and to be overcome by charity. For this reason, in order that love might conquer humanity more easily, it first overcame God, bringing God bound in its chains, bringing God wounded with its arrows, so that it would be more shameful for humans to resist charity, once they saw that charity had triumphed over God. For no chain would have bound Him to the column, had the chain of charity been absent.' So Hugh says.[16]

---

[13] *De naturis rerum* 2.74 (172).
[14] *Polic.* 5.6 (PL 196:551).
[15] Cf. Virgil, *Ecloga* 10:69, and for Pan and Syrinx, see Ovid, *Metamorphoses* 1.689–712.
[16] *Ibid.* (PL 176:974).

Augustinus eciam, loquens de ista caritatis uictoria, dicit quod 'sola caritas est que uincit omnia, et sine qua nichil ualent omnia'.

[5] Quinta pars picture est de Iouis induccione. Pingitur enim a poetis indutus tunica aurea. Unde de ista tunica loquens, poeta Ouidius dicit, 'Quattuor niueis aure[u]s ibis equis'. Alloquitur enim poeta uictorem redeuntem de prelio cum triumpho. Apud enim Romanos mos fuit quod talis uictor indueretur tunica aurea dei Iouis et poneretur in curru, quem currum trahebant quattuor equi albi, et sic ducebatur ad Capitolium. Ista autem induccio aurea bene conuenit uirtuti amoris et caritatis. Nam ut docent auctores, scilicet philosophi et alii, aurum dicitur forma omnium metallorum, et caritas est forma | omnium aliarum uirtutum. Unde sine caritate omnis uirtus informis reputatur a sanctis.

Habet eciam \aurum proprietatem quod ipsum ductilius est omnibus aliis metallis. Et [significat]/ latitudinem caritatis, que se extendit ad Deum, ad seipsum, ad amicum et ad inimicum, et ideo latum dicitur habere indumentum. Unde de ista caritatis dilatacione, [loquitur] Gregorius, 10 *Moralium*, ubi dicit quod 'caritas studiosa sollicitudine ad cuncta uirtutum facta dilatatur. Que caritas a duobus preceptis incipit, sed ad innumera se extendit'. Propter quam latitudinem et extensionem meretur de condigno auream ind[ucc]ionem.

[6] Sexta pars picture est [de] dei Iouis hillaritate. Pingitur enim Iubiter a poetis cum uultu hillari et ameno, sicut de hoc tractat Uirgilius, ut recitat Alexander Neckham in sua *Mythologia*. Astrologi eciam dicunt Iouem preesse sanguini; unde sanguinei sunt Iouis filii. Que complexio naturaliter est iocunda, et conuenit proprietas ista caritati, que cunctis est placida et nullis penitus est molesta. Et de hoc Bernardus in quadam epistola: 'O bona mater caritas, que siue foueat \infirmos/, siue exerceat prouectos, siue arguat inquietos; diuersis diuersa exhibens, sicut filios tamen diligit uniuersos. Cum te arguit, mitis est; cum blanditur, simplex est. Pie solet seuire, sine dolo [mulce]re, pacienter nouit irasci, humiliter indignari'.

---

137 aureus] aureis IOL   138 prelio] bello A   143 omnium] aliorum L   144 fol. 89rb
   145 reputatur a sanctis] *om.* L
147 significat] figurat O   148 extendit] ostendit I   150 loquitur] *om.* O
   151 uirtutum] *om.* I   152 preceptis] principiis I   154 de condigno] *om.* I, deus digno L • induccionem] indiuicionem O
155 pars] *om.* A • de dei] de AI, dei O   160 cunctis] *om.* I   penitus] que reperitur I
   161 Bernardus] bene A   163 arguat] aggrauet L   165 seuire] seruire AI, se iure O
   • sine … mulcere] sine dolore punire AIO, misericorditer punire L

Also Augustine, speaking of charity's victory, says that 'charity alone conquers all things, and without it, nothing has any power.'[17]

[135] [5] The fifth part of the picture concerns Jove's clothing, for the poets depict him clothed in a golden tunic. Speaking of this tunic, Ovid says, 'You will pass in your gold, with four snow-white horses.'[18] The poet here addresses a victor returning from battle in triumph. For among the Romans, it was the custom that such a victor should be clothed in the god Jove's golden tunic and placed in a chariot, drawn by four white horses, and he was led in this fashion to the Capitol. This golden clothing is appropriate for the virtue of love and charity. For as authors, both philosophers and others, teach, gold is called the underlying principle of all metals, and charity is the underlying principle of all the other virtues. For this reason, holy men account every virtue lacking charity featureless and unseemly.

[146] Gold has a further characteristic, that it is more malleable than all other metals. It thus indicates the breadth of charity that spreads itself out toward God, toward oneself, and toward one's friend and enemy. Therefore, charity is said to have a broad garment. For this reason, Gregory says in *Moral readings* 10 of this spreading of charity, 'Charity, through its eager concern, is spread out to encompass every virtuous action. It begins in two commandments, but it spreads itself out in innumerable actions.'[19] From this breadth and extension, charity appropriately earns golden clothing.

[155] [6] The sixth part of the picture concerns Jove's cheerfulness. For the poets depict Jove with a cheerful and pleasant face, as Virgil says and Alexander Neckam repeats in his *Mythology*.[20] Also astrologers say that Jove excels in blood; therefore sanguine people are Jove's children. This bodily temperament is naturally joyful, and this characteristic is appropriate for charity, which is pleasant toward everyone and disagreeable toward none at all. Bernard talks about this in a letter, 'O good mother charity, who fosters the weak, who exercises the aged, and who rebukes the restless; charity shows various things to various people, yet loves everyone as if they were its children. When charity rebukes you, it does so with meekness; when it flatters, it remains ingenuous. It customarily rages with pity, soothes without deceit, knows how to grow angry patiently and to be indignant in meekness.'[21]

---

[17] Sermo 354.6 (PL 39:1565).
[18] Ars amatoria 1.214–15.
[19] Moralia 10.6 (PL 75:922).
[20] VM3 3.3 (161/17–24), including citations of *Aeneid* 2.687 and 10.473.
[21] Epistola 2.1 (PL 182:80).

[7] Septima pars picture est de Iouis serenitate. Ad litteram enim pingitur a poetis cum facie relucente. Unde Iubiter a poetis dicitur Luce[c]ius uel Diespiter, id est 'diei claritatis pater'; *dian* enim Grece est Latine 'clarum'. Et bene conuenit | amori uel + caritati, quia nescit latere. Et ideo significanter Aristoteles, diffiniens ami[cicia]m, dicit quod est beniuolencia non latens. 'Si enim amor uerus fuerit, statim in opere se ostendit; operatur enim magna, si est; si autem operari renuit, amor non est', ut dicit Gregorius in omelia de Pentecoste. Unde notanda est illa narracio de philosopho Theofrasto, de quo narratur quod cum quidam sibi diceret de duobus hominibus, quod unus esset amicus alterius, quesiuit statim philosophus quomodo ergo est quod diues est unus et alter egenus. Uoluit enim Theofrastus per hoc innuere quod ibi non erat uera amicicia, ex quo ex una parte fuit copia et ex altera inopia siue penuria. Sicut enim recitat Ieronimus unum de potissimis preceptis Pic\ta/gorum fuit quod amicorum omnia debent esse communia. Unde de quodam legitur sapiente qui consueuit dicere se tantum diligere inimicum qui nichil facit mali sicut amicum qui nichil facit boni.

[8] Octaua pars picture est de Iouis fulminacione. Ista enim uerba, scilicet tonare, fulminare, sunt apud poetas excepte accionis, quia conueniunt Ioui et nulli alii. Qualiter ista fulminis iaculacio conueniat moraliter uirtuti amoris et caritatis, est notandum quod poete Iouis fulmen dicunt tri[f]idum, sicut patet per Remigium in commento super Marcianum. Sunt enim, secundum Plinium in libro *Naturalis historie*, fulmina triplicis differencie. Et de hoc eciam loquitur Seneca libro *Naturalium questionum*. Propter ergo istam triplicem differenciam fulminum, dicunt poete Iouem proiecere fulmen tri[f]idum, tripliciter scilicet fissum et uariatum.

---

169 Lucecius] Lucencius I, Lucessimus O • pater] *om.* I   170 fol. 89va 171 caritati] claritati OL • Aristoteles] *om.* I   172 amiciciam] animum O • beniuolencia] beniualencia uel benificium A, benificium L • latens] *adds* in contrapassis L   173 uerus] uersus A • statim ... ostendit] cito se comede(re) \ostendit/ I   174 renuit] *adds* caritas uel L   175 narracio] historia uel narracio A, opinio I   176 Theofrasto] quodam I   177 hominibus] amicis I • unus ... alterius] essent amici L   179 Theofrastus per] quod I • innuere] inuenire A   180 copia] uera copia A   181 inopia siue] *om.* A, parte L • inopia ... penuria] inopid I   181–83 Sicut ... legitur] *marg. to* 183 communia, *rest om.* I   183 Pictagorum] Pictagore A, Pictagoras I, Pitagorum *emended to* Pictagoreorum L

190, 195 trifidum] trisidum AIOL (*to first use, adds* uel triplum A)   196 fissum] scissum A

[167] [7] The seventh part of the picture concerns Jove's brightness, for in their texts, the poets depict him with a shining face. For this reason, the poets call Jupiter *Lucecius* 'the shining one' or *Diespiter* 'the father of day's brightness'; the Greek word *dyan* means 'shining' in Latin. And this is appropriate for love or charity, because neither knows how to hide itself. And Aristotle offers a significant definition of friendship in saying that it is an unhidden friendliness.[22] Gregory says in his sermon for Pentecost, 'If it is a true love, it immediately reveals itself in deeds. It takes on even great works, if that is necessary; but if it refuses to labour, it is not love.'[23] For this reason, one should notice this story about the philosopher Theophrastus, that when someone spoke to him about two men who were friends with one another, Theophrastus asked immediately why then one was rich and the other needy. Through this comment Theophrastus wanted to hint that it was not a true friendship, when there was abundance on one side and lack or poverty on the other.[24] Likewise, Jerome reports that one of the most powerful precepts of the Pythagoreans was that all friends' possessions ought to be held in common.[25] For this reason, we read of some wise man who was accustomed to say that he loved the enemy who did him no harm just as much as the friend who did him no good.

[186] [8] The eighth part of the picture concerns Jove's thunderbolts. The poets reserve the words *tonare* 'to thunder' and *fulminare* 'to loose a thunderbolt' for a particular action, appropriate to Jove and to no other person. To see how this casting forth a thunderbolt is appropriate in a moral reading to the virtue of love and charity, one should notice that the poets call Jove's thunderbolt three-pronged, as Remigius makes clear in his commentary on Martianus.[26] For there are, according to Pliny in his *Natural history*, three separate kinds of thunderbolt. Seneca also speaks about this in his *Natural questions*.[27] On account of this triple distinction between types of thunderbolt, the poets say that Jove throws out a three-pronged thunderbolt, that is one divided and varied in three ways.

---

[22] *Nicomachean Ethics* 9.11 (1171b).

[23] *Homeliae in evangilia* 30.2 (*PL* 76:1221).

[24] Also cited Holcot (on Ioel 2/310ff.), without the Theophrastus ascription; Seneca mentions him as an authority on friendship at *Epistula* 3.2.

[25] *Commentarii in Michaeam* 2.7 on Mi 7:5 (*PL* 25:1219, which actually doesn't quite say this).

[26] Not apparently Mart, but VM3 6.22 (187/11–12).

[27] *Historia naturalis* 2.138; *Quaestiones naturales* 8.2.1.

Et proporcionaliter triplex est genus dileccionum et
am[iciciaru]m, sicut eciam de hoc tangit Aristoteles, 8 *Ethicorum*,
scilicet amici|cia propter utile, propter honestum, et propter
delectabile. Et hec omnia continentur in amore uero, id est
in caritate et amicicia, que sola est uirtus uera. De qua pulcre
loquitur Augustinus in quadam epistola [et est] ad Macedonium:
'Talis enim amicicia caritate informata, que sola est uera uirtus',
ut ibi probat Augustinus, summe est utilis, summe est delectabilis,
et summe honestatis. Et ideo propter istam triplicem naturam ueri
amoris, merito amor dicitur fulmen proicere quod, ut dictum est,
triplicis [ponitur] nature.

    Sunt enim quedam fulmina, ut tangit Seneca, et concordat
cum Plinio: terebrancia, id est penetrancia; sunt eciam fulmina
dissipancia seu comminuencia, et sunt fulmina adurencia.
Primum est nature subtilioris, secundum est nature compaccioris,
sed tercium habet, ut dicit Seneca, plurimum materie terrestris.
Et proporcionantur ista tribus proprietatibus ueri amoris,
qui racione sue honestatis habet subtilitatem. Honestas enim
uirtutis res est subtilis, quia res mere spiritualis. Racione uero
sue delectabilitatis, quia scilicet est delectabilis, ideo similis est
fulmini, quod nature est compaccioris, quia delectacio causatur
ex quadam compaccione et coniunccione, scilicet conuenientis
cum conueniente, ut dicit Auicenna. Sed racione comoditatis
uel utilitatis, quam eciam habet amor uerus, assimiliatur amor
fulmini adurenti, cuius materia est magis terrest[r]is, quia [talis]
amor ad modum terre appetit commodum.

    Iuxta enim ymaginacionem poetarum, hoc est proprium
terre, ad illud quod est utile anelare, sicut patet in eius multiplici
nominacione. Nominatur enim | a poetis Ops ab opibus,
Berenthinthea, id est moncium dea, ab honoribus, et sic de
aliis. Dicta autem uaria sanctorum et philosophorum possunt
notari de ista materia, scilicet de istius uirtutis honestate,
complacencia, et commoditate. Nam eundo ad honestatem,

---

198 amiciciarum] amorem O   199 fol. 89[vb]   202 et est] *om.* O   206 merito] *om.* AI
    207 ponitur] *om.* O • nature] *om.* I
208–9 et ... Plinio] *om.* I   214–15 habet ... mere] *marg.* (quia res *om.*) I
    215 mere] materie L   216–17 similis est fulmini] singulis est fulmen L
    219 Auicenna] Seneca I   221 terrestris] terrestis O • talis] tunc O   222 ad
    modum] *om.* L • appetit commodum] ad illud quod est utile anelat (*from 224
    and repeated there*) A
223 ymaginacionem] ymaginem AI   224 terre] *om.* L   226 fol. 90[ra]   Berenthinthea]
    Uerendicia A, Berecinciam I, Berencia L • id est moncium] *over eras.* O

[197] Analogously, there are three kinds of loves and friendships, as Aristotle also discusses in *Nicomachean Ethics* 8: friendship for what is useful, for what is moral, and for what is delightful.[28] True love, that is charity and friendship, the single true virtue, encompasses all three. Augustine speaks neatly of these in a letter to Macedonius, 'Such friendship is informed by charity, which is the only true virtue', and Augustine proves there that charity is of the highest utility, the highest delight, and the highest moral standing.[29] Because of this triple nature of true love, love is appropriately described as casting forth a thunderbolt that, as I have said, is ascribed a triple nature.

[208] As Seneca, here in agreement with Pliny, says, there are several kinds of thunderbolt: those that bore in, that is penetrating ones; and there are also scattering ones or ones that break things apart, and there are burning thunderbolts. The first kind is more delicate in its nature, the second more compact in its, but the third has, as Seneca says, a great deal of earthy material.[30] These are analogous to three characteristics of true love, which from its virtuous nature, is delicate. The moral portion of a virtue is delicate, because it is a thing genuinely spiritual. However, because of its delightfulness, – and it is truly delightful – it is similar to the thunderbolt that is more compact in its nature, because delight is caused by a kind of compaction, pressing together, and joining, that is of one similar being with another, as Avicenna says.[31] But love for the sake of benefit or utility, also a property of true love, is like the burning thunderbolt, whose material is more earthy, for such a love desires something beneficial, in an earthly manner.

[223] According to what the poets imagine, it is characteristic of the earth to strive for what is useful. This is evident in the many names given to the earth. The poets call it *Ops* from the *opes* 'riches' it gives; Berecinthia, which means 'goddess of mountains', from the honours it grants; and so on. One should, however, attend to the various sayings of the saints and philosophers on this point, namely the moral status, pleasure, and benefit to be associated with friendship. For passing on to consider its moral standing,

---

[28] *Ibid.* 8.2 (1156ab).
[29] *Epistola* 155.4 (*PL* 33:672–73).
[30] *Historia naturalis* 2.137; ? *Quaestiones naturales* 2.40.
[31] Unfound.

230 Boycius, *De consolacione*, libro 3, prosa 2, attribuit amicicie maximam sanctitatem. Unde uocat amiciciam uirtut[em], sic inquiens, 'Amicorum quod sanctissimum quidem genus est? Non in fortuna, sed in uirtute, numeratur'. Hoc iste. Un[de] pro ista amicicie honestate dicit Tullius, quod hoc s[an]cire debet
235 lex amicicie, ut 'neque ab amicis res turpes rogemus, nec rogati faciamus. Turpis enim excusacio est, et minime acceptanda, cum quis amici causa peccauerit'. Et idem Tullius dicit, 'Hoc primum', inquit, 'sencio, nisi in bonis amiciciam non posse'.

  De complacencia et delectabilitate uere amicicie tractat eciam
240 idem Tullius, qui dicit quod 'caritate et beniuolencia sublata, omnis uit[e] aufertur iocunditas. Quid enim est dulcius', dicit Tullius, 'quam habere illum cum quo loqui sic audeas sicut tecum?' Ipsa enim amicicia, ut dicitur in libello qui *Speculum* intitulatur *amoris*, 'uirtutes omnes sua + condit suauitate; uicia omnia sua
245 perimit potestate; temperat aduersa, componit prospera, ita ut sine amico, nichil inter mortales poterit esse iocundum'. 'Nullius enim boni sine socio iocunda est possessio', dicit Seneca. 'Homo enim bestie comparatur non habens, qui sibi conlet[et]ur in rebus [s]ecundis, nec contristetur in tristibus; cui euaporaret, si quid
250 molestum | mens conceperit; cui communicet, si quid preter solitum sublime et luminosum accesserit. *Ue enim soli*, dicit Salomon, *quia cum cecid\er/it, non habet subleuantem se*. Solus omnino est qui sine amico est'.

  De commoditate eciam amicicie et eius plurima utilitate
255 loquitur idem Tullius. Dicit enim quod 'plurimas et maximas commoditates continet amicicia'. 'Res enim [s]ecundas amicicia facit splendidiores, et res aduersas, amicicia parciens et participans, efficit leuiores. Unde non aqua, non igne, pluribus locis utimur

---

231 uirtutem] uirtutis O   231–33 uirtutem ... iste] sanctissimam ubi autem sanctitas ibi honesta (honestatis A, honestas I) AIL   233 Unde] Unum O
234 sancire] sanitire A, scire O, sancciri L • sancire debet] est I
236 excusacio ... cum] accepcio non debet fieri ut I   238 non] *om.* IL
239 delectabilitate] delectacione A   241 uite] uita IO, uit\e/ L   242 tecum] *om.* I
244 condit] condidit O   245 prospera] *om.* L   248 conletetur] colloquetur A, collocetur I, consoletur O   249 secundis] facundis A, iocundis I, fecundis O, prosperis L   250 fol. 90rb 250–51 si quid ... accesserit] *om.* I   252 non ... se] *om.* I   253 amico] socio I
254 eciam] *adds* socii et A   254–55 et ... loquitur] *om.* I   256 commoditates] utilitates A • secundas] fecundas AO, prosperas IL   257, 258 amicicia] *om.* I
259–63 Res ... reperitur] *marg.* I (*omitting* 259 In ... loco, *and* 259–60 ut ... studio *scattered later in sentence*)

Boethius, *On the consolation* 3p2, ascribes to friendship the very greatest holiness. Thus he calls friendship a virtue, saying, 'What thing is more holy than one's friends? They are numbered among virtuous acts, not gifts of Fortune.'[32] So Boethius says. Cicero says one thing about the virtuous nature of friendship that the law governing friendship ought to confirm, that 'we should neither ask disgraceful things of our friends, nor, should we be asked, perform them. For it is a shameful excuse, and not to be accepted at all, that someone has sinned for a friend's sake.' Cicero also says, 'I think, first of all, that friendship cannot exist, except between good people.'

[239] Cicero also discusses the pleasure and delightfulness of true friendship, saying, 'If charity and friendliness were carried away, all the happiness of life would be removed as well. For', he says, 'what is more delightful than to have a person to speak with whom you hear just as if it were yourself speaking?'[33] As it says in the little book called *The mirror of love*, friendship 'seasons all virtues with its sweetness; its power suppresses all vices; it moderates bad times and calms good times, so that without a friend, nothing between mortals may be happy'. And Seneca says, 'One cannot possess anything pleasurable without a companion.'[34] [And Aelred continues], 'A person not having a friend is compared to a beast; he will lack someone rejoicing with him in favourable times and sharing his sorrow in sorrowful ones; someone to whom he may complain, if something has appeared vexatious to him; and with whom he may share, if something more lofty and brilliant than usual has befallen him. Solomon says, *Woe to him that is alone, for when he falleth, he hath none to lift him up* (Ecl 4:10). The person who is without a friend is completely alone.'[35]

[254] Cicero also speaks of the benefit of friendship and of its manifold usefulness. He says that 'Friendship contains very many, indeed the greatest benefits.' [And Aelred says], 'Friendship makes favourable times yet more brilliant, and in dividing and sharing harsh times, makes them easier to bear. For this reason, we don't use water or fire in more places

---

[32] *Ibid.* 3p2.9.
[33] Consecutively, *De amicitia* 40, 18, 19, and 22.
[34] *Epistula* 6.4.
[35] Aelred of Rievaulx, *De spirituali amicitia* 2 (*PL* 195:671).

quam utamur caritate uel amicicia. In omni enim loco', ut dicitur
in libello *De amicicia*, 'et in omni studio, in certis, in dubiis, in
quolibet euentu, in fortuna qualibet, in secreto et puplico, in
omni consultacione domi foris et ubique, grata est amicicia, et
amicus utilis reperitur'. 'Amici enim', ut dicit Tullius, 'uirtute
amicicie assunt absentes, quia amicicia facit eos presentes;
habundant eciam indigentes, ualent imbecilles et impotentes,
et quod mirabilius est, uirtute amicicie mortui sunt uiuentes';
quere de isto in Tulli *De amicicia*. Ista ergo sunt tria fulmina,
que iaculantur amicicia et caritas, que sola est uirtus uere. Que
habet maximam honestatem, quia sola facit animam Deo caram
et acceptam. Ipsa eciam habet summam commoditatem, quia
prestat eternam felicitatem summam, et habet iocunditatem, quia,
ut dicit Bernardus, 'omnis iocunditas | alia meror et tristicia'
est dicenda.

[9] Nona pars picture est de Iouis cibacione. Siquidem poete,
sicut tangit auctor ille antiquus Ig[i]neus, *De ymaginibus celestibus*,
pingunt et fingunt Iouem cibatum in puericia lacte capre. Quam
capram in celum Iouem fingunt pro mercede transtulisse et
signum Capricorni statuisse. Unum tamen cornu capre nutrici
Iouis dicunt Iouem in terris dimisisse, quod cornu repertum
ab Hercule. Fingunt poete Herculem dee Copie consecrasse.
Deam autem istam poete finxerunt, hoc cornu mediante, rerum
terrenarum habundancia[m] hominibus ministrasse, et ideo per
cornu consueuerunt copiam et opulencia[m] intelligere.

Patet ergo intellectus picture: cibatur enim Iubiter [et
reficitur] cornu capre per figuram sinodoche. Supponit enim
pars pro toto, quia cibatrix Iouis fuit capra cornuta, sed quia
istud cornu fuit consecratum dee Copie, ideo merito potest
ista Iouis cibacio applicari ad uirtutem amicicie. Uirtus enim
ista plena est omni copia, quia plenitudo legis dileccio. Unde
Augustinus, *De uera innocencia*, 'Quanta est caritas, que si
desit, frustra habentur cetera; et si assit, habentur omnia'.

259 quam ... In] *om.* L • caritate uel] *om.* AI 261 in fortuna] infortunio A
263 utilis] uerus A • ut dicit Tullius] *om.* I • dicit] asserit A 264 assunt]
adds licet A 267 tria] *adds* illa I, *adds* illa sublimia L 268 Que³] *add* caritas AL
270-71 quia ... quia] *after* 273 dicenda L 271-72 summam ... Bernardus] unde
bene I 272 fol. 90va
275 Igineus] Ignis A, Ingnis I, Ig|neus O 280 poete] *adds* hoc cornu L
282 habundanciam] habundancia O 283 opulenciam] epilenciam A,
epulenciam I, opulencia O
284-85 et reficitur] *om.* O 287 Copie] Capre A 291 cetera] omnia A

than we use charity or friendship.' As Aelred says in the little book *On friendship*, 'Friendship is welcome in every place and in any endeavour – in situations where we are secure or in ones where we are in doubt, whatever befalls or in whatever turn of fortune we may be, in public or in private, in every deliberation, whether a domestic matter or any sort of public one – and a friend is always useful.' Cicero says, 'Even though absent, through the power of friendship, friends are present to us, because friendship makes them so; friends make those in need rich, make those weak and powerless strong, and – it's the most wonderful thing of all – by the power of friendship, the dead live on'; you can seek more on the subject in Cicero's *On friendship*.[36] Therefore, these are the three lightning-bolts with which friendship and charity, truly the only virtue, are thrown. This virtue includes the greatest moral power, for it alone makes the soul dear and acceptable to God. It also includes the very greatest benefit, because it offers the greatest eternal happiness, and it includes joy, because, as Bernard says, any joy other than it should be called sorrow and sadness.[37]

[274] [9] The ninth part of the picture concerns Jove's being fed. For the poets, according to what the ancient author Hyginus says in his *On the heavenly signs*, present Jove as having been fed in his childhood with a goat's milk. They pretend that Jove moved that goat into heaven as a reward and thus established the sign Capricorn.[38] Nevertheless, they say that Jove left behind on earth one horn from the goat that nurtured him, and the horn was found by Hercules. The poets claim that Hercules consecrated that horn to the goddess Copia 'plenty'. Further, the poets pretended that she was a goddess and that she distributed to people the abundance of earthly things with the aid of this horn. Therefore the poets were accustomed to understand by a horn both plenty and riches.

[284] The meaning of the picture is evident. For Jupiter was fed and refreshed with a goat's horn as an instance of the figure 'synecdoche'. This substitutes a part for the whole, because Jove's serving-girl was a horned she-goat. Because this horn was consecrated to the goddess Copia (who distributes her plenty), Jove's feeding may properly be applied to the virtue friendship. For this virtue is filled with plenty for everyone, for the love of the law is fullness. For this reason, Augustine says in *On true innocence*, 'Charity is so great that, if it is lacking, one possesses other things in vain; but if it is present, one has everything.'[39]

---

[36] Combining *De amicitia* 23 and Aelred, *ibid*.
[37] *Epistola* 114.1 (PL 182:259).
[38] *De astronomia* 2.13 (although not the material on the cornucopia).
[39] Prosper of Aquitaine, *Sententiae ex Augustino* 327 (PL 45:1888).

Et Augustinus, in sermone suo de laude caritatis, dicit quod 'Diuinarum Scripturarum multiplicem habundanciam, latissimam doctrinam ille sine ullo errore comprehendit, et sine labore custodit, cuius cor plenum est caritate'. Hec est caritas, ut dicit Bernardus, sermone 18 *Super Cantica,* que | 'sola in rebus potest implere creaturam factam ad ymaginem Dei; solus autem Deus maior est illa'.

Istam autem copiam et uberem affluenciam amicicie tangit liber qui *Speculum amicicie* uocatur, dicens, '[Amicicia] diuitibus est pro gloria, + exulantibus est pro patria, egrotis pro medicina – *Amicus enim medicamentum uite est,* ut dicit sapiens – pauperibus est pro censu, imbecillibus est pro uirtute, mortuis pro uita, et sanis pro gracia'. Et sic finitur poetica pictura caritatis et amicicie sub ymagine dei Iouis. Nota quod in serie picture accipiat caritas et amicicia pro eadem uirtute, quia amicicia de qua locuti sunt philosophi non est dicenda uirtus, sed pocius uicium, nisi fuerit caritate Dei et proximi informata, sicut patet \per/ Augustinum in epistola ad Macedonium, ut tactum est prius.

292–95 Et ... caritate] *marg.* I   292 laude] *om.* L   294 latissimam] lasciuiam A   295 custodit] et tedio L   296 fol. 90vb
300 Amicicia] *om.* O, sic amicicia L   301 exulantibus] exultantibus O
307 dicenda] *om.* A

And Augustine, in his sermon in praise of charity, 'The person whose heart is filled with charity understands, without any error, the multiple abundance and the broadest teaching of Divine Scripture, and they preserve these without working at it.'[40] As Bernard says, *On the Song of Songs*, sermon 18, 'Among created things, only this charity can fill up a creature made in the image of God, for only God is greater than charity.'[41]

[299] The book that is called *The mirror of love* treats this plenty and abundant opulence of friendship, saying, 'Friendship is given to the rich for their glory, to those who are banished for their homeland, to the sick for their medicine – after all, the wise man says, *A faithful friend is the medicine of life* (Sir 6:16) – to the poor for their property, to the weak for their strength, to the dead for their life, and to the spiritually sound as grace.'[42] Thus ends the poetic picture of charity and friendship presented through the image of the god Jove. Notice that, in the sequence of this picture, charity and friendship should be taken to be the same virtue. For that friendship the philosophers spoke about should not be called a virtue – it's rather a sin – unless it has been founded on charity directed to God and one's neighbour. This is evident from Augustine's comments in his letter to Macedonius, as is discussed above.

---

[40] *Sermo* 350.1 (*PL* 39:1533).
[41] *Sermo* 18.6 (*PL* 183:862).
[42] Aelred, *ibid*.

[4]

Quarta mithologia Fulgencii est de dea Iunone, sub cuius ymagine poete solent depingere uirtutem memorie, que secundum Senecam et Tullium, est una de partibus prudencie. Nam partes prudencie, secundum Tullium in sua *Rethorica* sunt tres, scilicet preteritorum
5 memoria, presencium intelligencia, et futurorum prouidencia. Et ideo *83 questionum*, questione 31ᵃ, dicit Augustinus, 'Si prudens esse cupis, in futura prospectum intende que possunt contingere; animo tuo cuncta propone; nichil tibi subitum sit, sed totum ante conspicies. Presencia ordina; futura prouide; preterita recordare'.
10 Nota ergo quomodo poete fingunt | [Saturnum] istam triplicem prolem procreasse, scilicet Iunonem, quam ponunt loco memorie. Et significanter fingunt istam partem prudencie sexum habere muliebrem propter scilicet teneritudinem et fragilitatem organi uirtutis memoratiue. Nulla enim uirtus organica tam cito
15 solet in homine deficere sicut uirtus ista, dicente Seneca, libro primo *Declamacionum* in prologo, 'Memoria', inquit, 'est res ex omnibus animi partibus maxime delicata et fragilis, quam primum senectus incurrit'. Aliam prolem attribuunt Saturno poete, quam uocant Neptunum, deum marium, sub cuius ymagine
20 pingunt uirtutem intelligencie. Terciam prolem attribuunt Saturno, scilicet Plutonem, deum inferni, sub cuius ymagine fingunt uirtutem prouidencie, que est tercia pars prudencie. Unde quia apud eos Saturnus stat pro prudencia, ideo filii Saturni dicuntur isti, qui sunt prudencie partes, sicut proles est pars parentum.
25 Iubiter uero dicitur quarta proles, quia ex prudencia et sapiencia in intellectu consurgit bona et recta beniuolencia in affectu.
Notanda est ergo pictura poetica dee I[un]onis, que pingitur a poetis:
[1] uertice uelata,
30 [2] iride sertata,

---

1 dea] *om.* A 2 poete] philosophi I 7 in futura] [*blank*] A 8 totum] tunc A
10 fol. 91ʳᵃ • Saturnum] *om. at page-bound* O 11 procreasse] propagasse I
• Iunonem] Iouem A 13 habere] *om.* A • teneritudinem] temeritatem AI
14 organi] memorie (?) id est orgagani I 17 animi] *om.* L • quam] cuius
dampnum A 19, 21 deum] dominum A 20 Saturno] *adds* poete A, *adds* quod
uocant I 22 uirtutem] *om.* I • pars] *om.* L (*emended* L) 26 in intellectu] et
intelligencia AL, et intellectum I
27 Iunonis] Io\no/nis A, Iouis O

[4]

Fulgentius's fourth mythography concerns the goddess Juno. In her image, poets are accustomed to depict the virtue Memory, which, according to Seneca and Cicero, is one 'part' of prudence. For according to Cicero, in his *Rhetoric*, prudence has three parts, namely the memory of things past, the understanding of those present, and foresight about those to come. And therefore Augustine says, *83 questions* 31, 'If you wish to be prudent, concentrate your sight on those things that may befall in the future; attend to them all in your mind; then nothing may sneak up on you, but you will see everything before it happens. Organise present things; foresee those to come; recall past things.'[1]

[10] Therefore notice how the poets tell that Saturn fathered a triple offspring, particularly Juno, whom they offer in the position of memory. It is significant that they represent this part of prudence as a woman because of the weakness and fragility of the organ by which we have the power of memory. For no inbred power customarily fails in people so quickly, as Seneca the elder says in the prologue to book 1 of his *Declamations*, 'Memory is the most delicate and fragile of the parts of the soul, and the one old age attacks first.'[2] The poets ascribe Saturn a second child, named Neptune, the god of the sea; in his image, they depict the virtue Intelligence. They represent the virtue Foresight, the third part of prudence, in the image of the third child they ascribe Saturn, namely Pluto, the god of the underworld. For this reason, because they have Saturn stand for prudence, they call these parts of prudence Saturn's children, just as an offspring represents a part of its parents. Jupiter is said to be Saturn's fourth offspring, because the emotion of good and proper kindliness springs up from prudence and wisdom in the mind.

[27] One should notice the poets' picture of the goddess Juno, whom they describe as:

[1] with veiled head,
[2] garlanded with a rainbow,

---

[1] Cicero, *De inventione* 2.160; Augustine, *ibid.* (*PL* 40:20), but more directly Hugh of St Victor, 'De fructibus carnis et spiritus' 12 (*PL* 176:1002). For the Seneca reference, cf. *Epistula* 88.32–33.

[2] *Controversariae* 1.1.

[3] unguentis afflata,
           [4] sceptro decorata,
           [5] auro ligata,
           [6] Ioue maritata,
35   [7] Herculi irata,
           [8] auibus uallata,
           [9] humore rigata,
           [10] et luce lustrata. +
   Iste sunt decem partes picture qua poete solent istam Saturni
40 prolem de|pingere, et conueniunt bene uirtuti memorie, que
   ponitur una pars prudencie a Tullio.
       [1] Nam memoria peccati perpetrati bene ad modum Iunonis
   depingitur cum uelamine in uertice in signum pudoris et
   uerecundie quam quilibet discretus merito debet habere in peccati
45 recordacione. Quantus enim sit pudor peccati mortalis tangit
   Anselmus in fine *De similitudinibus*. 'Si hinc', inquit, 'peccati
   pudorem et illic cernerem inferni horrorem, et necessario uni
   eorum haberem immergi, prius me in infernum immergerem
   quam peccatum in me mitterem. Mallem enim purus a peccato
50 et innocens iehennam intrare, quam peccati sorde pollutus
   celorum regna tenere'. Peccator ergo ex peccati recordacione
   pudore confusus merito pingitur capite uelatus.
       [2] Secunda pars picture est de I\u/nonis coronacione.
   Secundum enim fincionem poeticam, istam coronam portat de
55 yride factam, de archu celesti in signum federis et reconciliacionis
   cum Deo, quam reconciliacionem homo consequitur per peccati
   perpetrati rememoracionem. Sicut enim docent doctores, et patet
   ex serie Scripture, archus iste celestis post diluuium fuit positus
   in signum federis inter Deum et homines, et in signum concordie
60 et reconciliacionis. Nam dixit Dominus ad Noe, *Archum meum
   ponam in nubibus celi, et erit signum federis inter me et terram.*
   Nichil aliud ergo per has | duas partes picture debemus intelligere,
   nisi quod memoria et recordacio culpe perpetrate pertingit per
   uelum uerecundie ad sertum, id est ad coronam reconciliacionis
65 et concordie.

   38 lustrata] *adds* Hec est pictura uirtutis memorie sub Iunonis ymagine O
   39 decem] *adds* proprietates uel A   40 fol. 91rb
44 merito] *om.* A   47 pudorem] inquit (*repeated*) A • inferni] *adds* dolorem et A
   49 quam … mitterem] *om.* A • purus] prius (*emended*) L   50 innocens]
   immunis A   52 pudore confusus] *om.* I
55 factam] *om.* IL   62 fol. 91va 63–64 per uelum] *om.* L

[3] wafting sweet smells,
[4] adorned with a sceptre,
[5] bound with gold,
[6] married to Jove,
[7] angered by Hercules,
[8] surrounded by birds,
[9] bathed in moisture,
[10] and irradiated with light.

These are the ten parts of the picture by which poets customarily depict this child of Saturn's, and they are appropriate for the virtue of memory – recall that Cicero identifies it as one part of prudence.

[42] [1] Juno is depicted with her head veiled as an appropriate way of showing the memory of sins one has perpetrated. She has a veil on her head as a sign of shame and modesty; any discreet person ought properly to be ashamed in recalling their sin. Alexander of Canterbury treats how great one's shame over mortal sin should be at the end of *On likenesses*, when he says, 'If I might know both shame for my sin here and the terror of hell in the next world, and if I should necessarily have to be immersed in one of them, I would prefer that I were sunk in hell rather than introduce sin into myself. For I would prefer to enter hell pure from sin and innocent than to rule all of heaven while soiled with the dirt of sin.'[3] Therefore a sinner, troubled with shame from remembering their sin, is properly depicted with a veiled head.

[53] [2] The second part of the picture concerns Juno's crowning. According to the poets' fiction, Juno wears a crown made from the heavenly rainbow as a sign of a covenant and reconciliation with God; this reconciliation is a consequence of a person's remembering the sins they have perpetrated. For, as learned men teach and as is evident from the scriptural narrative, this rainbow was placed in the heavens after the flood as a token of the covenant between God and humanity and as a token of harmony and reconciliation. For the Lord said to Noah, *I will set my bow in the clouds, and it shall be the sign of a covenant between me and the earth* (Gn 9:13). Therefore, from these two parts of the picture, we should understand nothing except that memory and recall of the guilt we have perpetrated extends from the veil of shame to the garlanding crown of reconciliation and harmony.

---

[3] Alexander (ps.-Anselm), ch. 191 (*PL* 159:701).

Nota in corona principium unitur cum fine, et moraliter loquendo, anima peccatrix, peccato deformata, inferior est omni creatura per memoriam. Et peccati uerecundiam unitur et reconciliatur cum principio, id est cum Deo suo. Notande autem
70 sunt alique auctoritates sanctorum ad propositum. Dicit enim Crisostomus in suo commentario super epistolam ad Hebreos quod 'Nullum delictorum inuenitur tale remedium sicut eorum continuata memoria, nec aliquid ita segnem reddit hominem ad nequiciam perpetrandam +'. Et subdit Crisostomus parum post,
75 'Si habueris in mente tua peccata continue, nunquam malum aduersum proximum tuum in corde retinebis. Aduersus enim nullum retinebis in corde malum, portans peccata in animo tuo, non irasceris, nulli detrahes, non sapies altum, nec redibis iterum ad peccandum, sed ad bona impetu uehemenciori consurges.
80 Intuere ergo quanta bona ex peccatorum recordacione generantur. Scio [enim] quod non + placet anime hec amara peccati memoria. Sed nos', dicit Crisostomus, 'debemus ad hoc animam cogere et compell\er/e. Melius quippe nobis est ut anima nostra mordeatur in presenti ex recordacione peccati quam in futuro tempore
85 supplicia senciat sempiterna. Nunc enim si recorderis peccatorum tuorum et frequenter ea in conspectu Dei pronunicies, et pro eis eius clemenciam depreceris, cicius ea delebis. Si autem nu[n]c | obliuiscaris peccatorum tuorum, tunc eorum recordaberis nolens, quando publicabuntur coram toto mundo in conspectu
90 tam amicorum quam inimicorum et sanctorum angelorum celestiumque uirtutum'. Hec Crisostomus.

[3] Tercia pars picture est de dee Iunonis inunccione. Pingitur enim ista dea a poetis redolens unguentis delicatis. Unde et unum de suis nominibus, sicut tangit Remigius in
95 commento super Marcianum, est Unxcia ab unguentorum habundancia. Et moraliter figurat spiritualem consolacionem quam homo consequitur post sui cum Deo reconciliacionem, ad quam attingit per peccati recordacionem. [Memor], dicit psalmista, *fui Dei mei,* scilicet reconciliati, *et delectatus sum et*
100 *defecit spiritus meus.*

---

74 perpetrandam] *adds* sicut eorum obliuio O   78 altum] *om.* A   • redibis] *corr. from* ridebis A, ridebis uel redibis L   80 bona] *om.* I   81 enim, placet] *om.,* placet I; quidam, placent O   • memoria] recordacio A   85 senciat] sustineat A   87–88 cicius … recordaberis] *marg.* I   87 nunc] nuc O   88 fol. 91vb 90–92 et … picture] *marg.* I

92 est … Iunonis] *om.* I   93 unguentis] congnentis I   96 figurat] significat I   97 sui] *adds* [blank] A   98 Memor] *om.* O

[66] Notice that in a crown, the beginning is joined to the end, and speaking of things in moral terms, the sinful soul, deformed by sin, becomes lower than any created thing through memory. And shame for sin is joined with and reconciled to its beginning, that is with God Himself. Moreover, one should notice the various authoritative statements of holy men on this point. For Chrysostom says, in his commentary *On Hebrews*, 'One can find no remedy for sins equal to remembering them continuously, nor does anything render a person so disinclined to perpetrate vice again.' And Chrysostom adds a little later, 'If you have had your sins continually in mind, you will never retain evil intentions toward your neighbour in your heart. In contrast, even if you are carrying sin in your soul, if you retain nothing evil in your heart, you will not grow angry, you will not slander anyone, you will not think yourself lofty, nor will you return again to sinful behaviours, but you will rise up to good things with a more vigorous motion. Therefore understand how many good things are produced, when one remembers one's sins. I certainly know that this bitter memory of sin will not be pleasing to the soul. But', Chrysostom says, 'we ought to coerce and compel our soul to remember. For it is indeed better for us that our soul should be gnawed with the memory of sin in the present than that it should feel eternal torments in time to come. For now, if you will recall your sins and frequently state them in God's presence, and pray that He grant you mercy for them, you will blot them out very quickly. If, however, you are now forgetful of your sins, then you will have to recall them against your will, when they will be exhibited before everyone, in the presence of both your friends and your enemies, as well as of the holy angels and the heavenly powers.' So Chrysostom says.[4]

[92] [3] The third part of the picture concerns the goddess Juno's anointing. For the poets depict this goddess smelling of sweet ointments. Also for this reason, one of her names, as Remigius mentions in his commentary on Martianus, is Unxia from her abundance of *unguenta* 'ointments'.[5] In moral terms, this image indicates spiritual consolation, which follows on after a person is reconciled with God, and they attain that reconciliation by recalling their sins. David says, *I remembered God*, that is, he was reconciled with me, *and was delighted, and my spirit swooned away* (Ps 76:4).

---

[4] Chrysostom, *in ep. ad Heb. Hom.* 31 (PG 63:216–17).
[5] Mart 63.16 (181/20–22).

[4] Quarta pars picture est de dee Iunonis sceptracione. Pingitur enim cum sceptro regio; unde a poetis dicitur Iuno regnorum dea, sicut tangit Alexander Nekham in sua *Methologia*. Et conuenit hec pars picture bene uirtuti memorie, quia per memoriam peccatorum redit peccator ad statum + regni prius perditum. Peccando enim amisit regimen sui ipsius, et peccati reminiscendo et de eo uerecundiam paciendo, recuperat pristinam potestatem ad cauendum peccati [per]uersitatem. Hec est autem maxima potestas et nobilissimum regimen, potencia regendi seipsum, sicut pulcre tractant poete et sancti eciam nostri. Unde ille poeta Claudianus in metro suo sic dicit:

> Tu licet extremos late domin[e]re per Indos, / [Te Medus, te mollis Arabs, te Seres adorent;] / Si metuis, si praua cupis, si duceris ira, / Seruicii paciere iugum; tolerabis iniquas / Interius leges. Tunc omnia iur[e] tenebis, / Cum poteris | rex esse tui'.

Et de ista eciam loquitur pulcre poeta Oracius in suis odis. Et ideo dicit significanter ille Prosper, quod 'ille non caret regia potestate, qui suo corpori nouit racionabiliter imperare. Uere dominator est terre qui carnem suam regit legibus discipline'. Et Seneca in quadam epistola, 'Si uis tibi omnia subicere, teipsum subice racioni; multos enim reges, si te racio rexerit'. Et de isto nota Origenem, *Super Iosue*; Augustinum eciam, libro 4 *De ciuitate Dei*; et Gregorium, libro *Moralium* in diuersis locis.

[5] Quinta pars picture est de Iunonis ligacione. Allegat enim hic Fulgencius auctorem illum Theopompum in suo carmine \e/pico, qui dicit Iouem ligasse Iunonem cathenis aureis. Et bene hoc conuenit hec pars picture uirtuti memorie, racione sue dignitatis et excellencie, stabilitatis, et permanencie. Unde Remigius, in commento super Marcianum, d[a]t causam quare memoria pingitur a poetis liga[ta uincul]is aureis, sic + inquiens, 'Omnia que uisu uel auditu percepimus, uelut quedam + nebule, euanescerent et elaberentur ab animo, nisi memoria uinculis

---

104 pars] *over eras.* O, *om. (with nom.)* L **105** statum] *om. (with acc.)* A • regni] regimen (*for* regiminis?) O **106, 109** regimen] regnum IL **108** peruersitatem] aduersitatem O **112** dominere] dominare AO, domineris L **112–13** Te¹ ... adorent] *marg.* I, *om.* O **113** adorent] adornant AI **115** omnia] anima I • iure] iura O • fol. 92ra

118 ille ... ille] ista pars picture A **119** racionabiliter] nobiliter A

126 Theopompum] Tetiposum A **128** conuenit] *om.* I **130** dat] dicit O **131** ligata uinculis] ligamentis O • inquiens] inquirens O **133** nebule] nebula siue quedam nebule O

[101] [4] The fourth part of the picture is of Juno's sceptre, for she is depicted with a royal sceptre. For this reason, the poets call Juno the goddess of kingdoms, as Alexander Neckam mentions in his *Mythology*.[6] And this part of the picture is appropriate for the virtue memory, because through memory of their sins, a sinner returns to that ruling state they had lost earlier. For by sinning, the sinner lost control of themselves, and by remembering sin and enduring shame for it, the sinner regains their original pure power, that is to avoid the perversion of sin. This is the greatest power and the most noble control, the power to rule oneself, as poets, as well as our holy people, treat beautifully. For this reason, the poet Claudian says in one of his poems:

> Although you command widely, as far as the distant Indians; / although the Mede, the effeminate Arab and the Chinese adore you, / if you are afraid, if you desire evil things, or are driven by wrath, / you will bear the yoke of slavery; you will endure evil / laws within. But you will control everything by right, / if you are able to be king over yourself.[7]

The poet Horace also speaks quite beautifully about this in his odes. And therefore Prosper of Aquitaine says significantly, 'The person who knows how to command his body through reason never lacks royal power. The person who rules his flesh with the laws of proper conduct is truly a world-conqueror.' And Seneca says in an epistle, 'If you wish everything to be subject to you, subject yourself to reason's rule; if reason has ruled you, you will rule many people.'[8] And on the same point, notice Origen, *On Joshua*; as well as Augustine, *On the city of God* 4; and Gregory, at various points in his *Moral readings*.[9]

[125] [5] The fifth part of the picture concerns Juno's binding. For Fulgentius refers here to the author Theopompus, who in his epic poem, says that Jove bound Juno with golden chains.[10] This part of the picture is appropriate for the virtue memory, because of its worthiness, excellence, stability, and permanence. For this reason, Remigius, in his commentary on Martianus, gives the reason why the poets depict memory bound with golden chains, saying, 'Everything we perceive by sight or hearing would fade or slip away from our mind, like clouds do, were they not

---

[6] VM3 4.5 (167/17–20).

[7] *Panegyricus de quarto consulatu Honorii Augusti* 257–62, followed by Horace, *Odes* 2.2.9–12.

[8] Prosper, *Sententiae ex Augustino* 242 (PL 45:1879), followed by Seneca, *Epistula* 37.4.

[9] Origen, *Homeliae super Joshuam* generally, cf. 11.6; *De ciuitate Dei* 14.19 (PL 41:427); *Moralia* 11.13 (PL 75:963).

[10] Fulg 1.3 (19/1–3).

\retinerentur. Quam uero preciosa sit [sana et perfecta] memoria ostendit poeta "uniculis/ aureis" dicens eam alligatam'. Hec Remigius. Unde notandum est quod aurum ceteris metallis est durabilius; ideo ad + innuendum quod memoria est de preteritis, ad hoc quod sit uera uirtus, oportet quod duret et sit permanens atque stabilis. Parum uel nichil ualet patrati sceleris recordari, et recorda[ti] continuo obliuisci. Ideo poete Iunonem [istam] fingunt cathenis non quibuscumque, sed aureis alligari. Unde uerbum notabile | [ad propositum] dicit Ieronymus in suo originali super Mattheum, 'Non', inquit, 'sepisse sed perfecisse uirtus est'. Et ideo dicit [Gregorius], libro primo *Moralium*, quod 'incassum bonum agit[ur], si ante uite terminum deseratur; quia frustra uelociter currit qui prius quam ad metas ueniat, deficit'.

[6] Sexta pars picture est de Iunonis desponsacione. Poete enim [f]ingunt Iouem plures habuisse pellices siue concubinas, sed uxor eius legittima fuit Iuno. Unde sicut tangit Seneca in \sua/ prima tragedia, ipsa est soror et uxor dei Iouis. Et bene conuenit [uirtuti] recordacion[is] siue memorie, nam peccator per peccati memoria[m] et memorati uerecundiam recupierat caritatem perditam et Dei pristinam beniuolenciam. Que caritas sub Iouis [ymagine] fuit prius figurata, et ideo uirtus ista memorie significanter pingitur Ioui mari\tata/. Nota ordinem: primo, peccati memoria inducit uerecundiam, figuratam per uelum capitis; et ex hoc, quod de peccato confunditur, Deo peccator reconciliatur. Sed in hoc, quod in ista confusione complacet et delectatur, permanet, et moratur hac complacencia, reducitur ad primam dignitatem et sui cum Deo pristinam familiaritatem.

[7] Septima pars picture est de Iunonis offensione. Pingunt enim eam nouercantem et si[ngulari]ter aduersantem Herculi, sicut de ista materia plura tangit Seneca in sua prima tragedia.

---

134 retinerentur] religarentur A, recluderentur I • sana et perfecta] sua O
137 innuendum] inueniendum IO, continuendum L   139 patrati] perpetrari A, *for* preteriti? • recordari] *om.* A   140 recordati] recor|da O • istam] *om.* O
142 fol. 92rb • ad propositum] *om.* O (*at column-boundary*)   143 perficisse] percepisse A   144 Gregorius] *om.* O   145 agitur] agit O
147 desponsacione] disposicione A   148 fingunt] pingunt O   151 uirtuti recordacionis] recordacionem O   152 memoriam] memoria O • recupierat] recipit A   154 Iouis] Iunonis A • ymagine] picture O   159 moratur] commoratur A, immoratur L   160 primam] pristinam AIL
163 nouercantem] [*blank*] A • singulariter] significanter O   164 materia plura] *om.* L • plura] *om.* A

retained by the chains of memory. The poet Martianus shows how truly precious a healthy and perfect memory is, when he says that it is bound "with golden chains".'[11] So Remigius says. For this reason, one should notice that gold is more longlasting than other metals; therefore, to hint that memory, insofar as it is a true virtue, concerns things past, it must necessarily endure and be permanent and stable. It is of little or no worth to remember a crime one has committed and then to continually forget what has been remembered. Therefore, the poets depict Juno as bound, not with just any chains, but golden ones. For this reason, Jerome says something worth noticing on this point in his commentary on Matthew, 'Virtue isn't a matter of beginning things, but of finishing them.' And therefore Gregory says, *Moral readings* 1, 'If a good ceases before the end of life, its actor performed it to no purpose; for a person runs quickly, but in vain, if he fails before he gets to the finish-line.'[12]

[147] [6] The sixth part of the picture concerns Juno's marriage. For the poets report that Jove had many mistresses or concubines, but Juno was legally his wife. For this reason, Seneca mentions in his first tragedy that she is both sister and wife of the god Jove.[13] And this is appropriate for the virtue recall or memory, for a sinner, through their memory of sin and their shame about what has been remembered, recovers the charity they had lost and God's original kindliness. I have already portrayed charity in discussing the image of Jove, and therefore this virtue memory is significantly depicted as married to Jove. But pay attention to the ordering of the image: first, the memory of sin induces shame, visualised as the veil on Juno's head; and from this, because troubled by sin, the sinner is reconciled to God. But because the sinner takes pleasure and delights in this troubled state, they remain in it, abiding with this pleasurable shame, and so they are drawn back to their original dignity and their original pure companionship with God.

[162] [7] The seventh part of the picture concerns Juno's offence. For the poets depict her as a wicked stepmother, and particularly as opposing Hercules; Seneca treats a good deal of this material in his first tragedy.

---

[11] Mart 8.17 (80/26–29).

[12] *Commentarii in evangelium Matthaei* 1 (on Mt 10:22) (*PL* 26:65); *Moralia* 1.37 (*PL* 75:554).

[13] *Hercules furens* 1–29; the reference at line 164 is to 214–15.

165 Et conuenit hec pars picture uirtuti memorie, nam Hercules interpretatur h[eroum], id est [magnorum uirorum], gloria. Qui ergo reducit ad memoriam uanam potenci[u]m et seculi gloriam, | merito ne et uirtuose irascitur et offenditur contra eam tanquam uanam et friuolam. Unde Galterius in suo *Alexandride*, de istius
170 glorie uanitate loquens, sic dicit:

> Quam friuola [gaudia] mundi, / quam rerum fugitiuus honor, quam nomen inane! / Magnus in exemplo est. Cui non suffecerat orbis, / sufficit excis[a], defossa marmore terra / quinque pedum fabrica[ta] domus, quam nobile corpus /
175 exigu[a] requieuit humo.

Et de ista memoria loquitur Augustinus in libro suo *De uera innocencia*, capitulo ultimo, dicens, 'Diuiciis flores et [de] maiorum nobilitate te iactas, et exultas de patria et pulcritudine corporis et honoribus qui tibi ab hominibus deferuntur. Respice teipsum,
180 quia mortalis es, [quia terra es], et in terram ibis. Circumspice eos, qui ante te fuerunt similibus fulcere splendoribus. Ubi sunt quos ante te ambiebant ciuium potentatus? Ubi insuperabiles [impe]ratores? Ubi qui conuentus disponebant et festa? Ubi equorum splendidi [inuec]tores? Ubi exercituum duces? Ubi
185 satrape? Ubi tiranni? Nonne omnia puluis? Nonne omnia fauille? Nonne in paucis [os]sibus uite eorum memoria est? Respice sepulcra eorum et uide, quis seruus, quis dominus, quis pauper, quis diues? Discerne, si potes, uinctum a rege, fortem a debili, pulcrum a deformi. Memor esto [nature], ne aliquando extollaris;
190 memor autem eris, si teipsum respexeris'. | Hec Augustinus.

[8] Octaua pars picture est de Iunonis stipacione, nam poete pingunt eam undique stipatam pauonibus. Hoc enim [genus] auis tutele dee Iunonis tradit[um] est, sicut [reci]tat Alexander Neckam in sua *Methalogia*. Et conuenit istud [moraliter] isti

---

166 heroum] herrori I, horror O • magnorum uirorum] magnatum A, mundanorum O 167 potencium] potenciam O • et seculi] *om.* AL
168 fol. 92va • ne] *om.* AIL • et offenditur] *om.* L 169 Galterius] auctor iste AIL 171 gaudia] *om.* O 172 exemplo] extremo A 173 excisa] exciso O
174 fabricata] fabrica O 175 exigua] exiguo O
177 Diuiciis] *om.* AL • de] *om.* O 179 et honoribus] *om.* A 180 quia^2 ... es] *om.* IO 181 ante te] *om.* AIL 183 imperatores] *emend.* L, oratores AIO, aratores uel oratores L 184 inuectores] nutritores AIOL 184–85 Ubi^2 ... tiranni] *om.* A 186 in] *adds* cibis et in A • ossibus] uersibus AIL, usibus O
189 nature] itaque AIOL 190 fol. 92vb
192 genus] *om.* O (*and thus later* tradita) 193 est] *adds* a diis L • recitat] tradit O
194 moraliter] *om.* O

And this part of the picture is appropriate for the virtue memory, for the name Hercules is derived from *heroum gloria*, that is 'the glory of great men'. Therefore the person who recalls the empty glory of powerful worldings, properly, indeed even meritoriously, grows angry with and is displeased by this excessively empty and frivolous glory. For this reason, Walter of Châtillon, in his *Alexandreis*, speaking of this vanity inspired by glory, says,

> How foolish are the joys of this world, / how fleeting the honour things bestow, how empty one's name! / The great Alexander stands as an example. The man for whom the world had not been enough, / now has enough from his burial in a house crafted / from marble, five feet long, / and his noble body has rested in a little dirt.[14]

[176] Augustine speaks about this memory in his book, *On true innocence*, the last chapter, where he says, 'You boast about your flourishing riches and your noble ancestry, and you rejoice about your homeland and your shapely body and those honours that people accord you. But look at yourself, because you are mortal, you are earth, and you will pass into the earth. Look around for those who preceded you and were strengthened by similar pomps. Where are those who before you walked about in command of citizens? Where are the invincible emperors? Where are those who managed assemblies and feasts? Where are the brilliant knights? Where are the leaders of armies? Where are the princes? Where are the tyrants? Aren't all these things dust? Aren't they all ashes? Isn't the memory of their life just a few bones? Look at their tombs and see: which one is a slave and which a lord? Which poor and which rich? Distinguish, if you can, a king from someone conquered, a strong person from a weak, one beautiful from one deformed. Remember your nature, lest you sometimes exalt yourself; for if you have examined yourself, you will remember.'[15] So Augustine says.

[191] [8] The eighth part of the picture concerns what surrounds Juno, for poets depict her surrounded on every side by peacocks. This kind of bird is said to be the guardian of the goddess Juno, as Alexander Neckam says in his *Mythology*.[16] This presentation is appropriate, in moral terms,

---

[14] *Alexandreis* 8.332–33, 10.448–50.
[15] Prosper, *Sententiae ex Augustino* 390 (PL 45:1897–98).
[16] VM3 4.5 (167/24–31).

195　uirtuti memorie, que optima [t]utrix est et custos uirtutum. Nam recordacio quam habet peccator de eius peccato et feditate, de uirtute eciam [et] eius honestate retrahit eum [a] recidiuo in peruersitate. Unde poeta Oracius in suis epistolis, 'Oderunt peccare boni uirtutis amore; / oderunt michi a
200　peccare formidinem pene'. Et de isto narrat Agellius, libro 14 *Noctuum Atticarum*, de philosopho Peregrino. 'Uidimus', inquit, 'philosophum Peregrinum nomine apud Athenas, uirum grauem atque constantem, in quodam tugorio extra urbem commorantem. Cumque ad eum frequenter ueniremus, multa
205　audiuimus eum dicere utiliter, inter que audiuimus eum dicentem uirum sapientem non debere peccare, etsi dii hominesque essent ignoraturi suum peccatum. Unde dixit uitandum esse peccatum, non timore pene uel metu infamie, sed iusti et honesti studio et officio'. Hec ille. Nota ergo applicando ad propositum, quod
210　uarietas et amenitas colorum in corpore pauonis figurat poetice diuersitatem uirtutum et bonorum morum que deputantur tutele uirtutis memorie. Quia reducendo ad memoriam criminum defe[cc]ionem et uirtutum perfeccionem, uitat homo transgressionem peccati.
215　　　[9] Nona pars picture est de Iunonis made|faccione. Pingitur enim a poetis dea ista sudore madefacta, sicut patet ex pictura qua depingitur a Marciano in suo libro *De nupciis*. Et bene conuenit uirtuti memorie, quia ex peccati memoria et eius considerata miseria consequitur lacrimarum inundancia. Ut enim dicit
220　Bernardus, peccator ad memoriam reducens se 'primam uocem omnibus similem emisisse plorantem et sic uallem lacrimarum ingressum, ubi malicie plurimum, sapiencie modicum, ubi omnia sunt uiciosa, lubrica, operta tenebris, et obcessa peccatorum laqueis, merito debet madere lacrimis'. Que lacrime figurantur
225　poetice per sudorem dee Iunonis, quia sicut sudor corporeus corpus purgat, sic fletus maculam peccati em[u]ndat. Lauant enim lacrime delictum, 'quod uoce pudor est confiteri', ut dicit Augustinus.

　　195 tutrix] nutrix O　**197** et] *illeg.* L, *om.* O　**198** a recidiuo in] a recidiuia A, a recidiuiacionis I, recidiuo in O, a recidiui L　**199** peruersitate] pertransite \ peruersitate/ I　**198–200** Oderunt ... pene] *om.* AIL　**200–9** Et ... ille] *om.* A　**203** constantem] *om.* I　**206** debere] *om.* I　**210** figurat] significat L
　　　213 criminum] peccatorum A　•　defeccionem] defensionem O, *over eras.* L
215 fol. 93ra　**216** madefacta] madida AL, iradiata I　**218** memoria] *om.* I
　　　219 miseria] memoria A　**223** lubrica] lugubra A　**225** corporeus] cooperiens A　**226** emundat] emendat O (*and* L *emend.*), mundat L

for the virtue memory, because it is the best instructor and guardian of the virtues. For the memory that a sinner has of his sin and disgrace restrains him, by this virtue, as well as its moral worth, from relapsing into his wickedness. For this reason, the poet Horace says in his epistles, 'Good men hate to sin through their love of virtue / But they hate me, since I avoid sin through fear of punishment.'[17] On this point, Gellius tells in *The Attic Nights* 14 about the philosopher Peregrinus. He says, 'I have seen a philosopher named Peregrinus, a serious and stable man, at Athens, where he lived in a shack outside the city. And when I visited him frequently, I heard him say a great many useful things, among which I heard him say that a wise person should never sin, even if neither gods nor people should ever know of his sin. For this reason, he said that one should avoid sin, not out of a fear of punishment or of ill fame, but out of duty and the pursuit of what is just and honourable.'[18] So Gellius says. Notice, in applying this to the matter at hand, that the pleasant range of colours in the peacock's body indicates, in poetic terms, the diversity of virtues and of appropriate behaviours that is assigned to the guardian of the virtue memory. For a person avoids transgressing and sin through recalling the defectiveness of sins and the perfection of the virtues.

[**215**] [9] The ninth part of the picture concerns Juno's soaking. For the poets depict this goddess soaked with sweat, as is evident in Martianus's portrayal in his *On the marriage*.[19] This is appropriate for the virtue memory, because a flood of tears follows upon the memory of sin and the consideration of its wretchedness. For, as Bernard says, 'A sinner, recalling how he first gave voice weeping – just like all people do – as he was just entering this vale of tears, should properly become wet with tears again. For in this vale, there is a great deal of evil, and only a small amount of wisdom, and everything is vice-laden, inconstant, covered in darkness, and obstructed with the snares of sin.'[20] The poets represent these tears as the goddess Juno's sweat, because, just as physical sweat purges the body, weeping cleanses the stain of sin. Tears wash a sin, because 'it shows shame to confess aloud', as Augustine says.[21]

---

[17] *Epistulae* 1.16.52–53.
[18] *Ibid*. 12.11.
[19] Mart 470.10 (2, 295/8–9).
[20] 'In feria iv hebdomadae sancte sermo' 6 + 'In Ascensione Domini sermo' 5.2 (*PL* 183:266, 316).
[21] Actually Ambrose, *Expositio evangelii secundum Lucam* 10.88 (*PL* 15:1825), although the surround is cited by Augustine, *De gratia Christi* 1.45.49–50 (*PL* 44:382–83).

[10] Decima pars picture est de Iunonis illustracione. Pingitur enim a poetis illustrata lumine. Unde, sicut tangit Remigius super Marcianum, poete Iunoni da[n]t plura nomina. Unde et a[b] eis uocatur Lucina uel Lucessia a *luce*, qua pingitur undique colustrata. Et bene conuenit uirtuti memorie, quia ex peccati miseria ad memoriam reducta, bene sequitur lacrima et cordis tristicia, [ex] quibus serenatur undique consciencia. Iuxta illud, in lacrimis tria sunt que multis cognita prosunt: 'Sunt lacrime clare, sunt salse, sunt et amare; / clarificat clarum, sal condit, purgat amarum'. Unde Hugo, *De claustro anime*, 'Sicut sol post pluuiam | clarior fulget, sic Cristus post lacrimarum irriguum benignior apparet, extendens radios sue cognicionis et illuminans corda uerbo consolacionis'. Sic igitur finitur quarta methalogia Fulgencii pro sensu morali. Et hic debet notari quod isti dii et dee gentilium uariis modis et diuersis apud eos depinguntur secundum diuersas ymaginaciones diuersorum poetarum. In isto igitur tractatu ponuntur non omnia ad picturam eorum pertinencia, sed aliqua que pro modo apparent utiliora.

---

229 Decima] *adds* et ultima I   231 dant] dat O   232 ab] ad O   235 ex quibus] ex quibus lacrimis AIL, quibus O • consciencia] *marg., later* I   236 cognita] condita A   239 fol. 93[rb]   242 dee] *adds* gentium uel L   244 ymaginaciones] ymagines AL   246 pro modo] *om.* A

[229] [10] The tenth part of the picture concerns the goddess Juno's radiance. For the poets depict her shining with light. For this reason, as Remigius mentions in his commentary on Martianus, the poets give Juno a great many names. For this reason, they call her Lucina or Lucessia, both names derivatives of *lux* 'light', because she is depicted as spread round with light on every side.[22] And this is truly appropriate for the virtue memory, because once one recalls the wretchedness of sin, tears and sorrow of heart follow directly, and through these, the conscience is brightened on every side. According to this distych, there are three things in tears, which, when known, are edifying in many ways: 'Tears are bright, salty, and bitter as well; / The bright gives light, the salt preserves, and the bitter cleanses.'[23] For this reason, Hugh of Fouilly, *The cloister of the soul*, says, 'Just as the sun shines more brightly after rain, after a flood of tears, Christ appears more welcoming; he spreads the rays that come from knowing him and enlightens hearts with a consoling word.'[24] Thus ends the moral reading of Fulgentius's fourth mythology. Here one ought to notice that these pagan gods and goddesses are depicted in various different ways, depending on how the various poets imagine them. Therefore, in this tract, I don't treat everything that might pertain to their depiction, but only some details that appear most useful for the occasion.

---

[22] Mart 63.12 (181/13).
[23] Not in Walther; also cited *Fasciculus morum* 460/54–56; Holcot 138/252–53.
[24] *Ibid.* 3.7 (PL 176:1095).

[5]

Sequitur quinta methologia de deo Neptuno, tercia prole Saturni. Sub cuius ymagine solent poete [depingere] secundam partem prudencie, uirtutem scilicet intelligencie, ad quam pertinet aduertere presencia, sicut ad memoriam pertinet preteritorum
5 recordacio seu reminiscencia. Est ergo pictura poetica dei Neptuni ista; depingitur enim:
   [1] cornutus,
   [2] opibus exutus,
   [3] Arpiis adiutus,
10 [4] statura leuatus,
   [5] mole grauatus,
   [6] canis dealbatus,
   [7] sale coronatus,
   [8] tridente sceptratus,
15 [9] Stigi maritatus.
Iste sunt nouem partes, quibus poete solent istam terciam prolem Saturni depingere, et bene conueniunt [secunde] parti prudencie, que dicitur intelligencia, sicut patet ex Tullio, libro 2 sue *Rethorice*.
   [1] Nam, sicut recitat Alexander Nekham in sua *Methalogia*,
20 deus iste marinus Neptunus depingitur cum cornibus, que quidem cornua bene conueniunt isti uirtuti predicte, scilicet intelligencie. Habet enim ipsa duo cornua, quibus potest se defendere. Unum cornu intelligencie est dictamen recte racionis; | aliud est libertas eleccionis. Istis cornibus potest ista uirtus se defendere contra
25 quoscumque insultus cuiuscumque temptacionis. Ex racionis dictamine, habet unde possit inter bonum et malum discernere, sed ex libertate uoluntatis habet unde possit malum respuere et bonum acceptare. Et de istis, possunt notari sentencie multe sanctorum et philosophorum. Nam Ieronymus, in epistola ad
30 Demetriadem, [et est] epistola \8/2, dicit quod in animis nostris

---

1 methologia] *add* Fulgencii AIL   2 depingere] *om.* O   6 ista] *add* nam iste deus AL   • depingitur enim] scripta I   9 adiutus] adiuctus A, adductus L (*emen.* L)   12 *line om.* A   • canis] canicie L *emen.*   16 nouem ... quibus] picture uel proprietates per quas A   • terciam] *om.* I (*after* i^{ta3} |)   17 secunde] tercie AIOL   • parti] *marg., later* I
20 marinus] *om.* A, marium L   23 recte] *om.* AI   • fol. 93va 24 uirtus] *om.* I
   27 respuere] respicere I   29 philosophorum] prophetarum I   30 et est] *om.* O

[5]

The fifth mythology follows; it concerns the god Neptune, Saturn's third offspring. In his image, the poets are accustomed to depict the second part of Prudence, namely the virtue Intelligence; this concerns paying attention to present things, just as memory concerns recollecting or remembering past ones. Therefore this is the poets' picture of the god Neptune, for he is depicted:
 [1] with horns,
 [2] stripped of riches,
 [3] aided by Harpies,
 [4] elevated in stature,
 [5] weighted down in bulk,
 [6] with white hair,
 [7] crowned with salt,
 [8] with a trident for a sceptre,
 [9] married to Styx.
These are the nine parts in which the poets usually depict this third child of Saturn. They are truly appropriate for the second part of prudence, which is called Intelligence, as is evident from Cicero, *Rhetoric* 2.[1]

[19] [1] For as Alexander Neckam tells in his *Mythology*, the sea-god Neptune is depicted with horns.[2] These horns truly are appropriate for this virtue intelligence. For Neptune has two horns, with which he can defend himself. One of intelligence's horns is the precept of right reason; the other is freedom of choice. This virtue can defend itself with these horns against any attacks of whatever temptation may befall. From the precept of reason, it has the power of discerning, so far as it is able, between good and evil, while from freedom of the will, it has the power of rejecting evil and taking up good, so far as it is able. Concerning these horns, one should notice the opinions of many holy people and philosophers. Jerome, epistle 82, to Demetriades, says that our spirits

---

[1] *De inventione* 2.160, again at line 73.
[2] Cf. VM3 5.7 (173/24–28).

est quedam [sanctitas] naturalis, que, uelut in arce animi presidens, exercet boni malique iudicium, et ut honestis rectisque actibus fa[uea]t, ista sinistra queque condempnat; atque ad consciencie testimonium diuersas partes domestica quadam
35 lege diiudicat. Nec ullo prors\us/ ingenio aut fucato aliquo argumentorum colore decipit, sed ipsis nos cog[it]acionibus fidelissimis et integ[erim]is sane testibus aut arguit aut defendit'. Hec ille. Istud ergo est unum cornu huius uirtutis, dictamen, scilicet recte racionis.
40 Et cum ista sentencia Ieronimi in epistola concordat Aristoteles, quia sicut ponit in nobis principia speculatiua, que nobis naturaliter sunt nota, sicut patet 2 *Methaphysice*, eciam sicut ianuam in domo, quam nullus ignorat. Ita ponit in nobis principia practica naturaliter nobis nota, quorum uirtute
45 possumus discernere inter uirtutes et uicia, sicut de hoc loquitur Ieronimus in eadem epistola prius allegata. Ubi dicit, 'Quod multos philosophorum audiuimus et legimus, et ipsi uidimus castos, pacientes, modestos, liberales, abstinentes, benignos, et | honores mundi simul et delicias respuentes, et amatores iusticie
50 non minus quam sciencie. Unde autem illis hec + bona, nisi de nature bono?' Hec Ieronimus. Et pro isto possit adduci processus apostoli, ad Romanos 2°, ubi dicit Paulus quod *gentes, que legem non habent, naturaliter que legis sunt faciunt, ostendentes opus legis scriptum in cordibus suis, testimonium illis reddente*
55 *consciencia ipsorum.*
De cornu uero altero, scilicet libertate eleccionis, satis loquitur Scriptura, Ecclesiastici 15, *Ab inicio Deus creauit hominem, et reliquit eum in manibus consilii, et adiecit mandata et precepta sua. Apposuit tibi ignem et aquam; ad quod uolueris*
60 *porrige manum tuam. Ante hominem uita et mors, bonum et malum; quod placuerit ei, dabitur ei.* Hec Scriptura. Et istud est secundum cornu huius uirtutis, scilicet libertas eleccionis. Ista ergo sunt cornua quibus uirtus intelligencie moraliter est armata,

---

31 sanctitas] sciencia O   33 faueat ista] faoim (?) ista I, [*blank*] facit ista O, sanet ita L • sinistra queque] si iusticiam I   33–36 ad … sed] *om*. L   35 diiudicat] dimicat I   36 cogitacionibus] cognacionibus O   37 integerimis] integris O
39 recte] *om*. AIL
43 in nobis] *om*. I   44 nota] *altered from* nota *to* nata A, nata L   47 et legimus … uidimus] *om*. A   48 fol. 93vb 50 hec] *adds* omnia O   52 ad Romanos 2°] *om*. AIL • Paulus] *om*. L
56 satis] sacra L   58 manibus] manu AIL • consilii] *add* sui AI   60 hominem] *adds* ponitur A   62 libertas] *adds* uoluntatis uel A

have a certain natural holiness; just like a ruler in the citadel of our spirit, it exercises judgement both of good and evil, and so that it may favour virtuous and proper actions, it condemns the perverse of whatever sort; it also distinguishes, following the witness of conscience, the different parts by a law native to itself. Nor indeed is it in any way deceived by cleverness or the artificial colouring of arguments, but it either reproves or defends us through the most accurate thinking and the most trustworthy evidence.'[3] So Jerome says. Therefore, that's one of this virtue's horns, namely the precept of right reason.

[40] And Aristotle agrees with this opinion from Jerome's epistle. For he likewise places speculative powers in us, naturally imprinted there, as is evident from *Metaphysics* 2, where he says it is just like a door in a house, which no one fails to recognise.[4] Likewise, he places in us practical powers, imprinted in us by nature; by virtue of these, we are able to distinguish between virtues and vices, just as Jerome says in the letter I have mentioned. Jerome says there, 'I have heard and read about many philosophers and have seen that they were chaste, patient, modest, generous, abstinent, kindly, rejecting both the honours and the delights of the world, and no less lovers of righteousness than they were of knowledge. But where did all these good behaviours of theirs come from, if not from a good provided by nature?' So Jerome says. On this point, one might adduce Paul's argument, Rm 2:14–15, where he says, *The gentiles, who have not the law, do by nature those things that are of the law, who shew the work of the law written in their hearts, their conscience bearing witness to them.*

[56] Scripture says plenty about the second horn, freedom of choice, for example, Sir 15:14–18, *God made man from the beginning, and left him in the hand of his own counsel. He added his commandments and precepts. He hath set fire and water before thee; stretch forth thy hand to which thou wilt. Before man is life and death, good and evil; that which he shall choose shall be given him.* So Scripture says. This is the second horn of this virtue, freedom of choice. Therefore, these are the horns with which the virtue of intelligence is armed morally,

---

[3] Pelagius, esp. 2–4 (*PL* 30:16–19) summarised; the subsequent citation from 3 (col. 18).

[4] 1.2 (982a).

quibus si usa fuerit, de ea nunquam uicii uiolencia triumphabit.
65 Sicut enim docet Ricardus, super illud Ysaie primo, *Omne caput languidum*, 'Liberum arbitrium non patitur dominium, nec pati potest, quia uiolencia[m] ei inferre nec creatorem d[e]cet, nec creatura potest'.

[2] Secunda pars picture est de Neptuni denudacione. Nam
70 sicut patet Marcianus in libro *De nupciis* depingit eum nudum et depauperatum, sicut patet per Remigium ibidem. Et illud bene conuenit uirtuti prudencie, ad quam pertinet potissime suam propriam nuditatem inspicere. Cum enim secundum Tullium, intelligencia, ut distinguitur a | memoria et prouidencia, sit proprie
75 rerum presencium, et ipse homo sit maxime pr[es]ens sibi ipsi. Consequens est quod actus intelligencie proprius est consideracio sui ipsius. Sed ut dicit Bernardus, libro 2° ad Eugenium, 'Consideranti tibi quid sis, occuret tibi homo nudus et pauper, miserabilis et miser, homo dolens quod sit homo, erubescens quod
80 nudus sit, plorans quod natus sit, [murmurans quod sit]; *homo natus ad laborem* et non ad honorem, *homo natus de muliere* et ideo cum reatu, *breui uiuens tempore* et ideo cum metu, *repletu[s] multis miseriis* et ideo cum fletu'. Hec Bernardus.

Et hic est notandum quod ista pars picture docet et describit
85 actum huius uirtutis, scilicet intelligencie, in rerum presencium appreciacione. Nam [uir] prudens uolens seipsum [uel] alium intelligere et de seipso uel de alio iudicare, debet se nudum, in terrenis diuiciis exutum, inspicere, sicut pulcre tangit Apulegius Madarensis in suo libro *De deo Socratis*, et Seneca eciam in
90 quadam epistola, et est epistola 78. 'Cum', inquit, 'uoles ueram hominis estimacionem inire et scire, qualis sit, nudum inspice. Deponat patrimonium, deponat honores et alia Fortune mendacia, corpus eciam ipsum exuat. Et tunc animum intuere, et tunc', ut dicit Seneca, 'uide[re poter]is, an suo bono an alieno, id est
95 extrinseco, sit magnus'.

Et de ista materia loquens, Apulegius in fine libri sui sic dicit, 'In emendis equis, phaleras non consideramus, et balthei

65 illud ... primo] *om.* AIL   67 uiolenciam] uiolencia O • decet] docet IO
71 per Remigium] Marcianum A   72 prudencie] intelligencie A   74 distinguitur a] directa L • fol. 94ra 75 presens] prouidens O   80 murmurans quod sit] *om.* IO
82 repletus] repletur IOL
86 uir] ubi O • uel] ad O   88-89 pulcre ... et] deducit A   91 scire] *om.* A
94 uidere poteris] intueri poteris A, uidebis O • an²] *add* bono IL
94-95 id ... extrinseco] *om.* L
96 de ... loquens] *om.* A • Apulegius] *add* quasi AIL

which, if they have been used, intelligence will never be defeated by the violence of vice. For this is just what Richard of St Victor teaches in discussing Is 1:5, *The whole head is sick*, 'Free will does not suffer any lordship, nor may it do so, because it is not fitting for the Creator to overwhelm it violently, and no created thing can so so.'[5]

[69] [2] The second part of the picture concerns Neptune's stripping. For, as Remigius makes clear there, Martianus in *On the marriage* depicts him as nude and impoverished.[6] This is appropriate for the virtue prudence, whose most powerful characteristic is to scrutinise its own bareness. For according to Cicero, since intelligence should be distinguished from memory and foresightedness, it should properly be a knowledge of things present, and a person should be most present to himself. As a consequence, the act most appropriate to intelligence is consideration of oneself. But as Bernard says, *On consideration* 2, 'By considering what you yourself are, you will discover yourself to be a bare and poor human, wretched and pitiable, a person sorrowing because one is human, ashamed because one is naked, lamenting and complaining that one was born and continue to be, *a human born to labour* (Iob 5:7) and not to honour, *a human born of a woman* and therefore with guilt, *living for a short time* and that in fear, *filled with many miseries* (Iob 14:1) and therefore with weeping.'[7] So Bernard says.

[84] Here one should notice that this part of the picture teaches and describes the act of the virtue intelligence, the assessment of things present. For where a prudent person wishes to understand themself or another and to judge themselves or another, they ought to inspect themself as if they were naked, stripped of all earthly riches, as Apuleius treats neatly in *On Socrates's god*, and Seneca as well in his epistle 78. There Seneca says, 'When you wish to determine and to know the true value of a person, what sort they are, examine them naked. Let them put aside their inheritance, put aside their honours and other lies of Fortune; let them strip themselves of their very body. Then examine their mind, and then', Seneca says, 'you can see whether they are great by virtue of their own goodness, or a foreign, external one.'[8]

[96] Speaking of this matter near the end of his book, Apuleius says, 'In buying horses, we don't consider their ornaments, and we don't look

---

[5] Richard of St Victor, *De statu interioris hominis* 1.3 (*PL* 196:1118).
[6] Mart 35.22 (133/12).
[7] *Ibid.* 2.9 (*PL* 182:753).
[8] *Epistula* 76.32, the conclusion paraphrase, and a further allusion at line 860.

116   John Ridewall, *Fulgencius metaforalis*

po|limi[n]a respicimus, nec ornatissime ceruicis contemplamur
diuicias, uidelicet si ex auro et argento gemmis monilia uarie gaze
100   dependent, si plena artis ornamenta capiti et collo circumiacent,
si frena celata, si epiphia fucata et si + cingula aurata sint,
sed istis [omnibus] exuuiis a[m]olitis, equum ipsum nudum
et solum corpus eius et animum contuemur, ut sit equus ad
speciem honestus, ad cursum [u]egetus, et ad uecturam ualidus.
105   \Similiter/', dicit Apulegius, 'in hominibus contemplandis, noli
aliena bona estimare, sed ipsum hominem penitus nudum
considera et ut meum pauperem Socratem, specta. Aliena uoco',
dicit Apulegius, 'que parentes + pepererunt et que Fortuna
largita est, quorum nichil laudibus mei Socratis admisceo, nec
110   enim inuenio in laude Socratis ullam generositatem, ullam +
prosapiam, ullos longos natales, ullas inuidiosas diuicias. Hec
enim cuncta aliena sunt'. Dicit Apulegius, '[Si] generosus est,
parentes laudas; si dixeris quod diues es[t], non credo Fortune;
sed si dixeris quod bonis artibus doctus et adp[rim]e eruditus est
115   et, quantum licet homini, sapiens, tandem ipsum uirum laudas.
Hoc non a patre hereditarium est, nec a casu pendulum, nec
a suffragio a[nnicul]um, nec a corpore caducum, nec ab etate
mutabile'. Hec Apulegius. Ex quibus contingit aduertere quid |
intelligitur poetice in hac secunda parte picture, in qua agitur de
120   istius uirtutis denudacione.

[3] Tercia pars picture est de dei Neptuni propagacione. Nam
poete fingunt Neptunum Arpias genuisse, sicut tangit Alexander
Nekham in sua *Methalogia*, que sibi sunt in auxilium in hac
Neptuni denudacione. Et nota Fulgencium, qui tractat in sua
125   *Mithologia* de istis Arpiis et earum descripcione, quarum poetica
pictura est ista:

97 fol. 94rb • polimina] po|||limia O • respicimus] consideramus A
98 gemmis] *om.* A   100 cingula] singula AIL, singula uel cingula O
102 omnibus] *om.* O • exuuiis] externiis A • amolitis] abolitis AIO, *om.* L,
L *emen.* amolitis   104 uegetus] \s/egetus O • uecturam] uictoriam A
105 hominibus] omnibus I   107 pauperem] *om.* AIL   108 parentes] *adds* non O
109 enim inuenio] enim misceo A, enim inuenio (? *over eras.*) I, inmisceo L
111 prosapiam] prosapienciam O • ullos … natales] *om.* L   112 cuncta] *om.* A
• Si] Si inquam A, Si enim I, *om.* O, Si enim dixeris L   113 est] es AO
• credo] crede IL   114 adprime] ad plenum AO   117 anniculum] annetulum I,
ad nuculium (?) O, amminiculum L   118 fol. 94va • secunda] *om.* IL
120 istius uirtutis] *om.* L
126 ista] *add* Siquidem in istis auibus AL (*at 129* Siquidem A)

closely at the polish on their bridles, nor do we consider carefully the riches of their unduly ornamented necks, whether their collars sag with jewels from various treasures made of gold and silver, if particularly artful ornaments surround their head and neck, if they have decorated reins, dyed saddles, or golden girths. We rather set aside all these things one could strip away and examine the bare horse itself, its body and its spirit alone, to see whether it is noble in appearance, energetic when it runs, and strong when it needs to pull something. Similarly', Apuleius says, 'in examining people, don't assess those goods that are foreign to the person, but consider and look at the person completely nude, just as I have done with my impoverished Socrates. I call those goods foreign', Apuleius says, 'that parents have conferred and that Fortune has bestowed, none of which I mix into the praises of my Socrates, nor indeed do I find in the praise of Socrates any good breeding, any high or lengthy lineage, any discreditable riches. For all these things are foreign.' Apuleius continues, 'For if you have said that someone is noble, you should praise their parents; if you have said they are rich, I don't trust in Fortune; but if you have said that they have been taught and fully instructed in good behaviours, and that they are wise, so far as that's allowed to humans, then at last you should praise this person. For this state is not one that one can inherit from one's parents, nor does it depend upon chance, nor is it granted through an annual vote, nor does it pass away from the body or change with age.'[9] So Apuleius says. From these things one should notice what the poets understand in the second part of this picture, which treats the stripping of the virtue intelligence.

[121] [3] The third part of the picture concerns the god Neptune's offspring. For the poets claim, as Alexander Neckam states in his *Mythology*, that the god Neptune gave birth to the Harpies, and they are aides to Neptune in his stripping. Notice what Fulgentius, who treats these Harpies and their description in his *Mythology*, says is their poetic picture:

---

[9] *Ibid.* 23.

Facies est grata, sed acies est serrata; scelerum sunt ultrices et fenorum contemptrices.
Siquidem Arpie, secundum poeticam ficcionem, sunt aues quedam rapaces, unguibus armate et uultu uirgineo decorate, \que a diis sunt ordinate/ a punicionem Phinei.
Iste enim Phineus filios proprios excecauit, propter quod Iubiter eum excecauit et excecatum Arpiis tradidit puniendum. Ista est series fabule.
Unde conuenit moraliter uirtuti intelligencie. Ista enim uirtute prediti sunt, [scilicet qui] prudenter et uirtuose presencia terrena estimant et intelligunt, et isti sunt ueri, sinceri, strenui, et seueri. Habent enim ueritatem in intencione; unde carent fumo duplicitatis, et ideo uultus eorum pingitur uirgineus, quia ueritas [uirgo] est expers corumpcionis. Similiter isti habent sinceritatem affeccionis, et ideo carent ueneno [cupiditatis], et ideo fenora et lucra terrena computant inter stercora. Et hac de causa, Arpie finguntur a poetis fedare cum stercoribus mensam Ph\i/nei. | Ut enim tangit Alexander in sua *Methalogia*, Phineus + dicitur a fenore, usura scilicet lucri deordinati cupiditate, quam prudens computat cum merda. Tales eciam grauitatem huius sceleris aduertentes, nec sunt nimis molles per muliebrem pietatem, nec sunt nimis segnes per pusillanimitatem. Et ideo aues iste + uirgines pinguntur, [unguibus] armate in signum strenuitatis \et ad scelerum ulcionem assignati in signum seueritatis/.
Ista [est] igitur triplex proles uirtutis, scilicet intelligencie, Aello, Celeno, et Occipite. Sic enim apud poetas nominantur Arpie, sicut patet per Fulgencium in textu. Unde secundum Fulgencium, Aello idem est quod 'aliena tollens', Occipite idem quod 'cicius auferens', Celeno Grece dicitur 'nigrum' Latine. Ueritas ergo, quam uirtus intelligencie habet in rerum consideracione et earum estimacione, tollit alliena, sicut patuit in secunda picture. Quia considerat sola bona merita et bonos mores hominis, et non bona fortuita (que, secundum Senecam,

127 serrata] superata L   128 fenorum] fimorum A   132 punicionem] *add* regis AL
134 puniendum] primum et fenorum contemptrices ostendendum A
137 scilicet qui] sunt quam O, scilicet si L   139 in intencione] et intelligunt A
• fumo] fuco AL   141 uirgo] ubique I, *om.* O   142 cupiditatis] *om.* O
144 fol. 94vb 145 Phineus] *adds* enim O   146 fenora] serena A   • scilicet lucri] *om.* A   149 iste] *adds* uirginee O   150 unguibus] *om.* O
152 est] *om. and adds* dure (for 'dicuntur'?) *after* intelligencie O   156 nigrum] magnum A   160 fortuita] fortuna AL

Harpies' faces are pleasant, but their glance sharp as a saw. They
avenge crimes and disdain profit.[10]

Indeed, the Harpies, according to the poets' fiction, are a kind of bird of prey

armed with talons and adorned with innocent women's faces, who
were ordered by the gods to punish Phineus.

Phineus blinded his own sons, and in return, Jupiter blinded him, and, once he was blinded, Jupiter sent the Harpies to punish him. That's the plot of the fable.

[136] For this reason, the image of the Harpies is appropriate, in moral terms, for the virtue intelligence. For those who have been endowed with this virtue assess and understand prudently and virtuously present earthly things, and they are true, sincere, active, and severe. For they have a true intention; for this reason, they lack the smoke of duplicity, and their faces are therefore depicted as virginal, because truth is a virgin free of corruption. Similarly, they have sincere feelings and lack the poison of desire, and therefore they account profit and worldly wealth as dung. For this reason, the poets represent the Harpies as fouling Phineus's table with dung. For as Alexander says in his *Mythology*, the name Phineus is derived from *fenus* 'profit', that is usury from a disordered desire for wealth, and prudent people account that just shit.[11] For such prudent people, when they notice the severity of this vice, are neither too forgiving through womanly pity nor too sluggish through cowardice. Therefore, these birds are depicted as virgins, armed with talons as a sign of their vigour and appointed to avenge crimes as a sign of their severity.

[152] Therefore, the virtue intelligence has three children, Aello, Celeno, and Occipite. For that is what poets name the Harpies, as is evident in Fulgentius's text.[12] For this reason, according to Fulgentius, Aello means 'carrying off foreign things', Occipite 'carrying away very quickly', and Celeno is a Greek word that means 'black' in Latin. Therefore, truth, which the virtue intelligence possesses in its consideration and evaluation of things, carries away foreign objects, as is evident in the second picture. For it considers only good things one has earned and a person's good behaviour, and not goods that come by chance – according to Seneca,

---

[10] VM3 5.5 (173/13–38), largely repetition of Fulg 1.9, 3.11 (21/15–22/7, 79/13–18).
[11] VM3 5.6 (173/39–40).
[12] Fulg 1.9 (21/20–22/3).

sunt penitus aliena), sed sinceritatem affeccionis, quam habet uirtus ista, quia prudens solum afficitur ad honestatem ueritatis. Ista autem Celeno, que 'nigredinem' significat in Latino, omnia ad que cupiditas usuraria intitulatur, reputat talia nigra et [computat]
165 inter stercora. Sed tercio, seueritas, cum strenuitate, quam habet ista uirtus intelligencie in scelerum et peccatorum grauium punicione, figuratur per Occipite, que stat | pro sceleritate, sicut patet Fulgencius.

[4] Quarta pars picture est de dei Neptuni proceritate.
170 Nam, sicut patet per Marcianum et Remigium, libro *De nupciis*, Neptunus pingitur a poetis in statura procera plurimum et eleuata. Et bene conuenit proprietas ista uirtuti intelligencie, que ad celum secundum ficcionem poeticam dicitur pertingere. Nam uirtus ista primo inclinat hominem ad sui ipsius consideracionem. Hec autem
175 consideracio seu noticia est \celica/. Nam fingunt poete quondam quesitum fuisse a deo Appolloine, que esset uia reccior et cercior per quam homines ad celum et ad beatitudinem peruenire possent. Qui respondit, 'Si teipsum', inquit, 'agnoueris'. Et de isto tangit Macrobius in suo commentario que dicitur *Sompnium Scipionis*.

180 [5] Quinta pars picture est de Neptuni magnitudine. Nam, sicut patet per Marcianum, sicut pingitur procere stature, sic eciam pingitur magnus in mole. Et molis magnitudo significat in uirtute intelligencie magnitudinem bonitatis et moralis perfeccionis, quam habet noticia, id est cognicio, sui ipsius pre
185 ceteris noticiis, sicut de hac materia tractat Augustinus, libro 14 *De trinitate*, et Hugo in libro suo *De anima*, ubi dicit quod 'melior es, si teipsum cognoscas, quam si, te neclecto, cursus syderum, uires herbarum, complexiones hominum, naturas animalium, celestium omnium et terrestrium scienciam habeas. Multi enim
190 multa sciunt, et seipsos nesciunt', cum tamen summa philosophia sit in sui ipsius | cognicione.

[6] Sexta pars picture est de dei Neptuni canicie. Sicut enim patet ex Marciano, deus Neptunus depingitur cum capite cano in signum honoris et reuerencie. Et bene conuenit

---

164 intitulatur] inclinatur L • computat] *om.* O 165 cum strenuitate] *om.* L 167 fol. 95ra
173 dicitur] *om.* A 175 quondam] *om.* I 176 uia] *om.* L 177 peruenire] pertingere L 178 Qui … agnoueris] *om.* AI, Qui legitur respondisse quod si quilibet seipsum agnosceret iam ad celum et ad beatitudinem peruenire posset L 179 Macrobius] Macrodius I
182 magnus] *om.* I 186 *trinitate*] ciuitate L 191 fol. 95rb • cognicione] noticia AL
192 canicie] *add* et capitis dealbacione AL

these are completely alien to the self; it rather considers sincere feelings. This virtue possesses those, because a prudent person is attracted only to the virtuousness of the truth. Celeno, whose name means 'blackness' in Latin, accounts all those things to which usurious desire is dedicated as if they were black and in the category 'shit'. Third, vigorous severity, which this virtue intelligence possesses in punishing crimes and grievous sins, is represented by Occipite. She stands for speedy action, as Fulgentius makes clear.

[169] [4] The fourth part of the picture concerns the god Neptune's height. For, as is evident in Martianus's *On the marriage* and in Remigius's commentary, the poets portray Neptune as very tall and as raised up in stature.[13] And this characteristic is truly appropriate for the virtue intelligence, since the poets' fiction says that intelligence extends to heavenly things. This virtue first influences a person to the consideration of themselves, and this consideration or examination is heavenly. For poets tell that the god Apollo was once asked what might be the most direct and certain way by which people might travel to heavenly blessedness. And he answered, 'If you would know yourself.' Macrobius treats this topic in his commentary called *Scipio's dream*.[14]

[180] [5] The fifth picture concerns Neptune's great size. For as Martianus shows, just as the poets depict Neptune as tall in stature, he is also depicted as of great mass. His great bulk indicates the large size of intelligence's goodness and moral perfection, for intelligence takes note of, that is it knows, itself before taking account of other things, as Augustine says, *On the trinity* 14, and Hugh of St Victor, in his *On the soul*. Hugh says there, 'If you know yourself, you are better, than if, having neglected yourself, you have knowledge of the paths of the stars, the properties of plants, the human complexions, and the natures of all the beasts, both heavenly and earthly.' 'Many people know many things and don't know themselves', but the very highest philosophy is in knowing oneself.[15]

[192] [6] The sixth part of the picture concerns the god Neptune's whiteness. For as Martianus shows, the god Neptune is depicted with a white head as a token of honour and reverence.[16] This is truly appropriate

---

[13] Mart 35.22 (133/13–19), as also the reference at line 181.

[14] Cf. *Commentarium* 1.9.2.

[15] Cf. *De trinitate* 10.12.19 (*PL* 42:984), followed by ps.-Bernard, *Meditationes* 5.14+1.1 (*PL* 184:494, 485) = MF consideratio sui af [ascribed to *De anima* 1.9].

[16] Mart 35.19 (133/1–2).

122 John Ridewall, *Fulgencius metaforalis*

195 uirtuti intelligencie, cui poete attribuebant honorem uaticinii et prophecie. Nam sicut docet poeta Iuuenalis, 'De celo *Notys olitos* dicitur descendisse'. *Nois olitos* in Greco est idem quod '[sui ipsius cognicio]' in Latino. Et uult + poeta dicere quod hoc genus noticie causatur in homine ex speciali Dei [inspi]racione, et ideo tales se
200 ipsos cognoscentes computandi sunt inter prophetas et uates.

[7] Septima pars picture est de Neptuni coronacione. Sicut enim patet per Marcianum, corona dei Neptuni est de lapide precioso salis albedinem pretendente. Et bene hoc conuenit uirtuti intelligencie, que hominem ad sui ipsius cognicionem habet
205 specialiter inclinare. Unde possumus hic notare quod in antiqua lege ordinat\um/ fuit de apponendo sale in quolibet sacrificio. Sic per uirtutem intelligencie premittitur in quocumque studio sui ipsius cognicio. Et de isto loquitur pulcre Hugo in suo libro *De anima*, ubi dicit sic, 'Disce ex tuo spiritu cognoscere quid de
210 aliis sp[iriti]bus debeas estimare. Hec enim est porta, hec enim est scala, hic est introitus, iste est ascensus; hac intratur ad intima, hac eleuatur ad summa. Ex hac, scilicet tui ipsius cog|nicione, proficis ad cognicionem omnium celestium, terrestrium, et infernorum'.
215 [8] Octaua pars picture est de dei Neptuni sceptracione. Secundum Marcianum et Ouidium, *De transformatis*, Neptunus iste portat pro sceptro uirgam tridentem, potestatem triplicem pretendentem. Et bene conuenit hec pars [picture] uirtuti intelligencie, ad quam pertinet potestas triplicis presidencie. Hec
220 enim uirtus habet cognoscere, et cognoscendo, dirigere uoluntates, affecciones, et sens\u/alitat[i]s surrepciones, et membrorum exteriorum exce[cu]ciones. Et istam ocupacionem circa sui ipsius consideracionem debet uirtus intelligencie cotidie exercere, sicut pulcre docet Seneca, libro 3 *De ira*, ubi narrat quandam
225 narracionem de quodam philosopho nomine Sixio. Qui cotidie posuit seipsum ad raciocinium, id est ad reddendum compotum de seipso, an scilicet illo die profecisset in moribus uel defecisset.

196 *Notys Olitos, Noisolitos*] Nothiolithos *and* Noth elitos A, *both* Nois olicos I, *both* Noisolitos L   197–98 sui ipsius cognicio] nosce teipsum O   198 poeta] poetam O   198 inspiracione] miseracione O
210 spiritibus] speb3 (= speciebus) O   212 fol. 95[va]
218 picture] *om.* IO   219 presidencie] consideracionis L   221 sensualitatis] sensualitates O • surrepciones] *om.* A   222 excecuciones] excecaciones O   223 consideracionem] cognicionem A • cotidie] continue L • cotidie exercere] *om. at page-boundary* A   225 quodam ... nomine] philosopho AL
226 seipsum] *om.* I   227 illo die] ille A

for the virtue intelligence, because poets attributed to it the honour of prediction and prophecy. The poet Juvenal teaches that '*Notys olitos* is said to have descended from heaven.'[17] The Greek *Nois olitos* means the same thing as 'Know yourself' in Latin. Juvenal wishes to say that a special divine inspiration causes this kind of knowledge in humans, and therefore those people who know themselves should be accounted among the prophets and seers.

[201] [7] The seventh part of the picture concerns Neptune's crowning. As Martianus explains, the god Neptune's crown is made from a precious stone of salt spreading out in whiteness.[18] This is truly appropriate for the virtue intelligence, since it requires that a person tend particularly to knowledge of themself. For this reason, I may notice here that in ancient law it was decreed that salt should be placed near any sacrifice. Likewise, through the virtue intelligence, knowledge of oneself should be put first in any study. Hugh of St Victor speaks fittingly on this point in *On the soul*, 'Learn from your own spirit to recognise how you should assess other spirits. For this is the gate, this the stairway, this the entry, this the means of ascent; by this, one enters the deepest secrets; by this, one is raised to the heights. Through this knowledge of yourself, you advance to the knowledge of all things, whether heavenly, earthly, or infernal.'[19]

[215] [8] The eighth part of the picture concerns the god Neptune's sceptre. According to Martianus and Ovid's *Metamorphoses*, Neptune carries as a sceptre a three-branched rod, the trident, and it spreads a triple power.[20] This depiction is truly appropriate for the virtue intelligence, because it has a triple governing power. For this virtue has the power of knowledge; through its knowing, it has the power to direct our wills, our desires, our feelings, the stealthy motions of sensuality, as well as our physical actions. The virtue intelligence should exercise daily this concern for considering itself, as Seneca neatly teaches in *On anger* 3, where he tells about a philosopher named Sextius. He set himself daily to taking account, that is to offering an account-book about himself, whether on that day he had advanced in his behaviour, or had failed to.

---

[17] *Satyra* 11.27.
[18] Unfound.
[19] Actually ps.-Bernard, *Tractatus de interiori domo* 36 (PL 184:545) [= MF consideratio sui ag, ascribed to *De anima* 1.31].
[20] *Metamorphoses* 1.283, 6.75; Mart 31.3 (123/8–11); cf. Fulg 1.4 (19/14–16).

Cotidie, inqu[it], animus ad racionem reddendam uocandus est. 'Faciebat enim hoc Sixius, ut consummato die, cum se ad nocturnam quietem [recep]isset, interrogaret animum suum, "Quod hodie malum moris sanasti? Cui uicio restitisti? Qua parte \melior/ es?" Per istum modum', dicit Seneca, 'desinet ira et moderacior erit, sciens quod cotidie sit ad iudicem ueniendum'. Et subdit Seneca, 'Quid ergo pulcrius hac consuetudine excuciendum [totum] diem? Qualis iste sompnus post recognicionem | sequitur, [quam] tranquillus, altus, et liber!' Hec Seneca. Hic est igitur tridens uirtutis intelligencie, quomodo animus regitur omni die pro triplici sua parte, scilicet inicio, medio, et fine.

[9] Nona et ultima pars picture est de Neptuni [marit]acione. Sicut enim patet per Marcianum et Remigium, Stix, nutrix et hospita deorum omnium, Neptuno datur in coniungium. Et bene conuenit hec pars picture uirtuti intelligencie, que per sui ipsius cognicionem, prebet uirtutibus omnibus nutrimentum. Et ideo Cassiodorus, super [psalmum], dicit quod 'Magna est utilitas seruo Dei propriam infirmitatem cognoscere, atque in suis uiribus aut meritis nullam fiduciam habere. Tunc enim incipit adesse uirtus diuina, quando incipit deficere presumpcio humana'. Ubi nota quod significanter Cassiodorus uocat uirtutem qu[id]dam diuin[u]m. Nam in estimacione paganorum, honestas uirtutis hominem parificat diis, sicut de hoc loquitur Seneca in quadam epistola, sicut prius fuit tactum. Et Tullius eciam dicit illud idem, sicut patet per quandam glossam Sapiencie 14, ubi dicit glossa quod Scichero dicit quod 'acuende uirtutis gracia, et ut homines libencius rei puplice gracia periculum adirent, optimos quosque uirorum forcium honore deorum inmortalium constat fuisse consecratos. Hinc Romani cesares consecrauerunt et deorum cathalogo ascripserunt et Ma[u]ri suos reges'. | Hec ille.

228 inquit] in qua O 229 hoc] et hoc frequencius A 230 recepisset] dedisset O 231 moris] inops I 233 iudicem] iudicium A 235 excuciendum] excufiendi I, *om*. L • totum diem] tunc diem AO, diuine (?) I, tunc dicit L 236 fol. 95vb • quam] quorum (?) A, *om*. O 237 tridens] triplex A • uirtutis] locutus I

240 maritacione] narracione O 241 Stix] Fax A 242 (and 262) hospita] hostia I 244 omnibus nutrimentum] omne incrementum A 245 psalmum] Romanos O 246 infirmitatem] uirtutem A 249 uocat] *om*. I 250 quiddam diuinum] quandam diuinitatem O 257 fuisse] *adds* sacratos id est L 258 Mauri] Mauei I, Maripi O • fol. 96ra

Seneca says that the spirit should be called to render a daily accounting. 'For Sextius did this, so that at the end of day, when he had begun his night's rest, he would ask his spirit, "Today, what defect in your behaviour have you cured? What vice have you resisted? To what extent are you better?" In this way', Seneca says, 'anger will come to an end and become more moderate, knowing that every day it will be obliged to come before a judge.' Seneca adds, 'What could be more beautiful than this practice of examining the whole day? What a sleep must follow such an inspection, peaceful, deep, and carefree!'[21] So Seneca says. This is the trident of the virtue intelligence, the way in which the mind is regulated every day through its triple division, that is the beginning, the middle, and the end.

[240] [9] The ninth and last part of the picture concerns Neptune's marriage. For, as Martianus and Remigius show, Neptune was given in marriage Styx, the nurse and hostess of all the gods.[22] This part of the picture is appropriate for the virtue intelligence, which, on the basis of its self-knowledge, offers nourishment to all the virtues. Therefore, Cassiodorus, speaking about a psalm, says that 'it is most useful to a servant of God to recognise their own weakness and to have no trust in their own powers or merits. When their human presumption begins to fail, divine virtue begins to be present to them.'[23] Notice there that Cassiodorus pointedly calls virtue something divine. For, as the pagans judged things, a virtuous quality renders humans equal to the gods, just as Seneca says in one of his letters, as I already discussed above.[24] Cicero also says the same thing, as is evident in a gloss on Sap 14, where it quotes Cicero as saying that 'thanks to the whetting of virtue, and so that people would more willingly enter dangers for the commonwealth, it came about that the very best among brave men were deified, given honour equal that of the immortal gods. For this reason, the Romans deified their emperors and wrote them into the list of the gods and the Moors did the same with their kings.' So he says.[25]

---

[21] *De ira* 3.36.1–2.
[22] Mart 36.2 (133/20–24).
[23] Actually Rufinus of Aquileia (?), *Commentarius in LXXV Psalmos* 7.3 (PL 21:669) [= *MF* consideratio sui ah, ascribed to Cassiodorus on Ps 6].
[24] *Epistula* 73.12–13, also cited at 2/11.
[25] *Ibid.*, 1480 edn, 2, 737b.

260   Sed queritur in proposito forte: que sit ista uirtus diuina, uirtuti intelligencie desponsata et que [deorum] omnium nutrix est et hospita? Dicendum quod hec est humilitas, \cuius primus gradus est cognicio sui ipsius, ut dicit Bernardus, *De gradibus humilitatis*/. Que uirtus humilitatis, ut ait Ieronimus in suo
265 originali *Super Mattheum*, est conseruatrix custosque uirtutum, et nichil est quod ita Deo faciat et hominibus gratum, quam si non uite merito magni, sed humilitate infimi uidea[m]ur. Et ideo significanter dicit Gregorius in quadam omelia quod qui sine humilitate, uirtutes congregat quasi puluerem in uento portat.
270 Sic ergo finita est [quin]ta mithologia Fulgencii de secunda parte uirtutis [prud]encie, descripta sub ymagine dei Neptuni.

260 in proposito] *om*. L   261 deorum] *om*. O   263-64 *De ... humilitatibus*] *om*. AIL   267 infimi] uisiui A, infirmi uel infimi L   •   uideamur] uideantur O   268 significanter] fi[guraliter A   270 quinta] sexta OL   270-71 de ... Neptuni] *om*. A   271 uirtutis prudencie] uirtutis intelligencie O, prudencie L

[260] But someone may ask on this point: what is the divine virtue betrothed to intelligence and nurse and hostess of all the gods? One should say that it is humility, the first step in which is knowledge of one's self, as Bernard says, *On the steps of humility*.[26] As Jerome says in *On Matthew*, this virtue humility preserves and guards the other virtues, and nothing makes one so welcome to either God or people than if we appear lowest in humility, rather than great in the merits of our behaviour. Therefore, Gregory says significantly in one of his homilies that the person lacking humility gathers virtues about as effectively as one carries dust in the wind.[27] Thus ends Fulgentius's fifth mythology; it describes the second part of the virtue prudence as an image of the god Neptune.

---

[26] *Ibid.* 1.1 (*PL* 182:942).
[27] Cf. Jerome, *Commentarii in Mattheum* 3 (on Mt 18:2–4) (*PL* 26:128); Gregory, *Homiliae in evangelia* 7.4 (*PL* 76:1103).

[6]

Sequitur sexta mithologia Fulgencii de tercio filio Saturni, scilicet de Plutone. Sub cuius ymagine describunt poete terciam partem prudencie, scilicet uirtutem prouidencie, que secundum Tullium, habet ad futura respicere, sicut intelligencia respicit presencia et memoria preterita. Et a poetis sic depingitur iste deus:
   [1] ebono coronatus,
   [2] opibus ditatus,
   [3] inferis prelatus,
   [4] Cerbero delatus,
   [5] E[c]ate ligatus,
   [6] Furiis armatus,
   [7] et Fatis uallatus.
Iste sunt septem partes picture dei Plutoni[c]e, quibus corespondent totidem proprietates prouidencie.

[1] Nam sicut patet per Marcianum et Remigium, libro *De numpciis*, iste Pluto, inuitatus ad nupcias Mercurii et Phi[l]ologie, uenit habens in capite sertum de ebeno, id est coronam regiam de talo ligno. Nota [ebenus est] quodam genus ligni inconbustibilis; | non enim potest igne consumi. Unde uersus, 'Ebenus est arbor, quod nullus concremat ardor'. Plinius autem in *Naturali historia*, libro 5, loquens de ebeno, dicit quod est arbor preciosissima, auro et ebore + comparabilis. Unde in Ethiopia solebat gens Ethiopum offerre ista tria imperatoribus pro tributo, [lignum] ebenum, ebur, et aurum. Unde regina Saba, que fuit regina Ethiopie, talia legitur Salomoni optulisse.

Et possunt ista applicari uirtute pr[oui]dencie. Hec enim uirtus reddit animum hominis impassibilem a quocunque, ut pulcre docet Seneca, epistola quadam, que in aliquibus libris 74. 'Nichil', inquit Seneca, 'pacieris, si tecum fuerit uirtus. Nichil', inquit, 'interest inter [pretu]ram Catonis et eius repulsam?

---

1 sexta] septima L   3 Tullium] cultum A   4 futura] *adds* prospicere uel L
• intelligencia] intellectus L   6 ebeno] ligno AIL   9 Cerbero] Cerebro AL
10 Ecate] Etati AL, Etate IO   13 Plutonice] Plutonie O
16 Philologie] Philo|gie A, Philosogie I, Phisiologie O   17 regiam] *add* factam AL
18 ebenus est] *om.* O   19 fol. 96rb 20–21 Plinius ... ebeno] *om.* A
22 comparabilis] incomparabilis O   23 lignum] *om.* O   24 legitur] *add* regi AI
26 (also 110, 126, 243 ...) prouidencie] prudencie O   29 Nichil ... Seneca] *marg.* I
• uirtus] *adds* prouidencie A   30 preturam] I *emen.* L, picturam AL, uictoriam O

[6]

Fulgentius's sixth mythology follows; it concerns Saturn's third son, Pluto. Through his image, the poets describe the third part of Prudence, that is the virtue Foresight. According to Cicero, this has the duty of examining things to come, just as intelligence examines those present and memory those past.[1] The poets depict this god as:

[1] crowned with ebony,
[2] plentifully enriched,
[3] the ruler of Hell,
[4] carried by Cerberus,
[5] bound to Hecate,
[6] armed with the Furies,
[7] and protected by the Fates.

These are the seven parts of Pluto's picture; they correspond to the same number of characteristics of foresight.

[15] [1] For as Martianus and Remigius show in *On the marriage*, Pluto, invited to the wedding of Mercury and Philology, came with a garland of ebony on his head, that is, with a royal crown made from that wood.[2] Notice that ebony is a variety of wood that won't burn, nor may fire consume it. For this reason, there is a verse, 'Ebony is a tree that no heat can burn up.' But Pliny, *Natural history* 5, speaking of ebony, says that it is the most precious tree, comparable to gold and ivory.[3] For this reason, the Ethiopians were accustomed to offer ebony, ivory, and gold to kings as tribute. Thus, we read that the queen of Sheba, who was queen of Ethiopia, offered these three to Solomon (cf. 3 Reg 10:2, 10–11).

[26] These details may be applied to the virtue foresight. For this virtue renders a person's mind incapable of suffering for any reason, as Seneca teaches in what's sometimes numbered epistle 74. 'You may suffer nothing', he says, 'if you have had virtue with you, for is there any difference between Cato's praetorship and his defeat?

---

[1] *De officiis* 1.11.
[2] Mart 35.19 (133/2–5).
[3] *Ibid.* 12.17, 19.

Nichil interest, utrum P[harsal]ica acie Cato uincatur aut uincat? Hoc est enim Catonis bonum quod uictis parti[bu]s, Cato uinci non potest. Eadem enim uirtute et mala fortuna uincitur et bona ordinatur'. Et patet ex serie epistole, quod specialiter
35 loquitur Seneca de uirtute prouidencie. Sicut ergo arbor ebanus est incremabilis, sic auxilio huius uirtutis, humanus redditur animus impassibilis.

Et ideo significanter Augustinus, in suo libello *De singularitate clericorum*, loquens de ista uirtute, dicit quod 'Prouidencia
40 frustrantur et deuincuntur uniuersa contraria. Ubi autem prouidencia necligitur, omnia contraria dominantur'. Et ideo dicit Gregorius in omelia | quod 'Minus iacula feriunt que preuidentur, et nos tollerabilius mundi mala suscepimus, si contra hec per prouidencie clipeum munimur'. Unde poete uirtutem
45 pro\uidencie/ dicunt esse scutum Palladis impenetrabile. De preciositate et utilitate istius uirtutis loquitur Seneca in quadam epistola, \dicens/ 'Prouidencia est ornamentum omnium uirtutum, custos oris, gubernacio accionis, temperancia cordis, moderacio lingue omniumque statera uerborum et ponderacio rerum'.
50 [2] Secunda pars picture est de Plutonis ditacione. Siquidem sicut patet per Remigium in commentario super Marcianum, Pluto iste a poetis et a paganis fingitur deus diuiciarum. Unde *Pluto* Grece idem est quod 'dis uel diues' L[atine], sicut dicit idem Remigius. Et bene conuenit uirtuti prouidencie, per quam homo
55 falsas diuicias deserit et ueras adquirit. Dicit enim Bernardus in quadam epistola, '*Utinam saperes et intelligeres ac nouissima prouideres*. Saperes, que Dei sunt; intelligeres, que mundi sunt; prouideres, que inferni sunt. Profecto, horreres infernum, superna appeteres, et que in mundo sunt contempneres'. Ecce quomodo
60 ex prouidencia sequitur horror inferni, amor et desiderium celi et rerum celestium, et contemptus mundi et rerum mundanarum. Quia ergo per istam uirtutem homo *thesaurizat* sibi | [ueras] *diuicias*, largiendo elemosinas et exercendo acciones alias

---

31 Pharsalica] far far salicia- I, Parthica O 32 est enim Catonis] dicunt Catonis (*later, over eras.*) I • partibus] Parthis O 33–34 Eadem … Et²] *om.* A
39 loquens … uirtute] *om.* AI 41 omnia] uniuersa A 42 in] *adds* communi L • fol. 96ᵛᵃ 44 prouidencie … munimur] proui [*blank*] A 45 Palladis] pallidum A 47 dicens] Bernardus eciam in quadam epistola dicit quod (*from lines 55–56*) L 49 statera] statura L
53 dis] diis I • Latine] legitur O 56–57 intelligeres … sunt²] *om.* A 58 superna] celestia A 59 appeteres] aspiceres L 62 fol. 96ᵛᵇ • ueras] *om. at page-boundary* O 63 elemosinas] electas L

Does it make any difference whether Cato was conquered by the vanguard at Pharsalia or conquered them? For it is Cato's virtue that, although conquered in some respects, Cato could not be conquered. For this same virtue both conquers bad fortune and makes preparations for good fortune.'[4] It is evident from the argumentative order of the epistle that Seneca speaks particularly of the virtue foresight. For just as an ebony tree cannot be burned, so a person's mind is rendered incapable of suffering through aid from this virtue.

[38] Therefore, Augustine says significantly in *On the singular state of clerics*, in talking about this virtue, 'Foresight frustrates and conquers everything that's contrary. But where someone neglects foresight, everything contrary reigns.' Therefore, Gregory says in a homily that 'Missiles that are foreseen strike with less force, and we endure the evils of this world more steadfastly, if we arm ourselves against them with the shield of foresight.'[5] For this reason, poets call the virtue foresight Pallas's impenetrable shield. Seneca talks about how precious and useful this virtue is in one of his letters, where he says, 'Foresight is the ornament of all the virtues, the guardian of our mouth, the director of our action, temperance for the heart and moderation for the tongue, and a balance beam that weighs all words and situations.'[6]

[50] [2] The second part of the picture concerns Pluto's wealth. For as Remigius shows in his commentary on Martianus, the poets and the pagans represent Pluto as the god of riches. For this reason, the Greek name 'Pluto' is the same as *dis* or *diues* 'rich' in Latin, as Remigius says.[7] This is truly appropriate for the virtue foresight, through which a person abandons false riches and acquires true ones. Bernard says in a letter, '*O that you would be wise and would understand and would provide for your last end* (Dt 32:29). You should *be wise* and know what things come from God; you should *understand* which are of the world; you should *provide*, that is foresee, which are hellish. Without a doubt, you should tremble at the thought of hell, you should long for the highest things, and you should disdain those of the world.'[8] See how the dread of hell follows from foresight, just as do the love and desire for heaven and heavenly things, and contempt of the world and worldly things. Therefore, by this virtue, a person *lays up* for themselves true *riches* (cf. Mt 6:19–21) by dispensing alms

---

[4] *Epistula* 71.7–8.

[5] Actually ps.-Cyprian (*PL* 4:866); Gregory, *Homeliae in evangelia* 35.1 (*PL* 76:1259).

[6] Cf. *Epistula* 5.8, an expanded citation version, since Seneca has only 'providentia, maximum bonum condicionis humanae'.

[7] Marc 5.18 (72/24–28).

[8] *Epistola* 292.2 (*PL* 182:498).

uirtuosas, fugiendo diuicias terrenas, que falso nomine uocantur diuicie. Quia, sicut dicit Seneca, 'Semper dimittunt hominem in maiori penuria et egestate'. Ideo hec uirtus sub ymagine dei dicitur 'opum affluere ubertate'.

Et possunt plura notari de ista diuiciarum diuersitate. De ueris enim diuiciis loquens, Gregorius in omelia dicit quod 'Sole ille diuicie uere sunt, que nos uirtutibus diuites efficiunt. Si ergo, fratres, diuites esse cupitis, ueras diuicias amate; si culmen ueri honoris queritis, ad celeste regnum tendite; si gloriam dignitatis diligitis, in illa superna angelorum curia ascribi festinate. *Ibi sunt reconditi thesauri* uirtutis prouidencie'. Unde bene exclamat Bernardus in quodam sermone de Aduentu, dicens, 'Filii Adam, genus auarum et ambiciosum, audite. Quid uobis cum terrenis diuiciis et gloria temporali, que neque uere neque uestre sunt? Aurum enim et argentum non[ne] sunt + terra rubia et alba, que solus error hominum facit, aut pocius reputat, preciosa? Denique, si uestra sint hec, tollite ea uobiscum. Sed homo, cum interierit, non sumet + omnia, neque descendet cum eo gloria eius. Uere ergo diuicie non opes sunt, sed uirtutes, quas secum portat consciencia, ut in eternum diues fiat'. Et de diuiciis talibus | prouidet sibi ista uirtus predicta, scilicet prouidencia; et ideo sibi in serie picture opum attribuitur affluencia.

[3] Tercia pars picture est de Plutonis prelacione. Siquidem poete pingunt eum deum inferni, sicut dicunt Neptunum deum pelagi et Iouem deum celi. Et bene conuenit hec pars picture uirtuti prouidencie. Actus enim debitus isti uirtuti est actus specialiter attributus diuinitati, sicut de ista materia tractatur in libro *Suda*, ubi allegatur ista auctoritas, Philonis narrantis, qualis sit opinio gentilium de Deo. 'Dixerunt', inquit, 'pagani gentiles Deum esse animal perfectum, immortale, intellectuale, existens in felicitate, mali nullius susceptiuum, mundi et eorum que in mundo sunt pro[uis]iuum'. Unde, secundum Damascenum, [libro] suarum *Sentenciarum*, 'Nomen Dei dicitur deriuari a *theaste*, quod est 'omnia considerare seu uidere', uel a *theo*, quod est

64 diuicias] *om.* L 66 dei] *add* huius AL
68 diuersitate] ubertate A 74 reconditi] reddite (*with dat.*) A 76 ambiciosum] ambiciosa gens AIL 77 temporali] corporali A 78 nonne] non AO • sunt] *adds* a O 79 hominum] *om.* AIL 80 uestra] uera A 81 sumet] *adds* cum eo O 81–82 neque ... eius] *om.* A 84 fol. 97[ra]
91 *Suda*] Iuda *corr. from* Suda I, Iuda L 92 pagani] *om.* A 94 mali] materiali L 95 prouisiuum] prouisissimum A, productiuum IO (*a corr.* I)
• libro] *om.* O

and performing other virtuous acts, and by fleeing earthly riches (called riches only under a false name). For as Seneca says, 'They always leave a person in greater poverty and need.'⁹ Therefore, this virtue, as depicted in the image of this god, is said 'to overflow with the fullness of riches'.

[68] There are many things to notice about this diversity of riches. For speaking of true riches, Gregory says in a homily, 'Only those riches that make us rich in virtues are true riches. If therefore, brothers, you desire to be rich, love true riches; if you seek the highest pitch of true honour, draw yourself toward the heavenly kingdom; if you love the glory that comes from high position, hasten to be enrolled in the highest court of the angels. In that court, *are hid all the treasures* of the virtue foresight (cf. Col 2:3).'¹⁰ For this reason, Bernard exclaims appropriately in a sermon for Advent, 'Sons of Adam, you grasping and ambitious race, listen to me. What is there for you in earthly riches and worldly glory, things that are neither true nor yours? For aren't gold and silver just red and white dirt that human error alone makes, or rather accounts, to be precious? Finally, if these are yours, carry them away with you. But people, when they have died, will not take everything with them, nor will their glory descend with them. Therefore, true riches are not riches, but virtues; these conscience carries with itself, so that it may be made eternally rich.' And this virtue foresight makes these riches available to itself; for this reason, this portion of the picture attributes an abundance of riches to it.

[86] [3] The third part of the picture concerns Pluto's lordship. Indeed, the poets depict him as the god of hell, just as they say that Neptune is the god of the sea and Jove the god of heaven. This part of the picture is appropriate for the virtue foresight. The action appropriate to this virtue is one specially attributed to divinity. That's the way this material is treated in the dictionary *Suda*, where it puts forward this authoritative view, explained by Philo, as to the views of pagan writers about God. Philo says, 'The gentile pagans said that God is a perfect being, immortal, intellectual, living in happiness, subject to no evil, having foresight of the world and all those things that are in it.' For this reason, according to Damascene in his *Sentences*, 'The name "God" is said to be derived from *theaste* "to consider or see all things", or else from *theo*

---

⁹ Cf. *Epistula* 119.9.
¹⁰ Gregory, *Homeliae in evangelia* 15.1 (*PL* 76:1132); Bernard, 'sermo 4 in Aduentu Domini' 1–2 (*PL* 183:47–48).

'omnia percurrere et omnibus prouidere'. Sicut ergo Deus prouidet hiis que sunt in mundo, ita uirtus prouidencie specialiter facit prouisionem contra ea que sunt in inferno. Unde sicut diuina prouidencia est circa mundi disposicionem, ita homo per uirtutem prouidencie uersatur c[ontr]a inferni declinacionem. Iste enim est actus proprius prouidencie, sicut patet per Tullium, 'ex presentibus futura perpendere et aduersus uenientem futuram calamitatem [se consilio] premuniri'. Considerat enim in presenti peccati perpetrati deformitatem et iam consulte, [se] premunit contra infernalis supplicii [futuram] calamitatem, penitendo de peccato et cauendo a recidiuo | et satisfaccionem faciendo.

Et essent plures circumstancie huius mithologie notande circa hanc uirtutem pr[oui]dencie, de quibus tractant poete. Siquidem uirtus ista sibi prouidet, ut + declinet famem et sitim Tantali, saxum Sisiphi, iecur Ticii, dolium filiarum Donaii, furorem + filiarum Cadmi +, rotam Ixionis, et cimbam Caronis. De hiis loquitur Seneca, tragedia prima, in qua agit de Hercule ad infernum descendente, narrans poetice quomodo Hercules hec omnia declinauit et de hiis omnibus et multis aliis triumphauit, nichil aliud uolens intelligere, nisi quod homo uirtuosus per uirtutem prouidencie potest de inferno et eius suppliciis uictoriam reportare, si peccata uoluerit declinare. Aliquando enim stat persona Herculis [in poetis] pro uiris uane gloriosis, aliquando pro hominibus uirtuosis.

[4] Quarta pars picture est de Plutonis deportacione. Nam, sicut patet per Fulgencium, poete pedibus dei \Plutonis/ subiciunt canem Cerberum. Nota quod canis iste Cerberus est a poetis dictus 'canis infernalis'; unde uocant eum ianitorem inferni. Et bene conuenit hec pars picture uirtuti pr[oui]dencie, nam poete per istum inferni canem dant intelligere cupiditatem mundi, quam intendunt depingere sub eius ymagine. Siquidem iste canis depingitur

cum tumultu, cum insultu;
pingitur stupendus et pingitur timendus.

---

101 circa] contra L   102 contra] circa AIO   105 se consilio] de consilio AI (de a corr. I), om. O   106 se premunit] premunitur O   107 futuram] om. O
108 fol. 97ʳᵇ • satisfaccionem] add debitam AL
109-21 Et ... uirtuosis] om., excepting 117-19 homo ... declinare A
109 circumstancie huius] circumstantes IL   111 declinet] declinent O
113 filiarum Cadmi] filiorum uel filiarum Cadmica dei O   117-18 per uirtutem] om. I   120 in poetis] om. O, in poeticis L
124 etc. Cerberum] Terberum A   127 inferni] Terberium A

"to survey everything and to foresee everything".[11] Therefore, just as God foresees the things that are in the world, the virtue foresight likewise makes special provision against the things that are in hell. For this reason, just as divine providence concerns the arrangement of this world, the virtue foresight turns a person away from swerving into hell. This is the action most appropriate to foresight, as Cicero shows when he says, 'It considers what things are to come on the basis of those present and, on the basis of its counsel, forearms one against approaching disaster.'[12] For it considers in the present the deformity of the sin one has committed and, having considered it, forearms one against the disaster to come, hell's punishment. It does this by repenting one's sins, taking care to avoid repeating them, and by performing works of satisfaction.

[109] And there may be many specific and noteworthy situations in this mythology that pertain to the virtue foresight and that are treated by the poets. Indeed, this virtue takes care so that it avoids Tantalus's hunger and thirst, Sisyphus's rock, Ticius's liver, the jars of Danaius's daughters and the frenzy of Cadmus's, Ixion's wheel, and Charon's boat. Seneca talks about these in his first tragedy, in which he treats Hercules's descent into hell. He tells, in his poetic fashion, how Hercules turned aside from all these and how he triumphed over them all, as well as many other dangers.[13] Seneca wishes one to understand only that a virtuous person, through exercising foresight, may return victorious over hell and its torments, provided they have wished to turn aside from sins. For sometimes in poems Hercules represents vainglorious people, sometimes virtuous ones.

[122] [4] The fourth part of the picture concerns how Pluto is carried about. For, as Fulgentius shows, the poets place the dog Cerberus beneath the god Pluto's feet.[14] Notice that the poets call this dog Cerberus 'hell-hound'; for this reason, they call him hell's gate-keeper. And this part of the picture is appropriate for the virtue foresight, for through this hell-hound, the poets want one to understand the desire for this world, and they intend to depict that through this image. Thus, this dog is depicted

> As something to be astonished at and feared / in its confusion and its attacks.

---

[11] For the *Suda*, see the Index fontium. L cites *De fide orthodoxa* 1.9; see the 'Index fontium'.

[12] Actually (ps.-)William of Conches, *Moralium dogma philosophorum* 1.A.1 ['De prouidentia'].

[13] *Hercules furens* 750–68.

[14] Fulg 1.6 (20/9).

Siquidem, sicut patet | per Senecam, tragedia prima, canis iste est tumultuosus. Unde dicit Seneca, 'Cum sono suo uasto et tumultuoso terrere umbras', id est animas mortuorum existentes in inferno et qualiter canis iste non solum concutit tumultum, sed eciam attemptat insultum. Sed patet ex nomine eiusdem canis interpretacione, nam Cerberus idem significat quod 'uorans carnes'. Qualiter eciam iste canis sit stupendus, patet ex eius monstruositate. Totus enim monstruosus est, et ideo plenus stupore et admiracione. Habet enim caput trinum et anum serpentinum, quia, ut Seneca describit, cauda Cerberi est draconi[na]. Et qualiter iste canis sit timendus, patet ex grauitate ueneni. Narrant enim poete, et tangit Ouidius et Boycius, et alii poete, qualiter [canis] iste tractus + ab Hercule de inferno, et ductus super terram, emisit super cautem, id est super lapidem, quandam saliuam toxicam et uenenosam, quod uenenum dicitur aconit[um]. De quo ueneno loquitur Ouidius, libro suo primo *De transformatis*, quando dicit, 'Lurida terribiles miscent aconita nouerce'. Iste ergo sunt quatuor partes istius picture, scilicet canis infernalis.

Et ut dictum est, per istum canem poete intelligunt mundanam cupiditatem quam uirtus prouidencie tenet et premit sub suis pedibus, calcando et contempnendo. Percipit enim uirtus ista quod hec cupiditas mundana abducit hominem a uirtutis honestate et | tandem perducit ad infernale supplicium. Unde hic poss[e]t notari quomodo cupiditas ista, ad modum canis inferni, facit tumultum et eciam insultum, quomodo ducit homines in stuporem, [eis eciam timorem] incutit et horrorem. Et de isto potest notari processus Crisostomi in suo libello, qui intitulatur *Quod nemo leditur, nisi a seipso*. 'In tantum', dicit Crisostomus, 'amor pecunie omnem animam fatigat, ut neque amicicie, neque propinquitatis, eciam interdum nec coniugis nec filiorum amori det locum, quibus affectibus inter homines nichil prefertur.

---

132 fol. 97va 135 et] *adds* notare eciam dicere potest L • concutit] excitat A, concidet I, concitet L 137 canis] *om.* A, et nominis L • significat] interpretatur A 139 Totus] Locus I 140–41 Habet … serpentinum] Habet … trinum *after* 143 draconina *and* caput serpentinum habet *after* 143 ueneni O 142 draconina] draconis O, draconia L 144 canis iste tractus] iste tractus sit O 147 aconitum] attonicum I, aconita O • ueneno] *om.* AI 148 miscent] pascent L

152 tenet et] *om.* A 155 fol. 97vb 156 posset] potest A, possent I, possunt O 158 eis … et] et incutit O • horrorem] errorem I

Indeed, just as Seneca shows in his *Hercules*, this dog is given to confusion, for he says, 'With his resounding and riotous noise to terrify the shades',[15] that is the souls of the dead living in hell, which shows how this dog doesn't just shake things into a confused state but also tries to attack. However, this is evident from this dog's name and its derivation, for Cerberus means the same thing as 'eating flesh'. Cerberus's monstrousness shows clearly why one should be astonished by him, for he is completely monstrous, and therefore full of shock and wonder. He has a triple head and the rear of a snake, for, as Seneca describes him, Cerberus has a dragonlike tail. Why one should fear this dog is evident from the severity of his poison. The poets tell – and both Ovid and Boethius, as well as other poets, treat this – how Hercules dragged this dog out of hell. Once he had been brought above ground, Cerberus spewed out on a rock his deadly and poisonous spittle, and this poison is called aconite. Ovid writes about this poison in *Metamorphoses* 1, where he says, 'The terrifying stepmothers mix pallor-inducing aconite.'[16] These are the four parts of the hell-hound's picture.

[151] And as I have said, the poets understand this dog to represent worldly desire. Foresight constrains this desire and treads it under foot, in trampling it showing its disdain for it. For this virtue perceives that worldly desire draws a person away from the nobility of virtue and, in the end, leads them to hellish punishment. For this reason, one should notice how this desire, in the same way as the hell-hound, both sows confusion as well as attacking, and how it leads people to bewilderment and also strikes them with dread and terror. On this point, one may notice Chrysostom's argument in his little book, *No one is harmed, except by themselves*, where he says, 'The love of money exhausts every soul to such a degree that it leaves no room for love of friends or care for one's relatives, even at times love for one's wife or children – and among people, no feeling is considered stronger than these.

---

[15] Cf. *Hercules furens* 783–85, (at line 141) 787.
[16] *Metamorphoses* 7.406–19, the citation at line 148, 1.147, *Consolatio* 4m7.19.

Amor tam[en] pecunie hec omnia humi deicit et pedibus
conculcat. Unde uelut quedam fera, crudelis domina possidet
omnium + corda, et tirannica dominacione subicit. Seuit ut
barbarus, [fertur] crudeliter ut tyrannus, debachatur inpudenter
ut meretrix, nusquam miseretur, nusquam pudet, adest ubique
\dura, ubique/ terribilis, + inclemens, inpia, truculenta, seuior et
ferocior lupis, ursis, et leonibus, acuens cotidie gladium et parans
hominibus foueam et precipucium'. Hec Crisostomus.

    Ex cuius processu patet mundane cupiditatis insultus et eius
tumultus, eius stupor et eius terror. Sed de istius canis triplici
capite specialiter possumus notare quod propter triplicem
cupiditatis morsum, poete attribuebant huic uicio caput ternum.
Primus morsus primi capitis est morsus laboris. Laborat enim
cupidus in adquirendo. Cuius | laborem describit Innocencius in
suo libello *De miseria condicionis humane*. 'Radix', inquit, '*omnium
malorum est cupiditas*; hec sacrilegia committit in furta, rapinas
excercet et predas, bella gerit et homicidia, symoniace uendit et
emit, [inique] petit et recipit, iniuste negociatur et feneratur, instat
dolis et iminet fraudibus, dissoluit pactum et uiolat iuramentum,
corumpit testimonium et peruertit iudicium'. Hec ille.

    Secundus morsus et secundi capitis est morsus timoris,
quia sicut habent laborem in adquirendo, ita habent timorem in
possidendo. Unde dicit Seneca quod 'Diues cupidus credit omnem
hominem esse latronem'. Et de isto loquitur Iuuenalis in poetria
sua, satira 5^a, ubi dicit sic:

    Pauca licet portes argenti uascula puri / Nocte iter ingressus,
    [gladium con]tumque timebis; / [Et ad] lumen mot[a]
    trepidabis arundinis umbram. / Cantabit uacuus coram
    latrone uiator.

Nota quod poeta uult [dicere] quod diues tantum in uia timet
predari quod motum arundin[is] credit esse motum lancee

---

164 tamen] enim A, tantum O   166 omnium] *add* mundanorum hominum IL, *adds* hominum mundanorum O   167 fertur] steruit (*marked for corr.*) A, furit O (*emen.* feruet L)   169 ubique ... terribilis] *om.* A • terribilis] *adds* dura I, *adds* domina O, *adds* dira L

175 poete ... ternum] *om.* A   177 fol. 98ra 180 excercet] exarset I   181 inique] necnon IO

184 morsus ... morsus] morsus I   187 poetria] quadam AIL   189 portes] partes A, potes I   190 gladium con-] can- A, tan- I, [*large blank*] O, gladium cinc- (*emen.* con-) L • Et] *om.* O • ad lumen mota] mote ad lumen A, nocte et lumen I, lumen mote O, motor ad limen (*emen.* mote ad lunam) L   193 dicere] *om.* O

194 arundinis] arundine O

Nevertheless, the love of money casts all these feelings to the earth and tramples them underfoot. For this reason, it's as if a great lady, wild and cruel, possesses everyone's hearts and subjects them to her tyrannical lordship. The love of money rages like a savage, behaves like a cruel tyrant, debauches shamelessly like a whore, never shows pity, never is ashamed, is present whenever there is anything harsh or frightful, merciless, pitiless, aggressive; more fierce and savage than wolves, bears, or lions; daily sharpening her sword and preparing a pit – and ultimate downfall – for people.'[17] So Chrysostom says.

[172] Chrysostom's argument shows worldly desire's attack and its confusion, and the astonishment and fear that accompany it. But I can specially single out that poets grant this vice a triple head because of the triple bite of desire. The first bite, associated with the first head, is that of labour. For an avaricious person works hard in acquiring things. Innocent III describes this person's labour in his little book *On the wretchedness of the human condition*, where he says, 'The desire of money is the root of all evils (1 Tim 6:10). This commits thieving sacrileges, engages in seizures and thefts, carries on wars and murders, buys and sells like Simon Magus, requests and receives wickedly, bargains and lends at interest unjustly, presses on and threatens deceitfully and fraudulently, dissolves agreements and breaks oaths, corrupts testimony and perverts justice.'[18] So he says.

[184] The second bite, associated with the second head, is one of fear. For just as avaricious people work hard in acquiring things, they are likewise fearful, while they possess them. For this reason, Seneca says, 'An avaricious rich man believes everyone else is a thief.'[19] Juvenal speaks about this in his satire 5, where he says:

> Although you may carry only a few small vases of pure silver, / when you go out on a night-time journey, you will fear the sword or the lance; / you'll shake at the shadow of a reed moved in the light. / A traveller carrying nothing will sing in the thief's face.[20]

Notice that the poet wishes to say that a rich person, while travelling, fears being robbed so much that he believes the motion of a reed is that of a lance

---

[17] *Ibid.* 6 (338/71–84).
[18] *De miseria* 2.2 (PL 217:717).
[19] Although often ascribed to 'Seneca', cf. Gregory, *Moralia* 15.23 (PL 75:1095), more fully at line 197.
[20] *Satyra* 10.19–22.

195 uel ensis. Sed uiator pauper, qui nichil timet amittere, securus erit, predone presente. De isto timore cupiditatis et auaricie, loquitur Gregorius in quadam omelia, 'Auarus et cupidus hic ardet estu concupiscencie, et postmodum ardebit igne iehenne. Si potenciorem uidet, timet raptorem; si inferiorem, suspicatur
200 furem. Infelix tanta | patitur, quanta pati timet'.

 Tercius morsus tercii capitis est morsus doloris, quia sicut cupidus adquisiuit cum + labore et custodiuit cum timore, ita in morte conquisita deserit cum dolore. Unde dicitur metrice,

 Diues diuicias non congregat absque labore,
205 nec tenet absque metu, nec deserit absque dolore.

O mors, quam amara est memoria tua homini iniusto *et pacem habenti in substanciis \suis/, etc.* Notari possent pro istis tactis uersus illi, quos ponit ille *Architrenius* de cupiditate, et est libro 5°, ubi dicit sic:

210 Iamque pererrato per plana, per aspera, mundo / Parte tenus magnum, monstrum reperitur [eunti] / Insolitus terror, nam celum uertice pulsat, / Et patulis terre digitis superocupat orbem / Et Phebe medium fraternos admouet ignes, / Et [Cristi] radios melioraque lumina tollit / Mater auaricie,
215 in sompnis ieiuna, cupido / Eternam + dampnata sitim producere, nulli[s] / Exsaciata bonis, lucri studiosa, rapinis +, / Artifices facta manus, u[i]sura recessus / Antipodum, noctisque dies, umbrasque sinistras / Ardentis secreta sinus, mollesque Sabeos / [Et] rigidos sine sole Getas, primeuaque
220 Pheb[i] / Limina cum scopulis, quibus exulat ultima Tile, / Ut uarias rerum species | em[ung]at, auari / Orbis opes, animi longo sudore secuta, / Ut tandem modico loc[ul]is de[s]eruiat ere.

---

195 uel ensis] et gladii A   196 cupiditatis et auaricie] cupidi A
200 fol. 98^(rb)
202 cum] *adds* dolore et O   203–5 Unde … dolore] *om.* A   205 tenet] habet I
• deserit] desit I   207 habenti] *om.* I   • etc.] *add* Ecclesiastici 41 AI; A *then om. to* 242 Hec   • tactis] *adds* de monstruositate istius cupiditatis mundane *and om.* de cupiditate L
210 tenus] per census L *(emen.)*   211 eunti] *om.* IO   214 Cristi] Phebi O
• melioraque] [*blank*] L   215 dampnata] dampnatam O   216 nullis] nulli O
• rapinis] *adds* uersus eorum dentes O   217 facta] factura IL   • uisura] usura IOL   219 Et rigidos] Frigidos O   220 Phebi] Phebo I, Phebe O
• Limina] Lumina IL   221 fol. 98^(va)   • emungat] emendat O   222 loculis] locis O   223 deseruiat] deferuiat I, deteruiat O

or sword. But a poor wayfarer, who fears losing nothing, will be safe, even in the presence of a thief. In one of his homilies, Gregory speaks about this fear associated with desire and avarice: 'Here an avaricious and desire-filled person burns with the heat of desire, and afterwards, they will burn with the fire of hell. If this person sees someone stronger, they fear being plundered; if someone weaker, they suspect them of being a thief. Unhappy, they suffer just as many things as they fear they will suffer.'[21]

[201] The third bite, associated with the third head, is the bite of sorrow. Just as an avaricious person has gained things with labour and has guarded them in fear, likewise they sorrowfully leave behind the things they have collected when they die. Thus, there is a verse:

A rich person doesn't gather their riches without labour,
Or hold them without fear, or leave them behind without sorrow.[22]
O death, how bitter is the remembrance of thee to an unjust *person that hath peace in their possessions, etc.* (Sir 41:1). And one might notice these verses concerning the subjects we are treating; *Architrenius* 5 says them about desire:

Now having wandered through calm and harsh places, to the whole great extent of the world, the traveller comes upon a monster, an unaccustomed fear, Mother Avarice. She's so tall that her head strikes the heavens, and she seizes the whole world from above with her outstretched fingers, drawing Phebus's friendly fires to the centre and leaving behind Christ's rays and His preferable stars. That's Mother Avarice, starved for sleep, a desire condemned to bring forth an eternal thirst, never sated by the goods she's stolen, eager for profit, deeds associated with her cunning hands. She will have seen the antipodeans' retreats, by night as well as by day, as well as the baleful shades, the secrets of her burning breast. She'll also have seen the effeminate Arabians and the stern Thracians, frozen since they are at the edge of the young sun's track, along with the rocks that strew the banished 'ultima Thule'. All this so that she may swindle all the various kinds of things, the world's riches, having pursued them with the sweat of a grasping spirit. But in the end, she has devoted herself to moneybags containing only a little brass.[23]

---

[21] *Moralia* 13.54 (*PL* 75:1016).
[22] Walther, *Sprich.* 6059.
[23] Ed. Thomas Wright, *The Anglo-Latin Satirical Poets*, RS 59.1/316 and 317.

142 John Ridewall, *Fulgencius metaforalis*

Nota quod uult poeta dicere et per ista describere quanto fatigatur
225 cupidus pro adquirenda parua pecunia, pro qua se exponit ad
[quecunque] pericula. Unde dicit postea:
   Dulcia sunt cupido lucrosa pericula, dulci / Eolus armatur
   [horrore], + Ceraunia fluctu, / Blanda Caribdis aqua,
   Forcis cane, [Sirtis] arena. / Emollit scopulos lucri dulcedo,
230   diurn[a]s / Absoluunt hyemes lucri momenta, labores / Expiat
   innumeros lucr[um] breue, sarcina lucro / [Fit] leuis, et rutilo
   sudor siccatur in auro.
Multa eciam alia tangit de cupiditatis tumultu et insultu, sic
dicens:
235   Hec Stigie superis infelicissima noctis / Filia fas abholit,
   cancellat iura, resignat / Federa, pacta mouet, leges abradit,
   honestum / Dampnat, amicicias rumpit, diuellit amorem.
   / Succi[n]ditque fidem; plena est discordia, questus / Ardor
   u[bi] pungnat; studio concu[rr]itur omni / [Ad loculos,
240   nam sola potest reuerencia nummi]: / Quodlibet ad libitum
   mundano + quolibet uti.
Hec est ergo ista cupiditas, que est iste canis infernalis
monstruosus et tumultuosus, quem uirtus pr[oui]dencie tenet
sub pedibus.
245   [5] Quinta pars picture est de dei Plutonis ligacione. Nam
poete fingunt eum ligatum uinculo coniugii E[c]ati, que alio
nomine | dicitur Proserpina. De ista Proserpina loquitur
Fulgencius in littera, dicens eam uocatam E[c]atem a numero
centenario, quia *e[c]aton* in Greco idem est quod Latine 'centum'.
250   Et conuenit istud coniugium uirtuti prouidencie, que declinando
inferni calamitatem, federat sibi celi felicitatem, per Proserpinam
figuratam, quia, sicut dicit Fulgencius, filia dicitur Cereris, id est
gaudii. Nam secundum Fulgencium, Ceres interpretatur 'gaudium'.
Ex gaudio autem et delectacione, qua homo delectatur in Deo,

---

224 poeta dicere] *om.* IL • quanto] *adds* labore L   226 quecunque] quodcunque
   (*with sg.*) I, omne O • postea] *adds* metrice L
227 Dulcia] Dubia I   228 horrore] [*blank*] O • Ceraunia] *extra minim* O,
   Ceremia L   229 Sirtis] Fortis O   230 diurnas] diurnos O   231 innumeros]
   immundos I • lucrum] lucra O, lucro L • Fit] Sic IOL • rutilo] iaccilo I
238 Succinditque] Scinditque I, Succiditque O, Scindetque L   239 ubi pungnat]
   pungnant, *corr. to* ut pu\n/gat O • concurritur] concurret I, concutitur O
   239-40 Ad ... nummi] *om.* O   241 quolibet] quodlibet I, quoslibet O
245 ligacione] ligamine L   246 Ecati] Etan AL, Etati IO   247 fol. 98vb
   248 Ecatem] Ethacon A, Etatem IO, Etaceo L   249 *ecaton*] ethacon A, etacio IL,
   eaton O   252 Cereris] celeris A

Notice that the poet wants to say, and to describe through these details, how much a desire-filled person exhausts themself in acquiring a little money, since they expose themselves to every sort of danger for it. For this reason, it says a little later:

> Desire finds profitable dangers sweet – Eolus armed with pleasant terror, the promontory Ceraunia with its current, Carybdis with her deceiving water, Phorcus with his dog [Medusa?], Syrtis with its sandbars. Profit's sweetness softens rocks, its persistent movement melts longlasting winters, a brief profit atones for labours beyond numbering, profit renders a heavy load a light one, and sweat dries up in the presence of red gold.

And he treats many other things about the confusion and attack of desire, when he says:

> This most unhappy daughter of Stygian night destroys what is proper in heaven; she cancels oaths, breaks contracts, adjusts agreements, erases laws, condemns what's virtuous, dissolves friendships, tears apart loves, and cuts down trust. She's stuffed with discord, having sought ardently places to contend; with all her energy, she gathers in her purses, because only coins deserve respect: whatever's pleasant to the world, she'll use it.

Therefore, that's what this desire is like; it's the monstrous and confusing hell-hound that foresight keeps underfoot.

[245] [5] The fifth part of the picture concens the god Pluto's binding. For the poets present him as bound in marriage to Hecate, who is also called Proserpina. In his text, Fulgentius talks about Proserpina; he says that she was called Hecate from the number one hundred, because *ekaton* in Greek is the same as *centum* 'one hundred' in Latin. And this marriage is appropriate for the virtue foresight, because in turning aside from the disaster of hell, it joins itself to the blissfulness of heaven. This is figured by Proserpina, because, as Fulgentius says, she is said to be the daughter of Ceres, that is of joy. For according to Fulgentius, Ceres means 'joy'.[24] For human blessedness springs from joy and delight, and through it, a person delights in God,

---

[24] Fulg 1.10 (22/9–16).

255 oritur hominis beatitudo, sicut dicit beatus Augustinus. Hec autem
pictura poetica illius Proserpine, nam pingitur
>a Cibele nata,
>litteris arrata,
>cithara letata,
260 >et luci[s] prelata.

Siquidem ista Proserpina fingitur filia dee Cibelis, que alio nomine dicitur Ceres, ut tangit Fulgencius. Cibeles, ut recitat Alexander Nekham in sua *Methalogia*, dicitur quasi *cubiles*. *Cubum* namque Grec[e] uocant 'solidum' Latin[e]; unde et numeri
265 solidi d[icunt]ur 'cubi' uel 'cubici'. Et est condicio potissime requisita ad felicitatem, scilicet quod sit solida et secura, sicut tangit Augustinus, 21° *De trinitate*, ['Esse enim certius quod semper erit in gaudio felicissimum erit'].

Item ista Proserpina pingitur inscriptis litteris arrata. Unde
270 super eius ymagin\em/ scribuntur multa nomina. Nam sicut tangit Fulgencius, uocatur + Lucina, uocatur Diana et Proserpina. Hiis tribus nominibus figurantur tres partes nostre beatitudinis, uidelicet per + Lucinam, claritas uisionis; per Dyanam, [intuitus] fruicionis. Amor enim penetrat usque ad intima + | amatorum,
275 et ideo dicit Augustinus super canonicam Iohannis, quod amor uult te unum facere cum amico. Et hac de causa Diana a poetis pingitur pharetrata, in qua pharetra portat sagittas et iacula medullas cordium penetrancia. Tercia uero pars beatitudinis, scilicet eternitas tencionis, figuratur per suum tercium nomen,
280 scilicet Proserpinam. Dicitur enim Proserpina a 'procul serpendo', et conuenit tencioni beatifice, cuius est perpetuo permanere.

Tercio uero ista Proserpina a poetis pingitur gaudere et delecta\ri/ in cithara. Unde ponunt eam primo coniunctam Orpheo in coniugio. Iste autem Orpheus pingitur a poetis
285 citharedus optimus, de cuius melodia efficaci plura tangit Boicius, *De consolacione philosophie*. Et bene conuenit ista complacencia in cithara cum beatitudine nostra, nam Rabanus docet in suo libro

---

260 lucis] luci O
264 Grece] Greci O • Latine] *om.* AL, *a later corr.* I, Latini O   265 dicuntur] dure O   267–68 Esse ... erit²] *om.* IO, *here from* A (certius] certus A, semper] sic L, in ... erit] hoc est beatissimum L)
269 inscriptis] in scripturis I   271 Fulgencius] [*blank*] A • etc. Lucina] Lucinia AO • et] *add* uocatur AL   273 intuitus] strenuitas O   274 intima] *adds* amoris|| O • fol. 99ra   276 amico] *adds* uel amatore A, amatore uel amato L   279 etc. tencionis] intencionis I
283 delectari] letari A • in cithara] *om.* AL

as Augustine says.[25] This is the poets' picture of Proserpine, for she is depicted

> born of Cybele,
> marked with letters,
> delighted with the lyre,
> displayed in light.

[261] Indeed, the poets represent Proserpina as the daughter of the goddess Cybele, who is also called Ceres, as Fulgentius mentions. The name Cybele, as Alexander Neckam says in his *Mythology*, is derived from *cubiles* 'cubelike'. For *cubum* in Greek means 'solid' in Latin; for this reason, 'solid numbers' are called *cubi* or *cubici* 'cubes' in Latin.[26] And the prerequisite most necessary for bliss is that it be solid and certain. As Augustine says, *On the trinity* 21, 'The most blissful state will be the one most certain that it will always be joyful.'[27]

[269] Also Proserpina is depicted as marked with inscribed letters. For this reason, many names are written above her image. For as Fulgentius mentions, she is called Lucinia and Diana, in addition to Proserpina.[28] These three names represent the three parts of our blessedness: through Lucinia, the brightness of vision; through Diana, our understanding of enjoyment. For love penetrates to lovers' very inmost parts, and therefore Augustine says in discussing John's general epistle that love wants to make you one with your friend.[29] And for this reason, the poets depict Diana with a quiver; in it, she carries arrows and missiles that can penetrate to the very marrow of hearts. The third part of blessedness, the stretching out of eternity, is represented by her third name, Proserpina. This name is derived from *procul serpendo*, that is 'creeping on to a great distance', and is appropriate for this blessed stretching, whose property is to remain forever.

[282] Third, the poets depict Proserpina as rejoicing and delighting in the lyre. For this reason, they state that she was first married to Orpheus. The poets depict Orpheus as the greatest player on the lyre; Boethius, in *The consolation of Philosophy*, speaks a great deal about his effective and affecting melody.[30] And this pleasure in the lyre is appropriate for our blessedness, for Rabanus teaches in

---

[25] Probably a general statement.
[26] VM3 2.3 (158/25–27).
[27] Cf. *ibid.* 1.13 (PL 42:843–44).
[28] Fulg 2.16 (57/16–17).
[29] Cf. *In epistolam Ioannis ad Parthos* 2.8–10 (PL 35:1993–94).
[30] *Consolatio* 3m12.6–19.

John Ridewall, *Fulgencius metaforalis*

De naturis rerum 'per hoc instrumentum musicum intelligitur communitas [ecclesie] et omnium electorum', 'quorum quilibet tantum gaudet de beatitudine alterius quantum de felicitate sui ipsius', ut pulcre docet Anselmus in suo *Proslogion*.

Quart[o], ista Proserpina pingitur lucis et nemoribus preposita et prelata. Unde a poetis uocatur dea nemorum et lucorum. Et significat hec pars picture delectacionis iocunditatem, quam habent bonorum anime in corporum resumpcione, quibus corporibus sicut [arb]oribus anime sunt prelate. Est enim notandum quod poete solent uocare corpus humanum lignum [e]uersum. Sunt enim capilli capitis | sicut radices, brachia et tibie sicut rami et frondes. Et ideo ista prefectura nemorum non est aliud nisi resumpcio corporum resurgencium.

[6] Sexta pars picture est de dei Plutonis armacione. Nam fingunt hunc deum Furiis infernalibus armatum. Unde notandum est, secundum Fulgencium, quod tres Furie finguntur a poetis isti deo Plutoni deseruire, quorum nomina ponit Fulgencius in littera. Prima est Allecto, secunda Tesiphone, et tercia Megera. Et conuenit bene hec pars picture uirtuti prouidencie, cuius moralis armatura est ira et indignacio uirtuosa, que quidem ira per has Furias supradictas moraliter est descripta.

Sed tamen notandum est quomodo tam sancti uiri, quam eciam philosophi et sapientes mundani, diuidebant inter iram uirtuosam et uiciosam. Crisostomus enim *Super Mattheum opus imperfectum*, [omelia 10], de hac ira que moraliter est bona sic dicit: '*Qui irascitur fratri sine causa reus est iudicii*; ergo qui cum causa, non erit reus. Nam si ira non fuerit, nec doctrina profi[ci]t, nec iudicia stant, uel crimina compescuntur. Iusta ergo ira mater est discipline, itaque non solum [non] peccat qui cum causa irascitur, sed e contra nisi iratus fuerit, peccat, quia paciencia irracionalis uicia [seminat], necgligenciam nutrit, non solum malos, sed eciam bonos, inuitat ad malum'. De hac materia loquitur Seneca in libris suis *De ira*. Applicando ergo ad propositum, uult ista poetica pictura dicere quod uirtutis | prouidencie hec est moralis armatura, irasci contra uicia et

---

289 ecclesie et] et eleccio O   291 docet] deducit AL
292 Quarto] Quartus O   296 arboribus] nemoribus O • anime] *adds* naturaliter L   298 euersum] transuersum O • fol. 99rb
309 uiri] nostri A   310 et] *om.* I   312 omelia 10] *om.* O • bona] uirtuosa A
   314 cum] sine A   315 proficit] profit OL   316 mater] magister A • non²] *om.* IO
   318 seminat] cecant O   321 pictura] scriptura A, *om.* I (*at line end*) • fol. 99va
   322 moralis] *adds* siue spiritualis eius A

On the natures of things that 'through this musical instrument, one understands the society of the church and of all the elect.' 'Each of them rejoices just as much in the blessedness of another as in their own happiness', as Anselm teaches neatly in his *Proslogion*.[31]

[292] Fourth, Proserpina is depicted as preferring and regarding favourably groves and woodlands. For this reason, the poets call her the goddess of woods and groves. This part of the picture indicates the delightful joy that the souls of good people have when they take up their bodies again, and those bodies are displayed as if they were the trees of the soul. For one should notice that poets customarily call the human body an inverted tree. The hairs on the head are like roots, the arms and legs like branches and boughs. Therefore, Proserpina's lordship over woods represents nothing other than the resurrected taking up their bodies again.

[301] [6] The sixth part of the picture concerns the god Pluto's arming. For poets represent this god as armed with the infernal Furies. For this reason, one should notice that, according to Fulgentius, the poets represent three Furies as serving this god. Fulgentius mentions their names in his text: first Allecto, second Tesiphone, and third Megera.[32] This part of the picture is appropriate for the virtue foresight, whose moral armament is virtuous wrath and indignation, and this wrath is described in moral terms through these three Furies.

[309] Nevertheless, one should notice how both holy men and philosophers and men wise in worldly subjects distinguished between virtuous and sinful wrath. For Chrysostom, in his *Unfinished work on Matthew*, homily 10, says of the wrath that is morally good, '*Whosoever is angry with his brother* without good cause *shall be in danger of the judgement* (Mt 5:22); therefore, the person who becomes angry for a good cause will not be in danger. For had he not become angry, teaching would not advance, nor would judgements stand, nor would crimes be restrained. Therefore, a just wrath is the mother of discipline, and for this reason, the person who becomes angry for a good cause does not simply not sin, but, on the contrary, if they hadn't become angry, they would sin, for a tolerance not governed by reason gives rise to vices, nourishes heedlessness, and invites, not just bad people, but even good ones, to evil.'[33] Seneca also discusses this matter in his book *On anger*. Applying this to our point, the poets, through this picture, wish to say that this is the moral armour of the virtue foresight, to grow angry

---

[31] Rabanus, *De universo* 18.4 (PL 111:498); *Proslogion* 25 (PL 158:241).

[32] Fulg 1.7 (20/20–21/5).

[33] *Opus imperfectum*, homily 11 (PG 56:690); the Seneca reference is fairly general, but cf. 1.6, 12, 14; 2.6.

peccata uirtuose. Nam per aliam uiam non poterit calamitatem inferni declinari et sibi deam Proserpinam, [felicitatem scilicet], copulare.

Possumus autem hic notare qualiter poete solent has Furias depingere. Siquidem alio nomine dicuntur Eumennides, id est bone dee.

Pinguntur enim ignite;
pinguntur infrunite;
pinguntur celeres et cite
et anguibus crinite.

Et di[cunt]ur a poetis animos hominum accendere et ignire. Et ideo pingi solent flamifere, sicut patet per Senecam in sua prima tragedia, qui pingit eas cum faculis ardentibus. Unde et prima Furia dicitur Alecto, id est 'sine lecto et quie[te]'. Unde Fulgencius dicit Alecto id est quod inpa[u]sabilis, et istud est ignis proprium nunquam quiescere, sed semper incendere, si habeat combustibile.

[Similiter] iste Furie pinguntur infrunite, id est discurrentes undique effrenate, sine freno discipline. Et propter hoc secunda Furia dicitur Tesiphone, id est secundum Fulgencium, 'uox irarum'. Uocis enim est undique se multiplicare et ad Furias [pertinet] ubique discordiam concitare. Unde a Seneca in prima tragedia d[icun]tur 'dee discordie'.

Tercio, iste [Furie sunt] depicte celeres et festine. Unde ille Claudianus depingit eas alatas. Unde loquens de Megera, concita[n]te sedicionem contra Rufini prodicionem, | + dicit, 'Pigraque ueloces per Tartera concutit alas'.

Quarto, iste Furie pinguntur cum crinibus serpentinis, sicut hec omnia tangit Seneca in sua tragedia prima et Ysidorus, 8 libro *Ethimologiarum*. Et conueniunt he\e/ partes huius picture ire laudabili et uirtuose, que posita est moralis armatura uirtutis prouidencie. Oportet enim quod t[alis] ira sit ad modum istarum

---

324 felicitatem scilicet] *om.* O (scilicet) *om.* I [*at page-boundary*])
327 Siquidem] *add* hee Furie que AL   327–28 Siquidem … dee] *after* 332 crinite O
333 (also 345 …) dicuntur] dure O   334 flamifere] flamescere A, flamigere L
335–36 qui … est] *marg.* I   335 faculis] flammis L   336 quiete] sine quiete I, sine requie O   337 inpausabilis] inpassabilis IO
340 Similiter] *om.* O   344 pertinet] *om.* OL
346 Furie sunt] dee *with* dicuntur *after* depicte O   •   et festine] *om.* L
348 concinante] concinate O   •   prodicionem] perdicator (?) I, *adds* uel | produccionem O   •   fol. 99vb 349 alas] *adds* festine L
350–52 sicut … Ethimologiarum] *om.* A   354 talis] tunc O

virtuously against vices and sins. For foresight might not swerve away from the disaster of hell and join himself to the goddess Proserpina, blissfulness, in any other way.

[326] Moreover, we can here set down how poets customarily depict the Furies. Indeed, they are also called by another name, Eumenides, that is 'the good goddesses'.

For they are depicted inflamed;
depicted as rash;
depicted swift and speedy;
and with snakes for hair.

The poets say that the Furies set on fire and ignite people's minds. Therefore, they are usually depicted bearing flames, as is evident in Seneca's first tragedy, where he shows them with burning torches.[34] Also, for this reason, the first Fury is called Alecto, that is *a lecto* 'without a bed' and 'without rest'. For this reason, Fulgentius says that Alecto means 'never pausing', for it is a property of fire never to rest, but always to burn, if it can find something that's capable of burning.

[340] Similarly, the Furies are depicted as rash, rushing violently about everywhere and unrestrained, lacking any rein of discipline. For this reason, the second Fury is named Tesiphone, which, according to Fulgentius, means 'the voice of angers'. It is a characteristic of the voice to echo in every direction and thus it's a property of the Furies to excite discord everywhere. For this reason, Seneca in his first tragedy calls them 'goddesses of discord'.

[346] Third, the Furies are depicted as swift and hastening. For this reason, Claudian depicts them as winged and when he speaks of Megera, stirring up unrest against Rufinus's treason, he says, 'And she beat her swift wings across drowsy Hell.'[35]

[350] Fourth, the Furies are depicted with snakes for hair, and Seneca says all these things in his first tragedy, as does Isidore, *Etymologies* 8.[36] The parts of this picture are appropriate for virtuous and praiseworthy anger, presented as the moral armament of the virtue foresight. For it is necessary that anger of this sort

---

[34] *Hercules furens* 87–89; the slightly inaccurate reference in line 345 is to 'discordem deam' 93; Fulg *ibid*.
[35] *In Ruffinum* 1.122.
[36] *Etym.* 8.11.95 (PL 82:324).

150 John Ridewall, *Fulgencius metaforalis*

355 E\umenidum/ flammifera, quia oportet quod fiat ex caritate fr[ater]na. Que quidem caritas ignis est, ut dicit Hugo in suo libello *De arra anime*. Et ideo dicit Gregorius, 5 *Moralium*, alia est ira quam impaciencia excitat, et alia quam zelus caritatis informat; illa ex uicio, hec ex uirtute generatur.

360 Secundo, hec ira uirtuosa ad modum illarum Eumenidum est infrunita, id est effrenata et nullis legibus [al]ligata. Docet enim Bernardus [in quodam omelia] *Super Cantica*, loquens de amore, quod 'ubi amor est, ibi effrenacio est'. Unde, sicut dicit, 'O amor preceps, uehemens, flagran[s], impetuose, qui preter te non sinis
365 aliud cogitare; fastidis [cetera], contempnis omnia preter te, teipso content[us]. Confundis ordinem, dissimulas + usum, ignoras modum totum quod oportunita[ti]s, quod racionis, quod pudoris, quod iudicii consiliiue uidetur; triumphas in temetipso et in captiuitatem | redigis'. Hec Bernardus.

370 Ex quo patet qualiter ira uirtuosa, amore inflammata, conuenienter pingitur infrunita et effrenata. Unde de tali ira loquens, Seneca, epistola 53ᵃ, sic dicit: 'Nunquam satis de uiciis litigammus que, [oro te], Lucili, persequere sine modo, sine fine, nam illis quoque nec modus nec finis est. Proice quecumque cor
375 tuum laniant, que si aliter extrahi nequirent, cor ipsum cum ipsis reuellendum est'. Hec Seneca. Dicit autem in primo libro *De ira*, 'Philosophus ille Theofrastus dicere consueuit quod non potest fieri ut bonus uir non irascatur malis; quanto enim quisquam fuerit melior, tanto hoc modo irascendi erit iracundior'.

380 [Tercio], hec ira uirtuosa ad modum Eumenidum festina pingitur atque cita. Unde dicitur habere alas ueloces. Amor siquidem nescit moras, et ideo ira que nascitur ex caritate caret mora cuiuslibet tarditatis. Unde notabiliter dicit \Bernardus/, *Super Cantica*, omelia 9ᵃ, 'Amor preceps est, iudicium non
385 prestolatur, nec concilio temperatur, nec pudore frenatur, nec racioni subiugatur'.

356 fraterna] frena O   359 uirtute] caritate A
360 uirtuosa] *om*. AL • Eumenidum] *adds* flammifera I   361 alligata] ligata O   362 in ... omelia] *om*. O   363 dicit] *adds* Seneca A   364 flagrans] flagrantis I, flagrante O, *illeg*. L   365 cetera] *om*. O   366 contentus] contento O • usum] uisum O   367 oportunitatis] oportunitas est AI, oportunitas O, oportunitatis est L   369 fol. 100ʳᵃ
371 conuenienter] communiter A   372–73 Nunquam ... modo] *om*. L   373 oro te] o mi OL   376 reuellendum] reuelandum AIL • est] erit AI, erat L • Dicit ... libro] *om*. A
380 Tercio] *om*. O

bears flames, like the Eumenides 'good goddesses' do, for it must emerge from brotherly charity. Indeed, charity is fire, as Hugh of St Victor says in his little book *On the soul's pledge*. And Gregory says, *Moral readings* 5, 'There is one anger that is incited by impatience, and a second that is informed by charity's zeal; the first is produced by vice, but the second by virtue.'[37]

[360] Second, this virtuous anger is rash, like the Eumenides are; it is violent and bound by no laws. For Bernard, in a sermon in *On the Song*, speaking of love teaches that 'wherever love is, rashness is also'. For this reason, he says, 'O love, sudden, violent, burning, impetuous, you don't allow one to consider anything apart from you; you dislike and disdain everything except yourself, content with yourself. You destroy order; you ignore what's customary, pay no attention to moderation, nor to what appears advantageous, reasonable, shameful, or proper to judgement or good counsel; you triumph over yourself and convert them into your slaves.' So Bernard says.[38]

[370] This shows why virtuous anger, inflamed by love, is appropriately depicted as rash and unrestrained. For this reason, Seneca discusses this anger in epistle 53, saying, 'We can never contend enough against the vices, I'd urge you, Lucillus, than to prosecute them incessantly without moderation, for they themselves likewise have neither moderation nor an end. Cast out whatever it is that wounds your heart, and if you don't know how to draw it out otherwise, then you should tear out your very heart along with the vice.' Seneca says this, and he also says in *On anger* 1, 'The philosopher Theophrastus used to say that one could not be a good person, unless one became angry about evils; indeed, the better a person is, the more angry he will be through this kind of virtuous wrath.'[39]

[380] Third, virtuous anger, the kind the Eumenides practice, is depicted as hastening and quick. For this reason, it is said to have swift wings. Indeed, love doesn't know how to delay, and therefore the anger that is born out of love lacks the delay that comes from any sort of slowness. For this reason, Bernard says notably, in *On the Song*, sermon 9, 'Love is sudden; it doesn't wait for judgement, nor is it moderated by advice, nor restrained by shame, nor put under reason's rule.'[40]

---

[37] *Ibid.* (PL 176:954); *Moralia* 5.45 (PL 75:726).
[38] *Sermo* 79.1 (PL 183:1163).
[39] Seneca, *Epistula* 51.13 and *De ira* 1.14.
[40] *Sermo* 9.2 (PL 183:815).

Quarto, hec ira uirtuosa contra uicia et peccata portare dicitur crines anguinos. Unde pingitur a[n]guicomina tercia Furia, que secundum Fulgencium, dicitur Megera, interpretatur 'lis uel contencio magna'. Unde assignans Fulgencius processum iracundie, dicit quod primum est non pausando iram concipere, secundum in uoce prorumpere, tercium iurgium procellare. Et iste actus appropriatur Megere, cuius come ideo sunt a\n/guine | propter uenenum anguinum irremediabile. Et isto modo debet uirtuosus cum uiciis semper contendere, scilicet continue sine cessacione, sicut prius patuit ex dictis Senece. Prelium enim cum uiciis non habet terminum quamdiu durat ista uita, quia *Milicia est uita hominis super terram* pugnare, scilicet cum eis quamdiu remanet super terram, sicut dicit Iob 7°.

[7] Septima et ultima pars picture est de Plutonis administracione. Fata enim famulantur isti deo, et ideo depingitur uallatus et stipatus Fatis, tamquam famulis et ministris. Quorum \nomina/ Fulgencius ponit in littera, dicens quod tria isti Plutoni destinantur Fata, et hoc ad Plutonis ministerium, ut tangit Alexander Nekham in sue *Methalogia*. Et sunt ista Fatorum nomina: prima Cloto, secunda Lachesis, et tercia Atropos. Que sorores sic pinguntur

onerate,
occupate,
obstinate.

[Unde, sicut tangit Alexander Neckham in sua *Methologia*], poeta enim Ho[meru]s depinxit primam sororem Cloto colum et fusum deferentem, hoc quoad onus. Idem eciam Homerus depinxit secundam sororem Lachesim filum extrahentem, hoc quoad opus et occupacionem. Depinxit eciam terciam sororem, scilicet Atropos, filum extractum et [im]placabiliter incidentem. Nec prece, nec precio, [nec fauore], nec amore, nec timore dimittit ista soror fili truncacionem.

---

388 anguicomina] aguiconica A, anguicona I, aguicomina O 388–90 tercia ... magna] sicut et Megera A, sicut et Megera, *but includes* secundum ... magna (dicitur *om.*) I 392 procellare] concelare A 394 fol. 100rb 395 semper] *om.* A 397 terminum] finem L 398 super terram] *om.* IL 399 dicit] dicit Scriptura L
402 Quorum] *add* Fatorum AL 406 Que] Fatorum autem poetica pictura est ista nam AL
411 Unde ... Methologia] *om.* O 412 Homerus] honores O 415 Depinxit] Similiter (Super L) idem Omerus depinxit AL 415–16 scilicet Atropos] *om.* L 416 implacabiliter] placabiliter O 417 nec fauore] *om.* O

[387] Fourth, this virtuous anger against vices and sins is said to have snakelike hair. For this reason, the third Fury Megera is depicted with snakelike hair. Fulgentius interprets her name as meaning 'a legal action' or 'a great dispute'. For this reason, Fulgentius describes anger as a progression and says that the first step is to conceive anger without any pause; the second, to burst into a voice (of rebuke); and finally, to beat off the quarrelling offender.[41] This final act is characteristic of Megera, whose hair is snakelike because of snakes' incurable poison. A virtuous person always ought to battle against vices in this way, continuously without stopping, just as I previously indicated from Seneca's words. For as long as this life lasts, the battle against the vices has no end, for *The life of man upon earth is* to battle in *warfare*, Iob 7:1, that is against the vices so long as we remain upon earth.

[400] [7] The seventh and last part of the picture concerns Pluto's government. For the Fates accompany this god, and therefore he is depicted defended and surrounded by the Fates, as if they were his servants and agents. Fulgentius gives their names in his text, saying that the three Fates are assigned to Pluto in order to carry out his will, as Alexander Neckam also explains in his *Mythology*.[42] The Fates are named in order Clotho, Lachesis, and Atropos. They are sisters and are depicted
    loaded down,
    busy,
    and stubborn.

[411] For this reason, as Alexander says, the poet Homer depicted the first sister, Clotho, as carrying a rod or a distaff, as if it were a load. Homer also depicted the second sister, Lachesis, as drawing out a thread, as if it were a labour and a profession. He also depicted the third sister, Atropos, as mercilessly cutting the drawn-out thread. This sister does not leave off her cutting the thread, whether by prayer, a bribe, or favouritism, whether from love or from fear.

---

[41] Fulg 1.7 (21/2–5).
[42] Fulg 1.8 (21/7–13) and VM3 6.23 (187/34–188/2).

Unde a poetis dicuntur iste tres sorores Parce per antifrasim,
420 id est per contrarium. Et conuenit specialiter istud uocabulum
isti Atropos, quia | [ipsa] nec parcit amico nec inimico, nec
extraneo nec propinquo, nec diuitibus nec pauperibus, nec alicui,
cuiuscumque fuerit status. Istud autem significatur per suum
nomen, scilicet Atropos, quod dicitur ab *a*, quod est 'sine', et *tropos*
425 'conuersio', quia non potest reuocari aliquo modo ab incepto. Et
quia sorores iste, et specialiter ista, noluit alicui parcere, nec ab
incepto desistere, ideo pinguntur obstinate. In cuius obstinacionis
signum, depinguntur aliqui circa ymaginem huius Atropos
munera offerentes, aliqui comminatoria intemptantes, alii
430 amicicias et proprinquitatem sanguinis ad memoriam reducentes,
alii nobilitatem generis et dignitatem status allegantes, et sic de
modis [aliis] plurimis quibus homines mundi solent allici et a
propositis suis retrahi. Sed ista soror tercia, non obstantibus hiis,
semper manet immutabilis et inpersuadabilis. Et ideo, racione sue
435 obstinacionis, uocabant eam poete isto nomine Atrapos, quod
sonat in carenciam conuersionis, quia idem significat Atropos
quod 'inuertibilis'.

Applicando ad propositum, possumus notare quomodo
sorores iste [sunt] uirtutis istius prouidencie famule et ministre.
440 Nam sub ymaginibus istorum trium Fatorum, intellexerunt poete
hominum statum mortalium. Unde secundum Fulgencium, Cloto
idem est quod 'euocacio', et significat mortis dissolucionem.
Nam in morte, anima euocatur a corpore. Post uero mortem,
anima recipit suam sortem, id est debitam remuneracionem iuxta
445 pristinam conuersacionem. Illud enim quod gessit in corpore sibi
post mortem erit | pro sorte. Et istud significat Lachesis, secunda
soror, que, sicut dicit Fulgencius, interpretatur 'sor[s]'. Sed quia
sors ista + manet \immutabilis/, quia erit eterna, siue bona siue
mala fuerit, ideo sequitur soror tercia, scilicet Atropos, que
450 inconuertibiliter incidit filum. Ipsa enim excludit omne remedium
euadendi malam sor[t]em; [excludit eciam omne dubium
amittendi bonam sortem].

---

419 Parce] porte A   **421** fol. 100va • ipsa] *om.* IO (*at page-boundary* O)
   423 autem ... per] sonat AL   **424** quod dicitur] *om.* AL • sine] sui A
   428 depinguntur] *om.* L   **432** aliis] *om.* O   **434** inpersuadabilis]
   insuperabilis AL   **436** conuersionis] condescencionis AL
439 sunt] sunt, *but also* scilicet *after* istius I, scilicet *after* istius O   **441** statum]
   fatum A • mortalium] *adds* et moriturorum A, *add* et mortuorum IL
   446 fol. 100vb **447** dicit] refert A • sors] sore O   **448** ista] *adds* semper O
   450 incidit] secat A, occat L   **451–52** sortem... sortem] sortem AI, sororem O

[419] For this reason, the poets call these three sisters *Parcae* 'the ones who spare', through *antiphrasis*, that is 'the opposite'. This name is especially appropriate to Atropos, because she spares neither friend nor foe, neither neighbour nor foreigner, neither rich nor poor, nor anyone, whatever may have been their state. Moreover, this is indicated by her name Atropos, which is formed from *a*, that is 'without', and *tropos* 'a change', for she may not be recalled in any way from what she has begun. Because these sisters, and especially Atropos, don't wish to spare anyone, nor leave off from anything they have started, they are depicted as stubborn. As an indication of their stubbornness, some people are depicted around the image of Atropos offering her bribes, others attempting to threaten her, others reminding her of friendships and blood relations, others alleging to her the nobility of their lineage or their lofty status, and so on – in the many various ways by which worldly people are accustomed to entice and draw others from what they've intended to do. But the third sister, in spite of their opposition, always remains unchangeable and unpersuadable. Therefore, because of her stubbornness, the poets called her Atropos, which refers to her lack of change, because Atropos means 'unchangeable'.

[438] Applying this to my point, I may note how these sisters perform as servants and agents of the virtue foresight. For in the images of the three Fates, the poets understood the state of all mortals. For this reason, according to Fulgentius, Clotho means 'calling', and indicates the dissolution that comes with death. For in death, the soul is called out of the body. After death, the soul receives its fate, that is the repayment it is due corresponding to its former behaviour. For whatever it has performed in the body will be its fate after death. The second sister Lachesis indicates this, as Fulgentius says, since her name means 'fate'. But because this fate remains unchangeable, because, whether it's a good or a bad fate, it will be eternal, the third sister, Atropos comes last and irrevocably cuts the thread. Thus, she excludes any remedy for avoiding a bad fate; equally, she excludes any fear of losing a good one.

Patet ergo qualiter iste tres sorores predicte famulantur uirtuti prouidencie. Nam onus prime sororis – ipsa enim pingitur onerata – uertitur in alleuiacionem. Corpus enim, quod corumpitur, aggrauat animam, et ideo anima uiri uirtuosi, a corpore exuta, alleuiatur, que tamen prius corpore onerabatur. Unde in signum alleuiacionis ipsius, qua uir uirtuosus alleuiatur quando moritur, Tullius, libro primo *Tusculanarum questionum*, dicit quod natura indidit cignis morituris cantum, quia solent exonerati ad cantum prouocari. Unde dicit Tullius sic, allegans dictum Socratis dicentis quod cigni, qui non sine causa Appollini sunt dicati, eo quod ab eo diuinacionem habere uidentur. Qui quasi prouidentes quid in morte boni sit, cum cantu ac uoluptate moriuntur. Et ut recitat Tullius, sic dicit Socrates, fore faciendum omnibus hominibus bonis et doctis. Sic ergo Cloto, prima soror, malis hominibus est in oneracionem, bonis est in alleuiacionem.

Secundo, opus [secunde sororis], scilicet Lachesis, que malis est ad pene calamitatem, bonis et uirtuosis cedit ad summam commoditatem, glorie scilicet felicitatem. Et de isto forent notanda multa, que sancti tangunt et philosophi pagani. Primo enim libro | *Questionum Tusculanarum* dicit Tullius duas notabiles narraciones de commoditate mortis. Quarum [un]a est de Agamede et Triphonio. Isti enim duo construxerant templum deo Appollini Delphico. Post templi uero edificacionem petebant isti duo constructores remuneracionem a deo. Petebant nichil determinatum, sed in generali petebant illud quod erat hominibus optimum. Acceperunt autem oraculum ab Appolline, quod oraciones erant exaudite et quod in tercio die forent opt[at]um munus accepturi. Die uero tercio illucente, ambo illi constructores templi mortui sunt reperti.

Narrat eciam idem Tullius ibidem de quadam paganorum sacerdotissa, nomin[e] Argie, que quadam die ad quoddam sacrificium solenne celebrandum curru ferebatur ad templum. Accidit autem iumenta currum trahencia fatigari et

---

457 alleuiatur] *om.* A   460 cignis] agnis A, annis (*emen.* animis) L
   463 diuinacionem] dominacionem A   464–65 ut … Tullius] *om.* A
468 opus] onus I • secunde sororis] *om.* O   469 pene] *om.* I   470–71 Et … pagani] *om.* A   472 fol. 101ra 473 una] prima O   474 Triphonio] Ephanio L
   475 deo Appollini] *om.* A (*at line-break*)   475 (and 476, 477) petebant] patebant I   476 duo] *adds* templi L   478 oraculum] responsum I
   479 optatum] optimum O
483 nomine] nomina O • die] uice AL   484 curru] *om.* A

[453] Therefore, it is evident how these three sisters serve the virtue foresight. For the burden of the first sister – recall that she is depicted as burdened – is turned toward relief. For the body, which is subject to corruption, weighs down the soul. Therefore the soul of a virtuous person is relieved when set free from the body, although it was previously weighed down by the body. As an indication of this relief, by which a virtuous person is relieved when they die, Cicero, in *Tusculan disputations* 1, says that nature has endowed swans about to die with song, because those found without guilt are customarily stimulated to sing.[43] Cicero says this, citing a statement of Socrates's, that swans are sacred to the god Apollo, appropriately so, because they appear to have powers of divination from him. As though they were foreseeing what might be good in death, they die in song and pleasure. And as Cicero reports that Socrates said, all people who are good and well instructed should do the same. Therefore, the first sister Clotho does likewise, burdening wicked people but relieving good ones.

[468] Second comes the labour of the second sister, Lachesis, who grants evil people the disaster of punishment, but good people the highest benefit, namely the happiness of glory. On this point, both holy men and pagan philosophers treat many things that one ought to notice. For in *Tusculan disputations* 1, Cicero tells two notable stories about the benefit of death. The first of these concerns Agamedes and Triphonius, who had built the temple for Apollo, god of Delphi. After the temple was built, the two who raised it asked the god for payment in return. They didn't ask for anything fixed, but offered a general prayer that they might get what was the best thing for humans. They received Apollo's oracle, that their prayers had been heard and that, on the third day, they would receive their chosen reward. When the third day dawned, both the temple-builders were found dead.

[482] Cicero also tells there the story of a pagan priestess named Argia; one day she was brought to her temple in a cart to perform a solemn sacrifice. However, it happened that the oxen drawing her cart grew weary,

---

[43] *Ibid.* 1.30.73–74.

sacerdotissa[m] a proposito impediri. Quod uidentes, duo filii
sacerdotisse, Cleobus et [Biton], ueste deposita, olio sua corpora
perunxerunt, et currui se iunxerunt et matrem Argiam ad phanum
perduxerunt. Que ad templum adducta, deam cuius erat sacerdos
490   exorabat, ut pro mercede daret filiis \premium/ maximum
possibile a diis dari hominibus. Adolescentes ergo, iste sacerdotisse
filii, cum matre sua, perfecto sacrificio, comederunt et post
prandium som\p/no se dederunt. Mane uero mortui sunt inuenti
in signum quod mors fuerat illud maximum premium quod per
495   deum posset dari hominibus.

Hinc concordant | Ambrosius, Augustinus, et Crisostomus,
et alii doctores catholici, sicut ex diuersis scriptis eorum plane
patet. Unde Ambrosius in libro suo *De bono mortis*, dicit quod
'omnifarie est [mors] bona', et probat quomodo omnibus modis
500   mors est bona. Et tangit unam racionem notabilem, scilicet istam,
quia 'mors diuidit compungnancia, ne inuicem se impugnent',
scilicet corpus et animam, inter que est pugna continua miserie
plena. Quia ergo per mortem finitur ista miseria, significanter
dicitur mors esse bona. Ista enim pugna [facit] peccatores
505   pugnatores; miseros reddit; *miseros autem facit populo\s/
peccatum*', dicit sapiens.

Magna est ergo bonitas mortis, per quam peccati miseria
non est possibilis +. Hec est ergo una racio quare mors est
bona et utilis, scilicet quia uite presentis est finis, que uita plena
510   est miseriis, sicut bene tangit Augustinus in quodam sermone,
sic dicens, 'O uita presens, quam multos decipis, que dum fugis,
nichil es; cum uideris, umbra + es; cum exaltaris, fumus es. Dulcis
es stultis, amara sapientibus; qui te amant, te non cognoscunt; et
qui te contempnunt, te intelligunt. Fugitiua est uelut sompnum;
515   uera non est uia quam ostendis. Aliis te ostendis longam, ut
perdas in finem; aliis ostendis te breuem, ut dum penitere uolunt,
non permittas; aliis latam, ut faciant quodcumque u[olun]t; aliis
angustam, ut non faciant bene; aliis tristem, ut non consolentur de
bono'. Et ibidem Augustinus [iterum] exclamat, 'O uita attrocissima,

486 sacerdotissam] sacerdotissa O   487 Biton] Pintotus A, Prenotus IO
490 premium] *om.* I
496–98 Hinc … patet] *om.* A   496 fol. 101rb 499 omnifarie] cumfaria A,
   multipharie *over eras.* I • mors] *om.* O   504 facit] *om.* O   505 miseros reddit]
   om. AIL • populos] plurimos A
507 bonitas] utilitas et libertas A   508 possibilis] *adds* uel passibilis O
   509 bona et] *om.* A   512 es^2] est O   515 ostendis^2] *om.* L   516 perdas] perdant AI,
   perdes L • ostendis] *om.* I   517 uolunt] ue[luit O   519 iterum] *om.* O

and the priestess was prevented from carrying out her plan. Seeing this, her two sons, Cleobus and Biton, having thrown off their garments, anointed their bodies with oil, hitched themselves to the cart, and dragged their mother Argia to the temple. When she had been drawn to the temple, Argia prayed to the goddess she served that the goddess should give to her sons as a payment the greatest reward possible for the gods to give to humans. Thus, the youths, the priestess's sons, once their mother had performed her sacrifice, ate with her and, after the meal, fell asleep. In the morning, they were both found dead, as an indication that death had been the greatest reward that might be given a human by a god.[44]

[496] On this point, Ambrose, Augustine, and Chrysostom, as well as other catholic doctors, agree, and it is thoroughly evident in their various writings.[45] For this reason, Ambrose in his book *On the good of death*, says that 'death is good in every way', and he proves how death is good in every manner. He discusses one noteworthy reason, that 'death separates combatants so that they may not fight one another', namely the body and the soul, between whom there is continual warfare, full of wretchedness. Because this wretchedness is concluded with death, he says significantly that death is good. For this battle makes sinners into warriors, and it renders them wretched; Solomon says, *Sin maketh nations miserable* (Prv 14:34).

[507] Therefore death is a great good, and through it, the wretchedness of sin is no longer possible. This is one reason why death is good and useful, because it is the end of our present life, filled with wretchedness. Augustine treats the point well in one of his sermons, saying, 'O present life, how many you deceive; which, so long as you flee, you are nothing; when you are seen, you are only a shadow; when you are raised up, you are just smoke. You are sweet only to the stupid, bitter to the wise; those who love you don't know you, and those who disdain you, understand you. You are fleeting, just like a dream; the way you show is not a true one. You show yourself as a long way to some, so that they may be lost in the end; you show yourself to others as a short way, so that, so long as they wish to repent, you will not allow it; to some, a broad way, so that they may do whatever they want; to some, a narrow way, so that they won't behave well; to others, a sad way, so that they may not be comforted about the good.' Augustine exclaims once more there, 'O most horrible

---

[44] Ibid. 1.47.113–14.
[45] Cf. Chrysostom, *in Matt. Hom.* 31.3-4 (PG 57:374–75); and Ambrose, *ibid.* 4.15 (PL 14:547).

520 quam honores tu|midant +, dolores exte[nu]ant, aeres morbidant, [esce] inflant, ieiunia macerant, ioci soluunt, tristicie consum\un/t, sollicitudo coartat, securitas enir[u]at, \paupertas eicit, iuuentus ex[toll]it, senectus incuruat, infirmitas/ frangit, meror marcidam facit'. Sed quia horum omnium mors est finis, ideo a sanctis, mors
525 ista omnifarie uocatur bona.

Unde narrat Augustinus in libro suo *De uisitacione infirmorum*, de philosophis, quomodo ordinauerunt quod in hominum [et] puerorum nataliciis, deberent homines ostendere signa meroris et tristicie, sed in morte hominum signa gaudii
530 et leticie. Et causa quare fuit ista, nam in hominis natiuitate inchoantur miserie prius ab Augustino descripte, sed in morte sunt iste miserie terminate. Et nota hic Augustinum in libello *De uisitacione infirmorum*, ubi maximam et singularem commendacionem facit de ista mor\tis/ commoditate. Quere
535 in originali. Ex quibus, seruicio et ministerio patet quomodo famulatur ista soror secunda, scilicet Lachesis, uirtuti prouidencie, que calamitosam occupacionem uertitit in finalem felicitatem.

Tercia uero soror, scilicet Atropos, que pingitur obstinata, ipsa ministrat uirtuti prouidencie de bono seruicio. Quia sicut prima
540 soror alleuiat ab onere et secunda b[eat]ificat pro quiete, ita ista tercia certificat de stabilitate. Unde istius Atropos obstinacio nichil aliud est quam felicitatis accepte securitas, ita quod non oportet ulterius hesitare de amissione. Et de ista | securitate, quomodo sit magna pars beatitudinis, pluries tractant, ut Augustinus et
545 Anselmus, et alii. Sic ergo finita est sexta mithalogia Fulgencii de uirtute prouidencie.

520 fol. 101va • tumidant] tu||tumidant O • dolores] colores A • extenuant] exterminant O   520–21 dolores … macerant] *om.* L   521 esce] escus IL, citus O   522 eniruat] enerciat A, enirat IO, eneruat L • iuuentus] inuentus A
523 extollit] exsoluit O
528 et] *om.* O   531 inchoantur] *adds* angustie et A   534 commoditate] cupiditate L   535–36 patet … famulatur] seruit AI   536 famulatur] fuerit L   537 felicitatem] leticiam uel felicitatem A, leticiam L
538 scilicet Atropos] *om.* AIL   540 beatificat] benificat O   541 certificat] rectificat L   542 securitas] assecuracio AL   543 fol. 101vb 545–46 sexta … prouidencie] undecima mithologia L   546 de … prouidencie] *om.* AI

life, which honours swell up, which sorrows weaken, airs infect, foods swell up, fasts make thin, jests slacken, sorrows eat up, care constrains, certainty makes weak, poverty casts out, youth praises, old age bends down, sickness shatters, sorrow withers.' But because death is the end of all these things, holy people call death good in every way.[46]

[526] For this reason, Augustine tells in his book *On visiting the sick* how philosophers decreed that on people's birthdays, even those of the young, people should show signs of sadness and sorrow, but signs of gladness and joy on people's deaths. The reason was that, at a person's birth, those occasions for wretchedness first begin, the ones that Augustine described above. But in death, these wretchednesses find an end. And notice further in Augustine's *On visiting* where he praises the very great, indeed unique advantage of death. Look in the text.[47] From discussions like these, it is evident how this second sister Lachesis supports the virtue foresight through her service and duties, for she turns disastrous business into final blessedness.

[538] The third sister, Atropos, who is depicted as stubborn, performs good service for the virtue foresight. For just as the first sister relieves one from a load and the second blesses one with rest, this third sister makes things certain through her stability. For this reason, Atropos's stubbornness is nothing other than the certainty of the happiness one has received, so that one needs no longer hesitate in worrying over losing it. Many authors, Augustine, Anselm, and others, treat this certainty, and how it is a great part of blessedness. So ends Fulgentius's sixth mythology, about the virtue foresight.

---

[46] Sermo 49 ad fratres in eremo (*PL* 40:1332–33).
[47] (ps.-Augustine) *ibid.* 1.6 (*PL* 40:1152).

[7]

Sequitur septima mithologia Fulgencii de Appolline dei Iouis prole. Fingunt namque poete Appollinem primum filium et precipuum dei Iouis. De ista prerogatiua dei Apollonis loquitur Marcianus libro *De nupciis*, uersus finem in oracione Philologie
5 quam facit ad Apollonem, quando dicit, 'Ignoti uis celsa patris et prima propago, etc.'. Nota quod Philologia in ista sua oracione uocat Apollinem \uirtutem dei Iouis, sicut nos Cristiani dicimus de Dei filio, quod est uirtus Dei patris, quia omnia per Ipsum facta sunt. Qui Iupiter ideo dicitur 'ignotus', quia hominibus est
10 incomprehensibilis. Uocat eciam Philologia Apollinem/ 'primam propaginem dei Iouis', id est precipuam eius filiolam.

Sub ymagine autem huius Apollonis, poete intendunt figuratiue depingere ueritatis ymaginem. A poetis siquidem iste deus Apollo depingitur
15 [1] iuuenis armatus,
[2] comis deauratus,
[3] quadriga delatus,
[4] equis agitatus,
[5] gemmis coronatus,
20 [6] literis aratus,
[7] Musis ministratus,
[8] in lauro locatus,
[9] et coruo curatus.

Iste sunt nouem partes picture, quibus poete solent deum
25 Apollinem depingere per quem intelligunt solem, ut dicit Fulgencius in litera.

[1] Qui sol pingitur iuuenis propter etatis calorem, armatus propter uirtutis uigorem, quem habet homo in sua iuuentute. Sicut enim in iuuentute habundat calor complexionis et uirtus
30 roboris, ita in planetis sol eciam magis hic inferiora | calefacit et plus uirtutis rebus hic inferius influit. Sicut de isto possunt adduci multa que tangit Marcianus in libro *De nupciis* et Remigius in commento et Ambrosius in *Exameron* et Plinius in *Historia naturali* et alii doctores diuersi.

1 septima] duodecima A • mithologia] *om.* I   2 prole] *om.* A   6 ista] isto? O
    7 Cristiani] Cristum? O   8 est] dicitur I   11 filiolam] sobolem A
21 Musis] musicis I   24 partes] uel decem A, *adds* uel decem I
30 fol. 102ra 31–34 Sicut … diuersi] *om.* A   34 doctores] auctores I

[7]

Fulgentius's seventh mythology follows; it concerns Apollo, son of the god Jove. For the poets depict Apollo as this god's first and most outstanding son. Martianus, in his *On the marriage*, speaks of this favour extended to the god Apollo, near the end, in Philology's prayer to Apollo when she says, 'You are the highest power of the unknown Father and his first offspring.'[1] Notice that in her prayer, Philology calls Apollo the power of the god Jove, just as we Christians say of God's son that He is the power of God the Father, for through Him, all things were made. For this reason, Jupiter is called 'unknown', because he is incomprehensible to humans. Philology also calls Apollo 'the first offspring of the god Jove', that is his outstanding little son.

[12] In the image of Apollo, the poets intend to depict, in a figurative fashion, an image of Truth. Thus, they depict the god Apollo as
 [1] an armed youth,
 [2] with gilded locks,
 [3] borne about in a chariot,
 [4] driven by horses,
 [5] crowned with jewels,
 [6] written over with letters,
 [7] served by the Muses,
 [8] placed in a laurel-tree,
 [9] and looked after by a crow.
These are the nine parts of the picture by which poets customarily portray Apollo. As Fulgentius says explicitly, they understand him to be the sun.[2]

[27] [1] The sun is depicted as a youth on account of the heat associated with that age and armed because a person has vigorous strength in their youth. For just as in youth a hot metabolism and strong power predominate, likewise among the planets, the sun heats lower things here more and more influences them here below in his strong activities. Many things may be adduced about this point; Martianus treats them in his *On the marriage* and Remigius in his commentary on it, as well as Ambrose in his *Hexameron*, Pliny in his *Natural history*, and various other learned people.[3]

---

[1] *Ibid.* 2.185 (= 73.10, 197/11–17).

[2] Fulg 1.12 (23/4).

[3] Probably intended as general references, but, for example, cf. Ambrose, *Hexameron* 4.1–3 (*PL* 14:187–91 passim).

35   Set eundo ad uirtutem ueritatis, hec uirtus poetice iuuenis depingitur in etate, quia ueritas nunquam deficit nec marcessit ex antiquitate; ymmo semper est recens et florida. Uirtus ista, sicut pulcre loquitur Seneca in quadam epistola, de uirtute ista dicens quod 'ueritas in omni parte sui eadem est, inmarcessibilis est; ea
40 uero que decipiunt nichil habent consolidi; tenue est enim \omne/ mendacium. Perlucet, si diligenter perspexeris'. Et psalmista dicit conformiter cum Seneca quod *Ueritas Domini manet in eternum.* Et Augustinus, *Super Iohannem,* dicit quod 'ueritas panis est que mentes + reficit, nec ipsa deficit', [immo] pocius floret semper et
45 uniformiter uirescit.

Non solum autem uirtus ueritatis depingitur a poetis iuuenis in etate pro iuuentutis flore, sed eciam pro illius etatis calore. Nam ueritas calefacit, hoc est allicit et afficit per amorem. Sicut de hoc pulcre loquitur Rabi Moyses Iudeus; libro 12, capitulo 7, dicit quod
50 'Creatori non placet, nisi ueritas, et non offendit eum, nisi falsitas'. Unde notandum est quod, sicut patet per beatum Augustinum, libro 14 *De ciuitate Dei,* et eandem s[ent]enciam *Super psalmos,* 'Duas ciuitates faciunt duo amores. | Ciuitatem Ierusalem + fundat et edificat amor Dei; ciuitatem uero Babilonie fundat amor
55 seculi atque sui. In una ciuitate \istarum/ seu communitatum ueritas perit, odium [regnat], puta in ciuitate Babilonie. Unde dicit Salustius, cuius auctoritatem recitat Ieronimus in suo comentario super epistolam Pauli ad Galatas, 'Obsequium amicos, ueritas odium \parit', sed in ciuitate Ierusalem est per oppositum.
60 Hec enim uirtus ueritatis in ista ciuitate allicit/ ad amorem et delectacionem. Unde dicit Augustinus in quadam epistola quod incomparabiliter est pulcrior ueritas Cristianorum quam Helena Grecorum. Et ideo uirtus ista ueritatis propter suam singularem pulcritudinem singulariter afficit mentes ciuium ciuitatis
65 Ierusalem per amorem.

Non solum autem pingitur Apollo iuuenis sed eciam armatus, ut enim poete solent fingere. Archus et sagitte sunt Apollonis armature; unde iste deus Apollo dicitur archum et sagittas portare.

---

37 recens] r̄c̄n̄s̄ (= ? rectus) O   38 de uirtute ista] *om.* A   42 conformiter] *om.* A, concorditer I   44 mentes] *adds* hominum O   • immo] sed O
51 sentenciam] scienciam O   53 fol. 102rb 54 fundat et edificat] fundauit et edificauit O   56 perit ... regnat] perit odium I, odium perit O   58 ueritas] ueritatis AI
66-67 Non ... poete] Sequitur secunda pars picture (Sequitur ... picture] Secunda pictatur I) de Apollinis armacione utpote AI   68 dicitur] pingitur habere *and om. later* portare AI

[35] But passing on to the virtue truth, poets depict this virtue as youthful because truth never fails, nor does it wither from old age; indeed, it is always fresh and blooming. Seneca says neatly of this virtue in one of his letters, 'Truth is always the same in every one of its parts, and it is incapable of withering; deceitful things have no substantial connection with it, and lying is utterly removed from it. Should you examine it carefully, it always shines forth.'[4] David agrees with Seneca, that *The truth of the Lord remaineth for ever* (Ps 116:2). And Augustine says, in *On John*, that 'Truth is the bread that refreshes people's minds, and it does not fail';[5] rather, it always flourishes and it keeps on growing.

[46] However, the poets depict the virtue truth, not just as youthful, a sign of youth's flowering, but also as a sign of the heat associated with that age. For truth heats things, that is, it entices and affects one through love. Rambam the Jew speaks neatly on this point; in 12.7 he says that 'Nothing pleases the Creator except truth, and nothing offends Him except falsehood.'[6] For this reason, one should notice that, as Augustine shows, *On the city* 14 – and the same opinion appears in his *On the Psalms* – 'There are two loves that construct two cities. The love of God founds and builds the city of Jerusalem; the love of the world and of oneself founds that of Babylon.'[7] In one city, or its constituent communities, namely Babylon, truth dies, and hatred rules. For this reason, Sallust says – Jerome repeats his authoritative opinion in his commentary on Galatians – 'Deference gives rise to friends, truth only to hatred',[8] but in the city of Jerusalem the opposite is the case. For this virtue truth in that city draws its friends to love and delight. For this reason, Augustine says in one of his letters that Christian truth is incomparably more beautiful than the Greeks' Helen.[9] Therefore this virtue truth, through its unique beauty, uniquely affects the minds of Jerusalem's citizens through love.

[66] However, as the poets customarily represent him, Apollo is depicted, not just as a youth but also as armed. Apollo's weapons are a bow and arrows, and so he is said to carry a bow and arrows.

---

[4] *Epistula* 79.18.
[5] *In Ioannis evangelium tractatus* 41.1 (*PL* 35:1692).
[6] *Dux neutrorum* 2.47 (p. 248).
[7] *De civitate Dei* 14.28 (*PL* 41:436), *Enarrationes in Psalmos* 64.2 (*PL* 36:773).
[8] Actually Terence, *Andria* 68, cited *Commentarii in epistolam ad Galatas* 2 (on Gal 4:15–16) (*PL* 26:382).
[9] *Epistola* 40.4 (*PL* 33:157).

Uocatur enim a poetis Apollo 'Phicius', eo quod cum sagittis interfecit serpentem quemdam, quem uocant Phitonem; de cuius interfeccione loquitur Ouidius, libro primo *De transformatis*. Nota quod 'Phicius' et 'Phiton' apud poetas, sicut patet per Alexandrum in sua *Methalogia*, interpretatur 'fidem auferens', et significat falsitatem exterminantem fidelitatem. Contra istum Phitonem pugnat Apollo, ueritas scilicet, et interficit serpentem istum cum sagittis. Una enim sagitta est ueritas uite; | secunda sagitta est ueritas iusticie; tercia + sagitta est ueritas doctrine.

De ista triplici ueritate loquitur Scriptura. De prima namque ueritate, scilicet uite, habetur Ysaie 38, quando Ezechias dixit, *Memento, queso, quomodo ambulauerim coram te in ueritate et in corde perfecto*. De secunda, scilicet ueritate iusticie, loquitur Salomon, Prouerbiorum 29, *Rex qui iudicat in ueritate pauperes, tronus eius in eternum firmabitur*. De tercia, scilicet doctrine, tangit Scriptura Matthei 22, *Magister, scimus quia uerax es et uiam Dei in ueritate doces*. Iste sunt tres sagitte quibus serpens Phiton, id est uicium falsitatis, interficitur.

Si ue[ro] sit falsitas in conuersando, quomodo omnes Cristiani qui male sunt uite dicuntur falsi et mendosi, sicut recitat Ambrosius in quodam sermone, \dicens/ quod 'non solum in falsis uerbis sed eciam in simulatis operibus mendacium est. Quia mendacium est se Cristianum dicere et opera Cristi non facere'. Mendacium est sacerdotem uel clericum se profiteri et contraria huic ordini operari. 22, questio 5, 'Cauite istam falsitatem in conuersacione'. Interfecit Apollo per primam sagittam, que est ueritas uite.

Si uero sit falsitas in docendo et predicando, illam interficit sagitta secunda Apollonis, scilicet ueritas doctrine. Si uero sit falsitas in iudicando, illam interficit Apollo per terciam sagittam, scilicet per ueritatem | iusticie. Bene igitur Apollo dicitur [cognomine] 'Phicius', nam ut dicit Fulgencius in littera, Appollo Grece sonat in Latino idem quod 'perdens uel exterminans'.

69 cum] ? tamen AO   74 fidelitatem ... Phitonem] felicitatem I   76 est ueritas] ueritatis est uirtus A   • fol. 102va 77 iusticie, doctrine] *trs.* AI   • sagitta] *an extra loop at the end* O
78–81 De ... perfecto] *after* 76 sagittis I   78 Scriptura] Scriptura ysid' A
  79 habetur ... 38] *om.* AI   81 De secunda] Similiter de AI   82 Prouerbiorum 29] *om.* AI   84 Matthei 22] euangelii AI
87 Si uero] Siue AIO   91 Quia mendacium est] *om.* I   93 22 questio 5] *om.* AI
  • Cauite] *om.* I (*at line-break*)
99 fol. 102vb 100 cognomine] cognomento A, *om.* O

For the poets call Apollo 'Pythius', because he killed Python the serpent with his arrows; Ovid speaks about this killing in *Metamorphoses* 1.[10] Notice that the poets' terms 'Pithius' and 'Pithon', as Alexander Neckam shows in his *Mythology*, mean in Latin 'bringing faith', and they figure faith's destruction of falsehood. Apollo, that is truth, fought against the Python and killed that serpent with his arrows.[11] For one of these arrows is truth in one's living; the second is the truth associated with justice; the third is truth in teaching.

[78] Scripture speaks about this triple truth. About the first kind of truth, that of one's living, there's Is 38:3, where Hezekiah said, *I beseech thee, O Lord, remember how I have walked before thee in truth, and with a perfect heart.* Solomon speaks about the second, the truth of justice, in Prv 29:14, *The king that judgeth the poor in truth, his throne shall be established for ever.* And Mt 22:16 presents the third, that is the truth of teaching, *Master, we know that thou art a true speaker, and teachest the way of God in truth.* These are the three arrows with which Apollo slew the serpent Python, that is the vice falsehood.

[87] If there is falsehood in behaviour, it's in the way that all Christians who live evilly are said to be false liars. Ambrose takes this up in a sermon where he says, 'Lying is not just a matter of false words but of feigned actions as well. For it's a lie to say that one is a Christian and then not perform Christ's works.'[12] It's also a lie to profess oneself a priest or cleric and then to perform actions contrary to the rules of clerical order. Gratian says, 'Beware falsehood in your behaviour.'[13] Apollo killed this form of falsehood with his first arrow, truth in one's living.

[96] If there is falsehood in teaching and preaching, Apollo kills it with his second arrow, truth in teaching. If there is falsehood in judging, Apollo kills this with his third arrow, truth in justice. Therefore Apollo is appropriately called by the nickname 'Pythius'. As Fulgentius says explicitly, Apollo in Greek means the same thing as Latin 'destroying or slaughtering'.[14]

---

[10] *Ibid.* 452–60.
[11] VM3 8.1 (200/6–13).
[12] Cf. *In psalmum David cxviii expositio*, sermo 11.20 (*PL* 15:1356–57).
[13] *Decretum* C.22, Q.2, c.16 (*CJC* 1:872).
[14] Fulg 1.12 (23/4).

Apollo igitur ideo 'Phicius' cognominatur, quia serpens Phiton, uicium scilicet falsitatis, per Apollinem, id est per uirtutem ueritatis, perditur et exterminatur.

[2] Sequitur secunda pars picture dei Apollinis, continens descripcionem crinium dei Appollinis. Nam ut docet Marcianus in libro *De numpciis*, Apollo iste pingitur auricomus, id est habens auream comam. Et bene conuenit ista proprietas uirtuti ueritatis. Hec enim uirtus, sicut habet defeccionis immunitatem, propter quod depingitur etate iuuenis; et sicut habet accionis strenuetatem, propter quod pingitur armatus iaculis, ita eciam habet delectacionis iocunditatem, et propter proprietatem istam, uirtus ista pingnitur comis deauratis. Nam aurum, ut docet Auicenna, est medicina cordialis; unde disponit hominem ad leticiam cordis. Quante eciam delectacionis sit uirtus ueritatis patere potest ex uerbis Augustini, 3º libro *De libero arbitrio*, ubi dicit quod 'tanta est pulcritudo iusticie, [t]anta est + iocunditas lucis eterne, hoc est incommutabilis ueritatis atque sapiencie, ut si non liceret in ea amplius manere quam unius diei [m]ora. Propter hoc solum, innumerabiles anni huius uite pleni deliciis et circumfluencia bonorum temporalium recte et merito contemp|nerentur'. Nota quod ueritas, que uirtus hic depingitur sub ymagine dei Apollonis, est quedam participacio illius ueritatis incommutabilis de qua in auctoritate loquitur Augustinus. Et ideo si tanta iocunditas est in lumine ueritatis incommutabilis, oportet quod participacio huius lucis sit delectabilis, in cuius figuram Apollo pingitur auricomus a poetis.

Et est hic notandum processus Senece in quadam epistola, que in libris aliquibus est 63, ubi tangit hanc materiam de complacencia uirtutis ueritatis. Ut enim dicit Seneca in epistola 74ª, Socrates dicebat uirtutem nichil aliud esse quam ueritatem, et e contrario, sed in sola uirtute est uerum gaudium; igitur de ueritate est solum gaudendum. Hec est deductio Socratis et Senece. Unde Seneca in epistola 62ª dicit, 'Cogita hunc sapiencie esse effectum gaudii iocunditatem. Talis enim sapientis est animus, qualis est

---

103 per ... per] per A
105 secunda] tercia A, alia I   106 dei Apollonis] *om.* AI   crinium] *expuncted from* crininum A   109 delectacionis] delecionis A   112 delectacionis] deleccionis I   116 libero] *om.* I   117 tanta] quanta O • iocunditas] iocunditatis O   119 mora] hora IO   120 innumerabiles] immutabiles A   121 fol. 103ra   122 uirtus] *adds* est et A, *adds* est (*at line-break*) I   124 est in] insit A
129 que ... 63] *om.* A   130 uirtutis] *om.* AI (ueritatis *over eras.* I) • in epistola 74ª] *om.* A   134 dicit] *om.* A • Cogita] *om.* I

Therefore Apollo is nicknamed 'Pythius', because he destroyed or slaughtered the snake Python, the vice falsehood, through the virtue truth.

[105] [2] Next comes the second part of the picture of the god Apollo, containing a description of the god's hair. For as Martianus teaches in his *On the marriage*, Apollo is depicted as golden-locked, that is having a golden head of hair.[15] This characteristic is particularly appropriate for the virtue truth. For this virtue, just as it is immune to loss – that's why it is depicted as youthful; and just as it has vigorousness in action – and thus is depicted armed with darts, also has happiness in delight, and because of this characteristic, it is depicted with golden locks. For gold, as Avicenna teaches, is a medicine that stimulates the heart,[16] and it thus disposes a person to have a joyful heart. Augustine's statement, in *On free will* 3, shows just how much delight may be associated with the virtue truth: 'Justice is just as beautiful as is the happiness of eternal light, that is the light of unchanging truth and wisdom, even if one were not permitted to remain in it longer than for the space of a single day. For this reason alone, one should properly disdain innumerable years in this life spent sated with delights and abundantly surrounded with worldly goods.'[17] Notice that truth, the virtue here depicted in the image of the god Apollo, is a sort of participation in this unchanging truth of which Augustine speaks in his authoritative statement. Therefore, if there is so much happiness in the unchanging light of truth, it necessarily follows that participation in this light is delightful, and it is as an image of this fact that the poets depict Apollo as golden-haired.

[128] And here one should notice Seneca's argument in one of his epistles, number 63 in some books, where he treats this material about the pleasure associated with the virtue truth. As he also says in epistle 74, Socrates said that virtue is nothing except truth – and the reverse. But true happiness resides in virtue alone; therefore one should rejoice in truth alone.[18] That's what Socrates and Seneca deduce. For this reason, Seneca says in epistle 62, 'Consider then that the happiness of true joy is the effect of wisdom. For a wise person's mind is just like the heavenly

---

[15] Mart 11.14 (88/19–23).
[16] Unfound.
[17] *Ibid.* 3.25 (*PL* 32:1308–09).
[18] *Epistula* 71.16.

mundus super lunam, semper enim illic, id est super lunam, serenum est. Et ita est de animo sapientis, quia nunquam sine gaudio est uerax sapiens'. Dicit Seneca, 'Plenus est gaudio, hilaris et placidus, inconcussus; cum diis ex pari uiuit'.

140 [3] Tercia pars picture est de dei Apollonis deportacione. Nam pingunt poete Apollinem deferri in quadriga. Et sicut quadriga inue[ct]itur quattuor rotis, ita uirtus ueritatis fundatur in quattuor mediis. Si autem queratur quare ueritas est exequenda, respondetur propter omnes uirtutes, et specialiter propter ipsius
145 honestatem, et illud est primum medium. Si queratur alia questio, an sit aliqua alia causa diligendi | ueritatem, certe respondetur propter falsitatis deformitatem. Nam si falsitas propter suam feditatem sit fugienda, ueritas propter suam honestatem est diligenda, et illud est secundum medium ueritatis.
150 Si queratur tercio an sit aliqua alia racio diligendi ueritatem, respondetur quod propter premii preciositatem. Uirtus enim ueritatis ad ueram perducit felicitatem, sicut probat Augustinus, *De ciuitate Dei*, et istud est tercium medium uirtutis ueritatis. Si queratur quarto, an sit dare quartum † racionem mouentem
155 ad ueritatem et eius dilectionem, respondetur quod propter supplicii seueritatem quam meretur falsitas, que est uicium ueritati oppositum propter suam deformitatem. Ista sunt quattuor dei Apollonis oracula seu responsa.

Est enim notandum quod apud poetas iste Apollo † fingitur
160 deus diuinacionis. Unde ad quattuor questiones in ista quadriga dat quattuor responsiones. Docet enim Augustinus in quodam sermone quod ad prophetam † pertinet iste quadruplex modus respondendi in colacione sua, ut responsio prophete sit de morum exhortacione, uel uiciorum prohibicione, uel suppliciorum
165 cominacione, uel de premiorum promissione. Unde uerba sancti Augustini sunt hec: 'Sancti prophete locuti sunt mouentes bona, prohibentes mala, terrentes de futuris tormentis, et promittentes de premiis'. Iste sunt rote quattuor quibus subuehitur currus ueritatis, scilicet hec quadruplex prius tacta consideracio.

142 inuectitur] inte[2] (= intelligitur) I, innititur seu uehitur O   144 omnes uirtutes] communis (omnis I) uirtutis AI   146 aliqua] autem A, *om.* I   • fol. 103[rb]
147–48 Nam ... honestatem] *om.* I   149 secundum] tercium I
150 racio] causa A   152 sicut] poret' | A   154 quartum] *adds* causam siue O
155 delectionem] delectacionem I
159 Apollo] *adds* depingitur et O   162 pertinet] pertinent O   163 sua] scilicet A, sic I   • responsio] r̄o (= ? racio) O   • sit] ut supra A   168 de] *adds* futuris A
• subuehitur] subuenitur I

world beyond the moon, for it is always calm there. And a wise person's mind is like that, for no truly wise person is ever without joy.' He further says, 'A wise person is filled with joy, happy and content, immune to disturbance, and such a person lives as an equal of the gods.'[19]

[140] [3] The third part of the picture concerns the god Apollo's transportation. For the poets depict Apollo borne about in a chariot. And just as a chariot is drawn about on four wheels, so the virtue truth is supported by four means. However, if one should ask why truth should be pursued, one would respond that it would be on account of all virtues, and particularly on account of truth's moral rectitude, and that's the first means. And if one would pose a second question, whether there might be some other reason for loving truth, the response would certainly be, on account of falseness's deformity. For if one should flee falseness because of its repulsiveness, one should love truth for its moral qualities – and that is the second means supporting truth.

[150] If one should ask a third time whether there is any other reason for loving truth, one would reply, because of the richness of its reward. For the virtue truth leads to true happiness, as Augustine proves in *On the city of God*,[20] and this is the third means supporting truth. And if one should ask whether one might provide a fourth reason that would impel one to truth and to loving it, the response would be on account of the gravity of the punishment that falsehood deserves – it's of course the vice opposed to truth because of its deformity. These are the four divine precepts or responses of the god Apollo.

[159] For one should notice that the poets represent Apollo as the god of divination. For this reason, he gives four responses to the four questions associated with this chariot. Augustine teaches in one of his sermons that a prophet has a fourfold way of responding when people are conferring with him. For a prophet's response may be one of exhorting to moral behaviour, or of forbidding vices, or of threatening punishments, or of promising rewards. Augustine's exact words are 'Holy prophets have spoken to impel men to good deeds, to forbid vicious ones, to frighten about punishments to come, and to promise coming rewards.'[21] These are the four wheels that draw along truth's cart, namely that fourfold consideration I have just treated.

---

[19] *Epistula* 59.16 and 14.
[20] E.g. *ibid*. 4.3 (*PL* 41:114).
[21] Not Augustine, so far as I can see; cf. Rufinus of Aquileia, *Commentarius in Oseam* 8 (*PL* 21:1000): Gildas, *De excidio Britanniae* 2.7.4 (*PL* 69:355).

170 Quarum una est de uirtutis honestate, alia de uicii uilitate, tercia de supplicii calamitate, qua homo reddit se dignum per uiciorum deformitatem; et quarta de premii felicitate, | ad quam homo pertingit ex uirtutis sinceritate. Ille enim qui considerat ista quattuor aptus est et habilis, ut sit auriga quadrige ueritatis.

175 [4] Sequitur quarta pars picture. Sicut enim ueritas pingitur in quadriga deportata, ita quadriga ueritatis pingitur equis agitata, quorum equorum nomina ponit Ouidius, libro 2º *De tra[n]sformatis,* ubi sic dicit, 'Interea uolucres Pirous, Eous, et Ethon, / solis equi, quartusque + Flegon hynnitibus auras / flamiferis inplent'. Est enim ad memoriam reducendum, sicut eciam patet per Fulgencium in textu, quod poete per Apollinem intelligunt solem, et ideo equi solis sunt equi Apollinis, et e contrario. Unde notandum est quod ex quattuor mediis prius tactis, quibus innititur uirtus ueritatis, concluduntur quattuor \conclusiones/ currum ueritatis agitantes. Et hee quattuor conclusiones sunt quattuor equi positi in quadriga Apollonis.

Primus equus est Pirous, ut dicit Ouidius, et est idem quod 'rubeus ad modum ignis'. Et significat hic equus pudoris ignominiam, que est contrario et sequela, que sequitur ad falsitatis indecenciam. Si enim falsitatis uicium sit indecens et deforme, sequitur quod pudor et ignominia debent hominem racionabiliter a falsitate retrahere. Iste igitur est tractus primi equi [qui] agitat quadrigam ueritatis.

Secundus equs in quadriga ueritatis uocatur Eous, et est idem quod 'lucens et clarus'. Et significat iste equs decoris uenustatem que est contrario, sequens ad ueritatis honestatem. Unde quia uir|tus ista ueritatis habet ingen[it]am uenustatem, sunt enim uirtutes iste de se pulcre et bone. Illud enim, ut dicit Ambrosius in libro *De Ysaac,* 'decorum est pulcrum, est speciosum, est in quo nichil est mali'. Tales sunt uirtutes, secundum Augustinum, cum ille sint de se bone, quibus non con[uen]it male uti, ut probat

---

170 uilitate] inutilitate (inu-*over eras.*) I   172 fol. 103ᵛᵃ   173 pertingit] potest pertingere AI
175 picture] *adds* de equorum deportacione A   177 equorum] *om.* I
   178 *transformatis*] trasformatis O • Interea] In terra I • Eous] Cous I
   179 solis] sol A • (and 213, 223, 258) Flegon] Flegron O • hynnitibus] hec mitibus A, habentibus I   186 quattuor] *om.* AI
189 contrario] questio A   190 sit] *adds* in se A   192 qui] *om.* O
194 ueritatis] Apollinis AI • uocatur] est A   196 contrario] cyculo (?) A
   197 fol. 103ᵛᵇ • ingenitam] ingenuam O   198 uirtutes] ueritates AI
   201 conuenit] contingit O

The first is the virtuousness of truth, the next the vileness of vice, the third the disaster of punishment – a person shows himself deserving of this by the deformity of his vices. The fourth wheel is the happiness of reward, which a person attains through his commitment to virtue. The person who thinks on these four is apt and able to be the charioteer of truth's chariot.

[175] [4] Next comes the fourth part of the picture. For just as truth is depicted borne about in a chariot, that chariot is depicted as moved by horses. Ovid sets down their names in *Metamorphoses* 2, where he says, 'Meanwhile the four swift horses of the sun, Pyrois, Eous, / Æthon, and Phlegon fill the air / with their fiery neighing.'[22] One should recall, just as Fulgentius also says directly, that poets understand through Apollo the sun, and therefore the horses of the sun are Apollo's horses, and vice versa.[23] For this reason, one should notice that through the four means I have already treated – they support the virtue truth –, one can derive four conclusions that drive truth's chariot. These four conclusions are the four horses yoked to Apollo's chariot.

[187] The first horse, as Ovid says, is Pyrois, whose name means 'red like a fire'. This horse indicates the ill-fame that comes from shame, which is the contrary and the conclusion that follows from the indecency of falsehood. For if the vice falsehood is indecent and deformed, it follows that shame and ill-fame ought to restrain a rational person from falsehood. Therefore, this is the impact of the first horse that moves truth's chariot.

[194] The second horse in truth's chariot is called Eous, whose name means 'shining and bright'. And this horse indicates the attractiveness of propriety, which is contrary to falsehood and leads to the virtuous behaviour of truth. For this reason, because the virtue truth has an innate attractiveness, these virtues that succeed it are also beautiful and good in themselves. As Ambrose says in his book *Concerning Isaac*, 'A thing that is fitting and beautiful has nothing evil in itself.'[24] According to Augustine, the virtues are like that, since they are good in themselves, nor is it appropriate that they be used in an evil cause. He proves this

---

[22] *Ibid.* 2.153–55.
[23] Fulg 1.12 (23/11–22) (running on to line 213).
[24] *Ibid.* 7.60 (PL 14:524).

Augustinus in 2º libro *De libero arbitrio*. Ideo sequitur quod honestatis et pulcritudinis decencia debet racionabiliter hominem retrahere ad usum istius uirtutis et cauendum bene [usum] falsitatis,
205 uicium ei oppositum. Iste est tractus et agitacio secundi equi.

Tercius equus in quadriga Apollonis est Ethon, et est idem quod 'ardens'. Et significat hic equus feruoris uehemenciam que est contrario, sequens ad felicitatis excellenciam ad quam perducit uirtus ueritatis. Quia enim uirtus ista finaliter hominem perducit
210 ad ueram felicitatem, ideo concluditur homini quod conformiter et feruenter tenetur agere inclinacioni istius uirtutis. Et iste est tractus tercii equi.

Quartus equs est Flegon quod interpretatur 'torpens uel tepens'. Et iste equs significat moraliter quartam conclusionem
215 que sequitur ex quarto medio cui innititur uirtus ueritatis. Quia enim falsitas, que est uicium oppositum uirtuti ueritatis, meretur supplicii calamitatem, racionabiliter debet [quilibet] homo inclinari ad usum ueritatis exequendum, et sic euadere possit supplicium debitum isti uicio. Et iste est tractus quarti equi. Sed
220 quia, ut probat Augustinus, homo magis debet allici ad bonum uirtutis eo fine, ut sequatur premium felicitatis, quam ut | uitet supplicium finalis calamitatis. Ideo quartus equus in quadriga Apollonis Flegon dicitur a poetis, id est torpedo et pigre trahens.

De istis quattuor conclusionibus trahentibus ad uirtutem
225 ueritatis et retrahentibus a uicio falsitatis, plura loquntur sancti et philosophi et historie gentilium. Unde de prima conclusione, scilicet [de] pudoris ignominia, patet in *Historia orientali*, ubi narratur de quadam gente Indie que habitat ultra locum in quo iacet corpus beati apostoli Thome, et uocatur terra Laceo,
230 quod supra modo omnes homines + de illa gente abhominantur mendacium, et pro nulla re uolunt mentiri, tante ignominie et [tante] pudoris est hoc genus uicii. Similiter de secundo equo et secunda conclusione ueritatis, que con[cerni]t ueritatis claritatem, tangit Crisostomus, *Super Mattheum*, quando dicit quod 'ille

204–5 bene ... oppositum] ad usum falsitatis uiciis apposicioni A, aliunde falsitatis uiciis oppositi I   204 usum] *om.* O
208 contrario] conclusio A
212 quod interpretatur] et significat Flegon I • torpens uel] *om.* AI
215–16 uirtus ... ueritatis] *marg.* I   215 uirtuti ueritatis] ueritati A   217 quilibet homo] quilibet AI, homo O   221 fol. 104ra
224–25 conclusionibus ... plura] *om.* I   227 de] *om.* O   229 Laceo] Lato A, Laeo I   230 homines] *adds* terre illius et O   232 tante] tanti A, *om.* O • uicii] *adds* apud eos A   233 concernit] continet AIO • ueritatis claritatem] ueritatem I

in *On Free Will* 2.[25] Thus, it follows that the decency associated with virtue and beauty ought to restrain rational people to use this virtue and especially to beware using falsehood, the vice that is opposed to it. This is the impact and the motion of the second horse.

[206] The third horse in Truth's chariot is Æthon, whose name means 'burning'. And this horse indicates the intense fervour against what is contrary that leads to truth's outstanding blissfulness. Because this virtue in the end leads one to true blissfulness, one should conclude that a person is required to direct their desire consistently and eagerly to this virtue. This is the impact of the third horse.

[212] The fourth horse is Phlegon, whose name means 'slowness or being luke-warm'. In moral terms, this horse indicates the fourth conclusion that follows from the fourth means supporting the virtue truth. Because falsehood, the vice opposed to the virtue truth, deserves only the disaster of punishment, any rational person ought to bend their path to follow truth's practice, so that they may avoid the punishment appropriate to this vice. And this is the impact of the fourth horse. But, as Augustine proves, a person ought more to be enticed to the good of virtue for that goal alone, so that they may attain the reward of blessedness – rather than that he just avoid the final disaster of punishment. Thus poets call the fourth horse in Apollo's chariot Phlegon, that is slowness and drawing slothfully.

[224] Holy people, philosophers, and pagan history talk a great deal about these four conclusions that draw people to the virtue of truth and that restrain them from the vice of falsehood. For this reason, as regards the first conclusion, the ill-fame that attaches to shame, the *Oriental history* shows that in India, beyond the place where St Thomas's body is buried, in the land called Laceo, a people dwell, all of whom unreservedly despise lying. They won't lie for any reason, because the ill-fame and shame associated with this vice are so great.[26] Similarly, with the second horse and the second conclusion of truth, which concerns truth's brightness: Chrysostom, in *On Matthew*, says that 'The person who

---

[25] *Ibid.* 2.18–19 (PL 32:1267–68), again at line 220.
[26] Marco Polo, *Il milione* 22.

235 clarus, ille nobilis, ille sublimis habendus est qui dedignatur seruire uiciis et ab eis superari'. Talem agitat + equus Eos.

De tercio equo et de tercia conclusione, que est de feruore ueritatis propter premium felicitatis, bene loquitur Anselmus, primo [libro *Cur*] *Deus homo*, capitulo 20, ubi dicit quod 'Tantus 240 debet esse in mortali uita amor et desiderium perueniendi ad gaudium, ad quod factus est homo, et dolor, quod nondum ibi es, et timor, ne non peruenias, ut nullam leticiam sentire debeas, nisi de hiis que tibi aut auxilium aut spem dant'. Illuc perueniendi talem hominem | ita feruentem ad felicitatem quam homo meretur 245 per ueritatem agitat et trahit tercius equs in quadriga Apollonis, scilicet Ethon quod est ardens.

De quarto equo et quarta conclusione, que est de timore supplicii quod homini debetur agenti deformiter [uirtuti] ueritatis, + loquitur Augustinus, *Super canonicam Iohannis*, ubi dicit quod 250 'Timor pene et supplicii locum preparat caritati. Cum autem caritas ceperit habitare, + pellit timor[em], qui ei preparat locum'. Quantum enim caritas crescit, tantum timor pene decrescit; + maior caritas, + minor timor. Ex ista deduccione Augustini, sequitur quod ille qui ex caritate feruenter esse desiderat cum 255 Cristo et eo fine uiuit, conuersando et agendo conformiter ueritati, quod timor pene et Iehenne eo est in ipso remissior, quo eius caritas est intencior. Et ideo timor suplicii, qu[i] est quartus equus trahens quadrigam Apollonis, significanter dicitur a poeta Flegon, id est torpens uel tepens.

260 [5] Quinta pars picture est de dei Apollonis coronacione. Nam sicut patet per Marcianum, libro *De nunpciis*, Apollo, per quem poete intelligunt solem, pingitur gemmis coronatus. Unde Marcianus, describens apparatum Apollonis illo tempore quo uenit ad nupcias fratris sui Mercurii, quando + desponsauit Philologiam, 265 dicit sic: 'Erat illi in circulum ducta fulgens corona que duodecim flammis ignitorum lapidum fulgurabat', et statim Marcianus ponit nomina lapidum. Et conuenit istud bene ueritati, que specialiter pre ceteris uirtutibus meretur coronari. | *Misericordia enim et*

---

236 agitat] *adds* secundus O
238 Anselmus] Augustinus A   239 libro *Cur*] capitulo O   243 Illuc] ad illam A, *om., eras.* I   244 fol. 104rb • ita] *om.* I
248 uirtuti] *om.* O • ueritatis] *adds* de qua conclusione O   251 pellit timorem] pellitur timor O   252 pene] *om.* I   253 maior, minor] maioratur, minoratur O
253–54 Augustini sequitur] *om.* I   257 qui] que O
264 desponsauit] des|sponsauit O   265 illi] ibi A • ducta] dicta A   266 fulgurabat] figurabatur A   268 fol. 104va

disdains to serve vices and to be overcome by them should possess what is bright, noble, and sublime.'[27] The horse Eous impels such an opinion.

[237] Anselm speaks well about the third horse and the third conclusion, the eagerness for truth on account of the reward of blissfulness. In *Why God became man* 1.20, he says that 'One should in this life have a great love and desire for passing to immortal joy, for that is what humans were created for. But one should also have an equally great sorrow because one is not yet there, and as great a fear, lest one not get there, so that one should feel joy only from those things that give one either aid or hope.'[28] The third horse in Apollo's chariot stirs and impels a person eagerly desiring to get to that blissfulness that one merits through truth. This is Æthon, that is 'burning'.

[247] The fourth horse and fourth conclusion concerns the fear of punishment due to a person who deforms the virtue truth in their actions. Augustine talks about this conclusion in *On John's epistle*, where he says that 'Fear of pain and of punishment prepares a place for charity. For when charity has begun to dwell in a person, it drives out fear, which opens a space for itself.'[29] For the more charity grows, the more the fear of punishment shrinks; the greater charity becomes, the smaller fear is. From Augustine's deduction, it follows that someone who, because of charity, eagerly desires to be with Christ and who lives for that end, behaving and working in conformity with truth, that, the more intense their charity is, the more subdued their fear of punishment and of Hell will become. Thus, Ovid significantly calls the fear of punishment, the fourth horse drawing Apollo's chariot, Phlegon, that is 'slowness or being lukewarm'.

[260] [5] The fifth part of the picture concerns the crowning of the god Apollo. For as Martianus's *On the marriage* shows, Apollo, through whom poets understand the sun, is depicted as crowned with jewels. For this reason, Martianus, describing Apollo's equipment when he went to the marriage of his brother Mercury to Philology, says, 'He had a shining crown drawn into a circle; it shone with the flames of twelve fiery stones.' Martianus immediately provides the names of the stones.[30] And all this is appropriate for truth, which particularly deserves to be crowned before all other virtues. As Solomon says (Prv 20:28), *Mercy and truth*

---

[27] Unfound.
[28] *Ibid.* (PL 158:392).
[29] *Epistola* 145.4 (PL 33:594).
[30] Mart 34.7–35.4 (129/1–31/17).

ueritas custodiunt regem, id est regiam coronam et roboratur
270 *clemencia tronus eius*, sicut dicit Salomon. Et per oppositum, ut dicit Ihesus filius Sirac in Ecclesiastico, *Regnum transfertur a gente in gentem propter iniusticias, iniurias, contumelias, et diuersos dolos.*

Et de isto nota bene Aristoteles ad Alexandrum, in epistola, capitulo 19, ubi dat causam destruccionis duorum regnorum, scilicet
275 Sitharum et Eubaliorum. Et causam dicit fuisse ui[o]lacionem istius uirtutis, scilicet ueritatis. Unde uerba Aristotelis sunt hec, 'Serua fideliter, o Alexander, promissa[m] fidem, quoniam omnem infidelem consequitur finis malus'. Et sequitur, 'Siquidem si quereres que fuit causa destruccionis duorum regnorum predictorum,
280 responderem tibi quod reges eorum utebantur iuramentis ad fraudem et decepcionem aliorum hominum et proximarum ciuitatum, et ideo equitas iusti iudicis non potuit eos amplius sustinere'. Quia igitur uirtus ueritatis custodit statum regie dignitatis. Ideo Apollo pingitur a poetis gemmis coronatus.

285 [6] Sequitur sexta pars picture de dei Apollonis inscripcione. Docet enim Fulgencius in littera quod iste Apollo apud poetas habet diuersa nomina, quorum aliqua ipse tangit et aliqua tanguntur ab aliis [auc]toribus. Uocatur enim Delius et Phicius et Phebus et Sol et Apollo et Licius; istorum nominum litteris fuit
290 ymago dei Apollonis exarata. Et conueniunt ista nomina uirtuti ueritatis, nam ex hiis nominibus ostenditur ueritatis efficacia, ueritatis | innocencia, ueritatis excellencia, ueritatis complacencia, ueritatis innotescencia, ueritatis displicencia.

Apollo enim, ut patet per Fulgencium sicut prius eciam
295 fuit tactum, interpretatur 'exterminans'. Et significat ueritatis potestatem efficacem. Nam ut dicit Ieronimus in suo commentario super Ieremiam, 'Ueritas uinci non potest, nec multitudine hostium terreri potest'. Ydeo sicut Seneca pulcre deducit in quadam epistola, 'Ui[s] ueritatis semper est magna, que contra omnia falsitatis
300 ingenia, calliditatem, solerciam, fictas hominum falsorum insidias per seipsam faciliter se defendit'. Hoc pro nomine Apollonis.

272 in ... iniusticias] *marg.* I • contumelias] *om.* I
274 dat] dicit A   275 causam] *adds* destruccionis A • uiolacionem] ui|lacionem O
277 promissam] promissa O • omnem] *om.* A, enim I   281 decepcionem] destruccionem I
288 auctoribus] doctoribus O • Delius] dolens A   289 Phebus] Plobus A
290 dei Apollonis] *om.* I   292 fol. 104vb 292–93 ueritatis^1 ... innotescencia] *om.* A   293 innotescencia] innocencia I
294–95 sicut ... tactum] *om.* A   299 Uis] Uie O   300 fictas] *om.* A, fucasque I
301 faciliter] finaliter A

preserve the king, and his throne is strengthened by clemency. And in opposition, Jesus son of Sirach says (Sir 10:8), *A kingdom is translated from one people to another because of injustices and wrongs and injuries and diverse deceits.*

[273] On this point, notice ch. 19 in Aristotle's letter to Alexander, where he gives the reason for the destruction of two kingdoms, those of the Scythians and the Eubalians. And he says that the cause was their transgression against the virtue truth. For this reason, his words are, 'Preserve faithfully, Alexander, the faith you have sworn, for a bad end follows every act of infidelity.' And he continues, 'If indeed you should ask what the cause of the destruction of those two kingdoms was, I would answer that their kings used oaths in order to defraud and deceive other people and neighbouring cities, and therefore the impartiality expected of a just judge might not sustain them any longer.'[31] Therefore the virtue truth preserves the state of royal dignity, and the poets thus portray Apollo as crowned with jewels.

[285] [6] Next comes the sixth part of the picture; it concerns the writing associated with the god Apollo. For Fulgentius teaches explicitly that among the poets Apollo has various names, ones which either Fulgentius or other learned men treat.[32] For he is called Delius, Pythius, Phebus, Sol, Apollo, and Licius. The letters of these names are written on the image of the god Apollo. These names are appropriate for the virtue truth, for the names show truth's active power, its innocence, its excellence, its pleasingness, its unfamiliarity, and its displeasure.

[294] For Apollo, as the passage from Fulgentius mentioned above shows, means 'destroying'. This name indicates the active power of truth. For as Jerome says in his commentary on Jeremiah, 'Truth cannot be conquered, nor can it be frightened by the great number of its enemies.'[33] Therefore, as Seneca elegantly puts it in one of his letters, 'Truth's strength is always great, for it easily defends itself through its own being against all falsehood's clever ideas, against cleverness, contrivance, people's deceits, and false peoples' onslaughts of lies.'[34] This explains the name Apollo.

---

[31] *Ibid.* 22 (p. 48).
[32] Fulg 1.14 (23/4–11); cf. Mart 15.7 (95/3–9); VM3 8.1 and 3 (200/2–22, 201/22–27).
[33] *Ibid.* 5, on Ier 24 (*PL* 24:830).
[34] Actually Cicero, *Pro Caelio* 63 [= *MF* veritas ad, ascribed to 'Seneca in epistola'].

Similiter uocatur iste deus Delius, a declaracione. Idem est enim Delius [quod 'declarator', et significat ueritatis innocencia que] omnia declarat et nichil occultat per calliditatis fraudulenciam. Et de hoc pulcre Ieronimus in quadam epistola ad Rusticum monachum: 'Ueritas', dicit Ieronimus, 'non [h]abet angulos neque querit susurriones'. Ydeo sicut dicit Bernardus in quodam sermone, 'Ueritas non amat angulos, nec ei placent diuersoria. In medio stat; communi uita, communi disciplina, communibus studiis delectatur'.

Tercium nomen Apollonis est Sol, quasi 'solus lucens' uel 'solus existens', sicut in littera tangit Fulgencius. Et conuenit hoc nomen uirtute ueritatis propter istius uirtutis excellenciam. 'Hec enim est ueritas que', secundum Bernardum in quodam sermone, 'sola saluat, sola liberat, et sola lauat'. Et ideo ueritas dicitur Sol, id est 'solus lucens' triplici radio, scilicet securitat[is], sinceritat[is], et libertat[is]. Et de hiis tractant Ambrosius et Seneca in suis epistolis. S[imilit]er ueritas dicitur Sol, quasi 'solus existens', nam sicut pulcre | deducit Augustinus, *Confessionum*, 'Omnia in quantum sunt uer[a], sunt, nec quicquam est falsitas, nisi cum putatur aliud esse cum nichil sit'.

Quartum nomen Apollonis est Phebus, et est idem quod 'nouus', \et significat ueritatis complacencia[m. Noua enim placent], sicut enim pulcre tangit Plinius/ in *Historia naturali*, libro 12, ubi dicit quod natura hominis est auida nouitatis. 'Arabia enim peregrinos mirre odores ab exter[n]is petit; tanta enim mortalibus suarum rerum est sacietas alienarumque auiditas'. Et isto modo est de ueritate, quia sicut [osten]dit Augustinus, 10 *Confessionum*, 'Omnes homines amant ueritatem lucentem, licet eam odiunt redarguentem'.

Quintum nomen Apollonis est Phicius, id est 'diuinator'. Unde, sicut tangit Alexander, Phicius descendit a uerbo Greco *phicio*, quod est idem in Latino quod 'interrogo'. Et bene conuenit ueritati, que ideo poetice fingitur d[iui]natrix. Quia ut dicit

302 declaracione] declinacione A   303 Delius] deliciis I • quod declarator] quod declinari A, a declaracione O   303-4 et … que] quia O   306 monachum] *om*. AI, *adds* Ut credo I   306-7 habet … querit] *trs. verbs* O
311 Tercium nomen] *om*. A   315 lauat] sanat A   316 securitatis (etc.)] securitate (etc.) O   318 Similiter] Semper O   319 fol. 105ra • deducit] dicit A   320 uera] uere O   321 cum] quod A, quam I
323-24 -ciam … placent] *cut away by binder* O   326 mirre] inire A • externis] ex terris O   327 sacietas] societas A   328 ostendit] dicit O   329 amant] habent A
333 *phicio*] phito A, phicon I   334 diuinatrix] dn̄at^{i}x (= ? dominatrix) O

[302] Similarly this god is called Delius, from his revelations. For Delius and *declarator* 'someone who reveals truths' mean the same thing, and the title indicates truth's innocence. For truth reveals all things and hides nothing through clever fraud. Jerome says this neatly in a letter to Rusticus the monk, 'Truth has no hidey-holes, nor does it seek to whisper.' As Bernard says in a sermon, 'Truth does not love hidey-holes, nor do kids' games please it. It stands forth openly, in the middle of things, and it is delighted by communal life, communal discipline, and communal studies.'[35]

[311] Apollo's third name is Sol 'the sun', as if he were 'shining alone' or 'existing alone', as Fulgentius says explicitly. This name is appropriate for the virtue truth on account of its excellence. Bernard says in a sermon, 'It is truth that alone saves, alone frees, and alone cleanses.'[36] Therefore, truth is called Sol, that is 'shining alone', because of its triple beam, that is for its security, its sincerity, and its freedom. Both Ambrose and Seneca discuss these things in their letters.[37] Similarly, truth is called Sol 'sun', as it were 'existing alone', just as Augustine argues nicely in the *Confessions*, 'All things, insofar as they are true, exist, and falsehood is nothing at all, unless something is thought to exist, while it is nevertheless only nothing.'[38]

[322] Apollo's fourth name is Phoebus, and it means the same as 'novelty' and indicates the pleasantness of truth. For new things are always pleasing, for as Pliny says in *Natural history* 12, it is human nature to be eager for novelty. 'People are so thoroughly sated with their own things and so eager for foreign ones that Arabia, with its scents of myrrh, draws travellers from far away.'[39] This eagerness for foreign things also refers to truth, for as Augustine shows in *Confessions* 10, 'Everyone loves shining truth, although they hate it when it rebukes them.'[40]

[331] Apollo's fifth name is Pythius 'prophet'. For this reason, as Alexander Neckam says, Pythius is a derivative of the Greek word *phicio*, which is 'I inquire' in Latin.[41] And this is appropriate for truth, which the poets therefore present as a seeress. For this reason,

---

[35] *Epistola* 125.19 (PL 22:1084); *Sermo in Ascensione Domini* 5.13 (PL 183:321).
[36] *Dominica prima post octavum Epiphaniae sermo* 2.6 (PL 183:161).
[37] Cf. *Hexameron* 4.1–3 (PL 14:187–91 passim); *Epistulae* 41.5 or 66.20.
[38] *Ibid.* 7.15 (PL 32:744).
[39] Unfound.
[40] *Ibid.* 10.23 (PL 32:794).
[41] VM3 8.1 (200/6–9; at line 341, 200/15–19).

335 Ambrosius in commentariis super epistolas Pauli, 'Omne uerum a quocunque dicatur a Spiritu Sancto est'. Et Augustinus, libro *Confessionum*, 'Si ambo uidemus uerum es[se] quod tu dicis, et ambo uidemus uerum es[se] quod ego dico, ubi, queso, illud uidemus? Nec ego utique in te, nec tu in me, sed ambo in ipsa que
340 supra mentes nostras est, incommutabili ueritate'.

Sextum nomen Apollonis est Licius et est idem quod 'lupus'. Et conuenit uirtuti ueritatis, que amare mordet et displicenter ad modum lupi. Unde Ieronimus, in suo dialogo quem edidit inter Atticum et [Crit]obolum, dicit loquens de ueritate, 'Ueritas amara
345 et rugose frontis, et tristis est; offenditque correptos, dicente apostolo ad Galatas, *Factus sum inimicus uobis ueritatem dicens?*'. Et ideo bene dicit Augustinus in quadam epistola | quod 'Ueritas habet dulcedinem et amaritudinem; dulcis est in parcendo, amara in castigando et corripiendo'.

350 [7] Sequitur septima pars picture de dei Appollonis ministracione. Nam poete fingunt Musas ministerio Apollonis deputatas, sicut in parte tangit Fulgencius in littera et Remigius in suo commento super librum *De nupciis*. Et bene conuenit uirtute ueritatis, nam sicut docet Remigius, et ad illud idem
355 Fulgencius in littera allegat Anaximandrum Lapsacenum, et Zenophanem et Pisandrum et alios auctores antiquos, dicentes quod nouem requiruntur ad formacionem humane uocis. Omnis enim sermo hominis ab hiis nouem + formatur rebus: a pulsu quattuor dencium, percussione duorum labiorum, plectro lingue,
360 concauitate gutturis, et adiutorio pulmonis. Iste sunt nouem Muse que seruiunt uirtuti ueritatis.

Sermo enim et loquela hominis indicium est huius uirtutis, sicut pulcre tractat Hugo in libro suo *De anima*. 'Uanus', inquit, 'sermo uane consciencie iudex est et sermo uerus consciencie
365 ueritatis. Mores enim hominis lingua pandit, et qualis sermo ostenditur, talis animus comprobatur'. Cui concordat [Seneca], dicens quod 'ymago animi sermo est; qualis enim est homo, talis est eius oracio'. Et ideo significanter poete fingunt

337, 338 esse] est O   338 uidemus²] *om.* I
342 displicenter] displicent I   344 Critobolum] Tricobolum O   345 et¹] est AI
    347 fol. 105ʳᵇ
352–53 sicut ... nupciis] *om.* A   355–56 allegat ... dicentes] *om.* A   358 formatur] formabitur O   360 adiutorio] agitacione A
366 Seneca] *om.* I, *blank* O   368 oracio] sermo A

Ambrose in his commentaries on Paul's epistles says, 'Every true thing, wherever it may come from, may be said to come from the Holy Ghost.'[42] And Augustine in his *Confessions*, 'If we both see that what you say is true, and if we both see that what I say is true, where, I ask, do we see this? For I neither see it in you, nor you in me, but we both see it in what is above both our minds, in unchanging truth.'[43]

[341] Apollo's sixth name is Licius, and it means the same as 'wolf'. And this name is appropriate for the virtue truth, because it bites sharply and unpleasantly like a wolf. For this reason, Jerome, speaking about truth in the dialogue he wrote between Atticus and Critobolus says, 'Truth is sour and sad, and has a wrinkled brow, and it puts off those whom it chastises, as Paul says to the Galatians (4:16), *Am I then become your enemy because I tell you the truth?*' And Augustine writes well in a letter that 'Truth is both sweet and sour – sweet when it spares, and sour when it chastises and corrects.'[44]

[350] [7] Next comes the seventh part of the picture, concerning Apollo's servants. For poets depict the Muses as assigned to serve Apollo, as Fulgentius explains explicitly in part, and Remigius in his commentary on *On the Marriage*. And this is appropriate for the virtue truth, as Remigius teaches.[45] On this point, Fulgentius cites directly Anaximander Lapsacenus, Zenophanes, Pisander, and other ancient authorities who all say that nine things are necessary to produce the human voice. Every human utterance is produced by these nine things: the striking of four teeth, that of the two lips, the tongue (like a musician's pick), the hollowness of the throat, and the aid of the lung. These are the nine Muses who serve the virtue truth.

[362] For human statements and speech are a sign of this virtue, as Hugh of St Victor explains eloquently in *On the soul*, 'Inane speech shows a conscience devoid of truth, and true speech a true conscience. For the tongue reveals a person's moral behaviour, and whatever speech reveals confirms that the mind is similar.'[46] Seneca agrees with Hugh, when he says, 'Speech provides an image of the mind; whatever kind of person they are, their speech is similar.'[47] Therefore, it is significant that the poets portray

---

[42] *In Psalmum David cxviii expositio* 18.36 (PL 15:1465).

[43] *Ibid.* 12.25 (PL 32:840).

[44] Jerome, *Dialogus adversus Pelagianos* 1.26 (PL 23:520); cf. Augustine, *Epistola* 53.3 (PL 33:199).

[45] Fulg (extensively, running to line 414) 1.15 (25/2–27/11); Mart 19.11 (101/27–102/14).

[46] Actually ps.-Bernard, *De modo bene vivendi* 30 (PL 184:1254–55) [= MF loquacitas t, ascribed *De anima* 2].

[47] Actually ps.-Seneca (ps.-Martin of Braga), *De moribus* 72–73 [= MF loquacitas ag, ascribed 'Seneca in proverbiis'].

Musas in ministerium Apollonis deputatas, nam sermo uerus et uirtuosus legatus est et nuncius uere et uirtuose conuersacionis; et per oppositum, uita et conuersacio uiciosa ante se premittunt in legacionem uanam et | uiciosam locucionem, dicente Crysostomus, *Super Mattheum*, omelia 42ª, 'Cum audieritis hominem perniciosa loquentem, ne estimes ei tantam solam [in]esse nequiciam quanta uerba demonstrant? Ydeo multo ampliorem interius cogn[osc]ite esse fontem, quod enim exterius dicitur esse superfluum eius est quod interius reconditur'.

Nota tamen in littera quomodo Fulgencius tangit suam propriam exposicionem de significacione istarum nouem Musarum. Uult enim Fulgencius per istas nouem Musas [sunt intelligenda nouem que requiruntur ad quamcunque scienciam. Unde dicit sic, 'Nos dicimus nouem Musas] nouem esse modos doctrine atque sciencie adquirende. In adquirendis enim scienciis requiritur primo studii diligencia, et istud significatur per primam Musam que dicitur Clio. Nam Clio interpretatur 'cogitacio'. Secundo, ad scienciam requiritur delectacionis complacencia, et hoc significatur per secundam Musam que dicitur Eutrope, id est 'bene delectans'. Tercio, ad scienciam requiritur meditacionis instancia, ut perseueret in studio, et hoc significatur per terciam Musam Melpomone, que interpretatur 'meditacionem faciens'. Quarto, requiritur ad scienciam concepcio et rei intelligencia, et hoc significatur per quartam Musam, scilicet Talian, que interpretatur 'capacitas'.

Quinto, requiritur ad scienciam memorie tenacitas, et hoc significatur per Musam quintam, scilicet Pollim[ni]a, que interpretatur 'memoria multa faciens'. Sexto, ad scienciam requiritur aduencionis subtilitas, que significatur per sextam Musam que dicitur Eratho, qu[e] interpretatur 'inueniens similem'. Ut enim dicit Fulgencius, post intelligenciam et memoriam, iustum est quod homo aliud simile de suo inueniat. Septimo, requiritur ad scienciam discussio + et | deliberacio de inuentis, et hoc significatur per septimam Musam

369 Appolinis] hominis A   372 fol. 105ᵛᵃ   374 inesse] esse O   375 cognoscite] cognite (?) AO
378 quomodo] qualiter AI   380–82 sunt … Musas] *om*. O   384 adquirende] *om*. AI   385 cogitacio] intelligencia A, *over eras*. I   387 Eutrope] Tentrepe A, *over eras*. I   389–90 ut … faciens] *marg*. I   389 studio] studii diligencia A
395 Pollimnia] P\e/limia A, Pollimia I, Pollima O   398 Eratho] Motio A • que²] quod O   399–400 Ut … inueniat] *om*. A   400 homo] *om*. I   401 discussio] *adds* seu discretio O • fol. 105ᵛᵇ

the Muses as assigned to serve Apollo, for true and virtuous speech is the ambassador and messenger of true and virtuous behaviour. By contrast, a vice-driven life and behaviour send out ahead of themselves, as if an embassy, vacuous and vicious speech. Chrysostom, *On Matthew*, homily 42, says: 'When you have heard a person speaking evil things, should you ascribe to him only that evil behaviour that his words display? Rather, recognise that there is within him an even greater fountain, so that what he says externally is just the overflow from what's hidden within.'[48]

[378] However, notice how Fulgentius offers explicitly his own explanation of the meaning of the nine Muses. For he wants the nine Muses to be understood as nine things that are required for any science. For this reason, he says, 'I argue that the nine Muses are nine ways of gaining any learning or science. In this process, one first requires diligent study, and this is identified with the first Muse, Clio, whose name means 'thought'. The next step in gaining knowledge requires pleasure in delight, identified with the second Muse, Eutrope 'delighting well'. Third, gaining knowledge requires promptness in meditation, so that one perseveres in study, and this is identified with the third Muse Melpomone 'producing meditation'. Fourth, one needs an idea and a knowledge of the thing itself, identified with the fourth Muse, Thalia, whose name means 'ability'.

[394] Fifth, knowledge requires a firm memory, identified with the fifth Muse, Polymnia, whose name means 'a memory producing many things'. Sixth, one needs subtlety in drawing things together, identified with the sixth Muse, Erato 'discovering likenesses'. As Fulgentius also says, after intellect and memory, it is appropriate that a person discovers something that is like himself. Seventh, one needs discrimination and assessment of the things one has discovered, identified with the seventh Muse,

---

[48] *Opus imperfectum* 43 (PG 56:378) [= *MF* ipocrisis an].

que uocatur Tresphecope, que interpretatur 'diiudicans instruccionem'. Ut enim dicit Fulgencius, post inuencionem
405 oportet discernere et diiudicare quid inueneris; igitur ad scienciam requiritur eleccio, ut scilicet post discussionem et deliberacionem de fugiendo uel de persequendo; de uero et de falso eligat quod eligendum est et dimittat quod est respuendum. Et istud significatur per octauam Musam, scilicet Uraniam, que
410 interpretatur 'celestis'. Ut enim dicit Fulgencius, [e]ligere utile et caducum respuere celeste ingenium est. Nonus, ad scienciam requiritur debita pronunciacio et scitorum conueniens expressio, et hoc significatur per nonam Musam que uocatur Kaliope, quod interpretatur 'optime uocis'.

415 [8] Sequitur octaua pars picture de dei Apollonis situacione. Nam ut fingunt poete, Apollo iste in lauro locatur, quia l[ectu]s dei Apollonis est laurus. Et de hoc tangit Fulgencius in littera, dans racionem quare laurus arbor deputatur a poetis in tutelam Apollonis. Et allegat [antiquos] auctores, uidelicet Amphionem
420 et Sarapionem Asco[l]onitam et Philetum et Arionem, qui in scriptis reliquerunt, quod [ad] capit[a] hominum [d]ormiencium tum apposita fuerat arbor laurus, tales in dormiendo sompniabunt uer[a] sompnia et non fantastica neque falsa. Et ideo quia Apollo est deus ueritatis, ideo Apolloni fuit consecrata laurus.

425 Et nota quomodo ad literam istud applicant philosophi ad uirtutem istam, scilicet | ad ueritatem. Nam qualis est hominis uita, talia sunt et eius sompnia, ut enim Auicenna deducit, 6° *Naturalium*, parte 5ª: 'Uerax homo habet, ut communiter, uera sompnia; pudicus pudica, et flagiciosus flagiciosa'. Et ideo
430 Aristoteles in fine primi *Ethicorum* bene reprobat quorundam opinionem dicencium quod mali homines non differunt a bonis, nisi secundum medietatem uite, hoc est tempore uigilie, et non quoad tempus dormicionis. Contra quam opinionem [se] opponit Aristoteles, probans eam esse falsam; nam fantasmata bonorum

---

403 Tresphecope] Tersicore, *expunged from* Terrisicore A, Tersecore I
410 eligere] coligere O   411 respuere] despicere A   412 conueniens] communis A   412-14 et ... uocis] *om.* I
416 lectus] locus O   419 antiquos] *om.* O   419-21 uidelicet ... reliquerunt] *om.* A   420 Ascolonitam] Ascobonicam I, Ascobo|nitam O   421 ad capita] si capitibus O • dormiencium] *a corr.* A, euncium dormitum IO   422 fuerat] sit A, fuerit I • dormiendo] sompniando I   423 uera] uere O   424 consecrata] *adds* arbor A
425 nota] *om.* A (*at page-boundary*), *possibly* non O   426 fol. 106ʳᵃ   430 in fine] *om.* A   431 bonis] *adds* hominibus A   433 quoad] primo ad A • se] *om.* O

Terpsichore, whose name means 'deliberating upon instruction'. For Fulgentius says that after discovery, one must discriminate and judge what one has found; thus knowledge requires choice, so that one knows after discrimination and thought what one should flee and what pursue. Between the true and the false, one should choose what is to be preferred and cast aside what is to be rejected. This process is identified with the eighth Muse, Urania 'heavenly'. For Fulgentius says that to choose what is useful and reject what is fleeting requires a heavenly intellect. Ninth, knowledge requires a proper pronunciation and appropriate expression of the things one has learned, and this is identified with the ninth Muse, Calliope, whose name means 'having the best voice'.

[415] [8] Next comes the eighth part of the picture; it concerns the location of the god Apollo. As the poets represent it, Apollo is placed in a laurel-tree, for the laurel is the god Apollo's bed. Fulgentius discusses the point explicitly, giving the reason why the poets assign the laurel as Apollo's guardian.[49] And he cites ancient authors – Amphion, Serapion of Ascalon, Philetus, and Arion – who said in the writings they have left, that if a sprig of laurel were placed next to the heads of sleeping people, while asleep, they will dream true dreams, ones neither fantastic nor false. And since Apollo is the god of truth, the laurel was sacred to him.

[425] And notice how philosophers apply this account to the virtue truth in a literal way. For a person's dreams are just like their way of life, as Avicenna proves in his *Natural things* 6.5: 'A true person most frequently has true dreams, and a modest person modest ones, but a criminal criminal dreams.'[50] Thus, at the end of his *Ethics* 1, Aristotle properly rejects the opinion of some who say that bad people are no different from good ones, except according to half their lives, that is during their waking hours, and not with regard to the time when they sleep. Aristotle opposes this opinion and proves that it is false, for the fantasies of good

---

[49] Fulg 1.14 (24/11–19).
[50] Unfound.

435 hominum et iustorum sunt meliora quam sunt fantasmata malorum. Ideo concludit Aristoteles quod uita iusti \differt/ a uita hominis uiciosi, non solum uigilando, sed eciam dormiendo. Et hec est racio secundum fincionem poeticam quare deus Apollo reclinatur in lauro.

440 [9] Nona pars picture est de dei Apollonis occupacione. Nam secundum fincionem poeticam, coruus + traditus est Apolloni in tutelam, sicut dicit Fulgencius in littera. Et istud conuenit bene uirtuti ueritatis. Unde dicit Augustinus super psalmum, 'Coruus rore celi pascitur et nutritur quando primitus propagatur', et
445 eodem modo ueritas, quando primo in homine generatur, a Deo celitus inspiratur. Sicut patet per Ambrosium, cuius auctoritas fuit tacta quando agebatur de \quinto/ nomine Appollonis. Et hec est fides nostra, scilicet quod in baptismo funduntur uirtutes in baptizatis, sicut exempla de summa Trinitate et fide | catholica,
450 libro 7 *Fidei catholice fundamento*. Unde notandum quod sicut coruus quamdiu in colore albus est, tamdiu reficitur rore celi, quia pro tempore sue albedinis, parentes corui renuunt eum pascere, sicut docet Augustinus. Ita tempore quo sumus dealbati, id est in sacramento baptismi iniciati et mundati, et ueste candita
455 [amic]ti, Deus nobis infundit graciam, uirtutem ueritatis. Sole enim uirtutes que a Deo sunt infuse sunt uirtutes uere. Alie autem uirtutes humanitatus adquisite non sunt dicende uirtutes uere, sed pocius [esse] uirtutis ymagines atque umbre, sicut de hoc loquitur [diffuse] Augustinus in suis libris *Contra Iulianum*, et *De ciuitate*
460 *Dei*, libro 29°, et in aliis multis locis.

Nota tamen quomodo Fulgentius tangit in litera sua unam causam propter quam coruus datur Apolloni in tutelam. Et allegat quendam uocatum Pindarum, et est ista causa, nam, sicut dicit, solus inter omnes aues, coruus habet 64 significaciones
465 uocum. Et conuenit ista suspicacio numerorum uirtuti ueritatis. Consurgit enim hic numerus \ex/ senario, ex denario, et ex quaternario. Dicit Bernardus in suo tractatu *De gradibus humilitatis* quod triplex est esse ueritatis, inqueritur enim,

---

436 malorum] *adds* hominum A
441 traditus] tradiditus O   446–47 Sicut … Appollinis] *om.* A   449 exempla] patet A • fol. 106rb   451 reficitur … celi] eum reficit ros celestis AI   452 corui] sui A   453 quo] *corr. from* quos (?) I   455 amicti] induti O • graciam] *om.* AI   456–57 uere … uere] uere A   458 esse uirtutis] uirtutum A, uere uirtutis O   459 diffuse] *om.* O   460 et² … locis] *om.* A
462–63 Et … Pindarum] *om.* A   464 habet 64 significaciones] 64 I   465 suspicacio] suppictacio A   467 Bernardus] H' A   468 inqueritur] inuenitur A

and righteous people are better than those of evil ones. Thus, Aristotle concludes that the life of a righteous person differs from that of a vicious one, not just when they are awake but when they sleep as well.[51] And this is why poetic fictions show Apollo lying down by a laurel-tree.

[440] [9] The ninth part of the picture concerns Apollo's work. For according to the poets' fiction, the crow was given to Apollo as a guardian, as Fulgentius states plainly.[52] This is appropriate for the virtue truth. For Augustine, discussing a verse from the Psalms, says, 'When it is first born, the crow is fed and nourished with the dew of heaven' (cf. Ps 146:9);[53] in the same way, truth, when it first springs up in a person, is inspired by God from heaven. Ambrose also shows this; I cited his statement above when I treated Apollo's fifth name. This heavenly knowledge is our faith, because in baptism, virtues are poured into those baptised, as shaping models for the highest Trinity and catholic faith, *On the foundation of the catholic faith* 7.[54] For this reason, one should notice that just so long as a crow remains white, it is fed with the dew of heaven, because, as Augustine teaches, during the whole time it is white, the crow's parents refuse to feed it. Likewise at the time when we are made white, that is initiated and cleansed in the sacrament of baptism, and dressed in a white garment, God pours his grace, the virtue truth, into us. For only those virtues that God has infused are truly virtues. Other virtues, acquired from a human source, should not be called true virtues, but rather images or shadows of true virtue. Augustine speaks of this at length in his books *Against Julian* and *On the city of God* 29, and in many other places.[55]

[461] Nevertheless notice how Fulgentius treats explicitly one reason why the crow is given to Apollo as a guardian. He cites someone called Pindar, whom he says alleges that uniquely among all the birds, the crow's voice has sixty-four different meanings. This suggestion of a number is appropriate for the virtue truth, for the number sixty-four is built up out of a combination of six, ten, and four. Bernard says in his treatise *On the steps of humility* that because truth ought to be treble, it should therefore

---

[51] *Nicomachean ethics* 1.13 (1102b).
[52] Fulg 1.13 (24/2–9).
[53] *Breviarium in Psalmos* CXLVI (PL 26:1256).
[54] Cf. Fulgentius of Ruspe, *Fidei catholicae instrumenta* 9, frag. 34 (PL 65:818–19).
[55] E.g., *De civitate Dei* 5.18 (PL 41:165).

ut dicit Bernardus, in Sui natura et in nobistipsis et in proximis nostris. Si enim ueraciter diiuidicamus nosmetipsos et facta propria, tunc inquirimus et quesitam inuenimus ueritatem in nobistipsis. Similiter ueraciter conpaciendo proximis nostris et eorum malis et infortuniis, inquirimus ueritatem in proximis, sed per mundacionem cordis perducimur ad contemplacionem ueritatis | in sui natura. Istum triplicem modum essendi ueritatis significat iste triplex numerus, scilicet senarius, denarius, et quaternarius. Nam sex sunt opera misericordie que exercere debemus circa proximum, sicut patet ex euangelio Matthei, et continentur in his uersubus, 'Uestio, cibo, poto, etc.'. Ideo ille senarius numerus correspondet ueritati quam + inquirere debemus in proximis.

Sed decem sunt precepta decalogi, ad quorum obseruanciam omnes sumus obligati. Et ille denarius numerus correspondet ueritati quam inquirere debemus in nobistipsis. Sed quattuor sunt affecciones nobis connaturales, que ex \nature/ [nostre] corumpcione, ad excessum sunt inclinate. Et ideo ad hoc quod [u]aleat ueritatem aliquis nostrum clare contemplari [seu cernere], oportet quod ille quattuor affecciones ordinentur et em[u]ndentur. Unde iste quaternarius numerus correspondet illi ueritati quam conspicimus in sui natura, postquam corde fuerimus em[u]ndati, secundum sentenciam Bernardi. Et pro isto satis ad propositum loquitur Boycius, libro primo *De consolacione*, metro ultimo, sic inquiens:

Tu quoque si uis / lumine claro / cernere uerum, / tramite recto / carpere callem: / gaudia pelle, / pelle timorem / spemque fugato / nec dolor assit. / Nubila mens est / uinctaque frenis / hec ubi regnant.

Propter istam differenciam numerorum, quam Fulgencius attribuit, secundum opinionem antiquorum, coruo et eius uociferacioni, uolebant ist[i] poete dicere quod coruus erat auis deputata deo Apolloni, sub cuius ymagine intendebant depingere uirtutem ueritatis. Et sic finitur septima mithologia Fulgencii.

---

469 ut dicit] ueritas secundum A   470 propria] nostra A   474 fol. 106va
476 quaternarius] quater|nam I   477 circa] *adds* ueram A   478–79 sicut … numerus] *om.* I • et … etc.] *om.* A   480 quam] *adds* incurrere| O
484 nostre] *om.* O   486 ualeat ueritatem] *after* contemplare O • seu cernere] *om.* O
487 emundentur, 489 emundati] e|mendentur, emen|dati O   488 quaternarius numerus] quaternus numerus A, quaternarius I   490–91 pro … loquitur] *om.* A
494 pelle pelle] pelle A   499 isti] iste O   500 depingere] describere AI
501 Et … Fulgencii] de que in littera loquitur (*corr. to* loquuntur) Fulgentius \et Ouidius de transformatis libro 2°/ A (*displaced from* 8/2–3), *om.* I

be sought in God's nature and in ourselves and in our neighbours. If we truly judge ourselves from our actions, then we seek and we discover the truth we have sought in ourselves. Similarly, we seek the truth in our neighbours, when we truly sympathise with them in their bad times and their misfortunes; but only through the cleansing of our heart are we led to contemplation of truth in its own nature.[56] This triple manner of being indicates truth's triple number, that is six, ten, and four. For there are six works of mercy that we are held to perform for our neighbour, as Mt 25:35–36 shows; these are contained in the verses, 'I clothe, I feed, I give drink … .'[57] Thus, the number six corresponds to the truth that we should seek in our neighbours.

[481] But there are ten commandments in the Decalogue that we are all obligated to observe. This number ten corresponds to the truth that we should seek in ourselves. But we also have four inbred affects or emotions; because of our natural corruption, these are inclined to excess. Therefore, in order that we may have the true power to contemplate and know God clearly, it is necessary that these four affects be regulated and purified. Thus, this number four corresponds to that truth that we gaze upon in its own nature, having first cleansed our heart, according to Bernard's dictum. And for the present purpose, it is sufficient to give what Boethius says, *On the consolation*, the final metre in book 1:

> Therefore you, if you wish / to know truth / with a clear sight / and to seize the way / in a direct path, / drive away both / joy and fear, / flee hope and / deny a place to sorrow. / Where these rule, / the mind is clouded, / conquered and in chains.[58]

Fulgentius, following the opinion of the ancients, attributes this distinction of numbers to the crow and to the sounds it makes. For this reason, poets wish to say that the crow was the bird assigned to the god Apollo, in whose image they intended to depict the virtue truth. This is the end of Fulgentius's seventh mythology.

---

[56] *Ibid*. 3.6ff. (*PL* 182:344), paraphrased.
[57] Not in Walther.
[58] *Ibid*. 1m7.20–31.

[8]

| Sequitur octaua mithologia Fulgencii de Phetonte, filio Apollonis, de quo in littera loquitur Fulgencius. Et poeta Ouidius hoc tractat magis diffuse, libro 2° *De transformatis*. Siquidem iste Pheton depingitur +, ut recitat Ouidius,

5
      [1] sole generatus,
      [2] curis inflammatus,
      [3] statu sublimatus,
      [4] in curru locatus,
      [5] litteris aratus,
10
      [6] loris occupatus,
      [7] mole minoratus,
      [8] timore turbatus,
      [9] honore priuatus,
      [10] morti condempnatus,
15
      [11] uersubus \ornatus/,
      [12] et fletu rigatus.

Iste sunt duodecim partes picture, quibus Ouidius et alii poete solent uicium ambicionis depingere sub ymagine Phetontis.

    [1] Unde primo, iste Pheton filius solis [f]ingitur; ut patet per
20 Fulgencium, per Apollinem enim poete consueuerunt intelligere solem. Et ille Pheton, quem Fulgencius dicit in littera filium esse Apollonis, Ouidius filium solis uocat. Unde dicit Ouidius, metrice narrans qualiter Pheton intrauit aulam solis et palacium, et quomodo sol, uidens Phetontem, alloquebatur eum, recognouit
25 eum filium suum; dicit sic, 'Sol oculis iuuenem, quibus aspicit omnia, uidet; / Que "que uie causa quid et hac" ait "ar[c]e petisti, / Progenies Pheton, non infici[a]nda parenti?"'. Nota quod sensus uersuum Ouidii est iste: ipse enim introducit solem alloquentem Phetontem ac eum pro filio suo recognoscentem. Applicando
30 igitur ad ambicionem, bene ambicio dicitur [esse] solis [proles], intelligendo per solem mundane glorie applicacionem. | Nam

---

1 fol. 106vb • Fulgencii] *om.* A • Apollonis] \solis/ A   4 depingitur] *adds* a poetis A, *adds* et fingitur O   6 curis] curiis I   7 statu] situ AI   18 partes] proprietates A • Ouidius] *adds* poeta I

19 fingitur] *om.* I, pingitur O   19–20 ut … poete] Isti A   23 et palacium] *om.* A. 26 arce] arte O   27 inficianda] inficienda AO, infacienda I • parenti] peccati I 28 uersuum] *om.* A   30 esse] *om.* O • proles] filius O   31 applicacionem] apparicionem A • fol. 107ra

[8]

Fulgentius's eighth mythology follows; it concerns Phaeton, Apollo's son, and Fulgentius speaks about him in his text. The poet Ovid treats the story at greater length in *Metamorphoses* 2.[1] Following Ovid's account, Phaeton is depicted as:
[1] born of the sun,
[2] inflamed with cares,
[3] raised in status,
[4] placed in a chariot,
[5] written over with letters,
[6] occupied with reins,
[7] reduced in weight,
[8] troubled with fear,
[9] deprived of honour,
[10] condemned to death,
[11] adorned with verses,
[12] bathed with weeping.
These are the twelve parts of the picture with which Ovid and other poets customarily depict the vice of Ambition through the image of Phaeton.

[19] [1] First, Phaeton is represented as the sun's son, for, as Fulgentius shows, the poets were accustomed to understand by Apollo the sun. And Fulgentius explicitly says he is Apollo's son, while Ovid calls him 'the sun's son' (1.751). For this reason, Ovid narrates in verse how Phaeton entered the hall and palace of the sun, and how the sun, seeing Phaeton, spoke to him, and acknowledged him as his son. He says, 'The sun, whose eyes look on everything, saw the youth, / and said, "What cause do you seek along the ways in this citadel, / Phaeton my son, one no parent should deny?"' (2.32-34). Notice the sense of Ovid's verses: he introduces the sun speaking to Phaeton and recognising him as his son. Applying this to ambition, it is properly called 'the sun's offspring', if one understands through 'sun' that it applies to worldly glory. For

---

[1] Fulg 1.16 (27/13-28/7); Ovid, *ibid.* 1.747-2.400 (lines cited are identified parenthetically within the text).

ab ista radice procedit ambicio, que nichil aliud est quam honorum deordinatus appetitus et libido dominandi, sicut de \hoc/ pulcre loquitur Crisostomus super Mattheum, *De opere imperfecto,* quando sic dicit, 'Tolle hoc uicium de clero, ut non uelint clerici hominibus apparere, et sine labore omnia uicia [res]ecantur. Ex hoc enim uicio nascitur ille defectus in clero, ut non uelint clerici inter se meliorem habere'.

Notari eciam potest alia racio huius partis prime picture Phetontis. Docet enim astronomi qui tractant de disposicionibus humanis, quibus solent homines affici uirtute planetarum in quorum dominiis sunt generati, quod genitus in dominio solis afficitur et inclinatur ad appetitum mundane honoris et seculari dignitatis. Sicut illud bene prosequitur episcopus et cancellarius Parisiensis in quodam suo tractatu quem edidit de utilitate methamatice, et specialiter de utilitate astronomie. Ibi enim distingit septem differencias amoris et affeccionis iuxta numerum septem planetarum: amorem saturnalem, 3ouialem, marcialem, solarem, uenerem, mercurialem, et lunarem. Et loquens de amore solari, dicit quod homines per illum amorem amant res ad uirtutem uitalem attinentes, utpote uiuere et uitam et uiuacitatem ipsiusque uirtutis, ualitudinem et longeuitatem. Odiunt autem homines et deuitant, secundum illum amorem solarem, mortem et omnia que mortem inducunt uel ad mortem disponunt. Loquendo autem de rebus extrincecis, homines per amorem istum solarem a|mant aurum regnare et predominare, et talia al[t]a et magnalia, et hec est causa naturalis quare Pheton iste, uicium scilicet ambicionis, proles dicitur esse solis.

[2] Secunda pars picture est de Phetontis solicitudine et curarum sua flagracione, de qua loquens Ouidius libro 2º *De transformatis* dicit sic, 'Solis erat monitus; dictis tamen ille, scilicet Pheton, repugnat / propositumque tenet flagratque cupidine currus'. Introducit enim Ouidius more poetico solem dissuadentem filio suo Phetonti ut desistat a peticione sua. Nam Ph\e/ton peciit quod uno die posset ducere currum solis, et sol statim dissuadet Phetonti, ne prosequatur peticionem propter

33 et libido] *om.* A   36 clerici] *om.* A   37 resecantur] refutantur A, ex|ecantur O
39 partis] *om.* I • prime] *om.* A   43 secularis] scandere A   49 uenerem] *om.* A
• mercurialem] mercinalem I   51 utpote] ut poete AI • uiuacitatem] unitatem A   52 -que uirtutis] per uirtutem I   54 uel ad mortem] ac I
56 fol. 107[rb] • alta] alia OI   57 naturalis] *om.* A
60 sua] suarum AI • flagracione] fagracione I   61–63 Solis ... currus] *after* 69 desistere AI   65 solis] sol enim sui I

ambition grows from this root; it is nothing except an unregulated appetite for honours and a desire to dominate, just as Chrysostom elegantly speaks about in his *Unfinished work* on Matthew, saying, 'Take this vice away from clerks, so that clerks don't wish to appear superior to other people, and all their other vices will easily be cut away. This vice gives rise to a particular defect in clerks, that they don't wish to have anyone better than they in their company.'[2]

[39] One can also notice another reason for this first part of Phaeton's picture. Astronomers treat human characters, on the grounds that people are customarily influenced by the strength of those planets in whose domains they were born. They teach that someone born in the sun's domain is affected by and inclined to a desire for worldly honour and dignity. The bishop and chancellor of Paris describes this well in a tract he composed to treat the usefulness of mathematics and particularly of astronomy.[3] He there distinguishes seven classes of love or desire, as these follow the rule of the seven planets: loves saturnine, jovial, martial, solar, venereal, mercurial, and lunar. Speaking of solar love, he says that people affected by it love those things that help them attain lively strength, that is to increase the life and liveliness of this strength, power and its persistence into a great age. Moreover, in accord with this solar love, these people hate and avoid death and all those things that bring on or dispose one to death. And to speak of external things, solar lovers desire to control and command gold, as well as other great and glorious things of that sort. This is a natural reason why Phaeton, the vice ambition, is said to be the sun's offspring.

[59] [2] The second part of the picture concerns Phaeton's anxiety and his burning desire for duties; Ovid speaks of this when he says, 'This was the sun's warning; nonetheless Phaeton rejected his words; / he held to his purpose and burned with desire for the cart' (2.103–4). Ovid introduces here, in his poetic fashion, the sun dissuading his son Phaeton, urging him to put aside his request. For Phaeton asked that he might direct the sun's cart for a single day, and the sun immediately dissuades him from

---

[2] Unfound.
[3] In fact, Roger Bacon, *Opus maius* 4 ('Mathematicae in divinis utilitas'), pp. 249ff., esp. 254 paraphrased.

periculum quod posset accidere. Sed Pheton iste fuit animatus uel inflamatus ardore honoris, quod nullo modo uoluit ab incepto desistere.

70 Et propriissime conuenit istud uicio ambicionis, nam ambiciosus est totus flagrans et sollicitus, sicut pulcre tangit dominus Innocencius in suo libello *De miseria condicionis humane* ubi dicit, 'Honores ambiciosus affectat, et ideo semper ambiciosus est pauidus, semper attentus, ne quid dicat uel faciat
75 quod in oculis hominum ualeat displicere. Humilitatem simulat', sicut Ouidius narrat Phetontem fecisse in principio peticionis sue. 'Ambiciosus autem honestatem mentitur, affabilitatem exhibet, benignitatem | ostendit; subsequitur et obsequitur, [cunctos honorat], cunctis inclinat, frequentat curias, uisitat optimates,
80 assurgit et amplexatur, applaudit et adulatur; promptus et feruidus, ubi se placere cognouerit; remissus et tepidus, ubi se putauerit displicere'. Hec dominus Innocencius, ex cuius processu patet ardor curarum quibus solet accendi animus ambiciosi.

[3] Sequitur tercia pars picture de Phetontis sublimacione.
85 Unde more poetico fingit Ouidius, libro 2° *De transformatis*, qualiter sol, uidens obstinacionem filii Phetontis, deduxit eum in altum ut uideret currum paternum. Unde sic dicit poeta in metro,
Ergo, quam licuit, genitor cunctatus ad altos / Deducit iuuenem Wlcania munera currus. / Aureus axis erat, themo
90 aureus, auretur cuncta; / Curuanturque rote, radiorum argenteus ordo.
Nota quod in hiis uersibus non uult aliud dicere nisi quod sol, quamdiu potuit, distulit peticionem filii sui. Sed quando uidit filii pertinaciam, tunc duxit eum ad uidendum currum solarem, quem
95 poete fingunt + factum soli a Wlcano fabro, qui est deus ignis, ut fingunt pagani. Et tunc narrat ultra Ouidius qualiter Pheton sublimatus ad contemplandum et considerandum currum solis, nichil aliud uidit nisi aurum et argentum et gemmas preciosas.

Et applicatur istud propriissime ad illum uicium, scilicet ad |
100 ambicionem, nam ambiciosus post suam sublimacionem

---

67 animatus uel] *om.* AI   68 inflamatus] armatus I • honoris] amoris A
74 attentus] accensus A   75 oculis] utilis I   78 fol. 107va 78–79 cunctos honorat] *om.* O   79 cunctis] uniuersis A   82 displicere] dispicere I
89–91 Aureus ... ordo] *om. at page-boundary* I   90 auretur ... Curuanturque] aurea summe curitatura A   93 filii²] *om.* A   94 duxit] *om.* A   95 fingunt] *adds* datum uel O   95–96 fingunt ... ut] *marg.* I   95 factum soli] factum A, *om.* I • fabro] *om.* AI   97 contemplandum] uidendum A   98 uidit] *om.* I
99 illum] predictum AI   99–100 scilicet ad ambicionem] *om.* A   99 fol. 107vb

pursuing his request because of the danger that might befall. But Phaeton was driven or inflamed with the desire for honour so that he didn't wish to leave off what he had started.

[70] This behaviour is most appropriate for the vice ambition. For an ambitious person is completely anxious and burning with desire, just as pope Innocent elegantly treats it in his little book *On the wretchedness of the human condition*: 'The ambitious person desires honours, and therefore is always fearful; such a person is always intent that he not say or do something that might arouse other people's displeasure. He offers a show of humility', just as Ovid tells that Phaeton did at the beginning of his request. Innocent continues, 'However, ambitious people only pretend to behave virtuously, display affability and show themselves as well-intentioned; they follow along and gratify others, they honour and defer to everybody, hang out around courts, visit all the best people, pop up to be embraced, applaud and flatter; they are prompt and eager where they know they will please, but behindhand and lukewarm where they think they will displease.'[4] In this passage, pope Innocent shows that desire for duties that customarily sets the mind of an ambitious person afire.

[84] [3] The third part of the picture follows; it concerns Phaeton's elevation. For in his poem, Ovid portrays how the sun, perceiving his son Phaeton's stubbornness, led him up on high so that he could see his father's cart. He says,

> Thus his father, delaying as was appropriate for him, led / the youth on high to the cart, Vulcan's great work. / The axle was gold, gold the traces – every bit of it gilded, / and the wheels were curved, their spokes arranged in silver. (2.105–8)

Notice that in these verses, Ovid wishes to say nothing more than that the sun, so long as he might, put off his son's request. But having seen his son's persistence, he led him to look at the solar cart. Poets claim that this was made for the sun by Vulcan the smith; pagans claim that he is the god of fire. Ovid further tells how Phaeton, raised up to contemplate and gaze at the sun's cart, saw nothing there but gold, silver, and precious stones.

[99] This description is most appropriately applied to the vice ambition, for the ambitious person after their elevation and

---

[4] *Ibid.* 2.26 (PL 217:727), as again in line 185.

et promocionem non habet oculum ad saluacionem animarum sed ad congregacionem pecuniarum et diuiciarum, sicut tractat istam materiam Bernardus, *Super Cantica*, omelia 33ª, 'Serpit hodie putrida + tabes per omne corpus ecclesie, et quo +
105 lacius, eo desperacius; eoque periculosius, quo interius. Omnes enim sunt ecclesie amici in apparencia, sed omnes enim sunt inimici in existencia; omnes necessarii, sed omnes aduersarii; omnes domestici, sed nulli pacifici; omnes proximi, et tamen omnes que sua sunt querunt, non que Ihesu Cristi. Ministr\o/s
110 se dicunt Cristi, et tamen seruiunt Anticristo; de bonis Cristi incedunt honorati, et tamen cui honorem debent non deferunt. De patrimonio enim Cristi prouenit iste quem cotidie uides – meretricius nitor, histrionicus habitus, regius apparatus. De patrimonio Cristi prouenit inde – aurum in frenis, in cellis, in
115 calcaribus – plus calcaria fulgent quam altaria. Pro huius uolunt esse et sunt ecclesiarum prepositi, decani, archidiaconi, episcopi, et archiepiscopi'. Hec Bernardus.

Eand[e]m sentenciam [fa]cit Hugo, *De duodecim abusionibus claustri*, capitulo ultimo, ubi dicit sic de ambiciosis ad ecclesie
120 dignitates promotis, 'Non oracionibus [uacant], sed lusubus insudant; legem Dei nec sciunt nec discunt; ocio uacant; comessacionibus et ebrietatibus student; terrenis inhiant; terrena sapiunt. Assidui in plateis, in ecclesia rari; tardi ad inuestigandum culpam peccatorum, parati ad in[quir]enda uestigia leporum.
125 | Uelociores ad congregandos canes quam ad conuocandos pauperes; libencius uolunt porrigere panem cani quam pauperi; plures ei seruiunt ad mensam, nulli ad missam. Hii sunt quorum thalamus est decoracior + quam ecclesia, mensa preparacior quam altare, ciphus preciosior calice, equus carior quam missale,
130 capa pulcrior quam casula, camisia delicacior quam alba'. Unde concludit Hugo, 'Ecce, *quomodo obscuratum est aurum,*

102 pecuniarum] pecuniam AI   102–3 tractat ... materiam] dicit A   103 Serpit] Sepit I   104 tabes] trabes AO   104–6 ecclesie ... ecclesie] ecclesie A   105 lacius] lasciuius IO   108 sed nulli] et nisi A • proximi] pacifici omnes A
109 sunt] *om.* I   110 dicunt] differunt I   111 honorati] onerati A • debent non] debitum A • deferunt] differant I   112 nitor] ultor I • habitus] habitilitus (?) I
114 inde] *om.* A • frenis] supernis I   115 Pro huius] Plus A
118 Eandem] Eandu' O • Eandem sentenciam] Et ad idem A • facit] bene facit I, dicit O • *abusionibus*] ambicionibus I   120 uacant] *om.* IO   121 insudant] exsultant AIO • sciunt] faciant I   124 inquirenda] inuenienda O   125 fol. 108ra
126 pauperi] paupi cano A   127 nulli] nullus AI   128 decoracior] decorior I, *adds* uel speciosior O

promotion is intent only on gathering money and riches, not on the salvation of souls. Bernard treats this subject in *On the Song*, sermon 33, 'Today there's a rotting disease that creeps through the whole body of the church; the more widespread it is, the more hopeless the situation is; and the further in it slips, the more dangerous it is. For all these people appear to be friends of the church, but they are all in essence its enemies. They all appear necessary to it, but all are its opponents; all appear its servants, but none of them its peacemakers; all brotherly neighbours, yet they all seek things that might be their own, not things that might be Christ's. They say they are Christ's servants, yet they serve Antichrist; they enter Christ's goods as honoured persons and yet don't defer to Him they should honour. You daily see this person benefitting from Christ's patrimony – glitter befitting a whore, a minstrel's garments, regal equipment. They benefit from Christ's patrimony everywhere – gold in their bridles, on their chairs and shoes; indeed, their shoes gleam more than Christ's altars! For things like these they want to be provosts, deans, archdeacons, bishops, and archbishops in our churches – and they become such.' So Bernard says.[5]

[118] Hugh of Fouilly makes the same point in the last chapter of his *On twelve abuses of the cloister*, where he says this about ambitious people promoted to high office in the church, 'They sweat over sports, rather than occupy leisure with prayers; they neither know nor teach God's law; they give themselves to leisure; they are eager for banquets and drunken sessions; they avidly seek earthly things and delight in them. They are constantly busy in town-squares, rarely in the church; slow to root out sinners' guilt, always ready to seek out the tracks left by hares. They are quicker at gathering their hounds than calling together the poor; they more willingly offer bread to their pup than to a poor person; many serve them at table, none at mass. Their bedroom is more adorned than their church; their dinner-table is more ready for use than their altar, their drinking-cup more precious than their chalice, their horse more expensive than their missal, their cape more beautiful than their chasuble, their shirt of more delicate cloth than their alb.' For this reason, Hugh concludes, *'How is the gold become dim;*

---

[5] *Ibid.* 33.15 (*PL* 183:959).

mutatus est color optimus prelatorum. *Obscuratum est aurum*', dicit Hugo, 'fuligine peccatorum, et mutatus est *color optimus* sanctitatis in feditate[m] uiciorum +'.

135 [4] Sequitur quarta pars picture de Phetontis cur[riz]acione. Narrat enim Ouidius in sua poetica ficcione quod p[ost]quam duxerat sol filium suum in altum ad uidendum currum suum, et noluit desistere a peticione, sol fecit Phetontem ascendere currum solarem et fecit Phetontem inungi unguento quodam
140 quod posset saluare se contra calorem. Unde dicit sic in hiis uersubus:

Tunc pater ora sui sacro medicamine nati / Contigit et rapide fecit paciencia flamme'. Et subdit Ouidius, 'Occupat is leuem iuuenili corpore currum / Statque super manibus datas
145 contingere habenas / Gaudet et inuito grates agit ille paterno.

Ubi nota quod moraliter Ouidius describit in hiis uersubus ambiciosorum elacionem. Currus enim cui insidet ambiciosus est currus superbie et elacionis. Istud pulcre describit dominus Innocencius in suo libello *De miseria condicionis | humane*, ubi
150 dicit quod 'ambiciosus, statim ut promotus est ad honorem, in superbiam extollitur et in iactanciam effrenatur. Non curat prodesse, sed gloriatur preesse. Presumit se esse meliorem, quia cernit se esse superiorem, priores + dedignatur amicos, ignorat notos, contempnit antiquos [socios]; uultu[m] auertit, ceruicem
155 erigit, fastum ostendit, grandia loquitur, sublimia meditatur'.

Currum autem istum elacionis portantem uicium ambicionis describit Hugo, *De claustro anime*, libro 2°, ubi describit rotas + currum sustinentes et equos currum trahentes. Unde dicit sic, 'Quattuor sunt equi qui trahunt currum elacionis: amor
160 dominandi, amor proprie laudis, contemptus, et inobediencia. Rote uero istius currus sunt iactancia, arrogancia, uerbositas,

---

132–33 mutatus ... Hugo] *om.* A 132 aurum] *om.* I 134 feditatem] feditates IO • uiciorum] peccatorum A, *adds* seu peccatorum O

135 Phetontis] fetentis I • currizacione] curacione O 136 postquam] pri|usquam O 137 sol ... suum] filium I • suum²] solis AI 138 et] *adds* fetori A 139 unguento quodam] *om.* A, unguento I 140 posset ... se] saluaret et perseruaret A, *over eras.* I 140–41 in ... uersubus] metrice [*with following blank line*] A, metrice I 142 Tunc] Sunt I 143–45 Et ... habenas] *om.* A, *marg.* I 145 paterno] pereuo A 147 elacionem] eleccionem I • insidet] inuidet A 148 superbie] superflue I 149 fol. 108ʳᵇ 151 in superbiam] et superfluam I • curat] *om.* I 153 dedignatur] dedignantur O 154 socios] *om.* O • uultum] uultus O 155 grandia] gaudia A

156 currum] curruum O 159 equi qui] que AI 160 laudis] elacionis A

the finest colour is changed (Lam 4:1) for prelates. *The gold* has become dim with the rust of sin, and *the finest colour* of holiness has changed into the filthiness of vice.'[6]

[135] [4] The fourth part of the picture follows; it concerns Phaeton's being placed in the cart. In his poetic fiction, Ovid tells how, after the sun had led his son on high to look at his cart, and Phaeton still would not leave off in his request, the sun made him climb up on the solar cart and had him anointed with an ointment that might preserve him from the heat. For this reason, Ovid says in his verse,

> Then the father touched his son's cheeks with a holy / drug and made them resistant to the rapid flame. And he adds, In his youthful body, he gets on the swift cart / and standing, takes in his hands the offered reins. / Rejoicing, he thanks his reluctant father. (2.122–23, 150–52)

In moral terms, notice that Ovid here describes ambitious peoples' vainglory. For the cart in which an ambitious person sits is that of pride and vainglory. Pope Innocent describes this very neatly in his *On the wretchedness*, 'Ambitious people, as soon as they are promoted to some honour, exalt themselves in pride and become unrestrained in boasting. They don't care about doing well, but exult in their pre-eminence. Because they see themselves as the very best, they presume that they are better and disdain their former friends, pay no attention to those they know, disdain their ancient companions; they avert their face from them, become stiff-necked, show their haughtiness, speak grandiloquently, consider only the highest things.'[7]

[156] Hugh, in *On the cloister of the soul* 2, describes this prideful cart that carries along the vice ambition, the wheels that hold it up, and the horses that draw it. He says, 'Four horses draw vainglory's cart: the love of commanding, the love of one's own praise, contempt, and disobedience. The wheels of the cart are boasting, arrogance, verbosity,

---

[6] *Ibid.* 2.23 (*PL* 176:1085–86).
[7] *Ibid.* 2.30 (*PL* 217:728).

et leuitas. Auriga in hoc curru est spiritus superbie, sed illi qui deferuntur in hoc curru sunt amatores huius mundi'. Et subdit Hugo, 'Equi currus istius sunt infrenes, rote sunt uolubiles, auriga peruersus, et qui portatur miser et infirmus'.

[5] Sequitur quinta pars picture de Phetontis inscripcione, nam depingitur cum uersubus descriptis super ymaginem ipsius. Narrat enim poeta Ouidius quomodo Apollo informauit filium suum Phetontem de regimine ipsius currus. Unde Ouidius ponit uerba Appolinis metrice,

'Utque ferant equos et celum et terra calores, / Nec [preme] nec + summum mollire per ethera currum. / Alcius egressus celestia tecta cremabis, / Inferius terras; medio tutissimus ibis'.

Nota quod sensus + | uersuum est quod si Pheton uelit bene regere currum patris sui, oportet quod teneat medium, quod nec nimis descendat ad terram, nec nimis ascend[a]t usque celum. Istam doctrinam patris sui quia Pheton non tenuit, ideo corruit et finaliter perditus fuit. Et optime conuenit ista doctrina ambiciosis. Duobus enim modis peruenit ambiciosus ad currum dignitatis et honoris, quia ascend[end]o uersus celum per ypocrisim \uel/ falsam sanctitatis simulacionem. Alius modus descend[end]o ad terram per rerum terrenarum oblacionem, munerum scilicet donacionem.

Et de istis loquntur doctores, ut \patet/ per dominum Innocencium in suo libello *De miseria condicionis humane*, sic dicentem, 'Uniuersis inclinat, scilicet ambiciosus, et improbat mala; detestatur iniqua ut iudicetur ydoneus, ut reputetur acceptus, ut laudetur ab hominibus, ut a singulis approbetur. Ambiciosus libenter agit de principatu quem ambit et dicit quando principabitur ille qui seuerus est in iusticia, pius in misericordia; qui non deuiet amore uel odio; qui non corumpatur prece uel precio; qui credat fidelibus et adquiescat simplicibus; qui sit

---

163 deferuntur] differ|untur I 164 sunt infrenes] in supernos A
168 enim poeta] *om.* A • quomodo] informandi modus quo A 171 Utque] Utique AI 171–72 preme nec] ymum (*over eras.*) nec I, per ymum nec per O
174 fol. 108ᵛᵃ • uersuum] uer||uersuum O 176 ascendat] ascendit O
177 quia] *adds* primus modus est A 180 ascendendo] ascendere A, ascendo O
181 uel falsam] et fallaciam *and adds* et *after* sanctitatis A 182 descendendo] descendo O 183 munerum] mundum I • donacionem] deᵃcionem A, \de/ⁱnacionem I
184 loquntur ... dominum] tangit (*with nom.*) A 186 dicentem] *adds* Ambiciosus humilitatem simulat sanctitatem mentitur cuntos honorat (*from 77-79*) A
187 ut iudicetur] est A 190 principabitur] principaliter I

and frivolousness. The cart's charioteer is the spirit of pride, and those who are borne about in this cart are the lovers of this world.' Hugh adds, 'The cart's horses have no reins, the wheels turn unsteadily, the charioteer is perverted, and the person who's conveyed is wretched and weak.'[8]

[166] [5] The fifth part of the picture follows, describing Phaeton's writing, for he is depicted with verses written above his image. Ovid tells how Apollo taught his son Phaeton about controlling the cart. For this reason, Ovid's verse reports Apollo's words,

> Let an even heat strike both heaven and earth. / Don't drive the cart and horses through either the airy depths or heights. / Passing too high you will burn the heavenly roofs, / too low the earth; you will pass most safely in the middle. (2.134-37)

Notice that the sense of these verses is that if Phaeton wishes to control his father's cart properly, it is necessary that he should hold to the mean. He should neither descend too near to the earth, nor ascend too high toward heaven. Because Phaeton wouldn't follow his father's teaching, he fell and in the end was destroyed. This teaching is particularly appropriate for ambitious people. The ambitious person attains the cart of dignity and honour in two ways. They either ascend toward heaven through hypocrisy or a false show of holiness, or they descend toward the earth through offering earthly things, that is by giving bribes.

[184] Learned people speak against these behaviours, for example pope Innocent in *On the wretchedness*, 'Ambitious people defer to everyone and condemn evils. They hate evils, but only so that people will consider consider them fit and will account them acceptable, so that people may praise them, so that all may approve of them. Ambitious people eagerly work at gaining office and seek support for it; they say that when they are given office, they will be rigorous in justice, but reverent in mercy; that they will not turn aside for love or hate, that they will not be corrupted by entreaty or payment, that they will believe those who are trustworthy and acknowledge the simple, that they

---

[8] *Ibid.* 1.6 (PL 176:1030).

h[um]ilis et benignus, largus et mansuetus, constans et paciens, sapiens et discretus'. Et extat bene ad propositum de Absalone; nota historia [blank] Regum. Isto igitur modo ambiciosus in celum adascendit, simulando se per ypocrisim sanctum et bene morigeratum.

Sed qualiter descendit ad terram, offerendo terrena munera, ostendit | idem Innocencius, sic dicens, 'Si forsan hac arte, scilicet per simulacionem sanctitatis, ambiciosus non proficit, tunc certe recurrit ad aliam, scilicet artem: aduocat Symonem, accedit ad Giezi, per hunc ab illo nititur emere quod per se non preualet obtinere. Supplicat et promittit, offert et tribuit – prodolor – graciam qua gratis adipisci non potuit, per fas et nephas nititur adipsci'.

Hii sunt duo motus qui prohibentur ab Apolline (qui a poetis fingitur deus ueritatis) in dignitatum adquisicione, et precipitur obseruacio medii ut, scilicet promouend[us] ad ecclesia[tica]s dignitates uiuat in medio, id est uirtuose, nam [uirtus] consistit in medio \et de medio/ obseruando. A talibus pulcre loquitur Gregorius in suo *Pastorali* quando sic dicit, 'Rect[or] discretus in silencio, utilis in uerbo, ne aut tacenda proferat aut proferenda reticescat, sed in medio se semper teneat. Quia sicut incauta locucio in errorem protrahit, ita indiscretum silencium hos quos erudire poterat in errore derelinquid'. Et sicut est seruandum medium locucionis et silencii, ita est de aliis, sicut ibidem deducit Gregorius per multa + exempla.

[6] Sequitur sexta pars picture de Phetontis occupacione. Unde poeta Ouidius fingit Appollonem alloquentem filium suum et tradentem sibi lora per que manu debuit equos regere. Unde dicit sic metrice, 'Corripe lora manu uel, si mutabile pectus / Est tibi, consiliis, non curribus utere nostris'. Nota ista lora per que promotus ad ecclesiasticas dignitates debet corripere sunt seueri|tas et lenitas, nam pro personarum qualitate debet prelatus ecclesiasticus nunc illos tractare cum seueritate, nunc illos regere cum misericordie lenitate, sicut patet per Gregorium, 20 *Moralium*, capitulo 7, quando dicit, 'Miscenda est lenitas cum

---

193 humilis] habilis AIO   194-95 Et extat ... Regum] *om.* AI   195 adascendit] ascendit AI
198 terrena] *om.* A   199 fol. 108vb
208 promouendus] promouendo O • ecclesiasticas] ecc^{as}| (= ? ecclesias) O
  209 uirtus] uertit O   211 Rector] Doctor rector A, Rectus et O   214 in errorem] merorem I   217 multa] *adds* per O
220-22 Unde ... nostris] *om.* I   224 fol. 109ra 225 nunc ... nunc] nec ... nec A

will be humble and pleasant, generous and meek, constant and patient, wise and discreet.'⁹ Absalom provides a good example of the point; look at his story in 2 Rg 15. In this way, ambitious people elevate themselves into heaven by hypocrisy, acting as if they were holy and of good moral character.

[198] But Innocent also shows how ambitious people descend to earth through offering worldly rewards. 'But if perhaps this art, namely the pretence of holiness, doesn't bring them profit, they certainly will turn back to another, contrary device: they follow Simon and give way to Giezi and through this action attempt to buy from someone else what they weren't strong enough to get through their own powers. They plead and promise, offer and give – disgusting to say – grace; what they could not freely gain, they attempt to get through any means, proper or sinful.'

[206] These are the two movements in acquiring honours that Apollo forbade – and recall that the poets represent him as the god truth – and he prescribed following a middle path. For example, someone who should be promoted to a dignity in the church should live in the middle, namely virtuously, since virtue lies in the mean and in adhering to that mean. Gregory talks well about such people observing the mean in his *Pastoral rule*, 'The priest should be discreet in his silence, useful when he speaks, neither offering things that should be kept silent nor being silent about things that should be offered, but should hold himself always in the mean. For just as incautious speech draws people into error, likewise an indiscreet silence abandons in error those whom he should have taught.'¹⁰ And just as one should preserve a mean between speech and silence, it's the same with other actions, as Gregory proves there through many examples.

[217] [6] The sixth part of the picture follows; it concerns Phaeton's occupation. For this reason, Ovid portrays Apollo addressing his son and giving him the reins with which he was to have controlled the horses with his hand. For this reason, his poem says, 'Seize the reins in your hand, or if you have / changed your mind, use my advice, not my chariot' (2.145–46). Notice that these reins, with which someone promoted to church office ought to correct others, are severity and leniency. For a prelate in the church ought, in accord with the quality of the person involved, at times treat some with severity and at other times control others with lenient mercy, as Gregory says, *Moral readings* 20.7, 'Leniency should be blended with

---

⁹ Continuing Innocent's discussion in 2.26 (217:727); the next paragraph, including references to Ac 8:18–24 and 4 Rg 5:20–27, is from 2.27 (*PL* 217:727).

¹⁰ *Ibid.* 2.4 (*PL* 77:30).

seueritate et facienda est ex utroque + temperamentum, ut neque
multa ex[ulc]erentur asperitate subditi, neque nimia benignitate
230 soluantur. Hinc Dauid ait, *Uirga tua et baculus tuus ipsa me
consolata sunt*; uirga percutimur, baculo sustentamur. Si igitur
est districtio uirge que feriat, sic eciam consolacio baculi qui
sustentet'. Sed non sic facit ambiciosus, sicut bene dicit dominus
Innocencius, 'Iste enim ambiciosus postquam promotus est,
235 subditis onerosus, concepta non differt, preceps et audax, [grauis]
et inportunus'. Et ideo, sicut tangit Ouidius in uersubus predictis,
melius foret + sibi ab officio prelacionis subtrahere quam in
officio permanere.
    [7] Sequitur septima pars picture de Phetontis [min]oracione.
240 Nam poeta Ouidius fingit quod iste Pheton non fuit ita ponderosus
sicut debuit fuisse, et ideo hoc percipientes, equi trahentes currum
solis inceperunt exorbitare. Unde dicit Ouidius sic metrice,
    Sed leue pondus erat, nec quod cognoscere possent / Solis
    equi solitaque iugum grauitate carebat. / Utque labant curue
245 iusto sine pondere naues / Perque mare instabiles nimia
    leuitate feruntur, / Sic onere insueto uacuos dat in aere saltus /
    Su[ccur]itur[que] alte similis[que] est currus inani.
Nota [in his uersibus] quod Ouidius uult dicere quod sicut nauis
carens sarcina proporcionali hinc et inde titubat et uacillat |
250 in mare, sic fuit de curru isto, qui propter defectum consueti
ponderis irregulariter trahebatur ab equis.
    Et conuenit istud moraliter istis ambiciosis, nam non
incumbunt + cure eis credite, nec gregem custodiunt cum debita
diligencia et solicitudine. 'Uolunt enim preesse, sed negligunt
255 prodesse', sicut dicit Gregorius. Et ideo currus, scilicet status et
dignitas pastoralis, uacua uidetur \penitus/ et inanis, et de ista

---

228 ultroque] *add* quodam IO 229 exulcerentur] asperentur AIO
230 soluantur] saluantur I • Dauid] dicendum I 232 districtio] d° (= ?
distinccio) A, descripcio I 233–34 sicut … ambiciosus] sed A 235 subditis]
subditus AI • onerosis] honorosus I 235–36 concepta … importunus] *om.* A
235 et audax] *om.* I • grauis] insanus AO, grauius I 236 sicut … predictis]
om. A 237 foret] *repeats* O • subtrahere] se trahere I
239 minoracione] immoracione IO 240 poeta] iste A 241 percipientes]
percuciantes A 242 exorbitare] exhortare A 244 solitaque] solitam AI
• grauitate] caritate A 246 dat] *om.* I 247 Sucurriturque] Sucurritur A,
Siccitutiturque I, Sumitur [*blank*] O • similisque] similis IO 248 in his
uersibus] *om.* O 249 sarcina] sarcinali A • fol. 109[rb] 250 de] in proposito in A
253 incumbunt] *adds* uel non intendunt O • credite] tradite I 255 sicut …
Gregorius] *om.* A • currus] *adds* solis A

severity and from both should be made a certain temperateness, so that one's subjects neither be wounded by great harshness nor dissolved by excessive kindness. Thus David says, *Thy rod and thy staff, they have comforted me* (Ps 22:4); God strikes us with the rod and sustains us with the staff. Therefore, if there's rigour in the rod that strikes, there is also the staff's sustaining consolation.'[11] But the ambitious person doesn't behave in this way, as pope Innocent says, 'After the ambitious person is promoted to office, a load for his subjects to bear, he rashly pursues whatever he's thinking, and he's forward and daring, pompous and oppressive.'[12] Thus, as Ovid says in the verses above, it would be better to take a prelate's duties from him than let him remain in the post.

[239] [7] The seventh part of the picture, concerning Phaeton's reduction, follows. For Ovid reports that Phaeton was not so hefty as he ought to have been, and the horses drawing the sun's cart perceived this and began to run astray. For this reason, Ovid's poem says,

> But the weight was light, and the horses of the sun were unable / to recognise it – their yoke lacked the accustomed heaviness. / And so, like unladen ships that slip out of their proper course / and unstable from excessive lightness are driven through the sea, / the chariot with its unaccustomed load gives empty leaps through the air, / and it rushed on high as if it were an empty cart. (2.161–66)

Notice that in these verses, Ovid wants to say that, just like a ship that lacks an appropriate cargo tosses here and there and swings about in the sea, so it was with the sun's cart. The horses drew it about erratically because it lacked the accustomed weight.

[252] And in moral terms, this is appropriate to the behaviour of ambitious people, for they neither devote themselves to the duty entrusted them, nor do they guard the flock with the proper diligence and care. 'Because they want only to be first, they avoid being good', as Gregory says.[13] Therefore the cart, that is the state and dignity of the priesthood, appears completely empty and light, and from this

---

[11] *Ibid.* 20.5 (PL 76:143–44) and *Pastoralis regula* 2.6 (PL 77:38).
[12] Cf. *ibid.* 2.30 (PL 217:728).
[13] E.g. *Moralia* 26.26 (PL 76:378, one of Gregory's oft-repeated proverbialisms).

uacuitate accidit mocio irregularis et exorbitacio [huius curris]. De qua loquitur Bernardus in exposicione regule beati Benedicti, parte 3ᵃ, capitulo 7°, exponendo illud Prouerbiorum, *Celum sursum et terra deorsum*, dicit sic, 'Negligencia et lenitas prelatorum tantam deordinacionem et confusionem induxit quod in eis terra est sursum et celum deorsum, pedes supra caput, et facies eius retro, interiora effusa sunt extra, Deus conculcatur [et] terra deificatur, diabolus honorifice recipitur, Deus contumeliose repellitur'.

Istas irregulares et deordinatas mociones que proueniunt in ecclesia Dei ex ambiciosorum lenitate et negligencia probat Bernardus + sic dicens, 'Ibi terra est sursum et celum deorsum, ubi terrena celestibus preponuntur. Ibi pedes sunt supra caput, ubi uiri spirituales despiciuntur, homines terrena sapientes in honore habentur. [Ibi est eciam facies retro, quando in operibus que bona fieri deberent intencione primo, intenditur utilitas terrena et postponitur merces eterna.] Ibi eciam interiora effusa sunt extra, quia bona spiritualia, que sunt intrinseca, negliguntur, et bona temporalia, que extrinsica sunt, diliguntur. Deus uero concultatur et terra deificatur, ubi deficit ca|ritas et regnat cupiditas. Diabolus honorifice recipitur et Deus contumeliose repellitur, quia ab istis ambiciosis raptores, usurarii, et lucris terrenis dediti, et potestate seculari prediti, cum honore recipiuntur et magnis expensis procurantur. Pauperes uero uel cum murmure sunt recepti uel totaliter expelluntur'. Iste est modus + diuersus quo, ut dicit Ouidius, succu[rr]it et subuertitur currus Phetontis.

[8] Sequitur octaua pars picture de Phetontis turbacione. Nam poeta Ouidius fingit istum Phetontem totum consternatum, et conturbatur ex timore postquam uiderat currum patris sui ita exorbitantem et irregulariter se mouentem. Unde sic dicit Ouidius,
Ut uero summo despexit ab ethere terras / Infelix Pheton penitus penitusque iacentes, / Palluit et subito genua

---

257 accidit] *om.* I • irregularis] irracionalis I • exorbitacio] exhortacio A • huius curris] *om.* O 259–60 in ... exponendo] exponens AI 260 sursum] cursum I 262 supra] sua I 263 et] in O
266 irregulares] irracionabiles A 267 Dei] *om.* AI 268 sic] sic | sic O • sursum] *om.* I 269 supra] sua I 271–73 Ibi ... eterna] *om.* O 273 sunt] *add* bona AI 276 fol. 109ᵛᵃ 278 lucris] aliis lucris A • dediti] dicati (*corr. from* de|dicati) A, detiti I 279 seculari ... expensis] *om.* A 281 modus] *adds* uel motus O 282 succurrit] succurritur I, succumbit O
285 conturbatur] turbatum AI 286 Ouidius] metrice AI 287 Ut ... terras] *after* 293 nam I 288 penitusque] positusque I

emptiness comes the cart's irregular motion and running astray. Bernard speaks of this in his explanation of the Benedictine rule 3.7, explaining the verse, *The heaven above and the earth beneath* (Prv 25:3). He says, 'The heedlessness and leniency of prelates brings on such great disorder and confusion that in them the earth is above and the heaven beneath, the feet above the head, and the face turned backward, the inmost parts spilled outside, God trampled on the ground and the earth made into a god, the devil honourably received and God driven away in scorn.'

[266] Bernard proves that these irregular and disordered movements spring up in God's church from the leniency and heedlessness of ambitious people, when he says, 'Where the earth is above and the heaven below, earthly things are preferred to heavenly ones. Where the feet are above the head, spiritual people are despised, and people worldly wise are held in honour. Also the face is turned backwards, when, rather than attending immediately to actions that should be done well, one rather attends to worldly usefulness and puts off eternal rewards. Also the inmost parts are spilled outside, because spiritual goods that are within are neglected, and external temporal goods are loved. God is trampled upon and the earth deified when charity is lacking and desire alone reigns. The devil is honourably received and God scornfully driven away, because these ambitious people then receive with honour thieves, usurers, those dedicated to earthly wealth, and those committed to secular power, and they draw them in at great expense. But poor people are received only grudgingly or they are completely driven out.'[14] As Ovid says, this is the diverse movement by which Phaeton's cart rushes about and is overturned.

[283] [8] The eighth part of the picture follows; it concerns Phaeton's distress. For Ovid describes Phaeton as completely distraught and troubled by fear after he had seen his father's cart moving so irregularly and out of its track. For this reason, Ovid says,

When poor Phaeton looked from high / in the air upon the earth lying far far away, / he turned pale and suddenly his knees

---

[14] = *MF* prelacio bl, ascribed to commentary 3.7.

[in]tremuere timore / Suntque oculis tenebre, per t[an]tum
lumen aborte, / Et iam mallet equos nunquam tetigisse
paternos.
Nota quod istud loquendo moraliter bene conuenit ambiciosis,
nam ex remorsu consciencie continue sunt in timore, et redeuntes
ad consciencam penes se, deliberant et iudicant eos melius fuisse
dignitate tali male adquisita semp[er] caruisse, quam ad eam per
modum talem illicitum ascendisse. Unde de ista pena timoris qua
laborant ambiciosi, et generaliter omnes mali, loquitur Seneca
in quadam epistola sic dicens, 'Scelera tuta esse non possunt.
Hee enim pene semper malam mentem premunt, timere semper
et | expauescere et de securitate diffidere'. Et subdit Seneca hic,
'Concenciamus Epicuro, dicenti malo facinore consciencam
flagellari, et plurimi illi tormentorum esse, eo quod ipsum
perpetuo sollicitudo urgeat et uerberet. Hoc enim est argumentum,
ut dicit Epicurus, nos a natura horrere scelera, eo quod sceleratis
timor est eciam inter tuta; multos enim sceleratos fortuna liberat a
pena sed neminem a metu'.

[9] Sequitur nona pars picture de Phetontis \de/gradacione.
Nam poeta Ouidius fingit istum Phetontem post istam timoris
consternacionem cecidisse de curru. Ait enim Ouidius sic metrice,
At Pheton rutilos flamma populante capillos / Uoluitur in
preceps longoque per + aera tractu / Fertur, ut interdum de
celo stella sereno / Etsi non cecidit, potuit cecidisse uideri.
Nota quod Ouidius hic comparat lapsum Phetontis [descensioni]
illi[us] impressioni[s] qu[e] uocatur 'assub', nam ad litteram
quando + impressio ista est descendendo uersus terram, uidetur
ac si stella descenderet de celo. Sed [quando aliquis uidet illam] de
prope materiam illius impressionis, + apparet eis abhominabilis
et multum uilis. Unde similis est muscilagini, id est corumpcioni
quam homo emittit per nasum. Et modo simili est de ambiciosis
qui simplicibus apparent clari pro tempore prelacionis. Tales enim
simplices non respiciunt nisi in superficie, et tamen sapientibus et

289 intremuere] tremuere IO • tantum] totum IO   293 redeuntes] reddentes I
294 fuisse] *om.* A   295 male] mole A • semper] semp| O   296 pena] poeta I
297 laborant] la|larant I   298 tuta] tua A, *over eras.* I   300 fol. 109vb
302-3 flagellari ... sollicitudo] *om.* A   305 tuta] *om.* (*after* in|ter) I
309 consternacionem] conseruacionem I   310 At ... capillos] *om.* I • rutilos]
   uitulos A   311 aera] ethera IO   313 hic] in hiis uersibus AI   313-14 descensioni ...
   que] illi impressioni qui O   314 assub] adulo I   315 quando] *repeats* O
316 stella] *om.* I • descenderet ... aliquis] *marg.* I • quando ... illam] si alias
   uideret O   316 apparet] appa\re/ret O • eis] *om.* A, res I   319 nasum] malum A

trembled in fear, / and his sight grew dim, destroyed by such
great light; / now he wishes that he had never touched his father's
horses. (2.178–82)

Notice that Ovid's language is quite appropriate, in moral terms, for ambitious people. Remorse of conscience constantly makes them afraid and returning to conscience within themselves, they deliberate and judge others, those who have always lacked that dignity so evilly acquired, better than themselves – and better as well, because they have not ascended through such illicit means. For this reason, in a letter, Seneca speaks of this fearful punishment that works upon the ambitious, and all evil people in general, 'They may not be immune to their crimes. For these torments always depress an evil mind: to be constantly fearful and unable to believe in any security.' And Seneca adds here, 'I agree with Epicurus when he says that the conscience is scourged for its misdeeds and that that is the very greatest of those torments, because worry impels and strikes that person continually. For Epicurus's point is that this is why we are naturally appalled by crimes, because even among healthy things, those who commit crimes are fearful; Fortune frees many criminals from punishment, but none of them from fear.'[15]

[307] [9] The ninth part of the picture follows; it concerns Phaeton's fall. For Ovid imagines Phaeton after his fearful dismay to have fallen from the cart. His poem says,

And Phaeton, with fire ravaging his now reddened hair, / twists
headlong and is borne in a long path / through the air, as sometimes a
star in the peaceful heavens, / even if it has not fallen, might appear to
have fallen. (2.319–22)

Notice that Ovid here compares Phaeton's fall to that impression of the air called 'assub' when it descends, for literally, when this impression is descending toward the earth, it appears as if a star were coming down from heaven. But when someone sees the matter underlying this impression from near at hand, it appears to them abominable and quite disgusting. For this reason, it is similar to mucus, the corrupt material a person sends out through his nose. It's similar with ambitious people, who appear glorious to the simple during the time of their advancement. For such simple people look only on the surface, whereas for the wise and

---

[15] *Epistula* 97.13–16.

discrete considerantibus, tales promoti per ambicionem in nullo sunt in gradu | quem occupant honorati, sed [potius] uituperati.

Sicut tangit Boycius in suo libro *De consolacione Philosophie*, unde narrat de quodam homine ambicioso promoto ad consulatum qui uocabatur Nonius. De quo sic promoto loquens, homo bonus et sapiens nomine Catullus, qui de promocione huius erat indignatus, uocauit eum Nonium 's[t]rumam' siue 'gi[b]bum'. Nota quod commentator dicit ibi, scilicet Gilbertus Poretanus, 'S[t]ruma siue gi[b]ba deturpat hominem gi[b]bosum et reddit eum non + honorabilem, sed pocius abhominabilem'. Et \consimili/ [modo], malus et indignus promotus ad dignitatem non ex hoc honoratur sed abhominabilior quam prius fuit efficitur, et sic ab hominibus sapientibus iudicatur. Et de isto nota Bernardus, libro 2º *De consideracione ad Eugenium*, ubi dicit quod 'monstruosa res est gradus summus et animus infimus, sedes prima et uita yma, lingua magniloqua et manus ociosa, sermo multus et fructus nullus, uultus grauis et actus leuis, ingens auctoritas et + nutans stabilitas'.

[10] Sequitur decima pars picture de Phetontis exterminacione. Nam Ouidius poeta fingit istum Phetontem de curru lapsum et cecidisse in flumen quoddam \nomine/ Eridanum, et ibi in flumine mortuum et submersum. Unde sic dicit Ouidius,

Quem procul a patria [diuerso] maximus orbe / Exipit Eridanus f[umanci]aque abluit ora. / N[a]ides Hesperie t[rif]ida fumancia flamma / Corpora dant tumulo, signant | quoque carmine [sax]um.

Nota quod Ouidius hic tangit duo genera mortis quibus interiit iste Pheton, scilicet ambiciosus. Nam fingit eum percussum fulmine et submersum in flumine et post a mulierculis traditum sepulture.

---

323 fol. 110ra • potius] *om.* O
325 quodam] *om.* A   327 huius] adds Nomie A, adds Nonie I   328 and 330 struma(m)] scruma(m) (*in the second use marked as* scrunia) O • gibbum, gibba, gibbosum] gil|bum, gilbum, gilbosum O   329 dicit] sicut notat A • scilicet ... Poretanus] Poretarius A   331 honorabilem] honorabiliorem O   331-32 consimili modo] \consimiliter/ O   333 fuit] *om.* A   hominibus] omnibus A   336-37 prima ... manus] *om.* I   338 uultus grauis] multus gradus I • nutans] mutans AO, micans I
341 Phetontem] *om.* I   342 flumen quoddam] fluuium quendam AI • Eridanum] Eudanum A   344 diuerso] dimisso A, diuiso I, diuisus O   345 fumanciaque] fumancia AI, fluentaque O • Naides] Eraiade I, Nides O   346 trifida] trifada A, tersida O   347 fol. 110rb   348 saxum] fatum AIO

those considering the matter with care, those put in high place through ambition, whatever rank they hold, should be satirised, not honoured.

[324] Boethius discusses this in his *On the consolation of Philosophy*, when he tells about an ambitious man Nonius who was promoted to a consulship. The good and wise Catullus, outraged at his promotion, gave him the name 'swelling' or 'pustule'. Notice that Gilbert of Poitiers, the commentator here, says, 'A swelling or pustule like that shames the person who has it and doesn't make him honourable, but rather abominable.'[16] Similarly, an evil and unworthy person promoted to a noble position isn't honoured by this but is made more abominable than he was before – and wise people judge him to be so. On this point, notice *On consideration to Eugene* 2, where Bernard says, 'It's a monstrous thing when the highest office and the lowest mind are joined – a leading place and the lowest conduct, a grandiloquent tongue and a slack hand, much talk and no profit, a serious countenance and frivolous behaviour, immeasurable authority and wavering stability.'[17]

[340] [10] The tenth part of the picture follows; it concerns Phaeton's destruction. For Ovid depicts Phaeton as having fallen from his cart and plunged into the river Eridanus, where he lay dead and submerged. For this reason, he says,

The river Eridanus receives him far from his homeland, / separated from it by most of the world, and it bathes his smoking cheeks. / The Hesperian nymphs give a tomb / to that triple thing – flame, smoke, corpse; / they also inscribe verses on his stone. (2.323–26)

Notice that Ovid here mentions two kinds of death that befell Phaeton, the ambitious person. For he describes him as struck by lightning and sunk in the river and only afterwards taken to his tomb by some young women.

---

[16] *Ibid.* 3.p4 in init.
[17] *Ibid.* 2.7 (*PL* 182:750).

Et bene conueniunt ista tria ambiciosis, nam ambicionis uicium hec tria consequntur, scilicet quod ambiciosi inperceptibiliter moriuntur. Nam quando credunt melius dominari, ex inopinato deiciuntur, sicut patuit de illo Aman Agagite, de quo Scriptura loquitur, Hester 6. Et de isto dicitur Iob 12, ubi ostendit quomodo ambiciosus imperceptibiliter deicitur: *Quare, inquid, inpii uiuunt? Subleuati sunt confortatique diuiciis? Semen eorum permanet coram eis, propinquorum turbe et nepotes in conspectu eorum.* [*Domus eorum*] *secure sunt et pa*[c]*ate, et non est uirga Dei super illos. Bos eorum concepit et non abortiuit; uacca peperit et non est priuata fetu. Egrediuntur quasi greges paruuli eorum, et infantes eorum exultant lusubus; tenent timpanum et citharam et gaudent ad sonitum organi.* [*Et ducunt*] *in bon*[*is*] *dies suos – et in puncto ad inferna descendunt.* Ecce quomodo isti ambiciosi et mundani honoris cupidi, de honore in quo fuerunt inperceptibiliter deiciuntur, quia *in puncto* decidunt et finaliter deficiunt. Et ideo poeta bene fingit tales percussos fulmine, quo solent animalia subito et inperceptibiliter perire.

Similiter de secundo, | quod Pheton ambiciosus [fingitur mersus in fluuium. Nam sicut ambiciosus] inperceptibiliter deicitur, ita celeriter honor et dignitas ambiciosi finitur. Et de hoc pulcre habetur Sapientie 5°, ubi tales elati et per ambicionem exaltati conqueruntur dicentes, *Quid nobis profuit superbia? aut diuiciarum iactancia, quid nobis contulit? Transierunt omnia illa tanquam umbra.* Et sequitur, *Spes impii quasi lanugo que a uento tollitur, et tanquam spuma gracilis* [*que*] *a procella dispergitur, et tanquam fumus qui a uento diffusus est, et tanquam memoria hospitis unius diei pretereuntis.* Hec Scriptura. Ecce quomodo celeriter deficit honor et dignitas ambiciosi hominis, et ideo significanter poeta fingit ambiciosum in flumine submersum.

---

354 Nam] Notandum I   355 deiciuntur] moriuntur A   356 Scriptura loquitur] *om.* A   356–57 Et … deicitur] Item Iob 12 de ambiciosis A   357 quomodo] *adds* uir iste I   358 uiuunt] uim I   360 Domus eorum] Domus I, *om.* O   361 pacate] parate AIO   362–64 uacca … citharam] etc. A   365 Et¹ … bonis] In bonum datum O   365-6 et² … descendunt] etc. A   367-8 deiciuntur quia] et A, quia I   370 inperceptibiliter] inconctibiliter (?) I

371 fol. 110ᵛᵃ   371–72 ambiciosus … ambiciosus] ambiciosus O   374 habetur] conqueritur (*and om. later use*) A, loquitur I   376 quid … contulit] etc. A, *adds* Et sequitur I   377 quasi] tanquam AI   378 spuma] spirina I   • que a] a a O   379 fumus] *om.* AI   381 deficit] transit A

[352] And these three things are appropriate for ambitious people, for this vice has a triple outcome. First, that ambitious people die without being aware of it. For when the ambitious believe that they are lording about most successfully, they are cast down unawares, as was evident in the case of Haman the Agagian in Est 6. Iob 21:7–13 talks about this and shows how the ambitious person is cast down unawares, *Why then do the wicked live? Are they advanced and strengthened with riches? Their seed continueth before them, a multitude of kinsmen and of children's children in their sight. Their houses are secure and peaceable, and the rod of God is not upon them. Their cattle have conceived and fail not; their cow has calved and is not deprived of her fruit. Their little ones go out like a flock, and their children dance and play. They take the timbrel and the harp and rejoice at the sound of the organ. They spend their days in wealth – and in a moment they go down to hell.* See how these ambitious people, desiring worldly honour, are cast down, without being aware of it, from their past honour, for *in a moment* they are cast down and fail in the end. For this reason, Ovid has cleverly invented the idea that such people are struck by lightning, for it usually kills animals suddenly and without their knowing it.

[371] Similarly with regard to the second point, that Ovid depicts the ambitious Phaeton sunk in a river. For just as an ambitious person is cast down without being aware of it, in the same way, the honour and high standing of the ambitious person come quickly to an end. Sap 5:8–9 speaks beautifully about how such puffed up people, exalted by their ambition, are conquered, *What hath pride profited us? Or what advantage hath the boasting of riches bought us? All these things are passed away like a shadow.* And it continues (5:15), *For the hope of the wicked is as dust which is blown away with the wind, and as a thin froth that is dispersed by the storm, and a smoke that is scattered abroad by the wind, and as the remembrance of a guest of one day that passeth by.* That's what Scripture says. See how quickly an ambitious person's honour and standing fail, and therefore Ovid significantly depicts the ambitious Phaeton sunk in a river.

Ad modum enim aque, impetuose et festine decurrentis, transit repentine dominium talis ambiciosi, iuxta illud poeticum, 'Omnia pretereunt more fluentis aque'.

Similiter tercio, sicut ambiciosi fulmine percuciuntur et in flumine submerguntur, ita a mulierculis sepeliuntur. Proprietas enim istius sexus est obstinacio, ut doce[n]t philosophi, Aristoteles et alii, et ideo, quia ut communiter, ambiciosi moriuntur obstinati. Ideo fingunt poete quod iste Pheton ambiciosus a mulierculis sit sepultus. Unde notari possunt uerba que dicit Bernardus in quodam sermone, [scilicet 80], de isto uicio ambicionis: 'Ambicio, dicit, subtile malum est, secretum uirus, pestis occulta, doli artifex, mater ypocrisis, liuoris parens, uiciorum origo, tinea sanctitatis, execatrix cordium'. Per hanc autem mentis | humane excecacionem, ambicio deducit hominem ad finalem obstinacionem.

[11] Sequitur undecima pars picture, que est de Phetontis adornacione. Nam Ouidius fingit sepulcrum illius uersubus + ornatum. Unde epita[f]ium Phetontis est tale, sicut recitat Ouidius, 'Hic situs est Pheton, currus auriga paterni, / Quem si non tenuit magnis, tamen excidit ausis'. Et bene conuenit istud ambiciosis et cupidis mundani honoris, quia nichil aliud portabunt finaliter de ambicione, nisi cupiditatem + et curiosam uanitatem sepulture, sicut bene tangit beatus Augustinus, *De uera innocencia*, in fine libri, et fuit auctoritas sua tacta superius in mithologia 4ª, de dea Iunone et uirtute memorie. Ibi enim Augustinus postquam dixit, 'Circumspicite eos qui ante uos similibus fulsere honoribus: ubi exercituum duces, ubi satrape, ubi tiranni'? et statim subdit, 'Nonne omnia puluis? nonne omnia fauille? nonne in paucis uersubus eorum memoria'? Uult enim Augustinus dicere quod istud est commodum quod in fine reportant ambiciosi: sumptuosa sepulcra uersubus adornata in memoriam mortui. Sed uana et misera est ista memoria, ut bene tangit Crisostomus,

---

383 aque] fluminis A, *om.* I 384 dominium talis] dominunculis A
• ambiciosi] ambientis AI
386 fulmine] flumine (?) I 388 sexus] *om.* I • docent] docet O 388–89 Aristoteles et alii] *om.* A 389 moriuntur] *adds* finaliter A 390 Pheton] *om.* I
391–92 Unde ... ambicionis] Bernardus sermo 80° A 392 scilicet 80] *om.* O
396 mentis] ueritas I • fol. 110ᵛᵇ • excecacionem] exsecantur I
399 uersubus] *adds* exaratum siue O 400 epitafium] epitalium AO, epicafium I
401 Quem] Omne I 403 portabunt] reporant A, deportat I 404 cupiditatem ... uanitatem] curiosam A • cupiditatem] curiositatem I, *adds* et ambisiosam O
405–7 in fine ... dixit] *om.* A 410 nonne in] in me I 413 sepulcra] sepultura AI

For the lordship of such an ambitious person passes away quickly, just like water rushing away vigorously and quickly. As the verse says, 'All things have passed away, just like a flowing stream.'[18]

[386] Similarly with regard to the third point, just as ambitious people are struck by lightning and immersed in a river, they are likewise buried by young women. For stubbornness is one attribute of this sex, as Aristotle and other philosophers teach. Similarly, it is common for ambitious people to die fixed in their stubbornness, and this is why the poets depict the ambitious Phaeton as buried by young women. For this reason, one should notice Bernard's words in sermon 80 about the vice ambition. He says that 'Ambition is a clever evil, a secret poison, a hidden disease, a craftsman of deceit, mother of hypocrisy, parent of envy, source of vices, a moth eating away at holiness, the woman blinding hearts.'[19] Moreover, through this blinding of a person's mind, ambition leads one to the ultimate stubbornness.

[398] [11] The eleventh part of the picture follows; it concerns Phaeton's adornment. For Ovid depicts his tomb as adorned with verses; this is his epitaph, as Ovid reports it, 'Here lies Phaeton, charioteer of his father's cart; / if he did not seize great things, he nevertheless was exceedingly daring' (2.327–28). This inscription is appropriate for ambitious people, those desiring worldly honour, for in the end they will carry away nothing of their ambition except their desire and the intricate vanity of their tomb. Augustine treats this well near the end of *On true innocence*, and I have already cited this authoritative statement above, in the fourth mythology on Juno and the virtue memory. For there, after Augustine said, 'Look around at those before you who sought to shine with similar honours: where are the leaders of armies now? Where are the princes? Where are the tyrants?', he immediately adds, 'Aren't all these things dust? Aren't they all ashes? Isn't their memory just a few verses?'[20] Augustine wishes to say that this is the reward that ambitious people carry off in the end – sumptuous tombs adorned with verses in memory of the dead. But this memory is empty and wretched, as Chrysostom states in

---

[18] Cf. Ovid, *Ars amatoria* 3.62, beginning 'Eunt anni' (the years pass away).
[19] *In psalmum XC 'Qui habitat'* 6.4 (PL 183:198).
[20] Prosper, *Liber sententiarum* 390 (PL 45:1897–98, 51:496) (L).

415 *Super Mattheum*, + 'O insipiens', dicit Crisostomus, 'quid tibi prodest ista memoria post mortem tuam, si ubi es, ibi cruciaris, et si hic, ubi non es, fallaciter commendaris'? Quasi diceret nichil.

[12] Sequitur | duodecima pars picture et est de Phetontis deploracione. Nam poete, sicut patet in littera per Fulgencium 420 et per Ouidium, fingunt sorores Phetontis deplorasse casum et exterminum Phetontis. Unde dicit Ouidius,

Nec minus Eliades lugent, et inania morti / munera, dant lacrimas [et cese] pectora palmis / Non auditur[um] miseras Phetonte querelas / Nocte dieque u[o]cant asternunturque 425 sepulcro.

Nota quod poeta hic uult dicere quod iste sorores Phetontis, quas uocat Eliades, id est solis filias, sicut Pheton fuit solis filius, lacrimantur pro morte Phetontis. Sed ille lacrime sunt infructuose Phetonti et carentes utilitate, et ideo uocat poeta 430 tales 'lacrimas inanes'. Et bene conuenit istud ambiciosis, nam [omnes] isti ambiciosi *edificant Syon in sanguinibus*, sicut dicit propheta Micheas, capitulo 3°. Expendunt enim bona ecclesie uel in consanguineis et eis secundum natiuitatem attinentibus, uel in focariis +, quas uerso nomine, solent suas sorores uocare. Et 435 ideo significanter pingitur poetice quod solum tales persone eis committere, uel per attinenciam sanguinis uel per lasciuiam carnis dolent de eorum morte. Aliis autem personis indifferentibus mors talium est gaudiosa, quia per mortem tollitur eorum prelacio perniciosa. Sic igitur finitur octaua mithologia Fulgencii, continens 440 picturam poeticam istius uicii supradicti, scilicet ambicionis, sub ymagine Phetontis, qui solis filius fingebatur.

---

415 O] O frater o O • insipiens] sapiens A
418 fol. 111ra   419–20 sicut … Ouidium] *om.* A   423 et cese] et terre AI, que terunt sibi O • auditurum] auditurus A, auditoro O   424 uocant] uacant O
431 omnes] *om.* O   433 secundum natiuitatem] carnaliter A   434 focariis] *adds* seu fornicariis O   436 lasciuiam carnis] attinenciam lasciuie A, lasciuiam I
437 dolent] debent I   439–41 Sic … fingebatur] *om.* A   439 finitur] facta I

On Matthew, 'O fool, what good is this memory for you after your death, since where you are now, you are being tortured, and here, where you aren't, you are honoured only with lies?'[21] It is as if he said that memory is worthless.

[**418**] [12] The twelfth part of the picture follows; it concerns the mourning over Phaeton. For poets, just as Fulgentius's and Ovid's texts show, report that Phaeton's sisters lamented his fall and death.[22] Ovid says,

> No less did the Heliades mourn and pour out their tears, / an empty tribute to the dead boy, and beat their breasts, / even though Phaeton would never hear the wretched outcry / they utter continually, as they cast themselves on his tomb. (2.340-43)

Notice that Ovid here wishes to say that Phaeton's sisters – they are called the Heliades 'daughters of the sun', just as Phaeton was his son – weep for his death. But these tears for Phaeton are fruitless, indeed lack any use at all, and the poet therefore calls these 'empty tears'. And this is appropriate for ambitious people, for all such, as Mi 3:10 says, *Build up Sion with blood*. For they spend the church's good either on their relatives or on those who were concerned with their birth, or on concubines, who (with a change of name) are usually called their 'sisters'. This is pointedly depicted in Ovid's poetry, because ambitious people consign themselves only to those who lament their deaths because they are attached to them by blood or else from lust of the flesh. But for other disinterested people, the death of the ambitious is an occasion for joy, because death has carried off their pernicious lordship. Thus Fulgentius's eighth mythology ends. It contains a poetic picture of the vice ambition in the image of Phaeton, whom poets represented as the sun's son.

---

[21] *Opus imperfectum* 25 (PG 56:761-62) [= *MF* veritas y].
[22] Fulg 1.16 (27/21-28/7).

[9]

| Sequitur nona mithologia de deo Mercurio, sub cuius ymagine poete fingunt uirtutem eloquencie. Siquidem Mercurius iste pingitur a poetis
    [1] sexu bifurcatus,
    [2] alis agitatus,
    [3] Fronesi ligatus,
    [4] cede cruentatus,
    [5] mercibus uallatus,
    [6] furum prelatus,
    [7] pillio uelatus,
    [8] et pacis legatus.

Iste sunt octo partes picture uirtutis eloquencie, quam uirtutem solent poete depingere sub ymagine dei Mercurii quem dicunt esse deum sermonis et facundie. Unde et alio nomine uocant eum, Hermetem, quod est uerbum Grecum et sonat in Latino idem quod uel 'disertum' uel 'eloquen[tem]', sicut de hoc facit mencionem Fulgencius in littera. Et hic est notandum quod Aristoteles, 4 *Ethicorum*, ponit affabilitatem inter uirtutes morales. Et propter hanc causam ego pono in proposito eloquenciam uirtutem et continetur sub uirtute iusticie, sicut patet ibidem.

[1] Applicando autem partes picture huius poetice ad uirtutem eloquencie, patet prima pars huius picture, scilicet qualiter eloquencia est sexu bifurcata. Notandum enim quod poete fingunt Mercurium androgenum, hoc est hermofroditum, habentem utrumque sexum, masculinum et femininum. Et hoc quia iste planeta Mercurius coniunctus cum planetis \est/ beneuolis [beneuolus] et cum maliuolis maliuolus. Et ita est ad litteram de ista gracia sermonis et + | facundie. Quando enim eloquencia et sermonis facundia associatur bone uite, tunc est bona et dicitur esse sexus masculinus. Quando enim coniungitur cum uita peruersa, tunc est sexus femineus et plena malicia. Unde de gracia eloquencie [uerificatur quod] dicit sapiens de muliere, *Non est malicia super maliciam mulieris.*

---

1 fol. 111rb • deo] onus I 6 Fronesi] frenesi AI 9 furum] furibus AI
    12 partes] *om.* A 14 facundie] eloquencie A 15 Hermetem] Ormetem A
    16 eloquentem] eloquencie| O 19 pono] *om.* I
27 beneuolus] *om.* O 28 et^1] *adds* facun|| O • fol. 111va 32 uerificatur quod] tunc ueritatis (?) I, *om.* O

[9]

The ninth mythology follows, that of the god Mercury. Through his image, the poets represent the virtue Eloquence. Thus the poets depict Mercury as

[1] divided in sex,
[2] moved about by wings,
[3] bound to Prudence,
[4] bloodied with a blow,
[5] surrounded by merchants,
[6] honoured among thieves,
[7] covered with a cap,
[8] and a messenger of peace.

These are the eight parts of the picture of the virtue eloquence. The poets customarily depict this virtue through an image of the god Mercury, since they say he is the god of speech and of elegant language. For this reason, they also call him by another name, Hermes, a Greek word that means the same as the Latin 'something skilfully expressed' or 'eloquence', as Fulgentius mentions explicitly.[1] One should notice that in *Ethics* 4, Aristotle places pleasantness among the moral virtues. And for this reason, in my composition I identify eloquence as a virtue, and it is part of the virtue Justice, as Aristotle shows.[2]

[21] [1] In applying the parts of this poetic picture to the virtue eloquence, the first part of the picture shows how eloquence is divided in sex. For one should notice that the poets represent Mercury as androgynous, a hermaphrodite, having both sexes, male and female. That's because the planet Mercury, when it is in conjunction with benign planets, is benign, and when with malign ones, malign.[3] And that's literally the case with this gift of speech and elegant language. For when eloquence and elegance in speaking are associated with a good life, then eloquence is good and is said to be male in sex. But when it is joined with a perverse life, then it is feminine in sex and filled with malice. One can prove this on the basis of Sir 25:26, which speaks about a woman and the gift of eloquence, *All malice is short to the malice of a woman.*

---

[1] Fulg 1.18 (30/2–4).
[2] ? *Ibid.* 4.13 (1126b–27a).
[3] So Albumasor, *Introductorius maior* 4.5.14b (1:389).

Dicente Tullio in sua rethorica, 'Me', inquit, 'diu cogitante, ipsa racio duxit in hanc ipsam potissimam sentenciam, ut existimem sapienciam sine eloquencia parum prodesse ciuitatibus; eloquencia uero sine sapiencia [nimi]um obesse plerumque et nunquam prodesse'. Et pro isto potest notari auctoritas Ieronimi super illud Ysaie primo, *Uinum tuum mixtum est aqua*: 'Omnis doctor', dicit Ieronimus, 'qui austeritatem Scripturarum, per quam deberent audientes corripi, uertit ad graciam et ita loquitur, non ut corrigat, sed ut audientibus placeat. Iste qui talis est uinum + Sanctarum Scripturarum uiolat atque suo sensu corumpit'. Ex isto patet qualiter, loquendo moraliter, uirtus ista eloquencia, ad modum istius dei et planete Mercurii, uariatur et mutatur ex bona societate et mala. Quia in homine bono hec uirtus est utilis et proficua et in malis hominibus est nociua, dicente Crisostomus in suo libello *De compunctione cordis*, 'Docere et non facere plurimum dampnum confert. Grandis enim condempnacio est componenti [quidem] sermo|nem suum, uitam uero suam atque opera negligenti.

[2] Sequitur secunda pars picture de dei Mercurii agitacione. Pingitur enim iste deus alatus et alis per aera agitatus. Unde et Stilbon appellatus est a poetis quod idem est quod 'celer' uel 'festinus'. Et bene conuenit hec pars picture uirtuti eloquencie, que efficax est in operacione et celer in expedicione. Solent enim audientes moueri et passionari per istam uirtutem secundum exigencia[m] \materie/, modo ad misericordiam, modo ad complacenciam, et modo ad penitenciam et modo ad acceptacionem et modo ad detestacionem, et sic de aliis passionibus, quibus oratores et predicatores uerbi Dei solent audientes mouere per uirtutem istam facundie et eloquencie.

Unde de istius uirtutis expedita efficacia tangit \Titus/ Liuius u[i]uam narracionem, libro 2° *De gestis Romanorum*, ubi narrat quomodo uulgus et populus Romanorum uersus erat in

---

34 cogitante] cogitantem AI (?)   37 nimium] minimum O   40 austeritatem] auctoritatem A   42 uinum] *adds* scienciarum uel O   43 corumpit] corripit AI
46 bona ... mala] bona societate A, uaria (*over eras.*) societate I   49 confert] facit A   50 quidem] *om.* O   • fol. 111vb
53 alatus] elatus A   54 Stilbon appellatus] Solon uocatus A   55 pars] *om.* I
56 et ... expedicione] celeriter enim et expedite AI (enim et] *om.* I)
57 audientes] gaudentes A   58 exigenciam] exigencia O   59 conplacenciam] contemplacionem AI   60 acceptacionem] exceptacionem A   62 istam] *add* predictam AI
64 uiuam] unam AO

[34] Cicero says in his *Rhetoric*, 'Having considered it for a long time, I think this problem leads to the utterly convincing precept that I assess wisdom without eloquence to be of little use to a commonwealth, but eloquence without wisdom to harm a great deal and never to be profitable.'[4] And on this point, one should notice Jerome's authoritative statement about Is 1:22, *Thy wine is mingled with water.* Jerome says, 'Every learned person who turns the severity of the Scriptures, through which they should be rebuking their audience, into pleasantry speaks, not to rebuke, but to please their audience. Such a person destroys the wine of the Holy Scriptures and perverts its sense.'[5] This argument shows how, speaking in moral terms, the virtue eloquence, just like the god and planet Mercury, wavers and changes when in good and bad company. For in a good person, this virtue is useful and profitable, and in bad people harmful, just as Chrysostom says in his little book *On compunction of heart*, 'To teach and not to do destroys in many ways. For one should condemn as guilty of a great fault a person who composes a sermon while paying no attention to their own life and actions.'[6]

[52] [2] The second part of the picture follows; it concerns Mercury's movement. For this god is depicted as winged and moving about through the air using his wings. For this reason, the poets also call him 'Stilbon', which means the same thing as 'swift' or 'hastening'.[7] This part of the picture is appropriate for the virtue eloquence, because it is effective in its working and swift in operation. For this virtue customarily moves and inflames the audience according to the needs of the situation – sometimes to pity, sometimes to acceptance, sometimes to penance, sometimes to taking up a cause and sometimes to hating one, and likewise with other passions. Speakers and God's preachers customarily move audiences to these emotions through this virtue, eloquence and elegance.

[63] Livy treats this virtue's effective operation in a lively story in *Roman histories* 2. He tells how the common people of Rome had been

---

[4] *De inventione* 1.1.
[5] *Commentarii in Isaiam* 1 (PL 24:38).
[6] *Ibid.* 1 (paraphrase of the opening argument, fols 106–14).
[7] Fulg 1.18 (30/11–15).

sedicionem contra maiores et potenciores ciuitatis. Uidentes autem
rei publice sapientes periculum iminere ciuitati, miserunt ad
sedandum sedicionem Meneneum Agrippam, uirum plurimum
eloquencie, qui produxit in medium parabolam et apologum
70 quamdam Esopi Frigii de dissencione quam quadam uice
omnia membra concitauerant contra uentrem. Dixerunt autem
[cetera] membra quod uenter et stomachus omnia consumebant.
Unde manus in hac conspiracione promittebant quod nichil ori
ministrarent; os autem promisit quod nichil intra se reciperet; |
75 dentes promittebant quod nichil molerent uel conterrerent quod
utile stomacho foret. Unde dum isto modo membra in sedicione
et dissencione contra uentrem et stomachum permanerent,
inceperunt omnia corporis membra deficere et ad extremam
tabem uenire. Et statim cepit ille orator Meneneus Agrip[p]a
80 apologum predictum applicare ad propositum et dixit quod simili
modo fuit de senatoribus et consulibus rei publice Romanorum
et de ipsa plebe. Auferre enim honores et alia que illis m[ai]oribus
rei publice erant consueta, cederet statim populo in exterminium
tocius communitatis. Unde ex ista Menenii oracione fuit statim
85 sedicio populi sedata et cum omni quietati, et cum consulibus
quos prius uolebant occidere concordati sunt. Propter igitur
repentinam et celerem efficaciam quam habet eloquencia in
passionando homines et mouendos ad [di]uersos mores, pingitur
iste deus Mercurius, qui est deus facundie, alis agitatus. Ideo dicit
90 Ieronimus significanter in epistola ad Paulinum, 'Nescio quid
latentis energie, hoc est uirtutis et efficacie, habet uiue uocis actus;
in aures discipuli de + auctoris ore transfusa forcius sonat'.

[3] Sequitur tercia pars picture de dei Mercurii confederacione.
Nam poete fingunt istum Mercurium desponsatum Philologie, que
95 fingitur ab eis filia Fronesis, id est Prudencie. Et istud sp[ec]ialiter
conuenit eloquencie | coniungi, scilicet cum racione et discrecione.
Unde scilicet loquens in loquendo consideret circumstancias
debitas, tam loci quam temporis, quam persone, et sic de aliis,
quia aliter loquendum est et perorandum coram una persona

---

67 ciuitati] communitati I   71 Dixerunt] Duxerunt I   72 cetera] *om.* O   74 os]
ut I • fol. 112ra 79 tabem] *om.* A • Agrippa] Agripta O   81–83 rei publice ...
rei publice] rei publice A   82 maioribus] minoribus O   84 communitatis]
ciuitatis A   85 sedata] quietata A • et cum omni] annonum I   86 quos ...
occidere] *om.* A   88 ad diuersos] ad|uersos O   91 uocis] cocos I   92 auctoris]
auctoritatis O

95 specialiter] spiritualiter O   96 fol. 112rb • coniungi] coniugi AI   97 loquens in]
om. AI   98 aliis] *add* circumstanciis AI

brought to a rebellion against the greater and more powerful citizens. But wise men of the commonwealth, who saw the danger that threatened the city, sent Menenius Agrippa, a man outstanding for his eloquence, to calm the rebellion. He put forward in his speech a fable and apologue of Aesop the Phrygian. This concerned the dissension that once arose when all the limbs had assembled against the belly. For the other limbs said that the belly and the stomach ate up everything. For this reason, in this conspiracy, the hands promised that they would give nothing to the mouth; in its turn, the mouth promised that it would receive nothing, and the teeth that they would neither bruise nor grind to bits anything that might be useful for the stomach. And so as long as the limbs remained in rebellion and at odds with the belly and stomach in this way, all the limbs of the body began to fail and to fall into the worst decay. The orator Menenius immediately began to apply this fable to the present situation; he said there was an analogy with the senators and consuls of the Roman commonwealth and the common people. For to take away the honours and other things to which the upper class was accustomed would immediately draw the people into the downfall of the entire community. For this reason, Menenius's speech immediately pacified the people's rebellion and, when it had been thoroughly quelled, the people were brought into accord with the consuls whom they had earlier wanted to kill.[8] Therefore because of eloquence's sudden and swift efficacy in arousing passions and convincing people to change their behaviour, Mercury, the god of eloquence, is depicted as moved by wings. And Jerome pointedly says in his letter to Paulinus, 'I don't know what hidden energy (the word means 'power' and 'efficacy') the action of the present voice has; but it sounds very strongly in a student's ears when it passes forth from an authoritative mouth.'[9]

[93] [3] The third part of the picture follows; it concerns Mercury's joining. For poets represent him as married to Philology, whom they suppose to be the daughter of Phronesis or Prudence. It is particularly appropriate that eloquence be joined with her, that is with reason and discretion. For this reason, when someone speaks, they should consider the appropriate 'circumstances', of place and of time and of person and of all the rest. For one should speak or orate in one way before one person

---

[8] *Ab urbe condita* 2.32.
[9] *Epistola* 53.2 (PL 22:541).

100 et aliter coram alia, et aliter in uno tempore et aliter in alio, et aliter in ista materia et aliter in alia. Et de isto tangit Gregorius Nazazenus, cuius auctoritatem recitat Gregorius papa in suo *Pastorali*, sic dicens, 'Longe ante nos reuerende memorie Gregorius Nazazenus edocuit quod non una eademque
105 exortacio cunctis congruit, quia nec cunctos par morum qualitas st[ring]it. Sepe namque aliis officiunt que aliis prosunt. Quia plerumque herbe que hec animalia nutriunt, alia occidunt; et leuis sibilus equos mitigat et catulos instigat; et medicamentum quod hunc morbum imminuit, alteri uires iungit; et pani\s/,
110 qui uitam forcium roborat, uitam paruulorum necat. Pro qualitate igitur audiencium formari debet sermo doctorum'. Et ideo significanter Mercurius fingitur iuisse matrimonium cum Philologia, hoc est cum racione et discrecione, quia secundum quod uariantur circumstancie oportet uirum eloquentem suum
115 sermonem uariare.

[4] Sequitur quarta pars picture de Mercurii cruentacione. Nam poete, sicut in littera tangit Fulgentius, fingunt quod iste Mercurius occidit Argum, pastorem dee Iunonis, qui Argus dicitur habuisse centum oculos. Et de ista interfeccione loquitur
120 Ouidius, libro primo *De transformatis*, ubi narrat quomodo | Argus iste habuit centum oculos et quomodo, dum una medietas oculorum dormiebat, alia mediatas uigilabat. Unde dicit sic, 'Centum luminibus cinctum caput Argus habebat; / Inde suis uicibus capiebant bina quietem, / Cetera seruabant atque in
125 stacione manebant'.

Ad istum Argum decipiendum, qui habuerat in custodia [Ion] filiam Inati, quam Iubiter mutauerat in uaccam, uenit Mercurius, qui cum fistula cepit canere et finaliter ita placenter contulit et alloquibatur illum Argum quod tandem reddidit illum
130 Argum in omnibus oculis saporatum. Quo dormiente, Mercurius gladium extraxit et Argum sopore depressum interficit. Unde sic dicit poeta,

100 alio] *add* tempore AI   104 edocuit] et docuit I   105 par] *om.* A
106 stringit] disting\u/it O • officiunt] efficiunt AI   109 imminuit] minuit AI
110 necat] uocat I   112 significanter] similiter I • iuisse] inesse I
118 Iunonis] Iouis A, Io[is] I   120–21 ubi … oculos] *om.* A   120 fol. 112[va]
121 quomodo dum] quando AI   123 cinctum] centum A
127 Ion] Iunonem I, *om.* O • filiam] similia A • mutauerat] *om.* I
130–31 Argum … depressum] eum A   131 depressum] depressit et I
131–37 Unde … una] *om.* A

and before some other person in another way, and one way in one time and a different way in another, and one way when treating one kind of material and another way when treating another. Gregory Nazianzen treats this matter, and pope Gregory repeats his authoritative views in his *Pastoral rule*, saying, 'Long ago Gregory Nazianzen of blessed memory taught us that a single identical sermon does not accord with everyone's needs, for not everyone is bound by identical behaviours. Often things that benefit others impede the audience addressed. There are many herbs that nourish one set of animals, but kill another; a soft hissing calms horses yet arouses cats; a drug that abates one disease makes a different one more virulent; and bread, which fortifies strong people, harms babies. Therefore learned men's sermons ought to be composed with an eye to the quality of the audience.'[10] And therefore it is significant that Mercury is said to have married Philology, that is reason and discretion, because an eloquent person must change their address to accord with changed circumstances.

[116] [4] The fourth part of the picture follows; it concerns Mercury bloodied. For the poets, as Fulgentius says explicitly, report that Mercury killed Argus, the goddess Juno's shepherd, who was said to have had one hundred eyes.[11] Ovid talks about this killing in *Metamorphoses* 1, where he tells how Argus had one hundred eyes and how, while half the eyes slept, the other half were on guard. For this reason, he says, 'Argus had one hundred eyes that girdled his head; / while half took its rest in its turns, / the others served and remained in their station.'[12]

[126] Now Argus had guarded Inachus's daughter Io, whom Jupiter had turned into a cow. Mercury came to deceive him and began to play on the pipe, and he conferred and spoke with Argus so pleasantly that he finally made all Argus's eyes sleepy. Once he was overcome with sleep, Mercury pulled out his sword and killed him. Ovid says,

---

[10] *Ibid.* 3.prol. (*PL* 77:49).
[11] Fulg 1.18 (30/18–31/6).
[12] *Ibid.* 1.625–27, followed at line 132 by 1.717–21.

Nec mora, falcato nucante[m] uulnerat ense, / Qua collo
est [conf]ine caput, saxoque cruentum / Deicit et maculat
135 preruptam sanguine rupem. / Arge, [iaces quod]que in tot
+ lumin[a] lumen habebas / Extinctum [est] centum[que]
oculos nox occupat u[n]a.

Et nota, sicut [tangit] Fulgentius in litera, Argus iste interpretatur
'uagus' et significat uirum insolentem et moribus immaturum.
140 Cuius insolenciam multiplicem et morum deformitatem
uir eloquens interficit et extingit per discretam et solertem
exhortacionem, sicut de hoc pulcre tangit Augustinus, et ponit
exemplum in quadam epistola de illo Polemone.

De quo [eciam] loquitur Ualerius Maximus, libro 6 *D[i]ctorum*
145 *et factorum memorabilium*, capitulo ultimo. Ubi dicit sic, 'Perdite
luxurie adolescens Polemo, neque illecebris tantummodo, sed
ipsa in|famia gaudens, cum e conuiuio, non post occasum solis
sed post solis ortum, surrexisset, domumque rediens, uidisset
hostium scole philosophi Zenocratis appertum, ipse uino grauis,
150 ungentis delubutus, amictus ueste perlucida, habens sertum in
capite, scolam Zenocratis intrauit et in scola residens, doctrinam
philosophi deridere cepit. [In]dignabantur discipuli Zenocratis de
impudencia Polemoni[s], sed Zenocrates, uultum suum semper in
eodem habitu, continuit et proposicionem de [qua] loqui ceperat
155 dimisit, et de temperancia et modestia disserere cepit. Cuius
sermonis maturitate Polemo delectatus, resipuit et primo sertum
de capite proiecit et paulo post brachium \intra/ pallium reduxit,
et ad ultimum totam luxuriam exuit. Et sic istius philosophi
eloquencia uarias in Polemone insolencias trucidauit'. Unde dicit
160 sic Ualerius, 'Ecce: ex infami ganione maximus philosophus factus
fuit'. Ecce: quomodo eloquencia Zenocratis Argum uagum in
Polemone interfecit.

---

133 nucantem] micante (*so marked*) O   134 confine] consciencie I, asine O
135 iaces quodque] iaces quod I, ratosque O • in] ut I   136 lumina] luminis
lumine O • est centumque] quoque centum O   137 una] uria O   138 tangit]
om. O   142 tangit ... et] Augustinus AI
144 eciam] *om.* O • *Dictorum*] doctorum O   145 *et factorum*] *om.* AI
147 fol. 112vb 150 amictus] amicus ? I   151 residens] rediens I
152 Indignabantur] Dedignabantur O   153 impudencia] imprudencia A,
impudicicia I • Polemonis] Polemonie O   154 proposicionem] proposito
rem AI • qua] *om.* O   155 dimisit] *om.* A   156 resipuit] respuit AI
157 brachium intra pallium] prandium intrat in brachium A   160 Ecce ...
ganione] postea A

No delay now. He wounded him with the curved sword as he nodded, / separating the head from the neighbouring neck, and cast down gore / on the stone, and stained the precipitous rock with blood. / Now you lie dead, Argus, even though you were lit by so many eyes; / now a single night possesses all hundred of them, extinguished.

Notice that as Fulgentius says explicitly, the name Argus means 'wandering' and it indicates an immoderate person, one who behaves immaturely. The eloquent person kills and extinguishes this multiple immoderate and deformed behaviour through prudently personalised and clever exhortation, as Augustine nicely discusses in one of his epistles, where he offers the example of a certain Polemon.[13]

[144] Valerius Maximus also speaks about him in *Memorable things about words and deeds* 6, the final chapter, where he says, 'The youth Polemon was abandoned in his luxuriousness – and not just to indecencies but rejoiced at the ill-fame they brought him. On one occasion, when he had risen from a banquet, not just after sunset but after sunrise, he was returning to his house. He saw the door to the philosopher Xenocrates's school open and entered, although drunk, smeared with oils, clothed in revealing garments, and with a garland on his head. Sitting down in the school, he began to mock the philosopher's teaching. Xenocrates's students were outraged by his insolence, but Xenocrates himself, constantly keeping a straight face, continued, and, setting aside the topic on which he had begun to speak, began to expound on temperance and modesty. Polemon, delighted by the maturity of his speech, came to his senses, and first threw off the garland from his head and a little later drew his arm inside his cloak and finally stripped himself of everything luxurious. Thus the eloquence of this philosopher killed off all Polemon's improper behaviours.' For this reason, as Valerius says, 'From a glutton of ill repute he was made the greatest philosopher.' See how Xenocrates's eloquence killed off the wandering Argus in Polemon.

---

[13] *Epistola* 144.3 (PL 33:592), followed by Valerius's account, 6.9.ext. 1.

[5] Sequitur quinta pars picture de Mercurii mercacione. Poete enim fingunt Mercurium esse deum mercatorum, et illud bene conuenit eloquencie uirtuose. Nam qui in negociis et mercacionibus occupantur, lucra et diuicias desiderant et uenantur. Ad hoc enim uacant mercacioni ut possint lucrari et ditari, | sed per istam eloquenciam peruenit homo ad ueras diuicias, sicut bene tangit Gregorius, 6º *Moralium*, ubi dicit quod 'Iste bene loquendi facundiam accipit qui s[in]um cor[dis] per recte uiuendi studia [extendit]. Nec loquentem conscienciam pre[pe]dit, cum linguam antecedit uita'. Nota Gregorius uult dicere quod nullus potest petere graciam eloquencie, nisi sit rectus et bonus in consciencia et uita, sed omnis talis ueris diuiciis est circumdatus et uallatus.

Probat enim Tullius quod sola uirtus facit hominem diuitem, et uicia faciunt eum pauperem et egentem. Unde dicit sic, 'Si isti rerum callidi estimatores prata et areas quasdam magni estimant, eo quod talibus possessionibus noceri non potest. Quia nec naufragio nec incendio talia amittuntur, quanti igitur estimanda est uirtus, que nec eripi nec surripi potest naufragio nec incendio, nec tempestatum nec temporum perturbacione mutari? Qui enim uirtute prediti sunt, illi soli diuites sunt. Soli enim possident res et fructuosas et sempiternas; soli eciam uirtuosi contenti sunt rebus et satis esse putant quod habent, nec ulterius appetunt. Hii soli diuites dicendi sunt. Nulla enim re egent; nichil sibi deesse senciunt; nichil requirunt. Inprobi eciam et auari, quoniam incertas atque casu positas possessiones habent et plus semper appetunt, nec eorum ad huc est inuentus. Quisquam cui quod haberet satis esset non modo, non copiosi nec diuites, sed pauperes et inopes dicendi sunt'. Hec Tullius. Ex quibus uerbis contingit deducere quod eloquencia | ueris diuiciis est uallata, quia oportet quod uirtutum insigneis sit ornata. Quia non est eloquencia, ut docet Tullius, nisi habeat hec duo, honestatem uiuendi et periciam loquendi. Sed honestas uite semper habet anexam ueram ubertatem et opulenciam. 'Sole enim diuicie uere sunt que nos uirtutibus diuites efficiunt', ut dicit Gregorius in quadam epistola.

---

168 fol. 113ra 170 sinum cordis] suum cor AO, suum cordis I   171 extendit] exstrudit I, instruit O • prepedit] prependit A, perpendit I, reprehendit O   174 consciencia] conuersacione A

177 eum] esse A   179 potest] *om.* A   184 contenti sunt] comtemptis A   188 casu] *om.* A   188–89 et plus ... appetunt] *om.* A   192 fol. 113rb 194 ut docet Tullius] *om.* A   196 opulenciam] subtilitatem A   197 epistola] omelia AI

[162] [5] The fifth part of the picture follows; it concerns Mercury's mercantile activities. For poets represent Mercury as the god of merchants, and that is quite appropriate for virtuous eloquence. For those who spend their time in business and mercantile operations desire and hunt for rewards and riches. Sometimes they even take a break from their mercantile operations to be further rewarded and enriched, but through eloquence a person comes to true riches. Gregory treats this well, in *Moral readings* 6, where he says, 'The person who opens out their heart's core in the studies of living well receives eloquence in speaking well. Nor when a good life precedes a ready tongue, does conscience hinder their speaking.'[14] Notice that Gregory wishes to say that no one can seek the gift of eloquence, unless that person is righteous and good in conscience and in behaviour, but every person of that sort is surrounded and fortified with true riches.

[176] Also Cicero proves that only virtue makes a person rich, and vices make them poor and needy. For this reason, he says, 'If people cunning about possessions consider their meadows and fields grand things, it's because harm may not befall so many possessions. But if neither shipwreck nor fire can bear away such things, how much more greatly should one value virtue, which can neither be snatched away nor stolen by fire or shipwreck, nor altered by the troubles brought on by storms or by threatening times? Only those who are endowed with virtue are truly rich. They alone own things both fruitful and enduring; only the virtuous are content with their things. For they think what they have enough, nor do they desire anything further. They alone should be called rich. They lack nothing; they feel nothing absent; they need nothing further. But vicious and avaricious people, both because the status of their possessions is uncertain and at risk, and because they always want more, are never found in this state. People for whom what they have now is not enough should not be called either prosperous or rich, but rather poor and needy.'[15] So Cicero says. From his words, one might well deduce that eloquence is surrounded by true riches, because it is necessary that eloquence be adorned with emblems of the virtues. For, as Cicero teaches, it's not truly eloquence, unless it has two things, virtuous living and skill in speaking. But virtuous living always has joined to it true fullness and wealth. As Gregory says in a letter, 'Only those riches that make us rich in virtues are true ones.'[16]

---

[14] *Ibid.* 6.36 (PL 75:759).
[15] *Paradoxa Stoicorum* 51–52.
[16] *Epistola* 7.29 (PL 77:885).

[6] Sequitur sexta pars picture [de] dei Mercurii prelacione. Nam ut tangit Fulgencius in littera, Mercurius iste est dominus furum et deus latronum. Proprietas furum et latronum est explorare et diligenter et callide locorum et temporum et aliarum circumstanciarum uicissitudines diiudicare, ut sic ad rem optatam optinendam possint pertingere. Et conuenit istud proprie uirtuti eloquencie, nam secundum Gregorium, *Super Ezechielem*, 'Doctor eloquens pensare debet et diligenter explorare quid sit loquendum et cui sit loquendum, qualiter loquendum, quantum eciam sit loquendum'. Et consimiles circumstancias oportet furem aduertere, si uelit in suis negociis expedire. \Et ponit ibi Gregorius de predictis exempla. Quid enim loquatur oportet doctorem aduertere +/, 'ut iuxta Pauli apostoli uocem, *sermo eius in gracia semper sit sale conditus*. Cui eciam loquatur oportet quod consideret, quia [sepe] una persona increpaciones admittit, altera respuit. Quando eciam loquatur oportet quod aduertat, sicut patet in exemplo de Abigail, que uirum suum Nabal existentem ebrium de culpa tenacitatis increpare noluit, quem tamen digesto uino, uerbis increpat[ion]is utiliter percussit. Qualiter eciam loquatur oportet quod penset, nam sepe uerba que alium ad | salutem reuocant, alium uulnerant. Quantum tunc loquitur oportet quod ponderet, ne si ei qui multa ferre non ualet exhortacionis uerba longe prot[ra]xerimus, auditorem ad fastidium pertrahamus'.

[7] Sequitur septima pars picture de dei Mercurii pilliacione. Nam [sicut] dicit Fulgencius in littera, Mercurius pingitur a poetis uelatus capite galero; uocat galerum 'pilium de corrio'. Uirtus autem ista [eloquencie] pingitur pilliata in signum ualoris et excellencie quam habet uirtus ista inter ceteras uirtutes, sicut de eius excellencia loquitur diffuse Quintilianus in suo libro

---

198 de] *om.* O   200 Proprietas] et I   202–5 optinendam … eloquens] quid I
  205 eloquens] loquendus | ad loquendum A   206 et cui sit loquendum] *om.* I
  208 in suis negociis] *om.* A   210 aduertere] *adds* si uelit in suis negociis (*marg., repeating 208*) O   211 uocem] *om.* I   212 sepe] se I, *om.* O   217 increpationis] increpatoriis O   218 penset] *adds* et ponderat A   218–20 nam … exhortacionis] *marg. (originally om. at page-boundary)* I   218 sepe] semper I   • fol. 113[va]
  219 quod] *adds* penset et A   220 ualet] potest A, potest uel non ualet I
  221 protraxerimus] pertrahimus A, protexerimus O
222 pilliacione] palliacione A   223 sicut] secundum A, sequitur O   224 corrio] *adds* sicut patet Papiam et alios gramaticos A   225 eloquencie] *om.* O
  226 et] *adds* eloquencie et A   226–27 sicut … excellencia] *om. (at column-boundary)* A

[198] [6] The sixth part of the picture follows; it concerns Mercury's lordship. For as Fulgentius says explicitly, Mercury is the lord and god of thieves.[17] It's a characteristic of thieves to explore and thereby to puzzle out, diligently and cleverly, variations of places and times and of the other 'circumstances' so that they may gain the very best way of attaining the goal they have chosen. This is very appropriate for the virtue eloquence, for according to Gregory, *On Ezechiel*, 'The eloquent teacher ought to consider and explore diligently what he should say and to whom he should say it, how he should say it, and how much he should say.' Analogously, thieves must pay attention to 'circumstances', if they wish to get ahead at their business. And Gregory offers there examples of these considerations. For a teacher must pay attention to what he should say, 'as Paul says: *Let your speech be always in grace seasoned with salt* (Col 4:6). Also it's necessary that the teacher should consider to whom he would speak, for often one person will accept rebukes while another will reject them. It's also necessary to pay attention to when one speaks, as the example of Abigail shows; since he was drunk, she did not choose to rebuke her husband Nabal for his persistence in sin, but once he had digested the wine, she struck him fruitfully with words of rebuke (1 Rg 25:37). Also it is necessary that one think about how one should speak, for often words that recall one person to salvation will only wound someone else. Finally, it is necessary that one consider how much one says, lest we protract words of exhortation excessively for someone who hasn't the strength to bear a great deal, since then we just drag the hearer along to the point where they're disgusted.'[18]

[222] [7] The seventh part of the picture follows; it concerns Mercury's headgear. For as Fulgentius says explicitly, poets depict Mercury with his head covered by a 'galerus', a word for a cap made out of leather.[19] The virtue eloquence is depicted with a cap as an indication of the strength and excellence it has among all the virtues. Quintilian, in his

---

[17] Fulg 1.18 (29/5–6, 30/9–11).
[18] *Homiliae in Ezechielem* 1.11.12–16 (*PL* 76:910–11).
[19] Fulg 1.18 (29/18–19).

De institucione oratoris. Unde dicit sic, 'Deus ille, princeps, pa[ren]s mundique fabricator, nullo magis hominem separauit a [ce]teris que qu[idem] mortalia sunt animalibus quam dicendi facultatem. Racionem enim precipuam nobis dedit eiusque nos socios esse cum diis immortalibus uoluit. Sed ipsa racio neque tam nos iuuaret neque tam esset in nobis manifesta, nisi que concepissemus mente promere eciam loquendo possemus. Quam eloquenciam magis deesse ceteris animalibus quam intellectum et cognicionem quandam uidemus. Namque mollire cubilia et [ni]dos texere et educare fetus et excludere, quin eciam reponere in yemem alimenta, opera eciam nobis quedam [inimi]tabilia, qualia sunt cerarum ac mellis efficere. Non nullius fortasse racionis est, sed, quia carent sermone que illud faciunt, muta atque irracionabilia uocantur'. Hec Quintilianus.

Et nota quod | Quintilianus uult probare quod uirt\us ista/ eloquencie est uirtus singularis excellencie, nam per istam graciam hominibus a Deo datam differt homo specialiter a brutis animalibus. Unde dicit quod alio modo plus apparet quod homo distinguitur a brutis per facundiam sermonis quam per iudicium racionis. Et ideo in signum \excellencie huius/, Mercurius deus eloquencie pingitur pilliatus in capite. Ei eciam propter hanc causam et eius tutele, poete attribuunt gallum, sicut patet in littera per Fulgencius, nam \g/alli incedunt capite cristati.

[8] Sequitur octaua pars picture de dei Mercurii legacione. Nam poete fingunt Mercurium legatum et nuncium deorum. Pingunt eciam Mercurium cum caducio, que uirga quedam est pacis et concordie. Quam uirgam Mercurius pingitur in manu portare, sicut patet \per/ Ouidium, primo *De transformatis*. Unde loquens de Mercurio et de eius apparatu, pro tempore quo missus fuit a Ioue ad interficiendum Argum, dicit sic,

Parua mora est alas pedibus uirgamque potentem /
Sompniferam sumpsisse manu tegumenque capillis. / Hec
ubi d[is]posuit, patria Ioue natus ab arce / desiliit in terras;

---

229 parens] pacis O   230 ceteris que quidem] terris quecunque O
232 immortalibus] mortalibus I   233 iuuaret] ipsa in|m°cret I   237 nidos] modos O   238 inimitabilia] immutabilia A, in mutabilia I, mutabilia O
239 cerarum ac mellis] terrenarum ac mollis I
242 fol. 113vb • uirtus] *om.* AI   244 homo] *om.* AI   244-46 brutis ... brutis] brutis A
251 pars] *adds* et ultima I   253 caducio] *adds* scilicet caduceo A   255 portare] porrigere I   258-62 Parua ... est] *om.* A   259 sumpsisse] soncisse I
260 disposuit] deposuit O • desiliit] defilit I

Institutes for orators speaks at length of this excellence, 'God, the prince, the parent and constructor of the world, separated humanity from other, equally mortal animals in no greater way than by the power to speak. In particular, he gave us reason and through it wished us to be companions of the immortal gods. But reason neither helps us so much nor is so obvious in us, unless we are also able to bring forth in speech those things that we have conceived in our minds. For we see that other animals lack eloquence more than they do either intellect or knowledge. They can make soft beds and weave nests and educate their young and drive them to independence, indeed even store away food for the winter, indeed some works that we cannot imitate, like making wax and honey. These are perhaps things done not without reason, but the animals that do these things, because they lack speech, are called mute and irrational.' So Quintilian says.[20]

[242] Notice that Quintilian wishes to prove that eloquence is a virtue of unique excellence, because through this gift that God gave humans, they are specially different from brute animals. For this reason, he says that there is another way in which man differs more from the animals than through his mode of thinking, and that is in eloquent speech. Therefore, as an indication of this excellence, Mercury, the god of eloquence, is depicted with a cap on his head. Also, as Fulgentius says explicitly, for this reason, poets assign him, as his guardian, a cockerel, for cockerels go about with a crest on their heads.[21]

[251] [8] The eighth part of the picture follows; it concerns Mercury's embassy. For poets represent Mercury as the messenger and herald of the gods. They also depict Mercury with the caduceus, a rod indicating peace and concord. They portray Mercury carrying the rod in his hand, as Ovid shows in *Metamorphoses* 1. For this reason, speaking of Mercury and of his equipment, at the time Jove sent him to kill Argus, he says,

With no delay, Mercury fixed his wings to his feet and took /
his rod, powerful in bringing sleep, in his hand, as well as the
covering for his head. / Having disposed all his things, Jove's
child leapt from his father's citadel / down to earth.

---

[20] *Ibid.* 2.16.12, 14–16.
[21] Fulg 1.18 (29/19–22).

illic tegumenque resoluit / Et posuit pennas, tantummodo
uirga retenta est.
Nota poeta hic uult dicere quod quando Mercurius parauit se ad
perficiendum mandatum patris sui Iouis de occidendo Argum,
tunc accepit secum alas suas et | galorum suum. Sed quando
descendit ad terram de celo, tunc retinuit solam uirgam, scilicet
caduceum, et dimisit alas et galerum. Nam uirga illa fuit
signum pacis, nam sicut docet Remigius in commento *Super
Martianum*, ideo dicitur uirga Mercurii 'caduceus', quia facit lites
et contenciones cadere, et ideo Mercurius pingitur a poetis nuncius
et legatus pacis.

Hoc enim proprium eloquencie est discordes pacificare,
amiciciam conseruare, et conseruatam multiplicare. *Uerbum
enim dulce multiplicat amicos*, ut dicit sapiens. Et de ista pacis et
concordie reformacione, qualiter fit mediante [ista uirtute, scilicet]
eloquencia, loquitur Augustinus pulcre, libro 4 *De doctrina
cristiana*, capitulo 7, ubi narrat de seipso quod quadam uice
'apud Cesaream Mauritanie + dissuadebat populo pugnam
ciuilem – ymmo plus quam ciuilem pugnam – quam uocabant
"cateruam". Neque enim ciues tantummodo, uerum eciam
propinqui, fratres, postremo parentes ac filii lapidibus inter se in
duas partes diuisi per aliquos dies continuos certo tempore anni
soleniter dimicabant, et quilibet quencumque poterat occidebat.
Egit igitur Augustinus, quantum ualuit, per eloquenciam et
modum dicendi quem rethores uocant grandiloquium, ut tam
crudele et inueteratum malum de cordibus et de moribus pelleret
ill[o]rum ciuium. Qui tandem, moti sermonibus Augustini, flere
ceperunt' et illam insaniam [et] pessimam consuetudinem penitus
dimiserunt et ad pacis unitatem omnes | concorditer redierunt.

Et de consimili materia ponit Ualerius, extra libro 8
Dictorum et factorum memorabilium, capitulo in quo agit de
potestate eloquencie, ubi narrat quod 'regibus exactis, plebs
dissidens a patribus, iuxta ripam fluminis in collo qui Sacer
appellatur armata consedit, eratque non solum deformis sed
eciam miserimus rei publice status, a capite eius c\e/tera parte

264 Iouis] r̄onis (= racionis) I   265 fol. 114ra 266 de celo] *om*. I   267 docet] *om*. I
271 pacis] pater A
275 ista … scilicet] *om*. O   278 dissuadebat] dissuadebant IO • populo] *om*. A
279 pugnam] *om*. A   281 postremo] *om*. A   286 illorum] illarum O • moti]
motus O   288 insaniam et] inanem et AI, insaniam O   289 fol. 114rb
290–300 Et … reformauit] *om*. A   291 et factorum] *om*. I   295 miserimus] in
miserime I • cetera] cum I

There he took off his cap / and laid aside his wings; he kept only his rod.[22]

Notice that Ovid here wants to say that when Mercury prepared himself to carry out his father Jove's commandment to kill Argus, he took with him his wings and his cap. But when he descended from heaven to earth, he kept with him only the caduceus, his rod, and put aside the wings and cap. For the rod was a sign of peace, for just as Remigius teaches in his commentary on Martianus, it is called 'caduceus' because it makes legal charges and strife *cadere* 'fall away'.[23] Therefore, poets depict Mercury as the ambassador and messenger of peace.

[272] For one characteristic of eloquence is to pacify discords, to preserve friendships, and, once they have been preserved, to multiply them. The wise man says (Sir 6:5), *A sweet word multiplieth friends.* Augustine talks neatly about this re-establishment of peace and harmony and how it comes about by means of the virtue eloquence, in *On Christian teaching* 4.7. There he tells that 'he was once in the Mauritanian city Caesarea and persuaded the people not to pursue a civil war – it was indeed a battle in excess of being civil – that they called "the swarm". Not just the citizens but indeed relatives, brothers, finally parents and their children, divided into two groups, fought each other with stones; this went on solemnly for consecutive days on end at a designated time of the year, and each side sought, so far as they were able, to kill one another. Augustine exerted himself against them, so far as he was able, through eloquence and that form of speech rhetoricians call "grandiloquence" to drive such a cruel and deeply seated evil from the hearts and behaviours of the citizens. At last, moved by Augustine's words, they began to weep', and they put aside completely their madness and most evil custom, and all returned to the harmonious unity of peace.[24]

[290] Valerius Maximus offers comparable material, in an appendix to *Memorable things about words and deeds* 8, in the chapter where he treats the power of eloquence. He tells that 'the kings having levied a tax, the people, dissenting from the senators, gathered armed on the hill "Sacer" next to the river bank. These were not just deformed but also the most wretched rank in the commonwealth, as it were a separate part of the body

---

[22] *Ibid.* 1.671–75.
[23] Mart 9.11 (82/15–20).
[24] *De civitate Dei* 4.24 (*PL* 34:115–16).

corporis pestifera sedicione diuisa. Ac nisi Ualerii subuenisset eloquencia, + spes imperii tanti in ipso pene ortu suo corruisset. Iste namque Ualerius populum, noua et insolita libertate temere gaudentem, oracione ad meliora et saniora [consilia] reuocatum
300   senatui subiecit' et inter discordes pacem et concordiam reformauit. Ideo significanter iste deus Mercurius, id est deus eloquencie, legatus pacis pingitur.

297 spes] $\overline{\text{spes}}$ (= species) O • in ipso] et non licet I   298 populum] *om.* I • insolita] insolida I   299 saniora] seniora I   consilia] *om.* O   302 pingitur] *adds* a poetis et sic finitur methologia 14ª Fulgencii A, *adds* a poetis I

severed from its head in pestilent rebellion. Had Valerius not intervened with his eloquence, the hope for so great an empire would have collapsed just at its beginning. For Valerius in his speech recalled the people, who were outrageously rejoicing over their new and unaccustomed liberty, to better and more healthy counsels, subjected them to the senate', and restored peace and harmony among those in discord.[25] Therefore Mercury, the god of eloquence, is significantly depicted as the ambassador of peace.

[25] *Ibid.* 8.9.1.

[10]

Sequitur decima mithologia [Fulgencii] de Dane, filia regis Acrisii, quam poete fingunt a deo Ioue stupratam sub specie aurei stillicidii. Sub ymagine igitur huius Danes uolunt poete [paraboliter] depingere uicium cupiditatis feminee, nam sicut patet per istos philosophos qui dicuntur sapientes mundani, sexus femineus magis communiter est ad hoc uicium inclinatus quam masculinus. Unde mulieres magis cupide sunt quam uiri. Danes igitur ista sic est picta:
    [1] situ sub|limata,
    [2] menibus uallata,
    [3] egestate sata,
    [4] agmine stipata,
    [5] prole fecundata,
    [6] et auro uiolata.
Iste sunt sex partes picture poetice huius uicii cupiditatis feminee.
    [1] Nam quo ad primam partem picture, isti poete fingunt quod Danes ista per patrem suum Acrisium in altissima turri et fortissima fuit collocata, quia timuit quod uiolenciam inferret iste fornicator Iubiter filie sue pro sua pulcritudine. Et conuenit moraliter istud pudicicie. Cristus enim, qui est uerus Acrisius, quia Acrisius dicitur ab *a*, quod est 'sine' et *crisis* 'aurum', quasi 'sine auro'. Cristus aurum non habuit nec argentum, sicut dicit Ambrosius in suis commentariis super Lucam; 'Cristus', inquit, 'noluit habere quod perderet, ut haberet diabolus quid auferret'. Et ideo, ut subdit Ambrosius, 'Ipse Cristus dicit, *Uenit enim princeps [huius] mundi et in me non habet quicquam*'. Ieronimus autem dicit in suo originali super Matheum quod dominus Ihesus fuit tante paupertatis quod unde pro se et suis apostolis redderet tributa non haberet. Cristus igitur fuit Acrisius auro orbatus qui filiam suam, pudiciciam scilicet, commisit feminis et eas honorauit et sublimauit honore sue ymaginis diuine. Quia utrumque sexum creauit Deus ad ymaginem suam, sicut patet ex Scriptura, Genesis 2°,

---

1 Fulgencii] *om.* O 2 stupratam] spupra|tam I 4 paraboliter] parabolice A, *om.* O
9 fol. 114va
17-18 Danes ... collocata] dacata I 20 pudicicie] *adds* et paupertati A
  24 ut haberet] ut non haberet A, *om.* I 26 huius] *om.* O 30 scilicet commisit] sciuit I 31 diuine] *om.* A 33 sicut ... Scriptura] *om.* A

[10]

Fulgentius's tenth mythology follows; it concerns Danae, the daughter of king Acrisius, whom poets claim was seduced by the god Jove in the form of dripping golden rain. Thus, poets intend to depict in this image an example of the vice, women's Greed. For as those worldly wise men who are called philosophers show, women are more commonly inclined to this vice than men. For this reason, women are greedier than men. Therefore Danae is depicted
 [1] in an elevated place,
 [2] walled in with fortifications,
 [3] filled with need,
 [4] closed off by crowds,
 [5] impregnated with a child,
 [6] and violated by gold.
These are the six parts of the poets' picture of the vice women's greed.

[16] [1] So far as the first part of the picture is concerned, the poets report that Danae was placed by her father Acrisius in a very high and strong tower, because he feared that the fornicator Jupiter would violently attack his daughter on account of her beauty. In moral terms, this detail is appropriate for Modesty. For Christ is the true Acrisius, because the name 'Acrisius' is derived from *a* 'without' and *crisis* 'gold', as if it were 'without gold'. Christ had neither gold nor silver, as Ambrose says in his commentary on Luke, 'Christ wished to have nothing that he might lose, lest the devil should have something that he might carry off.' And therefore, as Ambrose adds, 'Christ himself says, *For the prince of this world cometh, and in me he hath not any thing*' (Io 14:30).[1] Moreover, Jerome says in his commentary on Matthew that our Lord Christ was so very poor that he didn't have the wherewithal to pay tribute money for himself and his apostles. Therefore Christ was Acrisius, deprived of gold, who committed his daughter Modesty to women and honoured them and raised them up through the honour of his divine image. For God created both sexes in his image, as is evident from Scripture, Gn 1:27,

---

[1] *Expositio evangelii secundum Lucam* 4.39 (PL 15:1624), followed by Jerome, *Commentarii in evangelium Matthaei* 3 (on 17:26, PL 26:128).

et hec fuit maxima celsitudo, sicut satis patet per beatum
Augustinum in libello quem edidit *De dignitate et excellencia*
35 *huius ymaginis diuine.* Unde et glosa quedam super psalterium
dicit, 'Disce homo, quam grandis et preciosus es, et uilem te terra
demonstrat, sed gloriosum uirtus facit, fides carum, et ymago
Dei preciosum. Non est quicquam ita preciosum | sicut est ymago
Dei, quam dum retines, homo iure uocaris et nomen hominis non
40 amittis; cum uero eadem neclecta, in uicia cadis, non homo, sed
serpens aut wlpecula aut iumentum nominaris'. Sic igitur dignitas
ymaginis diuine est turris ista altissima in qua per Acrisium Danes
ista \fuit/ collocata.

[2] Quo ad secundum partem picture, patet quomodo
45 Danes ista fuit menibus circumdata [pariter] et uallata. *Nam
hominis anime et mulieris create ad suam ymaginem Deus dedit*
discrecionem et liberam eleccionem, que sunt anime humane pro
muro a dextris et a sinistris, ante et retro. Nam per discrecionem,
[anima] discernit quid sit conferens et quid nociuum, hoc quo ad
50 dexteram et sinistram. Per liberam eleccionem uero quam Deus
dedit uoluntati hominis, fugit homo et a tergo dimittit illud quod
est sibi nociuum, et consequitur illud quod est sibi conferens et
proficuum, hoc quo ad ante et retro. Ista sunt menia quibus Danes
ista, filia Acrisii, est uallata.

55 Et de isto bene loquitur Ricardus de Sancto Ui[c]tore in
suo tractatu quem edidit super illud Ysaie primo, *Omne caput
languidum et omne cor merens.* 'Habet libertas arbitrii ymaginem,
non solum eternitatis, sed diuine maiestatis. Uult[i]s', dicit
Ricardus, 'maiestatis similitudinem in ipsa prospicere, et quomodo
60 ad maiestatis ymaginem impressa sit, euidenter agnoscere?' Et
subdit, 'Deus superiorem non habet, nec habere potest, et liberum
arbitrium [domin]ium non patitur, nec pati potest, quia uiolencia
ei inferre nec Creatorem decet, nec creatura potest. Totus infernus,
| totus mundus, totus denique milicie celestis excercitus in unum
65 [con]currat, et hoc in unum coniuret, unum ex libero arbitrio

---

33 satis] *om.* A 34 excellencia] *adds* quam habet creatura racione A 35 glosa]
gl$\overline{\text{ra}}$ (= ? gloria) I 36 Disce] *om.* I • preciosus] speciosus A 37 carum]
rarum I 38 Non ... preciosum] *om.* A • Non est] An I • fol. 114vb
44 Quo] Similiter quo AI 45 pariter] *om.* O 49 anima] *om.* (*at line-break*) O
52 consequitur] prosequitur AI 53 menia] nenia I
55 Uictore] Uitore O 56 Ysaie] Ysidori A 58–59 Uultis ... maiestatis] *om.* A
58 Uultis] Uultus IO 59 prospicere] proficere I 61 Deus] *om.* I 62 arbitrium]
om. I • dominium] uim O 63 decet] docet I 64 fol. 115ra • denique]
diuineque I 65 unum¹] communi I • concurrat] currat O • libero] *om.* A

and this constituted the very greatest height. Augustine shows this sufficiently in his little book *On the dignity and excellence of the divine image*.[2] For this reason, there is also a gloss on a psalter-verse that says, 'Learn how great and precious you humans are; even though your earthiness shows you to be vile, your virtue makes you glorious, your faith makes you dear and your likeness to divinity makes you precious. For nothing is so precious as the divine image, and so long as you preserve it, you are properly called human, and you do not lose the designation human; but when you neglect it, you fall into vices, and then you should be called, not human, but a serpent or a little fox or a beast of burden.' Therefore, the dignity of the divine image is that highest tower in which Acrisius placed Danae.

[44] [2] As far as the second part of this picture, it shows how Danae was surrounded and walled in by fortifications. *For God gave to men's and women's souls, created in His own image*, discretion and free choice (cf. Sir 17:1–6). These two are like a wall protecting the human soul, on the right and the left, before and behind. For by discretion, the soul distinguishes what may be suitable and what harmful, the things that are on the right and the left. By the freedom to choose that God gave the human will, people flee and leave behind what's harmful, and they pursue what's suitable and profitable, the things that are before and behind. These are the fortifications with which Danae, Acrisius's daughter, is walled in.

[55] Richard of St Victor speaks well about this in his tract on Is 1:5, *The whole head is sick, and the whole heart is sad*. Richard says, 'Free will possesses an image, not just of eternity, but of God's majesty.' He continues, 'Don't you also wish to examine closely this likeness of His majesty and to recognise clearly how it has been imposed as an image of that majesty?' He further adds, 'God neither has, nor can He have, any superior, and free will does not suffer, nor can it, anything overpowering, because it is not fitting for the Creator to attack it violently, nor can a created being do so. Even should all hell, all this world, all the army of the heavenly host join together as a single group, even should they bond together as one, that's not strong enough to coerce an unwilling free will

---

[2] Not Augustine, but probably ps.-Bernard, *Meditationes* 1.2 (*PL* 184:485–86); followed by Ambrose, *In Psalmum David cxviii expositio* 10.10–11 (*PL* 15:1333).

consensum in re qualicunque inuito ipso extorquere non ualet'. Propter igitur istam liberi arbitrii inuiolabilem firmitatem, poete fingunt Danem istam muniri muris uallatam et circumdatam.

[3] Sequitur tercia picture pars, qua Danes ista pingitur
70 paupertatis nata. Quia ut prius tactum, ipsa dicitur a poetis filia regis Acrisii, qui est rex expers auri, sicut patet ex ethimologia uocabuli, et optime conuenit pudicicie uirginali. Nam sicut aurum et diuicie generant lasciuiam et luxuriam, sic per oppositum paupertas gignit mundiciam et pudiciciam. Et ideo dicit Gregorius
75 quod *in camino paupertatis* solent excoqui uicia carnis. De diuiciis autem, ut recitat Malmiberiensis in historia, solet esse prouerbium quod 'res est non pertrita, + sed coruo rarior albo, hominem habundare diuiciis et non lasciuire uiciis'. Uult dicere quod coruus albus est rara res, ita homo diues et non infectus lasciuia est res
80 que raro accidit, nec communiter est experta.

[4] Sequitur quarta pars picture de huius Danes stipacione, nam poete fingunt eam agminibus armatorum stipatam, et bene conuenit pudicicie. 'Semper enim', ut ait Ieronimus, 'angelis cognata est uirginitas'. Unde specialiter isti uirtuti[, scilicet
85 pudicicie] uirginali conuenit | quod dicit psalmista, *Angelis suis Deus mandauit de te ut custodiant te in omnibus uiis tuis*. Et de isto loquitur Ambrosius, libro primo *De uirginitate*, quando dicit, 'In uobis, uirgines, sp[eci]ale est presidium, que pudore intemerato sacrum Deum seruatis cubile; pro uobis enim, uirgines, angeli
90 militant, quia uos angelorum moribus militatis. Angelorum enim presidium uirgines merentur, quia uitam angelicam uirgines imitantur'.

[5] Sequitur quinta pars picture de istius Danes fecundacione. Fingunt enim Danem istam Perseo impregnata[m], sicut patet
95 per Ouidium, libro 3° de *Transformatis*, sic dicentem, 'Persea quem pluui[o] Dane conciperat auro'. Est autem notandum, sicut patet per Fulgencium, undecima mithologia, quam facit de Perseo, quod Perseus apud poetas stat pro uirtute quam generat puritas pudicicie, sicut pulcre tractat Augustinus in suo libello
100 *De duodecim abusionibus*. Iste tamen libellus traditur a multis

67 inuiolabilem] immobilem A 68 muniri] *om.* AI
74 gignit] signit I 77 pertrita] *adds* uel non experta O 79 albus] *om.* I
82 armatorum] armorum A 84–85 scilicet pudicicie] scilicet prudencie A, *om.* O 85 fol. 115rb 86 Deus] *om.* A 88 speciale] spirituale AO 89 angeli] *om.* I
94 impregnatam] impregnata O 96 pluuio] pluuia O 100 abusionibus] ambiciosis I 100–1 Iste ... Cipriano] *om.* A 100 traditur] creditur I

to consent to any extent.'³ Because of the inviolable firmness of free will, poets represent Danae as walled in and surrounded, protected by walls.

[69] [3] The third part of the picture follows. In it, Danae is depicted as born in poverty. For as I have said above, poets say that she is the daughter of king Acrisius. He is a king who lacked gold, as the etymology of his name shows, and this status is particularly appropriate for virginal modesty. For just as gold and riches give rise to sexual desire and lechery, the opposite, poverty, gives birth to purity and modesty. Therefore Gregory says that the vices of the flesh are customarily cooked away *in the furnace of poverty* (Is 48:10).⁴ Moreover, William of Malmesbury says of riches in his history that there's a common proverb, 'although it isn't a cliché, that for a person to abound in riches and not to run riot in vices is rarer than a white crow.'⁵ William intends to say that a white crow is a rare thing and likewise, that a rich person who is not infected with licentiousness is something that happens only rarely, nor is it something one routinely encounters.

[81] [4] The fourth part of the picture follows; it concerns Danae's being closed off. For poets represent her as closed off with crowds of armed men, and this is appropriate for modesty. As Jerome says, 'Virginity is always akin to the angels.'⁶ For this reason, what David says is especially appropriate for the virtue virginal modesty, *For God hath given his angels charge over thee to keep thee in all thy ways* (Ps 90:11). Ambrose talks about this, *On virginity* 1, 'There's a special protection for you, virgins, since you serve God's holy couch with unblemished modesty. For angels battle on your behalf, virgins, because you arm yourselves with angelic behaviours. For virgins earn angelic protection, since they imitate the angels' life.'⁷

[93] [5] The fifth part of the picture follows; it concerns Danae's impregnation. For poets represent Danae as impregnated with Perseus; Ovid shows this in *Metamorphoses* 3, when he says, 'Perseus, whom Danae had conceived in golden rain.'⁸ Moreover, one should notice, as Fulgentius shows in his discussion of Perseus, in his eleventh mythology, that, among poets, Perseus represents the virtue that modesty, with its purity, produces.⁹ Augustine discusses this in his little book *On the twelve abuses*. (Nevertheless, many people say that the book was

---

³ *De statu interioris hominis* 3 (*PL* 196:1118–19).
⁴ *Regula pastoralis* 3.2 (*PL* 77:52).
⁵ *De gestis regum Anglorum*, St Oswald (*PL* 179:1006), alluding to Juvenal, *Satyrae* 7.202.
⁶ Epistola 9.5 (*PL* 30:126).
⁷ *De virginibus* 1.8.51 (*PL* 16:202).
⁸ *Ibid.* 4.611.
⁹ Fulg 1.21 (33/9).

editus a Cipriano. Dicit igitur 'Sicut omnes bonos mores procurat et custodit in uiris p[ruden]cia, sic eciam in feminis cunctos honestos actus nutrit, fouet, et custodit pudicicia. Nam pudicicia auariciam refrenat, lites deuitat, iram mitigat, libidinem amputat,
105 cupidinem temperat, lasciuiam castigat, ebrietatem cauet, uerba non multiplicat, intemperanciam obpugnat, furtum omnino dampnat. Quid | plura? Omnia uicia restringit; uirtutes uero omnes et quicquid coram Deo et hominibus bonum est et laudabile fouet et nutrit'. Et hec est causa quare Perseum, quem
110 poete ponunt pro uirtute, fingunt genitum ab ista Dane.

[6] Sequitur sexta pars picture et ultima de Danes uiolacione. Nam poete fingunt Iouem seipsum transformasse in speciem gutte pluuialis auree, et sic intrasset cameram Danes, et in eius gremium descendisse, et eam post descensum corrupisse
115 et denigrasse. Et per istud nichil aliud uolunt poete intelligere nisi quod amor et pecunie cupiditas, ad quam inclinatur natura feminea, uiolat et destruit istam uirtutem, tot prerogatiuis, ut predicitur, insignitam. Et ideo dicit Fulgencius in littera, 'Dane ymbre aurato corumpta est, non pluuia, sed pecunia'. De ista
120 cupiditate fuit prius tactum in [sexta] mithologia, in qua actum fuit pictura Cerberi, qui \canis/ fingitur infernalis. Et ibidem fuit allegatus processus Crisostomi, in suo libello qui intitulatur *Quod nemo leditur, nisi a seipso*. Ubi sic dicit Crisostomus quod 'Amor pecunie omnia humi deicit et pedibus conculcat. Uelut
125 enim quedam fera et crudelis domina omnium corda possidet et tirannica dominacione deuin[c]it; seuit ut barbarus, [fertur] crudeliter ut tirannus, debachatur inpudenter ut meretrix. Nunquam enim pudet amor iste deordinatus + pecunie'.

[Ecce quomodo amor deordinatus et cupiditas pecunie]
130 uiolat et de|nigrat pudorem uirginalem pudicicie. Pudor enim et uerecundia, ut dicit Ambrosius in libro suo *De officiis*, 'comes est pudicicie'. Sed hanc uerecundiam corrump[i]t et

---

102 prudencia] pudicicia O   103 honestos] *om.* A   106 multiplicat] *adds* gule I
107 fol. 115va
111 et ultima] *om.* A   117 uirtutem] *adds* prudenciam (?) I   117–18 ut predicitur] *om.* A   119 aurato] amoto A, amato I   120 cupiditate] *add* pecunie AI
• sexta] 8 (= octaua) AI, quinta O   122 qui intitulatur] *om.* A   126 deuincit] deuixit I, deiunxit O   • fertur] furit O   127 debachatur] delatus I
128 Nunquam] Misera I   128–29 pecunie ... pecunie] pecunie A, Et cupiditas pecunie O
130 fol. 115vb 131 Ambrosius] Ieronimus AI   132 corrumpit] corrumpat O

written by Cyprian.) It says, 'Just as prudence gains and preserves all good behaviours in men, likewise in women, modesty feeds, nurtures, and preserves all virtuous acts. For modesty restrains avarice, avoids legal battles, moderates wrath, cuts away lechery, moderates desire, rebukes licentiousness, bewares of drunkenness, doesn't speak volubly, attacks intemperance, condemns theft completely. What more do you want? Modesty restrains all the vices, and it fosters and nourishes all the virtues and whatever is good and praiseworthy in the eyes of God and of other people.'[10] This is the reason why poets represent Perseus, whom they identify with virtue, as born of Danae.

[111] [6] The sixth and last part of the picture follows; it concerns Danae's violation. For poets report that Jove transformed himself into the shape of golden rainfall, and in this way he entered Danae's room and fell into her lap, and after this descent, he corrupted and disgraced her. And through this story, poets wish to understand only that the love and desire for money – and women's nature is bent that way – violates and destroys the virtue modesty, renowned for its many privileges, as I've described them above. Therefore Fulgentius says explicitly, 'Danae was ruined by a golden dew, and it wasn't rain, but money.'[11] I first discussed this avariciousness in the sixth mythology, in which I developed the picture of Cerberus, who is represented as a hell-hound. There I cited Chrysostom's argument, in his little book called *No one is ever harmed, except by himself*. Chrysostom says there that 'The love of money casts everything to the ground and tramples it underfoot. For just like a fierce and cruel dominatrix, it possesses all hearts and subjects them to a tyrannical lordship; it rages like a savage, comports itself like a cruel tyrant, debauches shamelessly like a whore. This disordered love of money is never ashamed.'[12]

[129] See how the disordered love of and desire for money violates and disgraces the virginal shame associated with modesty. For shame and restraint, as Ambrose says in *On duties*, 'are the companions of modesty'.[13] But the love of money corrupts and

---

[10] *Ibid.* (PL 4:873), the text now attributed to Gennadius of Marseilles.
[11] Fulg 1.19 (31/8–9).
[12] *Ibid.* 6 (338/74–79); the reference in the following paragraph to *ibid*. 79.
[13] *Ibid.* 1.18.69 (PL 16:44).

uiolat amor pecunie. Qu[ia] sicut dicit Cristostomus, nusquam pudet de ista auaricia quam Greci uocant *philargiriam*, id est
135 amorem pecunie. Qualiter uiolat, corumpit non solum uirtutem istam, scilicet pudiciciam, scilicet eciam omnem aliam, loquitur Prudencius quidam auctor in libro suo qui dicitur *Sichomachia*, sic dicens,

    Omne hominum genus mortalia cuncta / Ocupat inte[ritu],
140   non est uiolencius ullum / Terrarum uicium que tantis cladibus euum / Mundanum inuoluat populum dampnetque iehenne.

Et sic finitur decima mithologia Fulgencii sub ymagine Danes filia regis Acrisii.

---

133 Quia] que O • Crisostomus] beatus Ieronimus A   **134–44** de … Acrisii] *om*. A   **135** uiolat] et I   **137** quidam … in] *om*. I • *Sichomachia*] Siconiathia I   **139–42** Omne … iehenne] *om*. I   **139** interitu] intentum O   **143–44** sub … Acrisii] *om*. I

violates this restraint. As Chrysostom says, this love is never ashamed of the kind of avarice the Greeks call *philargiria* 'love of money'. It violates and corrupts not just this virtue modesty, but every other virtue as well. On this point, an author named Prudentius says in his book called *Psychomachia*,

> This sin seizes the entire human race; it busies itself / in death for every mortal thing; there's not / any vice on earth that's more violent, and it may enwrap / this worldly age in such great disasters that it condemns people to hell.[14]

This is the end of Fulgentius's tenth mythography that [shows desire] in the image of Danae, daughter of king Acrisius.

---

[14] *Ibid.* 493–96.

[11]

Sequitur mithologia undecima primi libri, sodomitici uitii
picturam continens sub ymagine Gaimodis, quem fingunt poete
\paticum seu cathamitum dei Iouis. Et uolunt poete/ sub ymagine
Ganimedis [pingere] uicii huius miseriam, hoc est innaturalis
commixtionis. Pingitur hic igitur Ganimedes sic pingitur a
poetis, ut
    [1] puer delicatus,
    [2] membris mutilatus,
    [3] aquila delatus,
    [4] a Ioue stupratus,
    [5] aquis + oneratus,
    [6] stellis sociatus,
    [7] et diis deputatus.
Iste sunt septem | partes picture huius uicii.
    [1] Nam quoad primam partem picture, poete fingunt
Gaimedem istum puerum fuisse tener[e]m et delicatum, sicut
consueuerunt esse filii regum. Nam iste fingitur filius regis,
et ideo a Ioue dilectus amore inordi[n]ato. Ad litteram, talem
molliciem puerilem et delicatam uenustatem appetunt isti
miseri qui exercent istius uicii feditatem, sicut bene tangit ille
uersifacator dicens,
    Intereant et eant, ad Tartara non redituri, / qui teneros
    pueros pro coniuge sunt habituri. / Regna nocencia, luce
    carencia uos habitetis, / qui puerilia queritis \ilio/que
    maculetis. / Quam prauus mos est pueros preferre puellis, /
    Cum sit nature Ueneris modus iste rebellis.
Consimili modo tractatur diffuse de isto in illo libro qui dicitur
Suda. Carnotensis in suo *Policraticon* eciam de hoc tangit,
libro 2º, capitulo 13, cum inquit, 'Lasciuientis diuitis luxus libidini
uota sua precingit, recumbentes pedes calamistratus comatulis
excipit, nitorem inuidens meretrici, histrionibus habitum, cultum
procis, uirginibus ornatum, triumphalem quoque principibus
apparatum, et in amborum aspectu pedes, et ne plus dicam,

---

1 on O fol. 134vb 1–2 sodomitici … Gaimodis] de Ganimede A   4 pingere] *om.* O
   • est] *adds* sodomitici et A   6 ut] septiformiter sic A   11 aquis] *adds* urnatus
   uel O   14 fol. 135ra • partes] *om.* A
16 tenerem] tenerum O   18 inordinato] inordiato O   20–36 sicut … ille] *om.* A

[11]

The eleventh mythology of the first book follows; it contains a picture of the vice Sodomy in the image of Ganymede, whom poets represent as the god Jove's passive partner or catamite. Poets wish to depict in the image of Ganymede the wretchedness of this vice, that is of unnatural sexuality. Therefore Ganymede is depicted here as he is by poets:

[1] a delightful boy,
[2] mutilated in his limbs,
[3] carried away by an eagle,
[4] defiled by Jove,
[5] burdened with water,
[6] companioned by stars,
[7] and appointed [to serve] the gods.

These are the seven parts of the picture of this vice.

[15] [1] So far as the first part of the picture, poets represent Ganymede as having been delightful and tender, the kind of youth that kings' sons customarily were. Indeed, they depict him as a king's son, and for that reason, loved by Jove in an immoderate fashion. As a literal statement, the wretched people who pursue this filthy vice desire boyish softness and delightful beauty. A versifier discusses this:

> May those who want to possess tender boys instead of wives / Die and pass to Tartarus, never to return. / You who seek boy-toys and would defile [them], / may you dwell in those harmful kingdoms, deprived of light. / What a depraved behaviour it is to prefer boys to girls, / Since this behaviour rebels against Venus's nature.[1]

This behaviour is treated in the same way, and at length, in the book called *Suda*. John of Salisbury also treats the subject in his *Polycraticus* 2.13, where he says, 'The person sumptuously living in lascivious riches girds himself up for [unbridled] action in accord with his sexual desires. With his curly locks, rivalling a whore's elegance, an actor's garb, wooers' smart clothes, virgins' ornaments, even princes' triumphal gear, he takes up the feet of the person lounging by him. As others look on, he caresses them with his soft hands and, should I say more,

---

[1] Walther *Sprich.* 12660, 23342 (cf. 31080); see the textual note.

teneris manibus tibias tractat. Ciroticatus enim incessit diucius,
ut manus sole subtractas emolliret ad diuitis usum. Deinde
licencia paululum procedente, totum corpus inpudico tactu
| oberrans, pruriginem scalpit, quam fecit, et ignes Ueneris
languentis inflammat'. Et subdit, 'Uerum hec abhominacio non
tam ostendenda quam conspuenda est. Puderet enim eam nugis
nostris esse in[ser]tam, nisi eandem apostolus, Romanis scribens,
uerbis manifestis expressisset, dicens quod *Femine eorum
mutauerunt naturalem usum \in eum/ qui est contra naturam,
set et masculi, relicto naturali usu femine, exarserunt in desideriis
suis, masculi in masculos turpitudinem operantes*'. Hec ille.

[2] Sequitur secunda pars huius picture de Ganimedis
mutilacione. Nam poete aliqui et multi pro maiori mollicie
fingunt eum castratum a Ioue. Et ad litteram isti nobiles diuites,
magni domini et potentes, solent pueros tales et iuuenes delicatos
castrare, ut castratis, barba non cresceret et ut diu iuuenes
apparerent et carne molliores et teneriores fierent, sicut et de hoc
loquitur Carnotensis in suo *Policraticon*, libro 2°, ubi prius, ponens
exemplum de 'Nerone, qui impiissimus imperator et luxurie
seuientis, puerum Spo[r]um, ex[c]ectis testiculis in muliebrem
naturam transformare conatus est'.

[3] Sequitur tercia pars picture de Ganimedis deportacione.
N[am] poete fingunt Iouem se in formam aquile transformasse
et puerum istum Ganimedem rapuisse, et raptum detulisse.
Secundum Fulgencium, in littera dicit quod Iubiter portauit in
uexillis suis bellicis | aquilam, et ideo, qua[si] uiolencia prelii, rapuit
puerum Gaimedem propter eius pulcritudinem. Ideo dicitur puer
iste Gaimedis pingi deportatus ab aquila. Tamen ad intellectum
moralem, poete per aquilam uolunt intelligere libidinis feruorem,
quo laborant isti miseri, qui hoc innaturali uicio sunt infecti. Nam
aquila est auis multum calida, in tantum quod, sicut auctores
dicunt et recitat Alexander Nekquam, *De naturis rerum*, libro
primo, capitulo 30, 'Aquila ouis suis, propter calorem sui, lapides
interponit frigissimos, ut sic caloris uehemencia oua non destruat',
admixtione frigoris temperata. Ad significandum igitur excessiuum
libidinis incendium, quo isti miseri incenduntur, qui sexu utroque,
tam femineo, quam masculino, ita bestialiter ab[ut]untur.

37 fol. 135rb
46 aliqui et multi] *om.* A   48 domini] *om.* A   53 Sporum] Sponsum O • excectis] excertis A, extectis O
56 Nam] Non O   59 fol. 135va • quasi] quia AO   62 libidinis] *adds* uehementem A
66 ouis] alis A   68 excessiuum] *om.* A   70 abutuntur] abducuntur O

the legs. He has customarily gone about wearing gloves, so that he might soften his hidden hands for this rich man's behaviour. Then, advancing little by little in his licentiousness, his shameless touch wanders over the whole body; it scratches the sexual itch he's aroused and inflames the fires of languishing Venus.' And he adds, 'Truly, this abomination shouldn't be shown, but rather spat upon. For it would have been shameful for it to be included among my trifles, were it not that Paul, writing to the Romans, had expressed the same plainly in his words, when he says that *Their women have changed the natural use into that use which is against nature. And, in like manner, the men also, leaving the natural use of the women, have burned in their lusts, men with men working that which is filthy*' (Rm 1:26–27).[2]

[45] [2] The second part of the picture follows; it concerns Ganymede's mutilation. For some, indeed many, poets report that Jove castrated Ganymede to preserve his softness. As a literal statement, noble rich people, great and powerful lords, are accustomed to castrate such boys and tender youths, so that, once they have been castrated, their beard may not grow, and they appear youthful for a longer time, and their flesh made softer and more tender. John of Salisbury writes about this in the same passage in *Polycraticus* 2, where he offers the example of 'Nero, the most wicked emperor, in his raging lechery having cut off his testicles, attempted to transform the boy Sporus into a woman.'[3]

[55] [3] The third part of the picture follows; it concerns Ganymede being carried away. For poets claim that Jove transformed himself into the shape of an eagle and seized the boy Ganymede, and having seized him, carried him off. Fulgentius says explicitly that Jupiter carried an eagle in his battle-standards, and therefore, as if in the violence of warfare, he seized Ganymede because of his boyish beauty.[4] Therefore, the boy Ganymede is depicted as carried off by an eagle. Nevertheless in the moral sense, poets wish to understand in the eagle the heat of sexual desire, which vexes those wretched people who are infected with this unnatural vice. For the eagle is a bird whose complexion is so extremely hot that, as authors say and as Alexander Neckam repeats, in his *On the natures of things* 1.30, 'On account of its heat, the eagle places very cold rocks between its eggs, lest the violent heat destroy them'[5] – the heat is moderated by this mixture with something cold. This should indicate the excessive fire of sexual desire, which burns these wretches, who so bestially abuse children of either sex, whether female or male.

[2] *Ibid.* 3.13 (PL 199:505).
[3] *Ibid.* 3.13 (PL 199:506).
[4] Fulg 1.20 (31/11–21).
[5] *Ibid.* 1.23 (71), although suppressing a different moralisation.

Depingitur Ganimedes iste deportatus al\is/ aquile. Et nota, ad detestacionem huius libidinosi ardoris, auctor[itat]em domini Innocencii in libro suo *De contemptu mundi*, ubi dicit sic, loquens de isto uicio maledicto, 'Pena docuit quid hec culpa promeruit: *Pluit enim Dominus super Sodomam et Gomorram sulphur et ignem de celo a Domino.* Noluit enim Dominus cuiquam angelorum uel hominum execucionem huius pene committere, sed sibi Ipsi uindictam huius sceleris reseruauit. Et ideo *pluit Dominus a Domino*, uidelicet a Seipso, non ymbrem aut rorem, sed sulphur et ignem. [Sulphur] propter | fetorem luxurie; ignem uero propter ardorem libidinis, quatinus pena esset similis culpe'.

Est autem et alia racio moralis quare Gaimedes iste fingitur a poetis ue[ctus et] delatus alis aquile, ut enim narrant auctores. Et Alexander Nequam recitat, ubi prius, 'Uirtus corrosiua inest naturaliter pennis aquile, in tantum quod, si penna aquile sit in sagittis, telis, uel iaculis, pennis aliarum auium sociata, penna illa aquile statim corrodit [alias pennas] aliarum auium et destruit'. Et consimili modo est de uicio isto diabolico, quod inficit et destruit omne collegium. De infeccione autem huius uicii, Auicenna, collacione 6, ut non luxurientur homines contra naturam, ibi dicit, 'Imperator, quod in regno in quo tale uicium habundat, in uindictam huius uicii, ueniunt in regno fames, pestilencie, terremotus, et tempestates alie, ex quibus accidit exterminum regni'. Istud est uicium ita uile quod polluit et fedat ora loquencium de predicto uicio uel aures oscultancium, sicut patet 32 questione, 4 per Ieronimum, et incipit canon, 'In eo forni[cato]r catholicus'.

[4] Sequitur quarta pars picture de Ganimedis stupracione. Nam poete dicunt et fingunt Iouem maculasse per stuprum istum predictum puerum Ganimedem. Ad litteram, istud genus uicii + antiquis temporibus inualuerit hominibus diuitibus et potentibus, quorum figuram gerit apud poetas et Iubiter. Dicit enim Albumasar in suo *Intro|ductorio maiori*, libro 9, differencia 4, quod 'Iubiter est significator diuiciarum et substancie et hereditatis mundane', et quia tales, antiquis temporibus, fuerant uiles sodomite, sicut patet ex historiis Romanorum de Octauiono, de quo narratur quod in tantum seruiuit libidini qu[od] inter

72 auctoritatem] auctorem O   79 a¹ ... seipso] *om.* A   80 Sulphur] *om.* O
• fol. 135vb 81 libidinis ... culpe] concupiscencie A
83 uectus et] uerius O   87 alias pennas] '*corr.*' *to* alas O   92 habundat] regnat A
94 et fedat] *om.* A   97 fornicator] formatur O
101 uicii] *adds* spiritus hec O   103 fol. 136ra 107 quod] quia O

[71] Ganymede is depicted carried away by an eagle's wings. And notice, to increase your hatred of this sex-driven heat, pope Innocent's authoritative opinion in his *On contempt of the world*, where he says of this cursed sin, 'He has taught what punishment this guilty behaviour deserves: *And the Lord rained upon Sodom and Gomorrah brimstone and fire from the Lord out of heaven* (Gn 19:24). The Lord did not wish to entrust inflicting this punishment to any angel or person, but He kept for Himself alone the vengeance for this crime. Therefore, *the Lord rained from the Lord*, that is from Himself – and he didn't send moisture or dew, but brimstone and fire. Brimstone on account of lechery's stench; fire on account of the heat of sexual desire, since a punishment ought to resemble the guilt.'[6]

[82] However, there is a further moral reason why poets depict Ganymede as transported and carried off by an eagle's wings, as authoritative writers tell. In the same passage I cited above, Alexander Neckam says, 'An eagle's feathers naturally include a corrosive power, to such a degree that if a single eagle's feather is joined in arrows, missiles, or spears, with feathers of other birds, that eagle's feather immediately eats away and destroys the feathers of the other birds.'[7] In just the same way, this diabolical vice infects and destroys an entire college or society. On the infection of this vice, to prevent people from seeking pleasure against nature, Avicenna says in collation 6, 'Emperor, in a kingdom in which this vice abounds, there come in revenge famine, pestilence, earthquakes, and other storms; from them, the kingdom is brought to an end.'[8] This vice is so disgusting that it pollutes and soils the mouths of those who speak of it, as well as their audience's ears, as is evident in *Decretum*, question 32.4, Jerome's canon that begins, 'A Christian who fornicates'.[9]

[98] [4] The fourth part of the picture follows; it concerns Ganymede's defilement. For poets say, feigning, that Jove stained the boy Ganymede by defiling him. In literal terms, in ancient times, this species of vice was particularly strong in rich and powerful people, and the poets use Jupiter as a figure for such people. Albumasar, in *The larger introduction* 9.4, says that 'Jupiter indicates riches and goods and worldly inheritances.'[10] In ancient times, such people had been disgusting sodomites, as Roman histories show. They tell about Octavian, so thoroughly devoted to sexual pleasure that

[6] *Ibid.* 2.25 (*PL* 217:726).
[7] *Ibid.* 1.23 (75), within a discussion of Jupiter's raping Ganymede.
[8] Unfound.
[9] Gratian, *Decretum*, C. 32, Q. 4, c. 12 (*CJC* 1:1130–31), indeed from Jerome.
[10] *Introductorius maior* 5.4.7 (1:460–61).

duodecim cathamos et totid[e]m puellas accubare solitus erat. Similiter de Nichomede, rege Bitinie, legitur et de Iulio Cesare, quod unus altero abusus fuerat. Qualiter Romani nobiles fuerint hoc uicio maculati satis patet ex poeta Iuuenali in diuersis satiris suis. Pro isto notandum est ad propositum, processus Crisostomi in suo libello qui initulatur *Nemo leditur nisi a seipso*, ubi loquens de diuiciis, dicit quod 'Diuicie uicia pro uirtutibus introducunt. Ipsarum enim diuiciarum sequaces luxuria, uanitas, intemperancia, furor, iniusticia, arrogancia, superbia, omnisque irracionabilis [motus] consequitur, etc.'.

[5] Sequitur quinta pars picture de Ganimodis oneracione. Nam poete fingunt quod iste Ganimedes teneat in man[ibus suis] duas amphoras aqua plenas, de quibus effundat aquam continue inferius uersus terram. Et moraliter loquendo, co[nuenien]ter applicatur ista pars picture ad uicium istud uile et detestabile, propter quod specialiter Deus inmisit diluuium super terram, sicut patet per Mechodium. Qui dicit, secundum quod Magister recitat in historiis, quod 'quingentesimo anno secundi ciliadis, | exarcerunt homines in a[dulteri]um coeuntes; septingentesimo anno filii Seth concupierunt filias Caym, et orti sunt gigantes; et post incepcionem tercii ciliadis cepit diluuium inundare'. Et ideo Ganimedes iste bene dicitur et fingitur a poetis aquis oneratus.

[6] Sequitur sexta pars picture de Ganimedis stellificacione. Sicut enim recitat Ig[i]nius, ille antiquus auctor, in suo libro *De celestibus ymaginibus*, poete fingunt Ganimedem esse illud sydus celeste quod nos uocamus Aquarium. Et uolunt per hoc poete describere errorem et insaniam hominum mundanorum, qui homines, peccatis uilibus et bestialibus maculatos et omni uirtute nudatos, crediderunt post mortem transire ad loca stellarum et ibidem beatificari. Unde sicut patet ex libris gentilium, post Campos Heliseos, debebant anime transferri ad co\m/es stellas, sicut et de Iulio Cesare, qui fuit unus de illis qui isto fuerant uicio irretiti. Fingit Ouidius quod fuit

108 totidem] to|tidium O   109–10 Similiter ... fuerat] *om.* A   111–12 in ... suis,
112 ad propositum] *om.* A   114–15 uanitas intemperancia] uanitates A
117 irracionabilis ... etc.] illicitus motus A • motus] *om.* IO
119 manibus suis] manu| O   121 conuenienter] $\overline{coi}$'| (= ? communiter) O   122 et
   detestabile, 123 specialiter] *om.* A   125 fol. 136rb 126 adulterium] alterutrum O
130 stellificacione] sollificacione A   131 Iginius] Ignius O   131–32 Sicut ...
   ymaginibus] *om.* A   134 insaniam] infamiam A   135 peccatis] *om.* A
   136 nudatos] mundatos A   137–42 Unde ... libri] *om.* A   139 comes] *corr. from*
   c<o>rp'es (?) O

he made a custom of going to bed with twelve catamites and an equal number of maidens. We read similar things about Nicomedes, the king of Bythnia, and Julius Caesar, that one of them had been abused by the other. The extent to which Roman nobles were stained by this vice is clear enough from various of Juvenal's satires.[11] On this point, one should notice Chrysostom's argument in his little book *No one is harmed, except by himself,* where, talking about riches, he says, 'Riches introduce vices in place of virtues. Riches' eager followers are lechery, vanity, intemperance, fury, injustice, arrogance, pride; any form of irrational impulse attends the rich.'[12]

[118] [5] The fifth part of the picture follows; it concerns Ganymede's burden. For poets represent Ganymede as holding in his hands two pitchers filled with water; from them, he continuously pours out water downward toward the earth. In moral terms, this part of the picture is appropriately applied to this disgusting and hateful vice, because God sent down the flood on earth particularly against it, as Methodius explains. He says that, according what Peter Comestor repeats in his *Histories,* 'In the fiftieth year of the second thousand-year cycle, people burned to join in adultery; in the seventieth year, Seth's sons desired Cain's daughters, and the giants rose up; and after the start of the third cycle, the flood began to flow in.'[13] Therefore, poets appropriately say that and depict Ganymede as burdened with waters.

[130] [6] The sixth part of the picture follows; it concerns Ganymede's being made a star. For just as the ancient author Hyginus says in his book *On heavenly figures,* poets depict Ganymede as the star in the heavens we call Aquarius.[14] Through this depiction, poets wish to describe that mad error of worldly people who believed that people, although stained with disgusting and bestial sins and stripped of every virtue, might, after their deaths, pass into the stars and be blessed there. For this reason, as books of the pagans show, after the Elysian Fields, their souls might be transported to the gracious stars, as happened with Julius Caesar, one of those who had been ensnared by this vice. Ovid claims he

---

[11] For Octavian, see Paul the Deacon, *Historia miscella* 7 (PL 95:861); for Caesar and Nicomedes, see *Polyc.* 3.14 (PL 199:508, citing 'jocularia carmina' from Suetonius); Juvenal, satyra 2, for example.

[12] *Ibid.* 7 (340/29–41).

[13] Peter Comestor, *Historia scholastica,* Genesis 31 (PL 198:1081); cf. ch. 25 (PL 198:1076).

[14] Hyginus, *De astronomia* 2.16, 29.

stellificatus et translatus ad stellam Ueneris, sicut patet in libro 15 *De transformatis*, quasi in fine libri. Et hic nota de miseria et insania Saracenorum, qui reputant actum talem bestialem et innaturalem meritorium uite eterne. Unde illi qui in lege
145 Machometi sunt reputati et uocati spirituales, et quasi pre ceteris uiri perfeccionis maioris, non reputant quod sodomia facta | cum brutis animalibus, et tamen bestiis, sit peccatum, sed pocius quod per hoc merentur. Unde et tales miseri sancti sunt in gente illa reputati.
150 [7] Sequitur septima pars \et ultima/ picture, et ultima de Ganimedis deputacione. Nam poete fingunt quod Ganimedes iste est comes indiuiduus \omnium/ deorum. Unde aliqui poete dicunt eum esse pincernam deorum; aliqui, camerarium deorum, et qui infundat aquam in manibus deorum. Et
155 uolunt per hoc innuere et describere fatuitatem diuitum huius mundi, qui credebant diuites propter diuicias transferendas fore ad societatem et parilitatem quandam deorum. Sicut de Octauiano legitur quod Romani uolebant eum adorasse pro deo, uidentes tantas eius diuicias, qui rem publicam de latericia
160 fecerat ma[r]moriam, et ipsemet gloriabatur, prout in cronicis Romanorum recitatur. Et hic potest ad propositum notari historia de Alexandro Magno, qui in principio regni sui gloriabatur se uocari filium [dei] Hamonis, sicut tangitur satis in *Historiis Trogi Pompei*. Et nota bene uersus magistri Alani, quos de
165 pla[n]ctu Nature composuit de isto uicio bestiali. Et ponuntur in principio libri sui, quem sic intitulauit *De planctu Nature*, quia ibi introducit Naturam plangentem istam innaturalem deformitatem, que fit in tali commixtione qualem poete fingunt Iouem exercuisse circa istum Ganimedem.

146 uiri, maioris, 147 animalibus] *om.* A   146 fol. 136[va]
152 indiuiduus] et induuduus A   155 innuere] inuenire A   157 parilitatem] paritatem A   160 marmoriam] mamoriam O   163 dei] *om.* O   165 planctu] plactu O   165–69 Et ... Ganimedem] Et sic finitur 16 methologia Fulgencii A

had been made a star and had passed to Venus's star, as he shows near the end of his book, *Metamorphoses* 15.[15] Here notice the wretched madness of the Saracens, who account such a bestial and unnatural act deserving of eternal life. For this reason, in Islamic law, those who have been accounted and designated 'spiritual people', as if they were of greater perfection than others, do not account sodomy performed with diverse animals, even brutes, a sin; indeed, they are made more deserving by it. For this reason, such wretched people are respected among that nation as if they were holy.[16]

[150] [7] The seventh and last part of the picture follows; it concerns Ganymede's final appointment. For poets represent Ganymede as the special companion of all the gods. For this reason, some poets say he is the gods' cupbearer; others, that he is their chamberlain and the one who pours water on the gods' hands. By this, they wish to hint at and describe the stupidity of rich people in this world, those who believed that rich people, on account of the wealth they expended, to be worthy of the companionship of and some kind of equality with the gods. Likewise, one reads of Octavian that the Romans wished him to be adored as a god, seeing that his riches were so great that he had made the commonwealth marble instead of the earlier brick, and that he himself exulted in this, as the chronicles of the Romans tell.[17] And here one can also relevantly point out the history of Alexander the Great, who, at the start of his reign, exulted in being called the son of the god Amon, as Pompeius Trogus states at sufficient length in his *Histories*.[18] And notice carefully the verses that Mr Alan of Lille composed, as Nature's lament about this bestial vice. These verses appear at the opening of his book, which is thus titled *On Nature's complaint*, for there he introduces Nature complaining about this unnatural deformity; it occurs in that sexual act that poets represent Jove as having performed with Ganymede.[19]

---

[15] *Metamorphoses* 15.745–820, continuing with the deification of Octavian/Augustus, mentioned in the next paragraph.
[16] See the textual note.
[17] Paul the Deacon, *Historia miscella* 7 (PL 95:856n, 862).
[18] Ibid. 11.11.
[19] Ibid. m1 (PL 210:431–32).

[12]

Sequitur duodecima mithologia Fulgencii de Perseo et filiabus
Forci regis, quas poete uocant Gorgones, quas eciam poete
fingunt tres sorores fuisse, sicut patet per Fulgencium in littera.
Et intendunt in ymagine Persei describere fortitudinis uirtutem
et audacie. Hic igitur Perseus sicut patet \per/ Ouidium, libro suo
De transformatis, pingitur
    [1] deo Ioue satus,
    [2] Pallade minatus,
    [3] egide uelatus,
    [4] ense recuruatus,
    [5] alis agitatus,
    [6] spoliis ditatus,
    [7] et diis sociatus.
Iste sunt septem partes picture poetice qua poete solent hanc
uirtutem depingere, scilicet fortitudinis et audacie. |

[1] Nam prima pars picture est de Persei generacione. Nam
poete dicunt eum filium dei Iouis, ut prius tactum fuit in tercia
mithographia, que est de Ioue. Poete enim sub ymagine dei
Iouis pingunt uirtutem amoris et amicicie, quam nos Cristiani
uocamus caritatem. Et ab ista caritate gignitur omnis uirtus alia,
quia ut in diuersis locis probat Augustinus, sicut patet in epistola
ad Macedonium et in libris contra Iulianum hereticum et in
suis omeliis super canonicam Iohannis, 'Sine caritate non est
alia uirtus uera'. Unde ista caritas est que dat formam omnibus
aliis uirtutibus, quomodo Deus et spiritus uitalis, sicut patet per
Aristotelem in suis libris *De [a]nimalibus*, dat formam fetui, matre
materiam administrante.

Et ideo significanter iste Perseus a poetis fingitur filius dei Iouis,
quia fetus ordinati amoris est uirtus uere fortitudinis. De isto amore
et eius prole, scilicet fortitudine, loquens, Bernardus in quadam
epistola sic dicit: 'Amoris fortitudinem nemo resistere potest;

---

1 returning to the continuous text, O fol. 115vb 2 Forci] certi A, fortis I   5 patet]
   om. I   7 satus] fatus I   9 uelatus] uallatus A   15 fortitudinis] uirtutis A
   • fol. 116ra
16 Nam^1] Siquidem AI   • Nam^2] *adds* quidam A   17 dei] *om.* I   19 quam] *add*
   uirtutem AI   21-22 sicut ... et^2] *om.* A   23 canonicam] canticam I
   25 quomodo ... uitalis] *om.* AI   26 *De animalibus*] Denimalibus O
27 filius] *om.* I

[12]

Fulgentius's twelfth mythology follows. It concerns Perseus and the daughters of king Phorcus, whom poets call the Gorgons. The poets represent them as three sisters, as Fulgentius says explicitly.[1] They intend in the image of Persius to describe the virtue Courage and Daring. Therefore Perseus, as Ovid describes him in his *Metamorphoses*,[2] is depicted as

[1] [seed] sown by the god Jove,
[2] driven on by Pallas,
[3] covered by the aegis,
[4] bent back with his sword,
[5] moved about by wings,
[6] made rich with his plunder,
[7] and a companion to the gods.

These are the seven parts of the picture in which poets usually portray this virtue, courage and daring.

[16] [1] The first part of the picture concerns Perseus's birth, for poets say that he was the son of the god Jove. I treated this in the third mythography, about Jove. For in the image of the god Jove, poets depict the virtue love and friendship; we Christians call it charity. Every other virtue is born out of charity. Augustine proves this in various places, for example in his epistle to Macedonius, and in his books against the heretic Julian, and in his homilies on John's canonical epistle. He says, 'Without charity, no other virtue is truly such.'[3] For this reason, charity gives 'Form' to all other virtues, in the same way that, as Aristotle shows in his books *About animals*, God and the vital spirit give Form to the offspring, while the mother provides the Matter.[4]

[27] Therefore poets significantly depict Perseus as the son of the god Jove, because the true virtue courage is the offspring of a properly ordered love. Bernard, speaking in a letter, says of this love and its child courage, 'No one can resist the force [*i.e.* courage] of love;

---

[1] Fulg 1.21 (32/2–33/7).
[2] *Ibid.* 4.610–803.
[3] E.g. *Epistola* 155.4 (*PL* 33:672–73), cited above at 3/202.
[4] *De generatione animalium* 1.2 (716a).

omnia sibi subicit; [amor] omnia suis profectubus seruire cogit; eciam inimicos amando superat et sibi amicos efficit inuitos. Amor, etsi habeat emulos, inimicos tamen omnino non habet. Nullum enim inimicum habere potest qui nulli nouit inimicari. Sicut enim amicicia non est, nisi inter duos, quia non est amicicia, nisi duorum amicorum; sic enim inimicicia, nisi duorum | inimicorum. Qui enim odit diligentem se non tam inimicus est dicendus quam [iniquis]'. Hec Bernardus.

[2] Sequitur secunda pars picture de Persei minacione. Siquidem poete pingunt Perseum in suis actibus et operibus deductum et ratum consilio dee Paladis seu Minerue quam poete dicunt deam sapiencie esse uel prudencie, nam sine sapiencia et discrecione aggredi terribilia, quod est proprium fortitudini, non esset uirtuosum sed temerarium. Unde de hoc bene tangit Bernardus, libro 2° ad Eugenium papam, 'Uides enim fortitudinis matrem esse prudenciam; uides in qua non esse fortitudinem sed temeritatem, quemlicet ausum quem non parturiuit prudencia'. Et ideo significanter Tullius in sua *Rethorica*, diffiniens fortitudinem, dicit quod est 'considerata periculorum suscepcio et laborum perpessio'. Et idem in libro suo *De officiis* dicit quod 'Sicut sciencia, quando remota est ab ea iusticia, pocius appellanda est calliditas + quam sapiencia, ita animus paratus ad pericula, cum non communi utilitate, sed sua cupiditate impellitur, audacie nomen pocius habet quam fortitudinis'.

Et pro ista minacione fortitudinis a Minerua bene potest notari processus Apulei in suo libro *De deo Socratis*, quasi in fine, ubi loquens de Ulixe, dicit quod 'Hac, scilicet Pallade seu Minerua comitante, Ulixes omnia horrenda subiit, omnia aduersa superauit, ea | quippe Minerua seu Pallade adiutrice. Ciclopis specus introiuit, sed egressus est; Solis boues uidit, sed abstinuit; ad inferos demeauit, sed ascendit. Ista enim Pallade Ulixem [min]ante, Scillam preternauigauit, nec areptus est; Caribdi eciam conceptus, se[d] non retentus est; poculum Circes bibit, nec mutatus est;

32 amor] *om.* O   36–37 quia … amicorum] *om.* A   37 fol. 116[rb]   39 quam iniquis] *om.* A, quam amicus O
42 ratum] r̄c̄m̄ (= rectum) A, iratam I   45 esset] *adds* proprie A   46–48 uides … prudencia] *om.* I   50 considerata] inconsiderata A   52 calliditas] *adds* siue fatuitas O   54 communi] omni I • impellitur] repellitur I
57 *deo*] dictis I   58 Ulixe] Urluxe A   58–60 Pallade … Pallade] Pallade I   60 fol. 116[va] • Minerua seu] desiderans sine/siue A • adiutrice] adnutrice I • Ciclopis] Sicoplicio I   61 Solis] solus I   62 minante] iuuante O   63 nec] et A   64 sed] seu O • retentus] renitentus A

it subjects everything to itself; it compels all things to serve its successes; it overcomes even enemies by loving them and makes them its friends, against their will. Love, while it may have rivals, nevertheless has no enemies at all. For a person who doesn't know how to be an enemy can have no enemy. For just as friendship does not exist, unless it is between two people – after all, there's no friendship without two friends – it's the same for enmity, which requires two enemies. For the person who hates someone who is loving them should not be called an enemy, but an evil person.'[5] So Bernard says.

[40] [2] The second part of the picture follows; it concerns the impetus Perseus received. Poets indeed depict Perseus as led and made strong in his acts and labours through the counsel of the goddess Pallas or Minerva. Poets say she is the goddess of wisdom or prudence, for to attack terrifying things, as it is proper for courage to do, without wisdom or discretion is not virtuous, but foolhardy. For this reason, Bernard treats the issue appropriately, in his book to pope Eugene 2, 'For you see that prudence is the mother of courage; and you see that whatever one dares that was not born of prudence isn't courage, but foolhardiness.'[6] Therefore it's significant that when Cicero defines courage in his *Rhetoric*, he says that it is 'the considered undertaking of dangerous things and persistence in difficult ones'.[7] And in his book *On duties*, he says that, 'Just as knowledge, when it is detached from justice, should be called cleverness rather than wisdom, likewise a spirit that is prepared to face dangers, if it is driven by personal desire, rather than usefulness for all, should be called daring, not courage.'

[56] And with regard to the impetus that Minerva gave to courage, one may notice Apuleius's argument in his *On Socrates's god*, near the end, where speaking about Ulysses, he says, 'With Pallas or Minerva as his companion and helper, Ulysses endured every sort of terrifying thing and overcame all his hardships. He entered the Cyclops's cave, but came out again; he saw the oxen of the sun, but didn't touch them; he passed to hell, but came back up again. With Pallas driving him on, Ulysses also sailed past Scylla and wasn't seized; was gobbled up, but not kept, by Charybdis; drank from Circe's cup, but wasn't transformed;

---

[5] ps.-Bernard, *Tractatus de charitate* 1.1 (*PL* 184:584).
[6] *De consideratione* 1.8.9 (*PL* 182:737).
[7] *De inventione* 2.163, followed by *De officiis* 1.63.

65   ad Lotofragos + accesit, nec remansit; Sirenas audiuit, nec accessit'.
      In isto processu Apulei, narratur qualiter Ulixes, qui fuit unus de
      Grecis obsidentibus Troiam, plura aggrediebatur terribilia, sed
      quia se in suis actibus per prudenciam regulauit, ideo feliciter et
      prospere finaliter ei accidit.

70   [3] Sequitur tercia pars picture de Persei uelacione. Nam poete
      fingunt quod Perseus, illo tempore quo iuit ad interficiendum
      Gorgones, + quod ipse habuit scutum Palladis. Et hoc scutum
      dicebatur a poetis *egis*, et fuit illud scutum totum cristallinum
      secundum ymaginacionem poetarum. Et uolunt poete per
75   hoc intelligere quod ad uirtutem fortitudinis requiritur uirtus
      perseuerancie. Nam Tullius in sua *Rethorica* dicit perseueranciam,
      quam ipse uocat constanciam, esse partem fortitudinis, et
      non qua[m]cumque sed principaliorem. Nam ut bene tangit
      Bernardus in epistola ad uirginem Sophiam, 'Persuerancia sola
80   meretur [u]iribus gloriam, uirtutibus coronam. Prorsus absque
      perseuerancia, nec qui pugnat uictoriam, nec qui | uictor est
      consequitur palmam'.
      Hec est perseuerancia quam poete figurant per egidem,
      scutum Palladis cristallinum, nam ut poete dicunt, scutum illud
85   est rotundum. Et bene conuenit istud uirtuti perseuerancie, tam
      pro materia, quam pro forma. \Cristallus/ est materia huius scuti,
      sicut autem patet per Aristotelem, 4 *Metheorum*, 'Cristallus est
      aqua congelata congelacione perpetua, ita quod non est spes
      ultra de eius resolucione'. Similiter figura rotunda, que est forma
90   scuti, caret termino siue fine. Et ista bene conueniunt uirtuti
      perseuerancie, ut potest bene accipi ex diffinicione illius Tullii
      quam ipse dat in sua *Rethorica*. Ubi dicit quod 'perseuerancia est
      in + racione bene cons[idera]ta stabilis et perpetua permansio'.
      Et de isto bene potest notari processus Augustini in suo libro
95   *De bono perseuerancie*.

---

65 Lot-] Golo- A • accesit] accensit O 66 Ulixes] Uilexes I 67 Troiam] terram I 68 regulauit] rogau [*blank*] I 69 prospere] aspere I • finaliter] s̄m̄r̄ (= ? semper *or* similiter) A

70 de] adds dei I 71 quod] fingunt quod O 73 egis] elus I • (and 84) cristallinum] cristallum I 74 ymaginacionem] ymaginem AI 78 quamcumque] quacumque O 80 uiribus, uirtutibus] *trs.* O • uirtutibus] *om.* I 81 fol. 116vb

86 pro forma] *om.* (*at line-break*) I • huius scuti] *om.* AI 89-90 que ... scuti] *om.* AI 90 uirtuti] *om.* A 91 illius Tullii] *om.* I 93 racione] oracione O • considerata] constituta AIO

he approached the Lotus-eaters, but didn't stay with them; he heard the Sirens, but didn't approach them.'[8] In his argument, Apuleius tells how Ulysses, one of the Greeks laying siege to Troy, attacked many horrifying things, but because he ruled himself and his behaviour by prudence, he came out of it all speedily and happily in the end.

[70] [3] The third part of the picture follows; it concerns Perseus's covering. For poets tell that Perseus, when he went to kill the Gorgons, had with him Pallas's shield. Poets called this shield 'the aegis', and they imagined it as made entirely out of the stone crystal. Poets wish to understand by this that the virtue courage requires also the virtue perseverance. For Cicero, in his *Rhetoric*, says that perseverance, which he calls 'constancy', is a part of the virtue courage, and not just any part, but the most prominent one.[9] For, as Bernard says appropriately in his letter to the virgin Sophia, 'Strength earns glory and virtues their crown through perseverance alone. Indeed, without perseverance, no fighter achieves victory, nor any victor the palm of triumph.'[10]

[83] The poets' emblem for perseverance is the aegis, Pallas's crystal shield, for, as they say, this shield is round. This is most appropriate for the virtue perseverance, because of both the shield's material and its shape. The material of this shield is crystalline, for as Aristotle shows in *Meteors* 4, 'Crystal is water frozen into an unchanging solid so that one cannot expect it to melt again.'[11] Similarly, a round figure, the shape of Pallas's shield, lacks any end. And these features are particularly appropriate for the virtue perseverance, as one may well understand from the definition that Cicero gives in his *Rhetoric*. There he says that 'perseverance is a stable and enduring persistence in a well-considered purpose'. On this point, one should particularly notice Augustine's argument in his *On the good of perseverance*.[12]

---

[8] *Ibid.* 24, repeating 2/86.
[9] *De inventione* 2.163, as in the next paragraph.
[10] *Epistola* 129.2 (*PL* 182:283), which is 'ad Januenses'.
[11] *Ibid.* 1.12 (347b).
[12] Probably 'ad fratres in eremo', sermo 8 (*PL* 40:1249–50)?

[4] Quarta pars picture de Persai recuruacione. Nam fingunt poete istum Perseum habuit in manu falcem, et cum false inuadentem Medusam et caput Meduse precidentem cum falce. Ubi notandum est quod usus falcis non communiter est, nisi racione alicuius specialis commodi uel utilitatis. Et ta[li] modo debet aggredi ardua et terribilia uir fortis, non ex temeritate uel mundane glorie cupiditate, sed pocius aut sua aut tocius rei publice utilitate, sicut de hoc loquuntur philosophi et uiri sancti. Unde Tullius, libro suo primo *De officiis*, dicit quod 'cauenda est glorie cupiditas. Eripit enim libertatem, pro qua libertate seruanda magnanimis uiris et fortibus omnino debet | esse contencio'. Et subdit Tullius in eodem libro, 'Fugiendum est illud, ne scilicet offeramus nos periculis sine causa, quo nichil esse stulcius potest. Sed cum tempus necessitatis expostulat, tunc mors seruitu[ti] turpitudini[que] anteponenda est. Quapropter in adeund[is] pericul[is] consuetudo medicorum imitanda est, qui leniter egrotantes leniter curant, grauioribus autem morbis periculos[as et ancipites] curas adhibere c[og]untur'. Et de isto tangit Seneca in quadam epistola, ubi dicit sic, 'Queris an omne bonum optabile sit. "Si bonum, inqui[s], optabile est [fortiter torqueri et magno animo uti et pacienter egrotare. Ergo ista erunt optabilia"'. Et respondit Seneca], 'Tormenta, inquit, [a me] abesse. Uolo sed si sustinenda fueri[n]t, ut me in illis fortiter, honeste, et animose geram, optabo. Uolo', dicit Seneca, 'non incidere bellum, sed si incid[ere]t, tunc et uulnera et \fa/mem et omnia que bellorum necessitas affert, generos[e] ut feram optabile est et pati fortiter'. Sic igitur patet quomodo et ex qua causa pingitur Perseus falce armatus; unde et cum ista falce precidit caput Gorgonis.

De quibus Gorgonibus est sciendum quod, iuxta ymaginacionem poeticam, Gorgones iste taliter sunt depicte: numero sunt trine,

---

98 Medusam] madulam I • Meduse] me inceduse I • precidentem] precindendo A, presidendo I   99 usus falcis] strenuitur antiquitus A • est] utebantur sua fortitudine A   100 tali modo] tantummodo O   102 cupiditate] uanitate AI   102–3 sed ... sancti] *om.* A   106 uiris] *om.* A • fol. 117ra 107 contencio] contradiccio I   108–9 nichil ... stulcius] uel esse fulcius I   110 seruituti turpitudinique] seruitus turpitudini O   111 adeundis periculis] adeundo pericula O   113 periculosas et ancipites] periculosisque anticipes O • coguntur] noscuntur O   115 inquis] iniquis A, inquit notabile O   115–17 fortiter ... Seneca] *om.* IO   117 a me] *om.* O   118 fuerint] sint A, fuerit O   120 incideret] incidere A, inciditis O   121 generose] generoso AO • ut feram] et forti A   122 et^1] sed et AI

[91] [4] The fourth part of the picture concerns Perseus's being bent backwards. For poets depict Perseus having a curved sword in his hand, and as attacking Medusa with his curved sword and cutting her head off with it. Here one ought to notice that using a curved sword isn't common, unless it's a matter of some special benefit or usefulness. A brave person should attack difficult and terrifying things in this way, not from foolhardiness or the desire for worldly glory, but rather from usefulness either for himself or for the whole commonwealth, a point discussed by both philosophers and holy men. For this reason, Cicero, in *On duties* 1, says, 'One should beware of the desire for glory. For it snatches away that freedom which brave and high-minded people should always strive to preserve.' And Cicero adds in the same book, 'We should avoid exposing ourselves to dangers without a good cause, for nothing could be more stupid. Yet when necessity demands it, then one should prefer death to slavery or shamefulness. For this reason, in approaching dangers, one should imitate the practice of physicians. They cure those who are suffering illnesses easily borne by easy means, but they are compelled to adopt dangerous and doubled cures for more serious illnesses.'[13] Seneca treats this point in one of his letters, where he says, 'You ask me whether one should choose to do every good thing. You say, "If it is a good, then one should choose to be gravely tortured, as to show a great spirit that might suffer in patience. Therefore one will choose to do these things."' Seneca answers, 'I'd choose to avoid torments. But I wish that if I must endure them, I will choose to do so, so that I might conduct myself bravely, virtuously, and courageously in them.' He continues, 'I don't wish there to be a war, but should one occur, then I would choose to bear nobly and suffer bravely the wounds, the starvation, and all those things that the necessity of wars brings.'[14] This shows how and why Perseus is depicted armed with a curved sword, and why he cut off the Gorgon's head with his curved sword.

[125] One should know that the poets imagine that these Gorgons are depicted as:
three in number,

---

[13] Respectively, 1.68, 1.83, and 1.81.
[14] *Epistula* 67.3–4.

　　　　　　　sanguine uicine,
　　　　　　　crine serpentine,
130　　　　　et uisu petrine.
　　　　　Siquidem Gorgones iste sunt in numero ternario, qua\rum/ ista sunt nomina: Stennio, Euriale, et Medusa. Siquidem, sicut patet per Fulgencium in litera, Stennio interpretatur 'debilitas', Euriale 'lata profunditas', | sed Medusa interpretatur 'obliuio'.
135　　Gorgones enim sunt idem quod terro[r]es; unde dicit Fulgencius *gorgor* interpretatur 'terror'. Tres igitur sunt Gorgones, quia tres sunt differencie terroris, \propter tres terro[ris]/ effectus. Unus effectus est debilitacio mentis et usus racionis, nam homo non habet sensum et iudicium racionis ita uiuaces tempore terroris
140　　seu timoris sicut habet aliis temporibus. Et iste effectus terroris per illam regis Forci filiam designatur que dicitur Stennio. Alius effectus terroris est stupor, scilicet quando homo, ex uehemencia timoris, incidet in stuporem mentis. Tunc enim, ut dicit Fulgencius, profundo quodam \timore/ mens hominis dispergitur. Et ille
145　　effectus timoris designatur per [E]uriale, que interpretatur 'lata profunditas'. Tercius uero effectus terroris est mentis obliuio et totalis sensuum caligo, et significatur iste effectus per Medusam. Nam Medusa interpretatur 'obliuio'.
　　　　　Propter istos tres terroris effectus sunt Gorgones iste depicte
150　　in numero ternario. Et istos Gorgones Perseus, id est uir fortis, inuadit cum falce, quia, licet uelit [non] se sponte et ex temeritate periculis exponere, tamen antequam incidat in aliquam trium predictorum, scilicet uel in mentis debilitatem uel in mentis stuporem et in racionis disp[er]cionem, uel eciam in racionis
155　　obliuionem et uisus caliginem, prius, inquam, uir | fortis congreditur et aggreditur, quodcunque terribile equanimiter sustinendo, et per pacienciam caput Gorgonis prescindendo, ut enim metrice dici solet, 'Nobile uincendi \genus/ est paciencia; / uincit qui patitur. Si \uincere/ uis, disce pati'. Et alius uersificator,
160　　　Excuciet pacem quam dat paciencia nullus / Armatamque
　　　　　　manum uincere sola potest. / Uir paciens forti melior minorque
　　　　　　triumphus / + urbis quam meritis dicitur esse minor.

132 etc. Euriale] Curiale A　**134** fol. 117rb　**135** terrores] terrones O　**136** terroris²] timoris A (*as again 149*), terro[*cut off*] O (*the same corr. marg.* I)　**138** usus] uisus A　**141** regis] *om.* A　• que dicitur] *om.* AI　**145** Euriale] Curiale O

151 non] *om.* AIO　**152** incidat] *om.* A　**154** dispercionem] dispō̄m (= disposicionem), *and repeats phrase* O　**155** fol. 117va

160 nullus] multis A　**161** melior] nulius (?) A　**162** urbis] uerbis AIO　• meritis] mentis AI

related by blood,
with snakelike hair,
and with a stony sight.

[131] Indeed, there are three Gorgons, and their names are Stennio, Euriale, and Medusa. Likewise, as Fulgentius states explicitly, Stennio means 'weakness', and Euriale 'a broad chasm', but Medusa means 'forgetfulness'. For the Gorgons are the same as terrors; for this reason, Fulgentius says that *gorgor* means 'terror'. Therefore there are three Gorgons, because there are three species of terror, because terror has three effects. One effect is the weakening of the mind and of its use of reason, for a person doesn't have so lively senses and rational judgement at a time when they are terrified or afraid as they do at other times. King Phorcus's daughter called Stennio indicates this effect of terror. The second effect of terror is bewilderment, namely when a person, on account of the violence of their fear, falls into a mental numbness. For then, as Fulgentius says, a person's mind is scattered by a kind of deep fear. Euriale, whose name means 'a broad chasm', indicates this effect of terror. The third effect of terror is an emptying of the mind and a complete darkening of the senses, and this effect is indicated by Medusa, whose name means 'forgetfulness'.[15]

[149] Poets depict the Gorgons as three on account of these three effects of terror. The brave person, that is Perseus, attacks these three Gorgons with their curved sword. Although they don't wish to expose themself to dangers voluntarily and from foolhardiness, the brave person nonetheless joins battle and attacks them before their threefold danger may befall them. (This danger involves mental weakness, or bewilderment and the scattering of their reason, or forgetting reason altogether, along with the darkening of their sight.) In this way, this person endures with equanimity whatever is fearsome and cuts off the Gorgon's head through the virtue patience. Thus, as the commonplace verse says, 'Patience is a noble species of triumph; / the person who suffers conquers. If you want to conquer, learn to suffer.' And another versifier says,

> No one will drive away the peace that patience gives, / And patience alone can conquer the armed hand. / A patient person is better than a strong one; it's a lesser triumph / over a city, for it is considered less in merit.[16]

---

[15] Fulg 1.21 (32/21–33/8).
[16] Walther 16974, followed by 8411 (cf. 32678) and 33547.

Nota quod uult dicere quod melius et nobilius triumphat ille de quocunque terribili qui est fortis moraliter, qualis est uir paciens, quam ille qui est fortis corporaliter. Paciencia quidem est una pars fortitudinis, que est uirtus moralis, sicut patet \per/ Tullium in sua *Rethorica*. Hec est paciencia que est f[al]x Persei recurua, quia ut tangit Cassiodorus in suo originali *Super psalmos* [blank], per istam uirtutem inclinatur homo ad aggrediendum ardua, non temerarie, sed racione alicuius honeste cause et necessarie. Unde Cassiodorus, diffiniendo pacienciam, sic dicit, 'Paciencia est honestatis atque utilitatis causa rerum arduarum ac difficilium uoluntaria atque diuturna perpessio'. Et hec est paciencia philosophorum, ut uult idem Cassiodorus, sed pacienciam catholicorum Cristianorum diffinit idem Cassiodorus, dicens quod 'Paciencia religiosi uiri est labor[um] et dolorum omnium spe futurarum rerum et amore [Dei] grata tollerancia'. Hec est paciencia, ut dicit idem | Cassiodorus, 'Que omnia uincit aduersa, non colluctando sed \tollerando/, non murmurando sed gracias referendo. Ipsa est que fecem tocius uoluptatis abstergit; ipsa est que limpidas animas Deo reddit'.

De istis autem Gorgonibus predictis, quare et qualiter sunt sanguine uicine, patet ex poetis, qui eas pingunt sorores fuisse. Non sicut ille dicuntur, sorores carnaliter, que genite sunt ab uno patre et ab una matre; ita ab una passione timoris [proueni]unt isti tres effectus prius descripti. Quare igitur istas Gorgones pingunt poete cum crinibus serpentinis hec est causa. Nam sedes mentis et iudicium racionis uiget in capite, ubi locus est crinium. Et ideo propter triplex uenenum timoris istius, tripliciter inficientem usum racionis, dicuntur iste sorores ferre crines serpentinos.

Sed de quarta parte picture Gorgonum, quare scilicet poete pingunt eas habentes uisum et aspectum per quem uidentes eas uertebantur in petras, hec est causa. Nam ut \prius/ dicit Fulgencius, timor reddit hominem timentem, obstinatum, et inpersuasibilem per modum lapidis induratum. Sicut patet de istis [h]ominibus auaris, qui credunt semper quod eis mundus deficiet, et ideo nulla possunt exhortacione seu predicacione conuerti,

---

163 et nobilius] *om.* I 165 corporaliter] totaliter A 167 est¹] uocatur A 168 falx] flax O 170 ardua] *om.* AI 171 diffiniendo pacienciam] *om.* AI 176 laborum] laboris O 177 omnium] cum A • Dei] *om.* O 178 fol. 117vb
185 proueniunt] fuerunt IO 188 in capite] *om.* A • ideo] non A
192 uidentes] occidentes A 194 timentem] timidum A, *adds* omnino I
   195 inpersuasibilem] insuperabilem A 195–96 istis hominibus] *om.* A, istis nominibus O

[163] Notice that this versifier wants to say that the person who is brave in moral terms, the patient person, triumphs more fully and more nobly over any terrifying thing than the person who is merely strong. Thus patience is a part of the moral virtue fortitude, as Cicero shows in his *Rhetoric*.[17] Patience is Perseus's curved sword, for, as Cassiodorus says in *On the Psalms*, through this virtue, a person is bent toward taking up hard things, not out of foolhardiness, but for the sake of some virtuous and necessary cause. For this reason, Cassiodorus, in a definition of patience, says, 'Patience is the willed and persisting suffering of harsh and difficult things for the sake of virtue or of usefulness.' This is the patience defined by the philosophers, as Cassiodorus points out, but he also defines the patience of catholic Christians, saying, 'The patience of a religious person is the thankful endurance of all labours and sorrows from the love of God and the hope of those things that are to come.' As he also says, 'Patience conquers all hardships, not struggling against them, but enduring them, and not complaining, but offering thanks. Patience washes away the shit of all desire; it makes our souls clear for God.'[18]

[182] Poets show why and how the Gorgons are related by blood, because they depict them as having been sisters. But they were not, as they say, sisters in the flesh, like those born from the same father and same mother. Rather, these three effects I have described spring forth from the single passion, fear. Here's the reason why poets depict them with snakelike hair. The mind, with its capacity to judge rationally, is located and is strongest in the head, which is also where hair grows. Because of the triple poison of their fear, which infects the use of reason in three ways, these sisters are said to have snakelike hair.

[191] As far as the fourth part of the Gorgons' picture, here's the reason why poets depict them as having a sight and appearance that turned those who looked upon them into stones. For as Fulgentius first says, fear makes a person fearful, stubborn, and incapable of being persuaded, just like the hardened form of a rock.[19] This is evident with avaricious people. They always believe that the world will fail to provide for them, and therefore they cannot be converted by any exhortation or preaching,

---

[17] *De inventione* 2.163.
[18] *In Psalterium expositio*, Ps 70 (which is citing Cicero, *ibid.*), Ps 7, and Ps 32 (*PL* 70:497, 73, 231), respectively.
[19] See the textual note.

nec plus quam petre possunt emolliri. Unde de ista petrina duricia auarorum loquitur dominus Innocencius, *De miseria condicionis humane*, ubi comparat duriciam auari duricie inferni. Unde sic dicit, 'Auarus + et infernus, | uterque commedit, sed \non/ digerit; recipit, sed non reddit. Auarus nec pacientibus compatitur, nec miseris subuenit nec miseretur, sed offendit Deum, offendit proximum, et offendit seipsum. Nam Deo detinet debita, proximo denegat necessaria, sibi ipsi subtrahit oportuna. Deo est ingratus, proximo est impius, sibi ipsi est crudelis'. Et hec omnia facit timor deordinatus et obstinatus. Hec est igitur causa moralis huius picture materialis de oculis istarum trium sororum, quarum uisus pingitur petrinus ab effectu quem timor deordinatus causat in omnibus taliter passionatis.

[5] Sequitur quinta pars picture de Persei agitacione. Siquidem poete pingunt eum habe\re/ alas, sicut patet Ouidius, libro 4° de *Transformatis*, fere in fine, ubi loquens de uolatu Persei dicit, 'A[er]a carpebat tenerum stridentibus alis'. Et moraliter nichil aliud uult poeta per alas Persei intelligere, nisi celeritatem fame que consequitur hominem fortem. Ex ista enim fama, poete fingunt eum alatum, quia fama boni hominis, eciam et mali, celeriter innotescit, nisi contingat ipsam famam bonam impediri per inuidiam, iuxta illud prouerbii, '[Fama] boni lente uolat, inuidia retinente; / Fama repleta malis leuibus deducitur alis', uel 'leuioribus euolat alis', quam autem famosa fuit. Apud gentiles incredulos uirtus ista fortitudinis patet ex eorum historiis, | et specialiter ex historiis Romanorum. Uideat lector in Tito Liuio, in Ualerio Ma[xim]o, et aliis + historiographis.

[6] Sexta pars picture est de Persi ditacione. Fingunt enim poete quod Perseus iste, ueniens cum capite Meduse quod absciderat cum ense suo, hoc est cum falce illa de qua prius in quarta parte huius picture facta est mencio, uenit per Athlantem regem Hesperie, qui habebat in orto suo arbores poma aurea deferentes, que Perseus abstulit et Athlantem in montem conuertit,

---

198 possunt] *adds* exhortacione A   199 auarorum] *om.* A   200 duriciam auari] talem duriciam A   201 et] id est O   • fol. 118ra 205 denegat] *om.* A
210 omnibus] hominibus AI

213 fere in fine, 213-14 dicit ... alis] *om.* A   214 Aera] Area O   215 celeritatem] celebritatem AI, cele|ritatem O   217 hominis eciam] *om.* A   219 Fama] *om.* O   221 uel ... alis] *om.* AI   222 fortitudinis] *om.* A   • fol. 118rb
224 Maximo] Magno AO   • et ... historiographis] *om.* A   • aliis] *adds* historiis O

227-28 illa ... mencio] *om.* A   229 regem] *adds* per regem I

nor may they be softened, any more than stones can be. For this reason, pope Innocent, in *On the wretched state of mankind*, speaks of the stony hardness of avaricious people and compares their hardness with that of hell. He says, 'Both an avaricious person and hell eat, but they don't digest; they receive, but they don't pay back. Avaricious people don't feel compassion for those who suffer, nor do they support or feel mercy for the wretched, but they offend God, their neighbour, and themselves. For they hang onto what is due to God, refuse their neighbour necessities, and deny themselves advantages. They are ungrateful to God, pitiless toward their neighbour, cruel to themselves.'[20] Unregulated and stubborn fear causes all these behaviours. This is the moral cause for the material picture of these three sisters' eyes. Poets depict their sight as stony from the effect that disordered fear causes in all those prey to this passion.

[211] [5] The fifth part of the picture follows; it concerns Perseus's motion. For poets indeed depict Perseus as having wings, as Ovid shows in *Metamorphoses* 4, near the end, where, speaking of Perseus's flight, he says, 'He pressed his way through the thin air on his rustling wings.'[21] In moral terms, Ovid wishes to understand by Perseus's wings only the speedy renown that results from a brave person's acts. For on the basis of this renown, poets depict Perseus as having wings, for the renown of both good and bad people is quickly recognised. Or it is so, unless a good person's renown is blocked by envy, in accord with the proverb, 'A good person's renown flies slowly, since envy restrains it, / But the renown for being thoroughly evil is drawn along by fleet wings', or 'it flies away on weaker wings', although it was once well-known.[22] Although they are not believers, the pagans display this virtue, courage, in their histories, especially in Roman histories. The reader should look at Livy, or Valerius Maximus, or other historians.

[225] [6] The sixth part of the picture concerns Perseus's wealth. For poets present Perseus passing with Medusa's head. (He had chopped it off with his sword, the curved one that I have mentioned in the fourth part of the picture.) He passed by Atlas, king of Hesperia, who had a garden with trees that bore golden apples; these Perseus carried off, and he changed Atlas into a mountain.

---

[20] *Ibid.* 2.11 (PL 217:721).
[21] *Ibid.* 4.616.
[22] Walther, *Sprich.* 8819.

sicut de isto tractat Ouidius 4 de *Transformatis*, ut dicit metrice, 'Tempus, Athla, ueniet [tua] quo spoliabitur auro / arbor, et hunc prede titulum Ioui natus habebit'. Ista, sicut tangit ibidem, fuit prophecia illius prophetisse Te[mis], qui fuit tempore Dedaleonis,
235 et fuit uerificata, ut dixerunt aliqui de Perseo. Alii dixerunt uaticinium illud uerificatum de Hercule.

Sed quantum spectat ad propositum nostrum, ficcio poetica nichil aliud intelligit, nisi magnitudinem et preciositatem premii quod debetur isti uirtuti, scilicet fortitudini. Nam premium
240 martirii est maximum, [sed bene de martirii premio loquitur] Ciprianu[s] in quadam epistola. Dicit enim quod 'Martirium est baptisma quod magis est in gracia, sublim\i/us in potestate, preciosius in honore'. Ad hoc autem sustinendum inclinatur homo, et specialiter disponitur per istum habitum uirtuosum. Unde
245 bene dicit | Ieronimus quod non nisi per istam uirtutem, scilicet fortitudinis, impletur quod Dominus dicit in euangelio, Matthei 2°, *Regnum [celorum] uim patitur et uiolenti rapiunt illud.*

[7] Sequitur septima pars picture de Persei [de]ificacione. Poete, sicut patet per Eginum, libro suo *De ymaginibus celestibus*,
250 stellificabant hunc Perseum, et reputabant eum de numero deorum, sicut de isto tractat Augustinus, *De ciuitate Dei*, libro 18, capitulo 13, ubi dicit quod 'Temporibus iudicum Israel, Perseus et uxor eius Andromada, postquam fuerunt mortui, credebant homines eos in celum esse receptos, ita quod ymagines eorum
255 stellis celestibus designarent'. Unde ymago eorum lucet in celo 24 stellis.

Sed ad propositum applicando, nichil aliud est per hoc moraliter intelligendum, nisi quod per istam uirtutem fortitudinis, homo fortis pertingit ad ueram felicitatem, que consistit in uisione
260 et fruicione Dei. Sed ille qui Deo fruitur in deum transformatur, sicut docet Augustinus super canonicam Iohannis. 'Si Deum diligis', dicit Augustinus, 'deus es'. Qui autem in deum est transformatus, iam est deificatus, sicut de hoc bene tangit Anselmus in suo libro

---

231-37 sicut ... spectat] sed A 232 tua] tuum I, *om.* O 234 Temis] Ten' O
• Temis qui fuit] *om.* I • Dedaleonis] Dentaleonis I
237 ficcio poetica] *om.* A 240-41 sed ... Ciprianus] sicut patet Ciprianum O
242 sublimius] liberius ? A 243 sustinendum] suscipiendum A 245 fol. 118[va]
247 celorum] Dei O
248 deificacione] edificacione AI 249 Eginum] Eu|genium I • sicut ... *celestibus*] *om.* A 251 de isto] *adds* expresse I 254 esse receptos] raptos A 255 eorum] Persei A
260 Dei] *om.* I 261-62 super ... es] dicens [blank] A

Ovid talks about this in *Metamorphoses* 4, where his verse reads, 'Atlas, the time is coming when your tree will be stripped / of its gold, and through this theft, Jove's son will have a claim to glory.'[23] As Ovid treats it there, this was a prophecy made by the seeress Themis – she was a contemporary of Daedalus's son Icarus – and this came to pass, as some people have reported about Perseus. But other people have said that this prophecy came to pass for Hercules.

[237] But so far as it pertains to my argument, this poetic fiction refers only to the great extent and the great value of the reward the virtue courage deserves. For the greatest reward is that a martyr earns, and Cyprian speaks well about the reward due martyrdom in a letter. For he says that 'Martyrdom is a baptism, but one greater than baptism in the grace it confers, more lofty in its power, and more valuable in the honour it confers.'[24] A person is inclined to endure it, and specially disposed to do so, by the virtuous behaviour of courage. For this reason, Jerome properly says that only through the virtue courage does one fulfil what the Lord says in the gospel, *The kingdom of heaven suffereth violence, and the violent bear it away* (Mt 11:12).[25]

[248] [7] The seventh part of the picture follows; it concerns Perseus's being made godlike. For, as Hyginus shows in his book *On heavenly figures*, poets made Perseus into a star and accounted him among the gods.[26] Augustine also addresses this point in *On the city of God* 18.13, where he says that 'In the time of Israel's judges, people believed that Perseus and his wife Andromeda, after they were dead, were received in the heavens, so that they traced out their images in stars in the sky.' For this reason, their heavenly image shines in twenty-four stars.

[257] But applying this to my argument, one should understand in moral terms only that through the virtue courage, a brave person attains true happiness, which consists in seeing and enjoying God. But the person who enjoys God is transformed into a god, as Augustine teaches in his commentary on John's canonical epistle. He says, 'If you love God, you are a god.'[27] Moreover, a person who is transformed into a god has been made a god right now, as Alexander of Canterbury argues in his

---

[23] *Ibid.* 4.644–45.
[24] *Epistola ad Fortunatum de exhortatione martyrii* Praef.3 (PL 4:654).
[25] Cf. *Epistola* 22.40 (PL 22:424).
[26] *De astronomia* 2.11–12, 3.10–11, etc., followed by Augustine, *ibid.* (PL 41:572).
[27] *Ibid.* 2.14 (PL 35:1997).

De similitudinibus, qui ponit exemplum de ferro ignito. Ibi enim ostendit Anselmus quod in celo uidendo et fruendo Deo, non solum erunt beati, sed deificati. 'Curabit', inquit, 'uos et sanitati restitutos, ornamentis perfecte iusticie et incorrupt[ibil]is ornabit, uos ad|ductos in filios, Sibi aboptabit, regni eciam Sui consortes efficiet et heredes, uocatos nomine Suo deos faciet. Enim Ipse dicit, *Ego dixi dii estis et filii Excelsi omnes*. Ipse tamen erit Deus deificans, et tu, homo, eris deus deificatus'. Hec Anselmus. Specialiter autem ad istum statum diuinitatis reputabant antiqui sapientes huius mundi hominem posse pertingere per istam uirtutem, scilicet fortitudinem. Quia ut recitat Tullius, 'In antiquis temporibus, nomen uirtutis fuit solius fortitudinis, ita quod in comparacione ad fortitudinem, non reputabant alios habitus dignos isto nomine, puta nomine uirtutis. Unde et a uiribus uirtus nomen accepit, et ideo antiqui illi per fortitudinem, tanquam per potissimam uirtutem, estimabant hominem perfectissime posse pertingere ad diuinitatem'. Undecima mithologia \et sic finit/.

264 quod] *adds* homines A   267 incorruptibilis] incorrupti^a tis I, incorruptis O   268 fol. 118vb   268–69 regni … uocatos] *om.* A   270 filii … omnes] *om.* A, *over eras.* I   271 deus²] *om.* I • Anselmus] Augustinus A   272–80 Specialiter … finit] *om.* A   277 nomine²] *om.* I   277–78 Unde … accepit] *marg.* I
280 Undecima … finit] Sic igitur finita est duodecima mithologia Fulgencii I

On likenesses, where he offers the example of iron set on fire. For Alexander shows there that by looking on heaven and enjoying God, worshippers will not simply be blessed, but deified. For he says, 'He will heal you, and having restored you to health, He will adorn you with ornaments of perfect and incorruptible righteousness, and having taken you on as His children, He will adopt you, will make you partners and heirs of His kingdom, and calling you by His own name, He will make you gods. For He Himself says, *I have said, You are gods, and all of you sons of the most High* (Ps 81:6). Nevertheless, He will be God creating gods, and you people will be a god made a god.'[28] So Alexander says. However, ancient wise men considered that a person of this world might attain to this state of divinity through the virtue courage. For as Cicero says, 'In ancient times, only courage was identified as a virtue, so that, in comparison with courage, they didn't consider other behaviours worthy of the name "virtue". For this reason, the noun "virtue" was also derived from *uires* "strengths", and therefore the ancients considered that, through courage, as the most powerful virtue, one might most perfectly attain the state of divinity.'[29] Here the eleventh mythology ends.

---

[28] *Ibid.* 56–57 (*PL* 159:640–41).
[29] Cf. *Tusculanae disputationes* 2.43.

[13]

Sequitur duodecima mithologia Fulgencii de Alcesta, uxore
Admeti. Et intendunt poete sub ymagine istius mulieris describere
uirtutem continencie coniugalis. Mulier autem predicta pingitur
   [1] a rege postulata,
5 [2] regi copulata,
   [3] precio donata,
   [4] Fatis uenundata,
   [5] inferis + allata,
   [6] sed Hercule saluata.
10 Iste sunt sex partes picture seu descripcionis poetice qua poete
solent depingere uirtutem continencie coniugalis.
   [1] Nam quoad primam partem picture, dicunt quod quidam
rex Grecie, Admetus nomine, quandam peciit | in coniugem
nomine Alcestem. Et per hoc uolunt poete intelligere unum quod
15 specialiter et principaliter requiritur ad istam continenciam
coniugalem. Requiritur enim mutuus consensus ad hoc, quod
usus iste et concubitus sit moraliter uirtuosus, scilicet quod
uir consenciat in mulierem, sicut in legittimam uxorem, et e
conuerso, mulier in uirum, sicut in legitimum maritum, non
20 quod uir consensu fornicario in mulierem consenciat uel
adulterino. Et de isto consensu ad istam continenciam coniugalem
requisitam, loquntur sancti uiri, sicut recitat magister Petrus
Lumbardus in suis *Sentenciis* et magister Hugo de Sancto Uictore.
Dicit enim Iohannes Crisostomus, *Super Mattheum*, quod
25 'Matrimonium non facit coitus, sed uoluntas et consensus'. Et
beatus Ambrosius dicit quod 'Non deflor\acio/ uirginitatis facit
+ coniugium, sed pactio coniugalis'. Dicit enim in suo decreto
papa Nicholaus quod 'Secundum leges, ad matrimonium solus
sufficit consensus; qui consensus, si in nupciis defuerit, cum coitu
30 celebrate frustrantur'.

3 pingitur] *adds* isto modo A   5 regi] *adds* p̄ia' (?), *over eras.* I   8 allata] uallata O
   10 partes] proprietates et A • descripcionis, depingere] *om.*, describere AI
13 nomine] *om. (at line-break)* I • quandam] *adds* mulierem A • fol. 119ʳᵃ   14
   intelligere] *om. (at page-boundary)* A   17 et concubitus] *om.* A   18 mulierem]
   uxorem A   19 mulier ... maritum] *om.* A   22 requistam] requisito AI • uiri]
   nostri AI • sicut ... magister, 23 in ... magister] *om.* A   25 facit] *adds*
   matrimonium seu O   29 cum] cetera cum ipso A, cum ipso I   30 celebrate]
   celebrata AI

[13]

Fulgentius's twelfth mythology follows; it concerns Alceste, Admetus's wife. Poets intend, through the image of this woman, to describe the virtue Marital Continence. This woman is depicted as:
  [1] asked for by a king,
  [2] having had sex with a king,
  [3] bestowed for a price,
  [4] sold to the Fates,
  [5] carried off to hell,
  [6] but liberated by Hercules.
These are the six parts of the picture or poetic description by which poets usually depict the virtue marital continence.

[12] [1] So far as the first part of the picture, poets say that a Greek king named Admetus once asked in marriage a woman named Alceste. Through this, poets wish to understand a single thing that is particularly and principally required for marital continence. For this custom and the sexual intercourse that goes with it to be morally virtuous requires a mutual agreement. Namely, the man should consent to the woman as his legitimate wife, and the reverse, the woman to the man as her legitimate husband, and not that the man consent to the woman as if they had agreed only to fornication or an adulterous relationship. Holy men speak about the consent required for marital continence, for example Mr Peter Lombard in his *Sentences* and Mr Hugh of St Victor.[1] For Chrysostom, *On Matthew*, says, 'It isn't sexual congress that creates a marriage, but will and consent.' And blessed Ambrose says, 'It isn't the deflowering of a virgin that creates a marriage, but a marital agreement.'[2] Also, pope Nicholas says in his decree, 'According to the laws, only consent is sufficient for a marriage, and those who celebrate a marriage with intercourse alone, that consent being absent, are deceived.'[3]

---

[1] *Ibid.* 4.27.2–3 (*PL* 192:910–11); Hugh, *Summa sententiarum* 7.6 or *De sacramentis* 2.11.4 (*PL* 176:158–59, 483–84).
[2] The Chrysostom unfound, followed by *De institutione virginis* 6.41 (*PL* 16:316).
[3] Cf. Gratian, *Decretum* C.30, q.1, c.3 (*CJC* 1:957, dated 858x67), but probably inherited (see the textual note).

Nota igitur quomodo consensum istum poete circumloquntur per regem Admet[u]m postulantem coniugium illius Alceste. Ut enim Fulgencius tangit in littera, iste Admetus stat apud poetas loco mentis; Admetus, secundum poetas, nuncupatus est, ut dicit Fulgencius, quasi 'qu[em] possit adire metus'. Passio enim timoris non est passio corporis [principaliter loquendo], sed pocius est passio anime. Et ideo Admetus dicitur | Alcestem in coniugium post\u/lare, nam oportet quod ipsa peticio uocis exterior procedat ex consensu interiori ipsius anime. Et eciam oportet quod ipsa peticio fiat cum timore racionabili, + qui est timor Dei. Aliter enim actus iste et usus mutuus corporum non erit usus uirtuosus et castus. Unde de isto habetur pulcher processus Tobie 6º, ubi narratur quod angelus Raphael dixit Tobie, *Audi me, et ostendam tibi qui sunt, quibus preualere potest dem\onium/ in eos. Hii namque qui coniugia ita suscipiunt, ut Deum et a se et a sua mente excludant, et sue libidini ita uacent, sicut equus et mulus, quibus non est intellectus, habet potestatem dem\onium/ super eos. Tu autem, cum acceperis eam, ingressus cubiculum, per tres dies continens esto ab ea. Et nichil aliud nisi oracionibus uacabis cum ea.* Et sequitur, *Transacta autem tercia nocte, accipies uirginem cum timore Domini.* Hec Scriptura ibidem. Ecce, qualiter iste qui postulat Alcestem in coniugium dicitur esse Admetus, qui scilicet 'poterit adire metus', ut dicit Fulgencius. Omnis enim talis qui uult coniu\g/ium inire Deum debet principaliter timere et cum eius timore coniugium petere.

[2] Sequitur secunda pars picture de Alcestes copulacione. Nam sicut poete dicunt, Alcestem postulatam ab Admete, ita dicunt quod copula Alcestis non est, nisi cum persona regis. Oportet enim quod ille qui uult esse coniugalis continens, quod sit moraliter rex, hoc est quod sciat se recte regere in usu actuali talis | copule. Ut enim dicit Ysodorus, libro 9, capitulo 3, et tangit Rabanus, *De naturis rerum*, apud ueteres tale erat prouerbium, 'rex eris si recte feceris, / sed si recte non feceris, rex non eris'.

---

32 Admetum] Admetem O   35 quasi quem] communia (?) quem A, quasi qui O   36 principaliter loquendo] *om.* O   37 fol. 119rb   40 fiat] *om.* A • racionabili] *adds* id est cum timore Dei uel O   45 Hii namque] Enim AI   47 intellectus] *adds* in hiis I   47–51 habet … ibidem] etc. A   48 super eos] *om.* I • eam] uxorem tuam I   49–50 ab … sequitur] *om.* I   51 accipies … ibidem] accipiens uxorem cum timore Domini I   53 qui scilicet] quem A, quia sibi I   54 debet] *adds* primo et A

59 coniugalis] coniugaliter AI   60 usu actuali] usuale A   61 fol. 119va   61–62 Ut … rerum] *om.* A   62 tale] talis copule A

[31] Notice how poets speak indirectly about consent in the figure of king Admetus asking to marry Alceste. For as Fulgentius says directly, among the poets, Admetus stands for the mind; as Fulgentius also says, according to the poets, he is called Admetus, as if he were 'someone who may *adire metus* "approach his fears".[4] For the passion of fear isn't, in its origin, a bodily injury, but rather a disease of the soul. Therefore Admetus is said to ask for Alceste in marriage, because the inner consent of his soul must necessarily precede his external oral request. It is also necessary that his request be made with rational fear, that is with the fear of God. For otherwise, this act and their use of each other's bodies will not be virtuous and chaste. And for this reason, Tob 6, where it tells what the angel Raphael said to Tobias, has an appropriately developed argument: *Hear me, and I will shew thee who they are, over whom the devil can prevail. For they who in such manner receive matrimony, as to shut out God from themselves, and from their mind, and to give themselves to their lust, as the horse and the mule, which have not understanding, over them the devil hath power. But thou, when thou shalt take her, go into the chamber, and for three days keep thyself continent from her, and give thyself to nothing else but prayers with her.* And there follows, *And when the third night is past, thou shalt take the virgin with the fear of the Lord* (6:16–18, 22). So Scripture says. See how the man who asks for Alceste in marriage is said to be Admetus, that is someone 'who might approach their fears', as Fulgentius says. For anyone who wishes to enter marriage should primarily fear God, and should ask for marriage with that fear in mind.

[56] [2] The second part of the picture follows; it concerns Alceste's sexual joining. For as poets say, after king Admetus had asked for her, Alceste's sexual joining was only to be with the person of a king. For it is necessary that a person who wishes to practise marital continence should be a king in moral terms, that is, should know how to rule themself properly in the physical activity involved in sexual joining. For as Isidore says in 9.3, and Rabanus mentions, *On the natures of things*, the ancients had a proverb, 'If you have acted properly, you will be a king; / but if you haven't acted properly, you won't be one.'[5]

---

[4] Fulg 1.22 (34/16–18).
[5] Isidore, *Etym*. 9.3.4 (*PL* 82:342); Rabanus, *ibid*. 16.3 (*PL* 111:446).

Recte enim faciendo regis nomen tenetur, peccando amittitur.
65 Et Adamancius in quadam omelia super Iosue dicit, 'Regem te esse [omnium] facit, si Cristus regnet in te. Rex namque a *regendo* dictus est, si igitur in te animus regnat et corpus obtemperat. Si concupiscencias carnis sub iugo imperii tui mittis, si viciorum gentes sobrietatis tue frenis arcioribus premis, merito rex diceris,
70 cum teipsum regere noueris'. Hec Origenes.

Uolunt igitur poete dicere quod ad continenciam coniugalem requiritur quod homo uxoratus tempore maritalis copule regatur recta racione. Aliter enim illa actualis copula erit [moraliter] uiciosa. Et ideo bene Hugo de Sancto Uittore in suo libello,
75 quem edidit ad quendam suum familiarem uolentem nubere, conqueritur in hunc modum, 'Heu, prothdolor! Ducuntur uxores hodie, non causa prolis procreande uel causa fornicacionis uitande, sed causa uoluptatis et luxurie [ex]plende, uel causa pecunie adquirende. Unde et Marcia Catonis filia iunior, cum
80 quereretur ab ea cur post amissum uirum [de nuo] non nuberet, respondit se non inuenire uirum qui se magis uellet habere quam sua. Quo dicto, eleganter ostendit', sicut dicit Hugo, 'diuicias magis in uxoribus solere eligi quam pudicici|am, et multos, non oculis sed digitis, ducere uxores'. Et tandem sic concludit Hugo,
85 'Optima sane res quam non auaricia consiliat et quam luxuria non copulat'. Ecce, qualiter oportet quod copula coniugalis sit copula regis, et quomodo regere se debuit homo ad hoc, quod talis copula sit moraliter uirtuosa. Et de isto bene potest notari processus Geronimi, *Contra Iouinianum*, ubi recitat uerbum 'Sixti
90 Pictagorici, dicentis in suis *Sentenciis* quod "Adulter est ille qui in suam uxorem est amator ardencior". Sapiens uir debet amare iudicio coniugem, non + effectu. Sed reget impetus uoluntatis, nec preceps feretur in coitum. Nichil enim fedius est quam uxorem amare tanquam adulteram'. Hec Ieronimus.
95 [3] Sequitur tercia pars picture de Alcestes dotacione. Ubi notandum est, sicut patet in littera per Fulgencium, quod poete fingunt quod pater huius Alcestes proposuerat tale edictum, quod si quis duas feras nature disperes suo currui iungeret,

---

65 Adamancius] Adamaticus A **66** omnium] *om.* O **68** mittis] admittis, *with the prefix expunged* (?) O
72 uxoratus] maritatus A • maritalis] carnalis A **73** moraliter] *om.* O
78 uitande] declinande AI • et luxurie] *om.* A • explende] implende O
80 de nuo] *om.* O **83** fol. 119vb **87** et quomodo] scilicet AI • debuit] scienciis AI **88–94** Et ... Ieronimus] *om.* A **92** effectu] effectum IO
97 pater huius] huiusmodi A **98** nature] sibi A

A king has that title through acting properly and loses it by sinning. Adamancius, in a homily on Joshua, says, 'If Christ rules you, He makes you king over all things. If your mind rules you and moderates your body, you are a king, since *rex* "a king" is derived from *regere* "to rule". If you put the desires of the flesh under the control of your mental lordship, and if you repress the alien vices with the very strict reins of your soberness, you will be properly called a king, since you have learned to rule yourself.' So Origen says.[6]

[71] Therefore the poets wish to say that marital continence requires that a married man be ruled by right reason when he has sex with his wife. For otherwise, the sexual act will be sinful, morally speaking. Therefore Hugh of Fouilly properly complains, in the little book he wrote to an acquaintance who wished to marry, 'Ah, alas! Today, people get married, not in order to procreate or to avoid the sin of fornication, but in order to fulfil their lecherous desires or to get money. It's for this reason that Marcia, Cato's younger daughter, when someone asked her why, after her husband's death, she hadn't remarried, answered that she hadn't found a man whom she wished to have more than herself.' As Hugh says, 'In saying this, she showed elegantly that wives are more usually chosen for their riches than their modesty, and many get married to please their fingers, rather than their eyes.' Hugh finally concludes, 'Truly, the best thing is what neither avarice counsels, nor what lechery joins.'[7] See, how it's necessary that marital sex be a royal joining together, and how a man ought to rule himself so that such joining is morally virtuous. On this point, one should notice Jerome's argument in *Against Jovinian*, where he cites the words 'of Sextus the Pythagorean in his *Opinions*, "The man who is too avid a lover of his wife is an adulterer". A wise man ought to love his wife with discretion, not with passion, and he should restrain onsets of desire, lest he be borne headlong into sex. For there's nothing more filthy than to love one's wife as if she were one's whore.'[8] So Jerome says.

[95] [3] The third part of the picture follows; it concerns legal arrangements for Alceste's marriage. Here one should notice, as Fulgentius says explicitly, that poets tell that Alceste's father had proposed a rule, that if anyone might join to his chariot two different species of wild beast,

---

[6] Origen, *Homeliae super Joshuam* generally, cf. 11.6.

[7] Hugh of Fouilly, *De nuptiis* 1.1 (PL 176:1206), mostly citation from Jerome, *Adversus Jovinianum* 1.46 (PL 23:275).

[8] *Ibid.* 1.49 (PL 23:281).

ille filiam suam Alcestem in coniugem reciperet. Admetus igitur,
100 qui Alcestem pecierat in uxorem, [consuluit] super isto [e]dicto
Herculem et Apollinem. Quorum unus fingitur deus ueritatis
[et intelligencie], Apollo scilicet; alius, scilicet Hercules, dictus
humilitatis et obediencie, ut fingunt poete. Nam, ut dicunt,
Hercules iste fuit miles et uassallus [Eureste]i regis, ad cuius
105 preceptum subiit Hercules illos duodecim graues labores, de
quibus facit mencionem Seneca in sua prima tragedia, et Boicius
libro 4 *De consolacione*, | metro 9°, quod sic incipit, 'Bella [bis
quin]is'. Isti igitur duo dii, scilicet Apollo et Hercules, iunxerunt
ad currum leonem et aprum, et ita accepit Admetus Alcestem
110 in coniugium.

Uolunt autem poete per hoc intelligere, sicut in littera tangit
Fulgencius, duplicem uirtutem requisitam ad castitatem siue
continenciam coniugalem. Nam, ut dicit Fulgencius, per leonem
datur intelligi uirtus animi et per aprum uirtus corporis. Portat
115 enim aper in corpore [quasi] quoddam scutum i[mpenetrabile].
Istud igitur duplex g\e/nus uirtutis + debent habere coniuges
in uiuendo, scilicet ut sint continentes et casti, immunes a
crimine adulterii, non solum corpore sed et mente. 'Nichil enim',
ut dicit Augustinus super psalmum, 'prodest caro integra et
120 mente corumpta'. Ydeo sicut dicit idem Augustinus, *De libero
arbitrio*, cuius auctoritas ponitur in canone 'De penitencia', +
distinccione prima, 'Si cui non contingat ubi sic habetur + facultas
concumbendi cum uxore aliena, planum tamen sit aliquo modo
e[a]m cupere, et si potestas daretur esse facturum, non minus est
125 reus quam si in ipso facto deprehenderetur'.

[4] Sequitur quarta pars picture de Alceste uenundacione.
Ubi notandum quod poete fingunt, et Fulgencius recitat in littera,
quod rex Admetus infirmabatur grauiter, et hoc usque ad mortem.
Quod ipse percipiens, deprecari cepit Apollinem, ut concederet illi
130 uitam et sanitatem. Cui respondit Apollo hoc fieri non posse,

99 reciperet] duceret A   100 consuluit] *om.* O • edicto] dicto O
102 et intelligencie] *om.* (*at line-break*) O   104 Eurestei (and 210 Euresteo)]
Oresti , Orestio O   107 fol. 120^(ra)   107–8 bis quinis] hiis que uis A, quisquis IO
108 duo dii] sunt dii A, duo filii I   108 iunxerunt] miserunt A
115 quasi ... impenetrabile] quoddam scutum in O   116 debent] deberent O
122 distinccione] d | di. O • ubi sic habetur] *om.* I, *adds* si cui non contingat O
123 uxore] coniuge AI • tamen] tibi AI • aliquo modo] *om.* AI   124 eam]
eum IO • facturum] in futurum A
129 cepit] *adds* dominum A, *adds* deum I   130 hoc fieri] se hoc facere AI

he would receive his daughter Alceste as his wife. Therefore Admetus, who had asked for Alceste as his wife, counsulted Hercules and Apollo about this condition.[9] Poets represent one of these, Apollo, as the god of truth and of intelligence; the other, Hercules, as that of meekness and obedience. For, as poets say, Hercules was a soldier and the vassal of king Eurystheus; at his command, Hercules underwent his twelve demanding labours – Seneca mentions them in his first tragedy, and Boethius in *Consolation* 4m9, which starts, 'A ten-year war'.[10] Therefore, these two gods, Apollo and Hercules, yoked a lion and a boar to the chariot, and in return, Admetus received Alceste as his wife.

[111] As Fulgentius says in his text, poets wish to understand by this that a double virtue is required for chastity or marital continence. For, as Fulgentius says, the lion gives the strength of a discerning mind and the boar physical strength.[11] After all, a boar's body has a kind of impenetrable shield. Therefore a married couple ought to display a double type of virtue in their behaviour, so that they are continent and chaste, immune to any accusation of adultery, not simply in their body but also in their mind. For as Augustine says on a psalter verse, 'A purified flesh, if it's joined with a corrupt mind, is of no value at all.'[12] Augustine also says, in *On free will*, a statement repeated in canon law, *On penance*, distinction 1, 'If it should happen that someone might not have the opportunity for having sex with another man's wife, it's nevertheless clear that, should he desire her in any way, and were he granted the power, would bring it about, he is no less guilty than if he were caught in the act itself.'[13]

[126] [4] The fourth part of the picture follows; it concerns Alceste's sale. There one should notice that poets relate – and Fulgentius says this explicitly – that king Admetus became seriously ill, to the point of death. When he perceived this, he began to pray to Apollo for relief, that the god would grant him life and health. Apollo answered him that this might not be,

---

[9] Fulg 1.22 (34/5–10).
[10] E.g. *Hercules furens* 30ff., 524ff., 780ff.; *Consolatio* 4m7.13–31.
[11] Fulg 1.22 (34/22–35/3).
[12] *Enarrationes in Psalmos* 99.13 (PL 37:1280).
[13] *Ibid.* 1.3.8 (PL 32:1225); Gratian, *Decretum* C. 33, Q. 3 ('De paenitentia'), d. 1, c. 33 (CJC 1:1125).

nisi Admetus | inueniret aliquem de suis qui se uellet offerri morti sponte loco Admeti. Igitur Admetus indicauit responsum Appolonis uxori sue Alceste, que statim optulit se ad moriendum loco uiri sui. Et ista de causa dicunt poete eam esse uenditam illis tribus Fatis, quas poete fingunt famulas dei Plutonis, de quibus prius fuit tactum in sexta mithologia. Ab istis enim Fatis credebant pagani quod + dependeat mors et uita cuiuslibet hominis.

Sed applicando ad propositum de Alceste et Admeto, poete per istam spontaneam oblacionem, qua Alcestes se optulit ad mortem, uolunt poete intelligere et circumloqui illam magnam et sinceram dileccionem que debet esse uxoris ad uirum suum. Dicit enim glossa quedam et est super Matthei 2° capitulo, quod tanto affectu uir et mulier debent copulari ut una anima in duobus corporibus esse uideatur, coniunctis spiritu et mente sociatis. Quia eciam naturaliter quodlibet membrum corporis seipsum exponit pro salute capitis et, ut [dicit] apostolus *Ad Corinthos, caput mulieris uir*. Ideo Alcestes pingitur se exponere morti pro salute uiri sui.

Et ideo bene Fulgencius in littera dicit, 'Sicut', inquit, 'benigna coniuge nichil est melius, ita infesta coniuge nichil crudelius. Sicut igitur coniux fidelis et benigna pro salute uiri sui animam suam ponit, pingnori sit coniux maligna. Negligit et contempnit mortem mariti, preeligens uitam propriam'. Igitur dicit Fulgencius, 'Quanto est uiro coniunccior, tanto | + est amoris dulcedine mellea, aut fellea malici[e] tox\i/ca; est quippe perpetuale refugium aut perhenne tormentum'. Est hic notandum iuxta ea que tangit Fulgencius in littera quod significanter hec coniugalis continencia nominatur Alceste, nam Alceste, ut dicit Fulgencius in littera, in lingua Actica et in lingua Greca interpretatur 'presu[m]pcio'.

Ista autem passio presumpcionis specialiter concomitatur passionem amoris et intense dileccionis, sicut de hoc multa loquntur poete et eciam sancti uiri. Unde Bernardus, exclamans

unless Admetus should find someone from his household who wished voluntarily to offer themself to death in Admetus's place. Therefore, when Admetus revealed Apollo's answer to his wife Alceste, she immediately offered herself to die, instead of her husband.[14] For this reason, poets say that Alceste was sold to the three Fates. Poets represent them as servants of the god Pluto, as I discussed above in the sixth mythology. The pagans believed that the life and death of every person proceeded from the actions of the Fates.

[138] But applying this to the discussion of Alceste and Admetus, through this voluntary sacrifice, in which Alceste offered to die for her husband, poets wish to understand and indicate indirectly the great and sincere love that a wife ought to have for her husband. For there's a gloss on Mt 2 that says that a man and his wife should be joined by such great affection that they appear a single soul in two bodies, joined in spirit and united in intention.[15] Moreover, it is natural for every limb of the body to expose itself to protect the head, and, as Paul says, *the head of the woman is the man* (1 Cor 11:3). Therefore, Alceste is depicted as exposing herself to death in exchange for her husband's health.

[149] And therefore Fulgentius says appropriately, 'Just as nothing is better than a kindly disposed wife, so there's nothing more cruel than a hostile one. For just as a faithful and kindly wife offers her own soul for her husband's health, a malicious wife treats him like a debt she's pledged. She'll pay no attention, indeed be unmoved, by her husband's death, preferring to live on without him.' Therefore Fulgentius says, 'The more closely she is bound to her husband, the sweeter her honeyed love – the alternative is poisoned and bilious hostility; indeed, marriages are either enduring safety or eternal torture.' One should notice here, among things Fulgentius treats explicitly, that marital continence is called Alceste significantly, because her name in Attic or Greek means 'anticipation'.[16]

[160] The passion of anticipation closely accompanies that of love, particularly when it's intense, and both poets and holy men speak a great deal about it. For this reason, Bernard, crying out

---

[14] Fulg 1.22 (34/10–14).
[15] *Glossa ordinaria* on Mt 19:5 (*PL* 114:148).
[16] Fulg 1.22 (33/21–34/4, 34/19–20, 34/20–22).

de hac amor\is/ presumpcione, dicit deuote, 'O amor uehemens,
o amor preceps et impetuose, flagrans, qui preter te aliud cogitare
165　non sinis, fastidis cetera, contempnis omnia preter teipsum,
content[us] teipso. Confundis ordinem, dissimulas usum,
ignoras modum. Totum quod oportunitatis, quod racionis,
[quod pudoris], quod iudicii, quod concilii uidetur, triumphas
in teipso et redigis in captiuitatem'. Hec ille. Et ista uidetur
170　fecisse Alceste, uxor regis Admeti, ex mariti excessiua dileccione,
postponendo uitam propriam [uite et] saluti uiri sui. Et
ideo nominatur isto nomine Alceste, quo nomine significat
'presu[m]pcio', sicut patet ex s[ent]encia illius poete Omeri, sicut
Fulgencius docet in serie littere.
175　[5] Sequitur quinta pars picture de Alcestes deportacione.
Nam poete fingunt quod Alcestem portabant ad infernum ista tria
Fata, postquam optulerat se sponte morti pro salute uiri sui. Istud
est enim unum de officiis Fatorum conducere et deducere homines
ad regnum Plutonis, cui famulantur. Qui Pluto | pingitur a poetis
180　deus inferni. Pro isto notandum est quod isti poete, ut in aliis
mithologis est tactum prius, fingunt tres filios Saturni occupare
tria sceptra mundi. Celi enim sceptrum occupat Iubiter; maris
\dominium/ occupat Neptunus; sed regnum infimum [et inferioris
honoris] est [regnum] inferni [et illud] occupat tercius filius,
185　scilicet Pluto.
Uolunt igitur dicere quod sunt tria genera castitatis, quia est
castitas uirginalis et isti debetur celum, quia est perfectissimus
modus continendi. Et est castitas uidualis, et ista est mediocris
gradus, quia minus perfecta quam sit uirginitas, et ideo hec
190　castitas uendicat sibi regnum Neptuni. Sed tercia, castitas
coniugalis, est inperfecior ceteris, et ideo a Fatis d[u]citur [ad]
regnum Plutonis, quod est infimum regnum. Et concordat
ista ymaginacio poetarum cum glossa super illud Matthei 13°,
Fructum facit aliud centisimum. Triplex est mulierum fructus:
195　centensi\m/us fructus uirginibus, sexagesimus uiduis et
continentibus, tricesimus sancto matrimonio deputatur.

166 contentus] contento O　168 quod pudoris] *om.* O　• concilii] filii ne A,
adds ne I　170 fecisse] *om.* I　171 uite et] *om. (at line-break)* O　173 presumpcio]
presupcio O　• sicut ... Omeri] *om.* A　• sentencia] scīa (= sciencia) O
174 serie] *om.* A
179 fol. 120vb　182 mundi] *om.* AI　183 occupat] habet I　183–84 et ... illud] id est
inferni O
188 ista] *adds* castitas A　191 ducitur ad] dicitur IO　193–96 super ... deputatur]
same information paraphrased AI

in a devout fashion about this loving anticipation, says, 'O violent love, o overwhelming and sudden love, burning love, you who allow thought of nothing except yourself, who dislike and disdain everything except yourself, being content with yourself. You destroy order, you ignore what's customary, pay no attention to moderation. You triumph in yourself over everything that appears advantageous, reasonable, shameful, or proper to judgement or good counsel, and you convert them into your slaves.'[17] So he says. Alceste, wife of king Admetus, appears to have behaved in this way, from her excessive love of her husband, treating her own life as of less importance than her husband's life and health. Therefore, she is called Alceste, a name that means 'anticipation'. This is evident, as Fulgentius teaches in the course of his text, from the poet Homer's saying.

[175] [5] The fifth part of the picture follows; it concerns Alceste's being carried away. For poets relate that the three Fates carried her to hell, after she had voluntarily offered herself to death in return for her husband's health. For it's one of the Fates' duties to gather people and lead them away to the kingdom of Pluto, the god they serve. Poets depict Pluto himself as the god of hell. On this point, one should notice that poets, as I have said in other mythologies above, represent Saturn's three sons as occupying the three lordships of the world. For Jove has the lordship of heaven; Neptune, that of the sea, but Pluto, the third son, has the lowest and least honoured kingdom, that of hell.

[186] Therefore, poets wish to say that there are three species of chastity. There's virginal chastity, and it merits heaven, because it is the most perfect form of continence. There's also a widow's chastity, and it is the middle stage, because it is less perfect than virginity, and therefore it can claim for itself Neptune's kingdom. But the third, marital chastity, is less perfect than the others, and therefore the Fates lead it to Pluto's kingdom, the lowest one of all. The poets' fantasy agrees with a gloss on Mt 13:23, *It yieldeth the one an hundredfold*. For women have a triple fruit: the hundredfold fruit is assigned to virgins, the sixtyfold to widows and those who practice restraint, and the thirtyfold to holy wedlock.[18]

---

[17] *Sermones in Cantica* 79.1 (*PL* 183:1163).

[18] *Ibid. PL* 114:131, citing Rabanus, *Commentarii in Matthaeum* 4.13 (*PL* 107:945–46); Jerome, *Commentarii in evangelium Matthaei* 2 (*PL* 26:89); Bede, *Homiliae* 13 (*PL* 94:68).

Sumitur ista glossa ab originali Ieromini *Super Mattheum*. Beda autem, loquens de ista triplici castitate, dicit sic, 'Bona', inquit, 'castitas coniugalis; melior est +', inquit, 'continencia uidualis; optima perfeccio uirginalis'.

[6] Sequitur sexta pars picture de Alcestes eleuacione. Sicut enim in littera tangit Fulgencius, poete fingunt Herculem illo tempore quo descendit ad infernum una cum Theseo et aliis uiris strenuis et robustis, | quo eciam tempore Hercules ligauit nexubus et uinculis adamantis Cerberum, canem inferni, de quo cane facta est mencio in precedentibus. Tunc, inquit, Hercules eleuauit istam Alcestem de inferno et adduxit eam secum. Per istam autem fabulam uolunt poete intelligere quod, licet continencia coniugalis sit gradus infimus castitatis, tamen Hercules, per quem intelligunt uirtutem obe\diencie/ et humilitatis – nam, ut dictum est, iste Hercules totus fuit humilis [et obediens] regi [Eureste]o, cuius fuit miles et uassallus – ita, inquam, uirtus obediencie eleuat Alcestem. Nam obediencia facit quod castitas et continencia coniugalis est equalis meriti coram Deo cum continencia uiduali seu uirginali.

Et de ista materia loquitur Augustinus ualde pulcre in suo libro *De bono coniugii*, ubi dicit quod pares in merito fuerunt castitas uirginalis in Iohanne et castitas \coniugalis/ in persona Abrahe. Et hec est racio Augustini: nam usus coniugalis, quem exercuit Abraham, non processit ex carnali lasciuia, sed ex Dei obediencia. Tunc enim actus [coniugalis] ille cadebat sub precepto de ista obediencia Abrahe. Loquitur pulcre Augustinus, 16 *De ciuitate Dei*, capitulo 25, ubi exclamando loquitur de contine[n]cia Abrahe, dicens, 'O uirum uiriliter utentem feminis, coniuge temperanter, ancilla obtemperanter, et neutra intemperanter'! Ubi notandum est quod, ut dicit Augustinus, *Contra Faustum*, 'Abraham ingrediebatur ad ancillam | Sare de uoluntate, tamen et precepto Sare, quia reuelatum fuit sibi quod uoluntas et preceptum uxoris sue Sare fuit uoluntas ipsius Dei et preceptum.

198–200 Sumitur ... uirginalis] *om.* A   199 est] *adds* melior | est O
201 sexta] *adds* et ultima I   204 et robustis] *om.* A   • fol. 121ra 205 adamantis] adamantinis A, adimantum I   205–6 de ... precedentibus] *om.* A
209 Hercules] exaltatur ab Hercule A   211 et obediens] *om.* O   214 meriti] *om.* A
215 ualde pulcre] diffuse A, pulcre I   218 est] *add* tota AI   220 coniugalis] *om.* O   222 continencia] continecia O   224 neutra] natura AI   226 fol. 121rb
   • Sare] Abrahe A, *add* scilicet Agar AI   228 ipsius ... preceptum] Dei A

This gloss is drawn from Jerome's commentary *On Matthew*. However, Bede, speaking of this triple chastity, says, 'Marital chastity is good, but a widow's self-restraint is better, and a virgin's the fullest perfection.'

[201] [6] The sixth part of the picture follows; it concerns Alceste's being raised. For just as Fulgentius states explicitly, poets claim that Hercules descended into hell in a group with Theseus and other active and strong men. This was also the occasion when Hercules bound Cerberus, the hell-hound, with chains and unbreakable bonds, as I have mentioned previously. Fulgentius says that then Hercules raised Alceste from hell and led her away with him.[19] Through this fable, poets wish to understand that, although marital continence is the lowest degree of chastity, nevertheless Hercules, in whom the poets understand the virtue obedience and meekness, raises up Alceste, because she was obedient. (As I've said, Hercules was thoroughly humble and obedient in his relation to king Eurystheus, and was his soldier and vassal.) At any rate, obedience makes marital chastity and continence equal to a widow or virgin's self-restraint in its merit before God.

[215] Augustine speaks quite persuasively on this subject in *On the good of marriage*, where he says that John the Baptist's virginal chastity and Abraham's marital chastity were equal in merit. Augustine's reasoning is that the marital behaviour that Abraham pursued didn't proceed from fleshly delight, but from obedience to God. For then Abraham's marriage fell under the command that he be obedient.[20] Augustine further speaks well about Abraham's self-restraint in *On the city of God* 16.25, when he exclaims, 'O what a man he was, having sex with women in a manly fashion – with his wife temperately, with her handmaid obediently, and with neither intemperately!'[21] One should notice there, as Augustine says in *Against Faustus*, 'Abraham approached Hagar, Sarah's handmaid, sexually at Sarah's request, indeed her command, because it was revealed to him that his wife Sarah's wishes and command were God's wish and command.

---

[19] Fulg 1.22 (34/14–16).
[20] A summary of *De bono conjugali* 21–22 (PL 40:390–92).
[21] *Ibid.* (PL 41:504).

Et ideo tantum meruit Abraham, sic obediendo Deo, sicut
meruisset [Iohannes] quod uirgo permansisset'. In libro eciam
suo *De bono coniugali*, loquens Augustinus de merito Abrahe et
de meritis uirginum, dicit sic, '[Sicut] non est i\m/par meritum
[paciencie in Petro, qui passus est, et in Iohanne, qui passus non
est, sic non impar meritum] continencie in Iohanne, qui nullas
expertus est nupcias, et in Abraham, qui filios generauit. Nam
et Iohannes celibatus et Abrahe connubium pro temporum
distribucione Domino militabant'. Uult Augustinus dicere quod
uterque, tam Iohannes quam Abraham, egerunt conformiter
uoluntati Dei, eo modo quo miles et uassallus facit, obediendo
i\m/periis domini sui. Et ideo uterque equaliter meruit, quia Deus
pro diuersis temporibus equaliter acceptauit factum unius et
factum alterius.

 Applicando igitur dictum Augustini ad istam ficcionem
poeticam de Hercule eleuante Alcestem de inferno, patet quod
continencia coniugalis, licet sit inferioris ordinis quam castitas
uirginalis, tamen uirtus obediencie, figurata per Herculem, eleuat
aliquando istam continenciam coniugalem et facit eam equalis
meriti cum continencia uirginali. Ymo in casu potest contingere
quod continencia coniugalis, circumstacionata per obedienciam,
sit magis meritoria quam quecunque continencia uirginalis,
sicut diffuse potest probari ex dictis beati Augustini in sermone
de obediencia, ubi dicit | quod 'Nichil sic Deo placet quomodo
obediencia. Una enim obediencia plus ualet quam omnes
uirtutes'. Sic igitur finitur duodecima mithologia Fulgencii et
commentarium super primum librum *Mithologiarum* eiusdem.

---

230 Iohannes] posito A, Po^{to} IO   232 Sicut] *om.* O   233-34 paciencie ... meritum] *om.* O

248-49 Ymo ... coniugalis] *om.* A   249 continencia] obediencia A   252 de] *add* bono (*with following gen.*) AI   • fol. 121va 257-55 et commentarium ... eiusdem] *om.* A

Therefore, by obeying God then, Abraham merited just as much as John had merited because he had remained a virgin.'[22] Also, in his *On the good of marriage*, Augustine says of the relative worth of Abraham and of virgins, 'It's just like the equal merit of Peter's and John's patience, even though Peter was martyred and John wasn't. The value of John the Baptist's continence – he'd never tried out marriage – and Abraham's, who sired sons, is equivalent. For both John in his celibacy and Abraham in his marriage were warriors for the Lord in accord with the distinction of the times in which they lived.'[23] Augustine wants to say that both John and Abraham acted in accord with God's will, in the same way that a soldier or vassal does in obeying the commands of his lord. Therefore, they both were equal in worthiness, for God affirmed the deeds of both equally, but in accord with the distinction of the times in which they lived.

[243] Therefore, one can apply Augustine's statements to the poetic fiction of Hercules raising Alceste from hell. For it is evident that marital continence ranks lower than virginal chastity. Nevertheless the virtue obedience, represented by Hercules, sometimes raises marital continence and makes it equal in merit to virginal self-restraint. Indeed, it may perhaps happen that marital continence, if it is surrounded by obedience, may be even more worthy than any virginal self-restraint. This view can be proven at length from Augustine's words in his sermon on obedience, where he says, 'Nothing so pleases God as obedience. For obedience alone is more powerful than all the other virtues.'[24] Thus, Fulgentius's twelfth mythology ends, and with it, my commentary on the first book of his *Mythologies*.

---

[22] Cf. *ibid.* 22.31 and 33 (*PL* 42:420–22)?
[23] *Ibid.* 21.26 (*PL* 40:391).
[24] ps.-Augustine, *Sermo de obedientia et humilitate* 1 (*PL* 40:1222–23).

\Liber secundus Fulgencii/

[1]

Liber secundus *Mithologiarum* Fulgencii incipit a pictura Paridis, qua solent poete istum Paridem depingere. Fuit enim Paris binomius; uocabatur enim Alexander et Paris. Sub ymagine eius Paridis consueuerunt po\e/te depingere uicium iniusticie et
5 iniquitatis. Huius autem pictura est talis, nam pingitur
      [1] natus regis,
      [2] pastor gregis,
      [3] lator legis,
      [4] amator mercedis,
10   [5] [auctor cedis],
      [6] proditor edis,
      [7] et subuersor sedis.
Iste sunt septem partes picture qua solent poete istum Paridem depingere.
15   [1] Nam quoad primam partem picture, poete dicunt Paridem istum fuisse filium regis Troie qui uocabatur Priamus, quem occidit Pirrus, filius Achillis, sicut docet Uirgilius, et idem recitat Augustinus, primo *De ciuitate Dei*. Ubi notandum quod, sicut tangit Augustinus, 3° *De ciuitate Dei*, poete fingunt istos reges
20 Troianorum fuisse periuros, nam dicunt isti poete quod La\o/medoun, qui fuit pater Priami et auus Paridis, pepigit cum Neptuno, filio Saturni et germano Iouis, cum Apoll[ine] eciam, quem fingunt filium dei Iouis, ad iuuandum eum in edifica\cio/ne ciuitatis + Troiane sub certa mercede. Et pactum initum inter
25 eos fuit firmatum per iuramentum. Sed postquam ciuitas fuit edificata, La\o/medoun noluit soluere illud | quod diis illis duobus, scilicet Neptuno et Apolloni, promiserat. Hec est autem fabula poetica.

---

2 qua ... depingere] *om.* A   5 nam pingitur] *om.* A, *adds* iste Paris I   10 auctor cedis] *om.* O

17 docet ... idem, 18–19 Ubi ... Dei] *om.* A   22 Apolline] Apolloni O   24 Troiane] Troie Troiane A, Troie siue Troiane O • pactum] factum AI • initum] non tamen A   26 fol. 121vb

[1]

Book 2 of Fulgentius's *Mythologies* begins with a picture of Paris; it shows how poets are accustomed to depict him. He was called by two names, both Alexander and Paris. Through Paris's image, poets customarily depicted the vice Injustice and Unfairness. This vice is depicted

[1] born of a king,
[2] shepherd of a herd,
[3] proposer of laws,
[4] lover of reward,
[5] creator of slaughter,
[6] traitor to his house,
[7] and overthrower of a throne.

These are the seven parts of the picture through which poets usually depict Paris.

[15] [1] So far as the first part of the picture, poets say that Paris was the son of the Trojan king Priam. As Virgil teaches, and Augustine, in *On the city of God* 1, says the same thing, Priam was killed by Pyrrhus, son of Achilles.[1] There one should notice that, as Augustine mentions in *On the city* 3, poets represent the kings of Troy as perjurers, for they say that Laomedon, Priam's father and Paris's grandfather, compacted with Neptune, Saturn's son and Jove's kinsman, as well as with Apollo, whom they represent as Jove's son, to help him in building the city of Troy. They entered into an agreement, with a particular stipulated reward, and it was confirmed through an oath. But after the city had been built, Laomedon did not wish to pay the two gods, Neptune and Apollo, what he had promised. However, this is a poetic fable.

---

[1] *Aeneid* 2.506–58; Augustine, *ibid.* 1.2 (*PL* 41:15) and 3.2 (*PL* 41:79–80).

Applicando autem ad propositum, poete ideo dicunt Paridem istum, per quem intelligunt iniustum iudicem et iniquum fuisse, de sanguine Troianorum, quia semper ista duo uicia sunt annexa iniquum iudicium et periurium. Quia omnis iudex obligatur, tamquam \a/strictus iuramento, ad faciendum iusticiam cuicunque sine quacunque personarum accepcione. De isto autem iuramento, quo astricti sunt iudices, loquitur dominus Carnotensis in suo *Policraticon*, libro quinto, capitulo 11°, 'Iudices sacramento legibus alligantur iurati, quod omni modo iudicium cum ueritate et legum obseruacione disponent. Ipso que iure traditum est, ut sacrorum euangeliorum scripture terribiles, ante sedem iudicialem deponantur'. Et ibidem, 'Ab inicio licium usque in finem permaneant, nec amoueantur, nisi sentencia recitata, qu[o] tocius consistorii latitudo, Dei ipsius repleta presencia, omnibus ad sacrosanctas scripturas metum incuciat et reuerenciam, et ab inquisicione ueritatis omnis iniquitas propulsetur. Omnis quoque carnis et sanguinis religio iudiciaria, propellat affectus, euacuans iram et odium, metum et amiciciam. Quia ut ait Iulius Cesar, "Haud facile animus prouidet uerum, ubi ista proficiunt". Hinc est illud prouerbium auctoris Cither[onis] apud antiquos celeberimum, "Exuit personam iudicis quisquis amicum induit". Equitas enim cui | iudex obsequium de[be]t, odii sinistram aut amoris dextram nescit'. Hec ille. Patet igitur quomodo iudex iniustus est periurus. Et ideo propter iniquum iudicium quod dedit, iste Paris fuit de genere La\o/medontis, quia filius Priam filii sui.

[2] Sequitur secunda pars picture de Paridis administracione. Fingunt enim poete quod Paris iste fuit a rege Priamo, patre suo, expositus in quadam silua morti statim postquam fuerat natus de matre sua. Et hoc fecit ille rex Priamus racione cuiusdam sompnii quod habuit Ecuba uxor Priami regis illo tempore quo fuit grauida, quando scilicet Paridem istum gestabat in uentre. Tunc enim so[m]pniauit se gestare facem ardentem, qua face fuerat incensa tota ciuitas Troie. Euigilans igitur Ecuba, et de sompno territa, referre cepit sompnium uiro suo, scilicet Priamo,

---

37 omni modo] omnino A   38 Ipso ... traditum] Ipsorum iuris A • traditum] tactum I   40 Ab ... licium] Que incolimen A   41 quo] per que O   42 tocius] cicius A   44 ueritatis] *adds* iunctat ? I • propulsetur] propelletur A, pulsetur I   48 Citheronis] Citherine O   50 fol. 122ra • debet] dedit O   51 amoris] ani|mi amens A • iudex] *adds* omnis A   53 Paris] *add* fingitur a poetis quod iste Paris AI
58 ille rex] pater suus A   61 sompniauit] sopniauit O   62 Troie] *om.* I

[29] But applying this to my argument, poets say that Paris was of this Trojan blood. Thus, they understand him to have been an unjust and unfair judge, for these two vices, injustice and unfairness, are always characteristics connected with an unjust and perjured judge. For every judge is obligated, as if he were bound by an oath, to do justice to everyone, without any regard for the persons involved. John of Salisbury, the bishop of Chartres, speaks in his *Polycraticus* 5.11 about this oath by which judges are constrained, 'Judges are bound to the laws by the oath they have sworn, because they should dispense justice on all occasions through truth and following the law. Those things that have been entrusted to such a person as law, like the terrifying writings of the holy gospels, should be preserved safely before the judicial seat.' And in the same passage, he adds, 'From the very beginning of a case to its conclusion, justices should remain steady, and should not be moved, except in offering their judgement; by this act, the full extent of the court is filled by the very divine presence; this instils in all a reverent fear for the divine scriptures and should expel all unfairness from the search for the truth. Also, all judicial reverence for flesh and blood should drive out the emotions, emptying the judge of anger and hatred, fear and friendship. For Julius Caesar said, "It's scarcely easy for the mind to see what is true where emotions gain ground." Therefore, this proverb of Cicero's was particularly renowned among the ancients, "Whoever clothes his friend strips the judge bare." For proper justice, to which a judge should defer, knows neither the left hand of hatred nor the right hand of love.'[2] So he says. Therefore, it is evident how an unjust judge is perjured. And therefore, because of the unfair judgement that he gave, Paris proved he was from Laomedon's tribe, because he was the son of Priam, Laodemon's son.

[55] [2] The second part of the picture, concerning Paris's management, follows. For poets report that his father, king Priam, exposed Paris to die in a wood immediately after his mother had given birth. Priam did this because of a dream his wife Hecuba had at the time she was pregnant, carrying Paris in her womb. For then she dreamed that she was carrying a burning bundle of sticks, through which the whole city of Troy had been set alight. When Hecuba awoke from her dream, terrified, she began to tell her dream to her husband Priam,

---

[2] *Ibid.* 5.12 (PL 199:570).

qui ad templum accessit, et dicunt aliqui quod ad asilum dee
Iunonis, cuius meminit Augustinus, *De ciuitate Dei* primo. Et ibi
quesiuit quid hoc sompnium uxoris sue pr[o]nosticabat, et fuit
sibi responsum quod uxor sua habuit in uentre puerum per quem
ciuitas Troie fuit per incendium peritura. Precepit rex Priamus
Eccube quod statim puer deberet interfici postquam foret natus.
  Statim igitur post natiuitatem pueri huius, traditus
fuit lictoribus ad deportandum in | Ydam siluam et ibidem
interficiendum. Qui accipientes puerum, portauerunt ad siluam,
sed moti pietate, noluerunt eum occidere, sed dimiserunt puerum
iacentem sub quadam arbore et redierunt ad regem Priamum,
nunciantes sibi puerum interisse. Uenit autem a casu pastor
quidam et inuenit puerum iacentem, quem cernens elegantis
forme, leuauit puerum et portauit ad domum suam et fecit
eum ab uxore sua educari, et educatum, adoptauit in filium.
Et postquam puer adoleuit, misit eum ad custodiendum pecora
cure sue commissa. Hec est historia quam narrant poete de
Paride, et eandem tangit Tullius, libro *De diuinacione*.
  Utrum autem ad litteram fuit, utrum istud poetice fictum,
nescio. Tamen possibile fuit [illud fuisse uerum], quia consimile
quidem narratur de Ciro, qui fuit imperator Persarum, sicut patet
per Trogum Pompeium, libro primo. Et de aliis eciam pueris sic
expositis, narrat Iustinus in *Abreuiacionibus* suis plura exempla.
Unde tangit de exposicione Remi et Romuli, qui fuerunt expositi
in Tiberim et tamen fuerunt saluati et nutriti a lupa, sicut tangit
libro 14. Similiter Iustinus recitat in libro 42 unam narracionem
multo mirabiliorem de quodam puero exposito, et tamen saluato
et educato a diuersis feris, et finaliter eum educauit cerua quedam
siluestris. Iste puer postmodum rex Hispanie fuit et uocabatur
Habidius. Posui istas historias hic pro probanda possibilitate
| istius quod narratur de isto Paride, primo morti exposito et
tamen finaliter saluato.

64–65 et ... Iunonis] ad consilium dee Iouis A   66 pronosticabat]
p'nosticabat O   69 deberet interfici] interficeretur I
71 lictoribus] *corr. from* latoribus ? I • fol. 122rb 73 occidere] interficere A
75 interisse] interfecisse A   78 eum] *adds* pastor iste A   81–83 et ... quia] et
quidam A
83 illud ... uerum] *om.* O   84 qui fuit imperator] rege A   85 Pompeium] *adds*
diffuse I   85–90 de ... mirabiliorem] narrat Iustinus A   86–87 Iustinus ...
fuerunt] *marg.* I   93 Habidius] Haludim A • probanda] uidendo AI
• possibilitate] *adds* ueritatis A   94 fol. 122va

who in turn went to the temple. Some say he went to the sanctuary of the goddess Juno, as Augustine recalls, *On the city of God* 1.[3] There he asked what his wife's dream foretold, and he was answered that his wife had in her womb a boy through whom the city of Troy was to be destroyed by fire. The king ordered Hecuba that the boy should be killed as soon as he was born.

[71] Therefore, immediately after the boy's birth, he was given to executioners for them to carry into the forest of Ida and to kill there. They took the boy and carried him to the wood, but, moved by pity, they didn't wish to kill him but left him lying under a tree and returned to king Priam, telling him that they had killed the boy. However, by chance, a shepherd passed by and found the boy lying there. He saw that the boy was beautiful, took him up, carried him to his home, made his wife bring him up, and once he was brought up, adopted him as his son. After the boy had grown up, he sent him to look after the livestock assigned him to care for. This is the story poets tell about Paris, and Cicero also treats it in *On divination*.[4]

[82] However, I don't know whether this actually happened, or whether it was invented by a poet. Nevertheless, it was possible that it was a true account, because a similar story is told about Cyrus, emperor of the Persians, as Pompeius Trogus shows in book 1.[5] Also Justinus, in his *Epitome* of Pompeius, gives many examples of other boys exposed in this way. For this reason, in book 14, he treats the exposure of Remus and Romulus, who were exposed by the Tiber and nevertheless were saved and fed by a she-wolf. Similarly, in book 42, Justinus recounts a much more wondrous story about a boy who was exposed, and yet saved and brought up by various wild beasts, and who was finally raised by a wild doe. Afterwards, this boy Habidius was king of Spain. I've put forward these histories here in order to prove that what's told of Paris, first exposed to death and nevertheless saved in the end, is possible.

---

[3] *Ibid.* 1.4 (PL 41:17–18).
[4] *Ibid.* 1.21.42.
[5] Justinus, *Epitome historiarum Philippicarum* 1.4–5, 43.2, 44.4 (which repeats the early references).

Applicando tamen ad propositum, sciendum est quod ideo poete fingunt Paridem istum, per quem intelligunt + omnem iniustum iudicem, esse pastorem gregis. Nam istud est unum officium pertinens ad iudicem, scilicet officium pastoris. Nam sicut pastor debet et tenetur lupos a gregibus arcere, ita iudex tenetur maliciis hominum obuiare, sicut dicit lex. Et nota de isto dominum Hostiensem, *Extra*, de eleccionibus, capitulo primo, 'Ne pro defectu', ubi ponit uersus quosdam in quibus patet multiplex et diuersum officium iudicis. Ad iudicem enim pertinet quod sit [doctor], ductor, medicus, miles, [cultor] et corrector. Unde uersus sunt hii:

Dux, doctor, preco, pastor, medicus, gladiator, / prefectus, uigilum, miles, nutrix, agricultor, / corrector, iudex, pater et speculum, speculator – / officium presulis prestat – [sacerque patronus].

In hiis uersubus quos iste doctor canonis ponit, patent uarii status quos pretendit persona iudicis. Tamen specialiter sibi co[nuen]it nomen pastoris. Propterea que ad officium pastoris pertinent describuntur Ezechielis 34; debet enim pastor intendere gregi[s] sibi credit[i] salutem et saluacionem, non propriam commoditatem; aliter enim dicendus est mercenarius, non pastor, et isto modo debet iudex facere in iudicio. Semper enim intendere debet equitatem et nullo modo aliquod emolumentum temporale. Et de isto | iudicis officio informauit Aristoteles Alexandrum in *Alexandride*, et sunt uersus isti:

Si lis accid\er/et te iudice, dirige libram / iudicii, nec flectat amor nec munera palpent, / Nec moueat stabilem persone accepcio, mentem. / Muneris arguitur accept[i] censor iniqus. / Munus a norma recti distorquet acumen / iudicis, et tetra inuoluit caligine mentem.

[3] Sequitur tercia pars picture de Paridis legis lacione, nam poete dicunt eum tulisse legem de coronando regem. Historia est ista, siue fuerit fabulosa uel ad litteram uera. Paris iste, quando taurus armenti, quod sibi fuit comissum, uicit taurum alterius armenti, tunc fecit sertum de floribus poni super caput tauri sui.

---

97 omnem] hominem O   98 iudicem] *adds* et iniquum A   103 Ne] Ue A
    105 doctor, cultor] *om.* O   107 prefectus] preses A   110 sacerque patronus] *a two-thirds line blank space* O   113 conuenit] copetit O • nomen] *adds* et officium A   115 gregis ... crediti] gregis ... traditi A, gre|gi ... credito O • saluacionem] sanitatem A   119 fol. 122vb • Aristoteles] *adds* regem I
    123 accepti] *a corr.* I, acceptor O   124 Munus] Minus I
127 regem] gregem I   128 siue ... uera] *om.* A   130 sertum] coronam AI

[96] Nevertheless, applying this to my argument, one should know that it's for this reason that poets represent Paris, by whom they understand every unjust judge, as a shepherd watching his flock. For a shepherd's duties are the same as those of a judge. For just as a shepherd ought, and is required, to drive wolves away from his flocks, likewise a judge is required, as the law says, to forestall people's evil acts. Notice on this point, Henry of Segusio, cardinal bishop of Ostia, commenting on the *Decretals*, 'on elections' 1, a canon that begins 'Lest on account of failure',[6] where he cites some verses in which he shows a judge's multiple and various duties. For it is appropriate for a judge to be learned, a leader, a physician, a soldier, a cultivator, and a corrector. For this reason, these are his verses:

> Leader, learned person, herald, shepherd, physician, swordsman, / governor, watchman, soldier, nurse, cultivator, / corrector, judge, father and mirror, sentinel – / a bishop is responsible for all these roles, as well as being a holy leader.

In these verses that this learned canonist presents, he shows the varied positions to which the role of judge extends. Nevertheless the noun 'shepherd' is especially fitting for such a person. On this account, Ez 34 describes those things that pertain to this position, for a shepherd ought to concentrate on the health and safety of the flock entrusted to him, not on his own advantage, since otherwise, he should just be called a hireling, not a shepherd (cf. Io 10:12). A judge should behave in this way in his judgements, for he ought always to concentrate upon what's just and never upon any worldly financial advantage. Aristotle taught Alexander about this duty of a judge in these verses from the *Alexandreis*:

> Should it befall you to judge a legal suit, rule things with justice's / scales, and don't let favour bend them nor rewards stroke them / nor allow preference for a person to sway your fixed intention. / A judge receiving rewards proves an unfair magistrate. / A reward twists a judge's acuteness / from the standard of rectitude, and vile things wrap the mind in darkness.[7]

[126] [3] The third part of the picture follows; it concerns Paris's proposing laws. For poets say that he proposed the law concerning crowning a king. This is the story, whether it is just a fable or a true account. Paris, when a bull from the herd of which he had charge conquered a bull from another herd, had a garland of flowers placed on the head of his bull.

---

[6] *Summa super titulis Decretalium* on *Decretales* 1.6 (de electione). The subsequent verses are not in Walther.

[7] *Ibid.* 1.105–10.

Si uero contingeret quod aliquis alius taurus uinceret taurum Paridis, statim Paris abstulit sertum de capite uicti et posuit super caput uictoris. Et propter istud paritatem quam ostendit, uocabant illum socii sui pastores Paridem. Per istud poete uolunt intelligere quod ad iudicem pertinet dictare legem et eius dictacione equitatem seruare. Unde *iudex* idem est quod 'ius dicens'. Et ideo dicit Cassidorus in quadam epistola quod 'Iudex quisquis tamdiu dicitur, quam[diu] ius dicit et iustus putatur'. Sed ut idem Cassiodorus dicit super psalmum, 'Iudex tamdiu est iustus, quamdiu seruat rectitudinem equitatis'. Nam ut dicit Cassiodorus, 'Iusticia nec nouit patrem nec matrem, sed solam ueritatem nouit'. Sic igitur causa huius picture, scilicet qualiter iste Paris pingitur, in figura legis latoris, patet sic ad | significandum equitatem iusticie quam iudex debet in iudiciis obseruare.

    Notandum hic est quod dicunt antiqui doctores unum esse librum intitulatum *De [pictu]ris antiquis* quem exposuisse dicunt Antistenem philosophum et alii Archimenidem. In quo libro describuntur tales modi depingendi ymagines uirtutum et uiciorum, sicut in proposita pictura Paridis. Nam pingitur Paris in ueste regali, quia inuoluitur purpura in signum quod fuit de stirpe regia. Similiter pingitur cum baculo pastorali in signum quod fuit pastor gregis. Tercio, pingitur *sedens pro tribunali* in signum quod fuit lator legis.

    [4] Sequitur quarta pars picture in qua agitur de Paridis redempcione. Unde poete fingunt eum eciam cum manu extenta, in signum quod est promptus [ad] recip[iendum] munera, que munera solent iudices specialiter excec[r]are. Unde est hic notandum de historia seu fabula quam tangit Fulgencius in littera de illis tribus deabus gentilium, scilicet de Minerua, Iunone, et Uenere, coram quibus residentibus in quadam planicie Yde silue, uenit dea discordie et proiecit coram eis pomum quoddam aureum, in quo sic fuit scriptum 'Pulcrior uestrum me habebit'. Qua scriptura uisa, ceperunt inter se iste dee contendere de

---

135 intelligere] *om.* A • et] et in AI   138 quamdiu] quam| O   144 fol. 123ʳᵃ • iusticie] *om.* A
146 doctores] auctores I   146–50 unum ... Nam] quod ymagines uirtutum et uicorum solebant depingi A   147 picturis] li|bris O   151 fuit de] *om.* A
155 in qua agitur] *om.* A   157 promptus] *adds* et paratus A • ad recipiendum] recipere O   158 excecrare] exercere A, excecare I, excecar'| O   160 tribus] duabus A   161 coram] *expunged* I

And if it happened that another bull had conquered his, Paris immediately removed the garland from the head of the vanquished bull and put it on the victor's head. On account of the *paritas* 'evenhandedness' that he showed, his fellow herdsmen called him Paris. Through this story, poets wish to understand that it is a characteristic of a judge to pronounce what the law is and to preserve justice in accord with this pronouncement. For this reason, the noun *iudex* 'judge' means *ius dicens* 'someone stating what the law is'. Therefore, Cassiodorus says in one of his letters that 'A person is called a judge only so long as they speak justly and are considered to be just.'[8] But as Cassiodorus himself says on a psalm, 'A judge is just only so long as they preserve that right action associated with justice.' For, as [Augustine] says, 'Justice recognises neither father nor mother, only truth.'[9] Likewise, the reason for this picture, the way Paris is depicted as an image of someone proposing laws, explicitly indicates that equity in justice that a judge should observe in his judgements.

[146] One should notice here that ancient learned men say that there is a book called *On ancient images*. They say it was written by the philosopher Antistenes, and others say by a follower of Archimedes. The book describes ways of depicting images of the virtues and vices, just as in the instant picture of Paris.[10] For Paris is depicted in royal garb, for he is dressed in purple to indicate that he came from the royal line. Similarly, he is depicted with a shepherd's staff, to indicate that he was shepherd of a flock. Third, he is depicted *sitting in the place of judgement* (Mt 27:19) to indicate that he was proposer of laws.

[155] [4] The fourth part of the picture follows; it treats Paris's judgement corruptly purchased. For this reason, poets also describe him with his hand extended, to indicate that he is eager to receive bribes; judges are accustomed to particularly detest bribes like that. For this reason, one should notice here the history or fable that Fulgentius treats in his text.[11] This concerns three pagan goddesses, Minerva, Juno, and Venus; while they were staying in a meadow in the forest of Ida, the goddess of Discord approached them. She threw among them a golden apple, on which was written, 'The most beautiful of you will possess me.' Once they saw this writing, the goddesses began to vie among themselves

---

[8] *Variae* 3.27 (*PL* 69:591), but the next citation is actually Rufinus of Aquileia (?), *Commentarius in LXXV Psalmos* 14.2 (*PL* 21:695) [= *MF* iusticia et iustus y, ascribed to Cassiodorus on Ps 14].

[9] *Enarrationes in Psalmos* 14.3 (*PL* 37:1967).

[10] Cf. Fulg 3.3 (62/20), 'Anaximenes, qui de picturis antiquis disseruit …'.

[11] Fulg 2.1 (36/6–19).

165 pulcritudine, et raciones uarias allegare. Tandem conuenerunt inter se de iudice, et placuit omnibus quod Iubiter daret iudicium, que earum haberet pomum. Sed Iubiter excusauit se, nec uoluit se de ista contrauersia | intromittere. Sed tamen ipse eis dixit quod adirent Paridem pastorem, et el[igere]nt eum in iudicem.
170 Uenerunt igitur tres dee ad Paridem, et quelibet earum promisit Paridi certum munus, eo pacto quod Paris fieret sibi fauorabilis in iudicio pomi. Minerua sibi promisit quod faceret eum uirum sapientissimum tocius orbis terre; Iuno promisit ei quod faceret eum ditissimum, sed dea Uenus quod haberet uxorem
175 pulcherrimam. Igitur Paris, uictus concupiscencia carnis, neclecta sapiencia Palladis et diuiciis Iunonis, dedit iudicium [de pomo] pro parte Ueneris.

Ista est fabula poetica, et nichil aliud per hanc fabulam uolunt poete intelligere, nisi describere tria munerum genera. Quia est
180 unum munus a manu, secundum a lingua, et tercium ab obsequio, que subuertere solent rectum iudicium. Nam beatus Gregorius in quadam omelia distinguit ista tria genera munerum. Iuno igitur, quam poete fingunt deam diuiciarum, ipsa promisit Paridi munus a manu, quia promisit diuicias et pecuniam. Sed Minerua, dea
185 sapiencie, promisit munus a lingua, quia sapienciam et famam, que sequela est sapiencie. Est enim lingua speciale organum sapiencie, sicut de hoc pulcre tangit Tullius. Uenus autem promisit Paridi munus ab obsequio, promittendo sibi uxorem pulcherrimam. In actu enim carnali sexus muliebris obsequitur
190 sexui uirili. Sic igitur patet misterium huius fabule | poetice. Nam inter omnia que subuertunt uerum iudicium, scilicet racionis, u[ene]num speciale peculancia carnalis delectacionis. Nec habet [delectator ali]um mercedem, nisi illam breuem et miserabilem delectacionem. Et hec est illa merces, cuius mercedis
195 dicitur am\at/or esse Paris.

---

165 uarias allegare] uariare A   167 haberet] deberet habere A   168 fol. 123rb
169 eligerent] elegerunt O   171 fieret] foret AI   173 tocius ... terre] *om.* AI
(*following* Iuno *over eras.* I) • promisit ei quod] *om.* I   174 eum] *adds* uirum A
• Uenus] *adds* promisit sibi A   176 de pomo] pro pomum I, siue sentenciam O
179–80 Quia ... obsequio] *after 182* munerum A   183 ipsa] \plura/ (*over eras.*) I
183–85 munus ... promisit] *marg.* (*and adds* Paridi) I   184–86 Sed ... sapiencie]
munus a lingua quia promisit ei sapienciam A   187 sicut ... Tullius] *om.* A
189 muliebris] mulieris I   190 fol. 123va 191 subuertunt uerum] peruertunt AI
192 uenenum] unum O • carnalis] *adds* siue A   193 delectator alium] luxuria ullum O   195 esse] iste A

about their beauty and to put forward all sorts of arguments [as to who was most beautiful]. Finally, they agreed among themselves about a judge, and they all agreed that Jupiter should pronounce judgement on which of them should have the apple. But Jupiter excused himself and did not want to get involved in this dispute. Nevertheless, he said to them that they should approach the shepherd Paris, and should choose him as their judge. Therefore, the three goddesses came to Paris, and each of them promised him a specific reward, on the condition that Paris would be favourable to that one in his judgement about who should have the apple. Minerva promised that she would make him the wisest man in the whole world, and Juno promised that she would make him the richest, but Venus that he would have the most beautiful wife. Therefore Paris, conquered by lust of the flesh, and having neglected both Pallas's wisdom and Juno's riches, gave his judgement about the apple to Venus's side.

[178] This is a poetic fable, and poets wish to understand by the fable only a description of three types of rewards. For one reward comes from the hand, the second from the tongue, and the third from subservience. But all three customarily subvert proper judgement. In one of his homilies blessed Gregory distinguishes these three types of rewards.[12] Therefore Juno, whom poets represent as the goddess of riches, promised Paris a reward from the hand, because she promised him riches and money. But Minerva, the goddess of wisdom, promised him a reward from the tongue, because she promised both wisdom and the renown that accompanies it. For the tongue is the special organ of wisdom, as Cicero says neatly.[13] However, Venus promised Paris a reward from subservience, when she promised him the most beautiful wife, for in the sexual act, the female sex defers to the male sex. This shows the hidden meaning underlying this poetic fable. For among all the things that destroy true and rational judgement, the wantonness associated with fleshly delight is particularly poisonous. Nor does a lover receive any actual payoff, except for the brief and wretched pleasure in the act. This is the payoff that the poets say Paris desired.

---

[12] Cf. *Homeliae in evangelium* 10.6 (*PL* 76:1112–13).
[13] Probably proverbial.

[5] Sequitur quinta pars picture de Paridis interuencione. Ubi notandum est quod poete fingunt et historie, quoad aliquid in hoc conueniunt, quod iste Paris fuit causa illius maxime stragis que fiebat in Troia. Unde poete aliqui loquntur de ista strage, quasi de interuencione. Est enim interuencio bellum de quo nullus euadit, et tempore quo Troia fuit incensa a Grecis. Omnes quasi Troiani fuerunt ebrii et dormientes, quasi sepulti sompno et uino, sicut dicit Uirgilius 2º *Eneydis*, 'Inuad[un]t urbem sompno uinoque sepultam'. Et ideo nullus quasi euasit quin fuit occisus uel ductus captiuus, excepto Enea et aliis paucis. Et ideo fingunt istum Paridem in effigie hominis + homicide, nam propter \H/elenam, quam iste Paris fretus, auxilio dee Ueneris, rapuit, Troia obcessa fuit a Grecis. Et in ista obsidione fuerunt strages facte maxime, sicut patet ex historia Daretis Frigii, ubi narrantur prelia diuersa, credo plura quam triginta. Narratur eciam ibi numerus interfectorum in quolibet prelio, et auctor omnium istorum homicidiorum fuit iste Paris pro \raptu suo/. |

Sed notandum est quod per hoc poete uolunt describere quantum malum accidit de iniquo iudice. In lingua enim iudicis pendet uita et mors +. Homicidium autem est maximum peccatum, e[ciam] in reputacione paganorum, sicut pulcre tangit Aristoteles in epistola ad Alexandrum Magnum, ubi dicit, 'O Alexander, monui te frequenter et ad huc moneo, parce sanguinem humanum effundere, quia hoc soli Deo conuenit, quia oculta nouit hominum et secreta cordium. Caue igitur, quantum potes, sanguinem humani generis effundere, quia egregius doctor Hermogenes scripsit dicens, "Quando creatura interfecit creaturam sibi similem, uirtutes celorum clamant ad diuinam maiestatem dicentes, 'Domine, seruus tuus uult esse Tibi similis, quod si iniuste interficiat eum'. Respondit Creator, 'Permittite eum, quia qui interficit interficietur; *michi uindictam, et ego retribuam*'. Et tociens uirtutes celorum representabunt in suis laudibus mortem interfecti donec uindicta sumatur de interficiente, qui erit unus de perseuerantibus in penis eternis'". Hec Aristoteles.

197-98 et ... conueniunt, 199-200 Unde ... interuencione] *om.* A   197 quoad aliquid] eciam alie I   203 Inuadunt] Inuadit O   206 homicide] homicidie O   212 fol. 123vb

214 malum] *om.* A • iudice] iudicio AI   215 mors] *adds* hominis O   216 eciam] et O   218 parce] ne (*with later* effundas, *both over eras.*) I

[**196**] [5] The fifth part of the picture follows; it concerns Paris's interference. Here one should notice that both poets and histories report, insofar as they agree on this matter, that Paris was the cause of the greatest destruction that ever occurred in Troy. For this reason, some poets speak of this destruction, as if it came about through interference. For this interference was war, which no one avoids, at the time the Greeks burned Troy. All those in Troy were drunk and asleep, as if they were buried in sleep and wine, as Virgil says in *Aeneid* 2, '[They] invade the city, buried in sleep and wine.'[14] Therefore, no one avoided either being killed or led captive, except for Aeneas and a few others. For this reason, poets represent Paris as the image of a murderer, because the Greeks besieged Troy on Helen's account – Paris, confident because he had Venus's aid, had abducted her. In this siege, the greatest destructions occurred, as Dares the Phrygian's history shows. He tells of numerous battles, I think more than thirty of them, and also tells there of the number slain in each battle.[15] Paris, in abducting Helen, was the instigator of all these killings.

[**213**] But one should notice that through this account, poets wish to describe how much evil comes about through an unfair judge. For people's life and death depend upon a judge's tongue. Moreover, murder is the greatest sin, and even the pagans considered it so, as Aristotle neatly puts it in his letter to Alexander the Great, where he says, 'O Alexander, I often warned you, and I'm warning you once again, avoid shedding people's blood, an act that is appropriate to God alone, since He knows what people try to hide and the secrets of their hearts. Therefore, beware, so far as you are able, of shedding people's blood. For the famous learned man Hermogenes wrote, "When one creature kills another like themselves, the powers of heaven cry out to the divine ruler, saying, 'Lord, your servant wishes to be like You, because he killed him so unjustly.' The Creator answers, 'Let him be, because the person who has killed will be killed; *vengeance is mine, and I will repay* (Rm 12:19).' The powers of heaven will often put forward in their praises of God a murdered person's death, until He takes vengeance on the killer, and the killer will be one of those enduring eternal punishments."' So Aristotle says.[16]

---

[14] *Ibid.* 2.265.

[15] Actually not Dares, but a general reference to Guido della Colonne; see the textual note.

[16] *Ibid.* 21 (p. 46).

[6] Sequitur sexta pars picture de Paridis prodicione. Poete enim + pingunt Paridem cum nota prodicionis. Ubi notanda est historia quam de eo narrant poete, nam Paris, postquam adiudicauerat pomum dee Ueneris, statim fretus consilio Ueneris, iuit + in Greciam et ibi loquebatur cum Helena, uxore regis Monelay, et tandem prodicio[s]e abduxit eam de Grecia in Troiam. Et ideo uocabatur iste Paris | 'proditor edys', hoc est aule regie. Uenit enim pacifice ad loca ubi mansit iste rex Grecie Menelaus, sed finaliter egit prodicio[s]e, sicut patuit quando per nauigium clam uxorem regis abduxit.

Et hic est notanda historia de lege hospicii obseruata apud antiquos. Nam consuetudo fuit talis: iuit enim hospes ad hostium, ibique pedem posuit super pedem hospitis sui, et manum suam in manu hospitis sui. Et ibi uterque iurauit alteri quod seruarent mutuo fidelitatem et uitarent omnem prodicionem. Sed istud non obseruauit iste Paris, et ideo dicitur a poetis 'proditor edys', id est hospicii et hospitis sui regis, scilicet Menelay +. Et de ista prodicione loquitur Uirgilius, 4 *Eneydos*, quando dicit 'Et federa soluere furto'. Et per hoc nichil aliud uolunt intelligere, nisi quod omnis iudex iniquus et iniustus proditor est aule regie maiestatis, \a qua iudex receperit officium iudicis, et est proditor ueritatis et equitatis.

Unde/ sicut patet ex antiquis historiis, iudices tales iniqui tanquam proditores erant puniti. Fuit enim antiquitus sanccitum quod proditores deberent excoriari, sicut fuit de Cambise rege, qui fuit filius Ciri. Narrat enim Ualerius Maximus, libro 6°, capitulo 3, quod rex Cambises mali cuiusdam iudicis pellem e corpore detractam selle iudiciarie extendit, et filium eius post

---

232 enim] *adds* fingunt et O • prodicionis] perdicionis I   234 pomum] *adds* esse I   235 iuit] iuitum O   236 Monelay] Melanai I • (and 239) prodiciose] prodicione O   237 fol. 124^(ra)   238 ad loca] *om.* A
244 seruarent] obseruaret A   247 Menelay] *adds* regis O   247-49 Et de ista ... furto] *om.* A   250 iniquus] impius I   250-51 maiestatis ... ueritatis] id est regie potestatis A
254 sanccitum] statutum A   255 rege] iudice I   255-56 sicut ... Ciri] *om.* A
257-65 rex ... datus] AI *have rather*:
cum iudex quondam (quidam iniquus fuisset A) de iudici iniusto (in quo A) accusatus et conuictus, rex precepit eum excoriari et pellem detractam selle iudicarie superextendi ad sequencium cautelam, uolens prouidere ne alii iudices futuri declinarent a rectitudine (*adds* iudicii A), reducentes ad memoriam acerbitatem supplicii.

[231] [6] The sixth part of picture follows; it concerns Paris's treachery. For poets depict Paris with a mark of treachery. Here one should notice the history that poets tell about him, for, after he had awarded the apple to the goddess Venus, Paris, made confident by Venus's advice, immediately passed into Greece. There he spoke with Helen, king Menelaus's wife, and at last, kidnapped her treacherously from Greece and brought her to Troy. Therefore, Paris was called 'traitor to the house', that is, to the king's court. For he went in peace to the place where Menelaus, king of Greece, lived, but in the end performed a treacherous act, as is evident when he secretly kidnapped the king's wife and sailed off with her.

[241] Here one should notice what historians tell about the law of hospitality the ancients followed. Their custom was that when a guest came to the door, he there put his foot on his host's foot and his hand in his host's hand. Then each swore to the other that they would keep faith with one another and avoid all treachery. But Paris did not respect this custom, and therefore the poets call him 'traitor to the house', that is both to hospitality and to his host, king Menelaus. Virgil speaks about this treachery in *Aeneid* 4, when he says, 'and to break a bond by theft'.[17] And poets wish to understand by this only that every unfair and unjust judge is a traitor to the royal hall of the divine majesty, from which a judge has received his responsibility as a judge, and he is a traitor to both truth and justice.

[253] For this reason, as ancient histories show, such unfair judges were punished as if they were traitors. For from ancient times, it was ordained that traitors should be flayed, as was done by king Cambyses, Cyrus's son. For Valerius Maximus tells in 6.3 that king Cambyses spread out in the judgement hall the skin he had stripped from the body of an evil judge, and he commanded the judge's son to

---

[17] Cf. *ibid*. 4.337, 'neque ego hanc abscondere furto'.

    patrem suum in ea iudicaturum sedere iussit, ut | paterne pene
260 memoria eum a iudicio peruerso + retrahet. Istos autem uersus
    dicunt quidam in loco illo eum scribi fecisse, uel saltem istorum
    uersuum sentenciam:
      Sede sedens ista, iudex, inflexibilis sta; / a manibus reuoces
      munus, ab aur[e] preces; / sit tibi lucerna lex, lux pellisque
265   paterna, / qua resides natus, pro patre sponte datus.
    Qualiter autem tales iudices sunt proditores patet ex uerbis
    Crisostomi, *Super Mattheum*, ubi sic dicit: 'Non solum est
    proditor ueritatis qui mendacium pro ueritate loquitur, sed qui
    non libere pronunciat ueritatem quam pronunciare oportet, aut
270 non libere defendit ueritatem quam defendere oportet'. Sed iudex
    tenetur ad utramque, scilicet ad pronuncia[cione]m et ad ueritatis
    defencionem. Et ideo semper quando pronunciat sentenciam
    continentem falsitatem, ipse nequiter p[ro]dit ueritatem.
    [7] Sequitur septima pars picture de Paridis subuersione.
275 Poete enim pingunt Paridem subuersorem regie sedis patris sui
    Priami. Unde sicut pingunt eum habe[ntem] manum extentam ad
    munera, ita in alia manu pingunt eum habentem sedem regiam
    regni et subuertentem eam. Et per hoc uolunt poete intelligere
    quam periculosum et perniciosum sit iniquum et iniustum
280 iudicium, quia ex tali iudicio prouenit quandoque subuersio et
    translacio regnorum. Unde Ecclesiastico scribitur *Iudex sapiens*
    iudicabit populum suum | et principatus + sensati stabilis erit. Et
    sequitur, *Execrabilis coram Deo omnis iniquitas gencium*, et statim
    subdit *Regnum a gente in gentem transfertur propter iniurias,*
285 *iniusticias, et contumelias et diuersos dolos*. Et ut narrant historie
    gentilium, ita accidit ad literam circa Priamum, qui fuit pater
    istius Paridis. Perdidit enim ipse regnum Troianum et potestatem
    regni sui propter iniquum iudicium filii sui. Et sic finita est prima
    mithologia secundi libri.

---

259 fol. 124[rb] **260** retrahet] retrahent O **264** aure] auro| O **266** iudices sunt] iniqui iudices sunt ueritatis AI **269** libere] *adds* pro ueritate I
269–70 oportet ... oportet] oportet A **271** pronunciacionem] pronunciandum O **273** prodit] perdit O
274 septima] *add* et ultima AI **276** habentem] habere O **277** pingunt eum] *om.* A **279** sit] *add* istud uicium scilicet AI • iniquum et] *om.* A
280 iudicio] uicio I • quandoque] aliquando AI **282** fol. 124[va] sensati] seu status O **283–85** gencium ... iniusticias] *om.* I **285** et[1] ... dolos] *om.* A
287–88 potestatem ... sui[1]] posteritas sua A **288** sui[2]] *adds* filii uenerabilis uiri I

sit on it, when he was to offer judgement, having succeeded his father. In this way, the memory of his father's punishment would restrain him from making perverted judgements.[18] Moreover, some people say that he had these verses written in that place – or at least the substance of these verses:

> Sitting in this seat, judge, remain rigorous. / You should send back from your hands, gifts; and from your ears, entreaties. / The law should be your guiding light, and your father's skin another light / – you sit on it as newly born, and as deliberately appointed in your father's place.[19]

Chrysostom shows in *On Matthew* how such judges are traitors. He says, 'It's not just the person who speaks a lie instead of the truth who's a traitor to the truth. This is equally true of the person who doesn't freely proclaim the truth when it's necessary to do so, or the one who doesn't freely defend the truth when it's necessary to do so.'[20] But a judge is required to do both, namely to pronounce and to defend the truth. Therefore, when he gives a judgement containing a falsehood, he always evilly betrays truth.

[274] [7] The seventh part of the picture follows; it concerns Paris's overthrowing. For poets depict Paris as the person who overthrew the royal seat of his father Priam. For this reason, just as they depict him having a hand extended to receive bribes, they likewise depict him holding in his other hand the royal throne of the realm and overturning it. Through this image, poets wish to understand how dangerous and perverse unfair and unjust judgement is, because through such judgement, the overthrow and passage of kingdoms sometimes come to pass. For this reason, Sir 10:1 says, *A wise judge shall judge his people, and the government of a prudent man shall be steady.* There follows (v. 7), *All iniquity of nations is execrable before God*, and he adds immediately (v. 8), *A kingdom is translated from one people to another, because of injustices, and wrongs, and injuries and divers deceits.* And, as pagan histories tell, it literally happened in that way to Priam, Paris's father. For he lost the kingdom of Troy and all his power on account of his son's unfair judgement. Here the first mythology of the second book ends.

---

[18] *Ibid.* 6.3.ext.3. Both the citation and the following verses also appear at *Fasciculus morum* 500/80–88.

[19] Walther, *Sprich.* 27839.

[20] Unfound.

[2]

Sequitur seconda mithologia, et est de pictura Palladis seu Minerue, sub cuius ymagine uolunt poete depingere statum uite contemplatiue, secundum ymaginacionem Fulgencii, ut patet in serie littere. Dicit enim Fulgencius quod 'philosophi uoluerunt
5   tripartitam esse [humanitatis] uitam; unam uocabant theoricam seu contemplatiuam, aliam dixerunt uitam practicam seu actiuam, terciam uitam uocabant Greci *philargeam*, quam \nos/ Latini uocare possumus uoluptariam uitam'. *Philos* enim Grece sonat in Latino idem quod 'amor', et ideo qui uiuunt
10 conformiter secundum ea que amant et appetunt, ipsi istam uitam terciam ducunt.

    Qui autem sunt status hominum qui ducunt ha[s] uitas diuersas explanat Fulgencius in littera, dicens quod 'Uitam primam, que dicitur uita contemplatiua seu theorica, ducunt
15 episcopi, sacerdotes, et monachi apud Cristianos, et apud paganos ducebant istam uitam philosophi'. Nam ut dicit Fulgencius, philosophos | nulla lucri cupiditas, nulla furoris insania, nullum fe[r]uoris + toxicum, \nullus/ uapor libidinis, sed tantum indagande ueritatis contemplande iusticie cura macerat, fama
20 ornat, et spes pascit'.

    Secundam uero uitam, quam Fulgencius uocat actiuam, ipse sic describit. Dicit enim quod 'est comodi auida, ornatus petax, habendi insaciata, rapiendi cauta, seruandi solicita; plus eciam semper cupit quam habeat, nec curat quid sapiat, nec considerat
25 quid expediat, sed semper anelat quid rapiat. Denique hec uita', ut dicit Fulgencius, 'non prestat quicquid stabile, quia nullus eam ducens uiuit honeste'. Et sicut dicit Fulgencius, 'Apud antiquos incredulos hec uita quam uocauit practicam uel actiuam fuit uita tirannorum; sed modernis temporibus', ut dicit Fulgencius,
30 'uitam istam ducit totus mundus'. Hec Fulgencius de istis duabus uitis.

3–4 secundum ... littere] *om.* A   5 humanitatis] *om.* O   8 uoluptariam] uoluntariam A   11 terciam] triplicem A

12 has] hac O   14–16 ducunt ... istam] *om.* I   15 episcopi] ipsi A   17 fol. 124vb
    17–18 nullum ... toxicum] *om.* A   18 feruoris toxicum] feuoris intoxicum O

22 auida] *adds a repetition of 21* uero ... uitam A (*following first word on a new page*)   30–31 Hec ... uitis] *om.* A

[2]

The second mythology follows; it concerns the picture of Pallas or Minerva. In her image, poets wish to depict the state of Contemplative Life, as Fulgentius imagines and shows in the sequence of his text. For Fulgentius says that the philosophers wished there to be three distinct ways of human life; they called one theoretical or contemplative, the second practical or active, and the third what the Greeks call *philargea*, which we Latin speakers can call the life of delight.[1] The Greek word *philos* means the same as 'love' in Latin, and therefore those who live in conformity with those things that they love and desire follow this third way of life.

[12] In his text, Fulgentius explains the human states that follow these various lives. He says that, 'among Christians, bishops, priests, and monks follow the first life, the contemplative or theoretical, and among the pagans, philosophers'. For, as Fulgentius says, 'only the care of seeking out truth and contemplating justice worries philosophers – not desire for money, nor mad rage, nor passion's poison, nor transitory licentiousness. As a result, renown adorns them and hope feeds them.'

[21] Fulgentius also describes the second life, which he calls active, saying, 'It's eager for any benefit, striving for ornament, incapable of having enough, secretive in theft, careful about saving; it always wants more than it has, doesn't care what it knows, never considers what's appropriate – it just always yearns for what it may steal. In the end, this life does not excel at anything that's lasting, for none of its adherents lives virtuously. Among the ancients, who lacked the faith, this life that they called practical or active was the life of tyrants, but these days, the whole world follows its course.' So Fulgentius says about these two lives.

---

[1] Fulg 2.1 (36/2–5, the following two paragraphs from 36/9–22).

Sed applicando ad propositum, notare possumus uarias partes picture quibus istam Palladem seu Minueruam poete solent depingere. Siquidem hec Minerua depingitur

[1] Ioue generata,
[2] iuuentute grata,
[3] ueste uariata,
[4] armis exornata,
[5] [uertice] cristata,
[6] sidere signata,
[7] pectore grauata,
[8] pudore probata,
[9] curis onerata,
[10] in arce locata,
[11] preliis p[rel]ata,
[12] et pace dotata.

Iste sunt duodecim partes picture qua Mineruam istam poete solent depingere.

[1] Unde quoad | primam partem, sicut patet ex Marciano in suo libro *De nupciis*, isti poete dicunt quod ipsa Minerua fuit nata de uertice dei Iouis, et uolunt per hoc poete intelligere excellenciam singularem uite contemplatiue. Tactum enim est prius in tercia mithologia qualiter per Iouem intelligunt isti poete uirtutem caritatis, [et nos intelligimus per Iouem uirtutem caritatis], que caritas habet duas partes. Inclinat enim ad dileccionem Dei et proximi, sed principalior pars est, quasi caput et uertex caritatis, dileccio Dei, per quam homo inclinatur ad uitam contemplatiuam ducendam. Et hec est causa quare Minerua, sub cuius ymagine depingitur uita ista contemplatiua, dicitur nata de uertice Iouis, quia uitam contemplatiuam ducat uirtus caritatis ex parte illa qua inclinatur ad dileccionem Dei.

Ista enim est pars melior quam elegit Maria, secundum illud, *Optimam partem elegit sibi Maria*. Et de ista preeminencia uite contemplatiue super omnem aliam uitam quam uiator posset ducere in hac uita, loquitur Gregorius in diuersis locis, sicut patet in *Moralibus* et in suo *Registro* et in suis *Omeliis super Ezechielem*. Dicit enim in libro 6° *Mo\ralium/*, uersus finem,

---

39 uertice] uirtute O   43 curis] turris A   45 prelata] parata O
49 fol. 125ra partem] *add* picture AI • sicut] *om.* A   54 caritatis] dileccionis A
54–55 et ... caritatis] *om.* O   57 caritatis] *add* est AI • quam] *adds* dileccionem A   61 inclinatur] inclinat AI
62–63 secundum ... Maria] *om.* A, *the full verse cited* I   66–67 Moralibus ... enim] *om.* A

[32] But applying this to my topic, I may notice the various parts of the picture through which poets usually depict Pallas or Minerva. Truly Minerva is depicted
   [1] born from Jove,
   [2] thankful for youth,
   [3] various in clothing,
   [4] adorned with arms,
   [5] with a crested head,
   [6] marked by a star,
   [7] weighted down in her breast,
   [8] tested in modesty,
   [9] weighed down with cares,
   [10] placed in a citadel,
   [11] prepared for battles,
   [12] with a dowry of peace.
These are the twelve parts of the picture by which poets usually depict Minerva.

[49] [1] So far as the first part is concerned, as Martianus shows in his book *On the marriage*, poets say that Minerva was born from the very top of the god Jove's head,[2] and through this detail, they wish to understand the unique excellence of the contemplative life. I have already treated above, in the third mythology, how poets understand by Jove the virtue charity, and how, with them, we understand Jove to represent charity. Charity has two parts, for it attends to love of God and of neighbour, but the most important part is that the head and peak of charity is the love of God, and by this, a person is disposed toward following the contemplative life. This is why Minerva, whose image depicts contemplative life, is said to have been born from the top of Jove's head. For the virtue charity, insofar as its second part is disposed to the love of God, directs contemplative life.

[62] This is the better part that Mary Magdalen chose, according to the verse, *Mary hath chosen the best part* (Lc 10:42). In various places, Gregory speaks about the pre-eminence of the contemplative life over every other life that a pilgrim might follow in this life; there are clear discussions in his *Moral readings*, in his *Register*, and in the *Homilies on Ezechiel*. For he says in *Moral readings* 6, towards the end,

---

[2] Cf. Mart 7.11 (76/20–77/12).

loquens de ista uita contemplatiua, 'Uita contemplatiua minor quidem est tempore quam actiua, sed tamen | maior est merito, sicut de sacris uerbis euangelii ostenditur, in quo due mulieres egisse referuntur diuersa. Maria quippe uerba redemptoris nostri audiens, ad pedes illius residebat; Martha corporalibus ministeriis insistebat. Cumque contra Marie ocium conquereretur, audiuit *Martha, Martha solicita est, etc.* *Mariam optimam, etc.*'. Dicit ergo Gregorius quod uita contemplatiua exprimitur/ per Mariam; per Martham uita actiua designatur. 'Marthe cura non reprehenditur a Cristo, sed Marie ocium plus laudatur, quia magna sunt uite actiue merita, sed contemplatiue pociora'. Hec Gregorius. Sic igitur patet prima pars + picture Palladis, quare scilicet dicitur nata de uertice dei Iouis. Ad istam enim uitam excercendam inclinat pars principalior caritatis, ut enim dicit Gregorius, *Super Ezechielem*, 'Amor Dei pertinet ad uitam contemplatiuam, sed amor proximi ad actiuam'. Hic autem amor Dei est quasi uertex caritatis, que est pars potissima ipsius.

[2] Sequitur secunda pars picture de Palladis iuuentute. Pingunt enim aliqui poete ymaginem Minerue in etate iuuenili, et aliqui in etate media, que ut patet 2° *Rethorice* uocatur ab Aristotele acme, uel etas consistencie alio nomine, in qua etate melius se habet natura hominis. Et per hoc uolunt poete intelligere quod status uite contemplatiue non admittit defectum duracionis nec corumpitur per lapsum temporis, sicut de senibus et rebus antiquis fieri consueuit. Et de ista + con|dicione uite contemplatiue tangit Gregorius, ubi supra, 6 *Moralium*, exponens illud *Maria optimam partem elegit*: 'Auferri', inquit, 'non dicitur pars Marie, quia actiue uite opera cum corpore transeunt; contemplatiue autem gaudia melius ex fine conualescunt'. Hec est causa quare unum nomen Palladis est Minerua uel Athane. Ubi notandum quod Pallas sonat in nouitatem; interpretatur enim Pallas 'noua'. Minerua [nomen] sonat 'immortalitatem'; *min* enim est idem quod 'in' apud Latinos. *Erua* uero significat 'mortalem'; inde

68 loquens ... contemplatiua¹] *om.* A • Uita contemplatiua²] *om.* I
69 fol. 125ʳᵇ 71–75 Maria ... quod] *om.* A 73 conquereretur] quereret I
76–78 Marthe ... Gregorius] *om.* A 79 picture] pictuture MS 80 inclinat] *adds* prima I
85 pars picture] *om.* I 88 acme uel etas] Athene uel ethas A • alio nomine] *om.* A
91 nec corumpitur] *om.* I 92–93 Et de ... tangit] *om.* A 92 fol. 125ᵛᵃ
• condicione] con||condicione O 93 Maria] Marti A 95 opera] *om.* A
97 nomen] autem O 98 sonat] significat A 100 significat] interpretatur idem quod A

speaking of contemplative life, 'Although it is lesser in its attention to opportunity than the active life, nevertheless its merits are greater. This is shown in the holy words of the gospel, in which two women are described as behaving in different ways. For Mary remained sitting at our Redeemer's feet, listening to His words; Martha set about physical duties. And when Martha complained about Mary's leisure, she heard, *Martha, Martha, thou art careful, [and art troubled about many things]. Mary hath chosen [the best part, which shall not be taken away from her]*' (vv. 41–42). Therefore Gregory says that Mary expresses the contemplative life, and Martha indicates the active. 'Christ does not rebuke Martha for her duties, but he praises Mary's leisure more highly, because the merits of the active life are great, but those of the contemplative life more powerful.'[3] So Gregory says. This explains the first part of Pallas's picture and why she is said to have been born from the top of the god Jove's head. The more important part of charity is disposed to pursuing this life, as Gregory says in *On Ezechiel*, 'The love of God pertains to the contemplative life, but the love of neighbour to the active.'[4] For the love of God is like the very pinnacle of charity and its most powerful part.

[85] [2] The second part of the picture follows; it concerns Pallas's youth. For some poets depict Minerva as youthful, and some in middle age, which, as Aristotle says in his *Rhetoric* 2, is the pinnacle or age of unchanging persistence; put otherwise, human nature is at its best in this age.[5] Through this, poets wish to understand that the state of contemplative life is not harmed by its persistence, nor is it corrupted by the passage of time in the way that old people and ancient customs usually were. Gregory treats this characteristic of the contemplative life in the passage from *Moral readings* 6 cited above, in his explanation of *Mary hath chosen the best part*. He says, 'Mary's part cannot be taken away, because the works associated with the active life pass away along with the body, but the joys of the contemplative life become stronger and better in the end.' This is why among Minerva's names are Pallas or Athena. On this point, one should notice that 'Pallas' indicates newness, because the name Pallas means 'new woman'. However, the name 'Minerva' indicates immortality, for *min* means in 'not' in Latin, and *erva* means 'mortal'. Thus, their compound

---

[3] *Ibid.* 6.37.61 (PL 75:764), cited through the following paragraphs.
[4] *Homiliae in Ezechielem* 2.9 (PL 76:954).
[5] *Ibid.* 2.12 (1389a).

Minerua quasi 'immortalis'. Ut enim dicitur libro Sapiencie, *Clara est et nunquam marcescit sapiencia*. Et ideo contemplatiua uita, que est solius hominis sapientis, sicut docet Fulgencius in littera, depingitur a poetis sub ymagine dee Minerue, que apud eos dicitur esse immarcessibilis et immortalis.

Nota quemadmodum docet Augustinus, 14 *De trinitate*, loquendo proprie de sapiencia, 'Ad eam solam pertinet noticia diuinarum rerum, et circa talia uersatur uita contemplatiua'. Et ideo sub ymagine dee Minerue, que est dea sapiencie, depinxerunt poete statum uite contemplatiue, quod sicut dicit Fulgencius in littera, 'Sapiencia nec potest mori aut corumpi', et eodem modo uita contemplatiua nec moritur nec corumpitur. Ydeo in morte hominis contemplacio perficitur, sicut prius patuit per Gregorium, ubi fuit allegatus 6° *Moralium*, ibi enim dicit quod pars Marie nunquam ab ea auferri dicitur, quia actiue uite opera cum corpore transeunt, sed contempla|tiue uite gaudia melius in fine conualescunt.

Et de isto, scilicet quomodo sapiencia, circa quam uersatur uita contemplatiua, semper durat, nec potest per mortem ab homine auferri, plura loquntur philosophi, sicut patet per Senecam in suis epistolis. Unde in quadam epistola, que in libris aliquibus est 74, [probat] quod 'Nichil aduerse potest accidere sapienti. Stat enim sapiens rectus sub quolibet pondere, nulla res sapientem potest minorare'. Unde, sicut recitat Seneca in quadam alia epistola, 'Philosophus Sex[t]us solebat dicere Iouem non posse plus quam uir sapiens et uirtuosus'. Et pro ista pictura Minerue, que dea dicitur sapiencie a poetis, potest notari hic processus Augustini, libro 2° *De libero arbitrio*, ubi ostendit quod sapiencia 'nec tempore peragitur, nec migrat locis, nec nocte intercipitur, nec umbra intercluditur, sed omnibus eam diligentibus est proxima et omnibus sempiterna'. Et ideo in serie picture Minerua depingitur iuuentute grata, quia nunquam deficit ex senectute. Ymo in ista etate, id est in senectute, hominis sapientis sapiencia est maioris uirtutis et efficacie, sicut tractat Tullius, libro *De senectute*. Unde

---

107 proprie] *om.* A • eam solam] eum solum AI   111 Sapiencia] *om.* I
  114–17 ubi … conualescunt] *om.* A   114–15 ibi … pars] *om.* I   116 fol. 125vb
  • uite] *om.* I
118 uersatur] conuersatur I   120–21 plura … Unde, 121–22 que … est] *om.* A
  122 probat] *om.* O   123 quolibet] omni A   124–26 Unde … uirtuosus] *om.*
  125 Sextus] Sexius OA   126 quam] *adds* possit I   131 in … picture,
  132 ex senectute] *om.* A   134–39 sicut … sapiencia] *om.* A   134–39 Unde …
  sapiencia] *om.* I

'Minerva' means 'immortal'. For Sap 6:13 says, *Wisdom is glorious, and never fadeth away*. Therefore, as Fulgentius teaches explicitly, poets depict contemplative life, the property of the wise person alone, through the image of Minerva; they say that this state cannot waste away and is immortal.[6]

[106] Notice what Augustine teaches, *On the trinity* 14, where he is properly speaking about wisdom, 'To it alone belongs the ability to inspect divine things, and contemplative life is directed toward them.'[7] Therefore, in the image of Minerva, the goddess of wisdom, poets depicted the state of contemplative life, because, as Fulgentius says explicitly, 'Wisdom can neither die nor be corrupted.' In the same way, the contemplative life neither dies nor is corrupted. Therefore, contemplation becomes perfect when we die, as Gregory shows in the passage I cited above, in *Moral readings* 6. He says that 'Mary's part may never be taken from her, because, while the works of active life pass away with the body, the joys of contemplative life become stronger and better at the end.'

[118] On this point, namely how wisdom – and contemplative life is directed toward it – always endures and cannot be taken away from a person by death – the philosophers speak a great deal, as is evident from Seneca's letters. For this reason, in one of them, numbered 74 in some books, he proves that 'Nothing can unfavourably affect a wise person. For a wise person remains upright under any load, and nothing at all can diminish a wise person.' For this reason, Seneca says in another letter, 'The philosopher Sextus used to say that Jove could do no more than a wise and virtuous person.'[8] And with regard to this poetic picture of Minerva, whom the poets call the goddess of wisdom, one ought to notice Augustine's argument, in *On free will* 2, where he shows that wisdom 'is not shaken by time, nor does it depart from its place, nor is it cut off or shut out by night or darkness, but it is near and longlasting for all those who love it'.[9] Therefore, in the sequence comprising her picture, Minerva is depicted as thankful for her youth, because wisdom never fails on account of old age. Indeed, in old age, a wise person's wisdom is greater in its strength and capacity, as Cicero teaches in *On old age*.[10] For this reason,

---

[6] Fulg 2.1 (38/10–13), paraphrasing, *inter alia*, the citation in the next paragraph.
[7] Paraphrasing 13.20.25 (*PL* 42:1025), or summary of 9.11–12 (ibid. 969–72).
[8] *Epistula* 71.26, followed by *ibid.* 73.12.
[9] *Ibid.* 2.14.38 (*PL* 32:1262).
[10] E.g. *ibid.* 26.

135 Ieronimus, epistola 33, dicit quod 'philosophus Themistodes uel Themistocles, cum expletis 107 annis, moreretur; dixisse fertur se dolere quod tunc egrederetur de uita, cum sapere cepisset', quasi innuens quod tunc primum, scilicet in etate senili, uigeret in eo sapiencia.

140 [3] Sequitur | [tercia] pars picture de Minerue induicione, de qua Fulgencius, loquens in littera, dicit istam Palladem habere triplicem uestem propter eius triplicem cognicionem. Unde a Remigio uocatur *Triconia* uel *Trieina*, hoc est trina noticia. Nam uita contemplatiua uersatur circa Creatorem
145 uel circa creaturam, et ita est duplex, quia una est corporea, alia incorporea, sicut anima racionalis et angelus. Iste igitur est triplex modus contemplacionis diuine. Potest enim uiator Deum contemplari in suo uestigio, et hoc pertinet ad creaturam corpoream. In omni enim re corporali potest uiator Deum
150 contemplari, sicut in quodam uestigio. Unde Bernardus, omelia 13 *Super Cantica*, dicit, 'Tanta hec formarum uarietas atque numerositas specierum in rebus conditis quid aliud sunt quam quidam radii deitatis, monstra\ntes/ et quia uere sit ille a quo sunt, non tamen dicunt quid sit'?
155 Potest eciam uiator Deum contemplari in sua ymagine, et hoc pertinet ad animam et creaturam incorpoream. Angelus enim et anima racionalis sunt facti ad ymaginem Dei. Et de isto modo contemplandi Deum [per suam ymaginem], loquitur Anselmus, *Monologion*, capitulo 66, ubi ostendit quod 'mens racionalis,
160 quanto studiosius ad seipsam cognoscendam intendit, tanto efficacius ad Dei contemplacionem ascendit. Et quanto seipsam intueri necgligit, tanto a Dei contemplacione deficit et descendit'.
De tercio uero modo conte[m]plandi Deum [est in seipso, sine omni ymagine uel uestigio. Et de isto tercio modo contemplandi]
165 tractat | liber beati Dionisii intitulatus *De mistica theologia*, ubi alloquens Thimiotheum, dicit sic, 'Tu autem, amice Thimiothe, circa misticas uisiones, for[t]i contricione, sensibiles derelinque et intellectuales operaciones et omnia sensibilia et intelligibilia et

---

140 fol. 126ra • tercia] secunda O   143 a Remigio] et armiger A • uel] contraria ? A • *Trieina*] Triconia A, Trioina I   145 est²] *add* creatura AI
150 quodam] *adds* Dei A, *adds* diei I
156 et ... incorpoream] increatam et incorruptam A   158 per ... ymaginem] *om.* O • Anselmus] Augustinus A   160 seipsam] *adds* contemplantum uel A
161–62 ad Dei ... a Dei] a Dei A
163 contemplandi] conteplandi O   163–65 est ... contemplandi] specialiter IO
165 fol. 126rb   167 forti] formi] IO • sensibiles] sensus A

Jerome, in letter 33, says that 'Themistocles the philosopher, having lived for 107 years, was about to die; people report that he lamented that he was about to pass from life just when he had begun to be wise.'[11] It was as if he was hinting that only then, in old age, had his wisdom first flourished.

[140] [3] The third part of the picture concerns Minerva's clothing. Of this, Fulgentius says explicitly that Pallas has triple clothing on account of her threefold way of knowing things. For this reason, because she knows things in three ways, Remigius calls her *Triconia* or *Trieina*.[12] For contemplative life is directed toward the Creator or toward created things, and so it is double, since one of these is bodily, and the other is incorporeal, like the rational soul or an angel. Therefore there is a triple form of contemplating God. For a pilgrim in this world can contemplate God through his traces, and this pertains to bodily created things. A pilgrim can contemplate God in every bodily thing, as it were in a trace He's left. For this reason, Bernard, *On the Song*, sermon 13, says, 'What else might so great a variety and number of images of forms in created things be, other than flashing rays from the godhead, showing that they are true because of where they emanate, and yet not speaking clearly what He is?'[13]

[155] A pilgrim can also contemplate God in His image, and this pertains to the soul and to a created thing that's incorporeal. For both an angel and the rational soul were made in God's image. Anselm, in *Monologion* 66, speaks of this way of contemplating God through His image; he shows that 'the rational mind, the more industrious it is in trying to know itself, the more readily it ascends to contemplating God. Correspondingly, the more it avoids examining itself, the further it fails and falls from contemplating God.'[14]

[163] The third way of contemplating God is in Himself, without any image or trace. Blessed Dionysus discusses this third form of contemplation in his book *On mystical theology*. Speaking to Timothy there, he says, 'However, you, my friend Timothy, with regard to mystical visions, by a powerful stripping away, leave behind anything that can be perceived by the senses, as well as working with powers of intellect and everything that is either available to the senses or the intellect or

---

[11] *Epistola* 52.3 (PL 22:529).
[12] Fulg 2.1 (38/3–5), Mart 7.3 (75/25–29, also the source of lines 97–98), supplemented by VM3 10.1 (221/27–22/3), who ascribes his material to Remigius.
[13] *Ibid*. 31.3 (PL 183:941).
[14] *Ibid*. (PL 158:213).

exercicia omnia, et sicut est possibile consurge ad Eius
170 contemplacionem, qui est super omnem substanciam et eius
cognicionem'. Super quem locum dicit dominus Robertus
Lincolniensis, 'Mistica theologia est cum mens transcendit omnes
creaturas et seipsam, et ociatur ab omnibus actibus uirium, quibus
solent res create apprehendi, desiderans uidere et tenere Ipsum
175 qui est super omnia, et expectans in caligine cum Moyse, donec
manifestat se Desideratus, quant[u]m nouit conuenire, desiderantis
dignitati et suscepta[bilita]ti'. Hec ille.
  Nota modum loquendi Dionisii et commentatoris sui, et
est difficilis et obscurus. Tamen si uelint loqui de isto genere
180 contemplacionis diuine, qui fit per raptum et extasim et mentis
excessum, tunc patet clare quid uelint dicere. Tunc enim
contemplator nec utitur uestigio Dei, nec ymagine Dei, ad
contemplandum Deum, sed Deus, per graciam suam, dat sibi
unam aliam noticiam de Deo, perfecciorem quam fuit illa quam
185 prius habuit per uestigium Dei uel per ymaginem Dei. Ista
igitur est uestis triplex, qua uestiri dicitur Minerua, scilicet dea
sapiencie, per quam uita designatur contemplatiua. Et de ista
materia plura possunt notari que | tangit Ricardus in suis libris
de contemplacione.
190   [4] Sequitur quarta pars picture de Palladis armacione.
Siquidem poete fingunt eam cum galea in capite, cum egide in
latere. Scutum enim Palladis uocatur egis a poetis. Tercio pingunt
eam cum hasta uel lancea in manu, sicut de isto patet ex processu
Fulgencii in littera. Unde pro misterio huius picture, debet notari
195 contemplatorem Dei tripliciter ab hoste infestari. Uellet enim
diabolus intellectum eius decipere per errorem et ignoranciam,
et contra istam infestacionem, Minerua portat galeam lucentem
discrecionis et intelligencie in capite. Secundo, diabolus uellet
effectum destruere et inficere per maliciam, et contra hoc,
200 Minerua portat scutum dileccionis et caritatis in sinistro latere.
Istud enim scutum Palladis a poetis fingitur rotundum, et
significat caritatem propter sui perpetuitatem, quia caritas

170 omnem] *om.* A   173 omnibus] omnium AI   176 quantum] quantam O
177 susceptabilitati] suscepati O
178–85 Nota … Dei²] *om.* A   178 commentatoris] *om.* I   187–89 Et …
contemplacione] *om.* A   188 fol. 126^(va)
193–94 sicut … littera] *om.* A   194 debet] potest A   196 intellectum] mentem A
  199 effectum] *the more explicit* affectum A   • destruere et] contemplatoris A,
  contemplacionis I   202 quia] ut satis patet quia (*from here to* 209 cristacione
  same hand in a space originally blank) I

to their use. In this way, it is possible to rise up to contemplate God, who is beyond anything with a substance and any way of knowing such a substantial thing.' Robert Grosseteste, bishop of Lincoln, says of this statement, 'Mystical theology is when the mind transcends all created things, as well as itself; and when it takes a break from all those powers by which we are accustomed to perceive created things. Then the mind desires to see and grasp Him who is above all things. It waits in the darkness with Moses, until the desired one reveals Himself, to the degree that He knows will be appropriate to the worthiness and the receptiveness of the one who desires Him.'[15] So he says.

[178] Notice Dionysius's manner of speaking and that of his commentator Grosseteste, for it is difficult and obscure. Nevertheless, if they wish to speak of this kind of contemplation of divinity, which comes about through rapture, ecstasy, and being released from one's conscious mind, then what they wish to say becomes perfectly clear. For then the contemplative leaves off using either God's traces or His images to contemplate Him; rather, through His grace, God gives him a different indication of divinity, more perfect than the one he had previously, either from God's traces or his image. Therefore, this is the triple clothing in which Minerva, goddess of wisdom and image of contemplative life, is said to be dressed. Richard of St Victor treats many noteworthy things concerning this material in his books about contemplation.

[190] [4] The fourth part of the picture follows; it concerns Pallas's armament. For poets indeed portray her with a helmet on her head and the aegis, the name poets give Pallas's shield, on her side. Third, they depict her with a spear or a lance in her hand, as Fulgentius shows explicitly in his argument.[16] For this reason, so far as the meaning hidden in the picture, one ought to notice that someone contemplating God is attacked by the ancient enemy in three ways. For the devil wishes to deceive them intellectually through error and ignorance; against this attack, Minerva wears a shining helmet of discretion and intelligence on her head. Second, the devil wishes to destroy and infect their love through malice; against this attack, Minerva carries on her left side a shield of love and charity. Poets depict Pallas's shield as round, and that indicates charity on account of its perpetuity, for charity

---

[15] Ps.-Dionysius's prologue and Grosseteste's comment, pp. 21, 23.
[16] Fulg 2.1 (37/27–38/2, 38/5–6).

nunquam excidit. Tercio, diabolus inpedire nititur et abscindere
operis effectum, ne scilicet contemplator exerceat se in bono opere.
205 Sed contra hoc, Pallas portat et uibrat in manu hastam sedulitatis
et diligencie, per quam iugiter instat operacioni sancte et meritorie.
Ista est igitur triplex armatura dee Palladis seu Minerue, per quam
status describitur uite contemplatiue.

[5] Sequitur quinta pars picture de Minerue cristacione. Sicut
210 enim tangit Fulgencius in littera, super galeam quam Minerua
portat in capite est quedam crista eleuata. Et bene conuenit hec
pars pic|ture statui uite contemplatiue, ut enim dicit Prosper
in suo libro *De uita contemplatiua*, 'Contemplator sola celestia
[medit]atur, separatur a terrenis, a turba carnalium cogitacionum
215 longe positus, dulces carnis refugit affectus, uagos sensuum motus
restringit, in Domino delectatur, angelica dulcedine fruitur, legit
et in libro uite'. Et propter istas proprietates uite contemplatiue,
crista super galeam quam Minerua portat in uer[t]ice leuatur.

[6] Sequitur sexta pars picture de Palladis seu Minerue
220 stellificacione. Unde notandum quod isti poete, prout recitat
Alexander Nekham in sua *Methalogia*, attribu[un]t signa celestia
et sydera diuersis diis et deabus. Unde et Minerue attribuunt
signum Arietis, et ex hac causa finxerunt Mineruam Grecos
p[uni]isse, eo quod sub illo signo perclitati fuerunt, ut narrat
225 Alexander hec. Est autem hic notandum quod Greci redierunt
de Troia cum uictoria circa equinoctium uernale, quo tempore
sol ingreditur signum Arietis, et in rediundo fuerunt isti
Greci fatigati in mari diuersis tempestatibus, et causam istius
uexacionis fingunt poete fuisse deam Mineruam, que fuit
230 offensa cum Grecis duplici ex causa. Una causa fuit propter
eorum luxuriam, nam uirgo Cassandra, filia regis Priami, fuit
ab eis uiolenter oppressa. Fuit Minerua offensa propter eorum
superbiam et ingratitudinem, nam propter eam habuerunt
uictoriam de Troianis, | et tamen noluerunt hoc recognoscere,
235 nec Minerue, sicut decuit, sacrificare. Et ideo ipsa puniuit eos

203 nititur] conatur AI • abscindere] abscondere A 205 portat] *adds*
lanceam I 206 meritorie] contemplatiue I 208 describitur] intelligitur I
211 quedam … eleuata] cristata et eleuata uertice I 212 fol. 126^(vb) 214 meditatur]
contemplatur O • cogitacionum] cognacionum AI 215 motus] *om.* A
218 uertice] u'ice O
221 attribuunt] attribuit O 224 puniisse] posuisse O 225 hec] *om.* A, idem I
228 Greci] *om.* I • diuersis] uariis AI • tempestatibus] temptacionibus A
230 offensa] *adds* cum Grecis A 234 fol. 127^(ra) • tamen] *adds* in superbia A

never is lost. Third, the devil tries to hinder and cut off the good effect of one's deeds, lest the contemplative exert themself in good works. But against this attack, Pallas carries and shakes threateningly in her hand the spear of attention and diligence, through which she continually presses on in holy and worthy deeds. Therefore, this is the triple armament of the goddess Minerva or Pallas; through these arms, poets describe the state of contemplative life.

[209] [5] The fifth part of the picture follows; it concerns Minerva's crest. For, as Fulgentius says explicitly, there's a crest raised on top of the helmet that Minerva wears on her head.[17] This part of the picture is particularly appropriate for the state of contemplative life, for as Prosper says in his book *On the contemplative life*, 'A contemplative person thinks only of heavenly things and is separated from earthly ones; they're placed far away from the mob of carnal thoughts, flee the sweet desires of the flesh and restrain the wavering motions of the senses; they are delighted in God and rejoice in angelic sweetness, and read from the book of life.'[18] The crest is raised at the very top of the helmet Minerva wears on her head on account of these characteristics of contemplative life.

[219] [6] The sixth part of the picture follows; it concerns Pallas or Minerva's being made a star. For this reason, one should notice that the poets, as Alexander Neckam tells in his *Mythology*, assign heavenly zodiac signs and stars to the various gods and goddesses. For this reason, they assign to Minerva the sign Aries, because they related that Minerva had punished the Greeks by exposing them to danger at the time of this sign, as Alexander tells there.[19] Here one should notice that the victorious Greeks returned from Troy just around the spring equinox, the time when the sun enters the sign Aries, and in their return, the Greeks were harassed by many storms at sea. The poets ascribe all this trouble to Minerva, who was offended with the Greeks for two reasons. One was their lechery, for they violently raped Cassandra, the virgin daughter of king Priam. Minerva was also offended by their pride and ingratitude, for they conquered the Trojans through her aid, yet did not wish to acknowledge this or to make sacrifices to her, as was fitting. Therefore Minerva punished them

---

[17] Fulg 2.1 (37/27–38/3).
[18] Actually Hugh of Fouilly, *De claustro animae* 3.1 (*PL* 176:1087).
[19] VM3 10.6 (225/8–22).

per tempestates, sole existente in signo Arietis, quod est signum attributum dominio huius dee.

Sed quantum spectat ad propositum nostrum, possumus notare quod astro[nom]i, sicut ille Misael et alii, consueuerunt
240 attribuere diuersa membra hominis diuersis signis celestibus. Unde collum in homine attribuunt signo Tauri, et estimant illud membrum corporis humani esse de complexcione illius signi. S[imili]ter humeros et brachia hominis credunt esse de [complexione] Geminorum; s[imilit]er tibias in homine attribuunt
245 signo Aquarii, et estimant eos esse de complexione illius signi. Et isto modo dicunt de signo Arietis et de capite hominis. Dicunt enim quod caput hominis attribuitur isti signo et est de complex[i]one illius.

Et loquendo moraliter ad intellectum poetarum, ymaginem
250 Minuerue describencium, nichil aliud per hoc debet intelligi, nisi quod prelati et illi qui sunt capitanei aliorum specialiter sunt obligati ad istum actum, scilicet contemplacionem di[ui]norum, sicut de hoc loquitur Gregorius in suo *Registro*, et eciam in suo *Pastorali*, ubi sic dicit, 'Tantum debet accionem populi accio
255 transcendere presulis et prelati quantum distare solet uita pastoris a grege. Sic ergo, sicut necesse \est/, prelatus [sit] cogitacione mundus, accione [precip]uus, discretus in silencio, utilis in uerbo, + singulis compassione proximis, scilicet sed pre cunctis contemplacione suspensus'. Hec Gregorius. Ecce quod potissime
260 ad sta|tum capitis pertinet accio contemplacionis, et ideo bene iuxta ficcionem poeticam uendicat sibi Minerua signum Arietis.

[7] Sequitur septima pars picture de Palladis oneracione. Siquidem poete fingunt eam portare caput Gorgonis in pectore. Significat hec pars picture quod status uite contemplatiue semper
265 ante se debet habere *spiritum timoris Domini*, sicut pulcre docet Bernardus, libro 5 *Ad Eugenium*. Ubi notandum quod, sicut

---

237 dominio] *om.* A
239 astronomi] astrologi O • sicut ... alii] *om.* A   240 diuersa ... hominis] partis corporis humani A, \diuersa/ I • diuersis] *adds* figuris et A   241 estimant] autumant AI   243 Similiter, 244 similiter] Super, super O   244 complexione] *om.* O   248 complexione] complexone O
249 intellectum] modum A   252 actum] intellectum I • diuinorum] dinorum O   253 in ... in] in A   256 sit] debet esse A, *om.* O   257 precipuus] strenuus O   258 singulis] singularis O   260 fol. 127[rb] • accio] actus AI
262 oneracione] honoracione A   263 in pectore] *om.* I   265–66 sicut ... quod] libro ... Eugenium *after* 270 Bernardus A   266 Eugenium] *adds* de consideracione I

with storms, while the sun was in the sign Aries, which is assigned to the lordship of this goddess.

[238] But, so far as pertains to my argument, I may note that astronomers, Messahala and others, customarily assigned humans' various limbs to various heavenly signs. For this reason, they assign a person's neck to Taurus, and they think that the 'complexion' of that body part is that of this zodiacal sign. Similarly, they believe that the human shoulders and arms follow Gemini's 'complexion', and likewise, they assign the lower legs to Aquarius and think that their 'complexion' is the same as that sign's. They speak in the same way about Aries and the human head. For they say that the head is assigned to this sign and has the same 'complexion'.[20]

[249] Speaking in moral terms about what the poets mean when they describe the image of Minerva, one should understand from this that only prelates and those who are leaders of others are especially bound to this action, the contemplation of divine things. Gregory speaks of this both in his *Register* and in his *Pastoral rule*; in the latter, he says, 'The behaviour of a bishop or a priest ought to exceed that of his people to the same degree as a shepherd's life usually is distinguished from that of his flock. Thus, as is necessary, a priest should be pure in thought, vigorous in action, discrete in his silence, useful when he speaks, compassionate to each of his neighbours, but, before anything else, raised up in contemplation.'[21] So Gregory says. See: contemplative behaviour is particularly appropriate to the social rank of the head, and therefore, in accord with poetic fiction, Minerva appropriately claims for herself the sign Aries.

[262] [7] The seventh part of the picture follows; it concerns Pallas's burden. Poets indeed represent her as carrying the Gorgon's head at her breast. This part of the picture indicates that the state of contemplative life ought always to have before it *the spirit of the fear of the Lord* (Is 11:3), as Bernard teaches eloquently in *On consideration* 5. Here one should notice that, as

---

[20] Unfound; see the textual note.
[21] *Ibid.* 2.1 (*PL* 77:25–27).

patet in littera per Fulgencium, Gorgo idem est quod 'terror' uel 'timor', et talis debet esse omnis Dei contemplator. Scrutator enim temerarius, scilicet maiestatis, oprimetur a gloria, et ideo
270 bene dicit Bernardus, 'Hominem sanctum et Dei contemplatiuum sanctum facit affeccio sancta, et talis affeccio est gemina, scilicet timor Domini sanctus et amor sanctus. Hiis perfecte affecta anima, ueluti quibusdam [duobus] brachiis suis comprehendit, amplectit, et stringit. [Et] tenet +, et ait *Tenui eum et non*
275 *dimittam*'. Et sequitur, 'Quid tam timendum quam potestas, cui non potes resistere? [Quid eciam tam timendum] quam sapiencia, cui abscondi non potes? Poterat minus timeri Deus, alterutro carens. Nunc autem perfecte oportet, ut timeas Illum, cui nec oculus deest, omnia uidens, nec manus, omnia potens'.
280 Hec Bernardus. Istud igitur est caput Gorgonis quod pendet in pectore Palladis, scilicet dee sapiencie, quia *Inicium sapiencie timor Domini*.

[8] Sequitur octaua pars picture de Palladis probacione. Fingunt enim poete Wlcanum petisse a deo Ioue Palladem in
285 uxorem. Sed Pallas renuit, nec Uulcano misceri uoluit, sed contra | Uulcanum armis se defendit uiriliter. Et significat hec pars picture contemptum et destestacionem qua Dei contemplator detestatur ardorem uolumptatis et luxurie. Stat enim Uulcanus pro ardore carnalis uolumptatis. Unde et a poetis Uulcanus fingitur maritus
290 dee Ueneris.

Ista autem Pallas defendere se dicitur contra Uulcanum per arma sua, ut enim prius tactum est. Pallas portat in capite lucidam galeam discrecionis; portat eciam in latere scutum sincere dileccionis, et hastam uibrat in manu recte operacionis.
295 Et per hec tria genera armorum se defendit contemplatiuus diuinorum contra Uulcanum, id est carnalis lasciuie uoluptatem. Ubi notandum est quod sicut patet per Remigium, Uulcanus iste fingitur claudus. A poetis dicitur eciam alio nomine 'Lemnus', id est lutosus. Dicitur eciam Uulcanus, quasi 'uolitans candor'.

269 enim] *adds* omnis ? I   **270** sanctum] *om.* AI   **272** sanctus²] Dei sanctus A, *om.* I   • Hiis] *add* affeccionibus AI   **273** quibusdam duobus] duobus AI, quibusdam O   • suis] spiritualibus AI (*add* Deum *after* 273 comprehendit *and* 274 et¹ AI)   **274** Et tenet] Tenetis O   **275** sequitur] subdit AI   **276** Quid ... timendum] *om.* O   **278** alterutro] altero AI   • ut ... Illum] timere Illum A, timere I

284 Wlcanum] Elcanum I   **285** fol. 127va **286** armis se] carminis se ui A
292 enim prius] *om.* A   **296** uoluptatem] concupiscenciam A   **298** Lemnus] Lasciuus A, Lemnius I   **299** Uulcanus] Lucanus A

Fulgentius states explicitly, the name Gorgon means the same thing as 'terror' or 'fear', and everyone who contemplates God should be like that.[22] For someone presumptuously inspecting God's majesty will be driven down from glory, and therefore Bernard says appropriately, 'A holy person who contemplates God is made holy by their holy emotions, and those are twofold, namely holy fear of the Lord and holy love. The soul that has been moved perfectly by these these two, as if they were its two spiritual arms, includes, embraces, presses God. This person holds Him and says *I held him, and I will not let him go*' (Ct 3:4). Bernard continues, 'What should one fear so much as a power that you are unable to resist? Or a wisdom from which you cannot be hidden? The person who lacks either of these fears God less. Now, however, it is necessary that you fear Him completely, since He doesn't lack an eye to see all things, nor a hand to rule all things.' So Bernard says.[23] Therefore, this is the Gorgon's head that hangs on Pallas, goddess of wisdom's breast, because *The fear of the Lord is the beginning of wisdom* (Sir 1:16).

[283] [8] The eighth part of the picture follows; it concerns Pallas's testing. For poets report that Vulcan asked the god Jove for Pallas as his wife. But Pallas refused, nor did she wish to be joined sexually to Vulcan, but she defended herself against Vulcan spiritedly with her arms. This part of the picture indicates the contempt and disgust with which someone contemplating God hates the heat of sensuality and lechery. For Vulcan represents the heat of fleshly sensuality. For this reason, poets represent Vulcan as the goddess Venus's husband.

[291] Poets say that Pallas defends herself against Vulcan with her arms, which I discussed above. Pallas wears on her head the shining helmet of discretion; she also carries at her side the shield of true love, and she shakes threateningly in her hand the spear of proper deeds. Through these three kinds of armament the person who contemplates divine things defends themself against Vulcan, that is the sensuality associated with fleshly delight. Here one should notice that, as Remigius shows, Vulcan is depicted as lame. Poets also call him by another name, Lemnis, which means 'defiled with mud'.[24] He's also called Vulcan, as if it were derived from *uolitans candor* 'a flickering brightness'.

---

[22] Fulg 2.1 (37/25–27).
[23] *De consideratione* 5.14.30 (*PL* 182:805–06).
[24] Mart 8.4 (79/7–14).

300   Et ista eius tria nomina significant triplicem proprietatem consequentem carnalem uolumptatem. Nam talis feruor carnalis uolumptatis habet duracionis breuitatem, \quoniam significat Uulcanus, qui sic dicitur a 'uolando' et propter suam breuitatem/. Pallas, per discrecionem quam portat in capite,
305   contempnit uoluptatem.

      Secundo, uoluptas carnalis semper habet sibi annexam feditatem, quam significat Uulcanus qui dicitur Lemnus, id est lutosus. Et ideo Pallas, per sinceram affeccionem quam portat in latere, se defendit contra Uulcanum et suam deformitatem
310   contempnit. Tercio, feruor carnalis uoluptatis habet annexam obliquitatem, scilicet peccati peruersitatem, quam significat Uulcanus qui claudus fingitur a poetis. | Unde Ysodorus in suis *Soliloquiis* dicit, 'Deordinacio uolumptatis est maius peccatum omnibus aliis peccatis, et uniuersa uicia antecedit'. Et contra istam
315   luxurie iniquitatem Pallas se defendit per hastam suam, scilicet per boni operis rectitudinem siue equitatem. Sic igitur patet octaua pars picture de Minerue pudore et eius probacione. Si enim contingat contemplatorem diuinorum temptari et probari per motus carnis, statim motibus talibus contradicit, et ista armatura
320   triplici contra carnis illecebras spiritualiter [se] defendit.

      [9] Sequitur nona pars picture de Palladis administracione. Dicit enim Fulgencius in littera quod noctua attribuitur cure et tutele dee Palladis seu Minerue. [Unde ista est administracio Minerue] curare de custodia noctue. Est autem noctua, ut dicunt
325   auctores, auis lucifuga. Unde auis ista communiter non apparet de die, et hanc legem + debet uerus contemplator diuinorum custodire, ut scilicet nolit hominibus apparere, sicut desiderare solent ypocrite. Istud enim g[e]nus uicii, scilicet ypocrisis et simulacio sanctitatis, specialiter repugnat sanctitati uere, et ideo
330   nullo modo stat cum contemplacione uel statu uite contemplatiue. Et ideo bene dicit Crisostomus in suo libello *De compu[n]ccione cordis*, quod 'Nemo illorum, qui presentibus et caducis delectatur, celestia ac spiritualia contueri potest. Qui uero ista contempserit

---

   304 breuitatem] *add* in durando AI
306 semper] *om.* A   307–8 quam ... lutosus] *om.* AI   311–12 quam ... poetis] *om.* AI   312 fol. 127vb 312 Deordinacio] *add* carnalis AI   314 peccatis] *om.* I   318 temptari] contemplari AI   320 se] *om.* O
322 noctua] nociua A   323–24 Minerue ... Minerue] Minerue O   325 auctores] Isidorus et alii A, *adds* et alii I   326 debet] deberet O   • contemplator] cultor A   328–30 Istud ... contemplatiue] *om.* A   328 genus] gnus O   331 *compunccione*] compuccione O   333 contueri] gustare A

His three names indicate a threefold characteristic that results from fleshly delight. For this eagerness for fleshly delight lasts only a short time. This indicates the god Vulcan, who is called that from *uolando* 'flitting about' and refers to this brevity. Pallas disdains sensuality because of that [helmet,] discretion, she wears on her head.

[306] Second, filthiness is always associated with fleshly delight; Vulcan indicates this because he is called Lemnis 'defiled with mud'. Therefore Pallas, with that [shield,] true love, that she carries at her side, defends herself against Vulcan and disdains his deformity. Third, the heat of fleshly delight is associated with being twisted, that is with sin's perversity, which poets indicate by representing Vulcan as lame. For this reason, Isidore says in his *Soliloquies* that 'The disorder produced by sensuality is a greater sin than all the rest and precedes all the other vices.'[25] Against this sin of lechery, Pallas defends herself with her spear, that is the uprightness and justice of good works. Therefore, the eighth part of the picture reveals Minerva's modesty and the way in which it was tested. For if it should happen that a person who contemplates divine things is tempted and tested by the influences of the flesh, they should immediately oppose those influences and defend themself spiritually with this triple armament against the enticements of the flesh.

[321] [9] The ninth part of the picture follows; it concerns Pallas's duties. For Fulgentius says explicitly that the owl is given to the goddess Pallas or Minerva's care and protection. For this reason, it's Minerva's business to take pains at guarding the owl. For as authors say, the owl is a bird that flees light. For this reason, this bird doesn't usually appear in the daytime, and a person truly contemplating divine things ought to follow this rule, that they not wish to appear before people, as hypocrites usually want to. For this kind of vice, hypocrisy and simulated holiness, particularly battles against true holiness, and therefore it has no place at all with contemplation or the state of contemplative life. Therefore, Chrysostom says appropriately in his book *On compunction of heart*, 'None of those people who are delighted with unstable present things can contemplate heavenly and spiritual things. The person who has disdained these things

---

[25] *Synonyma* 2.9 (PL 83:487).

et uelut umbram, hec hominum preconia ac puluerem duxerit,
335 uelocius ad ista spiritualia contemplanda perueniet'.
   [10] Sequitur decima pars + picture de Palladis locacione.
| Poete enim fingunt Palladem locatam in arce, loco scilicet
eminenciori et securiori. Unde de ista Palladis locacione loquitur
Uirgilius in suo *Eneyde*, cuius uersus tangit Augustinus, primo
340 *De ciuitate Dei*, capitulo 2, 'Nonne', inquit, 'Diomedes et Ulixes
   [P]alladi[um] cesis summe custodibus arcis, / corripuere
   sacram effigiem + manibusque cruentis / uirgineas a[u]si diue
   contingere ui\t/tas'?
Uult dicere Uirgilius quomodo ymago dee Minerue fuit a Troianis
345 collocata in supprema arce ciuitatis Troiane, de quo loco Ulixes
et Dyomedes, qui fuerunt Greci, abstulerunt ymaginem istam
furtiue. Quamdiu enim illa ymago Palladis fuit in ciuitate, non
fuerunt Troiani deuicti, sicut dicit Uirgilius ibidem. Sed tamen
hinc contradicit Augustinus, ubi supra, dicens quod postea
350 uicerunt Troiam. De ista autem Palladis collocacionem in loco
eminenciori satis meminit Marcianus in libro *De nupciis*.
   Sed applicando ad propositum, nichil aliud uolunt poete
intelligere per istam loci sublimitatem, nisi uite contemplatiue
quietem et securitatem. Ut enim dicit Ambrosius in sua
355 epistola ad ecclesiam Uerssellentem, 'Hec est uita tuta et secura
pariter, quia in ea nichil est quod timeas. Hec enim uita ocio
non sustentatur, alienis molestiis non ocupatur, nec humanis
discursibus + urgetur'. Et de ista eciam securitate loquitur quedam
glosa Prouerbiorum 28, ubi dicit quod 'Iusti hominis et ueri
360 contemplatoris securitas leoni comparatur, quia, cum quoslibet
| insurgere conspicit, ad mentis sue confidenciam redit, et sc[it,
quia] uincit, quia illum solum diligit quem nemo inuitus amittit'.
Hec glosa. Et de ista uita contemplatiua et de eiusdem locacione
loquitur deuote Bernardus, *Super Cantica*, omelia 15, exponens
365 Canticorum *Adiuro uos filie Ierusalem per capreas*, 'Magna',
inquit, 'et stupenda Dei dignacio quod quiescere facit animam
contemplantem in sinu suo'. Ecce: Dei sinus \turris/ dee Palladis

   334 duxerit] fugerit A   335 ista] *add* celestia et AI
336 pars] pars | pars O   337 fol. 128ra 338–51 Unde … nupciis] *om*. A
   341 Palladium] Palladem I, scilicet Palladis *after* effigiem O
   342–43 uirgineas … uittas] *om*. I   342 ausi diue] assidiue O
353 loci] *om*. I   354–58 Ut … Et] *om*. A   358 urgetur] purgetur IO   359 ueri] Dei AI
   360 contemplatoris] contemplacionis I   • quoslibet] quodlibet animal A
   361 fol. 128rb 361–62 scit quia] sic que ? I, sic O   363 uita … locacione] uite
contemplatiue collocacione AI

as simply darkness, and who has treated people's flatteries as if they were dust will pass more quickly to contemplating spiritual things.'[26]

[336] [10] The tenth part of the picture follows; it concerns Pallas's location. For poets report that Pallas was placed in the citadel, that is in a higher and safer place. For this reason, Virgil speaks about Pallas's location in his *Aeneid*, and Augustine cites his verses, *On the city of God* 1.2, 'Didn't', he says, 'Diomedes and Ulysses

> once they had slaughtered the guards of the highest citadel, / seize the holy image – it was of Pallas – and with bloodstained hands, dare to touch the goddess's virgin headbands?'[27]

Virgil wishes to tell how the Trojans had placed the statue of the goddess Minerva in the highest citadel of the city. The Greeks Ulysses and Diomedes carried away the statue from this place by theft. For so long as Pallas's statue was in the city, the Trojans will not have been conquered, as Virgil says there. Yet Augustine contradicts this and says that they conquered Troy afterwards. In *On the marriage*, Martianus gives adequate information about Pallas's being kept in a very prominent place.[28]

[352] But applying this to my argument, poets wish to understand by the surpassing height of this place only the peace and security of the contemplative life. For as Ambrose says in his letter to the church of Vercelli, 'This is a life both safe and secure, for there is nothing in it you should fear. For this life is not preserved by leisure, does not concern itself with external annoyances, is not threatened by people's bustling about.'[29] A gloss on Prv 28 also speaks about this security, 'The security of a righteous and truly contemplative person can be compared to a lion, because, when they see anyone rise against them, they withdraw into their confident mind, and know, and thus conquer, because they love only that thing that no one would voluntarily lose.'[30] So the gloss says. Bernard speaks devoutly about contemplative life and its location, in *On the Song*, sermon 15, where he is explaining the verse *I adjure you, daughters of Jerusalem, by the roes* (Ct 2:7, 3:5), 'It is a great and astounding regard that God shows, when he makes the contemplative soul rest in his bosom.' See: God's bosom is the goddess Pallas's tower

---

[26] *Ibid.* 2 (fol. 117rb).

[27] *Aeneid* 2.166–68, cited *ibid.* (*PL* 41:15).

[28] Mart 48.11 (157/5–17).

[29] Cf. *Epistola* 63.82 (*PL* 16:1211).

[30] *Ibid.* (*PL* 113:1111), from Rabanus, *Expositio in Proverbia Salamonis* 3.28 (*PL* 111:77).

est insuper, ut dicit idem Bernardus, 'Deus custodit contemplantem ab infestantibus curis, protegitque ab inquietubus accionum et
370 molestiis negociorum, nec animam talem contemplantem omnino patitur suscitari, nisi ad ipsius anime uoluntatem'. Hec Bernardus.

[11] Sequitur undecima pars picture de Palladis prelacione. Ipsa enim fingitur dea bell\i/. Unde et nomen Palladis sumitur a Greco ydiomate ab 'haste uibracione seu contussione',
375 quemadmodum uiri bellatores solent facere. Et de isto tangit Alexander Nec[kam] in sua *Methalogia*, et bene conuenit hec pars picture uite contemplatiue, que ut prius tactum est, uibrat hastam recte operacionis, et per eam penetrat omnem hostem cuiuscunque male uel deordinate temptac[ion]is. Qualiter autem
380 Dei contemplator prelietur et, in prelio triumphando, prosperetur, tangit beatus Gregorius, *Super Ezechielem*, ubi dicit quod 'Pler\u/mque contingit quod ille qui plus in contemplacione rapitur, amplius in | temptacione fatigetur'. Ecce: contemplancium dominacio. Et subdit Gregorius quod 'Licet temptacio aggrauet,
385 ne contemplacio per elacionem contemplantem inflet, tamen contemplacio contemplantem faciliter eleuat, ne eum temptacio demergat'. Ecce: contemplancium triumphus et uictorie reparacio.

[12] Sequitur duodecima pars picture de Minerue pacacione. Nam sicut patet ex eius descripcione, non solum depingitur
390 preliis prelata, sed pace dotata. Unde dee isti, scilicet Palladi seu Minerue, consecratur et dedicatur a paganis arbor oliue, que, sicut de diuersis paganorum historiis patet, quod fuit arbor pacis. Unde et Romanorum historie narrant de Enea, eorum patre et principe, quod illo tempore quando uenit primo in Ytaliam, locuturus
395 cum rege Ewandro et uidit Palatem filium Ewandri. Statim Eneas cepit leuare ramum arboris oliue, uol\en/s ostendere eis se uenisse pacificum.

Sed applicando ad propositum Cristianorum, qualiter Pallas ista seu Minerua, uita scilicet contemplatiua, sit pace dotata,

---

372 prelacione] prel\i/acione I   374 contussione] concussione AI   375–76 Et ... *Methalogia*] om. A   376 Neckam] Nec| O   378 recte] racione A
379 temptacionis] temptacois O   383 fol. 128ᵛᵃ   384 dominacio] dimicacio A, deicacio (*over eras.*, = ? deificacio) I   386 contemplantem ... temptacio] om. A
387 reparacio] reportacio AI

388 pacacione] *blank* A   392 paganorum] om. A   394 primo] om. A
395 Palatem] Palladem A, preliantem (*over eras.*) I • Ewandri] *adds* qui fuit gigas fortissimus uenire sibi obuiam in prelium una cum a[l]iis uiris bellicis A
397 pacificum] *add* et (ut I) narrant historie Romanorum AI

on high, as Bernard says, 'God preserves the person contemplating Him from cares that attack them, and protects them from the turmoils of actions and the annoyances of business, nor does he allow such a contemplative soul to be disturbed in any way, unless that soul itself wishes to be.'[31] So Bernard says.

[372] [11] The eleventh part of the picture follows; it concerns Pallas's precedence. For she is depicted as the goddess of war. For this reason, the name Pallas is also derived from a Greek term for the shaking or pounding of her spear; warriors are accustomed to do this as a warning. Alexander Neckam discusses this in his *Mythology*,[32] and this part of the picture is quite appropriate for contemplative life. As I discussed above, Pallas shakes her spear of performing righteously, and with it, she pierces every enemy that may be associated with any evil or disordered temptation. Moreover, blessed Gregory discusses how someone contemplating God will do battle and, after triumphing in battle, will prosper. In *On Ezechiel*, he says, 'It often happens that, the more a person is rapt in contemplation, the more they may be exhausted by temptation.' See: this is the lordship associated with contemplative people. Gregory adds, 'Although temptation may weigh the contemplative person down, lest they swell up in pride, nevertheless contemplation easily raises up the contemplative, lest temptation drown them.'[33] See: this is the triumph of contemplatives and the recovery their victory confers.

[388] [12] The twelfth part of the picture follows; it concerns Minerva's peacefulness. For as is evident from her description, Minerva is depicted, not just as in the front line in battle, but also as endowed with peace. For this reason, the pagans consecrated and dedicated the olive tree to Pallas or Minerva. As various histories of the pagans show, the olive was the tree of peace. For this reason, Roman histories also tell that Aeneas, their common ancestor and leader, at the time when he first came to Italy, was to speak to king Evander but first saw Pallas, Evander's son. Aeneas immediately began to raise an olive branch, because he wished to show that he had come to them with peaceful intent.[34]

[398] To apply this detail to something useful for Christians, how Pallas or Minerva, contemplative life, is endowed with peace,

---

[31] *Ibid.* 51.10 (*PL* 183:1029).
[32] VM3 10.1 (221/29–32).
[33] *Homiliae in Ezechielem* 2.2.3 (*PL* 76:950).
[34] Cf. *Aeneid* 8.115–16.

400 pulcre *Super Cantica* loquitur Bernardus, omelia 42. Nam [sicut] uide[mu]s corporaliter inter catholicos obseruari, fideles morituri oleo solent oliuarum iniungi, sed uiri omnes contemplatores [s]unt, ut ibi docet Bernardus, spiritualiter mortui et finali pace dotati, dicente Iohanne [in Apocalypsi], *Beati mortui qui in*
405 *Domino moriuntur. Amodo iam dicit | spiritus ut requiescant a laboribus suis.* Et Paulus apostolus dicit, *Mortui estis et uita uestra obscondita est cum Cristo in Deo.* Super quo uerbo dicit Bernardus, 'Ego spon[s]e extasim non absurde uocauerim mortem. Hac autem morte utinam frequenter cadam, ut sic
410 euadam laqueos mortis, ut non senciam uite luxuriantis mortifera blandimenta, ut obstupescam a[d] sensum libidinis, et ad e[s]tum auaricie, ad stimulos iracundie et inpaciencie, ad + angores sollicitudinum molestiasque curarum. Moriatur anima mea morte iustorum, ut nulla eam [fraus] illaqueet, nulla iniquitas
415 oblectet. Bona mors, [que uitam non aufert, sed transfert in melius. Bona mors], qua corpus non cadit, sed anima subleuatur. Talis', dicit Bernardus, 'opino[r] excessus aut tantum, aut maxime, contemplacio dicitur'. Hec ille. Ecce: quies et tranquilitas pacis, qua dotata est Pallas et uita contemplatiua. Et sic finitur secunda
420 mithologia secundi libri.

400–1 sicut uidemus] uides O   401 corporaliter] cor\pora/ I   402–3 contemplatores sunt] contemplanti sunt AI, contemplatores dicunt O   404 in Apocalypsi] *om.* O   405 fol. 128vb 408 sponse] sponte IO • absurde] absconde A
411 ad sensum] assensum O • estum] effectum O   412 angores] langores AO, hangores I   414 eam fraus] causa fraus A, ea fraus I, eam ficcio O
415–16 mors ... mors] mors O   417 opinor] opinionem A, opinioni O
419–20 Et^2 ... libri] *om.* A

see what Bernard says elegantly in *On the Song*, sermon 42. For we see the custom observed among Catholics that the faithful, when about to die, are physically anointed with olive oil. But, as Bernard teaches there, all contemplative people are spiritually dead and endowed with final peace. John says in Apc 14:13, *Blessed are the dead who die in the Lord. From henceforth now, saith the Spirit, that they may rest from their labours.* And Paul says, *For you are dead, and your life is hid with Christ in God* (Col 3:3). Bernard says of this verse, 'There's nothing absurd in my having called the bride's ecstasy death. Would that I might frequently fall into such a death, so that I might avoid the snares of death, so that I might not feel those death-bearing allurements of this riotous life, that I might be insensible to desire being aroused, or avarice's burning, or being goaded into anger and impatience, or to anxious cares and their nuisances. May my soul die the death of the righteous, so that no deceit ensnares it, that nothing sinful delights it. That's a good death, one that doesn't carry away life, but changes it into something better. It's a good death, one in which the body does not fall, but the soul is raised up. Such best defines contemplation, even if it's a view excessive or too much.'[35] So he says. See; this is the rest and the tranquil peace with which Pallas and contemplative life are endowed. This is the end of the second mythology of the second book.

---

[35] *Ibid.* 52.3–5 (*PL* 183:1031).

[3]

Sequitur tercia mithologia secundi libri de dea Iunone, que fuit una de illis deabus certantibus coram Paride, filio regis Priami, de pulcritudine. Historia fuit tacta mithologia prima huius secundi libri. Fuerunt tres dee in silua Yda sedentes, coram
5 quibus dea discordie proiecit pomum, hanc habens scripturam, 'Pulcrior uestrum me habebit'. Una autem istarum dearum fuit Minerua, dea sapiencie, sub cuius ymagine, ut dicit Fulgencius, poete et philosophi + des|cripserunt statum uite contemplatiue. Sed alia istarum dearum fuit Iuno, sub cuius ymagine, ut dicit
10 Fulgencius, poete et philosophi consueuerunt depingere [statum] istius uite quam communitas hominum mundanorum consueuit communiter ducere. Quam uitam Fulgencius in littera uocat uitam actiuam.

Et tamen hic aduertendum quod, licet iste uir uenerabilis
15 Fulgencius fuit uir catholicus et fidelis, tamen utitur uocabulo 'uite actiue' equiuoce, et ad alium intellectum quod usi sunt sanctus Augustinus et alii doctores ecclesie. Nam Augustinus docet expresse quod uera uita, tam actiua quam contemplatiua, est uirtuosa et uite eterne meritoria et Deo accepta. Unde Gregorius,
20 6 *Moralium*, dicit, ut tactum est prius in mithologia precedente, quod magna sunt uite actiue merita, sed contemplatiue pociora. Sed Fulgencius utitur isto termino ad malum, et ideo dicit in prologo huius secundi libri quod uitam actiuam ducebant tiranni, sed apud modernos, eam ducit totus mundus. Ideo utendo isto
25 uocabulo ad intellectum quem modo habet, Fulgencius oportet dicere quod uita actiua stat hic pro modo uiuendi et uita quam seruat communitas mundi, et planum est quod ista uita mala est. *Mundus enim in maligno positus est*, ut dicit Iohannes apostolus.

Istam igitur uitam actiuam mundi, scilicet uanam et malam,
30 describunt poete sub ymagine dee I[un]onis. Siquidem Iuno pingitur

3–6 Historia … habebit] *om.* A   4 Yda] *adds* Frigie I   8 fol. 129ra • descripserunt] des‖descripserunt O   9–10 ut … philosophi] *om.* A   10 statum] *om.* O
14–22 licet … Sed] *om.* A   17 sanctus Augustinus] sancti Augustinus scilicet I
    22–23 in … libri] *om.* A   23 ducebant] apud antiquos I   24–25 utendo … Fulgencius] *om.* A   25 modo] *canc.* I   27 seruat] ducit A • uita] *om.* A
29 scilicet] *adds* uitam I • uanam et malam] malam uitam actiuam A
    30 Iunonis] Iouis O   30–31 Siquidem … pingitur] que est ista A

338

[3]

The third mythology of the second book follows. It concerns the goddess Juno, who was one of those goddesses contending about their beauty before Paris, Priam's son. I treated this story in the first mythology of this second book. The three goddesses were sitting in the forest of Ida, when the goddess of discord threw an apple before them; it had written on it, 'The most beautiful of you will have me.' One of these goddesses was Minerva, the goddess of wisdom, in whose image, Fulgentius says, the poets and philosophers described the state contemplative life. The second of these goddesses was Juno, through whose image, as Fulgentius says, poets and philosophers usually depicted that state of life that the community of worldly people most commonly follow. In his text, Fulgentius calls this Active Life.[1]

[14] However, one should notice here that, although the venerable Fulgentius was a faithful Christian, he nonetheless uses the phrase 'active life' ambiguously, and in a sense different from that used by St Augustine and other doctors of the church. For Augustine teaches explicitly that a true life, whether it's active or contemplative, is virtuous, deserving of eternal life, and accepted by God. For this reason, Gregory, in *Moral readings* 6, says, as I discussed in the preceding mythology, that the deserts of active life are great, but those of contemplative life more powerful.[2] However, Fulgentius uses this term in a pejorative sense, and therefore he says in the prologue to the second book that tyrants pursued the active life, but that these days the whole world pursues this life. Therefore, because he uses the word in the sense that it has today, Fulgentius needs to say that active life here represents that manner of living and the life that the community of this world serves, and that this life is obviously evil. As the apostle John says, *The whole world is seated in wickedness* (1 Io 5:19).

[29] Therefore, poets describe this active life of the world, empty and evil, in the image of the goddess Juno. Indeed, Juno is depicted

---

[1] Fulg 2.1, as 2.1/n.11 and 2.2/n.1 above.
[2] As 2.2/n.3 above. The reference to Augustine is probably general, but cf. ps.-Augustine, 'De vita heremitica' 41 (*PL* 32:1464).

[1] opibus ditata,
[2] uiribus orbata,
[3] uestibus aurata,
[4] pauonis curata,
[5] Iride | lustrata,
[6] capite uelata,
[7] in sublimi sita,
[8] et unguento lita.

Iste sunt octo partes picture quibus solent poete Iunonem depingere, per Iuno[nem] uolentes uitam mundanam, que communiter est mala, intelligere. Unde notandum est quod poete aliquando utuntur eadem re in bonum et in malum, sicut et nos fideles exponendo Sacram Scripturam facere consueuimus. Et isto modo fecerunt poete de ista dea Iunone. Nam, sicut fuit tactum mithologia quarta primi libri, per Iunonem intellexerunt unam partem prudencie, que dicitur memoria. Hic autem in toto libro 2°, depingitur sub ymagine dee Iunonis uita mundialis, quam Fulgencius uocat uitam actiuam.

[1] Est autem notandum pro prima parte picture quod ideo ista Iuno pingitur opibus ditata. Nam dicunt poete eam promisisse Paridi, filio regis Priami, habundanciam diuiciarum, [eo pacto quod Paris ille adiudicaret sibi pomum. Similiter ista dea Iuno dicitur dea diuiciarum, que] est uxor dei Iouis. Et Iubiter, ut dicit + Albumazar in suo *Introductorio maiori*, est significator substanciarum. Notandum est igitur quod, sicut sunt octo partes huius picture, ita sunt octo condiciones male quibus, ut [communiter] dicitur, ista Iuno est infecta, uidelicet cupiditas, infirmitas, curiositas, emulacio, circumuenc[i]o, ambicio, adulacio, simulacio. Quia igitur uita actiua plena est rerum cupiditate, ideo Iuno ista depingitur opibus ditata.

De hac cupiditate, qua infecta est uita ista actiua, loquitur | beatus Ambrosius in suo libro *De bono mortis*. 'Quid boni', inquit, 'est homini in hac uita, qui in umbra uiuit, nec expleri potest

---

36 fol. 129ʳᵇ   39 unguento] urgentis A
41 Iunonem] Iuno| O   43–44 sicut ... consueuimus] *om.* A
52 filio ... Priami] *om.* A   52–54 eo ... que] quia Iuno O   55 dicit] *adds* u O
56, 57 octo] septem A   58 ut ... Iuno] uita que communiter ducitur in hoc mundo A • communiter] *om.* O   59 curiositas] *om.* A, *a corr.* I
• circumuencio] circumuenco O
62 actiua] *om.* A • fol. 129ᵛᵃ   63 libro] *add* qui intitulatur AI   64 homini] *om.* A

[1] plentifully enriched,
[2] deprived of strengths,
[3] golden in her clothing,
[4] looked after by peacocks,
[5] lighted by Iris,
[6] with veiled head,
[7] placed on high,
[8] and smeared with ointment.

These are the eight parts of the picture by which poets customarily depict Juno; they wish to understand through Juno earthly life, which commonly is evil. For this reason, one should notice that poets sometimes use the same thing both with a good signification and with an evil one, just as we faithful have customarily done in explaining Holy Scripture. The poets did the same thing with the goddess Juno. For, as I discussed in the fourth mythology in book 1, through Juno, they understood Memory, one part of Prudence. However, here and throughout book 2, the image of the goddess Juno depicts worldly life, what Fulgentius calls active life.

[50] [1] With regard to the first part of the picture, one should notice that Juno is portrayed as plentifully enriched. For poets say that she promised Paris, king Priam's son, an abundance of riches, on the condition that Paris would award her the apple. The goddess Juno is likewise said to be the goddess of riches, since she is the wife of the god Jove. Jupiter, as Albumasor says in his *Larger introduction*, is the figure identifying substances.[3] Therefore, one should notice that, just as there are eight parts in this picture, there are likewise eight evil characteristics with which, it's often said, Juno is infected. These are desire, weakness, curiosity, rivalry, trickery, ambition, flattery, and deceit. Therefore, because active life is filled with the desire for things, Juno is depicted as plentifully enriched.

[62] Blessed Ambrose speaks about this desire – it poisons active life – in his book *On the benefit of death*, saying, 'What good is there for people in this life, since they live in darkness and cannot satisfy the demands

---

[3] *Introductorius maior* 5.4.7 (1:460–61).

65 cupiditatibus? Et tamen si expleatur diuiciis, ad huc fructum amittit quietis, quia cotidie cogitat quomodo posset custodire quod misera cupiditate adquisiuit, et sic miserabilius ea possidet, [que sibi] non possunt prodesse. Quid enim miserius quam istarum rerum to[r]queri custodia, quarum nichil prodesset
70 habundancia'? Nulli enim cupido prodesse poterit habundancia, quia quo magis habundauerit, eo magis indigebit.

Unde et dominus Innocencius papa, alludens fabule poetice de Tantalo, sic dicit, 'Tantalus sitit in mediis undis, et cupidus eget in mediis opibus, cui tantum est quod habet, quantum est quod non
75 habet. Nunquam enim cupidus utitur adquisitis, sed semper inhiat adquirendis, dicente Salomone, *Est quasi diues, cum nichil habeat; et est quasi pauper, cum tamen in multis diuiciis sit.* Cupidus et infernus uterque comedit, sed n[euter] dige[ri]t; + recipit, sed non reddit'. Sicut prius fuit tactum, hec est igitur prima miseria, qua
80 inficitur uita mundana, quam Fulgencius in littera uitam uocat actiuam. Et ideo dea Iuno, sub cuius ymagine pinxerunt statum ipsius uite actiue, pingitur ab eis opibus ditata.

[2] Sequitur secunda pars picture, quomodo Iuno ista depingitur uiribus destituta et orbata. | Unde sicut tangit Alexander
85 in sua *Mithologia*, poete semper fingunt Iunonem penuriam pacientem et impotentem ad expediendum propria negocia. Unde sicut patet ex Uirgilio, primo *Eneydos*, illo tempore quando Iuno ista uoluit submersisse naues Enee in uindictam Paridis, qui negauerat sibi pomum. Statim aduocauit auxilium E[ol]y, qui
90 fingitur deus uentorum, rogans eum quod ipse uellet procellas in mari concitare et naues Enee submergere. [Unde dicit sic Uirgilius:
Eole, namque tibi d<iuo>m pater atque hominum rex / Et mulcere dedit fluctus et tollere uentos, / Gens inimica michi Tirenum nauigat equor, / Ili[u]m <in> Italiam portans uictosque
95 penates, / Incute uim uentis, sub<mer>sas obrue puppes. Hec fuit] oracio autem dee \Iunonis/ [quam fecit] ad deum uentorum ad inducendum eum ad submergendum naues Troianorum.

---

65 Et tamen] partim A   65–66 diuiciis ... custodire] *marg.* I   66 cotidie] continue A, que I   67 possidet] custodiat et possideat A, possideat I
68 quo sibi] quo si O   69 torqueri] toq̄|ri O   70 poterit] *adds* diuiciarum I
74 cui] cupido enim A   78 neuter] non O • digerit recipit] \in/diget re|recipit O
79 Sicut ... tactum] *om.* A • prius] in fine 17ᵃ mithologie I
83 ista] *add* semper AI   84 fol. 129ᵛᵇ   87 patet] *om.* A   89 Eoly] Eolon A, Eloy O
91–96 Unde ... fuit] *om.* O   (92 diuom] dominum AI; 94 Ilium] Yleon et Yleam A, Iliam I • in] et AI; 95 submersas] submissas AI)   96 quam fecit] fuit O

put by their desires? Yet if someone should be satisfied with riches, they lose any benefit that peace might bring, because they would think daily how they might preserve what they have acquired through their wretched desire. Thus, they possess them in yet greater wretchedness, since those things cannot be of benefit to them. For what is more wretched than to be tormented with guarding things, whose abundance confers no benefit?'[4] For abundance may be of no benefit to a desirous person, because the more they have gathered together, the more needy they will be.

[72] For this reason, pope Innocent, alluding to the poetic fable of Tantalus, says, 'Tantalus is thirsty amid all the waters, and a desirous person feels lack in the midst of riches, since however much they may have, there's just as much they don't have. For a desirous person never uses what they have gained, for they always gape greedily after further acquisitions. As Solomon says, *One is as it were rich, when he hath nothing; and another is as it were poor, when he hath great riches* (Prv 13:7). Both a desirous person and hell eat, but they don't digest; receive, but don't give.'[5] As I said above, this is the first wretchedness that poisons worldly life, which Fulgentius calls in his text active life. Therefore, poets depicted the state of active life through this image, in which the goddess Juno is plentifully enriched.

[83] [2] The second part of the picture follows; it shows how Juno is depicted abandoned and deprived of strengths. For this reason, as Alexander Neckam says in his *Mythology*, poets always depict Juno as suffering want and powerless to resolve her own disputes.[6] Virgil shows this in *Aeneid* 1, from the occasion when Juno, as revenge on Paris, who had refused to grant her the apple, wished to have sunk Aeneas's ships. She immediately called for aid from Aeolus, who is depicted as the god of the winds. She asked him to stir up storms in the sea and sink Aeneas's ships. Virgil reports her words:

> Aeolus, since the father of the gods and ruler of mankind / Has granted you power to still the tides and to raise the winds, / A people, my enemies, sail the Tyrrhenian sea, / bearing Troy and its conquered household gods into Italy; / strike up your winds to full strength, sink and drown their ships.

This was Juno's prayer to the god of the winds to encourage him to sink the Trojans' ships.

---

[4] *Ibid.* 2.4 (PL 14; 541).
[5] *De miseria* 2.11 (PL 217:721).
[6] VM3 4.1 (165/22–27); *Aeneid* 1.34–80 (verses 65–69 cited).

Et uolunt per hoc poete intelligere imbecillitatem et
100 inpotenciam hominum mundanorum et hominum cupidorum.
Quando enim magis indigent, tunc diuicie eis magis deficiunt. Pro
exemplo istius potest notari una narracio que ponitur in *Historia
noua orientali* quam fecit compilari dominus Marcus de Ueneciis.
Ibi enim dicitur quod ciuitas illa, que in libro Hester dicitur Susis,
105 uocatur modo Baldach, ubi habitat magnus prelatus Saracenorum,
quasi esset papa uel patriarcha eorum. Anno ab incarnacione
Domini M^{mo}CC^{o}l, quidam rex Tart\ar/orum obsedit hanc
ciuitatem Susis, et per potenciam cepit eam. Iste autem calephus,
rex et dominus ciuitatis, habuerat unam turrim plenam auro
110 et argento et lapidibus preciosis rebusque \innumeris/ immensi
ualoris. Sed quia ist[e] caliphus | fuerat cupidus et auarus, ideo de
sufficienti milicia sibi non prouiderat, nec munera statum suum
decencia suis militibus largitus fuerat. Et ideo confucioni patebat.
Cepit enim ipsum rex iste Tartarorum et captum fecit includi
115 [in] illa propria sua turri, in qua fuit tanta copia auri et argenti et
lapidum preciosorum. Negato sibi omni cibo et potu, dixitque ei
rex Tartarorum, 'Quia thesa[u]rum habes auare et auide, et sicut
cupidus et tenax, non seruasti teipsum et tuam communitatem,
quam saluasse potuisses, nu[n]c adiuuet te thesaurus tuus, quem
120 tam auide dilexisti'. Quarto uero die sequenti, fame periit diues
ille. Sic igitur patet secunda pars picture, quomodo Iuno opibus
ditata, uiribus tamen est destituta et orbata.
  [3] Sequitur tercia pars picture de dee Iunonis induicione.
Fingunt enim poete, sicut prius fuit tactum, quarta mithologia,
125 per Fulgencium, quod Iuno fuit a Ioue ligata auro. Hoc est
quod [uitte et] fimbrie + uestium et indumentorum dee Iunonis
fuerunt auree. Et hec pars picture significat unam aliam miseriam
quam consueuit infici uita mundana, que a Fulgencio uita actiua
uocatur, et est uicium et miseria curiositatis in sumptuositate
130 uestium et indumentorum corporalium. De qua indumentorum
curiositate loquitur dominus | papa Innocencius in libro

---

100 hominum] domini A   102–4 una ... enim] historia A   105 uocatur ... Baldach] *om.* A • Saracenorum] unus A   108–9 et per ... plenam] *om.* I   110 rebusque] aliisque rebus A   111 iste] ista O • fol. 130ra • cupidus et auarus] nimis cupidus A   112 milicia] malicia I   115 in] intra A, et O   115–16 in qua ... preciosorum] *om.* A   117 thesaurum] *om.* A, thesarum O   119 nunc] nuc O   120 uero ... fame] uel quinto A   121 Iuno] *om.* I
126 uitte et] *om.* O • uestium] uestimentorum O   127 significat] figurat AI   130 indumentorum¹] *adds* sumptuosa I   130–31 indumentorum curiositate] *om.* A   131 fol. 130rb

[99] Poets wish to understand through this episode the weakness and powerlessness of worldly and desire-filled people. For when they need riches most, they most lack them. As an example of this, one might notice a story that appears in *The new history of the East* that Sir Marco Polo the Venetian had someone write down for him. He tells there that the city that's called Susan in Est 1:2 is now called Baldach or Baghdad. A great Muslim prelate lives there, one of a status equivalent to being their pope or patriarch. In the year 1250, a Mongol king laid siege to the city of Susan and captured it by force. The caliph, king and lord of the city, had a tower filled with riches, with gold and silver and precious stones and innumerable things of immense value. But because the caliph had been filled with desire and was covetous, he hadn't provided himself with a sufficient military force, nor had he been generous to his soldiers with rewards appropriate to someone of his status. This became evident in his downfall. For the Mongol king captured him and ordered him shut as a prisoner in his very own tower, in which there was such a great abundance of gold and silver and precious stones. Having denied him all food and drink, the Mongol king said to him, 'Because you have gathered treasure covetously and eagerly, and, as someone desire-filled and niggardly, you have preserved neither yourself nor your community, which you should have been able to have saved. So now let your treasure help you, since you have loved it with such eagerness.' This rich man died of hunger after four days.[7] Thus, the second part of the picture shows how Juno, although plentifully enriched, is abandoned and deprived of strengths.

[123] [3] The third part of the picture follows; it concerns the goddess Juno's clothing. For poets tell, as Fulgentius reported in the fourth mythology above, how Jove bound Juno with gold. This is because the headbands and the fringes of Juno's clothes and wraps were golden. This part of the picture indicates another wretchedness that has usually poisoned worldly life, what Fulgentius calls active life. This is the vice and wretchedness of undue ornateness in sumptuous dress and bodily clothing. Pope Innocent speaks about this excessively ornate clothing in his book

---

[7] *Il milione*, chs 7 (only lines 543–44) and 8.

De miseria condicionis humane, sic dicens, 'Primis parentibus
fecit Dominus perizomita post peccatum, sed diues mundanus,
ut uide[atur magnificus], satagit duplicibus uestiri, mollibus indui,
135   preciosis ornari. Sed quid aliud est homo uestibus preciosis et
deauratis ornatus, nisi *sepulcrum foris dealbatum, intus autem
omni spurcicia plenum*? Ibi enim iacintus et purpura, coctus et
bissus in limo putrescunt; aurum et argentum, lapides et gemme
in luto sordescunt; dignitas et potestas male iacent in puluere;
140   honor et gloria male sordent in cinere. Quare ergo, diues, inaniter
curiose *philateria tua dilatas et magnificas tuas fimbrias*? *Diues
iste, qui induebatur purpura et bisso, sepultus est in inferno.
Holophernes, qui sedebat in conop\eo/, quod erat ex purpura et
auro et smaragdo et lapidibus preciosis intextum*, iugulatus est a
145   Iudith. Audi ergo diues, super isto consilium sapientis, *In uestitu
ne glorieris umquam*. Et apostolus dicit, *Non in ueste preciosa*,
[et] prima Petri 3°, *ne sit extrinsecus capillatura, aut circumdacio
auri, aut indumenti uestimorum cultus*'. Hec Innocencius. Sic
igitur patet tercia pars picture, et tercia miseria qua uita ista
150   actiua est infecta.

[4] Sequitur quarta pars picture de dee Iunonis occupacione.
Ut enim dicit Fulgencius in littera, poete attribuunt pauum uel
pauonem | tutele siue custodie huius dee. Hec autem pars picture
significat quartam calamitatem seu miseriam consequentem uitam
155   mundanam, quam Fulgencius uocat actiuam uitam, et est miseria
emulacionis et inuidie, que a mundi miseri primordio incepit inter
homines uiuentes mundialiter habundare, dicente Petro Rauennate
in quadam omelia, scilicet 4, 'Inuidia fecit et emulacio ut mundi
tocius esset du[o]bus [fratribus] angusta latitudo'. Ista emulacio et
160   inuidia, sicut dicit idem Petrus, omelia 14, 'Primo contaminauit
terras fr[ater]no sanguine. Ipsa est que ex\ci/tauit germanos
germanum uendere; ipsa Moysen [fugauit, et Aaron] in fratris
iniuriam incitauit. Ipsa eciam Mariam, sororem Moysy, [liu]ore
germani propri maculauit. Hec eciam emulacio et inuidia ad Cristi
165   sanguinem peruenit'. Hec Petrus Rauanensis.

134 uideatur magnificus] uidetur O   136 foris] *adds* deauratum et A
137-38 coctus et bissus] *om*. A   143 conopeo] tentorio I   144 et smaragdo]
om. A   146-48 Et ... cultus] *om*. A   146-47 apostolus ... 3°] sapiens dicit I
147 et prima Petri 3°] prima Petri 3° *after* dicit AO   148 indumenti] *om*. I
152 pauum uel] *om*. A   153 fol. 130ᵛᵃ   154 quartam] quatriplicem A   157 habundare]
om. A   158 4] *add* in numero AI   159 duobus] duobus, diuitibus O • fratribus]
om. IO   161 fraterno] freno O   162 uendere] uenundare I • fugauit et Aaron]
om. O   163 liuore] amore O   164 propri] propinqui A

On the wretchedness of the human condition, and says, 'The Lord made our first parents aprons after they had sinned, but a worldly rich person, in order to appear splendid, strives to dress themself doubly, to be wrapped in soft things, and to be adorned with costly ones. But what else is a person adorned with costly and golden garments, except *a whited sepulchre on the outside, but within filled with every kind of impurity?* (Mt 23:27). For in the grave, blue and purple cloth, scarlets and fine linens rot in the mud; gold and silver, precious stones and gems grow dirty there, too; majesty and power, ill used, lie in the dust; honour and glory, ill used, grow dirty in ashes. Therefore, why do you rich, to no profit, *make your* ornate *phylacteries broad and enlarge your fringes?* (Mt 23:5). Such *a rich man, who was clothed in purple and fine linen, was buried in hell* (Lc 16:19, 22). *Holofernes, who sat under a canopy, which was woven of silver and gold, with emeralds and precious stones* (Idt 10:19), was slaughtered by Judith. Therefore, listen rich person, to the wise man's counsel on this point, *Glory not in apparel at any time* (Sir 11:4). And Paul says, *Not with costly attire* (1 Tim 2:9), and 1 Pet 3:3 adds, *Let your adorning not be the outward plaiting of the hair, or the wearing of gold, or the putting on of apparel.*'[8] So Innocent says. The third part of the picture is explained in this way, as well as the third wretchedness with which active life is poisoned.

[**151**] [4] The fourth part of the picture follows; it concerns Juno's business. As Fulgentius says explicitly, poets assign the peacock to the protection and keeping of this goddess.[9] This part of the picture indicates the fourth disaster or wretchedness resulting from worldly life, which Fulgentius calls active life. That's the wretchedness of rivalry and envy; from the very beginning of this wretched world, it began to flourish among people living in a worldly fashion. Peter Chrysologus of Ravenna says in sermon 4, 'Envy and rivalry brought it about that the whole breadth of the world is too narrow for two brothers.'[10] As he also says in homily 14, 'Rivalry and envy first infected the earth with a brother's blood (Gn 4:10–11). They also incited brothers to sell their brother (Gn 37:18–28); they drove Moses into exile (Ex 2:11–15) and incited Aaron to injure his brother – on the same occasion as Miriam, Moses's sister, was spotted with leprosy for her envy of her own brother (Nm 12:1–12). This rivalry and envy extended to the shedding of Christ's blood.' So Peter says.

---

[8] *Ibid.* 2.37 (PL 217:732).
[9] Fulg 2.1 (38/22–39/4, much recast).
[10] *Ibid.* (PL 52:195), followed by sermo 48 (PL 52:336).

Hec autem miseria emulacionis figuratur in pauonis custodicione. De quo loquens, Plinius libro [*blank*] *Naturalis historie*, dicit quod pauo, postquam egesserit fimum suum, statim iterum sorbet et reincorporat fimum suum prius egestum. Scit enim pauo, per nature instinctionem, fimum suum utile esse et necessarium usibus hominum. Et ideo, cauere uolens humanam utilitatem, fimum quem egesset iterum transglutit. Bene igitur in tutelam dee Iunonis tribuitur ista auis. Uita enim mundana, cuius Iuno est figura, plena est emulacione et miseria, et inter ceteros homines huius mundi, isti homines diuites solent et esse | ad inuicem inuidentes.

Dicit enim Augustinus, *De uerbis Domini*, quod 'Nichil est quod sic generent diuicie quomodo superbiam. Omne enim pomum, omne granum, omne frumentum, omne lignum habet uermem suum. Alius est uermis mali, alius piri, alius tritici. Uermis autem diuiciarum superbia est'. Sed ut deducit idem Augustinus in diuersis locis, ad superbiam sequitur inuidia et emulacio. 'Est enim', ut dicit Augustinus, 'inuidia specialis filia superbie; mater autem ista nescit esse sterilis'. Et ideo si uis filiam non habere, oportet te primo \matrem/ suffocare. Ut dicit idem Augustinus, *De disciplina Cristiana*, 'Superbia', inquit, 'est mater inuidie. Superbia enim + inuidos facit. Suffoca ergo matrem, et non erit filia'.

[5] Sequitur quinta pars picture de Iunonis illustracione. Pingitur enim a poetis Iuno ista Yride lustrata. Eo modo, scilicet quo a famulis et seruientibus, solent domini et domine circumdari et stipari. Unde poete uocant Yridem famulam Iunonis, sicut patet ex Ouidio et aliis, et idem tangit Alexander in sua *Methalogia*. \Similiter/ dicit in littera Fulgencius quod huic Iunoni yrim, quasi archum pacis, adiungunt, scilicet poete. Significat autem hec pars picture [unam aliam] miseriam consequentem, ut communiter, uitam istam mundanam quam Fulgencius uocat actiuam, et est simulacio dileccionis et amicicie. Ut enim prius tactum est, Iuno ista pingitur a poetis opibus ditata. Unde et in eorum estimacione dicitur dea diuiciarum.

---

166 figuratur] *adds* et inuidie I **167** [*blank*]] suo AI **170** instinctionem] instruccionem A **173** mundana] *add* siue actiua AI **174** emulacione et] emulacionis AI **175** diuites] mundi A • fol. 130vb
178 sic] \cicius/ I • generent] germinent A • quomodo] sicut A, quam (*over eras.*) I **183** Augustinus] *adds* in diuersis locis A **187** enim] *adds* omnino O
192 stipari] stirpari A, stapari I **192–94** sicut … dicit] *om.* A **196** unam aliam] *om.* O **197** uocat] *add* uitam AI

[166] This wretched rivalry is figured in Juno guarding the peacock. As Pliny says, *Natural history* X, the peacock, after it has expelled its dung, immediately eats it again and takes back into its body the dung it had previously expelled. For the peacock knows, by a natural instinct, that its dung is useful and necessary for human purposes. Therefore, wishing to avoid people using it, it gobbles down again the dung that it had expelled.[11] Therefore, this bird is appropriately placed in the goddess Juno's guardianship. For worldly life, which is figured by Juno, is full of wretched rivalry, and, among all the people of this world, rich people especially are customarily envious of one another.

[177] Augustine says, in *On the Lord's words*, 'There is nothing that riches produce so much as pride. Every apple, every seed, every grain, every tree has a worm in it. There's a worm for the apple, another for the pear, yet another for grain. However, the worm appropriate for riches is pride.' As Augustine argues in various places, envy and rivalry follow upon pride. For, as Augustine says, 'Envy is pride's favourite daughter, for her mother doesn't know how to be barren.' Therefore, if you don't wish to have this daughter, it's necessary for you to stifle her mother first. For Augustine says in *On Christian discipline*, 'Pride is the mother of envy, for pride makes people envious. Therefore, stifle the mother, and there won't be a daughter.'[12]

[189] [5] The fifth part of the picture follows; it concerns Juno's illumination. For poets depict Juno as being suffused with light by Iris. In the same way, lords and ladies are usually surrounded and hemmed in, that is by their household and servants. For this reason, as Ovid and others show, and Neckam says the same thing in his *Mythology*, poets call Iris Juno's servant.[13] Similarly, Fulgentius says explicitly that poets join Iris the rainbow, that is a bow of peace, to Juno. However, this part of the picture indicates a further wretchedness that commonly follows this worldly life that Fulgentius calls active life, and that is the pretence of love and friendship. For, as I have already pointed out, poets depict Juno as plentifully enriched. For this reason, she is, in their opinion, called the goddess of riches.

---

[11] Cf. 10.22.

[12] *Sermones de scripturis* 61.9 (*PL* 38:412–13), followed by *Sermones de diversis* 354.5 (*PL* 39:1565) and *Sermo de disciplina Christiana* 7 (*PL* 40:673).

[13] *Inter alia*, *Metamorphoses* 11.585; followed by VM3 4.6 (167/32–39) and Fulg 2.1 (39/4–8).

Sed | diuites isti non habent ad aliquem hominem ueram
amiciciam, sed tantum simulatam, sicut de isto pulcre loquitur
Carnotensis in sue *Policraticon*, libro 3°, capitulo 22, ubi dicit
quod 'diues utique familiaris esse nouit, amicus nunquam uel
raro'. Unde recitat ibidem quod apud antiquos fuit dubitatum
et quesitum an esset possibile quod aliquis de numero diuitum
esset alicui amicus, loquendo proprie et utendo termino 'amicicie'
ad uerum intellectum. Et tandem fuit finaliter determinatum
pro parte negatiua, scilicet quod apud diuites nunquam uel raro
inuenitur amicicia proprie dicta. Et racio antiquorum, ut tangit
ibidem dominus Carnotensis, erat 'quia contraria in eodem
esse non possunt. Sed cupiditas et caritas sibi inuicem maxime
contrariantur. Sed diuites plurum habent cupiditatem; ergo
minimum caritatem'.

Sed deficiente caritate, necesse est ueram amiciciam deficere,
sicut deducit Augustinus in sua epistola ad Macedonum. Et
addit ibidem ad propositum alia multa dominus Carnotensis ad
probandum quod uera amicicia non est in cordibus diuitum,
maxime illorum qui ducunt istam uitam actiuam, de qua in ista
mithologia loquitur Fulgencius. Quia sicut patet ex prologo huius
secundi libri, 'ista uita actiua est habendi insaciata, rapiendi cauta,
seruandi sollicita; plus semper cupit quam habeat; nec considerat
quid expediat, sed semper anelat | ut rapiat'. Sed ubi sic cupiditas
unitur, uera amicicia, uera caritas exulat et proscribitur.

Istam igitur fictam et fucatam \simulacionem/ amicicie,
que inter ducentes istam uitam actiuam solet habundare, poete
uolunt intelligi per yridem. Nam impressio ista pretendit pacem
et amiciciam, quia penes nos est curuatura illius archus, et penes
celum est gibbositas seu conuexum. Sed qui archu utitur ad
pugnandum solet facere e contrario, nam penes sagittarium arcus
curuatura et concauitas est, sed uersus hostem est gibbositas seu
conuexum. Et ideo theologi dicunt quod Deus inposuit istum
archum in nubibus in signum federis et reconsiliacionis Dei et
hominis, sicut patet Genesis 12.

Sed quia in ista yride est uarietas in apparicione, nam nunc
apparet in oriente, nunc in occidente, nu[n]c in septemtrione,

---

201 fol. 131ra   hominem] *om.* A   210 racio] fuit responsio A, fuit racio I
   211 erat quia] sub hiis uersubus I   213 contrariantur] aduersantur AI
219 maxime ... qua] sed contra A   223 fol. 131rb   • cupiditas] *om.* I   224 unitur]
   uiuitur AI
225 fucatam] fugatam I   227 uolunt intelligi] solent intelligere AI   228 nos] *om.* A
235 uarietas] *adds* colorum A   236 nunc²] nuc O

[201] But rich people don't have true friendship with anyone, only pretended friendship. On this point, John of Salisbury speaks eloquently in *Polycraticus* 3.22, saying, 'Certainly, a rich person knows how to be familiar, but rarely or never how to be a friend.' For this reason, he tells there how, among the ancients, it was questioned and debated whether it is possible that any rich person might be a friend to anyone, were one to speak properly and use the term 'friendship' in its true sense. In the end, question was decided in the negative, namely that one seldom or never finds friendship in the strict sense among rich people. And the reason the ancients gave, as the bishop of Chartres presents it there, was that 'because contraries cannot exist in the same thing. And avariciousness and charity are completely opposed to one another. But rich people are extremely desirous, and therefore they have the least amount of charity.'[14]

[215] But where charity is lacking, true friendship is necessarily lacking, as well. Augustine argues out the point in his letter to Macedonius.[15] And John of Salisbury, in the passage I've already mentioned, adds many other things that are to the point. These go to prove that true friendship doesn't exist in rich people's hearts, and most particularly in those that follow the active life, about which Fulgentius speaks in this mythology. For, as he shows in the prologue of his second book, 'Active life is incapable of having enough, secretive in theft, careful about saving; it always desires more than it has, nor does it consider what's appropriate – it just always yearns after what it may steal.'[16] Wherever desire is joined to active life in this way, true friendship and true charity are exiled and proscribed.

[225] Poets wish to understand this pretended and dark imitation of friendship – it flourishes among those who are accustomed to follow active life – through Iris, the rainbow. For this phenomenon pretends to offer us peace and friendship, because the curved arc of this bow faces us, and its bulge or convex side faces heaven. But when someone uses a bow in combat, they are accustomed to point it the other way, for the curvature of a bow, its concave face, is toward the archer, and its bulge or convex curve is toward the enemy. Therefore, theologians say that God placed this bow in the clouds as a sign of a covenant and reconciliation between God and humans, as is evident in Gn 9:13.

[235] But because the rainbow is various in its appearances – sometimes it appears in the east, sometimes in the west, sometimes in the north,

---

[14] *Ibid.* 3.12 (*PL* 199:501), mostly summary, rather than citation.
[15] *Epistola* 155.1.1 (*PL* 33:667).
[16] Fulg 2.1 (36/15–19).

sed nunquam in meridie, ubi calor habundare consueuerit, est eciam breuitas in huius yridis duracione. Parum enim consueuit durare et quasi subito euanescere. Et propter hoc, poete uolunt intelligere per yridem fictam et simulatam dileccionem. Unde dicunt nomen *yridis* deriuari ab *eris* Grece, quod idem est quod 'lis' Latine seu 'dissencio'. Talis est enim simulata dileccio, que non est dicenda amicicia, sed ficcio est pocius reputanda, et lis et contencio quam amicicia et dileccio. Et de isto, nota Carnotensem in capitulo preallegato | tercii libri sui *Policratici*, ubi recitat sentencias [Cris]pi et Tulli Citheronis.

[6] Sequitur sexta pars picture de Iunonis uelacione. Pingunt enim poete deam istam Iunonem capite uelatam, ut enim dicit Fulgencius in littera. Uelato capite Iunonem pingunt, eo quod diuicie omnes semper sunt absconse, et possimus per istam diuiciarum absconsionem conuenienter intelligere omnium mundanorum diuiciis inherencium callidam circumuencionem. Et sequitur ista proprietas ex precedenti, eo quod enim sunt simulati et ficti amici; consequens est quod sunt fraudulenti proximis suis et uicinis. Ille enim qui decipit et circumuenit illum cui dicit se amicum, non est timendum quin circumueniret et deciperet uicinum suum.

Unde hic potest notari processus Gregorius, 10 *Moralium*, ubi ostendit quomodo tales homines deceptores et fraudulenti reputantur apud homines uitam istam actiuam ducentes sapientes et industr[i]. Ibi enim doctor iste, expondendo illud uerbum Iob 12, *Deridetur iusti simplicitas*, dicit sic, 'Huius mundi sapiencia est cor machinacionibus tegere, sensum uerbis uelare, que falsa sunt uera ostendere, que uera su[n]t falsa demonstrare. Hec nimirum prudencia usu a iuuenibus scitur; hec a pueris precio discitur; hanc qui sciunt ceteros superbiendo despiciunt; hanc qui nesciunt subiecti et timidi eam in aliis mirantur, quia ab eis hec eadem duplicitas industrie nomine palliata diligitur, dum mentis peruersitas urbanitas uocatur'. Hec Gregorius. Et subdit Gregorius,

238 huius yridis] eius A   241 nomen] *om.* I   243 ficcio] *om.* A   244 contencio] dissencio A   244-46 Et[2] ... Citheronis] *om.* A   245 fol. 131[va]   246 Crispi] Sippi O   Crispi ... Citheronis] de li[s] (= ? litteris) tam Cripsi historia quam eciam Tulli et Cheroni I
247 uelacione] uolacione A   251 omnium] hominum A   257 uicinum suum] amicum I
258 hic ... processus] *om.* A, *adds* uenerabilis doctoris beati I   260 uitam] *om.* I   261 industri] industros O   262 *Diridetur*] Dirigetur AI (*and* A *only at* 668)   264 sunt] sut MS

but never in the south, where it's usually quite warm –, the rainbow also appears for only a short time. For it usually has lasted for only a short while and suddenly disappears. For this reason, poets wish to understand by the rainbow a love that is fake and simulated. For this reason, they say that the noun *iris* 'rainbow' is derived from the Greek word *eris*, in Latin the same as 'quarrel' or 'dispute'.[17] Pretended love is like that, and it should not be called friendship, but rather accounted a fake, and more closely resembling a quarrel or dispute than love and friendship. On this point, notice what John of Salisbury says in the chapter from *Policraticus* 3 I've cited above, where he repeats the opinions of Crispus and Cicero.

[247] [6] The sixth part of the picture follows; it concerns Juno's veiling. For poets depict the goddess Juno with a veiled head, as Fulgentius says explicitly. They depict Juno with her head covered, because riches are always hidden;[18] we might appropriately understand through this hidden nature of riches the cunning trickery of all worldly people's grasping for riches. This characteristic follows from the preceding one, since they are also fake and pretended friends; it follows that they are deceitful with their neighbours. For one should not be in any doubt whether a person who deceives and tricks a person whom they say is their friend, may not also trick and deceive their neighbour.

[258] For this reason, one should here notice Gregory's argument, *Moral readings* 10, where he shows how such deceitful and fraudulent people are esteemed as wise and diligent among people who follow active life. There the learned Gregory, in explaining Iob 12:4, *The simplicity of the just man is laughed to scorn*, says, 'The wisdom of this world is to hide one's heart in scheming, to cloak one's meaning in other words, to show false things as true, and to prove true ones to be false. It's no wonder that youths know to use this "prudence", or that boys learn that it brings rewards; those who know it, in their pride, despise others, and those who don't, fearful subordinates, marvel at it in others. For its practitioners delight in calling this duplicity by the cloaked name "diligence", and also describe a perverse mind as "elegant".' Gregory adds,

---

[17] VM3 4.6 (167/34–38).
[18] Fulg 2.1 (38/19–20).

270 | '*Iustorum simplicitas deridetur*, quia uirtus ueritatis ab huius mundi sapientibus fatuitas creditur. Omne enim quod innocenter agitur ab eis proculdubio stultum reputatur, et quicquid in opere ueritas app[ro]bat carnali sapiencie fatuum sonat'. Sic igitur patet causa sexte partis picture de Iunonis \uelacione.

275 [7] Sequitur septima pars de Iunonis sublimacione/. Poete enim fingunt istam deam Iunonem deam regnorum, sicut docet Alexander in sua *Methalogia*, et ideo depingitur in sublimi sita. Unde in signum regalis dominii, pingitur a poetis Iuno ista portare sceptrum regale. Et significat hec pars picture uicium ambicionis,
280 quo solent laborare homines uitam actiuam ducentes, intelligendo, sicut intelligit Fulgencius, per uitam actiuam illam quam dicimus mundanam et inter homines huius mundi frequencius usitatam.

Et sequitur ista proprietas septima dee Iunonis ex sexta parte picture ipsius. Nam ex quo homines mundani, qui uitam ducunt
285 actiuam, sunt fraudulenti eciam dolosi, consequens est quod sunt ambiciosi et aspirantes ad dignitates huius mundi. Unde de hoc loquitur beatus Gregorius, 10 *Moralium*, ubi dicit quod 'Huius mundi sapiencia, [que dolo plena est et fraudulencia, precipit sibi obsequentibus honorum] culmina querere, adepta temporalis
290 glorie uanitate gaudere, irrogata ab aliis [mala] multiplicius reddere, cum uires suppetunt nullis resistentibus cedere, cum uero uir[tutis] possibilitas deest, quicquid per maliciam explere non ualet, hoc in pacifica | bonitate simulare'. Hec ille. Et de isto bene loquitur Bernardus, libro primo *Ad Eugenium*, 'Plena est', inquit,
295 'ambiciosis ecclesia. Non est quod iam \ex/horreat in studiis et molicionibus ambiciosis, non plus quam spelunca latronum in spoliis uiatorum'.

[8] Sequitur octaua pars picture de dee Iunonis linicione. Pingitur enim a poetis unguentis uariis delibuta seu delinita.
300 Unde propter ista unguenta, uocatur a poetis alio nomine *Unxia*, sicut tangit Alexander in sua *Methalogia*. Et significat hec pars picture uicium adulacionis, quo infecti sunt [communiter] homines huius mundi, quorum uita, secundum Fulgencium, uocatur actiua.

---

270 fol. 131vb 273 approbat] apparebat O   273–74 Sic ... uelacione] *om.* A
276–77 sicut ... Methalogia] *om.* A   279 picture] iste A
287 Gregorius] *adds* in loco prius allegato I   288–89 que ... honorum] est huius mundi O   298 honorum] bonorum A • adepta] ex illa A   290 mala] *om.* O
291 reddere] credere I   292 uirtutis] ueritatis A, nec ueritatis I, uirium O
293 fol. 132ra 293–97 Et ... uiatorum] *om.* A
298 Iunonis] *om.* I   300 unxia] unxta *over eras.* I   300 sicut ... Methalogia] *om.* A
302 communiter] *om.* O   303 huius mundi] isti mundani AI

'*The simplicity of the just is laughed to scorn*, because these worldly wise believe that virtuous truth is stupidity. For there's no doubt that they account anything that's done innocently as stupidity, and to the wisdom of the flesh any act that truth approves of gets called folly.'[19] That's the explanation of the sixth part of the picture, which concerns Juno's veiling.

[275] [7] The seventh part, about Juno's elevation, follows. For, as Alexander Neckham teaches in his *Mythology*, poets represent the goddess Juno as the goddess of kingdoms, and therefore, she is depicted in an elevated place. For this reason, as an indication of her royal power, the poets depict Juno as carrying a royal sceptre.[20] This part of the picture indicates the vice ambition, for which people following active life customarily labour. (Recall that, as Fulgentius understands it, active life is what we call worldly life, the one most often used among people of this world.)

[283] Juno's seventh characteristic follows from the sixth part of her picture. Since worldly people, those who follow active life, are given to fraud and treachery, it follows that they are ambitious and aspire to worldly honours. For this reason, Gregory speaks of this in *Moral readings* 10, saying, 'The wisdom of this world is filled with fraud and treachery. It instructs its adherents to seek worldly eminence with its honours, to rejoice in having achieved vain worldly glory, to return injuries inflicted on them by others multiply; so long as they have strength to do so, to give way to no one who resists them; and when they lack the capacity to use strength, so that they have no power to fulfil their malice, then they dissimulate peaceful goodness.' So he says. Bernard speaks appropriately about this in *To Eugene* 1, 'The church is filled with ambitious people. There's no one today who shudders at ambitious pursuits and labours, any more than one does at robbing travellers in a den of thieves.'[21]

[298] [8] The eighth part of the picture follows; it concerns Juno's anointing. For poets depict her as stained or smeared with various ointments. For this reason, because of these ointments, poets call her by the alternate name *Unxia* 'anointing goddess', as Neckam says in his *Mythology*.[22] This part of the picture indicates the vice flattery, which routinely poisons worldly people, those whose life Fulgentius calls active.

---

[19] *Ibid.* 10.29 (*PL* 75:947), continuing in the next paragraph but one.
[20] VM3 4.5 (167/17–20).
[21] *De consideratione* 1.10 (*PL* 182:741).
[22] VM3 4.3 (166/13–16).

Et regnat istud uicium specialiter in curiis diuitum. Iuno autem ista dea fingitur diuiciarum, sicut patet ex prima parte picture. Unde, ut ibi fuit tactum, poete fingunt quod Iuno ista promisit Alexandro Paridi copiam opum et habundanciam diuiciarum, eo pacto quod ipse uellet Iunoni, tanquam dee pulcriori, adiudicare pomum illud a dea discordie proiectum in presencia illarum trium dearum.

De isto autem adulacionis uicio, qualiter solet specialiter regnare in curiis diuitum, loquitur Alanus in suo libello *De planctu Nature*, ubi sic dicit, 'Huius pestis adulacionis, scilicet pestilencia, percuciuntur principum laterales, palatini canes, adulacionis artifices, fabri laudis, figuli falsitatis. Hii sunt qui magniloqua commendacionis tuba in | auribus diuitum citharizant, qui mellite [adul]acionis fauos foras eructuant, qui – ut emungant munera – capita diuitum oleo adulacionis inungunt, prelatorum auribus puluinaria laudis subiciunt, qui ab eorum palliis aut ficticium excuciunt puluerem aut uestem sophistice deplumat in plumine'. Hec ille. Et i[de]o bene dicit Petrus Blesensis in quadam epistola quod 'Adulacio in palaciis diuitum eliminat ueritatem; illi enim soli, scilicet adulatores, in diuitum et magnatum graciam admittuntur'. Hec ille. Sic igitur patet octaua pars picture de Iunonis linicione, etc.

305–6 sicut ... tactum] Unde A   307 Alexandro] *om.* A   308–10 adiudicare ... dearum] etc. sicut prius A
311 specialiter] *om.* I   697 scilicet] *om.* A   316 fol. 132rb 317 mellite] mollite I
• adulacionis] palpacionis AO, palpac[i]uus I   318 capita] rapina I
320 ficticium] bitumine A   321 plumine] puluine A, *a large addition* AI (*see the Appendix*)   • ideo] io O   321–23 Et ... ille] *om.* A   323 scilicet adulatores] *om.* I   324 admittuntur] *a large addition* I (*see the Appendix*)   325 etc.] et sic finitur tercia methologia secundi libri A, et sic finita est in ordine proxima mithologia Fulgencii et tercia secundi libri I

This vice rules particularly in the courts of rich people. Moreover, Juno is represented as the goddess of riches, as the first part of the picture shows. For this reason, as I said there, poets tell that Juno promised Alexander Paris plenty and abundant riches, on the condition that he would choose to award the apple – remember that the goddess Discord threw it into the vicinity of three goddesses – to Juno as the most beautiful goddess.

[311] Alan of Lille, in his little book *On Nature's complaint*, speaks about the vice of flattery and how it especially rules in rich people's courts. He says, 'This plague of malicious flattery strikes princes' sidekicks, dogs of the palace, craftsmen of flattery, smiths of praise, potters of falsehood. They're the ones who make music on the grandiloquent trumpet of praise for rich people to hear, who belch forth sweet honeycombs of flattery; they're the ones who anoint rich people's heads with the oil of flattery so as to extort rewards, the ones who lay down pillows of praise under prelates' ears, the ones who knock imaginary dust from their cloaks or speciously de-feather a garment that has none.' So he says.[23] And Peter of Blois says appropriately in one of his letters that 'In the palaces of rich people, flattery eliminates truth, for only flatterers are admitted to the favour of the rich and powerful.' So he says. Therefore I have explained the eighth part of the picture, concerning Juno's anointing, etc.

---

[23] *Ibid.* p7 (*PL* 210:469), followed by Peter, *Epistola* 77 (*PL* 207:238).

[4]

Sequitur quarta mithologia de dea Uenere, que fuit tercia dea de numero illarum dearum que certabant coram Paride de pulcritudine. Sub cuius ymagine, philosophi, secundum quod dicit Fulgencius in littera, consueuerunt depingere ymaginem uite
5   uoluptuose. Ut autem dicit \Fulgencius/, contrauersia fuit inter sectas de ista uita uoluptuosa. Nam Epicurei dixerunt uoluptatem esse rem bonam et laudabilem; unde et in uoluptate constituebant felicitatem. Sed secta Stoycorum dixerunt oppositum; Sto\y/ci enim dixerunt quod uoluptas est res nulla, quia est res mala, et malum
10 non est, nisi boni carencia. Unde uerba Fulgencii in textu sunt hec, 'Terciam deam Uenerem in similitudinem uite uolupt[u]arie posuerunt, quam uolumptatem Epicurei dixerunt rem bonam, sed Stoyci rem | nullam. Epicuri enim uoluptatem laudant; Stoyci uoluptatem dampnant. Epicuri libidinem colunt, sed Stoyci
15 libidinem nol[u]nt'. Hec Fulgencius.
    Eundo igitur ad seriem \picture/ huius dee, sciendum est quod, sicut patet per Fulgencium in littera et per Alexandrum in sua *Metalogia*, a poetis solet depingi [sub hac forma]:
      [1] corpore nudata,
20   [2] in mari deportata,
      [3] cute dealbata,
      [4] floribus sertata,
      [5] unguentis afflata,
      [6] Graciis stipata,
25   [7] uirore placata,
      [8] et concha locata.
    Iste sunt octo parte[s] picture quibus solent philosophi et poete deam Uenerem depingere. Et significant iste partes picture mala que concomitantur et consequntur uitam istam quam Fulgencius
30 uocat uoluptuariam seu uoluptuosam.

1 dea²] *om.* AI   2–3 de pulcritudine] *om.* A   3 philosophi] poete A (*but cf.* 12)
    6 de … uoluptuosa] *om.* A   •   dixerunt] asserunt A   8 enim] esse I
    9 nulla] \uana/ ? A, uana *over eras.* I   10–12 uerba … quam] ipsam I
    11 uoluptuarie] uoluptuose A, uoluptaarie O   12 posuerunt] *adds* philosophi A
    13 fol. 132ᵛᵃ   •   nullam] malam A   14 libidinem] *om.* I   15 nolunt] nolentes O
17–18 et … Metalogia] *om.* A   18 sub hac forma] *adds* pingitur enim A, *om.* O
    20 in mari] \<.>ani/ I   •   in mari deportata] equore delata A   27 partes] parte O

358

[4]

The fourth mythology, about the goddess Venus, follows. She was the third of those goddesses who contended about their beauty before Paris. According to Fulgentius's text, in her image, philosophers customarily depicted the Life of Pleasure. However, as Fulgentius says, there was a dispute between the philosophical sects about the life of pleasure. For the Epicureans said that pleasure was a good and praiseworthy thing; for this reason, they placed true happiness in pleasure. But the Stoics said the very opposite, for they said that pleasure was nothing at all, for it is an evil thing, and evil is only the absence of good. For this reason, Fulgentius says, 'They discussed the third goddess Venus as a likeness of the life of pleasure, and the Epicureans said pleasure was a good thing, but the Stoics that it was nothing at all. For the Epicureans praise pleasure, and the Stoics condemn it. The Epicureans cultivate pleasure, but the Stoics want nothing to do with desire.'[1] So Fulgentius says.

[16] Therefore passing to the sequence of this goddess's picture, one should know that, as Fulgentius's text and Alexander's *Mythology* show, poets usually depict her in this image:

[1] with her body bare,
[2] carried about in the sea,
[3] with white skin,
[4] crowned with floral garlands,
[5] blowing out ointments,
[6] surrounded by the Graces,
[7] pleased by growing plants,
[8] and placed in a seashell.

These are the eight parts of the picture by which philosophers and poets usually depict the goddess Venus. These parts of the picture indicate the evils that accompany and follow the life that Fulgentius calls pleasurable.

---

[1] Cf. Fulg 2.1 (36/22–37/5).

[1] Prima igitur pars picture de dee Ueneris denudacione significat indigenciam et paupertatem, que communiter solet consequi carnalis lasciuie uoluptatem. Dicente Augustino, libro *De doctrina Cristiana*, 'Luxuria, inquit, + inimica uirtutibus, [inimica] Deo, perdit omnem substanciam, [et pro presenti uoluptate luxuriosi deliniens, futuram eam non sinit cogitare paupertatem]'. Et de ista opum oblacione, que sequitur ex uoluptatis deordinacione, dicitur metrice, 'Tollit opes, famam, sensum uiresque libido'. Et ideo significanter dicit [sapiens], Ecclestiastici 9, *Ne des fornicariis animam tuam in ullo*, [*ne perdas te et animam et hereditatem tuam*]. Exemplo filii prodigi, de quo habetur in euangelio Luce 15, quod dissipauit substanciam suam, uiuendo luxuriose. Et de ista nuditate luxurie loquitur Ambrosius in suo libro *De ieiunio*, ubi dicit quod 'luxuria seminarium est et origo omnium uiciorum. [Nec', sicut ipse ibidem declarat, 'est huiusmodi dictum suum contra apostolum, qui dicit quod *cupiditas* et auaricia est *radix omnium malorum*], quoniam ipsa luxuria est mater auaricie. Postquam enim exhauserit quis proprias facultates luxuri|ando, tunc postea querit auar[a] compendia'. Hec Ambrosius. Sic igitur patet prima pars picture.

[2] Sequitur secunda pars [picture] \de/ dee Ueneris deportacione; siquidem poete eam pingunt nauigantem in mare. Et significat hec pars picture amaritudinem et remorsum consciencie que semper consequntur hanc deordinacionem uoluptatis et carnalis lasciuie. Unde de hoc bene loquitur Boycius, libro 3º *De consolacione*, prosa 7ª dicens sic, 'Quid loquar de corporis uoluptatibus, quarum appetancia est anxietatis plena, earumque sacietas est plena penitenci[e]? Tristes enim esse uoluptatum exitus, quisquis reminisci libidinum suarum uolet, euidenter intelligit'.

Et de isto dicto Boicii potest notari illa narracio Agellii, libro 10 *Noctium Atticarum*, de philosopho Demostene et

---

31 significat] figurat AI 34 inimica] inimicicia O 35 inimica] et IO
  35–37 et ... paupertatem] etc. O 36 uoluptate] uoluntate A, uoluptatem I
  • luxuriosi] *adds* graciam A • deliniens] declinans I • sinit] sunt I 39 dicit sapiens] dicitur O 40 ne ... tuam] etc. O 41–43 de ... luxuriose] Luce 15 A
  42 habetur] narratur I 44 *ieiunio*] remedio A 45–47 Nec ... malorum] *after* 44 ieiunio A, *om.* IO 49 fol. 132ᵛᵇ • auaricie] auara AI 50 Sic ... picture] *om.* A, *adds* de dee Ueneris nudacione I
56 *consolacione*] confessione A 57 anxietatis] anxietatibus A, anxietas I
  58 penitencie] penitencia AIO
62 libro ... *Atticarum*] *om.* A • philosopho De-] \de/ I

[31] [1] Therefore, the first part of the picture, concerning the stripping of the goddess Venus, indicates the need and poverty that commonly are accustomed to follow the pleasure of bodily wantonness. Augustine says in *On Christian teaching*, 'Lechery is the enemy of the virtues and of God; and it loses all it possesses. Lecherous people, soothing themselves with present pleasures, don't allow themselves to consider their approaching poverty.'[2] On this theft of one's riches, a result of pleasure's lack of regulation, there's a verse, 'Sexual desire carries away riches, one's good name, one's sense and one's strengths.'[3] Therefore, the wise man pointedly says in Sir 9:6, *Give not thy soul to harlots in any point, lest thou destroy thyself and thy inheritance.* Take as an example the prodigal son in Lc 15:11–32, who wasted all his goods in living riotously. Ambrose speaks about lechery's bareness in *On fasting*, where he says, 'Lechery is the seminary and source of all the vices, because it's the mother of covetousness. Nor', as he asserts there, 'is this conclusion contrary to Paul's statement when he says *The desire of money*, avarice, *is the root of all evils* (1 Tim 6:10), because lechery is the mother of avarice. For after someone has poured out all his own resources in living riotously, they afterwards still seek profits through covetousness.'[4] So Ambrose says. Therefore this explains the first picture.

[51] [2] The second part of the picture follows; it concerns the goddess Venus's carriage. Poets indeed depict her as sailing in the sea. This part of the picture indicates the bitterness and remorse of conscience that always follow the disorder of pleasure and fleshly delight. For this reason, Boethius says appropriately, in *On the consolation* 3p7, 'What should I say about bodily pleasures, since the desire for them is filled with worry, and their fulfilment with remorseful penance? Anyone who chooses to recall their sexual desires, clearly understands that all the conclusions to delights are sad ones.'[5]

[61] And, regarding Boethius's statement, one should notice the story that Gellius tells in *Attic Nights* 10 about the philosopher Demosthenes and

---

[2] Not *De doctrina*, but rather Jerome, *Epistola* 21.9 (PL 22:383).
[3] Walther 31449a.
[4] *De Elia et jejunio* 19.69 (PL 14:722).
[5] *Ibid.* in init.

de Tayde meretrice. Carnotensis \eciam/ tangit eandem sentenciam, libro 6 *Policraticon*, capitulo 20, ubi dicit quod 'Uoluptatis finis est penitencia. Si modo non credis, D\e/mesten[i crede], qui satis urbane hoc Tayde dicitur respondisse'. Apud Corinthum enim fuit meretrix quedam famosa, Tays uel Lays nomine, que in antiquis libris Agellii uocatur Lays per 'l'. Ad istam autem meretricem, propter suam singularem pulcritudinem, accedebant maiores et p[otenc]iores Grecie, dantes sibi pro mercede quam illa uolebat petere, ita ut communiter ista Tays nullum \accepit/ uel ad concubitum admisit, nisi pro quinquaginta libri argenti, ad quam se extendit medietas maioris talenti. Uenit igitur ad eam Demostenes philosophus, petens ab ea + | temptatiue concubitum, et Tays ab eo peciit dimidium talentum, sicut ab aliis recipere consueuit. Quo audito, Domeste[ne]s se auertit et ab ea recessit, et in suo recessu Taydi respondit, 'Ego, inquit, tanti penitere non emo'. Hoc est dictum, ex quo ista uoluptas carnalis non est sine penitencia et displicencia in fine. 'Nolo eam emere ita care', et subdit Carnotensis in suo *Policraticon*, 'Inicia [cup]idinis dulcia sunt super mel et fauum, sed eius nouissima quouis absinthio sunt amariora'. Et ideo merito Uenus ista depingitur in mare deportata.

[3] Sequitur tercia pars picture de dee Ueneris dealbacione. Poete enim solent eam depingere dealbatam in cute. Unde a poetis Fulgencius in serie littere dicit Uenerem istam uocari Affrodissam, quod nomen bene conuenit isti albedini cutis quam habere dicitur dea Uenus. Nam nomen Affrodisse deriuatur a uocabulo isto Greco *afros*, quod in Latino est idem quod 'spuma', et specialiter stat pro spuma marina, que simul habet annexam et albedinem et inpuritatem. Et ideo bene + conuenit nomen Affrodosse uoluptati uenere[e], eo quod licet in meretrice appareat exterius pulcritudo cutis, tamen interius sub cute est maxima habundancia impuritatis et spurcicie. Unde bene recitat Boycius ad propositum, libro [blank] *De consolacione*, prosa [blank], | auctoritatem Aristotelis dicentis, 'Si Linceis oculis homines uterentur, ut eorum uisus obstancia queque +

---

65 Demesteni crede] D\e/mesten O   67 famosa] *add* et formosa AI
67–68 uel ... l] nomine A   70 potenciores] pulcriores IO   74 fol. 133ra
• temptatiue] temptare I, te||temptatiue O   • concubitum] *om.* A
76 Demostenes] Domestes O   78 dictum] d̄cu A, dictu I   79 eam] *om.* AI
80 cupidinis] libidinis O   81 quouis] conclusionis A   82 in mare] *sic* AI
84–91 Unde ... ueneree] *om.* A   90 bene] *adds* contingit O   91 ueneree] uenere|
(*followed by* eo) O   94, 95 blank] *om.* AI   95 fol. 133rb

the whore Thais. John of Salisbury also treats the account in *Polycraticus* 6.20, where he says 'Penance is the end of pleasure. If you don't believe now, believe Demosthenes, who is reported to have responded quite wittily to Thais.' For there was a famous whore in Corinth, named either Thais or Lais (in the older copies of Gellius, she is called Lais, with an 'l'). On account of her unique beauty, the greatest and most powerful men of Greece sought her out. They gave her in payment whatever she wanted to ask, so that Thais routinely accepted no one nor allowed him in her bed, unless he paid fifty pounds of silver, and her price went up as high as half a greater talent. Demosthenes the philosopher came to her, tentatively seeking to sleep with her, and Thais demanded from him half a talent, just as she usually received from others. Having heard this, Demosthenes turned away and left her, and, as he went, he answered Thais, 'I won't buy penance at so great a price.' He said this because fleshly pleasure doesn't come without penance and displeasure in the end. 'I don't wish to buy penance so expensively.' The bishop of Chartres adds, 'The beginnings of sexual desire are sweeter than honey or its comb, but the last things everywhere associated with it are more bitter than wormwood.' Therefore, Venus is deservedly depicted as carried in the sea.[6]

[83] [3] The third part of the picture follows; it concerns the goddess Venus's whitening. For poets usually depict her with a white skin. For this reason, Fulgentius, in the course of his discussion, says that poets call Venus Aphrodite, a name that agrees well with the whiteness they attribute to her skin. The name Aphrodite is derived from the Greek word *afro*, which means the same thing as *spuma* 'foam' in Latin.[7] The word specially refers to sea-foam, which includes both whiteness and impurity at the same time. Therefore, the name Aphrodite is appropriate for sexual pleasure, because, although there may appear to be external beauty in a whore's skin, nevertheless inside, under the skin, there's a great plenty of impurity and filth. For this reason, Boethius speaks to the point in the *Consolation*, citing the authority of Aristotle, 'If people might use Lynceus's eyes, so that their sight might

---

[6] Gellius 1.8; *Polyc*. 6.23 (*PL* 199:622).
[7] Fulg 2.1 (39/14–18), differently moralised.

penetraret, nonne + introspectis uisceribus, illud Taydys corpus, pulcherrimum in superficie, turpissimum uideretur'?, quasi diceret ymmo ita appa\re/ret. Et ideo bene dicit Crisostomus in suo libello
100 *De reparacione lapsi*, 'Si diligenter consideres que sunt, que inter illam cutem que tibi formosa uidetur lateant, que eciam sunt, que inter nares tegantur, que infra fauces, que intra uentrem, nichil aliud pronunciabis esse istam cutis pulcritudinem et corporis, nisi *sepulcrum* quoddam *dealbatum*, quod foris apparet hominibus
105 decorum, sed intus plenum est sordibus et immundiciis'. Hec Crisostomus.

[4] Sequitur quarta pars picture de dee Ueneris adornacione. Siquidem poete solent istam Uenerem depingere rosis coronatam. Hec enim dea portat sertum roseum in capite in signum
110 ruboris et uerecundie ignominose que consequitur feditatem et immundiciam huius peccati, scilicet luxurie. Et de ista ignominia que consequitur luxuriam bene loquntur pagani et eciam doctores nostri Cristiani. Dicit enim Agellius, libro 10 *Noctuum Atticarum*, quod 'uoluptas ista carnalis, quando nimia est, \scilicet/ quando
115 est uiciosa, est omnium rerum fedissima. Unde et eos qui se isti uicio beluino dederunt, "grauissimi uicii" uocabulis Greci appellant, nos | autem incontinentes dicimus'. Hec Agellius. Et ibidem recitat Agellius super hoc sentenciam [So]cratis et Ypocratis. 'Ypocrates', inquit, 'uir diuine sciencie, existemabat
120 coitum uenereum esse quondam partem morbi te[terim]i, quem Latini uocant morbum comicialem'. Nota quod morbus comicialis est morbus caducus, et iste philosophus Ypocras reputauit quod omnis luxuriosus est computandus inter epilenticos. Quia sicut epilenticus pro tempore passionis priuatur
125 usu racionis, ita et luxuriosus pro \tempore/, quo est in ista feditate delectacionis, [et nulla racio et nulla discrecio], dicente Augustino, 14 *De ciuitate*, capitulo 16, 'Libido siue luxuria totum commouet hominem, ita ut momento ipso temporis, quo ad eius peruenitur extremum, pene omnis acies et quasi omnis uigilia
130 racionis obruatur'. Et ideo Crisostomus in suo originali

97 penetraret] penetret A, penetrarent O   99 appareret] *om.* A
100–1 inter ... que²] *om.* A
112–13 pagani ... Cristiani] infideles pagani A   116 uocabulis] *om.* A   117 fol. 133va
118 Socrates et] *om.* AI, Xenocratis et O   119 diuine] magne I   120 teterimi] tet'i|mi A, t'riui I, temeriui O   122 philosophus ... reputauit] Ypocras existimabat A   125 et luxuriosus] luxus A, in luxurioso I   126 et nulla¹ ... discrecio] *om.* O   128 momento] mouendo (*with abl.*) A

pierce whatever's placed between, wouldn't Thais's body, so very beautiful on the surface, once its inner organs were examined, appear particularly shameful?'[8], as if to say it would indeed appear so. Therefore, Chrysostom properly says in his little book *On the restoration of the fallen*, 'If you should carefully consider what the things are that may also be hiding under that skin that seems beautiful to you, the things that might be covered in the nostrils, or within the jaws or the belly, you would never assert that this beauty of skin and body was anything other than a *whited sepulchre* (Mt 23:27) that might appear, on the outside, pleasing to people, but that is filled with dirty and unclean things within.' So Chrysostom says.[9]

[107] [4] The fourth part of the picture follows; it concerns the goddess Venus's ornament. For poets indeed customarily depict Venus crowned with roses. This goddess wears a garland of roses on her head to indicate her redness, the disgraceful shame that results from the dirtiness and uncleanness of the sin lechery. Both pagans and our Christian learned men speak appropriately about the disgrace that follows lechery. For Gellius says, in *Attic Nights* 10, that 'Fleshly pleasure, when it is excessive, namely when it is a vice, is the filthiest of all things. For this reason, the Greeks identify those who have devoted themselves to this monstrous vice by the words "the most grievous vice", what we Latin-speakers call "incontinent people".' So Gellius says. In the same place, Gellius repeats the opinion of Socrates and Hippocrates on the point. He says, 'Hippocrates, a man of divine learning, considered sexual congress as if a part of the disease called *teterimi*, which Latin speakers call *morbus comicialis* "epilepsy".'[10] Notice that epilepsy is the 'falling sickness', and the philosopher Hippocrates thought that every lecherous person should be considered among the class 'epileptics'. For just as an epileptic is deprived of the use of reason during the time of a seizure, likewise a lecherous person lacks all reason and discretion during the time they spend in the filth of delight. Augustine says, *On the city* 14.16, 'Desire or lechery agitates the entire person, so that, at the moment in which it approaches its climax, nearly all mental sharpness and, as it were, all the watchfulness of reason are overwhelmed.'[11] Therefore, Chrysostom in his commentary

---

[8] Ibid. 3p8.10. Also cited, with a reference to Aristotle, *Fasciculus morum* 650/31–36.
[9] Ibid. 14 (298/68–74).
[10] Ibid. 19.2.1–2, 7–8.
[11] Ibid. (PL 41:424–25).

Super Mattheum, omelia 57ᵃ, dicit quod 'Luxuria facit luxuriosum esse porcum. Quod', inquit, 'malam non operatur luxuria? Porcos enim de hominibus facit, ymmo porcis deteriores'. Propter igitur ruborem uerecundie que consequitur uicium et peccatum luxurie, merito dea Uen[u]s coronata est rosis.

[5] Sequitur quinta pars picture de dee Ueneris inunccione. Nam poete depingunt eam aromatibus et unguentis delibutam. Unde sicut recitat Alexander Necham in sua *Methalogia*, a Cipro, insula unguentorum et aromatum feracissima, | accepit dea Uenus nomen C[iprid]is. Uocatur enim a poetis Cipris, sicut patet ex Ouidio et Uirgilio, ac Marciano in suis libris *De nupciis*. Ubi narrat qualiter Sillenius, id est Mercurius, fuit lactatus, hoc est allectus, Cipridys, id est dei Ueneris illecebris. Et idem patet ex aliis poetis, qui fingunt istam deam Uenerem natam in Cipro propter istius dee aromata et unguenta.

Et significat hec pars picture fetorem luxurie, pro cuius fetoris occultacione necesse est, quod isti luxuriosi utantur unguentis et aromatibus. Unde notanda est illa descripcio poetica luxurie sub ymagine chimere de qua facit mencionem Ualerius [in *Epistola*] *ad Rufinum, de non ducenda uxore*, ubi alloquendo Rufinum dicit, 'Desiderio tuo totus inflamaris, et speciosa nobilitate capitis seductus, chimeram nescis miser esse quod petis. Sed et scire deuoues, id est negligis, quod triforme illud monstrum insigni uenus\te/tur facie leonis, olentis, id est fetentis, maculetur uentre capre, uirulente armetur cauda uipere'. Ualerius uul[t] dicere quod uoluptas carnalis in hac effigie fuit antiquitus descripta a poetis, scilicet in effigie leonis, nam luxuria habet ardorem in principio; in effigie capre, quia habet uicium luxurie fetorem in medio, hoc est in opere et actuali exercicio; et in effigie | uipere, qui[a] habet dolorem in fine et suo termino, sicut tactum est ex Boycio.

Et ideo bene exclamat contra istam uoluptatem Ueneris dominus Innocencius in suo libello *De miseria condicionis humane*, 'O', inquit, 'extrema libidinis turpitudo, que non

---

131 omelia 57ᵃ] *om*. A, morali I • facit] *om*. A 135 Uenus] Ueneris IO
• coronata] *add* depingitur AI
138 recitat] *om*. A, *marg*. I 139 feracissima] fertilissima A • fol. 133ᵛᵇ
140 Cipridis] Cupidis I, Cupidinis O 140–41 Uocatur ... nupciis] *marg*. I
140–43 Uocatur ... illecebris] *om*. A
148 descripcio] \picture/ I • luxurie] *om*. A 149 in *Epistola*] *om*. O 150 ubi ... Rufinum] sic A 153 deuoues id est] *om*. AI 155 uult] uul O 159 et² ... uipere] *om*. A • fol. 134ʳᵃ • quia] qui O
163 turpitudo] turpedo A

On Matthew, homily 57, says, 'Lechery makes a lecherous person a pig. What evil won't lechery perform? For lechery makes people into pigs, indeed worse than pigs.'[12] The goddess Venus deserves to be crowned with roses because of the red blush of shame that follows the vice and sin of lechery.

[136] [5] The fifth part of the picture follows; it concerns the goddess Venus's anointing. For poets depict her as smeared with spices and ointments. For this reason, as Alexander Neckam tells in his *Mythology*, the goddess Venus received the name Cypris from Cyprus, an island extremely productive of spices and ointments.[13] For poets, as Ovid, Virgil, and Martianus in his *On the marriage* show, call her Cipris. Martianus tells how Cyllenius, that is Mercury, 'was enticed', that is drawn on, by Cipris, that is 'by the allurements of the goddess Venus'. Other poets show the same thing, for they represent the goddess Venus as born in Cyprus, on account of the spices and ointments associated with her.

[146] And this part of the picture indicates the stench of lechery, since lecherous people use ointments and spices, because it is necessary to hide this stench. For this reason, one should notice this poetic description of lechery through an image of the chimera. 'Valerius' mentions this in his *Letter to Rufinus that one shouldn't get married*, when he says, addressing Rufinus, 'You are totally inflamed with your desire, and seduced by the beauty of a fair head, you, wretch, don't know that what you are seeking is a chimera. But you are devoting yourself to knowing (that is, you are ignoring) that this three-shaped monster is ornamented with the visible face of a lion, but besmirched with the belly of a smelly, that is stinking, she-goat, and armed with the tail of a poisonous viper.'[14] Valerius wishes to say that, from antiquity on, poets described fleshly pleasure through this figure, that is, in the figure of a lion, because lechery is eager at the beginning; in the figure of a she-goat, because it stinks in the middle, that is in the deed itself; and in the figure of a viper, because it is sorrowful at the very end, as Boethius discusses.

[161] Therefore, pope Innocent appropriately cries out against Venus's pleasure in his little book, *On the wretchedness of the human condition*, when he says, 'O the surpassing shamefulness of sexual desire! It doesn't

---

[12] Unfound.
[13] VM3 11.1 (229/17–18), followed by Mart 22.16 (107/23–25), and cf. 3.13 (69/7–9).
[14] JBWW 1:125/27–31.

solum maculat animam, sed fedat personam; que non solum
[m]ores eff[emina]t, sed corpus + eneruat; semper illam precedit
ardor et petulencia; semper eam comitantur fetor et immundicia;
et eciam semper sequntur dolor et penitencia. + *Fauus enim
distillans labia meretricis, et nitid[i]us oleo guttur eius; nouissima
autem eius amara quasi absinthium et acutus quasi gladius biceps'*.

[6] Sequitur sexta pars picture de dee Ueneris stipacione.
Depingitur enim dea Uenus stipata Graciis. Ubi notandum quod
poete fingunt tres deas Charites, quas nos uocamus 'Gracias'
in Latino, et dicunt eas assistere isti dee Ueneri et eam ambire
et stipare, eo modo quo familia circa matremfamilias domus
solet facere. Et hec sunt nomina harum Gr[acia]rum, sicut tangit
Seneca in suo libro *De beneficiis* et Remigius in commento suo
super *Librum de nupciis*, et Alexander prosequitur diffuse in sua
Methalogia, scilicet Pasi[t]hea, Eugiale, et Euprosine. Et significat
Pasi[t]hea attraccionem; intepretatur enim '\at/trahens'. Eugiale
significat blan|dicionem, et interpretatatur 'demulcens'. Sed
Euprosine significat detencionem, quia interpretatur 'retinens'.

Et bene conuenit hec pars picture luxurie et carnis
uolumptati. Istis enim tribus modis decipitur homo ab hoc
uicio, sicut tangit Carnotensis in suo *Policraticon*, ubi ponitur
ab eo quidam uersus metrice continens fraudes et decepciones
uoluptatis. Et iste uersus, 'Uisus et alloquium, contactus et oscula,
factum'. Ubi notandum quod duo prima, scilicet uisio et loqucio,
attrahunt hominem ad uoluptatem, et ista duo correspondent
prime + Carithi Pasi[th]e. Sed alia duo, scilicet contactio et
osculacio, demulcent hominem post attraccionem, et ita illa duo
pertinent ad secundam Carithen, scilicet Eugiale. Sed tercium,
facti et operis consummacio, hominem + detinet captiuum
et miserum, et significatur per terciam sororem que dicitur
Euprosine, quod interpretatur '\de/tinens'.

165 mores effeminat] mores effectant I, memores | efficit O • corpus] *adds* semper O   167 Fauus] Faunus O   168 nitidius] nitidus O   169 acutus] *adds* sermo A
174 matremfamilias] matrem famulos I   175 Graciarum] gre'orum O
176 Seneca ... et] *om.* A   177–78 et ... scilicet] *om.* A   178 etc. Pasithea] Pasiphea O   180 fol. 134rb
183 decipitur] deti² (= detinetur?) I   189 Carithi Pasithe] Carithi Palithee I, Carithis Pasiphie O • contactio et] contractio de A   191 tercium] quintum AI
192 detinet] detinent IO

just sully the soul, but soils the person; it doesn't just render one's behaviour effeminate, but weakens the body; eagerness and wantonness always precede it; it's always accompanied by stench and uncleanness; and it's also always followed by sorrow and repentance. *For the lips of a harlot are like honeycomb dropping, and her throat is smoother than oil. But her end is bitter as wormwood and sharp as a two-edged sword'* (Prv 5:3–4).[15]

[170] [6] The sixth part of the picture follows; it concerns Venus being surrounded. For the goddess Venus is depicted as surrounded by the Graces. Here one should notice that poets tell about three goddesses, the *Charites*, whom we call 'Graces' in Latin; they say that they help the goddess Venus and encircle and surround her, in the same way as a household is accustomed to do around the lady of the house. The Graces are named Pasithea, Eugiale, and Euphrosyne, as Seneca discusses in his *On gracious deeds*, Remigius in his commentary on *On the marriage*, and as Alexander Neckam in his *Mythology* treats at length.[16] Pasithea indicates attraction, for her name means 'drawing towards'. Eugiale indicates flattery, for her name means 'stroking'. But Euphrosyne indicates imprisonment, because her name means 'retaining'.

[182] This part of the picture is quite appropriate for lechery and the pleasure of the flesh. For a person is deceived by this vice in three ways, as John of Salisbury discusses in his *Polycraticus*. There he offers a line of poetry that contains pleasure's deceits and deceptions, the verse, 'Sight and speaking, touch and a kiss, the deed itself.'[17] Here one should notice that the first pair, vision and speech, attract a person to pleasure, and these two correspond to the first Grace, Pasithea. But the next two, touching and kissing, soothe a person after they have been attracted, and so these two belong to the second Grace, Eugiale. But the third, the fulfilment of the deed itself, holds a person as a wretched prisoner, and this is identified with the third sister Euphrosyne, whose name means 'holding as a prisoner'.

---

[15] *Ibid.* 2.21 (*PL* 217:725).
[16] Seneca, *De beneficiis* 1.3; Mart 4.2 (69/25–34); VM3 11.2 (229/19–35).
[17] *Ibid.* 6.23 (*PL* 199:622), citing Walther, *Sprich.* 33819.

370   John Ridewall, *Fulgencius metaforalis*

195   Adamantinis enim uinculis tenet ista uoluptas carnalis hominem alligatum, sicut tangit Remigius in commento super Marcianum. Est enim adamas lapis quasi infrangilis, et ualde difficile est homini se a uoluptatis uinculis liberare. Et ideo bene consueuit imperator Iulius Cesar dicere, [cuius dictum] Iohannes
200   in suo *Policraticon*, libro 4, capitulo 4, recitat, quod 'in bello corpora hominum uulnerantur gladiis, sed in tempore pacis uulnera[n]tur uoluptatibus'. Et subdit Carnotensis, 'Senserat', inquit, 'gencium triumphator uoluptatem | nullo modo tam facile superari quam fuga, eo quod ipsum, qu[i] gentes do[muera]t,
205   Ueneris nexibus innodauit mulier impudica'. Hec ille [testatur, libro 4° sui *Policraticon*, 14 capitulo].

    [7] Sequitur septima pars picture de dee Ueneris placacione. Sicut enim recitat Alexander Necham in sua *Methalogia*, fingitur a poetis ista dea Uenus placata ueruenis, hoc est immolacione illius
210   herbe que dicitur ueruena. Et non sine causa, nam ad litteram, isti malifici et ydolatre consueuerunt in pluribus maleficiis et supersticionibus habere usum herbe predicte, scilicet ueruene. Et hoc ideo quia demones, quibus seruiunt specialiter et immediate isti malefici et ydolatre, gaudent singulariter in peccato luxurie.
215   [Significanter] et ideo non sine causa fingitur ista dea Uenus placari ueruenis. Et de ista notanda est glossa super [*large blank*] Leuitici, que dicit quod 'cum de omni peccato gaudent demones, specialiter et familiarius famulari uotum lux[ur]ie'. Et ideo bene per ueruanam herbam maleficam et supersticiosam placari dicitur
220   dea Uenus. Consueuit ab infidelibus et inc[redu]lis procurari maleficiis delectacio deordinata lasciuie carnalis, ut patet ex Uirgilio et aliis poetis.

    [8] Sequitur octaua pars picture de dee Ueneris locacione. Sicut enim tangit Fulgencius in littera, dea ista pingitur collocata
225   in concha marina. Unde dicit sic, 'Concha marina eam portari pingitur, eo quod huius generis animal toto corpore simul

---

196-97 sicut … Marcianum] *om.* A   **198** uoluptatis] *adds* uicio et A
   199 consueuit] conueuit A   **200** bello] libello A   **202** uulnerantur] uulneratur O
   203 fol. 134va **204** fuga] \debellare/ (*over eras.*) I • ipsum qui] ipsum A, inique I, ipsum quando O • domuerat] dami'erat A, dormierant IO
   205-6 testatur … capitulo] *om.* O
208 enim recitat] pulcre tangit et uocat I   **209** Sicut … Methalogia] *om.* A
   211 pluribus] pulueribus A   **213** quibus … specialiter] arguuntur sordescere et totaliter in sordibus delectari et I   **215** Significanter] *om.* O • causa] *adds* et racione A, racione I   **216** *blank*] *om.* AI   **218** luxurie] luxuriantis A, luxuriosis I, luxie O   **220** incredulis] incru|delis O

[195] For fleshly pleasure holds a person bound with 'adamantine chains', as Remigius says in his commentary on Martianus. *Adamas* is a rock that's, as it were, unbreakable,[18] and it is very difficult for a person to free themselves from pleasure's chains. The emperor Julius Caesar used to appropriately say, as John of Salisbury recalls in *Polycraticus* 4.4, that 'In warfare, people's bodies are wounded with swords, but in peacetime, with pleasures.' And the bishop of Chartres adds, 'That conqueror of many peoples had perceived that the only easy way to overcome pleasure is flight, because he himself, although he had tamed many peoples, was bound up in Venus's nets by a shameless woman.'[19] So he says, in *Polycraticus* 4.14.

[207] [7] The seventh part of the picture follows; it concerns propitiating Venus. For, as Alexander Neckam says in his *Mythology*, poets represent this goddess Venus as placated with shoots of verbena, that is through sacrificing to her this plant verbena. This is reasonable, because, according to Neckham, sorcerers and idolaters were accustomed to use this plant in many charms and superstitious acts, and this was because these sorcerers and idolaters particularly and immediately serve devils, who especially rejoice in the sin of lechery.[20] So it's reasonable, and significantly so, that the goddess Venus is represented as propitiated with shoots of verbena. On this point, one should notice the gloss on Lv 18:24, that says, 'Although devils rejoice over every sin, they are most particularly and most closely joined to desire for lechery.'[21] Therefore, the goddess Venus is properly said to be propitiated with this magical and superstition-laden plant verbena. As Virgil and other poets show, it was customary for infidels and unbelievers to gain the disordered delight of fleshly riotousness by using charms.

[223] [8] The eighth part of the picture follows; it concerns the goddess Venus's location. For as Fulgentius says explicitly, the goddess is depicted placed on a seashell. For this reason, he says, 'She is depicted as carried on a seashell, because animals of this kind

---

[18] Mart 9.1 (81/15–16).
[19] *Ibid.* 4.3 (PL 199:518); Caesar's aperçu is also cited from John at *Fasciculus morum* 660/72–74.
[20] Vaguely (no mention of verbena) from VM3 11.12 (235/27–36/17).
[21] *Ibid.* (PL 113:348).

aperto in coitu misceatur, sicut [I]uba phisiologus refert'. |
Et significat hec pars [picture] luxurie obstinacionem, nam
sicut concha marina in mari uersatur, et quo diucius in mari
230 moratur, eius testa eo multiplicius induratur, sic et peccator qui
per luxuriam maculatur, licet sicut in secunda parte picture
tactum est, amaritudinem displicencie respergatur. Quia
ut dicit Innocencius, 'Libidinem semper dolor et penitencia
concomicantur; hoc tamen non obstante, luxuriosus illo
235 dolore non emendatur, sed in malo [potius] obstinatur'. Dicit
enim Gregorius quod 'ex quo luxuria mentem alicuius semel
occupauerit, uix eum ad bona desideria conari permittit, nam
luxurie desideria omnino sunt uiciosa. Ex suggestione enim
luxuriosa oritur luxuriosa cogitacio; ex cogitacione, delectacio;
240 ex delectacione, consensus; ex consensu, operacio; ex operacione,
consuetudo; ex consuetudine, desperacio; ex desperacione, peccati
defencio; ex peccati defencione sequitur gloriacio de peccato, et
ex tali gloriacione sequitur finalis dampnacio'. Sic igitur finiuntur
Mithologie primi libri et secundi.

227 aperto] apto A • Iuba] ruba O • sicut ... refert] *om.* A • fol. 134vb
228 picture] *om.* O   230 multiplicius] multiformius A   231 secunda] prima I
235 potius] magis I, *om.* O   237 conari] corporari A   243-44 Sic ... secundi] Et
sic finitur 22^a methologia Fulgencii in ordine et quarta libri secundi AI

join for sex with the whole body wide open, as Juba the writer on animals says.'[22] This part of the picture indicates the stubbornness of lechery, for just as a seashell is tossed about in the sea, and the longer it remains in the sea, the harder its shell gets, likewise a sinner who is stained by lechery [only becomes more hardened in it], even though they may be sprinkled with displeasing bitterness, as I discussed in the second part of the picture. For, as Innocent says, 'Sexual desire always has sorrow and penance for companions, yet not withstanding, that sorrow doesn't produce a lecherous person's improvement, but they are made more stubborn in pursuing their evil.'[23] For Gregory says, 'Insofar as lechery once seizes someone's mind, it scarcely permits them to try to gain virtuous desires, for those desires associated with lechery are completely vice-ridden. For from a lecherous suggestion springs a lecherous thought; from that thought, delight; from delight, assent; from assent, the deed itself; from the deed, its habitual practice; from practice, despair; from despair, defending the sin; exulting in the sin follows from that defence; and from that exultation, final damnation.'[24] So Gregory says. Here both books of the *Mythology* end.

---

[22] Fulg 2.1 (40/21–24).
[23] Cf. *Sermones de diversis* 7 (*PL* 217:684).
[24] Cf. *Moralia* 4.18 (*PL* 75:654).

Appendix: Two inserted discussions

After 2.3/321 plumine, AI add (in form of I):

'Quid igitur est adulacionis inunccio, nisi do[n]orum emunccio? Quid commendacionis allusio, nisi prelatorum delusio? Quid laudis derisio, nisi potentum derisio? Adulatores enim a uoluntate uultum, ab animo uerbum, a mente linguam, ab
5   intellectu loquelam amplo + discecionis interuallo diff[i]bulant. Plerumque [enim] illo[s] exterius plausibiliter applaudando coll[a]udant quos interna [mentis deris]ione subsa[n]niant. Foris uultu applaudant uirgineo, intus scorpionis pungunt aculeo; foris adulacionis mellitos compluunt ymbres, intus detraccionis
10 euomunt tempestates'.

After 2.3/324 admittuntur, I alone adds:

'... qui eos palpant blandiciis et aures fame bibulas calicibus inebriant Babilonis'. Et subdit, 'Bene diuitibus et magnatibus ageretur, si eis gracia donaretur distinguendum inter adulacionem et ueram laudem, sed seca laudis ambicio, plus credent alii de
15 seipso quam sibi, utrumque recipit indistincte'. Tales enim adulatores isti diuites in magnates decernere. 'Ille est adulator mordatissimus destructor in absencia, proponens in hominum presencia que existimat complacere. *Uerba oris eius iniquitas et dolus*'. 'Cum enim sal correccionis in omni sacrificio acciditur
20 a Domino, m[e]l palpacionis in omni sacrificio rep[rob]atur'. Hec ille.

1 donorum] domorum I   2 derisio] diffusio A   3 derisio¹] *adds, repeating,* 2 Quid ... delusio A   5 discesionis] discensionis AI   • diffibulant] dissibulant A, difabulant I   6 enim illos exterius] si exterius illo I   6–7 applaudando collaudant] applicando applaudant A, applaudando colludant I   7 interna ... derisione] interna | deylione I   7 subsanniant] *a minim short* I
20 mel] mal I   • reprobatur] repleatur I

after 2.3/321 plumine:

What, then is the ointment of flattery, if it's not defrauding someone in the hope of gifts from them? What is this hinting at praise, if it's not deceiving prelates? What is the smile of praise, if it's not mockery of the powerful? Flatterers detach the countenance from the will, the word from the soul, the tongue from the mind, the speech from the thought – and they do so by interposing a wide space between them. For many, in their actions, convincingly praise and applaud openly those whom they mock inwardly and mentally with laughter. On the outside, they applaud with a virginally innocent face, while within they pierce with a scorpion's sting; on the outside, they rain down honeyed showers of flattery, while within they spew forth storms of backbiting.[1]

after 2.3/324 admittuntur:

'[… only flatterers are admitted into the favour of the rich], those who stroke them with sweet words and make their ears, thirsting for drinks of fame, drunk from Babylonian cups'. And he adds, 'It would be a good thing for rich and powerful people, if they were given the power to distinguish between flattery and true praise, but the blind eagerness for praise, believing more what others say than what one knows as true of oneself, receives both without distinction.' Flatterers like these declare that all rich men are great ones. 'Such a flatterer, when he's absent, is a truly caustic destroyer, but in his target's presence, he puts forward only what he imagines is going to please. *The words of his mouth are iniquity and guile* (Ps 35:4).' 'Since God accepts the salt of correction in every sacrifice, one should reject the honey of stroking in every sacrifice.'[2]

---

[1] Later in Alan, *De planctu* p7 (*PL* 210:470).

[2] Initially, the conclusion of the preceding citation, followed by citations from both later and earlier in *Epistola* 77 (*PL* 207:238–39); the final sentence from Peter's prologue/epistola 1 (*PL* 207:2–3).

Textual notes

In the individual headnotes below, I have supplemented references to the materials Ridewall found in Fulg with the relevant brief descriptions from the prologue to his commentary on *DCD*, C1 fols 1ᵛ–3: 'On this point, one should notice that these idolaters and worshippers of many gods, rather than a single one, used to extol their gods and to speak of them as great for various reasons.' He summarises his extensive presentation, 'These twenty-two (!) kinds of gods correspond to the twenty-two books here so that each book corresponds to a single god, and Augustine condemns that god's worship in spiritual terms, as my argument will show. In all these ways, Augustine shows that the single God of Christians is greater than all these gods. For our God surpasses all the pagan gods in the priority of his origin, since he is the creator of all heavenly, earthly, and hellish things. He also surpasses all the pagan gods in every power that the idolaters earlier attributed falsely to their lying false gods.'[1]

With Ridewall's listing, cf. Mart 1.42 (Lutz 114/27–115/25), citing a verse from Ennius on the twelve great Olympians; Ridewall cites and discusses it at C2 fols 47ᵛ–48, on *DCD* 6.7.1 (col. 184). Ridewall also commented on a Varronian list of 20, discussed in *DCD* 7.2–3 (esp. cols 194–95), to which he refers here, immediately following my first citation above; see further 1/51n.

---

[1] 'Pro quo notandum est quod isti ydolatre et cultores non unius Dei, sed multorum deorum solebant deos suos magnificare et eos magnos predicare ex multiplici racione' (C1 fol. 1ᵛ); and 'Ista uiginti duo genera deorum correspondent istis uiginti duo libris, ita quod cuiuslibet de istis uiginti duo libris correspondet unus deus, cuius cultus spiritualiter ab Augustino reprobatur, sicud in prosecucione ostendetur. Omnibus autem hiis modis ostendit Augustinus quod Deus Cristianorum, qui solus est deus, numerus unice et singulariter, est magnus super omnes deos. Deus enim noster deos omnes gentilium transcendit originis prioritate, quia est creator omnium celestium, terrestrium, et infernorum. Transcendit eciam omnes deos gentilium modis omnibus prius mendatis et diis falsis falso ab ydolatris attributis' (C1 fol. 3).

[1] Idolatry

Ridewall follows Fulg's account closely at the head (to about line 100), but Fulg offers no guidance for the *pictura*. Obviously, the account is unusually thin, but the central detail *orbata* (and its near similes in the division) have been stimulated by Fulg 16/4–5: 'the son, when he was carried away by Fortune's hostile attacks, which had left the father a cruel epitaph mourning a double loss (geminae orbitatis)'.[2] Most other divisions play upon the idol's falseness under the trope of the whore, who only feigns affection (206n), but one detail seems distinctly 'medieval' (231n). For an analogous instance, cf. *Fasciculus morum* 504/133–34, an *ymago* of Injustice 'might be shaped in the form of a fornicating whore with wandering eyes and open and dissolute hands'.[3]

1–2 *sub tegmine*: The term 'a covering' is routine in discussing classical myth. It indicates that 'the poets' intended their fictions to convey inobvious meanings, whether of a 'philosophical' stripe that referred to natural processes or, as Ridewall insists, offering moral instruction. Cf. 10/4 *parabolice*.

3 *appositarum*: *oppositarum* elsewhere, but this is a widely attested Anglo-Latin variant form.

13 *sensuit*: To represent L censuit, an example of persistent back-spellings following the fusion of classical *s/c/sc* in medieval Latin.

19 *angustiator*: Transparent, but the word is unnoted in dictionaries.

21 *originate*: O's terminal *-te* probably represents *-ti*.

48, 62: Although A's *inserere* appears the harder reading, Fulg 16/20 confirms the *inferre* of the other copies.

51 *uarie deorum differencie*: This distinction has been derived from Varro's *De rebus diuinis* (= *De antiquitatibus*, books 26–41), substantial portions quoted or summarised in *DCD* 6–7. Ridewall offers it as an original explanation of the three forms of worship mentioned by Fulg (16/19–20). He introduces Varro's classification at C2 fol. 19, commenting on the end of *DCD* 6.3 (col. 179), and continues, 'But one should notice about the principal and "select" gods that this species of god differs from the other gods I have numbered previously as common and less common. ... The gods whom

---

[2] '... qui [the son] dum adversis fortunae incursibus raperetur, quo patri crudelem geminae orbitatis derelinquisset elogium'.

[3] 'ymago potest formari ad modum meretricis fornicarie cum oculis vagis et manibus apertis et dissolutis'.

the Romans called "select", that is *seorsum electi* "chosen apart from the rest", according to Varro's account, were twenty in all, namely Janus, Jupiter, Saturn, Genius, Mercury, Apollo, Mars, Vulcan and others whom Augustine enumerates at the start of book 7.'[4]

66, 77 Notice the two examples of 'doublets of doubt' in L.

71ff. For the Stoic four 'affects', see Commentary, pp. 427 n.1, 430. This set of vices appears, as I indicate there, persistently as an analytic tool in Ridewall's discussions of pagan religion and the creation of idols, for example at C1 fols 64ᵛ–65 (on *DCD* 2.10, col. 55), to ascribe the Greek tolerance for staged lampoons to *timor deordinatus*, or at C2 fol. 14 (on *DCD* 6.2, col. 178), to argue that in his support for pagan cult, Varro, who in fact knew better, was driven alternately by fear (of punishment for breaking Numa's religious laws) and by hope/ambition. ('He wanted to perpetuate his memory and have praise and glory among his fellow-citizens for the zeal which his words showed he had'.)[5] See the discussion, Smalley 1960, 129–30.

90 I have accommodated the *textus receptus* to John of Salisbury's *nota* and *inurunt* + acc. In both cases, these seem to me errors likely to have been made in the transmission.

105 *ista*: The word should balance *talia* in the following clause, and O has misinterpreted a form like *iᵃ*. In the following sentence, Augustine confirms LAI's subjunctive (although late medieval usage may have been indifferent to mood in constructions like this).

120 *reserantur*: Although Hugh, like L, has *referantur*, the gate-opening metaphor suggests it is wrong, a confusion of the similar *f* and *s*, aided by the relative familiarity of the root *fero*.

183 *finxisse ... artem fingendi statuas*: Of course, the relatively neutral physical usage, 'to shape', which is unique in the text. Much more usually, the verb appears in constructions such as 2/20 *poete fingunt*; while the verb here carries strong connotations of its modern English derivative 'feign', 'to

---

[4] 'Set de diis precipuis et selectis notandum est quod istud genus deorum differt ab aliis diis prius iam enumeratus, sicud communis et minus commune. ... Dii quos Romani uocabant selectos, id est seorsum electos, erant uiginti in numero secundum computacionem Marci Uarronis, scilicet Ianus, Iupiter, Saturnus, Genius, Marcurius, Appollo, Mars, Wlcanus, et sic de aliis quos in principio libri 7ⁱ enumerat Augustinus' (C2 fol. 20ᵛ). The full list of twenty is also cited in Mart 26.15 (115/8–18).

[5] 'ad perpetuendum memoriam suam et ad habendum laudem et gloriam inter ciues suos propter zelum quem in uerbis ostendit se habere'.

(lyingly) fabricate', I have customarily adopted less incendiary translations, usually 'represent'.

198 O *auctorum* is probably an echo/dittography stimulated by unqualified *aliorum*; cf. 204 antiquos] aliquos, where the repetitious context has produced dissimilated readings.

206 The sexualised image, esp. the feminisation, follows from *Inicium fornicacionis* (Sap 14:12), cited in line 155.

207 *orbata*: On absence/deprivation, a feminisation aligned with immorality, cf. C2 fols 56ᵛ–57, on the castrated priests of Cybele/Berecinthia, with a citation from *De uetula* 2 [= *DCD* 6.7.3, col. 185], and again fol. 60. But also cf. the reading *in bono* (Saturn castrated) at 2/212ff.

213 *fornicarie*: Another transparent form not recorded in dictionaries.

228–29 *cornu uentilata*: This division apparently describes a medieval charivari, in which a community derides and expels a member deemed criminous. Traditionally, this is a punishment for sexual misconduct, which looms large in Ridewall's description.

230 *timor seruilis*: A technical term, 'love for God only from fear of punishment' (as opposed to *timor filialis*); see the Augustine cited at line 150.

239 *amor ereos*: See further Morrisey, the most recent treatment of this 'excessive love', with abundant further references.

[2] Saturn/Prudence

The entire division (including 35 'Pollucis', preceding the division; see the note to that line), except points [5] and [7], is derived from the opening of Fulg's account (17/10–12). For point [7], see 263n. Cf. Ridewall on *DCD* 6.7, 'Saturnus senex' (col. 184): 'Saturn's effigy or simulacrum was this, as Martianus and his commentator make clear: The poets depict the god Saturn as advanced in years, white-headed, with a face sorrowful and sad [the added point 5], dressed in a green garment, in his left hand bearing a sickle and in his right a flaming dragon that's eating its own tail. This was the simulacrum of Saturn that was placed in temples, and mimes depicted a similar one in theatres, when Saturn's acts were recited in songs made by poets.'[6] Ridewall treats Martianus's extra detail (cf. 'proprietates ... plures

---

[6] 'Eius autem effigies seu figura fuit ista, sicud patet per Marcianum libro de nupciis et per commentatorem suum Remigium: depingebatur enim a poetis deus Saturnus etate senex et capite canus et wltu mestis et tristis et glauco amictu

sibi attribuat' 80–81), the dragon, in a discussion of Varro's 'dei incerti', those with monstrous attributes, at C2 fol. 20ᵛ (on *DCD* 6.3, col. 179); this figure, according to Mart 33.8 (127/4–10, followed by VM3 1.6), represents the year, which, at its end, has consumed what it has earlier produced.

In his prologue to *DCD*, Ridewall says: 'Some were called gods, first, because of their antecedent origin, as is evident with Saturn and Cybele, whom the unbelievers called great, because they believed that the other gods were born from these two.'[7]

35 *Pollucis*: Helm prints *Polluris* (17/10, 17), but the more obvious *Pollucis* appears in one family of his manuscripts and is the reading at VM3 1.9, with Fulg's etymology (156/12–14). *Polluris* itself is actually a scribalism, for *Telluris*, gen. of the name of Saturn's mother, Tellus 'the earth'.

38–45 Cf. VM3 Prooem. (153/8–10), citing Varro, for the distinction between *homo* 'body' and *sapiens* 'soul'.

50 *Cum calcitres ut azinus*: an allusion to the proverbial ass that resists the harp, e.g. Boethius, *Consolation* 1.p2.

65 *est in aliquibus libris 78*: There was considerable variation in the text of the *Epistulae* (including separable transmission of parts of the text as if the whole); for details, see L. Reynolds.

94 *Caribdi*: I have adjusted O's word-order to follow the source, which O reproduces accurately in the reprise of this quotation at 12/64. The scribe skipped on the repeated clause-ending 'est', but quickly recognised the error and reasserted the reading he had omitted.

105–10 See 253n, and the usual moralisation Ridewall represses there.

112 *celeritate*: In A only, confirmed by Cicero; the *celeritatibus* of the other copies has been attracted to the inflected *corporis*.

126 *Alexander Nekham in suis* Methologiis: On the ascription here, commonplace in the Middle Ages, even among some very sophisticated readers (e.g. Salutati 1:299), see Hunt 1984, 24, 148 (and Sharpe 53). This ascription appears to be derived from Neckam's commentary on Macrobius, where large chunks of VM3 are cited without acknowledging the source

coopertus, in una manu ferens falcem, scilicet in sinistra, et in manu dextra ferens flaminem draconem caudam propriam deuorantem. Hec fuit ymago dei Saturni posita in templis, et consimilis erat illa que representabatur a mimis in theatris, quando de eo erant recitata carmina facta a poetis' (C2 fol. 44ᵛ).

[7] 'Primo ex originis prioritate, sicud patet de deo Saturno et dea Cibele, qui in numero deorum sunt ab incredulis dicti magni, quia credebant quod ab istis duobus fuerunt dii alii procreati' (C1 fols 1ᵛ–2).

and as if original (see esp. 1–62). Although surviving in only two MSS, the commentary would appear to have had a wider circulation than now visible, as is also evidenced by isolated glosses from it in one standard commentary on the beginner text *Ecloga Theoduli*.

Elliott-Elder, the only published list of MSS of VM3, is incomplete and filled with errors; there are least 60 extant copies. Their account of insular copies overlooks the MS here designated I and an excerpt from an expanded version of the prologue (not in Bode's edition) at BL, MS Burnley 305, fols 75–77^v, while Durham Cathedral, MS Hunter 45, contains only notes, s. xvi.

132 *sacerdotes*: The O interlineation is not integral to the text, but a gloss indicating a more familiar synonym.

148 *discernunt*] decernunt AL (= Vulgate); similarly **157** *posuit*] proposuit AL (=Vulgate): Since the Bible includes variant readings, one cannot be certain which is Ridewall's. I assume that scribes will revert to established forms and thus that readings varying from the *textus acceptus* are more apt to be correct. Similar logic guides my handling of 5/58–60.

154–55 *colore ... 'confirmacio'*: The sense, which is commonplace in rhetorical handbooks, does not appear in dictionaries. As the Greek Ridewall cites would indicate, *confirmatio* is a form of personification, the introduction of a speech by a normally speechless subject, here the abstract noun *sapiencia*.

156 *illud*: conuiuium AIL, arguably representing split transmission of authorial *illud conuiuium*.

170 *uultus ... seu*: O's small omission has probably been stimulated by -s...s. (= scilicet).

172 *enim*: O intrudes a second example, an echoic error. However, the text is laden with such repetitive, potentially dittographic readings, and I have generally let them stand. Cf. further 5/142 *et ideo ... et ideo*, where only L varies, reading *unde* for the second use, surely a response to the repetition. But in 5/145, the second use of *enim* appears only in O, and I have removed it as echoic. Other examples appear at 7/102 *igitur ideo*; 9/128–29 and 2.3/208 *finaliter ... tandem*; 13/138–40 *poete ... poete* (similarly 2.1/19–20); 2.3/14–15 *tamen ... tamen*.

183ff. Cf. the analogous discussion, from a Dominican exemplum collection, s. xiii ex., Herbert 500 (no. 270).

199 *Flentem autem Cristum frequenter inuenies*: Most famously at Io 11:35, but also Lc 19:41, implicitly Mt 26:38–39.

205–6 Alluding to Mt 5:5 and Lc 6:21, 25. In 205, O has misunderstood an abbreviated form.

253 *aliam esse Uenerem*: For what is implicitly the *in malo* reading of Saturn's castration, see 2.4/83–106.

263ff. *proprios filios in cibum assumpsisse*: Fulg mentions the episode (18/1–2), but probably more relevant to the account here is Augustine's critique of 'philosophical theology''s sanitising reading at *DCD* 6.8 (col. 186). In his comment on the passage, Ridewall uses the noun *physiologia* 'a conclusion relating to natural science/philosophy' to describe the received reading (available in Cicero's *De natura deorum*, and elsewhere); the term does not appear in dictionaries. Ridewall has, of course, managed to work in this moralisation earlier at 105–10, although denatured from the horror Augustine ascribes it.

266 *filius ... 'fit ut ille'*: An etymology, deriving *filius* from *fio*.

276-77 *Et sic ... mithologie*: Throughout the text, these concluding statements appear (and disappear) frequently across all the manuscripts. Given that there is no evidence for any divisions between the mythographies, other than initials, these may be the remnants of an earlier set of rubrics, variously taken up or ignored by individual scribes.

[3] Jupiter/Love and Friendship

This chapter is largely Ridewall's free invention. The analogous discussion in Fulg is devoted to the marriage of Jupiter and Juno, and develops a 'philosophical'/'physiological' reading, the marriage of fire and air. A single detail from that discussion is developed in Ridewall's treatment of Juno; see the headnote to chapter 4 and 4/33 etc. below.

1 (and cf. 4/1, 2.3/1): In his prologue to *DCD*, Ridewall comments, 'Second, others were also called great gods from their excellent honour, as is evident with the god Jupiter and goddess Juno. The idolaters worshipped him as the king and leader of all the gods and her as their queen, in addition to being Jupiter's wife and sister. Augustine and Seneca, in *Hercules furens*, treat this topic.'[8]

12 The reference here to Heraclitus reinforces the approval extended to his weeping in 2/183–221. In his discussion of *DCD* 6.5.2 (col. 181), Ridewall comments on his identification of fire as ruling principle:

Moreover, Heraclitus's opinion was well taken, because fire is

---

[8] 'Secundo, fuerunt eciam alii uocati dii magni, excellenti dignitate, sicud patet de deo Ioue, quem coluerunt ydolatre tanquam deorum omnium regem et principem, et de dea Iunone, deorum et dearum omnium regina et dei Iouis coniuge et sorore, sicud tangit Augustinus et Seneca, prima tragedia' (C1 fol. 2).

the origin and beginning of heat. Heat is the origin of life in an animate body, and God is the origin and cause of all living things, whether it was a spirit or bodies. For this reason, Varro did not reject Heraclitus's opinion, for as Isidore says, 'Varro agreed with Heraclitus in part, for Varro called fire the world-spirit, because fire controls everything that is in the world.' Everything in the world is produced through the power of fire and heat. 'And this is true of us, so far as our spirit is concerned, because so long as our spirit is in us, we live and are controlled by it. And when it has left us, then we die.' It is the same with God in his relation to all beings, for He created all things, and once he had created them, he preserved their being and controlled them. ... Therefore, Varro called fire a god, because *In God, we live, move, and are* [Ac 17:28], as the poet Arator says; this is evident in Bede's gloss on Acts. Unless God preserves things in being with His hand, everything would decline into nothing, as Augustine states elsewhere.[9]

19 *ad presens* (O): Clearly otiose and probably echoing an abbreviated form for *possumus* (*presens* might be represented by $\overline{pns}$).

33ff. In his lengthy comment on the concluding sentences of *DCD* 6.3 (col. 179), Ridewall draws attention to Jupiter's humanoid Roman depiction: In the Capitol, the effigy of Jupiter presented the image of a king sitting on a royal throne with a crown and sceptre. The reason for this was, as has been said in book 4, that the Romans thought Jupiter was the king of all the gods. For the Romans called

---

[9] 'Istud autem dictum Eracliti bene poterat intelligi, quia ignis est fons et principium caloris. Calor est principium uite in corpore animalis, et Deus est principium et causa uite omnium uiuencium, siue fuit spiritus siue corpora. Et hec fuit una causa quare Uarro non reprobauit opinionem Eracliti. Immo sicud dicit Isidorus, "Marcus Uarro concordauit in parte cum Eraclito, nam ipse Uarro uocauit ignem animum mundi, eo quod ignis omnia gubernat que sunt in mundo". Res enim mundi omnes generantur et producuntur per uirtutem ignis et caloris. "Et isto modo est de nobis quantum ad nostrum animum, quia quamdiu animus est in nobis, per ipsum uiuimus et gubernamur. Qui cum a nobis recesserit, tunc emorimur". Et simili modo est de Deo respectu omnium encium. Ab eo enim omnia creantur, creata conseruantur in esse et gubernantur ... Et ideo Uarro uocauit deum ignem, quia *in Deo uiuimus, mouemur, et sumus*, ut dixit poeta Aratus, ut patet in glossa Bede, Actuum xuiii° capitulo. Nisi enim Deus manu teneret res in esse, cuncta decederunt in nihil, sicut alibi declarat Augustinus' (C2 fol. 29). The citation from Isidore is *Etym.* 8.6.20–21 (*PL* 82:307), but although Bede frequently cites Arator here, he does not in this chapter (*PL* 92:980).

Jupiter the god of kingdoms, because they believed that through him human kingdoms and empires were ruled and governed. ... Nevertheless, other kingdoms understood otherwise about Jupiter's image, for some depicted Jupiter in the form of a ram, and he was worshipped in this form in Lybia, because Jupiter sometimes had appeared in this form in the sands of Lybia. Others depicted Jupiter in the form of an eagle and worshipped him in this form, because Jupiter represented himself as an eagle when he abducted Ganymede. Others depicted Jupiter in the form and likeness of a bull, because there was a rumour that Jupiter had abducted Europa in that shape.[10]

57 *Ergo ... quia*: The initial *Quia ergo* probably anticipates the subsequent use of *quia*; I *quia ... cum* is secondary dissimilation.

94-95 *uniuersalis uis*: Ridewall comments on *DCD* 6.3 (col. 178): 'The number five was dedicated to Jupiter, because, as Aristotle says in the *Secreta secretorum*, this is the universal number, and it was therefore assigned to Jupiter. For as Remigius teaches in his commentary on *On the marriage*, Jupiter is the same thing as universal power.'[11]

98 *palmeo*: Another transparent form (and, in this case, a classical one) not recorded in dictionaries.

112 *Grecos*: This is an etymology, and OL have been attracted to the preceding phrase and the repeated mention of 'poets'. I have not included AI's subsequent 'et uictum' in the text, since it may simply be an effort to balance the subsequent 'captum amore'. However, the variation is very apt to be linked, not independent, and AI also an authorial reading.

---

[10] 'In Capitolio Iouis simulacrum representabat effigiem regis residentis in trono regio cum diademate et sceptro. Et racio istius fuit, nam, ut 4º libro fuit dictum, Romani putabant Iouem fuisse regem omnium deorum. Uocabant eciam Romani Iouem deum regnorum, quia per eum credebant regi et administrari regna et imperia hominum. ... Alie tamen naciones aliud senserunt de ymagine dei Iouis, nam alique depinxerunt Iouem in effigiem arietis et per hunc modum colebatur in Libia, quia Iupiter in arenis Libie aliquando apparuerat in tali effigie. Aliqui uero depingebant ymaginem dei Iouis in forma aquile et sic eum colebant, nam in figura aquile Iupiter se representabat quando rapuit Ganidem. Alii uero Iouem et eius effigiem depinxerunt eciam in forma et figura tauri, quia in tali specie fuit fama Iouem rapuisse Europam' (C2 fol. 20ᵛ).

[11] 'Numerus autem quinarius fuit consecratus deo Ioui, quia ut deducit Aristoteles in epistola ad Magnum Alexandrum, iste numerus est numerus uniuersitatis, et ideo de Ioue fuit iste numerus deditus. Quia ut docet Remigius in commento suo super librum *De nupciis*, Iouis idem est quod uniuersalis uis' (C2 fol. 16ᵛ).

31–32 *Nullum ... defuisset*: om. AIL (and not in Hugh). I include it as a possible memory of Hugh's *De archa Noe mystica* 1–2 (*PL* 176:681–85 passim), and it may have fallen out of the other copies through an auditorily motivated skip between *-phasse* and *-fuisset*.

137 *aureus*: Following Ovid; the majority reading has been attracted to the surrounding ablatives.

152 *duobus preceptis*: The two great commandments of Mt 22:37–40, echoing Dt 6:5.

165 *sine dolo mulcere*: The received reading *sine dolore punire* 'punishes without sorrow' isn't particularly sensible, as L's guess *misericorditer* indicates. I have inserted Bernard's reading (cf. L *mis'icor-* with his *mulcer-*, i.e. *ml'cer-*); the first two members of this sentence parallel the two clauses of the preceding.

168–69 *a poetis dicitur Lucecius*: Although I have emended the epithet in accord with the majority received form, the text is still probably wrong. L cites VM3 3.1 (160/33–35), the source of Ridewall's information here; this reads, in part, 'qui lingua Oscorum a luce, quem hominibus praestare putatur, *Luccejus* [nuncupatur]' (who, because he was considered superior to men, was named *Lucceius*, a derivative of *lux* 'light' in Oscan).

195 *trifidum*: While there is a British Latin *trisceles, triscilis* 'three-legged', *trifidus* is the usual epithet for Jupiter's thunderbolt, e.g. Ovid, *Metamorphoses* 2.325, a passage from which Ridewall cites at length in chapter 8.

243 *Speculum ... amoris*: Ridewall has confused two Aelred works with similar titles; there is also a *Speculum charitatis*. *condit* may be an error for Aelred's *ostendit* (routinely abbreviated $\overline{ondit}$), but the sentence has been partially paraphrased. **249** *secundis* is Aelred's reading.

276 *pingunt et fingunt*: Although I have retained this reading, universal in my copies, it is almost certainly a doublet of doubt from early in the tradition. Or perhaps one could translate 'both depict and narrate that'?

fingunt Iouem cibatum: Ridewall's very extensive comment on DCD 6.7.1 (col. 184) begins: 'On this point, one should notice that an image of the god Jupiter had been placed in the temple on the Capitoline, and next to it, an image of his nurse, the goat Amalthea, from whose milk the poets claim Jupiter was nourished. For this reason, the poets report that Jupiter transferred the goat who nursed him into heaven and made it a constellation', with a further discussion, as here, from Hyginus.[12] Ridewall's

---

[12] 'Pro quo notandum quod in templo illo fuerat positum simulacrum dei Iouis et iuxta istum deum Iouem positum erat simulacrum nutricis sue capre scilicet

discussion there proves excessively lengthy, because usually it is not the goat that was named Amalthea, but the nymph who owned it (cf. Ovid, *Fasti* 5.111–28), and Ridewall seeks to reduce this 'diuersitas apud istos poetas'.

280 *fingunt poete*: In *DCD* 4.8 (col. 118–19), although Augustine launches a witty assault on the Roman propensity for identifying a god to be in charge of everything (the door-hinge, as well as the threshold), he doesn't take up Copia. Ridewall's prologue, however, presents two completely fictive comparable deities: 'Twenty-first, there were also further gods considered great because they restored abundance, as is evident with the god Abundance and the goddess Fullness; the pagans exalted them, since they believed that from these gods, plenty grew among people, through the provision of luxurious foods.'[13] There is, of course, a certain humorous quality to this comment: filling the slots suggested by Augustine's 22 books produces the kind of deific overkill Augustine himself deprecates.

[4] Juno/Memory

See the headnote to chapter 3; at this point in the text, Fulg indulges in 'theologia philosophorum' and offers but a single useful detail (19/1–6), 'They say Juno was bound by Jupiter with golden chains', the source of point [5]. (Ridewall ignores the continuation, 'and weighted down with anvils of iron'.)[14] Ridewall constructs his depiction by borrowing details from the later account of Juno as worldliness (2.3). There he depicts, in order, Juno as goddess of kingdoms, here part [4]; veiled [1], with tutelary peacock [8], and served by Iris [2]. In the later account, of course, these are attributes presented *in malo*, in accord with the *versus* used for the division there; here they are converted to attributes *in bono*.

26 *in intellectu*: O's reading balances the later *in affectu*.

112–13 *Te … adorent*: marg. I, om. O. Unlike the examples cited in the Introduction, pp. 18–19, which show I's affinity with A, here, in a passage where I suggest that I originally was following a manuscript like O, it has been corrected to provide readings of A.

Amalthee, de cuius lacte poete fingunt deum Iouem fuisse nutritum. Unde propter hanc causam poete fingunt Iouem capram suam nutricem in celum transtulisse et translatum stellificasse' (C2 fol. 46ᵛ).

[13] 'Uicesimus primus, fuerunt eciam dii reliqui reputati magni ex recreacionis saturitate, sicud patet de de[o] [MS de] Habundio et de dea Sacia, quos pagani magnificabant, credentes ab hiis numinibus prouenire inter homines copiam dela[t]is [MS de|lantis] et delicatis cibariis' (C1 fol. 3).

[14] 'ait Iunonem ab Ioue uinctam catenis aureis et degrauatam incudibus ferreis'.

143 *sepisse*: As quite regularly, the medieval Latin fusion of *c/s/sc* renders the reading, a representation of classical *coepi-*, routinely in the text *cepi-*, a little opaque.

183ff. *imperatores*, etc.: I have accommodated the textus receptus to the readings of the source, obscured by a number of small scribal misperceptions. Key here is 186, O's homeograph *usibus* for correct *ossibus*. *Inuector* for the epic epithet 'breaker (of horses)' is otherwise unrecorded, but *nutritores* isn't particularly sensible (horse-breeders?), a complaint also to be lodged against later *itaque*.

194 *Neckam*: Although, unlike Ridewall, he offers the usual moralisation of the peacock *in malo*, as the tainted rich, a reading Ridewall reserves for 2.3/151–88.

195 *tutrix*: O has settled for a fixed phrase prominent in citations from patristic discussions.

198 *a recidiuo*: Much of the variation appears to reflect the fact that, although morphologically an adjective, *recidiuus* is recorded as a noun 'relapse' frequently in Anglo-Latin.

199–200 For the second line, Horace reads 'tu nichil admittes in te', rather than 'oderunt michi a peccare' (although the citation in this form, with 'mali' for 'michi', appears elsewhere).

225–26 *corporeus corpus*: Very likely an archetypal doublet of doubt or other dittography. A *cooperiens* 'covering' recognises the difficulty, and just possibly does reflect the headword of 215 'madefaccio/madefacta'.

[5] Neptune/Intelligence

Again, Fulgentius offered only a single detail for this discussion, point [8], and even this is given a naturalistic allegorisation there. The remainder of the account mainly depends upon materials Ridewall collected from Remigius's commentary on *De nuptiis*. The punishing Harpies have been removed from Fulg's discussion of Pluto, in accord with comments in Ridewall's prologue to *DCD*: 'Fifteenth, there were other gods who were accounted great on account of the rigour of their justice, as is evident with the god Neptune. Poets depict him as the god of rigour and punitive justice, because through him, they say the flood washed over the world to avenge and punish sinners. This occurred in the time of the god "Icabo" and Pyrrha, his wife, and Augustine also treats this.'[15] (The 'dei Icabonis' of the MS is surely a scribal stab at 'Deucalionis'.)

---

[15] 'Quinto decimo, fuerunt et dii alii reputati magni ex iusticie seueritate, sicud

17 *secunde*: *tercie* has been attracted to the earlier *terciam prolem*.

23, 39 *recte*: perhaps O's automatic intrusion.

29-30 *Ieronymus ... ad Demetriadem*: Ridewall knows the ascription is erroneous, 'ut Beda dicit in opere suo *Super Cantica*, non fuit Ieronimi, set fuit facta a quodam oratore Cristiano qui tamen fuit infectus heresi Pelagiana' (C2, fol. 22, on *DCD* 6.4, cols 179-80). This is a lengthy discussion of the power of the human *dictamen*, dismissed by Augustine; for the (accurate) reference to Bede, see *PL* 91:1073.

70-71 *sicut patet ... sicut patet*: The second of these two uses has probably generated the first, but, however awkward, the reading is universal.

86 *appreciacione*: Another transparent form that has escaped lexicographers.

99 *uarie gaze*: I've accommodated several variants to the source text. However, Apuleius reads *variegata*, but this reading, which strikes me as *durior*, is a widely occurring variant. In 102, A *abolitis* is an intensifier for Apuleius's *amolitis*, and I've followed L in correcting the text. In 107, O alone reproduces Apuleius's *pauperem*. 109-10 *nec ... Socratis* is Ridewall's connective, as is L's *dixeris* after *Si* in 112. In Apuleius's original, the whole is presented as a question and response.

101 *cingula*: Although all the scribes write forms indicating their participation in the fusion of earlier *c* and *s*, they remain capable of being confused by the resulting ambiguous forms.

152 *Ista est ... intelligencie*: In contrast, O reads, *Ista ... intelligencie dure*. Assuming that, as elsewhere, O has represented *dicitur/dicuntur* by *dure*, retaining something like the copy-text may be the preferable: 'This threefold offspring are called ... '. The other copies would then have suppressed a verb indicating naming before *nominantur* in the following sentence.

167 *sceleritate*: In a context in which *scelerum* has just appeared, this is the universal reading. But the form represents, as the etymology 'cicius auferens' indicates, *celeritate*.

186 *Hugo in libro suo* De anima: On the status of this text – and that Ridewall knew it only through MF's citations – see the Index fontium.

patet de deo Neptuno, quem poete fingunt deum seueritatis et iusticie punitiue, quia per eum dicunt diluuia ducta in mundum ad uindictam et punicionem peccatorum. Sed patet de tempore dei Icabonis et Pirre, coniugis sue, et de isto eciam tangit Augustinus' (C1 fol. 2ᵛ). The concluding reference is to *DCD* 18.10 (col. 568).

197 *Notys olitos*: Juvenal, of course, reads the Greek γνῶθι σεαυτόν 'gnothi seauton', but this is a routine medieval Latin approximation.

221 *surrepciones*: The form is not recorded in dictionaries, and is probably a derivative of *subrepo*, not of *subrapio* (that form, recognised in dictionaries, means 'theft').

254 *acuende*: In fact a sophistication (I ac<.>uende, *with eras.*) for Cicero's *augendae*. Cicero has *memoriam* after *forcium*. But Ridewall's readings are inherited from the *glossa*. The passage is cited again, in a discussion of euhemerism, at C2 fol. 65 (on *DCD* 6.8, col. 187). There, Ridewall reads *acuende*, includes 'quisque memoriam uirorum forcium memoria' (although within a certain amount of paraphrase) and reads *Mauri*. In Cicero, this concluding noun refers to the Alabandans in south-west Turkey.

[6] Pluto/Providence

This chapter groups what Fulg presents as six separate discussions, his 1.5–10, all particularly brief. Only the first, responsible for Ridewall's points [2] and [3], directly addresses Pluto. Ridewall reorders and disposes Fulg's chapters among his 'partes' of the argument: Cerberus [4 = Fulg 1.6], Proserpina/Hecate [5 = Fulg 1.10], the Furies [6 = Fulg 1.7], the Fates [7 = Fulg 1.8]. Fulg's 1.9, on the Harpies, has already appeared in the previous mythography, and the brief 1.11 on Ceres is simply ignored, but for the etymological note at 253. Ridewall manages to incorporate nearly all Fulg's sketchy detail, but his ample augmentations are a great deal more striking.

Ridewall's description of Pluto in the prologue to his commentary on *DCD* runs:

> Twelfth, there were other gods who were called great because of their excessive wealth, as is evident with the god Februus or Pluto. He was extolled by the pagans for his riches. They claimed that Pluto or Februus was the god of riches, as Remigius shows in his commentary on *On the marriage*, where he says that the Greek name Pluto is the same as Latin Dis and 'rich person'.

In this account of the gods, Ridewall again ignores Ceres altogether; the closest analogue he mentions is 'Seventh, there were other gods accounted great because of the profusion of what they produced, as is evident with the god Genius, whom pagans claimed was the god of nature and of generation.'[16]

---

[16] 'Duodecimo, fuerunt et alii dii uocati magni ex opulencie ubertate, sicud patet de deo Februo seu Plutone. Qui fuit ab ipsis paganis magnificatus pro suis diuiciis. Fingunt enim istum Plutonem siue Februum deum esse diuiciarum, sicud patet Remigium super librum *De nupciis*, ubi dicit quod Pluto Grece idem est quod Dis et

29 *uirtus*: The A addition *prouidencie* is an overspecification; as lines 33–34 indicate, Seneca describes a monadic Stoic 'virtus'.

74 Ibi ... *prouidencie*: This concluding sentence, with its biblical allusion, is Ridewall's addition.

79 *rubia*: perhaps a small error, shared by all the copies, for Bernard's *rubra*.

90ff. The same authorities and much the same material appear in the commentary on *DCD* 6.5.2 (col. 181), following the material cited at 3/12n. The one notable variation, appropriate to the discussion of Heraclitus there, is an additional etymology ascribed to Damascene, 'or *theos* is derived from *ethin* "burning", for God is a fire that consumes all malice' (uel *ethin*, id est ardens. Deus enim ignis est consumens omnem maliciam, C2 fol. 29). Like Ridewall's citations from *Suda*, this again indicates his access to Robert Grosseteste's rare translation of Damascene, available at Oxford Greyfriars.

102 Confusion between *circa* and *contra*, which can be represented by the identical abbreviated form, c^a, is endemic in Latin texts.

132–34 Cf. Seneca's 'Here the savage hell-hound terrifies the shades; he guards the kingdom with his triple head, shaking it with his huge outcry' (Hic saevus umbras territat Stygius canis, / qui terna vasto capita concutiens sono / regnum tuetur). **135** *concutit* suggests that the original quotation may have been more exact.

138 *uorans carnes*: the etymology is from VM3 6.22 (187/1–3).

142 *draconina*: The Anglo-Latin dictionary has but a single citation, from an analogous description of the chimera (cf. 2.4/148–60).

166 *omnium*: I have suppressed the following, unnecessarily specifying qualification (*mundanorum*) *hominum*, which appears neither in Chrysostom's original nor in the partial reprise of this passage at 10.125. After 168 *terribilis*, *domina* is also alien to the original and is probably a second-generation echo of the earlier usage (stimulated by preceding *dura*). In the reprise *subicit*, here the universal reading, reads instead *deuincit*.

174–75 *triplicem cupiditatis morsum*: This introduces a commonplace reading of avarice, cf. the *versus* cited at 204–05, or the extensive comparison of the avaricious with a poisonous spider, Malachy 755–94.

190 *Et ... mota*: Juvenal reads, 'et mota ad lunam'. I've corrected in part, although *lumen* appears the (inexact) archetypal reading.

"diues" Latine' (C1 fol. 2ᵛ). And 'Septimo, fuerunt dii alii reputati magni ex produccionis fecunditate, sicud patet de deo Genio, quem pagani finxerunt deum nature et generacionis' (C1 fol. 2).

226 *quecunque*: O *omne* is, of course, ungrammatical, but it may imply that O's exemplar, like I's, read the singular *periculum*.

246-47 *Ecati ... Proserpina*: In his prologue to DCD, Ridewall offers only the briefest reference to the 'triple goddess': 'Twentieth, there were other gods considered great from the pleasure associated with their job, as is evident with the goddess Diana. The pagans extolled her, considering her to be the goddess of the woods and of hunting.'[17]

261 *filia dee Cibelis*: The lure of a telling etymology seems to have drawn Ridewall here. He apparently forgets or suppresses the basic grammar-school text, Claudian's *De raptu*, where Ceres is Cybele's daughter; the appropriate information appears in both Fulg (22/9-10) and VM3 7.1 (197/9). The etymological reading, however forced it may seem, is commonplace; see Peter Comestor 1/93-97, 2/55 (pp. 46-47, 66). Holcot also alludes to it in a discussion of patient/solid charity at *Robert Holcot*, 126-27/81-96.

269ff. Cf. Ridewall's comment on the end of *DCD* 6.3 (col. 179), a discussion of Diana as a god 'incertus', because having multiple images: 'Likewise, Diana's idol is depicted with three faces, following Virgil's verse, "The three faces of the virgin Diana"' [*Aeneid* 4.511].[18]

342 *irarum*: Fulg reads *istarum* (21/2), but, given the turn to discord in the next two sentences, this is a plausible enough reading. Cf. Fulg's further description of Tisiphone, 'in vocem irrumpere' (21/4-5).

345 A slightly inaccurate reference to Seneca's *discordem deam* 93 ('the goddess Discord').

376 *reuellendum est*: *reuelandum* AIL is surely a substitution.

450 *incidit*: *occat* L, like A *secat*, an effort to dissimilate the reading from the preceding word in *inc-*, has been suggested by the common *versus*, Walther *Sprich*. 2879b: 'Clotho colum baiulat, Lachesis net, Attropos occat'.

510ff. The citation appears to be a set-piece of ps.-Augustinian materials; in addition to the sermon I cite, further examples appear at *Meditationes* 21 (*PL* 40:917) and *Speculum* 1.30 (*PL* 40:981). There are a great many variants, most predictable scribalisms, from any of the printed versions: 518-19 *aliis tristem ... bono* has no parallel in 'Augustine'; 520 *honores* corresponds to *humores* in the source; 520 *extenuat/exterminant* to *aestuant*; 522 *eniruat* to

---

[17] 'Uicesimo, fuerunt eciam dii alii uocati magni ex occupacionis amenitate, sicud patet de dea Diana, quam pagani magnificabant, estimantes eam esse deam nemorum et uenacionum' (fol. 3).

[18] 'Similiter de ymagine Diane que depingebatur cum triplici facie iuxta illud poete Uirgilii, "Tria uirginis ora Diane"' (C2 fol. 19).

hebetat; 523-24 *marcidam facit* to *consumit*, and the concluding sentence is mainly paraphrase. While that final detail may imply that this was always paraphrase, the variation suggests that this example, at least, is derived from a citation version or a *florilegium*, not *originalia* (although notice the directive at 534-35). However, the source was not *MF* uita humana presens g; it agrees with the *PL* texts, although misascribed 'in originali tractans illud Iacobi IIII'.

[7] Apollo/Truth

As with Pluto, Fulg displays the discussion over multiple chapters, 1.12-15, 17: Apollo, the crow (Ridewall's part [9]), the laurel (Ridewall's [8]), the Muses (Ridewall's [7]), Apollo's youth and his arrows (Ridewall's [1]), respectively. Virtually all Fulg's material is absorbed here – the discussion of the Muses as extensive direct quotation. However, in part [4], while the Ovidian account substitutes for Fulg's rather unusual nomenclature, the explanation is largely Fulg's. In contrast, although Apollo's various names in part [6] are ascribed to Fulg, he offers only 'sol'/'solus', and the discussion is entirely predicated on Mart and VM3, a point also emphasised in the prologue to *DCD*: 'Eleventh, there were other gods whom the pagans called great because of their obscure thought, as is evident with the god Apollo. The pagans extolled him, because he gave answers and made doubtful things clear. For this reason, they called him Delius for his revelation of doubtful things, and Remigius treats this in his commentary on *On the marriage*, as Augustine also does in this book.'[19] See further 4n.

1 *septima*: But *duodecima* A (variation henceforth ignored in the collations). At the chapter-break, A reads: '//Finita autem 6ᵃ mithologia Fulgencii, sequitur 12ᵃ methologia Fulgencii de Apolline' (fol. 48ᵛᵇ), but cf. the L variant *undecima*, cited in the collations to 6/545-46. In A, this numbering runs to the end of the text, in both that MS's regular running titles and in the text's references, and with double numbering (e.g., both '1' and '19') for bk 2. One might further notice that A's table of chapters (fol. 78ᵛᵇ) runs unproblematically from 1 to 6, but the scribe then originally wrote '7', cancelled it immediately and replaced it by '12', with the rest in sequence 13-22.

The variation reflects a confusion between Ridewall's 'mythologies' and the chapters of Fulg's book 1. There, Fulg devotes seven chapters, 1.5-11,

---

[19] 'Undecimo fuerunt dii alii ab istis gentilibus dicti magni ex innotescencie mente (?), sicud patet de deo Apolline, quem pagani magnificabant, quia ipse responsa dabat et quecunque dubia declarabat. Unde uocabant eum Delium a declaracione dubiorum, et de isto tangit Remigius super librum *De nupciis* et eciam Augustinus in isto uolumine' (C1 fol. 2ᵛ).

to Pluto and his companions, and, thus, Apollo is chapter 12. However, this numeration imposed on A's rendition equally ignores Fulg's further chapter divisions. As my headnote indicates, Fulg treats Apollo, like Pluto, in multiple chapters, including, in the fourth such, a discussion of Phaeton. This second possibility for multiple numbering was probably precluded by Ridewall's offering an independent account of Phaeton, rather than one subordinated, as in Fulg.

Nearly identical treatment appears in Q, as well as in the other MSS that share its 12-chapter version of the text, Berlin and Royal. These MSS run unproblematically through 1.6, and their early divisions are much as those in I. Although Q does not number its Apollo chapter, Royal here reads more or less as A, 'Sic igitur finita est ui^a mithologia Fulgencii. Sequitur xii^a mithologia Fulgencii'. Excepting its omission at the head of Apollo, Q agrees with A and the others in presenting mythologies numbered 13–17 (where the text ends with Perseus). This agreement implies that all three copies represent the presentation in β. (The Berlin rubric at the end of 1.6, 'Sic igitur finitur ista mithologia Fulgencii, et est *ultima*, etc.', offers no evidence for a truncated authorial text, but is rather a scribal misunderstanding of L's *undecima*.)

The situation is more complicated in I. The forms in this MS are decidedly mixed, often inconsistent, and subject to correction, completed or intended; the relevant deviant examples include:

8/1 'Sequitur mithologia 8 <*over eras.*> Fulgencii <13 *erased*> de Fetonte … ' [marked marginally as 'Octaua metho'].

8/439–41 as O, with variants: 'sic igitur … fingitur a poetis. Sequitur 13^a de onus [sic] Mercurio … '.

10/1 'Sequitur [*blank*] mithologia Fulgencii de Dane … '.

10/143–44 + 12/1 '…et sic finitur 15^a mithologia Fulgencii sequitur. Sequitur 11^a mithologia Fulgencii de Perseo … ' [Recall that, at this point, I lacks authorial 1.11.]

12/280–13/1 ' … sic igitur finita est 12^a mithologia Fulgencii. [a blank line, a more emphatic division than the usual mid-line lombardic capital that customarily marks chapter openings in this MS] Sequitur 18 (?) mithologia Fulgencii de Alceste … '.

13/254–55 ' … et sic igitur finita 18^a mithologia Fulgencii et commentarium in librum primum mithologiarum eiusdem'.

2.4/243–44 ' … sic igitur 22^a finita methologia in ordine Fulgencii tam quarta (?) 2^i libri quod Stocton'.

The wavering between authorial numeration and that present in β copies further testifies to I's probable conflation/multiple manuscript consultation described at Introduction pp. 18–20.

4 *uersus finem*: Perhaps the phrase 'libri 2' has dropped out.

12 In the commentary on *DCD*, Ridewall describes Apollo's cultic image on several occasions, e.g. on *DCD* 6.7, 'Apollo ephebus' (col. 184): 'Apollo was depicted in temples as youthful and completely beardless, with golden hair and a crown with twelve precious stones on his head, as well as carrying a bow and quiver with arrows. Ancient authors and poets discuss these attributes, Martianus and his commentator Remigius, as well as Fulgentius and Ovid.'[20]

24 *partes*: But uel decem A, *adds* uel decem I (and Royal). As the AI variant in line 66, 'Sequitur secunda pars ...', would indicate, the reading ignores 15 'iuuenis *armatus*' and reflects a sense that Ridewall's part [1] should treat youth exclusively. AIQ and Royal continue this misnumbering through the account.

76–86 This discussion forms a model sermon division, introduced by a triplet rhyming on classical -æ, presented as such in I, and succeeded in the following paragraph by 'proof-texts' that offer biblical warrant for the argumentative division, three verses indicating appropriate contexts for *ueritas*, one for each of the proffered divisions.

87 *Si uero*: *Siue* is the unanimous reading, perhaps dittography for Siue si 'put otherwise, if'. However, as the parallel lines 96 and 97, it should surely read *Si*. I've assimilated the reading to those parallels.

97–98 *secunda ... terciam*: Inadvertently reversing the order established in the division above.

117 *tanta*, **119** *mora*: Both readings confirmed by Augustine's text.

130 *uirtutis ueritatis*: AI share, in motivation, the same original misprision and have dropped one of the two genitives (either a small skip or haplography). However, the readings suggest, even in I's illegibility, that each had omitted a different one of the pair, *uirtutis* in A, *ueritatis* in I. The I correction probably comes from consultation of the β copy available to its scribe Stockton.

142 *inuectitur*: Although the sense is rare (there are two figurative uses in the Anglo-Latin Dictionary), all copies witness initial *in-*, rather than the common simple verb (clearly a guess in O).

---

[20] 'Depingebatur enim in templis etate iuuenis et totus imberbis, cum crinibus et capillis aureis, coronam habens in capite de xii lapidibus preciosis, portans eciam archam cum pharatram [sic] et sagittis, sicud de istis tangunt antiqui auctores et poete, scilicet Marcianus et commentator suus Remigius. Similiter Fulgencius et poeta Ouidius' (C2 fol. 44ᵛ). Similar discussions appear at C2, fols 19ᵛ, 20ᵛ, and 45ᵛ–46. The last contrasts the image of the armed Apollo, described as angry-faced, with the benign image of the life-giving sun, when the god appears 'cum wltu hilari et cum cithara aurea in manu'.

162 *pertinet*: O's plural probably reflects the possible confusion introduced by a form like A pertīet.

174 *ut sit auriga quadrige ueritatis*: Unlike Phaeton in the next mythography.

213 *torpens uel*: Although this appears O's doublet of doubt (*om*. AI), one should note 223 *torpedo* and that, in the reprise at line 259, AI preserve the doublet.

227 *in* Historia orientali: From Marco Polo's description of the legendary *gymnosophisti* 'naked wise men', the Brahmans. Ridewall also knew the more expansive account offered by the Brahman sage Didimus to Alexander the Great, and cites at length its attack on pagan polytheism from *De preliis Magni Alexandri* at C2 fol. 35 (on *DCD* 6.6, cols 182–83).

233 *concernit*: Although the unanimous reading, *continet* is not sensible.

249 *loquitur Augustinus*: From a passing comment on 1 Io 4:18.

266–67 *et statim Marcianus ponit nomina lapidum*: They are, of course, the signs of the zodiac, through which the sun passes on its annual course. Cf. also VM3 8.7–13 (203/3–207/44).

275 Aristotle has 'Abraycorum et Scitorum'.

290–93 Another rhyming *distinccio*, inviting elaboration from the pulpit and more extensive than that in 76ff. It is presented as a *distinccio*, the parts yoked with brackets, in AI and subjected to amplification in the following paragraphs.

307, 308 *angulos*: Perhaps alluding to Prv 7:12?

350ff. In his commentary on *DCD*, C2 fol. 27^{rv}, on 6.5.1 (col. 181), Ridewall develops his own mythographic account to undermine 'poetic theology' (cf. Plato constructing 'the dream of Er', after decrying the excesses of the poets):

> *Another from drops of blood.* Augustine introduces Varro's third example; in it, Varro rejects poetic or fabular theology. In this example, Varro mentions the horse Pegasus, which the poets report was born from bloody drops from the Gorgon Medusa, when Perseus slew her. Ovid retells this fable in the *Metamorphoses* [4.785–86, 5.250–68]. Poets claim that this horse was turned into a star and put in the heavens, as Hyginus tells in *On the heavenly images* [*De astronomia* 2.17]. Because of this stellification, this horse was worshipped as a god by credulous pagans.
>
> For poets claim that the horse Pegasus, immediately after it was born, struck the earth with its hoof. From his blow, sprang a fountain, sacred to the nine Muses, because the water from

this fountain had the property of filling those who drank it with wisdom. For this reason, Persius recalls the story, when he says, 'I didn't wash my lips in the nag's fountain' [*Satyrae*, Prol.1]. Taking this literally, people who weren't very good at the art of poetry were accustomed to come to that fountain to drink and to sleep next to it. They thought that in their sleep they would miraculously receive poetic gifts. Because of this effect, some people worshipped Pegasus as if the horse were a god.

That's what Varro appears to have understood in the words that Augustine cites. However, Varro opposed the divinity of Pegasus by two sorts of arguments I have already cited. This kind of poetic theology detracts from divinity both its proper dignity, as well as its eternality and immortality. For the horse Pegasus was born at a specific time and of disgusting matter, from the blood of the terrifying monster Medusa. But every true god is eternal and immaterial. Thus, it's unbefitting to ascribe any true god any bodily image. It's even more unbefitting that any true god be figured in the likeness of a brute animal. Therefore, Varro said significantly that poetic theology includes many made up things opposed to the dignity and nature of God, and particularly as to how the poets' gods had been depicted.[21]

[21] 'Ibi *Aliis ex guttis sanguinis*. Ponit Augustinus tercium exemplum Marci Uarronis, per quod Uarro improbauit theologiam poeticam seu fabularem. Et facit in hoc exemplo Uarro mencionem de equo Pegaso, quem poete fingunt genitum de guttis sanguinis Gorgonis, id est Meduse interfecte a Perseo, quam fabulam tangit Ouidius libro suo *De transformatis*. Iste equus fingitur a poetis stellificatus et in celum translatus, sicud tangit Yginius in suo libro *De ymaginibus celestibus*. Et racione istius sui stellificacionis, equs iste predictus pro deo colebatur ab incredulis et paganis. ... Nam poete fingunt quod iste equs Pegasus, statim quando fuit natus, [fol. 27ᵛ] percussit terram cum pede. Ex qua percussione, fons erupit qui nouem Musis fuit consecratus, eo quod aqua fontis illius fuit talis nature quod bibentes repleuit sciencia. Unde de isto meminit Persius in poesi suo quando dicit, "Nec fonte labra prolui caballino". Ad litteram enim consueuerunt aliqui minus experti in arte poetica ad illum fontem accedere et de fonte haurire et iuxta fontem obdormire; in quo somno putabant se recipere miraculose artem poeticam, et racione huius effectus iste equs Pegasus ab aliquibus colebatur sicud deus.

Et istud Marcus Uarro uidetur intelligere in uerbis suis que in littera recitat Augustinus. Contra istam autem diuinitatem istius Pegasi se opposuit Marcus Uarro per illa duo media superius posita. Derogant [sic] enim huiusmodi poetice tam dignitati diuinitatis quam eciam sue eternitati et immortalitati. Iste enim equs Pegasus fuit natus ex tempore et de uili materia, quia de sanguine illius horrendi monstri, scilicet Gorgonis seu Meduse. Deus autem omnis uerus eternus est et immaterialis. Indignum est eciam aliqui uero deo attribuere quamcumque figuram

398   John Ridewall, *Fulgencius metaforalis*

Leaving aside the objections ascribed to Varro (whom Ridewall can have known only through citations), his invented account would deny poetic myth any efficacy in pursuing supernal truth. In this account, as the lawyers say of illegal searches, myth is indeed 'the fruit of the poisoned tree'. The poets' inspiration is quite literally an effusion of monstrous blood.

360 *adiutorio*: Although A's *agitacione* A is attractive, Mart 101/30 supports O.

383 *adquirende*: Supported by Fulg 26/2ff.

419-20 Reproducing Fulg 24/16-18, a list of those 'qui de somniorum interpretatione scripserunt' (those who have written about the interpretation of dreams) as 'Antiphon, Filocorus et Artemon et Serapion Ascalonites'.

447 *fuit tacta*: at lines 334-35.

468 *Triplex est esse ueritas*: The passage I have cited at 3/94-95n continues: 'This was the reason why those who administered the ceremonies for the gods under the priests and augurs had been established as five in number, namely fifteen of them, which make five groups of three.' Ridewall associates the number three with Amor/Cupid on the basis of Virgil, *Ecloga* 8.74 ('numero deus impare gaudet'), and as a number praising the creator on the basis of Aristotle's prologue to *De celo*. Much the same information recurs in Ridewall's comment on *DCD* 6.5.2 (col. 181), on 'philosophical theology', where Ridewall recounts Pythagoras's opinion that number was the universal principle: 'Pythagoras specially attributed the number three to God, because it is the number dedicated to love. ... Because God ought to be loved by people before anything else, Pythagoras established that in prayers, sacrifices, and other things that worship God, worshippers should always use the number three.'[22]

---

corporalem. Et multo indignus est quod alius uerus deus effigietur in similitudine bruti animalis. Et ideo signanter dicebat Uarro quod in theologia poetica fuerunt multa ficta contra dignitatem et naturam Dei, et specialiter quantum ad hoc quod dii poetici erant sic figurati.'

[22] 'Hec ergo fuit causa quare qui sub pontificibus et auguribus administrabant sacra deorum fuerant in isto numero [five] ordinati, scilicet quindecim et idem faciunt quinquies terni'. And: 'Deo autem attribuebat Pytagoras specialiter numerum ternarium, quia iste numerus fuit consecratus amori. ... Quia igitur Deus est summe ab hominibus diligendus, ideo Pytagoras ordinauit quod in sacrificiis et oracionibus et aliis quibus colendus deus, semper cultores uterentur numero ternario' (C2 fol. 29).

Textual notes: [8] Phaeton/Ambition 399

479 The *versus*, which actually has seven members, concludes ' ... redimo, tego, colligo, condo' (I ransom, I cover/shelter, I gather/visit, I bury'). The last member, 'burying the dead' was imported from Tob to bring the number to the magical seven.

[8] Phaeton/Ambition

Uniquely in this chapter, Ridewall owes virtually nothing to Fulg. His presentation offers only details that inspire Ridewall's division [12], largely with attention to the Ovidian transformation of the Heliades. Instead, the entire discussion overtly comes from Ovid's account. Difficulties in accurately rendering his sophisticated verse spill over into a very sloppy rendition of the whole.

1 *Apollonis*: I leave O's form for *Apollinis* as a plausible spelling.

27 *inficianda*: To represent Ovid's *infitianda*.

67 *animatus uel*: May represent O's effort at glossing the metaphor.

95 *Wlcano fabro*: He appears among the great gods Ridewall discusses in the prologue to *DCD*: 'Seventeenth, there were some gods who were called great from their subtle artifice, as is evident with the god Vulcan, whom the poets depict as Jupiter's smith. Ovid speaks of his subtle artifice in the *Metamorphoses* [most notably at 4.167–89], as does Augustine.'[23]

114 425 *cellis*: Representing *sellis* 'seats'.

118 *Hugo*: The citation includes gloriously untranslatable wordplay, e.g. *mensa/missa* or *leporum* 'bunnies'/*leprosorum*.

128 *decoracior*: decorior I, *adds* uel speciosior O, perhaps an error for Hugh's *ornacior*. 128–29 *mensa ... calice* has no parallel in Hugh.

149ff. In general, Ridewall's citations correspond to the texts offered by *PL*. This is equally true of a substantial portion of the citations from Innocent. However, such is not the case with a series of adjacent citations from *De miseria* (others at 185, 199, and 234), most particularly this one. In this case, matters are further complicated by a conjunction of the transmitted readings with the presentation at *MF* ambitio u. Not only do the two accounts share readings, but both Ridewall and *MF* edit the passage similarly; both agree in suppressing a full sentence and one

---

[23] 'Septimo decimo, fuerunt eciam aliqui dii dicti magni ex artificii subtilitate, sicud patet de deo Wlcano, qui fingitur a poetis fas (*l*. faber?) dei Iouis. Et de istius artificis subtilitate loquitur Ouidius, libro suo *De transformatis* et eciam de eo loquitur Augustinus' (C1 fol. 2ᵛ).

clause. Conversely, *MF* includes two readings equivalent to the *PL* text; for 153–54 *ignorat notos, contempnit antiquos* [*socios*], *MF* reads *notos ignorat hesternos, comites contemnit antiquos*.

Given that elsewhere Ridewall accurately cites the *PL* Innocent, and that his citations include materials not paralleled in *MF*, I consider this coalescence accidental. A wider conspectus of the manuscript tradition of Innocent's text, provided by Lewis's edition, indicates that the agreements, and the variations from the *PL* text, simply reflect widespread readings, many probably correct, as the *PL* rendition is not. For this passage, see 183/30.1–9 and the collations, where Lewis's text accords with Ridewall's, except in reading *ignorat, extraneos nouit, comites* [and *nouit* om. in many copies]. Lewis's evidence would suggest that the only difficulty in Ridewall's citation would be *socios*, which may represent AIL's clarifying scribal supply. His account indicates the potential for abundant variation in a text of virtually universal appeal. See further the notes to 185ff., 199ff., and 234ff.

183 *donacionem*: de^acionem (= ? deificacionem) A, \de/inacionem I. As its only partial correction indicates – notice I's retention of O -*na*- – this represents a reading I has conflated in from its β exemplar.

185ff. This citation is one of several not paralleled in *MF*. See Lewis, *De miseria* 178/26.14–17, 24–31, and the collations. 191 *deuiet* is Lewis's preferred reading; 188 *hominibus* and 193 *simplicibus* are variants widely dispersed in the transmission (for correct *omnibus* and *supplicibus*). I have emended the received 193 *habilis* to Lewis's *humilis*, since it probably reflects difficulties with an abbreviated form that might occur in Ridewall's transmission; however, I retain what may be a synonymous substitution 194 *discretus* (Lewis *astutus*).

199ff. See Lewis, *De miseria* 179/27.1–6, and his collations. All Ridewall's variations from Lewis's and *PL*'s text reproduce widely disseminated variants: 199 *forsan* (for *forte*), 203 *prodolor* (for *proh pudor*), and the intruded 204 *fas et nephas*.

201–3 Simon magus, of course, gives his name to 'simony', the purchase of church office (Ac 8:18–24). The less familar Gehazi, Elisha the prophet's servant, takes money for his master's healing powers after his master has refused reward; he is stricken with leprosy for his venality (4 Rg 5:15–27).

229 *exulcerentur*: Gregory's reading; *exasperentur* has been assimilated to the following word.

234ff. See Lewis, *De miseria* 183–85/30.11–13, and his collations. Although the reading is somewhat compromised by the MS's adjacent errors, I take *grauius* in I to indicate that Ridewall's original reading corresponded to Lewis's text and was not the *insanus* of the other copies.

338 *nutans*: Bernard's reading, subjected to an added minim to create a considerably more familiar partial synonym in most copies.

377 *quasi lanugo*: So O, as opposed to the universal *tanquam* in the Vulgate. The reading is very likely to represent dissimilation, although I have let it stand.

406 *tacta superius*: At 4/176.

434 *solent suas sorores uocare*: This is apparently accepted, although not recognised, Middle English usage; cf. 'The Bargain of Judas', Cambridge, Trinity College, MS 323, line 7, 'Imette wid is soster þe swikele wimon.'

[9] Mercury/Eloquence

Most of the description (parts [2], [4–7]) relies on Fulg's attribute-centred account. Part [1] is a submerged moralisation of the caduceus (explained otherwise under part [8]), and part [3] has been inspired by one of Ridewall's persistent mythographic sources, Mart.

Ridewall also describes Mercury in his prologue to *DCD*: 'Thirteenth, there were gods called great because of the sweetness of their eloquence, as is evident with Mercury or Hermes, whom the idolaters extolled, attributing to him power because of his speech and eloquence. Remigius treats this at length in his commentary on Martianus.'[24]

20 *continetur sub uirtute iusticie*: See the Commentary, p. 429.

22ff. Ridewall offers a similar account in his comment on the end of *DCD* 6.3 (col. 179, at C2 fol. 19ᵛ), a description of Mercury as a 'deus incertus' whose gender shifts in representations, with an analogous astronomical explanation.

41 *uertit ad graciam*: Jerome identifies this action, in a phrase Ridewall suppresses, as resembling those of the Pharisees.

80–81 *simili modo*: The whole account, of course, forms a *mise en abyme*, an analogue to Ridewall's own removing the danger from myth through moralisation.

85 *et cum omni*: But annonum I. Although ungrammatical (the noun is feminine), a provocative reading, perhaps 'the people, pacified through an *annona* "grain-dole"'. This would be appropriate, because the anecdote

---

[24] 'Tercio decimo, fuerunt dii alii dicti magni ex eloquencie suauitate, sicud patet de deo Mercurio seu Hermete, quem magnificabant ydolatre, attribuentes ei uirtutem per oracionis et eloquencie, sicud de istis tractat diffuse Remigius super Marcianum' (C1 fol. 2ᵛ).

deals with a riot over Roman grain supply (and Menenius's intervention was thoroughly cynical, since the people were the empty stomach, rioting over local shortages).

97 *circumstancias*: In classical rhetoric, these were the properties of the person and the action that every argument was to address. The standard medieval set included 'quis, quid, cur, quomodo, ubi, quando, quibus auxiliis?' These categories were particularly prominent in the Middle Ages not as injunctions for forensic orators but as penitential questions, to be addressed both in the penitent's preparation and the priest's confessional interrogation. Similarly, in a discussion, based upon Aristotle and Cicero, analysing the requirements for a moral act at the end of *DCD* 6.4 (col. 180), Ridewall proposes 'qui agant, ubi agant, quando agant, et quid agant' (C2 fol. 16). On the rhetorical background, see the index entry *circumstantiae* at Copeland–Sluiter 924; and on widespread confessional use, Robertson.

139 *uagus*: The edited Fulg 31/2 reads 'uacuus', but Helm's collation identifies *uagus* as a prominent variant.

156 *resipuit*: A normal Anglo-Latin form for Valerius's 'resipiscuit'.

159 *trucidauit*: literally 'slaughtered', an appropriate punchline, matching Argus's spilt blood, as the final sentence makes clear.

170 *sinum cordis*, **171** *prepedit*: Both emendations reflect Gregory's text.

224 *galerum*: Fulg 29/18–19 reads 'Galere enim coperto capite pingitur, quod omne negotium sit semper absconsum' (he is depicted with a helmet covering his head, because all trading ought to be hidden). Ridewall puts the word into a different declension, and ignores Fulg's moralisation, as he does with the moralisation of the cockerel at line 250.

[10] Danae/Modesty and Women's Greed

Fulg 1.18–20 (31/4–9) appears to represent a lacuna in the text. Ridewall's source concludes with Mercury's bloody deception of Argus, ascribed to cunning overcoming even the most careful caution. He continues, 'Solet igitur adludere his speciebus et honeste mendax Grecia et poetica garrulitas semper de falsitate ornata, [XIX. De Danae] dum et Danae imbre aurato corrupta est non pluuia, sed pecunia.' Although the introduction emphasises 'women's greed', Ridewall's account mainly addresses the 'astuta falcataque cautela' that served neither Argus nor Acrisius, and Danae's longstanding modesty. For such ambiguities in the myth, see Kahr, esp. 43–45, 46 n.18.

Of course, Ridewall's prologue to *DCD* limits itself to gods, not to the human figures of myth, but cf. (as also with 13/1): 'Tenth, there were other gods who were accounted great because proof against corruption and

Textual notes: [11] Ganymede/Sodomy 403

virginal in their wholeness, as is evident with the goddess Vesta, whom the idolaters extolled for her pure modesty. For they believed the goddess Vesta to be a figure of virginal modesty. For this reason, only virgins were allowed to serve in Vesta's temple, as Augustine also discusses.'[25]

7 *mulieres magis cupide*: Protracted discussion of this proposition is reserved for Juno's second appearance in 2.3, as a figure for 'worldly life'.

20 *Cristus enim, qui est uerus Acrisius*: Of course, a pun on the name 'Christ', the true gold. Cf. Ridewall's earlier comments about on true 'Son-ship', e.g. 2/262–76, 3/158–61, more distantly 9/199–204.

77 *sed coruo rarior albo*: A witty reversal of Juvenal's comparison of a chaste woman with a black swan, *Satyrae* 6:165.

97 *undecima mithologia*: See the Introduction, p. 4 n.11. But see also the next note.

120 *prius tactum*: At 6/122–244. I have adjusted O *quinta* to reflect the appropriate division of the text; AI *octaua* corresponds to neither Ridewall nor Fulg.

143 *sub ymagine*: Apparently, a qualifying phrase has dropped in all the copies. (Pembroke here has the same truncated form as does I, and Q includes no equivalent to the sentence.)

[11] Ganymede/Sodomy

Fulg provides material only for Ridewall's part [3]; the remainder of the account is predicated on his customary mythographic sources.

1–2 On the transmission of this chapter, and its placement in O, which I take up here on fol. 134vb, see the Introduction p. 4.

22ff. Dinkova-Bruun 2012, 332 n.25, discusses a fuller version, and the last couplet opens a poem, with similar material, edited Boswell 389–92.

59 *quasi*: A small misperception shared by AO, who have *quia*.

89 *collegium*: At this point CUL Ii.2.21 has an extra sentence, possibly authorial: 'Quin eciam obnubilat et obfuscat, propter suam innaturalem et inenarrabilem turpitudinem, ut comuniter merita bonorum' (Furthermore,

---

[25] 'Decimo, fuerunt dii alii reputati magni ex infeccionis immunitate et incorrupcionis integritate, sicud patet de dea Uesta, quam magnificabant ydolatre pro sue pudicicie puritate. Credebant enim Uestam deam esse uirginee pudicicie. Unde solis uirginibus fuit concessum in templo dee Ueste ministrare, sicud tangit eciam Augustinus' (C1 fol. 2^{rv}).

because of its unnatural and unspeakable foulness, it routinely clouds and darkens the deserts of good people).

95 *oscultancium*: For *auscul-*, not a form recorded in dictionaries.

115-16 *uanitas intemperancia*: for Chrysostom's 'ira intemperans'; A reads 'uanitates'.

142-49 A familiar piece of anti-Islamic invective. Generally, Muslims are presented as if oversexed because of their tolerance of polygamy and the prophet's alleged misbehaviour. On the charge, see Daniel 164-69. For one likely local source, although much less virulent than the materials here, see Roger Bacon, *Opus maius* 7, IV, d.2.13 (219): 'Their prophet was the filthiest of men in his conduct, because he was the worst adulterer, as is written in the Qūrān; he seized every beautiful woman from her husband and raped her.'[26]

166 *in principio libri sui*: There the charge is spoken in the poet's voice; Nature begins her comparable complaint only in p4 (*PL* 210:449). Ridewall cites from the opening, m1/11–18+the concluding couplet, at C2, fol. 59^v, on *DCD* 6.8.1 (col. 186).

[12] Perseus/Courage

Fulg dismisses the myth as too well known, on the basis of Lucan and Ovid's accounts, to bear repeating (32/4-7). Ridewall shapes what he knows from these sources in the light of Cicero's (and *Moralium dogma*'s) partition of Fortitude. In refusing to retell the myth, Fulg concentrates instead upon the Gorgons, and Ridewall's lines 125–236 depend on his account.

17-20 *prius tactum fuit*: E.g. in 3/2-6, etc.

51 De officiis: Where Cicero says he is quoting Plato.

77 *constanciam*: The nomenclature here is not, in fact, Cicero's. His comparable virtue of persistence is 'perseverantia'. However, ps.-William of Conches, *Moralium dogma philosophorum* I.C offers instead 'constantia', defined as 'stabilitas animi firma et in proposito perseuerans'.

93 *considerata*: From Cicero's account.

94-95 Augustine cites the Ciceronian definition at *De diversis quaestionibus LXXXIII* 31.1 (*PL* 40:21).

---

[26] 'Legis lator fuit vilissimus in vita, nam pessimus adulter fuit, sicut in libro Alchoran scribitur; omnem enim mulierem pulcram ipse a viris eorum rapuit per violenciam et violavit'.

97 *falcem*: The point seems to be that Perseus wasn't, in killing Medusa, precisely aggressive, but rather bowing toward a greater necessity or good. The *falx* does not appear in Fulg, and is only mentioned, not moralised, at VM3 14.2, 'cum ... harpe, quod genus est teli falcati' (251/5–6). Ridewall knew the *harpe* from Ovid, *Metamorphoses* 4.666, and Mercury uses the same implement to kill Argus at 1.717 (cf. 9/116–43). Lucan, *Pharsalia* 9.659–84 says that Mercury gave his *harpe* to Perseus along with his winged shoes for this adventure. Cf. Ridewall's other moralisations of curved items, 2/139–69 on Saturn's *falx* and 2.3/225–34 on Iris and the rainbow.

135–36 While Fulg most extensively associates the Gorgons with terror ('id est tria terroris genera', 32/22ff.), his etymology (32/9–12) is otherwise. He connects the name with the root *georg-* and agriculture, and VM3 14.1–2 repeats this doubled information (251/10–12, 23–33). Contrast the rather strange account of the Gorgons, derived from Albertus Magnus, at *Fasciculus morum* 658/60–660/72.

194–95 *timor reddit hominem ... obstinatum et inpersuasibilem*: I don't find that Fulg 1.21 says any such thing, beyond associating the Gorgons with fear. Nor is the information from VM3 (see the previous note) or Remigius (50.16, 161/14–162/5), largely repetitions of Fulg's information.

234 *tempore Dedaleonis*: Ovid's report of that other flyer, in this case a fallen one, Icarus, appears at *Metamorphoses* 8.183ff.

255–56 *ymago eorum lucet in celo 24 stellis*: Hyginus's 3.10–11 say that Andromeda has 20 stars, and Perseus 19. A *Persei* might be attractive, as roughly corresponding to Ridewall's figure.

[13] Alceste/Marital Continence

Ridewall's divisions and mythological detail closely follow Fulg's account.

22–25 Both citations are probably from Peter Lombard's 4.27.4 (col. 911), where the Chrysostom is ascribed to 'homilia 32 ad cap. 19 Matth.'. Both also appear in the first quotation from Hugh, as does the citation from Pope Nicholas – in the same form, not that of the published *Decretum*, that Ridewall cites.

45 *Hii namque*: O has the usual Vulgate reading. Following my argument at 2/148n, one might wish to insert *Enim* AI.

92 *effectu*: Representing *affectu*. The form recurs at 2.2/200, where A has the explicit *affectu*.

136 *prius fuit tactum*: At 6/400–545.

158–59 *ut dicit Fulgencius*: Fulg cites Homer, *Iliad* 3.45 'a strong brave mind', which includes the Greek *alkē* 'prowess, courage', mentioned again in line 173.

162 The Bernard has appeared above, at 6/362.

181 *est tactum prius*: At 4/10–26; the Cerberus reference at line 206 is to 6/124ff.

197 Super Mattheum: As Jerome says there, he's engaged in self-plagiary, from the more famous discussion at *Adversus Jovinianum* 1.3 (*PL* 23:213–14).

205 *adamantis*: A's adjectival *adamantinis* is an equally plausible reading.

215ff. Augustine's point, as the subsequent citations clarify, is that both Abraham and John had the same 'habitus' (mental inclination) to chastity, but not the same 'opus' (physical expression). The emphasis on Abraham's obedience connects the discussion to the previous account of Hercules and Alceste's deserved release from hell.

224 *obtemperanter*: Following Gn 16:2, Augustine says Abraham slept with Hagar at Sarah's insistence.

230 *Iohannes*: The variation – all three copies provide related absurd forms: *posito* A, *Po^{to}* IO – probably reflects difficulty with a *littera nobilior* followed by an abbreviation. The complementary error, *P* with mark of abbreviation rendered as *L*, or secondarily *I*, occurs in some copies of Walter Map's *Dissuasio Valerii* in renditions such as *Licia* or *Itia* for the unfamiliar name *Periccion* (from Jerome's *Aduersus Jovinianum* 1.42, *PL* 23:273). In these examples, the majuscule *P* has apparently dissolved into two separate strokes, one associable with a character having a high loop, as does *I*.

2.1 Paris/Injustice

Ridewall's account, focusing on Paris the judge, is largely alien to Fulg's, the greater part of which is deferred here to the head of 2.2. Likewise, the depiction does not rely upon conventional histories of Troy such as Dares and Guido della Colonne. Cicero, cited in line 59, is certainly the source of the first part (and provides a lengthy citation from Ennius). The Idan materials probably rely upon Ovid's *Heroides* 5 and 16; there the goddesses appear to Paris *in propria persona*, not, as in Trojan histories, in a dream. So far as I can tell, part [3] is completely fictive, Ridewall's invention; one might note the particular insistence early in Ridewall's presentation that the story is entirely fabular, not historical.

15–28 Although the point is not elaborated here, the gods deceived emphasise the roots of the Trojan line in injustice. For Neptune as a figure of strict justice see the headnote to chapter 5, and Apollo's 'ueritas' is one 'part' of the virtue *iustitia* in Cicero's influential account.

124 *tetra* (classical taetra): Should require a plural verb, but this is Walter's text.

141 *Cassiodorus*: The ascription of this citation, actually Augustine, may have been carried over from the preceding one and should perhaps be emended.

146–50 As the footnote to my translation indicates, Ridewall, in an off-the-cuff reference to Fulg 3.3 (62/20), here rather 'bares the device', indicating the dependence of his depictions upon what he takes to be classical practice. The identical citation appears at VM3 7.3 (198/37), where it is invoked to describe Actaeon's unfortunate sight of Diana and his subsequent death. In VM3, this introduces a rationalising reading, implicitly of a *pictura*, of Actaeon as a fearful and unwilling hunter slain by his dogs, who are starving because he has provided them with no quarry. Cf. also VM3 11.5 (231/14–20).

176 *de pomo*: O's *siue sentenciam* appears to be a doublet of doubt; I assume that, in what appear to have been difficulties over the preceding noun, the scribe has inadvertently dropped this phrase.

181 *beatus Gregorius*: Gregory offers a particularly ironic counterpoint, since he is there describing the gifts of the Magi. He offers no distinction to parallel the one Ridewall presents. Of course, gold (= wisdom) corresponds to Minerva, but the other gifts, incense and myrrh, for Gregory represent prayer and the memory of our mortality, respectively. These two are particularly ironic, since, in Gregory's account, prayer is supposed to still carnal thoughts and myrrh to produce abstinence, eradicating bodily desire altogether.

209 *Daretis Frigii*: These details do not actually appear in Dares, *De excidio Troiae historia*. Rather, they are prominent features of Guido della Colonne's *Historia Troiana*, the most popular late medieval version. Down to book 28, Guido has at least 21 numbered battles, the last of which is said to be of a month's duration (p. 216); the list of those slain by heroes appears in 'liber ultimus' (35, pp. 274–75), where Guido might be understood as ascribing the information to Dares.

241ff. *de lege hospicii*: Ridewall's invocation of hospitality here is his original addition, not in accord with either the poetic accounts mentioned above or the *Historia Troiana*. While no one should wish to exonerate Paris, elsewhere he never meets Menelaus, but takes advantage of his absence to approach Helen at a temple festival. Ridewall's invention represents an 'historicising' detail, relying upon numerous accounts of hospitality in classical poetry.

246 *proditor edys*: I don't find the phrase itself in 'the poets'. In a text Ridewall cites elsewhere, Claudian, *In Ruffinum* 1.319 has 'proditor imperii', and 'proditor rei puplicae' occurs several times in Cicero's prose. The subsequent reference to Virgil is to the verb at *Aeneid* 4.431; Dido's view that Aeneas has betrayed (*prodidit*) their marital vows certainly addresses violated hospitality. The root also appears at Ovid, *Metamorphoses* 8.56, 115 to describe Scylla's betrayal of her father.

256 *Ualerius*: He describes this as a barbaric innovation. In the unusual paraphrased passage at 257–65, most of O more closely replicates Valerius than do the readings of AI.

[2] Minerva/Contemplative Life

The lengthy opening (lines 1–31) is direct quotation from Fulgentius 2.1. The remainder largely expands upon Fulg's rather listlike sequence of Minerva's attributes, and only Ridewall's parts [6] and [12] are entirely independent of his account.

In the prologue to *DCD* Ridewall presents Minerva: 'Sixth, there were other gods who were called great because of the great extent of their lives, as is evident with Minerva, whom the pagans extolled for her immortality, just as Augustine says. For the name Minerva means "immortal".' Further details appear in a discussion of euhemerism, commenting on the end of *DCD* 6.8 (col. 187): 'People also accounted others as gods, thanks to their having discovered arts, for example Minerva. For the ancient pagans believed that Aesculapius discovered the art of medicine and that Minerva had also discovered diverse arts. For this reason, she invented the art of war and the art of pipe-playing, as Ovid reveals in the *Fasti* and *On the art of love*. For this reason, both Esculapius and Minerva were worshipped as gods after their death.'[27]

---

[27] 'Sexto, fuerunt dii alii dicti magni ex duracionis diuturnitate, sicud patet de dea Minerua, quam magnificabant pagani pro immortalitate sua, sicud eciam tangit Augustinus. Interpretatur eciam Minerua "immortalis"' (C1 fol. 2). And 'Fuerunt eciam aliqui qui erant dii ab hominibus reputati ob graciam arcium repertarum. Exemplum de Minerua. Credebant enim antiqui pagani quod Esculapius fuit repertor artis medicine et quod Minerua fuerat eciam repertrix aliarum arcium diuersarum. Unde ipsa adinuenit artem preliandi et artem fistulandi, sicud patet per poetam Ouidium libro *Fastorum* et libro eciam *De arte*

4–8 Fulg's account echoes the traditional classical discussion of three kinds of theology. Minerva's contemplative life corresponds to 'philosophical theology'; Juno's active life to 'civil theology', and Venus's life of delight to 'poetic theology'.

135–36 *Themistodes uel Themistocles*: I take this doublet of doubt to be authorial, since it depends on the ambiguous reading of a twelfth-century manuscript written with 'erect *d*', thus in an unfamiliar name legible as 'd' or 'cl'. The scribe, after all, has access to, at best, a fourteenth-century copy, where this will not have been a difficulty in either anglicana or textura.

163–64 *est … contemplandi*: A is vastly more prone to abbreviating material (particularly the identification of Ridewall's citations) than to add. Here that reading is clearly preferable, as a fuller introduction and exemplification of Ridewall's division. The other copies have clearly dropped this material through homeoteleuthon. In line 167, A *forti* is also supported by the *forti attritione* of the source. For another example of a fuller correct A reading, see 2.4/45–47.

240 *diuersa membra*: These identifications are conventional, allusions to the frequently depicted 'zodiac man'.

270–79 In spite of the plethora of variants, O generally reproduces Bernard.

292 *ut enim prius tactum est*: At lines 190–208.

334 *hominum preconia*: Apparently Ridewall's insertion; Chrysostom's construction is *hec uelut umbram ac puluerem* '[disdained] these things as if they were darkness and dust'.

362 *inuitus*: For Rabanus's *intuitus* 'contemplative person'. But 372 'nisi ad ipsius anime uoluntatem' implies that Ridewall had the scribal reading.

377 *ut prius tactum est*: At lines 192ff. above.

379–87 A discussion probably predicated on 2 Cor 12:7–9, the 'stimulus carnis' that accompanies Paul's vision of the third heaven.

395 *Palatem*: Ridewall probably expects one to notice the pun connecting the goddess and Evander's son.

411 *ad sensum*, **412** *angores*: Both readings are confirmed by Bernard's text.

---

amandi, et hiis ex causis post mortem colebantur Esculapius pro deo et Minerua pro dea' (C2 fol. 64ᵛ).

[3] Juno/Worldly Life

As I've indicated in the headnote to 1.4, many of these discussions have already appeared *in bono* as part of the description of Juno there. Here, their original position in Fulg, they appear, as Ridewall explicitly notes, *in malo*. Ridewall's discussion is driven by an apparently subsidiary eight-part rhyming jingle, introduced in lines 56-60. Fitting the description to this pattern leads him to multiply details associated with wealth (parts [1] and [3]; [7] is implicit in Fulg's account), and part [8] is largely inspired by a detail in VM3.

3 *fuit tacta*: At 2.1/158-77 above. As I point out at Introduction pp. 7-8, repetition of materials responds to potential selective consultation of the text. Were one seeking materials about unjust judges, one would have found the materials there with ease; however, if looking for a comparable discussion of active life, one would have missed the account.

20 *ut tactum est*, **22-23** *ideo dicit in prologo*: Cf. 2.2/74-78 and 27-30, respectively.

66 *quia ... custodire*: This passage looks to have swelled in all the MSS with a sequence of echoic intrusions; Ambrose reads only 'quia cogitur custodire'. The expansions align the account with the earlier discussion of Avarice as Cerberus's 'three bites', 6/172-207.

77-79 Previously cited at 12/201.

94 *Ilium*: Assimilated to the following placename in I (partially so in A).

124 *sicut prius fuit tactum*: At 4/125-46.

152-53 *pauum uel pauonem*: Probably not a doublet of doubt; Fulg uses *pauum* universally, whereas Ridewall uses the more frequent late medieval form.

161 *fraterno*: Peter of Ravenna's *germano* supports AI against O *freno*, that copyist having overlooked a suspension.

193 *ex Ouidio*: Cf. *Metamorphoses* 11.585, 'Juno said, "O my Iris, the most faithful messenger for my word", ('"Iri, meae", dixit [Iuno], "fidissima nuntia vocis"').

220 *ex prologo*: As cited above, 2.2/21-25.

317 *adulacionis*: The reading *palpacionis* seems to me to introduce a ridiculously mixed metaphor, and I have restored Alan's reading. The received text has probably stumbled over a form where one of the vowels was indicated by a tick on *l*.

[4] Venus/The Life of Pleasure

As in 2.2, the opening involves extensive quotation from Fulg. Although their order has been adjusted, Ridewall works in most of Fulgentius's list of attributes (some as verbatim quotation), but see 137n.

In his prologue to *DCD*, Ridewall describes Venus: 'Fourteenth, there were other gods who were esteemed great from their joyous pleasure, as is evident with the goddess Venus, whom the idolaters extolled, believing her to be the goddess of love and pleasure, as well as of joy and licentiousness.' Commenting on *DCD* 6.3 (col. 179), and following Isidore, *Etym.* 18.42–51 (*PL* 82:657–59), Ridewall presents her and Bacchus as the dedicatees of the theatre since she 'is the goddess of pleasure and fleshly wantonness, and dissolute gestures and soft licentiousness follow her'.[28]

6 *Epicurei*: Epicurean theology was especially distasteful, not simply because of its prioritisation of pleasure but because of its underlying materialism (Democritan atomism) and its view of God as a creator only (not a continuing immanent power). A lengthy discussion appears in the commentary on *DCD* 6.5.2 (col. 181) at C2 fol. 30^{rv}, partly predicated on Isidore, *Etym.* 8.6.15 (*PL* 82:306–07), and Ridewall certainly knew the derisive account in Cicero's *De natura deorum*.

9, 13 *nulla(m)*: Especially given the intervening material, I have retained the O reading. However, one should note Fulg 39/12 'uanam rem'. In the first of these readings, AI offer *uana* as a correction (and in I the text presumably read originally as O). In the second, A alone provides *malam*, which is surely wrong.

33 *dicente Augustino*: The citation is not from *De doctrina*, although Palmer 2005, 222 n.90, cites Thomas of Ireland so ascribing it [= *MF* luxuria e]. It is rather Jerome, epistola 21.9 (*PL* 22:383). *MF* includes the erroneous *voluntatem* for Jerome's reading 36 *uoluptate*. 36 *luxuriosi* is an insertion into Jerome's text (and absent from the citation in *MF*), and its grammar is unclear; A *graciam* is an attractive variant, but may simply be responding to the problem.

37 *oblacione*: Another medieval variant spelling for the classical form *ablacione* AI.

40–41 *Ne ... tuam*: One needs the full biblical verse to make the point.

---

[28] 'Quarto decimo, fuerunt et dii alii reputati magni ex complacencie iocunditate, sicud patet de dea Uenere, quam magnificabant ydolatre, credentes eam esse deam dileccionis, delectacionis, et leticie ac lasciuie' (C1 fol. 2^v). And 'est dea uoluptatis et carnalis petulancie qua sequitur dissolucio gestus et mollicies lasciuie' (C2 fol. 18^{rv}).

45 *uiciorum*: Ambrose actually paraphrases, rather than citing Paul's verse directly; his reading *uiciorum* for concluding 47 *malorum* indicates that this is eyeskip.

55 *loquitur Boycius*: Ridewall's commentary on Walter Map's *Dissuasio*, in a passage he will cite below at line 149, also includes this quotation at *JBWW* 71/203–06.

63 *Tayde*, 67 *Tays uel Lays*: Ridewall apparently inherited this doubt from his MS of Map's *Dissuasio*, where a large number of early copies have confused Lais with the repentant Alexandrine prostitute; see *JBWW* 1:139/228 and the collations there. Similarly, in his commentary on Map's text, Ridewall repeats this identification (*JBWW* 107/709–17), and again refers to her as Gellius's *Thays* at C2 fol. 51.

65 *modo*: For John of Salisbury's *mihi*. I've retained the reading, clearly down to differing perceptions of abbreviated m^i/m^o, and potentially an error in Ridewall's source MS or one he made himself.

67 col *et formosa*: A doublet of doubt.

73 *medietas maioris talenti*: John of Salisbury reports that the amount requested was equivalent to 'denarii viginti millia': i.e., just over £83. The exact amount actually appears in neither Gellius nor John, who read 'nimium quantum'.

74 *temptatiue* : Corresponds to John's *clanculo* 'in secret' (and Gellius's *clanculum*).

95 *Linceis*: Lynkeus, the farsighted Argonaut. The relevant *Thais* appears instead of Boethius's Alcibiades.

115 *grauissimi uicii*: Gellius glosses the Greek terms he cites, *akrateis* and *akolastous*, as 'incontinentes uel intemperantes', as well as confirming *Socratis*, rather than the various MS readings in line 118.

128 *momento ipso temporis*: Augustine's reading.

137 *Alexander Necham*: Although overtly cited only here, most of Ridewall's divisions and their moralisations are paralleled there, as well as in Fulg.

165 col *semper*: A scribal intensifier, echoing the subsequent uses, and not paralleled in Innocent.

204 *qui gentes domuerat*: I have emended the MSS to accord with John of Salisbury's text.

216 *glossa*: As Ridewall's discussion would indicate, the gloss links lechery with idolatrous practice.

218 *specialiter ... luxurie*: Expanding the gloss 'praecipue tamen fornicatione et idolatria'. In all the copies 'familiarius' appears to have been generated by the following verb.

221–22 *ut patet ex Uirgilio*: A great deal of VM3's subsequent discussion of various forms of divination, 11.14–16 (237/3–38/38), is derived from references in Virgil.

Appendix

It is probably no surprise to find scribes adding in extra bits from these two texts, since both are widely distributed and were standard authorities in Oxonian dictaminal training. For Alan's *De planctu* as an Oxford grammatical staple, see Camargo 1994, 176 (esp. nn.41–42) and the table at 185–86; and Camargo 1999, 937–38. There are 21 records in the *MLGB3 Corpus*, with five from Cambridge and one from Oxford (the surviving Merton College, MS 113). Camargo does not list Peter of Blois among those local classics, which also include Guido's Trojan history (cf. 2.1/209n). However, Peter's may well be the outstanding English letter-book, with something like 200 surviving manuscripts. For an indication of the wide general circulation, see Lawler 2013, 55–60; and further Wahlgren and Southern, who give special attention to Peter's presentation of the collection as a dictaminal model. There are 46 records in *MLGB3*, three of these from Cambridge (including the surviving St John's College, MS C.5, originally from Peterhouse) and four from Oxford (including a book in William Reed's donation to Merton College in 1374 and a copy in a New College inventory c. 1386). Given that I believe these non-authorial materials, I've largely retained the *textus receptus*.

3 *derisio*[1]: diffusio A (arrisio Alan); I have translated to follow Alan's *arrisio*.

5 *discesionis*: discensionis AI; corrected to follow Alan's *discessionis*.

7 *interna ... derisione*: interna | deylione I, but Alan 'contradictoria derisione'. *subsanniant* corresponds to Alan's *defraudant* and has apparently been assimilated to the same root earlier in Alan's sentence.

12 *diuitibus et*: does not appear in Peter's text.

13ff. *Si ... donaretur*: for Peter's *si scirent*; *credent* has replaced his *credens*; and if I indeed reads *decernere*, it's a minim short.

14 *seca*: To represent *ceca*.

19 *acciditur*: For Peter's *accepteur*; one might read 'accipitur'. I have emended I's clearly erroneous *mal* and *repleatur*.

The A tabula

This *tabula*, although in some respects erratic, seems to offer unusually detailed access to Ridewall's text. Certainly, the whole appears unusual in its extent; it includes around 400 entries and approaches in length about 5 per cent of the text it describes. On the other hand, unusually for s. xv, entries appear to be alphabetised only by the first letter. It appears as if the indexer set up single-letter headings and then read over text in sequence, putting relevant items under each letter, perhaps sometimes leaving spaces for additional entries (but sometimes, it would appear, not doing so). However, he shows no attention to further alphabetisation or to grouping like entries together, and, late in the alphabet, intruded a small number of repeated nearly identical references in close proximity to one another.

Medieval *tabulae* are predicated upon a selectiveness alien to our expectations based upon modern indexes. That is, they tend to ignore what we might think major textual features, the subjects of chapters or divisions in a clearly ongoing argument (or the explanations of specific passages in a consecutively written commentary). The people who construct *tabulae* assume an intelligent reader can find those discussions in a scan of the text or by using a table identifying chapter rubrics (also supplied in this MS; see 7/1n).

In accord with this convention, a modern reader may be surprised by the avoidance in this *tabula* of mythographic materials. But those, the attributes assigned individual divinities, are readily available to any reader first through a chapter index, then through Ridewall's carefully outlined textual divisions at the head of each mythography. Rather, this *tabula* indexes topics, moralised or moralisable bits, with a few entries devoted to clear concordance (moral discussions of beasts, things, objects). It encourages readers to use the text in accord with Ridewall's opening statement, that theologically minded readers, i.e. Christians, should heed not mythographic detail but its inherent moral implications (1/5–7).

Such an emphasis further accords with Ridewall's practice throughout. The mythic information he provides is actually fairly commonplace, while, in contrast, the expansive Christian 'metaphorisation', laden with provocative citations and anecdotes, is frequently far from such. The *tabula* has been constructed to aid a user seeking provocative *moralitates* or *integumina*, not immediately identifiable as associated with any particular mythographic detail. Particularly in its apparent redundancies, double entries – e.g. 'celestia signa' under 'C' and 'signa celestia' under 'S' – it provides, as I argue elsewhere (pp. 7–8, 2.3/3n), 'cue-links' based upon differing topics or words a user might be searching for. In contrast to a frequent (mis)reading that emphasises Ridewall's pictorialism as the construction of 'memory-diagrams', this *tabula* presupposes that subordinated detail remains too multifarious to be remembered. Its author imagines what one might describe as 'normal research procedures' and facilitates a user seeking relevant topical material with the book in hand. One supposes that this indexer seeks to aid preachers pursuing materials for the exemplaristic amplification of sermon topics, a group of users I have documented above (pp. 10–11).

In the MS, the tabula identifies its referents by notations such as 'M 1 pic 3': i.e., the third part of the picture in the first chapter 'Idolatry'. I have reduced these to the form '1/3', etc. However, I have left intact the chapter numeration of this copy (see 7/1n). This capitulation is easily matched with the text above: after chapter 5, this MS's chapter-numbering adds five to that of the printed text *and* continues consecutively through Ridewall's book 2, where chapters 1–4 are here 19–22. I have retained the indexer's sporadic added comments following the identification of locus indexed.

I should note one sporadic quirk, exemplified by the entry 'Passiones quattuor', indexed as '1 ante picturam d'. Although these notations are not marked in the margins of the MS itself, they must refer to the opening six columns of the text, fols 35ra–36rb, those that precede the pictorial division at the head of fol. 36va. This represents a modest hangover of an Oxfordian indexing system, prominent c. 1250–1320, in which indexing referred to columns and lines numbered in Arabic.

I have not attempted to correct wrong references or to fill in the blanks I note in the transcription below, although it is relatively easy to do so. For example, 'Homo differt a brutis sola facundia [*blank*]' can readily be identified with 9/8 (or, in the table's numeration, 14/8).

[fol. 76va]
Amor deordinatus   1/pic [*blank*]
Amores duo   1/pic [*blank*]
Adulator: quod omnis adulator sit idolatra   1
Adulacio fuit execatrix idolarie   1/3
Adulator est clauis in oculo   1/2
Adulterium est in coniugio luxurioso   14/2
Amor ordinatus ignis et uita est   3/p' ante picturam Iouis

Amoris pictura   3/1 de Ioue et amicicia
Amicus probatur in necessitate   3/2 de eodem
Amicus non est querenda in aula   3/2 de eodem
Amor uincit omnia et Deum   3/4 de eodem
Amor uel caritas quid fecit optime nota (?)   3/4 ut supra
Amor est principium bene operandi   3
Amoris signum est iris   21/5
Amicicia est propter tria   3/8
Sine amicicia totus mundus non uidelicet/usque   3/8
Sine amicicia homo comparatur bestie   in eodem
Attributa signa celestia humano corpore   20/pic de Pallade et contemplacione
Amicicie commoditas   3/8
Anima compellitur ad dolendum pro peccatis   4/2
Aurum ceteris metellis est durabilius   4/pic [blank]
Agere bene parum usque nisi consummet'   4/5
Anima in nostra est quedam sanctitas naturalis   5/1
Appm' (?) pictura   5
Animus quomodo est regendus triplici parte Dei   5/9
Aurum et argentum quid est   6/2
Anime sunt prelati corporibus   6/5
Amor uelox est et alatus   6/6
Aurum causat in homine leticiam cordis   12/3
Ambicionis pictura   13/1
Ambicio quid est   13/1
Ambiciosorum currus   13/4
Contra ambiciosos et uiros ecclesiasticos (?)   13/3
[fol. 76rb]
Ambiciosi duplex mors   13/10
Ambiciosi semper languent   13/8
Assub: nota de eo   13/9
Ambicionis diffinicio   13/10
Ambiciosi cruciatus et sepultura   13/11
Aurea gutta   15/6
Aquile condiciones   16/3
Amor omnia sibi subicit   17/1
Auari duricia   17/4
Aurei pomi   17/6
Amor ardens   18/4
Amor contemplacionis   18/4
\[later, marg.] Arma contemplacionis   20/4/
Arma Palladis tria contra luxuriam   [blank]/8
Arbitrium liberum   15/1
Abraham quomodo meruit   18/6

418 John Ridewall, *Fulgencius metaforalis*

Amicicia diuitum est simulata   21/5
Adulator: contra adulatores   21/8
Audacia et fortitudo pingitur   16/1
Auarus et infernus comparantur   17/5
Alexander uel Parides significant iniusticiam   19 per totum
Aper et leo   18/3
Amor et dolor sunt duo motus cordis   1/ante picturam
Alios debet regere qui nouit se regere   4/4
Aggredi non debemus ardua propter uanitatem   17/4
Arbor oliue   20/12

Boni sunt aliqui naturaliter   5/1
Bruta animalia loquuntur operibus   14/7
Boni et mali differunt uite   12/10
Bona uxore nichil melius   18/4

Canis inferni Terberus   6/4
Cibus auget nutrit comfortat   3/7
Caritas est principium bene operandi   3/ante picturam
Caritas est uirtus capitalis   3/1
Caritas fugat demones   3/3
Caritas assimilatur auro   3/5
Caritatis latitudo   3/5
Caritas sola facit animam Deo caram   3/8
Caritatis signum est iris   21/5
De caritatis laude   3/9
Cognicio sui ipsius premittitur in quolibet studio   5/7
Compotum reddendum de seipso   5/8
Cupiditas multa mala facit   6/4
[fol. 76va]
Cupiditatis triplex morsus   6/4
Canis Terburus habuit tria capita   6/4
Cingnis quomodo moritur   6/7
Caritas quomodo pellit timorem   [blank]/5
Coruus quomodo pascitur   12/10
Consummacio est uirtus bone accionis   4/5
Condicionis humane miseria   5/2
Celestia signa attribuuntur humano corpori   ../6 [i.e. 20/6 = 2.2/219]
Corona ueritatis   12/6
Cor mouetur amore et dolore   1/ante picturam
Cupiditatis pictura   19/1
Sine caritate nulla est uirtus   17/1
Continencie coniugalis pictura   14/1

Continencia coniugalis   ibidem
Coniugium luxuriosum   [*blank*]/2
Castitas requirit duplicem uirtutem   18/3
Continencia corporis parum uidelicet   [*blank*]
Coniuges se mutuo debent diligere   18/4
Castitatis tria genera et triplex fructus   14/5
Castitas coniugalis saluat ab inferis   18/6
Castitas uirginalis et uidualis possunt esse eiusdem meriti   ibidem
Creatura quando interficit creaturam   19/5
Creatura potest Dominum contemplari   20/3
Cruciatus et sepultura ambiciosi   13/11
Contemplacionis arma   20/4
Contemplacionis status   20/5
Contemplacio est hasta dimicans (?)   20/11
Contemplacio est mors suauis   20/12
Cupidus similatur inferno   21/1
Contemplacionis status   20/de (*the word expunged*)
Currus elacionis per quattuor trahitur   13/4
Curiositas uestium nocet   21/3
Contempnuntur omnia propter moram unius diei in celo   12/3
Cura medicorum quomodo est   17/4
Cristallus erat scutum significatque constanciam   17/3
Corpori humano attribuuntur signa celestia   20/[*blank*]

Detestacio peccati mortalis   4/1
Deorum tria et tres differencie   1/ante picturam b
Diis tria fieri consueuerunt   1/ante picturam b d
Dolor pro peccatis unit cum Deo   4/2
Dolor peccatoris quot bona generat et facit   4/2
Dolor peccati seruat a residiuo   4/4
Diuicie uere que sunt   6/2
[fol. 76vb]
Diuicie uere sunt uirtutes   6/2
Dignitas hominis   15/1
Discrecio et liberum arbitrium   15/2
Diuites sunt lasciui   15/3
Dolor et amor sunt duo motus cordis   1/ante picturam
Diuicie sunt uirtutes hominis   14/5
Diuicie competunt eloquencie   [*blank*]
De dea discordie et de pomo aureo   19/[*illeg., in the gutter*]
Deus quare sit timendus   20/7
Diues non potest habere caritatem   21/5
Diuicie faciunt hominem fraudulentem   21/6

Diei unius mora in celo facit contempnere omnia   12?/[*illeg., in the gutter*]
Dissencio figurat per iridem   21/5

Equi empcione quid consideratur   5?/2
Exhortac[i]o prophete siue religiosi   12/4
Elacionis currum quattuor trahu[n]t   13/4
Eloquencie pictura (?) siue Mercurii   14/1
Eloquencia est efficax in operacione   14/2
Eloquencie graciam nullus habet nisi sit bonus in uita   14/5
Effectus ire   6/6
Eterna felicitas   12/5
Epilenticus est luxuriosus   22/4

Falce sceptratus est Saturnus deus prudencie   2/4
Filius dicitur quia sit ut ille   [*blank*]
Fulminum tria genera   3/8
Fortes fuerunt Deo consecrati   6/9
Fortitudo et audacia   17 per totum
Furie [*sic*] tria nomina   6/6
Fatorum tria genera   6/6
Fatorum pictura   6/7
Felicitas eterna   12/15
Fraus generatur de diuiciis   22/6
Falsitatis interfeccio   12/3
Falsitas uite   6/7
Fortitudo uel audacia pingitur   17/1
Fortitudo quomodo diffinitur   17/1 et 2
Fama bona et mala   17/5
Fortis homo peruenit ad felicitatem   17/7
Facundia est per quam homo differt a brutis   14/7
Furum proprietas siue latronum   14/6
[fol. 77[ra]]
Formacio humane uocis nouem requirit   [*blank*]/8

Gaudium est semper in sapiente   12/3
Gorgones   17 per totum

Homo habet quattuor passiones principales   1/8
Hominum studia et uicia sunt lacrimanda (?)   2/4
Homo debet pocius lacrimare quam ridere   2/4
Homo habet libertatem eleccionis   5/1
Homo non peccat nisi uoluntarie   5/1
Homo de quibus debet laudare   5/5

Humilitas est nutrix omnium uirtutum   5/9
Homo quanto fuerit melior tanto magis irascitur   6/6
Homo differt a brutis sola facundia   [blank]
De dignitate ymaginis hominis   15/1
Humane condicionis miseria   5/2
Humane uocis formacio nouem requirit   12/8
Hominis iusti uita differt a uita mali   12/18
Hominis sermo talis est qualis et uita   4/1
Homo fit solum diues per uirtutem   14/5

Inferni canis Cerberus   6/4
Intelligencia quomodo depingitur   5/1
Intelligencia habet duo cornua   5/1
Iudicare debet homo de seipso   5/2
Intelligencie triplex proles   5/3
Intelligencia inclinat hominem ad sui cognicionem   [blank]
Intelligencie attribuuntur honor et reuerencia   5/6
Intelligencie triplex potestas   5/8
Iram quid debet compescere   5/8
Intelligencia prebet nutrimentum uirtutibus   5/9
Ira: nota de ira et eius effectibus   6/6
Ira siue correpcio duplex   6/6
Iniusticia tollit regnum   12/6
Iurantes falsa et contra tales   12/6
[fol. 77rb]
Iusticie pictura siue Paridis   19 per totum
Iudices quales debent esse   19/1
Iudex debet quattuor obliuisci   19/1
Iudex omnis est pastor   19/2
Iudicis officium   19/2
Iustus iudex nullum debet agnoscere   19/3
Iudex malus est proditor aule regie   19/6
Indumenta curiosa nocent   21/3
Inuidia nota bene   21/4
Iusticie libra   19/2
Iusticie iudicium peruertitur per tria munera   19/4
Interfeccio falsitatis   12/4
Infelicius quid est uxore mala   18/4

Luxuria maxime opponitur prudencie   2/6
Luxuria est capitalis pestis hominibus   2/6
Lacrime lauant peccatum   9/9
Lacrime illustrant conscienciam   9/10

In lacrimis tria nota   9/10
Post lacrimas Cristus benignus apparet   [blank]
Latronum et furum proprietas   14/6
Loquendum est ex circumstancia   14/6
Liberum arbitrium   15/2
Leo et aper   18/3
Contra luxuriam   22/2
Luxuria est mater auaricie   22/2
Luxuria est amara   22/2
Luxuria est ignominiosa   22/2
Luxuriosus est epilenticus   22/4
Lasciuia est cum diuiciis   19/3
Luxuria conuertit hominem in porcum   22/4
Luxurie fetor   22/5
Luxurie descripcio   22/5
Ad luxuriam que attrahunt hominem   22/6
Luxuria uulnerat corpora   22/6
Luxuria eneruat   22/6
Luxuria inducit obstinacionem   22/8

Mala mors est infelicissimum [sic]   18/4
[fol. 77va]
Motus: motus cordis sunt duo   1/1
Memorie pictura   4 per totum
Memoria ligatur cathenis aureis   4/5
Memoria peccatorum reducit hominem ad pristinum gradum   4/6
Memoria peccatorum ducit hominem ad se   4/7
Memoria est custos et nutrix uirtutum   4/8
Memoria peccatorum trahit hominem a residiuo   4/8
Memoria peccatorum deducit lacrimas   4/9
Miseria condicionis humane   5/2
Mors: de morte   6/7
Mortale peccatum est detestabile   4/1
Mors est optimum quod potest hominem euenire   6/7
Mors est melior quam uita   6/7
Malorum mor\i/u\i/orum pena   6/7
Mors est optima et finis omnium malorum   6/7
Muse requiruntur in sapiencia   12/8
Pro mora diei in celo contempnerentur omnia   12/2
Memoriam (?) est semper tenendam   13/5
Mercurius habuit utrumque sexum   14/1
Mercurius quomodo interfecit Argum   14/4
Medici quomodo curant   14/4

Meritum: quomodo Abraham meruit   18/6
Munerum tria genera peruertunt iudicium   19/4
Metallorum omnium durabilius est aurum   4/5
Mali hominis et boni uita differunt [sic]   12/10

Neptuni pictura 5 per totum Triplex eius proles   [5]/3
Nouem requiruntur ad formacionem uocis humane   12/8

Obediencia plus placet Deo omnibus uirtutibus   18/6
Orto puero plorabant sapientes   6/7

Pacis uirga   14/7
Peccata quare fiunt   1 ante picturam c
Passiones quattuor principales in homine   1 ante picturam d
Prudencia est rectrix et auriga omnium aliarum uirtutum   2 ante picturam
Prudentes computabantur inter deos   2 ante picturam
Prudentem uirum Deus non uincit   2 ante picturam
[fol. 77vb]
Prudencia est rectrix omnium: nota bene   2/[blank]
Prudencie luce destituti non sunt homines sed bestie   2 ante picturam
Prudencie pictura   2 per totum
Prudencia subuenit et auxiliatur   2/1
Prudencia Ulixes multa superauit   2/1 et 17/2
Prudencie suffragia   2/1
Prudencie uirtus reperitur in senibus   2/2
Prudencia requirit magnum tempus   ibidem
Prudentes antiquitus incedebant uelato [an extra loop] capite   2/3
Prudens debet regnare et habet sceptrum ad modum falcis   2/4
Prudencie conuiuium (?)   2/7
Prudencie maxime nocet luxuria   2/6
Palma nullo oneri succumbit   3/4
Palma est signum uictorie   ibidem
Prudencie tres partes   4 ante picturam
Proles triplex Saturni   ibidem
Peccatum mortale est detestabile   4/1
Peccatorum amara recordacio est cuius remedium   4/2
Potestas nobilissima est regere seipsum   4/4
Principia practica sunt nobis nota eciam eciam [sic] speculatiua   5/1
Proles triplex Neptuni   5/3
Philosophia summa cognoscere seipsum   5/5
Philosophie exhortacio   12/4
Plutonis pictura uel prouidencie   6 per totum
Prouidencia reddit hominem impassibilem   6/2

Prouidencia est scutum   6/1
Prouidencie pulcra descripcio   6/1
Prouidencia plantat uirtutes   6/2
Prouidencia potest comparari Deo   6/3
Per prouidenciam homo potest declinare infernum   [blank]
Prouidencia assimilatur cani infernali   6/4
Prouidencia ligatur Proserpine per coniugium   6/5
Proserpina habet tria nomina   6/5
Prouidencie armatura dicitur irasci contra peccata   6/6
Pudicicia Cristi et puritas   15/5
Pugnandum est semper contra uicia   6/6
Pulcrum quid est   12/5
Paupertas Cristi   12/1
Puritas Cristi et pudicicia   15/5
Peruertitur iudicium per tria dona   19/5
Presens uita est quasi umbra   21/1
Practica et speculatiua principia sunt multa (?)   5/1
Perseuerancie condiciones   17/3
[fol. 78ra]
Paciencia et eius diffinicio   17/7
Pauonis condiciones   21/4
Porcus est luxuriosus in comparacione   22/4
Plorabant sapientes in ortu puerorum   6/7

Quadriga Apollinis uel solis, id est ueritas   12/4

Res corporalis informat contemplari Deum   20/3
Racio est summum bonum a Deo datum   2/ante picturam
Racione nichil est melius datum hominibus   ibidem
Regere alios dignus est qui nouit regere seipsum   4/4
Rex unde dicitur   18/2
Regibus tria offerebantur   6/1
Rex dicitur omnis qui bene facit   18/2
Residiuacio preseruabatur per dolorem peccatorum   [blank]
Religiosi et prophete exhortacio quadruplex   12/4
Recordacio peccati est remedium magnum   4/[blank]
Reconciliacionis iris est signum   4/2
    et est signum amoris   21/5

Scutum perseuerancie   17/3
Senectus dicitur laudabilis   2/6
Senectutis honor   2/3
Sepultura ambiciosi   13/11

Regi offerri solent tria   6/1
Sapientes plorabant in natiuitate puerorum   6/[7?]
Sol inter planetas (?) optinet principatum   12/1
Sagitte tres quibus Phicius interfecit falsitatem   12/2
Sapiens nunquam est sine gaudio   12/2
Sapiencia requirit nouem Musas   12/8
Strenuitas Ulixis   12/2
Strenuitas est in uita contemplatiua   20/10
Sompnia nota   16/9
Sodomitici uicii pictura   16 per totum
Sodomia fecit diluuium   16/5
Superbia et superbus: uide in uerbo ambicio
Strenui non debent aggredi ardua propter uanitatem   17/4
[fol. 78rb]
Sapienti nichil potest accidere aduersi   20/2
Signa celestia attribuuntur partibus humani corporis   20/6
Sedes Dei est sinus contemplanti   21/[blank]
Sapiencia huius mundi que est   21/6
Sceptrum prudencie est falx   2/4
Speculatiua et practica sunt nobis necessaria   5/1
Sermo est talis qualis est uita   14/1

Terroris tres differencie et tres effectus   [blank]

Uictor rediens de bello apud Romanos quomodo erat indutus   3/5
Ueritas tollit aliena   5/3
Uox et eius proprietas et Furis (?)   6/6
Uite falsitas   6/7
Ueritatis uel Apollinis pictura   12/[blank]
Ueritas pingitur iuuenis   12/1
Ueritatis laus   12/1
Ueritas et nichil aliud placet Deo   12/1
Ueritatis tres sagitte   12/2
Ueritatis uel Apollinis quadrige quattuor rote   12/4
Ueritas quare est diligenda   12/4
Ueritatis rote quattuor currus   12/4
Ueritatis quadrige nomina equorum quattuor   12/5
Ueritas pre ceteris uirtutibus meretur coronari   12/6
Ueritas uinci non potest   12/7
Uerum omne prolatum a Spiritu Sancto est   [blank]
Ueritatis discripcio   12/7
Uoci humane formande nouem requiruntur   12/8
Uerbum est index consciencie   12/8

Uita iusti differt a uita mali   12/10
Ueritas triplex   12/10
Uita hominis talis qualis est sermo   14/1
Uirtus sola facit hominem diuitem   14/5
Uirtus pacis   14/7
Ulixis strenuitas et prudencia   2/1
Uxore mala nichil infelicius   18/4
Uxore bona nichil melius   ibidem
Uite contemplatiue pictura   20 per totum
Uita triplex   20 ante picturam
[fol. 78^(va)]
Uita contemplatiua   20/1
Uita actiua   20 ante picturam
Uiator potest Deum contemplari in re corporali   20/3
Uita contemplatiua est secura   20/10
Uita presens est umbra   21/1
Uermis diuiciarum est superbia   21/4
Ueneris pictura   22 per totum
Uita bona solum habet eloquentem   14/5
Uoluptas Ueneris luxuria efficit porcum et multa consimilia   22/4
Ueruene herbe proprietas   22/7
Unius diei mora in celo contepmni facit omnia   12/3
Uanitas non faceret aggredi ardua   17/4

Ydolatria inter omnia peccata plus displicet Deo   1 ante picturam
Ydolatrie inicium et continuacio   1 ante picturam
Ydolatria quomodo intrauit mundum   1 ante picturam
Ydolorum tria genera   1 ante picturam b
Ydolum quid est   in eodem
Ydolatrie continuacio est adulacio   1 ante picturam
Ydolatrie executor est timor   1 ante picturam d
Ydolum cultum duo induxerunt   ibidem
Ydolatrie origo   1 ante picturam f
Ydolorum diuersa nomina   ibidem
Ydolatrie pictura   1 per totum
Ydolatria est ceca   1/2
Yris est archus reconciliacionis   21/5
Yris significat discencionem et condiciones eius   ibidem

Xpisti paupertas   15/1
Xpisti pudicicia et puritas   15/5

A brief commentary

As Morton Bloomfield showed very long ago, Christian conceptions of vice were fixed very early on, in a famous and ubiquitously cited passage from Gregory the Great's *Moralia*. In contrast, for the virtues, things were never so simple. Down to the mid-twelfth century, any variety of actions or emotions might be identified as such, e.g. 'oratio'; a biblical listing, like the 'fruits of the spirit' in Gal 5:22, was an open invitation to expansiveness. During the twelfth century, however, there was at least a substantial reduction of common possibility, although confusingly, to two sets of seven. On the one hand, there was biblical warrant for three prominent Christian virtues, Paul's faith, hope, and charity (1 Cor 13:13), and to those might be added the four 'cardinal' virtues that had been inherited from classical theory, most notably a lengthy discussion in Cicero's *De officiis* 1 and the more handy enumeration (with briefly defined 'partes') in *De inventione* 2.159–64. (The 'parts', while their precise relationship to the 'whole virtue' is often a little murky, gain support from the fact that Gregory had subdivided his sins analogously.) In contrast to this set of seven, there was a second seven, 'the contrary virtues', i.e. those opposed to and 'remediating' the sins.[1]

These two sets coexist, largely because their 'use-spheres' are rather different. The 'contrary virtues' are integral to popular instructional programmes, what is considered a 'septenary' treatment, a mnemonic of basic responsibilities, focused by repeated groups of seven (sins, beatitudes, petitions of the Pater Noster, etc.). While the 'four plus three' virtues (Paul's 'theological virtues' plus the 'cardinals') often appear in such a context, it is most usually as an excursus.[2]

---

[1] See e.g. Graf; numerous studies passim in Lottin; Houser; Tuve 57–143, with her enormously varied index entry 'Virtues and Vices' at 459–61; and Bejczy. Houser is particularly useful for his treatment of the Stoic 'four affects' at 23–24 and of *De inventione* (and its 'parts') at 25–30. Cf. also the tables of 'parts' across a range of prominent texts at Houser 228–33, Tuve 442–43, and Bejczy 291–96.

[2] Perhaps the most prominent early formulation of the septenary appears in Hugh of St-Victor, *De quinque septenis* (PL 175:405–14), explicitly cited by Holcot as a model. As an example of a rather inconsequent 'tucking-in' of the 'four plus

In contrast, the analysis of virtue as 'four plus three' is largely a learned pursuit. In the course of the early thirteenth century this presentation became the standard form of analysis within theological training. At least one major focus of these lucubrations, essentially a response to the early medieval proliferation of virtues (or 'virtuous activities'), was the demonstration of the 'sufficiency' of the cardinal virtues. Or, to paraphrase Lear's fool, 'The reason why the four virtues are no more than four is a pretty reason' – and, as in Aquinas's *Summa*, whether Cicero's identification of 'parts' formed a logically compelling division. A second focus, analogous to explanations of pride as the 'head-vice' and of Paul's 'the greatest of all is …', concerned whether the cardinal virtues might be ranked, whether one was more important than all the others. (Almost universally a[n unequal] contest between Prudentia and Iustitia.)

Allen discusses (1982, 222–27), as many other scholars have done, the patterning of Ridewall's opening chapters. He points out that four of the opening sequence of six mythographies rely (and elaborate) upon a pre-existing ethical system, Cicero's presentation of the virtue Prudentia and its division into 'parts'. In this, the virtue itself is represented by Saturn (1.2), and the subsidiary 'parts' as offspring, Saturn's children (1.4–6, cf. 4/10–26). This is sufficient for Allen's argument for late-medieval 'ethical poetics'.[3] However, in his edition, *John de Foxton*, Friedman, more helpfully, comments frequently on Ridewall's investment in the cardinal virtues. It is his suggestion, and Cicero's shorthand description at *De inventione* 2.159–64, that I develop here.

Ridewall's text certainly begins, as everyone has recognised, with an interrupted invocation of Cicero's ¶160, the subject of *Fulgencius* 1.2, 4–6: 'Prudentia est rerum bonarum et malarum neutrarumque scientia. Partes eius: memoria, intelligentia, providentia.' In traditional discussions, Prudence is the highest/lead virtue, broadly equivalent to 'sapientia', or the Phronesis of Martianus and Alan of Lille. However, the succeeding discussions rely not simply on Cicero's formulation but also on one that Ridewall, as is fairly common, apparently took to be an alternative Ciceronian statement. This is the *Moralium dogma philosophorum* often attributed to William of Conches. (Cf. the citation ascribed to Cicero at 6/103.)

I have described this presentation as 'interrupted', for Saturn's prudential 'proles' actually follow the introduction of Jupiter (1.3). Logically, one might

three virtues' in a universally popular septenary text for lay and parochial use, see *Somme le roi* 232–37.

[3] Equally, it appears to me the only sensible underlying logic for Chance's analysis, and her insistence that after 1.6, Ridewall's text lacks discernible pattern (cf. Introduction, p. 3 n.9).

have expected Ridewall to have associated the three parts with the three ruling sons. However, Jupiter, after all, the chief god, is reserved as special, a representative of 'amor et beneuolencie'; the discussion most frequently emphasises classical 'amicitia'. Yet the prominence of this portrayal is more or less directly a Christianisation; Ridewall's 'amor' directly reflects 'caritas', as the author clarifies at several later occasions for anyone who might have missed the point. The 'greatest virtue' deserves the greatest god.[4] Yet one should also notice that among ps.-William of Conches's reformulation of the Ciceronian 'parts', 'amicitia' appears as a subdivision of 'iustitia'. Ps.-William is probably following Cicero's definition of the part of 'iustitia' he calls 'gratia', 'which contains the memory of and the desire to reward other people's friendship and kindly deeds' (in qua amicitiarum et officiorum alterius memoria et remunerandi voluntas continetur).

The remainder of the virtues Ridewall describes have been derived from Cicero's divisions. Just as 'prudentia' has three parts, similarly, the six Cicero ascribes to 'iustitia' include 'religio', 'pietas', and 'veritas', i.e. cues for 2.3 (Minerva) and 1.7 (Apollo). Also explicitly 'part' of 'iustitia', although unnoted by Cicero, is 'eloquentia', 1.9 (Mercury).[5] Fortitude obviously is the subject of 1.12 (Perseus), and Ridewall there manages to work in references to three of the four Ciceronian 'parts', with an assist or confusion again from *Moralium dogma*.[6] And, finally, Cicero's 'temperantia' includes the parts 'continentia' and 'modestia', i.e. 1.13 (Alceste) and 1.10 (Danae, whatever the identification in the first paragraph, mainly a discussion of 'pudicitia').

Equally, as one would expect, the vices are in large measure opposites. This is most obvious in the case of 2.1 (Injustice = Paris) and in the intemperate sexuality of 1.11 (Ganymede) and 2.4 (Venus). The remaining pair, 1.8 (Phaeton) and 2.3 (Juno), are, like Jupiter as Charity, assimilable to the leading Christian vices, Pride and Avarice.[7] But equally, the first might be identified with Paris's negative justice – Cicero defines the virtue as 'habitus animi communi utilitate conservata suam cuique tribuens dignitatem' (that mental disposition preserving communal benefit and rewarding each person in accord with their worth), and Juno represents the negative of Jupiter's *gratia*.

[4] E.g. 12/18–27.
[5] See 9/17–20, ascribed to Aristotle as his virtue 'affibilitas'; but equally *Moralium dogma* I.B.2.b.I under that part of 'liberalitas', one of his 'partes', discussed as 'beneficentia'.
[6] See the textual note to 12/77.
[7] It's worth noting that the doubled presentation of Juno is balanced in 1.10 and 11 by a depiction of Jupiter *in malo*, his earlier 'amicicia' run amuck. Ganymede is only a victim (as is, implicitly, Danae).

Cicero may have provided topics for assigning the gods their various identifications, but the form of Ridewall's analysis is derived from elsewhere in learned virtue lore. The opening Idolatry chapter implicitly, largely by argument on its contrary, lays out an ethics. It is, of course, a particularly witty take on the 'invention of idolatry' parable: there lack or absence, the dead son, can only produce a compensatory excess – and the analysis interfaces with, or opposes, the discussion of Saturn's children, where wise behaviour produces children who represent virtuous acts. The argument insistently returns to 'immoderation' (the root *ordino*, usually with a privative prefix, appears 20 times in Ridewall's discussion of idolatry), and nearly so frequently to that self-regulation through reason that would avoid these excessive behaviours. This is one reason for the prominence of the four 'affects', extreme emotional states, a pair of polar opposites that undo the pursuit of virtue. Moreover, such a presentation is a persistent feature in Ridewall's analysis of pagan depictions in his commentary on *DCD*:

> The first example of how the gods the poets spoke about were enslaved by foolish and **unregulated** emotions and passions is Jupiter (C2 fol. 27^v) ... Apollo [served a mere mortal, Admetus because] enslaved by **unregulated** love for a king's daughter (C2 fol. 28) ... The goal for which cities had established theatres was the practice and presentation of plays; the citizens had arranged these to worship and honour their gods. But this goal was disgusting, **unregulated**, and morally evil, because, through these plays, many Romans were incited to vices and sins (C2 fol. 32) ... [of Pluto's rape of Proserpina] For it is blasphemy and superstition to think that any true god might be enslaved by **unregulated** love for any woman ... Concerning Venus's foolish and **unregulated** love for Adonis .... (C2 fol. 53^v, my emphases)[8]

---

[8] 'quomodo scilicet dii de quibus poete loquebantur erant captiuati fatuis et **deordinatis** passionibus et affeccionibus. Exemplum primi de deo Ioue ... Aliud exemplum tangit Uarro de deo Appolline, qui captus amore **deordinato** filie cuiusdam regis ... Nam finis quare ciuitates instituerant theatra fuit usus et exercitum ludorum scenicorum, qui ludi erant per ciues rei puplice ordinati ad cultum et honorem deorum. Set iste finis fuit uilis et **inordinatus** et moraliter malus, quia per illos ludos scenicos fuerunt multe persone rei puplice Romane ad uicia et peccata excitati ... Est enim blasfemium et superstitiosum sentire de aliquo uero deo quod sit captus amore **deordinato** cuiuscunque mulieris ... De amore illo fatuo et **deordinato** quo dea Uenus dilexit istum Adonidem.' Similar comments litter the mythographic passages in Ridewall's commentary on Map's *Dissuasio*, e.g. *JBWW* 77/300, 85/482, 99/598.

Material like this – or in Apollo's unheeded instructions to Phaeton, 'Alcius ... inferius ... medio tutissimus' (8/172–73) – obviously alludes to a differing but equally learned and school-disseminated version of moral theology. This is Aristotle's discussion of virtue as a mean. Ridewall returns frequently to Robert Grosseteste's translation of the *Nicomachean Ethics* as a guide to the nature of virtuous action.

Most relevantly, in 2.5, Aristotle invokes handicrafts as a model to which virtue should be analogous. (A perfect object is one to which nothing may be added or taken away.)[9] Moreover, throughout this portion of the *Ethics*, Aristotle relies on the example of fortitude – a mean between excessive 'audacitas' and defective 'pusillanimitas'. His discussion is carried over pretty much intact into Ridewall's chapter on Perseus (1.12). This begins with a bit of a shocker, the identification of the virtue as 'fortitudo et audacia', as if they were equivalent. But rather immediately, 'audacia' is largely eliminated as part of the virtue through warnings about 'temerarious' behaviour and concomitant assertions that proper fortitude is bravery for the common good (which derives from Cicero's *'considerata periculorum susceptio'*). Similarly, the extensive analysis of Perseus's foes, the Gorgons, insists on their capacity to instil one of the four affects, numbing terror.

I don't think Ridewall's presentation merely an automatic reflex of a university scholar (although that is where this discourse is most prominent), or merely 'popularisation', taking Oxford to the provinces. It is equally a historicist gesture. If mythography truly underpins moral philosophy through an *integumen* that the poets intended, those authors could only describe those virtues and vices known to them, that is the cardinals. Further, they could only generally describe their operations through equally contemporary theory, Aristotle's *Nicomachaean Ethics* on the mean (moderation or *ordinatio*). Such theory is to be instantiated through 'metaphor', the conventional preacherly use of similitudinous argument.

---

[9] See Aristoteles Latinus 26.2, 217 (= 1106b 8–28).

Indexes

My citations identify only the onset of frequently extensive citations.

Biblia

Gn 1:27   10/31
Gn 4:10–11   2.3/160 (from Peter Chrysologus)
Gn 9:13   4/60, 2.3/232
Gn 19:24   11/75 (from Innocent)
Gn 37:18–28   2.3/161 (from Peter Chrysologus)

Ex 2:11–15   2.3/162 (from Peter Chrysologus)

Nm 12:1–12   2.3/163 (from Peter Chrysologus)

Dt 32:29   6/56 (from Bernard)

1 Rg 25:37   9/215

2 Rg 15   8/94

4 Rg 5:20–27   8/201

Tob 6:16–18, 22   13/43

Idt 10:19   2.3/143 (from Innocent)

Est 6   8/355

Iob 5:7   5/80 (from Bernard)
Iob 7:1   6/399
Iob 12:4   2.3/261 (from Gregory)
Iob 14:1   5/81 (from Bernard)
Iob 21:7–14   8/356

Ps 17:25   3/64n
Ps 21:2   1/100
Ps 22:4   8/230
Ps 35:4   App/18
Ps 37:25   3/64n
Ps 76:4   4/101
Ps 79:17   1/104
Ps 81:6   12/270 (from Alexander)
Ps 90:11   10/85
Ps 116:2   7/42
Ps 146:9   7/443

Prv 5:3–4   2.4/167
Prv 8:4–5   2/160
Prv 8:15–16   2/147 (from John of Salisbury)
Prv 9:2–5   2/153
Prv 13:7   2.3/76 (from Innocent)
Prv 14:20 and 19:4, 6   3/64n
Prv 14:34   6/506
Prv 20:28   7/268
Prv 25:3   8/259
Prv 29:14   7/82

Ecl 4:10   3/251

Ct 2:7, 3:5   2.2/365 (from Bernard)
Ct 3:4   3.2/272 (from Bernard)

Sap 5:8–9   8/374
Sap 6:13   2.2/101
Sap 14:12–16   1/153

Sir 1:16   2.2/282
Sir 6:5   9/273
Sir 6:16   3/302
Sir 9:6   2.4/40
Sir 10:1, 7. 8   2.1/281
Sir 10:8   7/271
Sir 11:4   2.3/145 (from Innocent)
Sir 13:25   3/64n
Sir 15:14–18   5/57
cf. Sir 17:1–6   10/45
Sir 25:26   9/52
Sir 41:1   6/205

Is 1:5   5/65, 10/56
Is 1:22   9/39
Is 11:3   2.2/265
Is 38:3   7/79
Is 48:10   10/75 (from Gregory)

Lam 2:13   2/258
Lam 4:1   8/131

Mt 5:22   6/313 (from Chrysostom)
Mt 6:19–21   6/62
Mt 11:12   12/247 (from Jerome)
Mt 13:23   12/194
Mt 22:16   7/84

Mt 23:5   2.3/141 (from Innocent)
Mt 23:27   2.3/136 (from Innocent),
   2.4/104 (from Chrysostom)
Mt 25:35–36   7/478
Mt 27:19   2.1/153

Lc 10:42   2.2/63
Lc 15:11–32   2.4/41
Lc 16:19, 22   2.3/141 (from Innocent)

Io 14:30   10/25 (from Ambrose)

Ac 8:18–24   8/201

Rm 1:26–27   11/40 (from John of
   Salisbury)
Rm 2:14–15   5/52
Rm 12:19   2.1/226

1 Cor 11:3   13/146
1 Cor 13:13   3/41

cf. Col 2:3   6/74 (from Gregory)
Col 3:3   2.2/406
Col 4:6   9/211

1 Tim 2:9   2.3/146 (from Innocent)
1 Tim 6:10   6/178 (from Innocent),
   2.4/47

1 Pet 3:3   2.3/147 (from Innocent)

1 Io 5:19   2.3/28

Apc 14:13   2.2/404

Auctoritates

I have not included Fulgentius, persistently cited, and usually following his argumentative sequence.

'Adamantius', see Origen

Aelred of Rievaulx, *De spirituali amicitia* 2 (*PL* 195:671)   3/243, 300

'Agellius', see Gellius

Alan of Lille, *De planctu Naturae* m1 (*PL* 210:431–32)   11/166
    p7 (*PL* 210:469)   2.3/312
    p7 (*PL* 210:470)   App/1

ps.-Albrecht/'Alberic of London' (= VM3), *Scintillarium poetarum* (on the authorship, see Besson), Prooem. (152–53)   1/29
    cf. 1.1 (153/19) and 1.4 (154/30)   2/135
    2.3 (158/25–27)   6/263
    3.3 (161/17–24)   3/157
    4.1 (165/22–27)   2.3/84
    4.3 (166/13–16)   2.3/301
    4.5 (167/17–20)   4/103, 2.3/277
    4.5 (167/24–31)   4/194
    4.6 (167/32–39)   2.3/193
    4.6 (167/34–38)   2.3/240
    5.5 (173/13–38)   5/122 (largely repetition of Fulg)
    5.6 (173/39–40)   5/145
    cf. 5.7 (173/24–28)   5/19
    6.22 (187/11–12)   3/191 (ascribed Mart)
    6.23 (187/34–188/2)   6/405
    6.34 (196/9–28)   2/126
    8.1 (200/6–13)   7/72, 332
    8.1 (200/15–19)   7/341
    cf. 8.1 and 3 (200/2–22, 201/22–27)   7/286
    10.1 (221/27–22/3)   2.2/143, 376 (largely repetition of Remigius)
    10.6 (225/8–22)   2.2/225
    11.1 (229/17–18)   2.4/138
    11.2 (229/19–35)   2.4/177
    11.12 (235/27–36/17)   2.4/208

Albumasor, *Introductorius maior*, ed.tr. Keiji Yamamoto and Charles Burnett, *The Great Introduction to Astrology by Abū Ma'shar*, 2 vols (Leiden and Boston, 2018), 4.5.14b (1:389)   9/15
    5.4.7 (1:460–61)   11/103, 2.3/55

Alexander of Canterbury (ps.-Anselm, ? revised by Robert de Braci), *De similitudinibus* 56–57 (*PL* 159:640–41)   12/263
  191 (*PL* 159:701)   4/46

Alexander Neckam, *De naturis rerum*, ed. Thomas Wright, Rolls Series 34 (London, 1863), 1.23 (75)   11/65, 84
  2.74 (172)   3/103
  see also ps.-Albrecht (and 2/126n, pp. 381–82)

Ambrose of Milan, *De bono mortis* 2.4 (*PL* 14:541)   2.3/62
  4.15 (*PL* 14:547)   6/498
De Elia et jejunio 19.69 (*PL* 14:722)   2.4/43
De institutione virginis 6.41 (*PL* 16:316)   13/26 (from Hugh of St Victor?)
De Isaac 7.60 (*PL* 14:524)   7/98
De officiis 1.18.69 (*PL* 16:44)   10/131
De virginibus 1.8.51 (*PL* 16:202)   10/87
  cf. 3.5.23 (*PL* 16:226–27)   2/261
Cf. *epistola* 63.82 (*PL* 16:1211)   2.2/354
Expositio evangelii secundum Lucam 4.39 (*PL* 15:1624)   10/23
  10.88 (*PL* 15:1825)   4/228
Hexameron 1.8.8.31 (*PL* 14:140)   2/114
  cf. 4.1–3 (*PL* 14:187–91 passim)   7/33, 317
In psalmum David cxviii expositio 10.10–11 (*PL* 15:1333)   10/34
  cf. 11.20 (*PL* 15:1356–57)   7/89
  18.36 (*PL* 15:1465)   7/335

Anselm of Bec, *Cur Deus homo* 20 (*PL* 158:392)   7/239
  Monologion 66 (*PL* 158:213)   2.2/158
Proslogion 25 (*PL* 158:241)   6/291
  see also Alexander

Apuleius, *De deo Socratis* 23   5/96
  24   2/86, 12/57

Aristotle, usually cited from volumes of *Aristoteles Latinus* = AL
De generatione animalium 1.2 (716a); cf. Michael Scot's translation, ed. Hermann Stadler, *Albertus Magnus De animalibus libri xxvi...*, 2 vols (Münster i. W., 1916–2), 15.1.2 (2:993–94)   12/26
Metaphysics 1.2 (982a), translated Jacobus Veneticus, AL 25.1, 2   5/42
Meteora 1.12 (347b), translated William of Moerbeke, AL 10.2, 30   12/87
Nicomachean Ethics 1.13 (1102b), translated Robert Grosseteste, AL 26.1, 182–83   7/436
  cf. 2.2 (1104b), AL 26.2, 202, but also an extensive discussion, book 6   2/4
  ? 4.13 (1126b–27a), AL 26.3, 219–20   9/15
  6.8 (1142a), AL 26.2, 261   2/119

7.6 (1149b), AL 26.2, 283   2/216
8.2 (1156ab), AL 26.5, 114-15   3/198
8.3 (1156ab)   1/241
9.8 (1168b-69a), AL 26.6, 274   2/40
9.11 (1171b), AL 26.5, 118   3/171
Problemata 7, from John of Salisbury   3/109
Rhetorica 2.12 (1389a), translated William of Moerbeke, AL 31.2, 247   2.2/87
Topics 3.2 (117a), translated Boethius, AL 5.1, 54   2/103
    general reference   8/388

ps.-Aristotle, *Secretum secretorum*, Philip of Tripoli's translation, ed. Reinhold Möller, *Hiltgart von Hürnheim: Mittelhochdeutsche Prosaübersetzung des Secreta Secretorum*, Deutsche Texte des Mittelalters 56 (Berlin, 1963) [the Latin facing the German translation] 21 (p. 46)   2.1/217
    22 (p. 48)   7/273

Augustine, *Breviarium in Psalmos CXLVI* (PL 26:1256)   7/443
Confessiones 7.15 (PL 32:744)   7/319
    10.23 (PL 32:794)   7/328
    12.25 (PL 32:840)   7/336
    Contra Faustum cf. 22.31 and 33 (PL 42:420-22)?   13/225
De bono conjugali 21-22 (PL 40:390-92)   13/215
    21.26 (PL 40:391)   13/230
De civitate Dei 1.2 (PL 41:15)   2.1/18, 2.2/339
    1.4 (PL 41:17-18)   2.1/65
    3.2 (PL 41:79-80)   2.1/18
    e.g. 4.3 (PL 41:114)   7/152
    4.24 (PL 41:115-16)   9/276
    E.g. 5.18 (PL 41:165)   7/459
    6.1ff. (PL 41:193ff.)   1/52
    14.16 (PL 41:424-25)   2.4/127
    14.19 (PL 41:427)   4/123
    14.28 (PL 41:436)   1/23, 7/51
    16.25 (PL 41:504)   13/221
    18.13 (PL 41:572)   12/251
    cf. *De diversis quaestionibus LXXXIII* 31.1 (PL 40:20-21)   4/6
De dignitate et excellencia huius ymaginis diuine, probably ps.-Bernard, *Meditationes* 1.2 (PL 184:485-86)   10/34
    cf. *De gratia Christi* 1.45.49-50 (PL 44:382-83), actually citing Ambrose on Luke   4/228
De libero arbitrio 1.3.8 (PL 32:1225)   13/120 (also Gratian)
    2.14.38 (PL 32:1262)   2.2/128
    2.18-19 (PL 32:1267-68)   7/200, 220
    3.25 (PL 32:1308-9)   3/116

cf. *De trinitate* 1.13 (*PL* 42:843-44)   6/267
    cf. 10.12.19 (*PL* 42:984)   5/185
    13.20.25 (*PL* 42:1025), or summary of 9.11-12 (ibid. 969-72)   2.2/105
    15.18 (*PL* 42:1082)   3/39
Enarrationes in Psalmos 14.3 (*PL* 37:1967)   2.1/141 ('Cassiodorus')
    64.2 (*PL* 36:773)   7/51
    on Ps 79:17 (*PL* 36:1026)   1/103
    99.13 (*PL* 37:1280)   13/119
Epistolae 40.4 (*PL* 33:157)   7/61
    cf. 53.3 (*PL* 33:199)   7/347
    144.3 (*PL* 33:592)   9/142
    145.4 (*PL* 33:594)   7/249
    155.1 (*PL* 33:667)   2.3/216
    155.4 (*PL* 33:672-73)   3/202, 12/20
In epistolam Ioannis ad Parthos 2.8-10 (*PL* 35:1993-94)   6/275
    2.14 (*PL* 35:1997)   12/261
    5.4 (*PL* 35:2014)   2/272, 3/44
In Ioannis evangelium tractatus 41.1 (*PL* 35:1692)   7/43
    43.7 (*PL* 35:1708)   1/150
Sermones de diversis 350 (*PL* 39:1533-34)   3/42
    350.1 (*PL* 39:1533)   3/292
    354.6 (*PL* 39:1565)   3/133
Sermones de scripturis 61.9 (*PL* 38:412-13), followed by *Sermones de diversis* 354.5 (*PL* 39:1565) and *Sermo de disciplina Christiana* 7 (*PL* 40:673)   2.3/167
Sermones 'ad fratres in eremo', probably sermo 8 (*PL* 40:1249-50)?   12/94
    49 (*PL* 40:1332-33)   6/510
Soliloquia 1.10 (*PL* 32:878)   2/217
(ps.-Augustine, in fact Gennadius of Marseilles), *De duodecim abusionibus* 5 (*PL* 4:873)   10/99
(ps.-Augustine) *De visitatione infirmorum* 1.6 (*PL* 40:1152)   6/526
cf. (ps.-Augustine), *De vita heremitica* 41 (*PL* 32:1464)   2.3/17
(ps.-Augustine) *Sermo de obedientia et humilitate* 1 (*PL* 40:1222-23)   13/251
    see also Cyprian, Gildas, Hugh of St Victor, Jerome, Prosper, Rufinus
a general statement?   6/255

Aulus Gellius, Agellius, see Gellius

Averroes, 'the commentator' on Aristotle's *Nicomachaean Ethics*   1/241

Avicenna, all references unfound   3/219, 7/106
    6° *Naturalium*, parte 5ª   7/427
    collacione 6   11/90

Bede, *Homiliae* 13 (*PL* 94:68)   13/192

Bernard of Clairvaux, *De consideratione* 1.8.9 (*PL* 182:737)   12/46
 1.10 (*PL* 182:741)   2.3/94
 2.7 (*PL* 182:750)   8/334
 2.9 (*PL* 182:753)   5/77
 5.14.30 (*PL* 182:805–6)   2.2/270
De gradibus humilitatis 1.1 (*PL* 182:942)   5/263
 3.6ff. (*PL* 182:344), paraphrased   7/467
Epistolae 2.1 (*PL* 182:80)   3/161
 114.1 (*PL* 182:259)   3/272
 129.2 (*PL* 182:283)   12/79
 292.2 (*PL* 182:498)   6/55
In psalmum XC 'Qui habitat' 6.4 (*PL* 183:198)   8/391
Sermones de tempore
 'sermo 4 in Aduentu Domini' 1–2 (*PL* 183:47–48)   6/75
 'Dominica prima post octauum Epiphaniae sermo 2'.6 (*PL* 183:161)   7/314
 'In feria iv hebdomadae sancte sermo' 6 + 'In Ascensione Domini sermo
  5'.2 (*PL* 183:266,316)   4/220
 'Sermo in Ascensione Domini 5'.13 (*PL* 183:321)   7/307
Sermones in Cantica 9.2 (*PL* 183:815)   6/383
 18.6 (*PL* 183:862)   3/296
 31.3 (*PL* 183:941)   2.2/150
 33.15 (*PL* 183:959)   8/103
 51.10 (*PL* 183:1029)   2.2/368
 52.3–5 (*PL* 183:1031)   2.2/408
 79.1 (*PL* 183:1163)   6/362, 13/162
ps.-Bernard, *Tractatus de charitate* 1.1 (*PL* 184:584)   12/30
 see also (ps.-Bernard) Augustine, *De dignitate*; Hugh of St Victor,
  De anima
? *Exposicio regule beati Benedicti* 3.7   8/258 [= *MF* prelacio bl, ascribed to
 commentary 3.7]

Boethius, *Philosophiae consolatio* 1m7.20–31   1/135, 7/491
 2p5.24–29   2/47
 3p2.9   3/230
 3p4 in init.   8/324
 3p7.1   2.4/61
 3p8.10   2.4/94
 3m12.6–19   6/285
 cf. 4p3.15–23   2/47
 4m7.13–31   13/106
 4m7.19   6/143

Caecilius Balbus, from John of Salisbury   1/82

Cassiodorus, *In Psalterium Expositio* 21 (PL 70:153)   1/101
    on Ps 70, Ps 7, and Ps 32 (PL 70:497, 73, 231)   12/168
Variae 3.27 (PL 69:591)   2.1/137
    see also Augustine, Peter of Blois, Rufinus

'the chancellor of Paris', see Roger Bacon

Cicero, *De amicitia* 23   3/267 [= MF amicicia ax, but JR's paraphrase]
    40, 18, 19, and 22   3/234 [40 = MF amicicia bd, but JR's paraphrase; 22 = MF amicicia at, but citation there much more extensive]
    De divinatione 1.21.42   2.1/81
De inventione 1.1   9/35 [= MF eloquencia h]
    2.160   4/4; 5/18, 73
    2.163   12/49, 76, 91, 167, 172 (the last from Cassiodorus)
De natura deorum 3.50   5/252 (from the gloss)
De officiis 1.11   6/3
    1.63   12/51 [= MF fortitudo t, but Ridewall probably from *originalia*]
    1.68, 1.83, 1.81   12/104
De senectute 17   2/110 [= MF consilium i, but Ridewall from *originalia*]
    e.g. 26   2.2/134
    39–41   2/229
    40   1/62
Paradoxa Stoicorum 51–52   9/176
Pro M. Caelio 63   7/298 ('Seneca') [= MF veritas ad, ascribed to 'Seneca in epistola']
Tusculanae disputationes 1.30.73–74   6/459
    1.47.113–14   6/482
    cf. 2.43   12/274
probably proverbial   2.1/187
    see also ps.-William of Conches

Claudian, *In Ruffinum* 1:122   6/347
Panegyricus de quarto consulatu Honorii Augusti 257–62   4/111

'cronica Romanorum', see Paul the deacon

Cyprian of Carthage, *Epistola ad Fortunatum de exhortatione martyrii*
    Praef.3 (PL 4:654)   12/241
    ps.-Cyprian (and ps.-Augustine), *De singularitate clericorum* (PL 4:866)   6/38

Damascene, see John of Damascus

Dares the Phrygian, *De excidio Troiae historia*, see Guido

Decretales 1.6 ('de electione'), see Hostiensis

ps.-Dionysius the Areopagite, *De hierarchia angelica* 15.2, but a rather more general reference, ed. Declan Lawell *et al.*, *Corpus Christianorum, continuatio mediaevalis* 268 (Turnhout, 2015)   3/9
De mystica theologia, Prol. and comment, ed. Ulderico Gamba, *Il commnento di Roberto Grosseteste al "De mystica theologia"...* (Milan, 1942), 21, 23   2.2/165

cf. Fulgentius of Ruspe, *Fidei catholicae instrumenta* 9, frag. 34 (*PL* 65:818–19) 7/450

Gellius, *Noctes Atticae* 1.8   2.4/61
    12.11   4/200
    19.2.1–2, 7–8   2.4/113

Gennadius of Marseilles, see (pseudo-)Augustine

Gilbert de la Porrée, *The Commentaries on Boethius*, ed. Nicolaus M. Häring, Studies and Texts 13 (Toronto, 1966) unfound   8/329

cf. Gildas, *De excidio Britanniae* 2.7.4 (*PL* 69:355)   7/165

glossa ordinaria on Lv 18:24 (*PL* 113:348)   2.4/216
    on Ps 118, see Ambrose
    on Prv 28 (*PL* 113:1111)   2.2/359 (from Rabanus)
    on Sap 14:12 (*PL* 113:1178)   1/213
    on Sap 14 (1480 edn,, 2:737b)   2/10, 5/253
    on Mt 13:23 (*PL* 114:131)   13/193 (from Jerome and Rabanus)
    on Mt 19:5 (*PL* 114:148)   13/142

Gratian, *Decretum* C.22, Q.2, c.16 (*CJC* 1:872)   7/93
    C.30, Q.1, c.3 (*CJC* 1:957, dated 858x67)   13/27 (from Hugh)
    C. 32, Q. 4, c. 12 (*CJC* 1:1130–31)   11/96 (from Jerome)
    C. 33, Q. 3 ('De penitentia'), d. 1, c. 33 (*CJC* 1:1165)   13/120 (from Augustine)

Gregory the Great, *Epistolae* 7.29 (*PL* 77:885)   9/197
Homeliae in evangelia 7.4 (*PL* 76:1103)   5/268
    cf. 10.6 (*PL* 76:1112–13)   2.1/181
    15.1 (*PL* 76:1132)   6/69
    30.2 (*PL* 76:1221)   3/175
    35.1 (*PL* 76:1259)   6/42
Homiliae in Ezechielem 1.11.12–16 (*PL* 76:910–11)   9/209
    2.2.3 (*PL* 76:950)   2.2/381
    2.9 (*PL* 76:954)   2.2/81

Moralia in Job 1.37 (*PL* 75:554)   4/144
    cf. 4.18 (*PL* 75:654)   2.4/236
    5.45 (*PL* 75:726)   6/357
    6.36 (*PL* 75:759)   9/169
    6.37.61 (*PL* 75:764)   2.2/67, 2.3/19
    10.6 (*PL* 75:922)   3/150
    10.29 (*PL* 75:947)   2.3/261ff.
    11.13 (*PL* 75:963)   4/124
    13.54 (*PL* 75:1016)   6/197
    15.23 (*PL* 75:1095)   6/186 (often ascribed to 'Seneca')
    20.5 (*PL* 76:143–44)   8/226
    26.26 (*PL* 76:378)   8/255
Registrum general references   2.2/65, 253
Regula pastoralis 2.1 (*PL* 77:25–27)   2.2/253
    2.4 (*PL* 77:30)   8/211
    2.6 (*PL* 77:38)   8/226
    3.prol. (*PL* 77:49)   9/102
    3.2 (*PL* 77:52)   10/74

Gregory Nazianzen, from Gregory   9/102

Guido della Colonne, *Historia Troiana*, ed. Nathaniel E. Griffin, *Historia Destructionis Troiae* (Cambridge MA, 1936)   2.1/209

Haymo of Auxerre, *Homiliae in evangelia de tempore* 22 (*PL* 118:164) or *Commentaria in cantica aliquot*, 'Canticum Moysi' (*PL* 116:712)   3/76

'historiae Romanorum', see Paul the Deacon

Horace, *Epistulae* 1.16.52–53   4/198
Odes 2.2.9–12   4/117

Hostiensis, i.e. Henry of Segusio, essentially a mnemonic for a twelve-part distinction of the *officium prelati*, at *Summa super titulis Decretalium* (Augsburg: Hohenwang, 1477), fol. F 10[rv]   2.1/102

Hugh of Fouilly, *De claustro animae* 1.6 (*PL* 176:1030)   8/157
    2.23 (*PL* 176:1085–86)   8/118
    3.1 (*PL* 176:1087)   2.2/212 ('Prosper')
    3.7 (*PL* 176:1095)   4/238
De nuptiis 1.1 (*PL* 176:1206)   13/74 (citing Jerome)

Hugh of St Victor, *De archa Noe* 4.8 (*PL* 176:674)   1/9
De arrha animae (*PL* 176:951)   3/6
    (*PL* 176:954)   6/356
De fructibus carnis et spiritus 12 (*PL* 176:1002)   4/6 ('Augustine')

De laude charitatis (PL 176:974)   3/118

De sacramentis 2.13.3 (PL 176:527)   1/110

Expositio super regulam beati Augustini 1 (PL 176:883)   3/73

Summa sententiarum 7.6 or *De sacramentis* 2.11.4 (PL 176:158–59, 483–84)
13/23

ps.-Hugh, *De anima*, actually ps.-Bernard, *De modo bene vivendi* 30 (PL 184:1254–55), and earlier ps.-Augustine, sermo 3 ad fratres in eremo (PL 40:1239)   7/363 [= MF loquacitas t, ascribed to *De anima* 2]

actually ps.-Bernard, *Meditationes* 5.14+1.1 (PL 184:494, 485)   5/186 [= MF consideratio sui af, ascribed to *De anima* 1.9]

actually ps.-Bernard, *Tractatus de interiori domo* 36 (PL 184:545)   5/208 [= MF consideratio sui ag, ascribed to *De anima* 1.31]

On the status of this text, a congeries of chunks from ps.-Bernard and ps.-Augustine, see Rudolf Goy, *Die Überlieferung der Werke Hugos von St. Viktor*... (Stuttgart, 1976), 494. As Goy says, it 'stellt die Forschung vor gröszte Probleme. Sicher scheint das jedes Buch [of the four that comprise the text] ein eigenes Werk ist'.

Hyginus, *De astronomia* 2.11–12, 3.10–11, etc.   12/249
    2.13   3/275
    2.16, 29   1/131

Innocent III, *De miseria conditionis humanae* 2.2 (PL 217:717)   6/177
    2.11 (PL 217:721)   12/199, 2.3/72
    2.21 (PL 217:725)   2.4/162
    2.25 (PL 217:726)   11/73
    2.26 (PL 217:727)   8/72, 185
    2.27 (PL 217:727)   8/199
    2.30 (PL 217:728)   8/149, 233
    2.37 (PL 217:732)   2.3/131
cf. *Sermones de diversis* 7 (PL 217:684)   2.4/233

Isidore, *Etym.* 8.11.8–10 (PL 82:315)   1/180
    8.11.13–14 (PL 82:315)   1/42
    8.11.95 (PL 82:324)   6/351
    9.3.4 (PL 82:342)   13/61
    11.1.6 (PL 82:398)   2/42
    12.1.11 (PL 82:426)   3/36
Sententiae 3.29 (PL 83:702)   3/53
Synonyma 2.9 (PL 83:487)   2.2/312

Jerome, *Adversus Jovinianum* 1.46 (PL 23:275)   13/79 (from Hugh of Fouilly)
    1.49 (PL 23:281)   13/89
Commentarii in Ezechielem 1.1 (PL 25:22)   2/45

Commentarii in Ieremiam 5 (on Ier 24) (*PL* 24:830)   7/296
Commentarii in Isaiam 1 (*PL* 24:38)   9/38
Commentarii in Michaeam 2.7 (on Mi 7:5) (*PL* 25:1219)   3/181
Commentarii in evangelium Matthaei 1 (on Mt 10:22) (*PL* 26:65)   4/142
    2 (on Mt 13:23) (*PL* 26:89)   13/192 (glossa)
    3 (on Mt 17:26) (*PL* 26:128)   10/26
    cf. 3 (on Mt 18:2–4) (*PL* 26:128)   5/264
Commentarii in epistolam ad Galatas 2 (on Gal 4:15–16) (*PL* 26:382)   7/57
Dialogus adversus Pelagianos 1.26 (*PL* 23:520)   7/343
Epistolae 9.5 (*PL* 30:126)   10/83
    21.9 (*PL* 22:383)   2.4/33 (Augustine, *De doctrina*)
    21.13 (*PL* 22:384–86)   1/8
    cf. 22.40 (*PL* 22:424)   12/245
    52.3 (*PL* 22:529)   2.2/135
    53.2 (*PL* 22:541)   9/90
    125.19 (*PL* 22:1084)   7/305
    see also Gratian, Pelagius

John Chrysostom, *De compunctione cordis* 1 (paraphrase of the opening argument), ed. [Urach. c. 1483–85] (Bod-Inc J-122), fols 106–14 in the online copy from Munich   9/43
    2 (fol. 117rb)   2.2/331 [cf. *MF* contemplacio z]
De nemo laeditur 6, translated Annianus Celedensis, ed. A.-M. Malingrey, 'Une ancienne version latine du texte de Jeanne Chrysostome, "Quod nemo laeditur..."', *Sacris Erudiri* 16 (1965), 320–54, ch. 6 at 338/71–84   6/159
    at 338/74–79   10/122
    7 (340/29–31)   11/113
De reparacione lapsi 14, also translated Annianus, ed. Jean Dumortier, *À Theodore*, Sources chrétiennes 117 (Paris, 1966), 257–322, at 298/68–74   2.4/99
In epistola ad Hebraeos 31 (*PG* 63:216–17)   4/82
Cf. *In Mattheum Homiliae* 31.3–4 (*PG* 57:374–75)   6/496
    76 (*PG* 57:69)   2/195
unfound references to *Super Mattheum*, which may be the next, occur at 7/234, 372; 13/24 (from Hugh of St Victor), 2.1/267, and 2.4/130
(ps.-Chrysostom) *Opus imperfectum in Mattheum* 11 (*PG* 56:690)   6/310
    25 (*PG* 56:761–62)   8/414 [= *MF* veritas y]
    43 (*PG* 56:878)   7/372 [= *MF* ipocrisis an]
    unfound   8/34

John of Damascus, *De fide orthodoxa* 1.9 (L), unpublished; Grosseteste's translation appears at Oxford, Magdalen College, MS lat. 192, fols 155–200; see Sharpe 547–48 and S. Thomson 45–52   6/95

John of Hautville, *Architrenius*, *The Anglo-Latin Satirical Poets*, ed. Thomas Wright, Rolls Series 59.1 (London, 1872), 316 and 317 (5.239–53, 268–73, 254–62, respectively)   6/208

John of Salisbury, *Polycraticus* 3.4 (*PL* 199:481)   1/219
    3.12 (*PL* 199:501)   2.3/211
    3.13 (*PL* 199:505)   11/27
    3.13 (*PL* 199:506)   11/51
    3.14 (*PL* 199:507)   1/84; (*PL* 199:508, a 'jocularia carmina' from Suetonius)   11/209
    4.3 (*PL* 199:518)   2.4/199
    4.6 (*PL* 199:525)   2/145
    5.6 (*PL* 196:551)   3/107
    5.12 (*PL* 199:570)   2.1/35
    6.23 (*PL* 199:622)   2.4/63, 184

Justinus, *Epitome historiarum Philippicarum* 1.4–5, 43.2, 44.4   2.1/85
    11.11   11/164

Juvenal, *Satyrae* 7.202   10/76 (from William of Malmesbury)
    10.19–22   6/187
    10.32   2/176
    10.365–66   2/15
    11.27   5/196
    general reference (for example, satyra 2)   11/111

Livy, *Ab urbe condita* 2.32   9/63

Lucan, *Pharsalia* 9.511ff.   3/50

Macrobius, cf. *Commentarium in Somnium Scipionis* 1.9.2   5/179

Marco Polo, *Il milione* 7 and 8   2.3/102
    22   7/227

Martianus Capella, *De nuptiis Philologiae et Mercurii* (= Mart, usually references to Remigius's commentary, rather than the text itself) 4.2
    (69/25–34)   2.4/176
    5.18 (72/24–28)   6/51
    5.22 (73/3–11)   2/80
    7.3 (75/25–29)   2.2/143
    cf. 7.11 (76/20–77/12)   2.2/49
    8.4 (79/7–14)   2.2/297
    8.17 (80/26–29)   4/130
    9.1 (81/15–16)   2.4/196
    9.11 (82/15–20)   9/268
    11.14 (88/19–23)   7/106

cf. 15.7 (95/3-9)   7/286
19.11 (101/27-102/14)   7/352
22.16 (107/23-25), and cf. 3.13 (69/7-9)   2.4/141
31.3 (123/8-11)   5/216
34.7-35.4 (129/1-31/17)   7/261
35.19 (133/1-2)   5/193
35.19 (133/2-5)   6/15
35.22 (133/13-19)   5/70, 170, 181
36.2 (133/20-24)   5/241
37.4 (135/32-36/3)   2/252
48.11 (157/5-17)   2.2/351
63.12 (181/13)   4/230
63.16 (181/20-22)   4/94
73.10 (197/11-17)   7/4
470.10 (2, 295/8-9)   4/217
unfound   2/135, 5/202
see also ps.-Albrecht

Messahala; see Lynn Thorndike, 'The Latin Translations of Astrological Works by Messahala', *Osiris* 12 (1956), 49-72   2.2/239

ps.-Methodius, see Peter Comestor

Origen, *Homélies sur Josué*, ed.tr. Annie Jaubert, Sources chrétiennes 71 (Paris, 1960), paraphrasing the general theme of the whole, e.g. 11.6   4/123, 13/65

Ovid, *Ars amatoria* 1.214-15   3/136
    3.62   8/384
Metamorphoses 1.89-112   2/20
    1.147   6/141
    1.283, 6.75   5/216
    1.452-60   7/71
    1.625-27, 1.717-21   9/120, 132
    1.671-75   9/255
    1.689-712   3/113
    1.747-2.400   8/2 etc.
    2.153-55   7/177
    4.610-803   12/5
    4.611   10/95
    4.616   12/212
    4.644-45 (and cf. 8.183ff.)   12/231
    7.406-19   6/143
    11.585   2.3/193
    15.745-820   11.142

Paul the Deacon, *Historia miscella* 7 (*PL* 95:856n, 862) 11/158; (*PL* 95:861) 11/106

Pelagius (ps.-Jerome), 'Epistola ad Demetriadem' 2-4 (*PL* 30:16-19) summarised   5/29
   3 (*PL* 30:18)   5/46

Peter of Blois, *De amicitia Christiana* 1.14 (*PL* 207:885)   3/52 ('Cassiodorus') [= *MF* amicicia ai, ascribed to 'Cassiodorus in quadam epistola']
Epistolae 1 (*PL* 207:2-3)   App/19
   77 (*PL* 207:238)   2.3/321, App/11

Peter Chrysologus of Ravenna, *Sermones* 4 and 48 (*PL* 52:195, 336)   2.3/157

Peter Comestor, *Historia scholastica*, Genesis 31 (*PL* 198:1081); cf. ch. 25 (*PL* 198:1076)   11/124
   Genesis 40 (*PL* 198:1090)   1/166

Peter Lombard, *Liber sententiarum* 4.27.2-3 (*PL* 192:910-11)   13/22

Petronius, frag. 27.1   1/98 (from Fulg)
   frag. 80.9 (L)   3/55

Plato, *Timaeus* 21e-22b, ed. tr. John Magee, *On Plato's* Timaeus *Calcidius*, Dumbarton Oaks Medieval Library 41 (Cambridge MA, 2016), 22B (22-25)   1/196

Pliny, *Historia naturalis* 2.137   3/209
   2.138   3/192
   cf. 10.22   2.3/167
   12.17, 19   6/20
   unfound references   3/70, 7/324

Plutarch, *Memorabilia* 8   3/109 (from John of Salisbury)

Pompeius Trogus, see Justinus

Prosper of Aquitaine, *Sententiae ex Augustino* 242 (*PL* 45:1879)   4/118
   327 (*PL* 45:1888)   3/290 (Augustine, *De vera innocentia*)
   390 (*PL* 45:1897-98)   4/176, 8/405 (Augustine, *De vera innocentia*)
   see also Hugh of Fouilly

Prudentius, *Psychomachia* 493-96   10/137

Quintillian, *De institutione oratoris* 2.16.12, 14-16   9/227

Rabanus Maurus, *Commentarii in Matthaeum* 4.13 (*PL* 107:945-46)   13/192 (glossa)
De universo 16.3 (*PL* 111:446)   13/62
   18.4 (*PL* 111:498)   6/287

448   John Ridewall, *Fulgencius metaforalis*

Expositio in Proverbia Salamonis 3.28 (*PL* 111:77)   2.2/359 (glossa)

Rambam, *Dux neutrorum*; cf. *The Guide for the Perplexed*, tr. M. Friedländer, 4th edn (New York, 1904, frequently reprinted), 1.36 (p. 51)   1/14
   2.47 (p. 248)   7.49

Remigius of Auxerre, see Martianus

Richard of St Victor, *De statu interioris hominis* 1.3 (*PL* 196:1118–19)   5/65, 10/55
   general reference   2.2/188

Robert Grosseteste, see Aristotle, ps.-Dionysius, John of Damascus, *Suda*

Roger Bacon, *Opus maius* 4 ('Mathematicae in divinis utilitas'), ed. John H. Bridges, 2 vols (London, 1900), 1:249ff., esp. 254 (paraphrased)   8/44
Operis majoris pars septima seu moralis philosophia, ed. Ferdinand Delorme and Eugenio Massa (Zurich, [1953]), IV, d.2.13 (219)   11/143n

Rufinus of Aquileia (?), *Commentarius in LXXV Psalmos* 7.3 (*PL* 21:669)
   5/245 [= *MF* consideratio sui ah, ascribed to Cassiodorus on Ps 6]
   14.2 (*PL* 21:695)   2.1/139 [= *MF* iusticia et iustus y, ascribed to Cassiodorus on Ps 14]
? cf. *Commentarius in Oseam* 8 (*PL* 21:1000)   7/165

Sallust, see Terence

Saracenorum, de insania   11/143; see the note and Roger Bacon

Seneca maior, *Controversariae* 1.2   4.15

Seneca minor, *De beneficiis* 1.3   2.4/176
cf. *De ira* 1.6, 12, 14; 2.6   6/320
   1.14   6/372
   3.36.1–2   5/224 [= *MF* consideracio sui al]
De tranquilitate anime 15.2   2/179
Epistulae morales ad Lucilium 3.2   3/176
   cf. 5.8   6/46
   6.4   3/247 [= *MF* societas x, but only the first sentence]
   19.11   3/61 [cf. *MF* amicitia bt, but varies verbally]
   37.4   4/121 [= *MF* regimen siue regere ak]
   41.5 or 66.20   7/317
   51.13   6/372
   59.16 and 14   7/134 [59.14 only = *MF* sapiencia uel sciencia ax]
   67.3–4   12/114 [cf. *MF* fortitudo g]
   71.7–8   6/33
   71.16   7/128
   71.26   2.2/120

73.12–13   2/11, 5/251, 2.2/120
76.8–9   2/64 [= *MF* homo t]
76.32 (the conclusion paraphrase)   5/89, 160 [cf. *MF* honor x]
79.18   7/38
cf. 88.32–33   4/2
90.5   2/24
97.13–16   8/300
cf. 119.9   6/65
Hercules furens 1–29   4/149
e.g. 30ff., 524ff., 780ff.   13/106
87–89, 93   6/334, 345
214–15   4/164
750–68   6/114
cf. 783–85, 787   6/133, 141
Quaestiones naturales 2.40   3/208
8.2.1   3/193
ps.-Seneca (ps.-Martin of Braga), *De moribus* 72–73 [= *MF* loquacitas ag, ascribed 'Seneca in proverbiis']   7/366
see also Cicero, Gregory

Statius, *Thebaid* 3.661   1/100

Suda, tr. Grosseteste, ed. Tiziano Dorandi and Michele Trizio, '*Editio Princeps* del *Liber qui uocatur Suda* di Roberto Grossatesta', *Studia Graeco-Arabica* 4 (2014), 145–90, presumably from the lost ch. 1 'De deo'   6/91
presumably from the lost ch. 31 'spado'   11/27
Cf. Dorandi, '*Liber qui vocatur Suda*: La traduction de la *Souda* de Robert Grosseteste', *Aevum* 87 (2013), 391–440, at 425–26, with a citation from Ridewall's Apocalypse commentary, from the chapter on Hermes/Mercury, surviving at BodL, MS Digby 11, fol. 33.

Terence, *Andria* 68   7/57 (from Jerome)

Valerius Maximus, *Dicta et facta memorabilia* 6.3.ext.3   2.1/256
6.9.ext. 1   9/144
8.9.1   9/290

Cf. Virgil, *Aeneid* 1.34–80 (verses 65–69 cited)   2.3/91
2.166–68   2.2/341 (from Augustine)
2.265   2.1/203
2.506–58   2.1/17
2.687 and 10.473   3/157 (from VM3)
cf. 4.337   2.1/248
cf. 8.115–16   2.2/393
Eclogae 10.69   3/112

Walter of Châtillon, *Alexandreis*, ed. Marvin L. Colker (Padua, 1978) 1.105–10
 2.1/110
 8.332–33, 10.448–50   4/169

Walter Map, *Dissuasio Valerii*, ed. *JBWW* 1:125/27–31   2.4/149

Walther, *Sprich*. 6059   6/204
 8411 (cf. 32678)   12/159
 8819   12/219
 12660 (cf. 23342)   11/21
 16974   12/159
 23342 (cf. 31080)   11/22
 27839   2.1/263
 31449a   2.4/38
 33547   12/159
 33819   2.4/86 (from John of Salisbury)

(ps.-)William of Conches, *Moralium dogma philosophorum* 1.A.1 ['De prouidentia']   6/103 ('Cicero')

William of Malmesbury, *De gestis regum Anglorum*, St Oswald (*PL* 179:1006)
 10/76